THE POLITICAL THOUGHT

OF

PLATO AND ARISTOTLE

THE POLITICAL THOUGHT
OF
PLATO AND ARISTOTLE

BY

E. BARKER

DOVER PUBLICATIONS, INC.
MINEOLA, NEW YORK

Bibliographical Note

This new Dover edition, first published in 1959, and reissued in 2009, is a unabridged and unaltered republication. It is published through the authorization of Sir Ernest Barker and special arrangement with Methuen and Company. A revised edition of the first four chapters of this book was published by Methuen and Company in 1918 under the title of *Greek Political Theory: Plato and his Predecessors*, and was reprinted in a third edition in 1947. A translation of the *Politics* of Aristotle with an Introduction, notes and Appendixes was also published by the author in 1946, and may serve as an aid in the study of the last seven chapters of this book.

International Standard Book Number
ISBN-13: 978-0-486-20521-2
ISBN-10: 0-486-20521-5

Manufactured in the United States by Courier Corporation
20521510
www.doverpublications.com

PREFACE

THIS book began, some seven years ago, as an introduction to the *Politics* of Aristotle. I found, however, as I began to delve into my subject, that my introduction would itself need to be introduced by a preface of some length. It seemed to me necessary, first and foremost, to explain, as best I could, the political views of Plato. Aristotle had sat at his feet, and listened to his lectures; nor could he, if he had been pressed, have done otherwise than acknowledge Plato (as Laud afterwards acknowledged Aristotle) for "his master *in humanis*," and pre-eminently *in politicis*. But Plato in turn had his master, a master whom he always loyally and chivalrously acknowledged; and to speak of Plato without speaking of Socrates would only have offended Plato's ghost. On the other hand, Plato had also his enemies: he wrote not only to defend Socrates, but also to attack the Sophists. Some account of the Sophists, therefore, and of Sophistic views of the State, seemed necessary to explain the polemics, and even the constructive theory, of the *Republic*. When the matter had been pushed so far back, the result was inevitable, that I should, as Aristotle himself would say, "begin from the beginning," and, in defiance of Horace, commence my tale *gemino ab ovo*. Finally, reflecting on the later history of Aristotle, *Maestro di color che sanno*, and on his influence during the Middle Ages, I could not refrain myself from touching upon Aquinas and Marsilio, or from treating of the times of contempt of Aristotle, when Dryden could say:

> The longest tyranny that ever swayed
> Was that wherein our ancestors betrayed
> Their free-born reason to the Stagirite,
> And made his torch their universal light.

In this way the book grew to something wider than the original design. But its growth has seemed to me, if I may be allowed the expression, to bring it nearer to the spirit of Aristotle. The systematiser of Greek knowledge, he always regarded the contributions of his predecessors to that knowledge as matter for serious study, whether they were criticised and found wanting, or approved and adopted into the system. He saw in knowledge a development; and each of his treatises can only be properly studied in the light of the development of the subject with which it deals. We shall best understand his ideas when we see them growing from their simplest original expression to the technical shape which they assume in his system. Εἰ δή τις ἐξ ἀρχῆς τὰ πράγματα φυόμενα βλέψειεν, ὥσπερ ἐν τοῖς ἄλλοις, καὶ ἐν τούτοις κάλλιστ᾽ ἂν οὕτω θεωρήσειεν.

While thus "looking backward," I have, in a sense, attempted to look forward. While attempting to refer Aristotelian conceptions to their sources in past speculation, and to their basis in contemporary Greek politics, I have also attempted to discuss the value of those conceptions to-day, and the extent to which they can be applied to modern politics. I have taken, for instance, Aristotle's conception of citizenship, of democracy, and of distributive justice, and I have tried to show how far they can be used to illustrate, and what light they can be made to throw, on the conditions of modern citizenship, the problems of modern democracy, and the distribution of political power in the modern State.

The seven chapters (v.-xi.) which are directly concerned with the *Politics* have been arranged on the following scheme. Chapter v. is meant to sketch the background of the *Politics*—its relation to contemporary history and to Aristotle's philosophical system. In chapters vi. and vii. the two conceptions of "end" and "whole" are considered, and the results are deduced which follow upon their application to politics. Chapter viii. deals with the moral aspect of the life of a political association, and chapter ix. with its material or economic side; but since economics are considered by Aristotle from an ethical point of view, the moral life of the State really comes under discussion in both chapters. All these five chapters may be regarded as general "prolegomena": they are based on the first three books of the *Politics.* In the last two chapters particular States are considered. Chapter x. is occupied by a sketch of Aristotle's ideal State: its basis is the two books (vii. and viii. in the old order; iv. and v. in the new) in which Aristotle propounds his ideal. Chapter xi. is concerned with actual States—principally oligarchy and democracy, and with Aristotle's suggestions for their amelioration—especially the Polity; and here I have used the three books (iv., v. and vi. in the old order; vi., vii. and viii. in the new) in which Aristotle deals with contemporary politics.

My debts are many. My general conception of political science I owe to T. H. Green's *Principles of Political Obligation;* and it is with his teaching that I have contrasted, or (more often) compared, that of Plato and Aristotle. In chapter i. I am indebted to Professor Burnet's *Early Greek Philosophy*, and to his article in the *International Journal of Ethics* on the antithesis of φύσις and νόμος (vii., 328 *sqq.*); to Gomperz's *Griechische Denker*, volume i.; to Pfleiderer's *Sokrates und Plato*; to Dümmler's pamphlet, *Prolegomena zu Platon's Staat*; and to McCunn's article on the Cynics in the *International Journal of Ethics* (xiv., 185 *sqq.*). Both in this chapter and in the rest of the book, I have been helped by Hildenbrand's *Geschichte und System der Rechts- und Staatsphilosophie* (Band i., *Der klassiche Alterthum*, a consecutive history of the development of Greek political thought, somewhat external, and written from a modern point of view), and by Henkel's *Studien zur Geschichte der Griechischen Lehre vom Staat* (a book which says παῦρα μέν ἀλλὰ μάλα λιγέως). In the chapters dealing with Plato (ii., iii. and iv.), I have used Nettleship's lectures on the *Republic*, to which I owe whatever there is of any value in chapter iii., and Pfleiderer's *Sokrates und Plato*, which I found suggestive and stimulating. I have also used Pöhlmann's *Geschichte des Antiken Kommunismus und Sozialismus*,[1] the second volume of Gomperz's *Griechische Denker*, and Jowett's translation of the *Platonic Dialogues*, to which I am indebted for the rendering of most of the passages I have quoted from Plato. The chapters which are concerned with Aristotle (v.-xi.) may be regarded as τεμάχη τῶν Ὁμήρου δείπνων—fragments from Newman's great edition of the *Politics*, which has been constantly by me. Much as I owe to the introduction, I should also like to acknowledge particularly my debt to the notes. From A. C. Bradley's essay on the *Politics* in *Hellenica* I acquired my first interest in the *Politics*; and I believe that his method of dealing with Aristotelian conceptions in that essay has influenced me more than I consciously realise. To Oncken's *die*

[1] I may also refer to P. Natorp, *Platos Staat und die Idee der Sozialpädagogik*, which came to my knowledge too late to be used in chapter iii.

Staatslehre des Aristoteles I owe, as far as I know, but little: the book seemed to me vigorous, but erroneous. In chapter v. I am indebted to several books. In section 2 I have followed, with some reservations, von Wilamowitz-Möllendorff's *Aristoteles und Athen;* in section 3 I have used Eucken's *die Methode der Aristotelischen Forschung;* in section 6 I owe everything to Shute's *History of the Aristotelian Writings.* Professor Burnet's edition of the *Ethics* helped me in many places; and I should like to acknowledge the use which I have made of Congreve's edition of the *Politics.* My obligations to a number of other authors whom I have used I have tried to acknowledge in the text.

In conclusion I have to acknowledge, with very cordial thanks, the help which I have received from Mr. Wells, Fellow of Wadham College, who was kind enough to read chapter xi. and to suggest corrections and alterations; Mr. Ross, Fellow of Oriel College, who has read for me almost the whole of the book, and helped me greatly by his sound Aristotelian scholarship; Mr. Unwin, author of *Industrial Organisation in the Sixteenth and Seventeenth Centuries*, who read the Introduction and chapter i.; and Mr. Lennard, of New College, to whose kindness and diligence I am much indebted throughout, especially in matters of style and punctuation.

E. B.

August, 1906

CONTENTS

INTRODUCTION

CHAPTER I

THE PRE-SOCRATICS, SOCRATES, AND THE MINOR SOCRATICS

Proverbial Thought and the Philosophy of Nature

The State of Nature and the Social Contract

Socrates and His Lesser Followers

CHAPTER II

PLATO AND THE PLATONIC DIALOGUE: THE DEFENCE OF SOCRATES

The Life of Plato

THE METHOD OF PLATO

THE EARLIER DIALOGUES OF PLATO

CHAPTER III

THE *REPUBLIC*, OR *CONCERNING JUSTICE*

THE PLAN AND MOTIVES OF THE *REPUBLIC*

THE *PRIMA FACIE* THEORY OF JUSTICE

PLATO'S CONSTRUCTION OF THE STATE AND DISCOVERY OF TRUE JUSTICE

PLATO'S THEORY OF EDUCATION

COMMUNISM

CHAPTER IV

PLATO'S VIEW OF MONARCHY, AND OF THE MIXED STATE

THE ABSOLUTE MONARCH

PLATO'S CLASSIFICATION OF STATES

CONSTITUTIONAL CHANGE

THE LAW STATE AND THE MIXED CONSTITUTION

CHAPTER V

ARISTOTLE—HIS LIFE AND TIMES: THE PLACE OF THE *POLITICS* IN HIS SYSTEM

THE SOURCES OF THE *POLITICS*

The End of the State

CHAPTER VII

[*Politics*, III., c. i.-viii: VI. (IV.), c. iii.-iv.]

THE STATE AS A COMPOUND

The Units of the Compound

The Scheme of Composition

The Classification of States

CHAPTER VIII

[*Ethics*, V. *Politics*, II., c. viii.: III., c. ix.-xviii.]

ARISTOTLE'S CONCEPTIONS OF LAW AND JUSTICE

Nature and Sphere of Law

APPENDIX A

APPENDIX B

CHRONOLOGICAL TABLE OF EVENTS BEARING ON THE TEXT

B.C.

830-820. Date assigned by Thucydides (I. 18) to the legislation of Lycurgus.
683. Tyrtæus came from Athens to Sparta.
660. Zaleucus gave the Locrians the oldest written laws known in Greece.
640. Charondas gave laws to Catana.
620. Laws of Draco at Athens.
594. Solon's legislation.
589. Pittacus æsymnete at Miletus.
585. Thales *floruit.* (Anaximander is called by some his "companion," by others his "disciple".)
560. Peisistratus becomes tyrant at Athens for the first time.
543. Theognis *floruit.*
532. Pythagoras *floruit;* also Phocylides.
509. Constitution of Cleisthenes.
504. Heraclitus *floruit.*
490. First Persian War.
480. Second Persian War.
475. Organisation of the Delian League.
460. Pericles lessens the power of the Areopagus at Athens: introduction of pay for the jurors.
448. Anaxagoras *floruit.*
445-431. Peace between Athens and Sparta: Pericles' ascendency.
440. Protagoras *floruit.*
431-404. Peloponnesian War.
428. Birth of Plato.
427. Gorgias of Leontini comes to Athens: *στάσις* at Corcyra.
411. Revolution at Athens, led by Antiphon and Theramenes: polity of the 5,000.
404. End of the Peloponnesian War: the Thirty at Athens.
403. Restoration of the Athenian democracy.
401. Xenophon and the retreat of the Ten Thousand.
400. Aristippus of Cyrene and Antisthenes the founder of the Cynics pupils of Socrates.
399. Death of Socrates.
392. The Iphicratean peltasts defeat a Spartan mora.
387. Peace of Antalcidas: Plato's first visit to Sicily—after which, possibly, the composition of the *Republic* is begun.
384. Birth of Aristotle.

B.C.

371. Defeat of the Spartans at Leuctra: Spartan decline.
368. Plato's second visit to Sicily.
367. Aristotle comes to Athens, and studies under Plato.
361. Plato's third visit to Sicily; after which comes the composition of the *Laws*.
347. Plato's death: Aristotle leaves Athens for Atarneus.
343. Aristotle goes to Macedonia as Alexander's tutor.
338. Philip's victory at Chæronea, "fatal to liberty".
336. Congress at Corinth. Alexander "general plenipotentiary" of Greece: semi-federal constitution for Greece. Decay of the City-State.
335. Aristotle returns to Athens and founds a school. The *Politics* delivered as lectures. Archaizing revival at Athens under Lycurgus.
323. Death of Alexander: death (according to tradition on the same day) of Diogenes the Cynic.
322. Death of Aristotle.
264. Death of the Stoic Zeno. (He is said to have lectured in his school for fifty years.)
167. Date of Polybius' exile.
55 (*circiter*). Cicero's *De Republica*.

A.D.

400 (*circiter*). St. Augustine.
520 (*circiter*). Boethius' *De Consolatione Philosophi.*
600. Isidore made Bishop of Seville.
845-882. Hincmar Archbishop of Reims.
1156. The *Polycraticus* of John of Salisbury completed.
1244. Bracton one of the Justices Itinerant.
1260-1270. William of Moerbeke's translation of the *Politics* into Latin.
1264. *Song of Lewes.*
1274. Death of St. Thomas Aquinas.
1280 (*circiter*). The *De Regimine Principum* of Aegidius Romanus.
1302. Dante's exile. The *De Monarchia* composed in exile.
1324. Composition of Marsilio's *Defensor Pacis* (or perhaps 1342).
1373. Nicholas Oresme's *Tractatus.*
1430 (*circiter*). Lionardo Aretino's translation of the *Politics.*
1442. Fortescue Chief Justice of King's Bench.
1460. Ficino begins his translation of Plato.
1495-1498. First printed edition of the *Politics* (the Aldine Aristotle).
1516. More's *Utopia* published. Composition of Machiavelli's *Prince.*
1576-1580. Bodin's *De Republica.* The *Vindiciae Contra Tyrannos.*
1594. The first part of Hooker's *Ecclesiastical Polity* published.
1599-1626. Campanella imprisoned at Naples.
1651. Hobbes' *Leviathan.*
1676 Spinoza's *Tractatus Politicus.*
1680. Filmer's *Patriarcha* published (though written earlier).
1690. Locke's *Two Treatises on Civil Government.*
1748. *L'Esprit des Lois.*
1761. *Contrat Social.*

THE POLITICAL THOUGHT

OF

PLATO AND ARISTOTLE

THE POLITICAL THOUGHT OF PLATO AND ARISTOTLE

INTRODUCTION

POLITICAL thought begins with the Greeks. Its origin is connected with what may be called the secularity of the Greek mind. Instead of projecting themselves into the sphere of religion, like the peoples of India and Judea, instead of taking this world on trust, and seeing it by faith, the Greeks took their stand in the realm of thought, and daring to wonder about things visible, they attempted to conceive of the world in the light of reason. It is a natural instinct to acquiesce in the order of things presented in experience. It is easy to accept the physical world, and the world of man's institutions, as inevitable, and to raise no question either of man's relations to nature, or of the relations of the individual to institutions like the family or State. If any such questionings arise, they can readily be stifled by the answer out of the whirlwind: "Shall he that cavilleth contend with the Almighty?" But such acquiescence, natural in all ages to the religious mind, was impossible to the Greek. He had not the faith which can content itself with the simple reference of all things to God. Whatever the reason (whether it was due to the disturbing effect of early migrations, or to a civic organisation in many commonwealths, preventing the rise of one universal and majestic Church), the fact is indisputable, that the religious motive appealed little to the Greek.[1] Nor had he, therefore, that sense of the littleness of human thought and endeavour, which might induce him to regard himself as a

Origin of political thought in Greece

[1] Reverence for the local deities of the city springs from a political rather than a religious motive.

speck in the infinite. On the contrary, he attempted to conceive of himself as something apart and self-subsistent: he ventured to detach himself from his experience, and to set himself over against it in judgment. It may seem a little thing, and yet it is much, that this abstraction and antithesis should be made. It is the precedent condition of all political thought, that the antithesis of the individual and the State should be realised, as it is the task of every political thinker to reconcile and abolish the antithesis whose force he has realised. Without the realisation of this antithesis none of the problems of political science—problems touching the basis of the State's authority, or the source of its laws—can have any meaning: without its reconciliation none of these problems can have their solution. It is in this way that the Sophists, who seized and enforced the antithesis, are the precursors and conditions of Plato and Aristotle, by whom it is abolished.

A sense of the value of the individual was thus the primary condition of the development of political thought in Greece. That sense has its practical, as well as its theoretical results; and as issuing in action it may be said to involve the conception of free citizenship of a self-governing community—a conception which forms the essence of the Greek city-state. Whatever may be said of the "sacrifice" of the individual to the State in Greek politics or in Greek theory, the fact remains that in Greece, as contrasted with the rest of the ancient world, man was less sacrificed to the whole to which he belonged than he was elsewhere. The Greeks were never tired of telling themselves that while in their communities each man counted for what he was worth, and exercised his share of influence in the common life, in the despotisms of the East nothing counted but the despot, nor was there any common principle at all. In this peculiar State, in this community of men, "like" if not always "equal," and pursuing a like object in common, political thought found a natural soil. Here were individuals distinct from the State, and yet in their communion forming the State. What was the nature of the distinction, and what was the character of the communion? Was there any opposition between the natural instincts of the individual, and the constant claims of the State? Did the individual naturally regard as just some-

The Greek idea of the State

thing other than that which the State constantly enforced as such? If there was such a discrepancy, how had it arisen, and how had a communion come to be formed which enforced a conception of justice different from that of the natural man? Such were the questions which, it seems, would naturally arise (and which did arise in Athens during the fifth century) as a result of the peculiar character of political life in Greece. The detachment of the individual from the State, which is theoretically a necessary condition of political science, had already been attained in practice, in the life of the "city"; and the Greek citizen, thoroughly as he was identified with his city, was yet sufficiently independent, and so far a separate moment in the action of the community, that he could think himself over against it, and so come by a philosophy of its meaning. In other words, the Greek "city" depended upon a principle, unrealised but implicit, of rational coherence; and just because that principle was already implicitly there, it was the more easy for conscious reason to apply itself to the solution of the problem of political association.

Constitutional changes and political thought

In yet other ways did the existence of the city-state afford a basis for political thought. Unlike the States of the Oriental world, it was not stationary: it possessed a principle of growth, and had known a cycle of changes. Sparta was the one State of the Greek world which had maintained a steady tradition of unbroken continuity in its government: in other cities there had been a development which had almost everywhere followed the same order, from monarchy to aristocracy, from aristocracy to tyranny, from tyranny to democracy. These changes must have conduced in two ways to the growth of political thought. In the first place, they accumulated a number of data for inquiry. Instead of any single type of constitution, history presented a variety; and while speculation may be silent before a single instance, a number of types inevitably suggests comparison and discussion. But it may be suggested that the last of these types furthered the growth of political thought still more directly. Aristocracy had not given way to democracy without a struggle; and democracy had still to maintain itself against the claims of wealth and nobility. On the ground of theory, as well as in actual life, this struggle made itself felt.

The "few" found it easy to talk of the rights of property and of birth: the "many" had to discover a philosophic answer. Metaphysics would not be necessary, it has been said, if it were not for the existence of bad metaphysics. Similarly, it may be suggested, political science owed its existence in Greece to the need of correcting a false theory already in vogue. And thus it would appear, that Greek political thought began with democracy, and in the attempt of the "many" to answer by argument the claims of aristocratic prestige. In any case, it can hardly be doubted that the actual struggle of the Few and the Many must have given a great impulse to the development of theory, just as, in modern times, it has been actual revolts against monarchy which have produced or stimulated political theories like that of a social contract.

Variety of types leading to discussion

But not only did the city-state offer a number of historical data for comparison and discussion. By its very nature, the city-state was not one but many; and in Greece there were at any given time a number of different States, not only co-existent, but also in close contact. Men were forced to ask themselves questions about the real meaning of the State, when they saw so many different interpretations current. They were driven to ask themselves what a citizen really was, when Athens, Thebes, and Sparta imposed qualifications so various. Particularly would a question arise, which would almost seem to have had a peculiar charm for the Greek—What is the best State? which of existing forms is nearest to perfection, and by what degrees do other States successively recede from it? Just because the real was so manifold, the need of the conception of an ideal was vividly felt: the ideal State would serve as a standard, by which existing States might be classified and understood. And this search for the ideal was the more natural, as these different States exhibited not merely "constitutional" differences, in the modern sense of that word, but deeper and more fundamental differences of moral aim and character.[1] Small as was the city-state, its very size encouraged the rise of a local opinion of decency and propriety. Each city had its "tone" (ἦθος): each had evolved in the course of its history

[1] To Aristotle these differences would be constitutional, since the constitution represents the moral aim of the State.

a code of conduct peculiar to itself. Such a code found its sanction in the force of public opinion by which it had been created. Concentrated and intense, that opinion bore upon each individual with a weight which we can hardly imagine: where each knew his neighbour (and this is one of the conditions which Aristotle postulates for a proper city), and each was concerned about his neighbour's behaviour, it would be hard for any man to go against the tone and habit of his city's life. The city formed a moral being, with a set character of its own; and its members, as the funeral speech of Pericles shows, were conscious of the individuality of their city, and could contrast its character with that of others. A political consciousness had thus developed in the Greek States. Each was aware of itself as a rounded whole, possessed of a moral life, created and sustained by itself; and it expressed this sense in the conception of the "self-sufficingness" or *αὐτάρκεια* of each political unit. Because it was self-sufficing, each State claimed to be self-governing: *αὐτονομία* flowed inevitably from *αὐτάρκεια*; and an inherent right of independent existence was postulated for every city. No wonder, then, that men began to discuss the value of each of these distinct types, or that the political consciousness of a separate individuality issued in political reflection.

It would thus appear that the political condition of the city-state tended to produce a growth of political thought, first, because the city was a self-governing community whose relation to its members demanded investigation; secondly, because the city had gone through a process of growth which at once supplied the data for thought, and, in its last stage, administered an impulse; lastly, because the co-existence of different types of cities, each conscious of its own identity, suggested a comparison of types and the search for the ideal. But the political thought, which deals with the city-state, is inevitably coloured by the peculiar conditions of its subject. The πόλις was an ethical society; and political science, as the science of such society, became in the hands of the Greeks particularly and predominantly ethical. The constitution is to Aristotle the State; and the constitution is not only "an arrangement of offices," but also "a manner of life". It is more than a legal structure: it is also a moral

Greek political thought connected with Ethics

spirit. This is indeed its inward essence and its vital meaning. In treating of the State, therefore, a thinker must approach his subject from an ethical point of view. He must speak of political science in terms not of jurisprudence, as a later generation, taught by Rome, attempted to do, but of moral philosophy.[1] He must ask—What is the aim which a State ought to pursue, and what are the methods which it should use, in order to lead the right "manner of life," and to attain the true moral spirit? He must not ask whether political power should be concentrated or divided; he must not inquire into natural rights or the distribution of taxes: he must remember that he is concerned with a moral, not a legal community, and he must discuss the various aspects of its moral life. Political science must be for him the ethics of a whole society, which coheres in virtue of a common moral purpose: it must determine the "good" of such a society, the structure by which its "good" will best be realised, the action by which it will best be secured. Between political science thus conceived and ethics there is for Aristotle no difference. The good of the individual is the same as the good of the society; his virtue is the same as that of his State; there is no discrepancy between individual and social morality. And this being so, political science, as the science of a whole moral society pursuing the full good which can be realised by common action, is for Aristotle the supreme ethics. It is the science of the *whole* duty of man—of man in his environment, and in the fulness of his actions and relations. Aristotle has no word for or conception of ethics as a separate science. If he writes a treatise on ethics distinct from his treatise on politics, this does not mean that he is distinguishing a science of ethics from a science of politics: it only means that he is differentiating virtue as a static and psychological condition in the individual, from virtue as the dynamic energy of man in society. And thus to Aristotle there is a unity of political science with moral philosophy—and of both (it may be added) with jurisprudence; for the ethical code of the State is the same as law or right, nor is there any distinction between the theory of

[1] Political science, it may be said, has always had to borrow its vocabulary from other studies—ethics, jurisprudence, or biology; *cf. infra*, p. 246. Greek political science always spoke in terms of ethics.

public and that of moral law. Political science is a trilogy. It is the theory of the State; but it is also a theory of morals and a theory of law. It contains two subjects, which have since been removed from its scope, and treated as separate spheres.

Consequent peculiarities of Greek thought

From this conception of political science there flow certain differences between Greek political thought and our modern ways of thinking. The conception of the State as an ethical association for the attainment of virtue meant a conception of the relations of the State to the individual different from any which is current to-day. Although, as has been said, the Greek thought of himself as one who counted for what he was worth in his community—although he regarded himself as a moment in determining its action, the fact remains that in the political thought of Greece the notion of the individual is not prominent, and the conception of rights seems hardly to have been attained. It is, perhaps, precisely because the individual felt himself an influence in the life of the whole, that he did not endeavour to assert rights against the whole. Secure in his social value, he need not trouble about his individual "person". And hence, starting from an ethical point of view, and from the conception of the State as a moral association, Greek thought always postulated a solidarity which is foreign to most modern thinking. The individual and the State were so much one in their moral purpose, that the State was expected and was able to exercise an amount of coercion which seems to us strange. Both by Plato and by Aristotle the positive inculcation of goodness is regarded as the mission of the State. They start from the whole: they look for the means by which its life and purpose may be impressed upon the individual. To the modern thinker the mission of the State is preventive: its function is the removal of hindrances (rather than the application of a stimulus) to the moral life. We start from the individual: we regard him as possessed of rights (only too often of "natural" rights independent of social recognition), and we expect the State to guarantee those rights and, by so doing, to secure the conditions of a spontaneous growth of character. We are anxious that the interference of the State should not introduce too much automatism into the life of its members. Our motto is—Better the half of a good act done from within, than the whole enforced from without. The Greeks had little of this anxiety. They had little if any conception of the sanctity of rights. Plato indeed seems ready to abolish the most vital of them all, though Aristotle, here as elsewhere, is more conservative, and vindicates a right (just as in slavery he vindicates a wrong), if it can plead a prescriptive title.[1] Accordingly the mark of Greek political thought is rather a desire for the interference of the State, and an attempt to sketch the lines of its interference, than any definition or limitation of its province. Nor could it be otherwise with a theory which was the theory of a city-state. The city-state, it must always be remembered, knew no distinction between State and Church. Its sphere was not limited by the existence of an association claiming to be its equal or superior. It could not leave to that association the preaching of morality and the finding of sanctions for its truths: being itself both Church and State, it had both to repress original sin—the function to which mediæval theory restricted the State, and to show the way to righteousness—a duty which mediæval theory vindicated for the Church. And again the very size and political structure of the city-state entailed a corresponding difference between the theory of its action and modern theories of the action of the nation-state. Removed as we are in large States from the central government, we readily tend to feel its action as that of an alien force: "this thing is not of us, and we will have as little of it as possible". It was not so in the city-state. There it was easy for each citizen to feel that the State was but himself writ large, and to say, with some truth—"The State? I am the State, and why should I fear its action?" In a word, the smaller the community, the greater the solidarity of which it admits.[2]

πολιτική a practical science

The theory of the city-state is therefore a theory which admits readily the full action of the State, and inquires particularly into the proper methods of its exercise. It is a theory

[1] That Plato, and still more Aristotle, had a conception of "rights," is by no means denied, *cf. infra*, pp. 155, 225. Such a conception was involved in their teleological view of the world.

[2] See below, on Aristotle's perception of this truth, p. 398. It may be noticed that the modern Socialist can welcome State action for the same reason as the Greek citizen. He too may urge that the State is the sum of its citizens: and why should they be afraid of themselves?

of, and for, the legislator. The Greeks believed that the different tones and tempers of their States were due to the action of sages like Lycurgus or Solon, who had cast the moulds in which the lives of their fellows were ever afterwards shaped. The customs which had grown by quiet accretion from many minds, the institutions which the accidents of war and it might be conditions of climate had fashioned, the manners and habits which luck had suggested and imitation made inveterate—all these were to Greece the laws of a Lycurgus, or still more primitive Minos. It is indeed a natural and universal instinct to refer what has been the slow process of a people's mind to the fiat of the greatest of its sons; and if it gave Greece the figure of Lycurgus, it has also given England the figure of Alfred. But it is an instinct which would seem to have been particularly present in the Greeks. It may be, that their artistic temper demanded that institutions should appear as the rounded product of a single chisel: it is certainly true that the colonial expansion, which is so great a feature of Greek history, involved the action of real and historical legislators. In any case, the figure of the legislator seems to occupy the minds of political thinkers. They regard themselves as imaginary law-givers, drawing, as the first-born of their thought, the full plan of what should be, and sketching next the proper lines on which the given and actual may be rebuilt. If an actual legislator had thus made the past, why should not a philosopher make the present, moulding matter according to his will, as the legislator had done before? There is always this practical bent in Greek political thought. The treatises in which it issues are meant, like Machiavelli's *Prince*, as manuals for the statesman. Particularly is this the case with Plato. True to the mind of his master Socrates, he ever made it the aim of his knowledge that it should issue in action; and if the tales of his Sicilian experiences are true, he even attempted to translate his philosophy into action himself, or at any rate to induce Dionysius to realise the hopes of the *Republic*. Nor shall we do justice to Aristotle unless we remember that the *Politics* also is meant to be "the delight of whoso wisheth" to found a colony, or to reform a State. As the *Ethics* is intended to make men good, so the *Politics* is meant to preserve and improve States.

Political Science a Science or an Art?

But if this be the case, it may be asked, is not the political science of the Greeks an art, rather than a science? If its aim is to make, or at any rate to produce some alteration in the subject studied, can it be a science, seeing that science seeks merely to know the truth about a given subject of investigation? The answer to this difficulty lies in realising, that the sciences which treat of the operation of the human mind, whether in thought or in action, have a double aspect. Primarily, sciences such as logic, ethics, and politics attempt to determine the laws, by which the mind acts in their several spheres. They analyse their material in order to determine the general propositions which can be laid down with respect to its nature. But to understand the laws, by which reason has been acting, is not merely to lay down laws in the sense of general propositions: it is also to lay down laws in the sense of regulations. The discovery of the process of reasoning by logic is also an act of legislation for the right methods of reasoning. It is easy to over-rate the authority of the law thus promulgated, and to cramp the process of thought under the rules of a formal logic; and where this is done, a reaction is inevitable against the dictatorial aspect of the science of thought. But such an aspect it undoubtedly possesses; and such an aspect is also presented by the sciences of human action. The propositions which are true of the action of man in his political capacity are also rules for his action, because the subject of which these propositions are true is the healthy normal subject, just as the propositions of logic are true of normal and "regular" thought. Accordingly, such propositions as that "the aim of the State is its citizens' well-being," or that "justice means the requital of good for good and evil for evil," can be written in the imperative as well as in the indicative mood. A State *ought* to pursue the well-being of its citizens in the fullest and truest sense of the word: it *ought not* to make wealth, or power, or equality, its aim. A State *ought* to give honour and office to those who have given to it the virtue which furthers its aim: it *ought not* to put in authority the wealthy, merely because they are wealthy, or the poor, merely because they are poor. It is on this dictatorial aspect of science that the political thought of the Greeks chiefly concentrated itself. The Greeks wrote their political science in the imperative mood. But that does not mean that they had forgotten the indicative. To be able to know and to assert the truth is the aim of political science to Aristotle, even though he generally expresses himself in the imperative, and—by dividing science into theoretical and practical, and classifying politics as practical—emphasises the value of the science of politics as a director of practice.

Distinction of State and Society

We have now seen what were the main peculiarities of the political thought which the city-state produced. It was a thought which conceived the State as a moral association, and, as a result, approached its subject from an ethical point of view. It was a thought which was so closely allied with practice, that it always conceived itself as pre-eminently a practical study. One feature of Greek politics still presents itself, as of vital importance in determining the course of Greek political thought, a feature of the pathology rather than the physiology of the State, but one which, just because political thought was practical and medicinal, had all the greater effects upon the line of its movement. The Greeks, to use Hegel's terminology, never distinguished with sufficient clearness between "society" and "State" between the complex of economic classes, who by their different contributions form the social whole, but are immersed in individual interests, and the neutral, impartial and mediating authority of the sovereign, who corrects the individualism of society in the light of the common interest of which he is the incarnate representative. Much depends on keeping the State distinct from society, on preserving the mediatory and corrective authority pure and intact from the influence of the interests which it controls. To secure such a distinction, such an integrity, is as much a concern of the modern State as it was of the ancient. There is still the danger that some social class, some economic interest, may infect the purity of the State, and, capturing the powers of the Government, direct them to its private advantage. On the other hand, there is always a danger that the State may harden into a repressive crust, which prevents the free growth of society, as it may be said to have done in the later days of the Roman Empire, when such organs of society as the *municipium* or *collegium* were rigorously regimented and controlled. From this point of view it may be argued that the play of society ought to modify the action of government, and that the State ought to respond to new social developments. In a free political society like that of the Greeks, however, this modification or response came naturally; and we may still say that the real danger was the infection of the State by social motives. Such corruption is the plague of politics. It may attack great modern States, just because their size and immensity make it easy for a "machine" to use its organisation all the more secretly and effectively. But it was a disease to which the city-state would seem to have been especially exposed. A city, where the Government has for its subjects acquaintances, whose interests and passions it knows, and can at pleasure thwart or forward, can hardly expect a neutral government. Limited in its area, the πόλις could not develop a remote and majestic government, above the play of social motives: it could not specialise a political organ, full of the zeal of its own mission.[1] Society must be one with the State, because there is not room for differentiation. The very theory of "distributive justice" illustrates the point; for this theory presupposes that political power must be awarded, either to *each* of the social classes, in proportion to their several contribution, or to *one*, in virtue of its pre-eminent services. Thus, while the political theory of the Greeks realised the conception of a common good as the aim of every political group, it never attained a full conception of the right organ for securing that common good. It is always groping its way to such a conception: the very evils which the want of it produced were a sufficient stimulus. These evils were very real. If in theory men sought for a just distribution of office among the different classes, in practice they tended to make political authority the prize of the strongest class, and to use the prize when it had been won in the interest of the class which had conquered. Hence, at any rate by the fourth century, politics had become a struggle, a στάσις; and political power became an apple of discord, for which the rich vied with the poor. Accordingly, political thought was occupied with the problem of producing a *concordia ordinum,* just as, in the "pre-Adamite" days of the Mercantile System, political economy was concerned

[1] Much of this criticism of the πόλις must be modified, when it is applied to Sparta, as Sparta was in her great epoch. But in the fourth century, in which both Plato and Aristotle wrote, Spartan government also was corrupt.

with the problem of discovering a scheme, by which the different factors might work harmoniously, and manufacture and agriculture might both be protected, without any detriment resulting to either from the preference shown to the other. Such a *concordia ordinum* Plato sought to attain in the *Republic*, by the creation of a specialised class of governors detached from society by a system of communism—an attempt at once to differentiate "State" from "Society," and to discover an organ for the realisation of the common good. The same aim was pursued by Aristotle also, but by different means. In opposition to Plato, who sought to institute a human sovereign, Aristotle fled to the conception of neutral and dispassionate law as the true sovereign of the State. Realising, however, the need of human agency to enforce law, and alive to the truth that laws are what men make them by the manner of their enforcing, he sought in the "middle class" the mediator and arbitrator between contending factions. If neither extreme rules, but the middle class, which shares in the interest of both, is supreme, then in its supremacy the *concordia ordinum* is established, and the common good has found the organ of its realisation.

Athens and Sparta

So far we have regarded the city-state, and the general conditions of its life, as the material with which political thought was occupied, and to which it adjusted its conclusions. But it should be noticed, in conclusion, that there were two States in particular, which occupied the attention, and helped to determine the theory, of both Plato and Aristotle. The two were Athens and Sparta—pre-eminently and particularly Athens. In Athens Plato and Aristotle spent the best part of their lives; and Athenian conditions were those which they naturally observed. But it was not merely facts like these which make their political philosophy a philosophy of Athens: it was the fact that in Athens there was a highly developed political life, with its appropriate and regular organs, which had attained to full self-consciousness. Whether or no philosophers admired the development, here was a full and perfect specimen of its kind for their study: whether or no they agreed with its theory, they had a theory to examine. Freedom was here claimed as a birth-right; and by freedom men understood the right of "living as one liked" in social matters, and the sovereignty of the majority in political affairs. Equality was a watchword; and equality meant "Isonomy, or equality of law for all; Isotimy, or equal regard paid to all; and Isagoria, or equal freedom of speech".[1] Culture was not forgotten: Athens prided itself on being a *Kulturstaat,* and opposed the many-sided and versatile play of its interests to the close devotion to war which characterised Sparta. None the less Sparta had a great attraction for the philosopher, because, almost alone of Greek States, she enforced a "training" (ἀγωγή) which preserved the "tone" of her constitution, and because by this means she was able to teach each individual Spartan to regard himself as a part of the social organism. Here there was a principle adopted, and carried to its conclusion with what seemed a thorough and remorseless logic; and the philosopher could not but admire the philosophic State. Here the sense of "limit," which meant so much to the Greek, was a living and active thing: if Athens boasted of *εὐτραπελία,* Sparta could boast of her *εὐνομία*; while the stability of a constitution which had stood secure for hundreds of years was something to which the versatile Athenian was entirely strange. No wonder therefore that the *Republic* is, to some extent, a "Laconising" pamphlet—a critique of Athens, and a laudation of Spartan logic, Spartan training, and Spartan subjugation of the individual to the State. Athens had sinned, in Plato's eyes, in the want of training for politics which disfigured her politicians: she had sinned still more, because the spirit of self had invaded her politics, and the individual, in his claim for a false freedom and a false equality, had set himself up in arms against the State. Her salvation, and that of Greece, was to be found in following Spartan example, so far at any rate as to train a citizen for his work, and to inculcate upon him his duty to the State. But Sparta too had her faults, of which Plato is not unaware, and which Aristotle trenchantly exposes. The principle she had adopted was of the narrowest: she had made success in war the end and aim of her existence. Her training only produced a limited and stunted type of character; and underneath a fair show of ascetic loyalty to the State there lurked not a little self-indulgence. The width of Athenian, and the concentration of Spartan character needed to be blended, to form the ideal Greek; and the ideal city must reconcile the

[1] Schömann, *Antiquities of Greece,* E. T., p. 173.

expression which the individual attained in Athens, with the order and the unity which the State enforced in Sparta.

Connection of philosophy and practice

No political philosophy can be detached from its environment in history; and most of the great works of political thinkers, the *Prince* of Machiavelli, the *Leviathan* of Hobbes, the *Contrat Social* of Rousseau, have something of the nature of political pamphlets addressed to the conditions of their times. Plato and Aristotle show this tendency all the more strongly, because they had a conception of political science as a practical and remedial thing. Especially is it visible in Plato, who had more of the spirit of a prophet and reformer than had Aristotle, and was therefore led to address himself still more to actual tendencies and conditions. But in dealing with the works of both, we have always to remember, not only the general character of the city-state of which they spoke, but also the peculiar temptations and difficulties which it had to face; nor must we forget, that while they are speaking of city-states and their temptations, they have always in the back of their minds those two States, whose rivalry had distracted Greece in the Peloponnesian War, and whose opposing aims and traits so obviously challenged attention and comparison. Their philosophy is of the Greek, and for the Greek; nor was it until the city-state was being absorbed in the empire of Macedon that a new type of experience, more analogous to our own, suggested to the Cynics and Stoics a political theory, with which a modern mind can readily sympathise. From the theory of the city-state philosophy leapt to a theory of the world-state: from the theory of the world-state it has turned back in modern times to that of a nation-state. Yet through all its mutations it has retained a fundamental unity. Even if Greek philosophy is a philosophy of the Greek and for the Greek, yet the Greek was a man, and his city was a State; and the theory of the Greek and his πόλις is, in all its essentials, a theory of man and the State—a theory which is always true. The setting may be old-fashioned: the stone itself remains the same. We do not therefore come to the study of the philosophy of the city-state, as to a subject of historical interest: we come to the study of something, in which we still move and live. The city-state was different from the nation-state of to-day; but it was only different in the sense that it was a more vital and intense form of the same thing. In it the individual might realise himself more easily and clearly as a part of the State, because its size permitted, and its system of primary government encouraged, such realisation. In studying it we are studying the ideal of our modern States : we are studying a thing, which is as much of to-day as of yesterday, because it is, in its essentials, for ever.

CHAPTER I

THE PRE-SOCRATICS, SOCRATES, AND THE MINOR SOCRATICS

Proverbial Thought and the Philosophy of Nature

§ 1. THE beginnings of political and of moral philosophy in Greece are to be found in isolated apophthegms (*ῥήματα βράχεα ἀξιομνημόνευτα*, as Plato says), the product of the proverbial stage of thought, in which single aperçus are tersely expressed in a brief sentence. The time has not yet come for the reflection which sees life steadily, and sees it whole; but experience has taught, or inquisitive eyes have seen, some facet of the truth, and the sparkle which has thus been caught has been preserved for ever in some saying. Such sententious maxims were dear to the Greeks; and in the tragedies of the fifth century there are still many to be found. But the stage of proverbial thought appears in its purity partly in the sayings of the Seven Wise Men, partly in the writers of elegiac or even epic verse. Here we find something of a philosophy, sometimes marked by a crude utilitarianism, sometimes by homely expressions of a deeper truth. The Seven Wise Men were for the most part statesmen; and scattered among their ethical sayings, such as *μηδὲν ἄγαν*, we naturally find political truths like *ἀρχὴ ἄνδρα δείξει* ("Office will prove the stuff of which a man is made"). Plutarch, indeed, in the *Convivium Septem Sapientium*, introduces the Seven Sages in the act of discussing the conditions necessary to the greatest happiness of a State, and he professes to give the opinions held by each of the seven. Plato tells us that the fruits of their wisdom were dedicated by the seven in congress to the Temple of Apollo at Delphi.[1] The Ampictyons inscribed their sayings

Proverbial philosophy

[1] *Protagoras*, 343 B.

on its walls, and they might thus seem to acquire something of the sanctity of a divine revelation. "In these celebrated names we have social philosophy in its early and infantine state."[1] The political sayings of Homer or Hesiod must have acquired an equal reputation. Homer is a believer in the divine right of monarchy:

> οὐκ ἀγαθὸν πολυκοιρανίη· εἷς κοίρανος ἔστω,
> εἷς βασιλεύς, ᾧ ἔδωκε Κρόνου παῖς ἀγκυλομήτεω.[2]

Hesiod rebukes in advance the Sophistic view held by the "kings" of his generation; and to their philosophy, "Better be wicked than just," he answers by an appeal to Divine retribution.[3] Among writers of elegiac verse the two who turned their attention most closely to political things were Theognis and Solon. The one represents the views of an aristocracy, with its sharp antithesis of "the Good" and "the Bad". He laments the overthrow at Megara of a nobility of birth by a mob "wearing the skins of goats, and knowing nought of dooms or of laws".[4] Solon, the legislator of Athens,[5] whom Athenians afterwards regarded as the father of democracy, told in verse the story of what he had done. It was not democracy which he had founded, but a "Polity," as Aristotle would have said, a "middle constitution" which avoided the evils of the rule of the Good, and yet did not give absolute power to the Bad. "I gave the people such power as sufficed, neither taking from their due honour, nor giving yet more: I gave heed that men who had influence and were famous for their wealth should suffer nothing unseemly: I stood with my shield held aloft to guard both the rich and the poor, nor did I permit either to triumph wrongfully." Here first appears the conception of a neutral and mediating State, which the Greeks were to seek so long, and in so many different ways, in order to escape the strife which raged between the sections of society. Not only the poetry of Theognis and Solon, but that of Alcæus and Tyrtæus also, bears the mark of this civic strife. If Solon had guided the

[1] Grote, *History of Greece*, iv., 23.
[2] *Iliad*, ii., 204-5. "It is not good to have many masters: let there be one master, one king, to whom Zeus has given his throne."
[3] *Works and Days*, 248-64. [4] Theognis, vv., 350-51.
[5] He is also counted as one of the Seven Sages.

State into its desired haven, Alcæus "cannot comprehend the strife of winds" which buffets the ship of state at Mitylene, where Pittacus is ruling as dictator; and Tyrtæus' verse is not only a trumpet-call to battle, but a political sermon in praise of law-abidingness (*εὐνομία*).

§ 2. The next epoch in the history of Greek political thought is that which is marked by the influence of natural philosophy. Here we reach the age of reflection. Puzzled by the riddle of the physical universe, seemingly composed of many elements, yet liable to changes which transmuted each one of these into another, men cast about to find the one identical, the single substratum of matter which underlay all the elements, and from which they all proceeded. This single substratum of matter, however it might be conceived, they called *φύσις*—Nature. It is perhaps too readily assumed, that before Socrates men studied Nature alone, and that thinkers were first induced by his example to study Man (*ἤθη*).[1] But the conclusions at which the pre-Socratics arrived about Matter were not mere theories of physical scientists dealing with a problem of chemistry: they were, to those who propounded them, solutions of the riddle of the universe. As such, they applied to the life of man as much as they did to the life of the earth. Conclusions with regard to the elements of physical nature and their mutual relations involved similar conclusions about the elements of man's moral nature and the connection of those elements—about the elements of the State and the scheme by which they were united. This step from the physical truth to its moral counterpart was perhaps made most readily by the Pythagoreans of the fifth century, when they turned the ritual of Pythagoras into a system of philosophy. The unity to which they had reduced physical elements was not a material substance, such as was postulated by most of the Ionic philosophers, but the more immaterial[2] principle of number. Such a principle was easily extended to the moral world of man's conduct. The under-

Pythagoreanism

[1] Aristotle, however (on whose dicta this assumption is based, *cf. Met.*, 987 b 1-4, 1078 b 17-19), while he speaks of Socrates as *περὶ τὰ ἠθικὰ πραγματευόμενος*, does not say that he was the first to turn to Ethics, but that he was the first to introduce definitions, and that he introduced them in the sphere of Ethics.

[2] It is true that the Pythagoreans regarded number as extended in space.

lying principle of that world, it might be argued, was also one of number, or the observance of number.[1] In this way the Pythagoreans came on their conception of justice. Justice was a number ἰσάκις ἴσος: it was a number multiplied into itself, a square number. A square number is a perfect harmony, because it is composed of equal parts, and the number of the parts is equal to the numerical value of each part. If justice is defined as a square number, it follows that justice is based on the conception of a State composed of equal parts. A number is square so long as the equality of its parts remains: a State is just, so long as it is distinguished by the equality of its parts. Justice is the preservation of such equality. But how is such equality to be preserved? By taking away from the aggressor, who has made himself too great and his victim too small, all the profit of his aggression, and by restoring it in its integrity to the loser. Hence the further definition of justice by the Pythagoreans as requital (τὸ ἀντιπεπονθός): with what measure you mete, it shall be measured out to you again. As the aggressor has trespassed, so trespass shall be made upon the aggressor exactly equivalent to his own trespass. It is obvious that in this conception of justice there is much which was to influence profoundly the trend of later political thought.[2] Here is the idea of the State as a sum of equal members: here is the idea of its aim as consisting in a harmony or equipoise called justice, which preserves the nice adjustment of the members. In the *Republic* Plato adopts this conception of justice, and gives it a

[1] For such an extension one may compare Plato, *Gorgias*, 507 E-508 A. Plato argues that moral selfishness (πλεονεξία) contradicts the physical fellowship and friendship which holds together earth and heaven, and contravenes the principle of geometrical equality. Plato seems to be contending, that as, *e.g.* the planets are kept together in fellowship by the fact that each keeps its appointed place, and does not violate equality by trespassing on that of its neighbour, so men should abide in a fellowship secured by the fact that each keeps his appointed place, and does not violate equality by trespassing to "get more" (πλεονεκτεῖν). This is just the teaching of the *Republic.*

[2] Burnet, however (*Early Greek Philosophy*, p. 317), regards the definition of justice as a square, as "a mere sport of the analogical fancy". But the same might be said of Herbert Spencer's conception of the State as an organism—which is, none the less, a vital part of his system. And it is especially easy to apply mathematical analogies to justice: *cf.* Maine, *Ancient Law* (p. 58): "The equal division of numbers or physical magnitudes is doubtless closely entwined with our perceptions of justice; there are few associations which keep their ground in the mind so stubbornly or are dismissed from it with such difficulty by the deepest thinkers".

more spiritual content and a deeper truth. Justice is an adjustment, but an adjustment which gives to each of the spiritual factors which go to form the State—reason, spirit and appetite—its right and proper place. In Aristotle's theory of "particular" justice the formal and numerical aspect of the Pythagorean conception is still more obviously present. The theory of distributive and corrective justice in the fifth Book of the *Ethics*, and the application of a theory of justice to commerce in the first Book of the *Politics*, owe something to Pythagorean teaching.[1]

Pythagoreans in politics

Thus, then, had the Pythagoreans helped the growth of political science by their application of the principles of natural philosophy to the State. A later generation assigned to Pythagoras himself the tenets of his later disciples, and believed that Pythagoras had attempted to realise them in practice. Tradition told of a club of Three Hundred founded by Pythagoras at Croton, which consisted of young men trained, like the Platonic guardians, in philosophy, and, like them, governing the State in the light of their philosophy.[2] The Pythagorean principle *κοινὰ τὰ τῶν φιλῶν* ("The goods of friends are common property") was interpreted into an anticipation of the communism advocated by Plato. We may, however, regard these traditions and interpretations as a later reading of Platonic ideas into the mind of "the master": *ipse* non *dixit*. The Pythagorean order was in reality a body of Disciples, meeting both to hear the mysteries of ritual and taboo and to join in vegetarian syssitia (the basis of the supposed communism), and interfering in politics, as it did at Croton, only because its members formed an aristocratic club, and because any aristocratic club would naturally try to influence the State.[3] In this indirect way philosophy (such as

[1] Aristotle (*Ethics*, v., 1132 b 22) objects to the Pythagorean definition of justice as mere requital. Such a definition disregards motive, in the sphere of corrective justice; nor is it applicable to distributive justice (which awards offices), because it disregards differences of worth. But he holds that "*proportionate* requital" is the bond of the State. It serves the State as the standard of its correction and distribution: it regulates the general dealings of the citizens one with another: it is the basis of commercial exchange, the buyer giving the seller exactly as he has received.

[2] Hildenbrand suggests that the Three Hundred were taught that the world was an order (*κόσμος*) in virtue of number, and were meant to influence the State in the direction of Doric *εὐκοσμία*. But Pythagoras was an Ionian!

[3] *Cf.* Grote, iv., 329-32; Burnet, *Early Greek Philosophy*, 94-95.

there was) may have come to influence the State; and the history of the Pythagorean club might suggest to Plato the rule of philosopher kings. It is certain that Pythagorean ideas were vigorous in Plato's time. Thebes had come under their influence: the Pythagorean Lysis was the instructor of Epaminondas, who called him father; and Aristotle tells us that at Thebes, "as soon as the rulers became philosophers, the city began to flourish".[1] Archytas of Tarentum was a famous Pythagorean of the fourth century, who for a long time was supreme in his native city, and served seven times as its general, in spite of a law to the contrary. A man like Archytas, general of his city, and also teacher of philosophy to his disciples in his garden-precinct at Tarentum, must obviously have served as a model for the *Republic*, even if the original club under Pythagoras was not present to Plato's mind. When we remember that Archytas was living at Tarentum, and Epaminondas at Thebes, in the very days when Plato wrote, the *Republic* begins to assume a decidedly practical aspect.

When we turn from the Pythagoreans of Italy to the Ionic philosophers of Asia Minor, and attempt to discover how far they too applied their physical conclusions to political speculation, we enter upon an obscurer theme. To what extent the Ionic school touched upon human life in their teaching and writings it is difficult to discover. It is possible, and it has

Heraclitus

been suggested, that all the works entitled περὶ φύσεως dealt with politics. Heraclitus' work on Nature is certainly recorded to have been written in three books, one of which was concerned with politics.[2] Yet the recorded utterances of Heraclitus upon politics are rather of the nature of disjointed apophthegms in the manner of the Seven Sages, than indicative of a political theory. That sense of the physical laws of the universe which led him to say that the Furies would track down the sun if it

[1] Aristotle, *Rhetoric*, ii., 23, 11.

[2] *Diog. Laert.*, ix., 5, διῄρηται εἰς τρεῖς λόγους, εἴς τε τὸν περὶ τοῦ παντὸς καὶ πολιτικὸν καὶ θεολογικόν. Diogenes adds that one of the commentators, Diodotus, held the work to be not περὶ φύσεως, but περὶ πολιτείας: what was said περὶ φύσεως was in the nature of an example or illustration. This view, however erroneous it may be, is interesting: it shows that a commentator believed that Heraclitus had made the transition from physics to politics. Apparently Diodotus made Heraclitus' work a prototype of Bagehot's *Physics and Politics.*

left its course, finds its counterpart in the saying that the people must fight for their law as much as for their city's walls. This parallel between the law of the world and the law of the State appears also in Anaximander, when he speaks of the physical elements as "suffering sentence of *justice* and paying the penalty one to another for their *injustice*," and explains thereby the phenomena of change. But Anaximander is here arguing, not from Nature to man, but from what he regards as the inevitable law of human conduct to Nature;[1] and the same may be true of Heraclitus. Yet there is some ground for thinking that Heraclitus argued from physics to politics, and not from politics to physics. He held that truth lay in *τὸ ξυνόν*, the common and identical substance of reason.[2] To this "the thinker must cling, and not to his own wisdom, even as a city should to law". All the more should a city hold fast to the law which was its *ξυνόν*, and therefore the truth of its practical life, because "all human laws are sustained by the one divine law, which is infinitely strong, and suffices, and more than suffices, for them all". Thus are human laws explained by the physical law of the world: the physical law vivifies the laws of the moral world. Laws are emanations of that one law: they are embodiments of the common substance of reason, which is fire. This line of thought led Heraclitus to adopt an aristocratic temper. "Though wisdom is common, the many live as if they had a wisdom of their own"; but "what wisdom or sense have the masses? many are evil, few are good". "The Ephesians ought to hang themselves: they have expelled Hermodorus, the best man among them, saying 'Let there be no best man among us'." Yet "one man is as good as ten thousand to me, if he be the best". Here we see something of a Platonic character in Heraclitus: the one man who has clung to the common (who has seen, as Plato would say, the Idea of the Good) is better than any many-headed Demos. And yet again there is something in Heraclitus of the Stoic cosmopolitan: the "wise man" is wise by clinging to the common unity of reason which pervades all the world; and the ideal State of such a man will be, in the long run, a State which embraces the world.

[1] *Cf.* Professor Burnet, *International Journal of Ethics*, vii., 328 *sqq.*
[2] This substance Heraclitus conceived materially as fire.

Some of the Ionic philosophers exercised an influence in actual politics; and it is noteworthy that here, as in regard to the Pythagoreans, there is no divorce between theory and practice, between philosophy and politics. When Plato and Aristotle busied themselves with writing practical works on politics, and even (it may be) with actual attempts to influence politicians, they had many examples before them. Heraclitus, we are told, refused to take any part in public life at Ephesus, but he was at any rate "king" of Ephesus, the priest of a branch of mysteries; and Thales is reported to have urged the Ionians of Asia Minor to unite in a federation with its Capitol at Teos.[1] The report comes from Herodotus: the suggestion of a federal State is remarkable. Like Thales, the Eleatic philosophers also exercised an influence in Politics. Parmenides is said to have given laws to Elea: Zeno, his pupil, is recorded by Strabo to have deserved well of his State, and is said to have attempted to defend its liberty against a tyrant. A like activity is also recorded of Empedocles of Agrigentum. He would appear to have been a democratic leader in his native city, and a champion of equality: he destroyed the caucus of the Thousand, and was offered but refused the position of king.

Natural analogies in political thought at Athens

It is when we turn to the Athens of the later fifth century, that we first find any real political thought, existing as a substantive and independent fact. However much attention the physical philosophers may have paid to political life, their political theory was but an off-shoot of their cosmology, and an accident of their attempt to find a material substratum out of which the world of change was produced. When we attempt to discover what Athenians were thinking in the later fifth century, we seem to see men reflecting primarily about politics and the world of man's conduct and institutions: if they turn to physics, it is "by way of illustration," and to get examples (which, they fancy, will serve as proofs) for their political ideas. Physical science had come to Athens with Anaxagoras, during the ascendency of Pericles, who may have introduced the philosophy of Ionia to Athens as part of a policy of imparting to the Athenians "something of the flexibility and openness of mind

[1] Aristotle illustrates his practical wisdom, in the first book of the *Politics*, by the story of the "corner" in oil-presses.

which characterised their kinsmen across the sea ".[1] Archelaus of Athens, a disciple of Anaxagoras, and according to tradition the master of Socrates, was, we are told by Diogenes Laertius, the last of the physicists, and the first of the moralists, delivering lectures on law and justice. Under such impulses it would seem that at Athens, somewhere about 430 B.C. or soon afterwards, physical analogies began to be drawn by thinkers who wished to defend the existence of the State in general, and the democratic constitution in particular ; for, as it has already been suggested, the defence of democracy is the natural beginning of political thought. Nature was conceived by these thinkers on a teleological scheme—not, however, as fulfilling an immanent end, but as having for its aim and object the setting of an example to man. In this way, the transition would appear to have been finally made from physics to ethics. If matter was still considered, it was only considered in order to arrive at conclusions about man. The results of the philosophers of Asia Minor, who had postulated some one material substance as the basis of the physical world, were so far adopted, that men argued from the example of unity which appeared in Nature to the necessity of the State as the condition of human unity. This line of thought was naturally opposed to the views of those contemporary Sophists, who were preaching, as we shall see, that the State did not exist by Nature, but only by convention. Here, on the contrary, the example of Nature itself was used to explain the necessity of the State. But where, it may be asked, is evidence for this line of thought to be found ? In the plays of Euripides. A German critic has disinterred, and reconstructed from scattered hints in Euripidean plays, a political treatise which he would connect with the period and school of Antiphon.[2] The motive of this treatise was a parallel between the order of the State and the order of the world, by which a State under the sovereignty of law was justified, and government was proved to rest with a middle class (consisting apparently of peasant farmers), similar to that which the revolution of 411 attempted to put into power. That Euripides should have

[1] Burnet, *op. cit.*, p. 277.

[2] The main passages are *Orestes*, 917-22 ; *Supplices*, 399-456, 238-45 ; *Phoenissae*, 535-51 (Dindorf's text). See Dümmler, *Prolegomena zu Platons Staat*, Basel, 1891.

versified a treatise on political science may seem curious; and yet it is only parallel to his introduction of Anaxagoras' philosophy into his verse. From his reproduction of the treatise[1] we find that it contained a vindication of equality and democracy against πλεονεξία and tyranny. Democracy may be liable to selfishness:

> Full of fine words, but set on private ends:

its members may be too ignorant, or at any rate too busy, to think of the common weal (the very objections which, as we shall see, Plato brings against democracy); but only where there is an equal law is there equal treatment for rich and poor. Night and day interchange equally on their yearly course, each yielding place to the other: so should there be equality and interchange of office in the State. A parallel passage from *Troilus and Cressida* springs naturally to the mind, in which Shakespeare (arguing, it is true, for inequality rather than equality) defends rule and subordination by the evidence of Nature:—

> The heavens themselves, the planets and this centre
> Observe *degree*, priority, and place,
> Insisture, course, proportion, season, form,
> Office and custom, in all line of order;
> And therefore is the glorious planet Sol
> In noble eminence enthroned and sphered.
> . . . O, when *degree* is shaked,
> Which is the ladder to all high designs,
> Then enterprise is sick! How could communities,
> Degrees in schools, and brotherhoods in cities . . .
> But by *degree* stand in authentic place?

Nor is it only in Euripides that traces of this treatise appear. As it has been conjectured that Aristotle used a tract of Theramenes, the contemporary of Antiphon, in the Ἀθηναίων πολιτεία, so it is possible to discover traces of the treatise used by Euripides in the *Politics.* When Aristotle justifies slavery by examples of similar subordination in Nature, he is following the old method indicated already in the fifth century.[2] In Plato

[1] The passage in the *Supplices*, 399 *sqq.*, is an instance of Euripides' method. Theseus and the Theban herald are made to indulge in an argument, in which the one attacks the tyranny of Thebes, the other the ochlocracy of Athens, simply because the herald addresses Theseus as tyrant, a title which he hastens to repudiate.

[2] Dümmler suggests that a history of the genesis of the State formed the preface of the treatise; and he refers the first chapter of the *Politics*, in which

too there are some traces of this early method of using Nature by way of illustration; and we find more than once in the *Republic* the use of physical analogies to justify political views. But in Plato political thought has become part of a whole system; and the State appears as a necessary element in the scheme of the world. There is no argument from physical nature to things moral or political; the two are not independent entities, but united as embodiments of one Idea, which constitutes both.

"The State is by nature prior to the individual," said Aristotle; and it would certainly appear, from what we have seen, that discussion of the nature of the State preceded discussion of the individual. It was natural that men should turn from considering the riddle of the universe itself (for Greek thinkers began with the greatest first) to consider next the riddle of a smaller *κόσμος*, and the meaning of the State. Nor should we expect the Greeks, believing as they naturally did that the State was a moral being and each citizen a member thereof, to begin otherwise than with the State, when they turned from things physical to things human. But with the Sophists we seem to enter a new atmosphere. In their teaching (at any rate, in the teaching of those whom Plato discusses) there is a detachment and even a glorification of the individual. Political thought seems to be sufficiently developed to run into individualism. A new and revolutionary spirit begins to appear. Hitherto the conception of *φύσις* had been used in a conservative sense: it had served to justify the existing order of things, and to sustain the ancient *mos majorum*. Pythagoreans had found in their interpretation of "Nature" a basis for justice: Heraclitus had been led by his sense of the stability of "the common" to emphasise the majesty of human law: the Athenian thinkers who had used the conception of Nature had found therein a reason for the State's existence. When we come to the Sophists we still find *φύσις* a current term; but *φύσις* is now subversive. Opposed to *νόμος*, or convention, it supplies a standard by which

a similar history is attempted, to a fifth century model. He also suggests that the treatise contained suggestions about the salvation of constitutions, and about the different kinds of democracies, which Aristotle followed. But his evidence is not conclusive.

the State and its law are judged and found wanting. How had this great change come about?

The State of Nature and the Social Contract

§ 3. The natural tendency of early Greek thought was one which accepted the order of the State and the law which it enforced without murmur and without question. Men were born, and lived, and died, under old customary laws, whose origin no man knew. It was dimly felt that they were divine: it was certainly recognised that they were rigid and fundamental. Custom was Lord of all things, as Pindar sang and Herodotus repeated after him. The sense of an inevitable order of human life was so powerful, that by comparison the life of the earth, with all its flux and change, with its lightning and tempest, might well seem incalculable and indeterminate. In human life all was appointed. You did *this*, and *that* followed. It was not so in Nature. "Man lived in a charmed circle of law and custom, and all around the world was lawless."[1] It was possible, as we have seen, for a thinker like Anaximander to attempt to import order into the physical world, by showing that there was a principle of "justice" in all its changes—by arguing from the undoubted fact of man's law to the probability of a law in the world. On the other hand, when thinkers had detected a law in the world, it was natural that they should use this law to illustrate and to defend the similar and equally inevitable law of man. But the process of history was none the less slowly undermining the stability of human order. Colonisation, which led to the formation, by human hands, of new States with new laws, was tearing men loose from the old vesture of custom, and unsettling traditional stability. A new religious movement came: a fresh ritual, a system of "mysteries," appeared, resulting, sometimes in the growth of new religious societies independent of the State,[2] sometimes, as at Athens, in an alteration of the State religion, which admitted the new ritual into its pale. Legislators became active in many States: a Solon or a Charondas gave laws to Athens or to

Disturbance of ancient custom

[1] Burnet, *Int. Journ. Eth.*, vii., 328 *sq.*

[2] This was the original character of the Pythagorean club; but it ultimately interfered in politics.

Catana. Here was an obvious making of law by man: was all law of a similar institution? Had legislators everywhere laid down laws (νόμους τιθέναι): had peoples everywhere adopted laws (νόμους τίθσέθαι)? If so, the conclusion was natural, that the State and its law was either the creation (θέσις) of an enacting legislator, or the convention (συνθήκη) of an adopting people. The State was made by hands: it was either the work of a Lycurgus, or a "contract" of primitive man.

Anthropology

While the process of history was leading to such results, the growth of human thought was tending in the same direction. New knowledge had been collected by travellers and recorded by logographers. Much was known of the customs of different peoples and tribes, and considerable attention was devoted to anthropology, in the Athens of the fifth century.[1] The idyllic usages of Nature's children, the uncontaminated Hyperboreans or the unspoiled Libyans, served social reformers as arguments in favour of communism or promiscuity. If a study of anthropology led to any scientific conclusion, it must have driven men, contemplating the infinite variety of savage customs, to doubt the existence of any natural or universal law. The laws of Nature are the same to-day and yesterday, in Greece and in Persia: fire burns everywhere, and at all times. But here were ten or a hundred different customs of marriage, or burial;[2] nor was there any one thing, it might well be thought, which was "common and identical" everywhere. There could be nothing here which was the product of Nature: it must all be the product of man. Law was a convention: the State itself was based on a contract.[3] Thus, while the study of physics had worked towards the conception of a single underlying substratum of all matter, the anthropological study of the human world worked towards the conception of an infinite diversity of institutions. The old relation was inverted: Nature abode by one law, and

[1] Aristotle himself, in the next century, was to collect a record of savage customs.

[2] Herodotus notes the differences of custom with regard to burial: Euripides remarks on the manner in which some people make merry over a funeral, and some make lamentation.

[3] The same ideas were applied to the problem of language, and attempts were made on the one side to show that language had a natural origin (φύσει) in involuntary exclamations, on the other to prove that it was a code upon which men had agreed (θέσει) for ease of intercourse. See Gomperz, *Greek Thinkers*, E. T., i., 394 *sqq.*

men hovered between many. Physics and anthropology stood opposed to one another; and their opposition issued in the antithesis of *φύσις* and *νόμος*.[1]

A new movement of thought in the fifth century, which also tended to issue in the conception of man as the maker of institutions, is to be found in the *Aufklärung* headed by the Sophists. A great war of national defence, like the Persian wars, must in any case have given an impulse to freedom of thought, by increasing both national and individual self-consciousness. "Proud of their achievements," Aristotle says, "men pushed further afield after the Persians wars: they took all knowledge to be their province, making no distinction, but seeking wider and wider studies."[2] In Athens this awakening, comparable to that of Elizabethan England, was still more vigorous than elsewhere. Political change followed close on the war of independence. The hegemony of the Delian league intensified Athenian pride; while the political changes which took place within Athens itself opened a free field for popular discussion in the assembly and the courts of law, and attached a practical value to ability to think and capacity to express one's thoughts. It was the work of the Sophists at once to express this new self-consciousness, and to satisfy the practical demand both for new ideas and for words in which to clothe them.

The Sophists

Broad and general as was the new movement, so broad and so general was the work of the Sophists who sought to be its teachers. Some are philosophers. Some again are grammarians; and they raise the fundamental question of the origin of language—"Is it of human creation, or a natural thing?" Some are logicians, eager to discuss conceptions like "the Same" or "the Different," or to argue upon the nature of predication. Most of them, and pre-eminently Gorgias, are rhetoricians, for rhetoric is what the young politician desires; and most of them, again, have views about morals and politics, for everybody is

[1] The *Antigone* of Sophocles indicates another path by which men advanced to the distinction of *φύσις* and *νόμος*. The law of the State forbids Antigone to bury her brother: a higher law wills that she should. "The unwritten laws, whereof no man knoweth whence they come" (*Antigone*, 453-57; *cf. Œdipus Tyrannus*, 865 *sqq.*) must over-ride the laws of the State. The problem of a "conflict of laws" seems to have attracted Sophocles: it recurs in the *Ajax*.

[2] *Politics*, 1341 a 30-32.

interested in such things. But these views vary from hedonism to a defence of traditional morality, and from an apology for tyranny to a defence of the reign of law. The Sophists are versatile: "they are the historical romancers, the theosophists, the sceptics, the physiologists of their day".[1] The acme of sophistic versatility was Hippias of Elis, who once appeared at the Olympic games dressed in garments altogether made by his own hands, and who was poet and mathematician, mythologist and moralist, student of music and connoisseur in art, historian and politician, and a voluble writer in every capacity. It was not *what* the Sophists taught—(for they were far from forming a school, or from holding one set of opinions: they were free lances, one and all)—it was the *fact* that they taught, that they were the first professional teachers of Greece, and that their teaching was meant to give practical help in politics, which made them what they were. To go to the Sophists was to go to the university—a university which prepared men for their after-life, and which—since that life was to be one of politics—prepared them to be politicians, exactly as Plato hoped that the plan of education sketched in the *Republic* would prepare his guardians. The Sophists have been called half professors, half journalists;[2] they were half teachers and thinkers, half disseminators of things new and strange, paradoxical and astonishing, which would catch the ear. With something of the charlatan they also combined something of the philosopher. In any case it was much for the future history of Greek thought that they should have systematised subjects like rhetoric or politics into a "method," or course of instruction. Such a systematisation did two things. It helped the differentiation of subject from subject, and the division of labour in the field of knowledge. It gave the idea of a scientific handling, on the basis of its own principles, of each of the subjects treated. The Sophists who systematised their courses prepared the way for Aristotle.

Protagoras and Gorgias

The increased self-consciousness of Greek thought appears first in the mental philosophy which the Sophists, Protagoras and Gorgias taught: it appears next, by a natural extension, in new theories of the State and Society, which correspond to the

[1] Dümmler, *Prolegomena zu Platons Staat.*
[2] Gomperz, *Greek Thinkers*, i., 413, 414.

new views of the human understanding. The alteration which Protagoras made was apparently, to use Kant's simile, like that of Copernicus in astronomy.[1] Instead of first determining matter, and then allowing his view of man to be determined by some view of matter, he brought man to the fore-front, and declared that it was man who was the determinant of matter. "Man is the measure of all things": it is man's seeing things as he does which makes them what they are. This dictum was not meant to deny the possibility of knowledge, or to make it the play of man's subjectivity: it was intended on the contrary to widen the province of knowledge, and to show that it was not dry bones, but full of human life, and instinct with human reason. It was intended to inculcate the duty of teaching and learning, for the good measurer must set forth his measuring, and the ignorant receive it accordingly. The "climax" of Gorgias is the reverse side of this doctrine: it proves the impossibility of the existence, knowledge, or teaching[2] of "Being," and by implication suggests that the proper study of mankind is Man. But to have emphasised, as the Sophists in their *rôle* of universal teachers were naturally impelled to emphasise, the part which man plays in constituting the world of knowledge, inevitably leads, in the long run, to a similar emphasis of the part which the individual plays in constituting law, the State, and human institutions in general. No longer will the State stand as unquestioned as the eternal hills, or still more unquestioned than they: problems will arise in abundance.

Man the maker

How did man constitute it in the beginning? Did he constitute it rightly? Is it in need of reform? Such questions were not indeed raised by Protagoras, if the myth which Plato puts into his mouth in the dialogue of that name represents his real views. On the contrary he seems to have believed that the law of the State was not of man's enacting, but of God's ordinance, though he held that the primitive association of men in cities

[1] The way had been prepared by "that Janus-like figure," Anaxagoras, who introduced νοῦς (but a material and universal, not a spiritual or human νοῦς) into the world: *cp.* Aristotle, *Met.*, 984 b 15-18. In the view here taken of Protagoras and Gorgias I follow Pfleiderer, *Sokrates und Plato.*

[2] Gorgias, orator and teacher, cannot have held that *everything* was "incommunicable and inexplicable". It is more natural to suppose that he, like Protagoras, was only decrying the physicists, and showing that his own teaching was what was needed.

was of human origin and created for self-preservation. But other Sophists did raise such questions; and the answer they gave was that man did *not* constitute the State rightly, and that it *is* in need of reform. It does not answer, they felt, to the sense of self-consciousness which had appeared in Protagoras' dictum. "Measured" by man, it is found wanting. It does not satisfy his instinct for free expression and fulfilment: it represses and stifles the full play of activity which is the real principle of moral life, the *φύσις* of the human world. In this way men came to reject the State and its law as anathema. Such things do not exist by nature, but by convention; and convention is altogether wrong.[1] "Law, being a tyrant" (the Sophist Hippias is made by Plato to say in the *Protagoras*), "constrains man contrary to nature."

The antithesis of *φύσις* and *νόμος* in the mouth of these Sophists meant, that the moral content of tradition and custom and institutions was opposed to the ideal code of morality suggested by the fundamental principle of human life. This opposition, it has just been suggested, is based on the fact that the principle of life is regarded as consisting in self-assertion, while traditions and customs and institutions seem to rest on an opposite view. Another basis for this opposition has been suggested,[2] in the shape of a parallel between the efforts of the early physicists and their results, and these efforts of the early moralists and the conclusions to which they led. The early physicists, when they attempted to find a permanent basis underneath all the flux of the corporeal world, always attempted to discover it in a corporeal body. Even the Pythagorean "numbers" were extended in space: even the Anaxagorean *νοῦς* had substance. But if the permanent basis of the world is corporeal, and the world itself is also corporeal—if the two are thus *in pari materia*, then one of the two must be unreal. In the result, the world of actual perception was regarded as unreal: the new corporeal unity denied existence to the world of sense. The fault lay in the conception of the *φύσις* of things as corporeal: if it had been regarded as spiritual, something not outside the every-day

Meaning of nature in the sphere of morality

[1] The distinction between *φύσις* and *νόμος* is attributed to Archelaus: he taught that "the noble and the base exist by convention, not by nature" (Ritter and Preller, 8th ed., § 218 b).

[2] By Professor Burnet, *Int. Journ. Eth.*, vii., 328.

world, but immanent and indwelling as a principle of life, such a result would not have followed. Similarly, when the early moralists attempted to find a permanent basis (φύσις) underneath all the flux of the moral world of man's life and institutions, they sought, not a spirit, but a code, of like material with the many codes which it underlay. It followed on this procedure, that the permanent basis of morality which they sought was conceived as annihilating the many codes and laws of actual life.[1] The relation of the ideal code of morality to ordinary codes could only be one of opposition: the latter were so many backslidings, so many perversions, of the former. Here again, as in physics, the fault lay in making the permanent basis as material and objective as the facts which it underlay, and in conceiving the "Nature" of morality as external, and therefore inimical, to the ordinary "Custom" of moral life. What thought should have done was to find an inner spirit pervading the sphere of ordinary moral life equally with the sphere of ordinary physical existence. And this is what Plato attempted to do in the Idea of the Good, though even he was so far under the influence of ancient views, as to tend towards the objectification of his spiritual principle.

But what will be the character of the ideal code, which constitutes the "Nature" of ethical and political phenomena? It will be everything which the ordinary codes, to which it is opposed, are *not*. Just as the "Nature" of the material world, being conceived as the opposite of ordinary objects, came to be regarded as spatial extension, or as pure but materialised Reason, so the Nature of the moral world, being equally conceived as the opposite of the ordinary rules of social life, came to be regarded as the mere pleasure and satisfaction of the individual. Thus we return again to individualism as the characteristic of much of Sophistic thought. When "custom," the complex of historical institutions and sanctions and rules, is rejected, it is rejected to make room for the free play of the individual's will and his appetite for power and pleasure. It is possible that the teaching of Heraclitus may have helped to introduce this fashion of thought,

[1] "If we look for ethical reality in one code of rules which are really binding instead of seeking it in that which gives binding force to the moral codes which already exist, we are bound to regard the latter as arbitrary and invalid" (*Int. Journ. Eth.*, vii., 330).

and to give a definite content to the abstract conception of "Nature". The law which he postulated for the physical world may have been applied by some of the Sophists to the moral world.[1] Just as modern views of evolution, which teach the survival of the fittest, may lead some to conclude that might is right, so the Heraclitean doctrine, that "struggle and strife is at the bottom of that incessant motion which is the source and preservative of life,"[2] may have led to the Sophistic teaching that "justice is the interest of the stronger". This principle of strife Heraclitus called "father and king"; and he applied the principle himself to human life, saying: "Some it had proved gods, others men: some it has made slaves, others freemen". Whether Heraclitus' theory of the world influenced the Sophists or not, we have Plato's word for the view that conceptions of the physical universe underlay their conception of human life. It is a materialistic view of the world, as without God or reason, which produces the theory that "might is right".[3] It would appear therefore that conceptions of the physical universe were now being used to support absolutely different political views. One thinker defended law and the institutions of democracy by analogies from Nature: on the other hand, there were Sophists who, on the strength of Heraclitus' views, or at any rate of some physical conception, attacked law and democracy, and preached the doctrine of brute strength and individual will. "Nature and natural law were on one side the chosen shibboleth of the growing love of equality; and on the other side they served the aristocrats and the worshippers of a strong personality."[4]

Might is right

In various ways we have seen that individualism is the gospel to which men were tending by the end of the fifth century. We have seen that historical processes like colonisation, the growth of new rituals, and the action of legislators, tended to unsettle the old feeling of the city's stability: we have seen that the study of anthropology, by widening the circle of men's knowledge and opening their eyes to strange diversities, exerted a similar

[1] *Cf.* Gomperz, *Greek Thinkers*, i., 72, 405.

[2] The Common and Identical was a harmony that underlay a strife of warring opposites. Men seized on the idea of strife, and forgot that of harmony.

[3] *Laws*, 889 *sqq.*; *cf. infra*, pp. 205-7.

[4] Gomperz, *Greek Thinkers*, i., 407.

influence. We have seen that a new feeling of self-consciousness may be said to appear in the teaching of Protagoras, which emphasises human agency in thought, and which may be extended to emphasise human agency in politics and conduct: we have seen how the attempt to discover a "natural law" in the moral world leads to a conception of right as consisting in might. We may now ask—what was the political theory which this individualism produced? We have to rely almost entirely on the testimony of Plato; but, so far as we can see, the theory in vogue was that of a social contract. In this theory the individualism of the present projects itself into the past. Because men are to-day fully conscious of their individual will and its claims, they begin to ask how it came about that the men of the past, who are imagined to have been equally conscious, surrendered the free exercise of that will and the full assertion of those claims. Such a surrender, some will say, can only have been the result of a voluntary act, by which men abandoned a satisfaction limited by the weakness of individual strength for the advantages of co-operation. Here we get the conception of a voluntary contract of each with all, which Plato presents in the *Republic* by the mouth of Glaucon.[1] The State no longer seemed as ancient and as inevitable as the earth on which it stood. No longer was its origin referred to a divine act of union which man might not dissolve. It had sprung from the interested action of ordinary men. It had nothing of the inevitability of a natural order, nothing of the sanctity of a divine institution: it had only expediency to plead in self-defence. It had come to rescue men from a previous condition of Nature, in which they preyed upon one another, and were preyed upon by the beasts: it had come by convention, but the name of convention was blessed, seeing that by its power men had been rescued from a "nasty and brutish" condition.

Social contract

So far, individualism does not present itself in its extreme form. It involves only two conclusions, which may be regarded as moderate—that there was an original condition of Nature, in which men lived as individuals according to their own good pleasure, and that there was afterwards an act of contract by which these individuals surrendered, in a conscious bargain, the

[1] *Republic*, ii.; *cf. infra*, p. 99.

free exercise of their own wills in return for the protection and preservation of their lives. In this moderate form the theory of a social contract stated by Glaucon may perhaps have been a tenet of Democritus. There are several reasons for so thinking. In the first place, we know that Epicurus in later days held the theory of a social contract, and as he was in many respects a follower of Democritus, it seems natural to suppose that he was following Democritus in his political theory. Again, we know that Democritus maintained the conventional or artificial view of the origin of language; and we are told that he attributed secondary qualities like bitterness and sweetness to "convention". What he believed with regard to language and secondary qualities may well have been his belief with regard to the State.

But what was the theory of a pure and extreme individualism? A pure individualism must reject, or at any rate revolutionise, the State; and the theory which has just been stated justifies the State, even if it justifies it for individualistic reasons. It would seem that pure individualism gave the answer which we should naturally expect. Its tenet was still a social contract—but a social contract made by the weak, who instituted the State in their own interest, at the expense of the strong. In its present condition—so men argued—the State violated natural law: it was a conventional thing, utterly artificial, and to be utterly overthrown. The genesis of such a view might be somewhat as follows. "Man is the measure of all things"; and man measures his self-satisfaction highest, and self-satisfaction is therefore his standard of action. Or again, "the natural law of the moral world is something, which tradition and custom are not": tradition and custom repress the individual, and therefore the natural law is the emancipation of the individual to a full licence of self-satisfaction. If each has thus a right to satisfy himself according to his powers (as either of these lines of thought supposes), it follows that the strongest have the greatest right, because they have the greatest power. The "natural law" is the greatest right of the greatest might. In a state of Nature this would be the rule: each would get his satisfaction as best he could, the strong man fully, the weak man feebly or not at all. But an instinct of self-defence drives

Superiority of a state of Nature

the weak to combine, as small birds will unite against a hawk, in order to get greater satisfaction for themselves, and to secure that the strong shall have less. This is the origin of the State: these are the principles which underlie its action—to exalt the weak, and bring down the strong. To the pure individualist they are utterly erroneous principles. The right of individual might is everything; but here the individual who is weak gets more than his powers warrant (πλεονεκτεῖ), while the individual who is strong gets less. The State must be reorganised on the basis of the rule of the strong: the "natural" state is a tyranny, where the strong man in arms governs as he will. This is the view which Plato makes Thrasymachus expound in the *Republic*, and Callicles in the *Gorgias;* and though Plato may have been exaggerating, it seems none the less obvious, that he was handling —even if he was heightening—conceptions which were actually current.

The gospel of the strong man is by no means dead, though the strong man is now generally conceived as a saviour of society, which he disciplines into order.[1] We shall meet with a discussion of the value of that gospel, when we come to Plato. Meanwhile we may notice, that the individualism which refused to spare the State was equally destructive of other institutions and beliefs. The very gods became creatures of convention. Prodicus taught that the first gods to be worshipped were man's personifications of Nature's forces: Diagoras the "atheist" attacked the gods in a set treatise: Critias spoke in the Sisyphus of the gods as the invention of wise men for the better security of social life—for the fear of the gods stopped the secret imagining of evil, as the laws which wise men had equally instituted stopped its overt manifestation. Slavery too was condemned, as we may learn from the verse of Euripides:

General iconoclasm

> The name alone brings shame upon the slave; [2]

and the Sophist Alcidamas in the fourth century re-echoed the condemnation, when he maintained that no man was by nature

[1] It may be added that in regard to international relations, the "strong" nation has always its votaries; and a *Realpolitik* regards the "natural law" which regulates the comity of nations as the right of the strong man armed. *Cf.* the argument of the Melian dialogue, Thuc., v., 85-111.

[2] *Ion.*, 854.

a slave. The difference between a noble and a non-noble class was pronounced as artificial as the difference between freeman and slave. Euripides writes:

> The honest man is Nature's nobleman;[1]

and Lycophron is said by Aristotle to have denied the reality of any distinction of birth—just as, we are told in the *Politics*, he spoke of law as merely conventional, and as simply "a guarantor of men's rights against one another". But the age of enlightenment went still further. Not only did it attack the apex and the basis of Greek society, the noble and the slave, as both unnatural: it also laid hands on such institutions of every-day life as the family and private property.[2] The position of women is a problem that occupies Euripides. In the *Medea* he makes his heroine complain of the lot of women as compared with that of men:[3] she would rather fight in battle thrice than suffer the pains of labour once. In a fragment of the *Protesilaus*[4] he advocates community of wives. It is obvious that there was contemporary discussion with regard to the emancipation of woman; and the Platonic solution which lies in communism, and in giving to women the same work as to men, seems to have been already anticipated. It is indeed obvious that the *Republic* is much indebted to all the seething of opinion which characterised the end of the fifth century at Athens. If Plato attempted to remodel the Greek conceptions of religion, he had Prodicus, and Diagoras, and—it may be added—the religious doubts of Protagoras, for his forerunners. If he sought to remodel society by the abolition of property and the family, he had his precursors in this field too, as we learn from Euripides. The Collectivism (if it may be so called) of his politics is a natural reaction from previous individualism; and the philosopher-king is the "strong man" adopted, educated and transmuted. The *Republic* did not spring at once to life, self-begotten in Plato's brain: it had its prelude and its preparation in previous

[1] Fragm. 345 (Dindorf).

[2] Probably comparative anthropology furnished something of a basis here: the different customs of marriage and property would be particularly striking. Aristotle in the *Politics* (Bk. II.) refers to Libyan customs of marriage, and to the practices of "some of the barbaric tribes" in respect of property.

[3] *Medea*, 230 *sqq*.

[4] Fragm. 655.

thought.[1] And if we find Plato in constant antagonism to his precursors, let us not forget his indebtedness. Not only did they furnish him with a starting point and a stimulus: they gave him also some of the materials which he used.

The Sophists and the Encyclopædists

In all this one is instinctively reminded of the period before the French Revolution. Like Montesquieu, the sophists seem to have loaded their discourse with piquant items of anthropology, though rather with the idea of upsetting laws, than of proving their growth from peculiarities of climate or national character. Like Rousseau, they have an idea of a state of Nature: to some of them it is a state of golden inequality to which we ought to return; to Rousseau, in some of his moods,[2] it is a state similarly golden, but golden in its equality, and to him too it seems the proper goal of "retrogression". Like the encyclopædists, they attack contemporary religion: like them, they raise the cry of Reason. No French Revolution follows on their teaching—for the simple reason that there is no *ancien régime*. They did not fire the blood in the veins of a suffering people: they held witty disputations before "rich young rulers". Accordingly they spoke not of the rights of man, but of the rights of the strong man; and if they appealed to any circle, and added fuel to any political passions, it was to aristocratic clubs and coteries, and to the old murmurings against the rule of the "accursed Demos". Here their "hero-worship" would find ready hearers: here, perhaps, lay its dangers; for here there were men to be found like the "young lion" Alcibiades, who hardly needed to be told of their strength or their rights. But it must not be thought that all the sophists were encyclopædists or *illuminati*. This was by no means the case. As we have seen, the Sophists were no school; and there were among their numbers many placid conservatives. Prodicus, who wrote the apologue of the choice of Hercules, was a preacher of ethics: he was famous in antiquity for his discharge of all his civic duties. Protagoras, like Plato, wrote a *Republic;* and Protagoras, the greatest of the Sophists,

[1] This is the point made by Dümmler, *op. cit.* Ideal States had already been depicted before Plato's time, by Phaleas and Hippodamus, *cf. inf.*, p. 44.

[2] "In some of his moods"—but in his greatest work, the *Contrat Social*, the state of Nature is a non-moral state; and it is the coming of the State (*un être moral*) which first gives men their morals. Here there is the idea of progress *away from* a state of Nature.

would seem to have been a conservative. It is true that he is said to have been banished from Athens for a work denying the Gods; but his work probably denied only the possibility of knowing the Gods, and if we may trust Plato's picture, he believed that, while men gathered themselves into cities for reasons of self-preservation, it was God who gave law and order to their cities. Nor would a revolutionary have been employed, as Protagoras was, to help in the founding of an Athenian colony. Like Prodicus and Protagoras, Antiphon too was a conservative, and he defended the type of democracy in which the middle class was supreme. His treatise *On Concord* had for its theme "the desire to conciliate the good-will of one's fellow-citizens"; and yet he is counted among the Sophists. The author from whom Euripides borrowed in the *Phœnissæ* and the *Supplices* was a defender of existing order and democratic government against the attacks of revolutionaries. If there were Sophists who were the friends of the enemies of the Demos, there were also Sophists (and if we include Protagoras, still greater Sophists) who were the friends of its friends. Nor indeed could the majority have been otherwise: they had to earn their daily bread.

Whatever the divergencies of view among the Sophists, they were all at one in turning from Nature to man. Protagoras and Gorgias, as we have seen, made the transition easy, the one by showing the impossibility of the old physical conceptions, the other by emphasising the part which man plays in constituting the world; and following in their steps, many Sophists had pursued the study of man in all the manifestations of his activity—in his politics, in his law, in his language. For the future, this was to be the channel in which thought would flow. That thought could not but be pre-eminently political. Man was too much tied to the State for any discussion of individual ethics: any philosophy of human action must be a "political" philosophy. In the struggle of contemporary parties, again, questions would constantly arise, which called for an answer, and made political thought a vital and practical thing. The busy study of politics moved in various directions. It was partly historical; and here political thought clothed itself in historical narrations or disquisitions. It was partly ideal; and men imagined Utopias which did not seem visionary.

Finally in the mind of a Socrates, it was active, reformatory, insistent, a matter of prophesying, a gospel and a testimony.

In its historical aspect, political thought appears in various forms. It appears in the set history of Herodotus and Thucydides. Herodotus reflects on varieties of custom: he compares the merits of monarchy, aristocracy and democracy. Thucydides gives us the philosophy of Greek στάσις: in the speeches, where he gives free rein to political reflection, he makes Pericles sketch the picture of an ideal Athens, or Athenagoras defend the principles of popular government. But the political pamphlet concerns us more closely than history; and many political pamphlets were written at Athens towards the end of the fifth century.[1] The first of these was written by a *littérateur* from Thasos, Stesimbrotus, who composed a work which dealt with Themistocles, Thucydides, and Pericles—a work which some have regarded as an attempt to estimate Athenian democracy by its greatest statesmen, and which others have viewed as a mere collection of political scandals. There is still preserved a treatise on the Athenian Constitution, once attributed—but erroneously—to Xenophon. It is a treatise written by a member of the oligarchical party, who criticises what he describes, and yet seeks to understand what he criticises. The characteristics of Athenian democracy are shown to flow from the principles of freedom and popular sovereignty which it has adopted; and a close connection is drawn between sea-power and democracy. In both of his contentions the author anticipates the *Politics*;[2] and the extent to which he has made general principles inform his record of details has caused his treatise to be called "the earliest model of the deductive method as applied to society and politics".[3] Yet another pamphlet on the Athenian Constitution, written from a different point of view, has been attributed to Theramenes the trimmer; and it has been suggested that the Aristotelian treatise on the Con-

Political Pamphlets

[1] For an account of these *cf.* von Wilamowitz-Möllendorf, *Aristoteles und Athen*, i., 161 *sqq.*

[2] For the connection of democratic characteristics with the principles of freedom and popular sovereignty, *cf. Pol.*, viii. (vi.), c. 2, 1317 a 40—1318 a 10; for the connection of sea-power and democracy, *cf.* vii. (v.), c. 4. 1304 a 22-24.

[3] Gomperz (after Scholl), *Greek Thinkers*, i., 500.

stitution of Athens, which we now possess, was based on this pamphlet. In it Athenian democracy was discussed in the light of its leading statesmen; and from their history it was argued that Athens would do well to substitute a moderate constitution for the extreme democracy which the Periclean age had produced. This form of constitution the author endeavoured to identify with the old "ancestral" constitution of Solonian times; and Aristotle may have been led by his arguments to entertain that preference for a moderate democracy (or Polity) which he shows in the *Politics*.[1]

Ideal Constitutions.

Alongside of histories and pamphlets recording or judging the present or the past come the attempts to sketch the lines of the future. Not only did men attempt to elicit political ideas from existing constitutions: they also tried to embody political ideas in pictures of ideal constitutions.[2] Such pictures were a natural result both of the tendencies of thought and of the practical needs of the hour. The attack on things conventional, and the praise of things natural, inevitably led to the suggestion of ideal States possessed of "natural" institutions. The anthropology, which had helped to produce the attacks on institutions like the family and property, now served as the basis of positive construction. The first ideal States would naturally be based on travellers' accounts of Nature-peoples; and even in Plato's *Republic* some traces of this basis may be seen. The practical problem of colonisation made these sketches less visionary than they would otherwise have been. The great age of colonisation was indeed past: the boundless field for political experiment which had been presented by the incessant foundation of new communities was by this time restricted. Yet there were still cases of colonisation, and still room for experiment. In 443 we find Protagoras acting as legislator for the Athenian colony at Thurii: at the end of his life we find Plato laying down the "Laws" for an imaginary colony.

[1] Critias, one of the Thirty Tyrants, who did Theramenes to death, was also a political writer. He is said to have written in prose and verse, treating of the inventions of various lands for the comfort of life (*cf.* von Wilamowitz-Möllendorf, *op. cit.*, i., 175).

[2] Accordingly, in the second book of the *Politics*, Aristotle inquires into the ideas of previous thinkers, like Plato and Hippodamus, as well as the characteristics of constitutions like Sparta, Crete and Carthage.

The dramatist Cratinus first sketched an ideal State in a comedy called the *Πλοῦτοι*; but the two chief writers of "Utopias" were Phaleas and Hippodamus, who both belong to the end of the fifth century.[1] Their views are recorded by Aristotle in some detail, in the second Book of the *Politics*. Phaleas of Chalcedon started, we are told, from a conviction that it was economic troubles which led to civil dissension; and he accordingly proposed the equalisation of property in land. In the foundation of colonies, he thought, this could readily be secured: in an old State, it might be effected by the regulation of dowries. The rich might give dowries, but should not receive them: the poor might receive dowries, but should not give them. The proposal may remind us of Mill, who similarly proposed to remedy the inequalities of property, by limiting the amount "which any one should be permitted to acquire by bequest or inheritance".[2] But Phaleas not only proposed the equalisation of property: he was anxious that there should also be equality of access to a uniform education for every citizen. A further feature of his scheme was that he wished to make all the artisans public slaves, possibly in order to increase the revenues of the State, more probably in order to prevent the competition of men, who had acquired different degrees of wealth by industry, with a peasantry settled on equal holdings.[3]

A more ambitious scheme was propounded by Hippodamus, a native of Miletus who had settled in Athens. He was a man of some pretensions, as we learn from Aristotle. An innovator in architecture, he was the author of the plan of cutting cities into square blocks by a system of intersecting roads. He sought for effect in his personal appearance: he wore his hair long and set with ornaments: his clothing, made of cheap

[1] Phaleas' date is unknown, but he would seem to have been an older contemporary of Plato (*cf.* Newman, ii., 283) and a little later than Hippodamus (Gomperz, i., 578).

[2] *Political Economy*, II., ii., § 4. A similar proposal to that of Mill is made by Aristotle (1309 a 24): in an oligarchy whose preservation is desired, property should be transmitted by inheritance, not by will or gift, and one man should only receive one inheritance.

[3] Newman, ii., 294. For Aristotle's criticism of Phaleas' scheme, *cf. infra*, p. 397, note 1.

material but warm texture, served him in winter and summer alike. He was a man of learning in physics; and it accords with his somewhat pretentious temper that he should have been "the first man who was not a politician who tried to describe an ideal State". He anticipated Plato in his division of the State into three classes: he differed from Plato in that his three classes consisted of artisans, farmers and warriors, while Plato's three were formed of a single producing class, a class of warriors, and a class of philosophic rulers. Possibly there is some imitation of Egyptian castes in Hippodamus' plan: possibly, as his use of the number three suggests, he was under Pythagorean influences. As he divided the citizens into three classes, so he divided the land into three portions—one sacred, and reserved for religious purposes; one public, and assigned to the use of the warriors; a third private, and left to the farming class. That he should have made the land which supplied the needs of the soldiers public property again reminds us of Plato's scheme—though Plato pursued a different plan, and, assigning all the land to the producing class, imposed on them a tribute in kind which the soldiers and rulers consumed in common. Both in providing a special fighting class, and in making its property the property of the State, Hippodamus may be said to have aimed at instituting a reformed government, exempt from the vices of the times—a government freed from political incapacity by specialisation, and from political corruption by communism. But in one respect he did not depart from Athens. The three classes of his ideal State in conjunction formed "the people," and the people elected its rulers. Here Hippodamus differs widely from Plato, who will have nothing of the people, and proposes that the producing and fighting classes shall be governed by a class in whose appointment they have no part. The laws, like the citizens and the land, Hippodamus divided into three classes, according as they dealt with offences against honour, or property, or life; and he similarly distinguished the administration by the three subjects of its action—public matters, matters relating to resident aliens, and matters concerning foreigners. He advocated the institution of a Supreme Court of Appeal, composed of a number of the older citizens appointed by public election. Finally, he proposed rewards for men who found out inventions which were of service to the common weal.[1]

Socrates and His Lesser Followers.

§ 4. From these reformers we now may turn to study the great figure of Socrates. "It is with men's desires that one should deal," Aristotle objects to Phaleas, "and not with their properties." It is man's moral nature that must be reformed, and not external things. In Socrates a reformer of man's moral nature appeared, a reformer who sought to make men think strenuously, see clearly, and act according to the vision of the truth which strenuous thought had given. The tendency of the Sophists' teaching had been to inculcate the maxim—Assert yourself: the key of Socrates' life and work lies in the motto—Know thyself. Where they had taught men to let themselves go along the lines of instinct, and to take everything which they could grasp, Socrates taught men to discipline themselves into knowledge, and to control themselves by wisdom.

Know thyself

> Self-reverence, self-knowledge, self-control,
> These three alone lead men to sovereign power.

Yet in contrasting Socrates with the Sophists, we must remember that in many respects he was one of them; and indeed his age, and later ages, called him Socrates the Sophist. The age of the Sophists had conclusively shown both the need in which men stood of a teacher, and the need that such a teacher should give rules of action. There had been a systematisation in almost every branch of knowledge. Cookery had been made into an art, and that art had been made the subject of a treatise. Protagoras had discovered some of the rules of grammar; but, instead of making these rules follow the use of language, he had sought to make language conform to his rules; and in the matter

[1] For Aristotle's criticism of this last suggestion, *cf. infra*, p. 325. He criticises Hippodamus' division of the State into three classes on the ground that the soldiers will always be the most powerful section, and will always control the government, in spite of the "people's" rights of election. He argues that there is no necessity for a separate farming class, as the artisans will live by their industry, and the soldiers already have lands of their own. He raises the question of the cultivation of the common land: if the soldiers cultivate it, they will not have time to be soldiers; if the farming class, they will be overburdened with work; if a class separate from either, then there are four classes in the State.

of genders, which seemed to him irrational and in need of reform, he had attempted to change current usage. Like cookery and grammar, the sphere of human conduct had been brought under rules, and made into the subject of an "art"; but here too, the rules were to reform and not to explain, and the new standard of "self-assertion" was to sweep away as irrational the old maxims of conduct, as Protagoras' rules of grammar were to abolish the anomalies of ordinary speech. Socrates attached himself to this "art" of human conduct. He drove home hard and direct the lesson, that a man should live by known rules; and so far as this was the burden of his teaching, he was a Sophist of the Sophists. But he differed from the Sophists in not attempting to teach new canons of conduct. Far from endeavouring to preach a new rule of self-assertion, which should revolutionise old standards, he sought to elicit from the ordinary conduct of men a clear conception of the rules, by which they already acted. He wished men to analyse carefully the duties of life, and to arrive at a clear conception of their meaning: he did not wish them to bring a new conception, acquired from some other source, and remodel life by its aid. It is as if, in the sphere of grammar, he had said: "Get to know the rules by which you have all along been acting—unknowingly, and therefore imperfectly—and then you will write better Greek; but do not bring some Procrustean rule, and chop the language till it fits your scheme".

To find out clear conceptions, which could be shaped into general definitions, was thus Socrates' aim; and accordingly Aristotle speaks of him as the first to introduce general definitions. But it was for no mere intellectual purpose that he craved for definitions: it was always for a moral end. A man who had arrived at a general conception and expressed it in a definition had made explicit the rules on which he had hitherto been unconsciously and imperfectly acting; and his life would be the better for his acting by a known and explicit rule. "Virtue is knowledge," was Socrates' great maxim: he who has come to know the rules, which have always underlain his actions, will be a better man for his knowledge. With this moral aim before him, Socrates lived the life not of a philosopher, but of a prophet, in the old Hebrew sense of the word. He was a teacher; but he

Socrates a prophet

was a teacher of righteousness to his people, burning with the zeal of his mission. As to the prophets of old, so to him, there came the whisper of a still small voice (τὸ δαιμόνιον) to inspire his work. As the prophets of old had sought to raise the standard of morality of their generation, and to bring men back to the old clear vision of God, so Socrates laboured among the Athenians. We must never forget that Socrates is the prophet and missionary of his times; nor, when we come to Plato, must we fail to remember that he too was of the school of the prophets.

A prophet prophesies without price; and unlike the Sophists, who taught for money,[1] Socrates taught freely to all who would come. For, again unlike the Sophists, who had taught the young nobility of Greece, Socrates spoke to every Athenian, in the street or in the market-place—wherever men were gathered together. A craftsman himself (for he had learned his father's craft of sculptor), he never despised labour; and herein he showed himself free from the prejudice, which even Plato and Aristotle still shared.

ἔργον δ' οὐδὲν ὄνειδος· ἀεργείη δέ τ' ὄνειδος [2]

was his feeling: he is not far removed from the sentiment of the Benedictine motto—*laborare est orare*. And thus his exposition touched—and attempted to elicit the general conceptions which underlay—almost everything in the nature of an art. In so wide a range it would have been impossible to teach by way of imposing new rules; nor, as we have seen, did Socrates ever think of doing so. Not to put knowledge into a man, but to draw out the immanent and implicit idea of what a man already knew, was his endeavour. Every man knew, after all, the tricks of the art at which he worked, having received the tradition in his apprenticeship. What no man had done was to think them together into one conception, or to see them together as making for one end. And so by a cunning use of questions Socrates sought to produce such a synopsis, and to elicit a sense of the end and purpose of man's activity.

In a sense Intellectualism was the key to his life and in-

[1] This is made a reproach by Plato. But the Sophists, who gave men the knowledge and the intellectual dexterity which won success in practical life, were worthy of their hire.

[2] "To work's no shame: the shame were not to work."

fluence. Heraclitus had said, "I have researched into myself": what Socrates said to every man was "Research—research into yourself: know what is the purpose, the general conception, which underlies all your actions". Whatever the art at which a man worked, let him know, and know yet again, and always know, his art and its meaning. Borrowing one of Oliver Cromwell's fine phrases, we may say, that Socrates loved a plain russet-coated Athenian, who knew what he worked at, and loved what he knew. Now men *do* know their professions, partly because they dare not do otherwise, for a bungler's job finds no market, partly because they insensibly contract a zeal for the subject with which they have identified themselves, and push forward in its study in the strength of that zeal. To work at a profession truly and wisely is much; but it is a little thing in comparison with true work in the conduct of moral life, or wise action in the guidance of the State. Yet paradoxically enough, Socrates felt, men are content to conduct their lives in ignorance, and to leave the guidance of political affairs with men who know nothing of "political art". Accordingly he made it his effort to banish this paradox, and to induce men to make of moral or political life a "profession" in the noblest sense of that word.[1] Why should not the moral action of the individual and the political guidance of the State, be regarded as arts, for which a man needs preparation, thought, and wisdom? The grave duty of acting wisely, by known and realised rules, Socrates proved by the simplest examples. The analogy of the steersman readily occurred. Could a pilot attain excellence or virtue[2] as a pilot, if he knew not the Pole Star from Venus, if he was ignorant of the currents, if he did not know his ship, or how she would answer the helm? And must not a man in conducting his own life, if he was to attain virtue or excellence as a man, know the Pole Star of his life, the gusts and eddies of his passions? Must he not know

Scientific thinking

[1] The Secretary for War has bidden us to regard the army as a nationalised industry, and to apply to its guidance the energy, the calculations, the spirit which we should bring to a private concern. This is purely Socratic. Socrates is the apostle of scientific thinking. "Put the State on the lines of a business, and your conduct on the lines of a craft; and before you do either, be sure that you know your business and your craft."

[2] It is important to notice that the Greek word for excellence and virtue is one and the same—ἀρετή. This has an important bearing on Socrates' thought.

"himself," and how far he would answer to guidance? Above all, must not the steersmen of the ship of State, the *gubernatores reipublicæ*, make some study of their subject, in order to attain political virtue? Must they not have some inkling of the "dim port" to which they should steer, and of the application of pleasures and pains, punishments and rewards, which would enable them to steer their vessel and its crew into the haven?

The analogy is to some extent false. Life must be lived by faith rather than by knowledge: politics often demand instinct rather than scientific wisdom from the politician, and in any case he can only guide whithersoever his subjects have the will to follow. But the analogy lies at the root of Socrates' ethical and political teaching none the less. In his conception of ethics the need of living by rule found expression, as we have seen, in a saying which seems almost a paradox—virtue is knowledge. One may say "this is only a formal answer: what is the matter of the knowledge?" So far as Socrates gave any answer, it was this—that the knowledge which constituted virtue was knowledge of what was useful or pleasant.[1] Providence had so arranged its plan—the order of the world was so established—that man by knowing his utility found his excellence. The answer is open to an obvious criticism. Life does not show this unity between virtue and utility. "The good which I would, I do not: but the evil which I would not, that I practice." Knowledge will not deliver us out of the body of this death. Nor again did Socrates explain what utility he meant. Was it a private utility, or was it the utility of all? As Pfleiderer says—"He never answered in words; but he served others till his death". In truth, however, it is not any teaching of utilitarianism, whether applied to the individual, or to the greatest number, that is of importance here. Such teaching is secondary—we may almost say accidental.[2] The essential thing is the demand for knowledge, not the definition of the object known. Apply this

[1] Here again we must remember that in Greek τὸ εὖ πράττειν means both to "do well" (virtue) and to "do well by yourself" (happiness). But this is not the root of the matter. Socrates identified virtue with happiness, because for *him* true happiness lay in virtue. Because it was true for him, he simply assumed as an axiom what Plato has to prove strenuously by long argument in the *Republic* (Gomperz, *Greek Thinkers*, ii., 69-73).

[2] But in the hands of the minor Socratics, especially the Cyrenaics, it becomes of great importance.

Aristocratic tendency of Socrates' politics

demand to politics, and it issues ultimately in that advocacy of an aristocracy of intelligence, which is the basis and staple of most of Plato's political thought. Hence Socrates objected to the filling of offices by lot, because it left room for the rule of ignorance. You shall know the true ruler when he comes, so he taught, neither by lot nor by vote, but by the fact that he knows how to rule. In the same spirit he objected to the rule of a sovereign assembly, where tinker and tailor, cobbler and fuller, sat together, and ruled Athens, and yet had never given a single thought to the meaning of politics. The anti-democratic trend of his teaching is obvious; and it proves the Athenian democracy not to have been altogether mistaken in its dislike of Socrates. It is true that he preached the unselfish rule of the wise; but when men like Alcibiades and Critias came forth from his preaching, it was the despotism of an emancipated oligarchy which the people feared, and, under Critias, experienced. No wonder that he was accused of corrupting a youth, which had rather corrupted his teaching, or that Æschines could say, years after his death, that Socrates the Sophist was put to death because Critias had been educated by him. He might well seem to be the hierophant of an aristocratic coterie; and the parallel might readily occur of Pythagoras and that aristocratic club which, having found its *raison d'être* in his teaching, had interfered in politics against the side of the people. Yet the suspicion is fundamentally unjust. Kings were to Socrates shepherds of their people, chosen, not in order that they might be good stewards of their own interests, but that the welfare of their subjects might prosper in their hands. This is the conception inherited by Plato, and enforced in the *Republic*. Politics is an art; the statesman is an artist; and since he who practises an art must be wise in his art, and pursue it whole-heartedly for its own sake, so must the statesman be skilled in political art, and practise it for its own sake and the betterment of his subjects.

In the Athenian democracy such teaching could not but appear new and radical, whatever its nobility. Yet in many respects Socrates was a loyal son of Athens. He had served in its army: he had been a member of the Council, even though he must have passed to his membership through the avenue of the

Socrates a Conservative

lot. The laws of his country were to him a sacred thing, not to be disobeyed, except for righteousness' sake; nor would he leave the walls of the prison where he lay doomed, even when escape was easy, lest the laws should rebuke his flight. His teaching is the very opposite to that of the Sophists. For him there was no rule of natural justice outside the law: law is justice, he held, and what is just is simply what is commanded in the laws. As the Just was one with the Legal, so again it was one with the Useful. What is just for man, what is imposed upon him by social morality, is also what is useful for him individually: the law, which contains justice, enacts nothing except what is for the welfare of every single member of the State. To it both citizen and ruler are subject: it is not the servant of the ruler, as the Sophists said, but the sovereign of both. Accordingly Socrates defined law as "the written agreement of the citizens, defining what should be done, and what not done"; and he cursed as impious the man "who first divided the just from the useful". As virtue was to Socrates one with utility, so was obedience to the law, or political obligation, one with utility too. It was profitable to obey the law, and there could be no conflict between public duty and private interest. Here again there appears in Socrates a harmony only too readily assumed—a harmony to which Sophocles had already made Antigone give the lie, and which Socrates contradicted in his own person, when for righteousness' sake he refused to cease the preaching which the State forbade.

And yet a Radical

So he died the martyr's death, because he introduced new gods, and corrupted the youth. The Athenian democracy, always "somewhat superstitious," had already proved by its expulsion of Anaxagoras and Protagoras that it could not grant liberty of conscience. To a State like the ancient State—both Church and State in one—any new religious beliefs, or disbeliefs, resulting in the formation of hostile groups of opinion, were in reality dangerous; yet Socrates could not think his way to any "general conception" of the gods which harmonised with traditional or contemporary dogma. The intense solidarity of a city-state could not admit religious non-conformity; and he had to die. While in his religious opinions he had undermined the solidarity of the city-state, in his ethical tendencies he was ultimately the enemy of its stability, however loyal he may have been in practice and even in his immediate preaching. Socrates the Conservative would ultimately prove the parent of Radicalism; and to that extent he *was* "a corrupter of youth". To defend the State's laws and institutions on the ground of their utility to the individual is ultimately to lay them open to being rejected or at any rate reformed on the ground of inutility. It is good to stimulate men to think in order that they may see the *raison d'être* and the meaning of existing order; yet a stirring and active thought is an uneasy thing, before whose questions ancient order may be dumb and perplexed, and a traditional temper of action may crumble and disappear. Even in Socrates himself such questionings had already appeared. He had criticised the lot: he had spoken with scant respect of the assembly. Nor was he only the enemy of democracy; was he not in truth the enemy, unconsciously, unwillingly, of the city-state? The outburst of philosophic thought which flowed from him was too broad for its bonds. Reason is a universal, not a civic principle. The Cynics were descended from Socrates; and the Cynics were cosmopolitans, who found their own reason sufficient for their needs, and, craving no city, took the world to be their home.

The greatest lesson of Socrates' life, we may almost say, was his death. He taught thereby (and Plato has elicited the lesson for us in the *Apology* and the *Crito*), that for conscience' sake a man may rise up against Cæsar, but that, in all other matters, he must render unto Cæsar the things that are Cæsar's, even to the debt of his life. Of positive principles of political philosophy his life bequeathed but little. He had not analysed the basis of the State, except in so far as he had made it rest on individual utility: he had not built any superstructure of theory, except in so far as he had attempted some slight classification of States.[1] But he had taught one great lesson—that politics were a matter of thought, and government a concern of the wise. It is a lesson eternally true—as true in democracies as in aristocracies. In it are involved the two great principles of government, that those must rule who have prepared themselves for their work, and won knowledge of their

[1] *Cf. infra*, p. 174.

Over-intellectualism of Socrates' views

subject; and again, that those must *not* rule who are animated merely by a class interest, and understand only how to pursue its attainment. But yet, one feels, this emphasis on wisdom is an emphasis of only half the truth; nor can we afford to forget —what Socrates left out of sight—those elements of will and of instinct which count for so much in political affairs. To the Greek, it has often been said, knowledge was more than will; and Greek ethics in general bear the same mark of intellectualism, which distinguished the teaching of Socrates. But in ethics and in politics the element of will is always an element to be considered. For the proper conduct of his life it is good that a man's reason should be enlightened: it is also good that his will should be habituated by moral discipline. For the proper guidance of the State it is right and proper that the wise should rule; but for its safety and its unity it is necessary that the will of the people should be attuned to their rule. Both are necessary; and both are *equally* necessary. Mere will means ochlocracy—the government of ignorance in the interest of selfishness. Mere knowledge means in the long run an intellectual despotism —a Strafford and the rule of Thorough. And as the element of will must count in the conduct of human affairs, so must the element of instinct. There is necessarily much that is incalculable by reason in all human action; and the right instinct (ὀρθὴ δόξα) which springs from experience must always command a hearing. This instinct Plato discovers, and admits, in dialogues like the *Meno;* but he rejects it almost as soon as it is discovered—for it cannot be transmitted by instruction, and it avails no man except its possessor. Accordingly, in Plato the intellectualism of Socrates continues, and even increases; and in Plato, therefore, the defect of the master's quality reaches its zenith along with the quality itself. Yet in criticising Plato and Socrates we must remember their environment; and if we do, our criticism is silent. They spoke of knowledge to a people which already recognised, and more than recognised, the elements of will and instinct. They spoke to an Athenian democracy, where the popular will expressed itself in decrees contrary to fundamental law, and where statesmen like Cleon pleaded instinct because they had nothing else to plead. Little wonder if thinkers spoke of reason, and reason only, in such an environment. They stated the half of the truth which was neglected: they omitted its complementary truth which had little need to be stated.

§ 5. The future progress of Greek political thought was to follow the lines laid down by Socrates. Plato is thoroughly his disciple: Aristotle builds on Plato's foundations. But before we turn to Plato, we must first consider the teaching in matters political of minor followers of Socrates, some of whom carried his teaching to conclusions very different from those which Plato drew. In Xenophon, indeed, the master found a loyal exponent of his doctrines, who extended the gospel of capacity to such matters as horsemanship, generalship, and domestic economy. Like Plato, Xenophon was biassed against the Athenian democracy for its lack of capacity: unlike Plato, he sought a remedy not in a new and ideal government, but in making Athens conform to an existing type of government, nominally Persian, but in reality Spartan. This type Xenophon sketched in the *Cyropædia*, an historical novel, in which the career of Cyrus is made the vehicle for the exposition of Socratic ideas. The State, we are here told, must be like an army, if it is to be as efficient as an army: there must be a proper system of grades, and a thorough division of labour. Over all things the wise man must rule, and under him each must do the thing which he knows. The *Cyropædia* enunciates many ideas which appear again in Plato and Aristotle. Laws must not merely aim at preventing crime: education must not be left to mere private enterprise. It was not so in Ancient Persia. There law was positive and creative: it gave the citizens a spirit of righteousness, so that they had no inclination to commit an evil or dishonourable deed. There education was given by the State, and lasted all life long. "The Persian boys went to school to learn justice, as ours go to learn reading, writing and arithmetic"; and the mentors whom the State appointed for their training were the older citizens, who had gone through their own course with honour. Somewhat in the same way as Plato does in the *Republic*, Xenophon sketches the four stages of the life-long education of the Persians in moral and military excellence; and then he shows how in such an environment was developed the ideal ruler Cyrus—a man who was wiser and

Xenophon's *Cyropædia*

better than any of his people, and made his people wiser and better than they had ever been before. Thus in Xenophon the old Greek idea of the State as a moral association is developed in the light of Socratic ideas; and the result is the conception of an education in moral wisdom given by the State, and of the rule of an ideally wise man produced by that education. These are also the Platonic conclusions; and indeed the *Republic* may be termed a *Cyropædia* without the historical setting of Xenophon, a *Cyropædia* informed instead by a deep philosophy of man and of the world.[1]

As we turn from Xenophon to the Cynics and Cyrenaics, who also sprang from Socrates' teaching, we enter upon an absolutely different line of thought. If Xenophon had entertained and expanded the old Greek idea of the State, the schools which go by these names abandoned it altogether. In them we see the heirs of that cosmopolitan tendency which appears even in Socrates. The Cynics[2] based their position partly on the life, partly on the teaching of Socrates. If Socrates had gone barefoot, and had talked with every man, high or low, so did the Cynics. If Socrates had taught that a man should know himself, and act according to his knowledge, the Cynics pushed his teaching further, and taught that the wise man, who had attained knowledge, was sufficient unto himself. Following and exaggerating the life of Socrates, they developed into mendicant beggars, something after the pattern of the early Franciscans, but with this great difference, that they embraced poverty not because they loved the kingdom of heaven, but because they hated the

Cynic cosmopolitanism

[1] For the *Cyropædia*, *cf.* Henkel, *Studien*, p. 136 *sqq.* Xenophon also wrote a dialogue called *Hiero* (apparently commending a dictator somewhat after the positivist pattern), and two treatises, one on the Lacedæmonian constitution, and one on the Revenues of Athens, advocating the nationalisation of the merchant-shipping, and of inns and lodging-houses (*cf.* Gomperz, ii., 134-35). Like Xenophon, Isocrates had apparently come under the influence of Socrates (*cf.* Henkel, p. 147 *sqq.*), but there is little trace of Socratic influence in his speeches. He starts from Xenophon's ideas that law is positive, and education is moral; and he finds his ideal in Solonian Athens, and the instrument of its realisation in the *Areopagus*. He appears indeed as an enemy of the lot; but he objects to it on the ground that it contradicts a true conception of equality, and not on the ground that it is inimical to the rule of wisdom. A true conception of equality is one which gives to each his desert; and the use of the lot disregards all considerations of merit.

[2] *Cf.* McCunn, *Intern. Journ. Eth.*, xiv., 185 *sqq.*

kingdoms of the earth. Socrates had criticised some of the institutions of democracy: they revolted against the whole of society, with all its grades and its institutions. They became "equalitarians," if one may use the word—the enemies of property, family, city, and whatever else involved degree, priority or place. One man was as good as another, and one place was as good as another: "Why should I be proud of belonging to the soil of Attica with the worms and slugs?" Denationalised by this spirit of revolt—"professing no city, or home, or country," they fortified themselves in their *incivisme* by their interpretation of Socrates' teaching. "Virtue is knowledge": it is an inward thing, and only an inward thing. External things are not manifestations of virtue: they are of the nature of hindrances. A man must leave all things and follow virtue: she alone is free. "External institutions are obstructions: all social interests are distractions." "He taught me," said Diogenes, speaking of Antisthenes, the founder of the school, "that the only thing that was mine was the free exercise of my own thoughts." The wise man, self-poised in his own *αὐτάρκεια*, thus became their ideal: the Cynic was sufficient to himself, and independent of everything outside himself.[1] To him all things were indifferent; and the State was a meaningless thing. If he acknowledged any citizenship, it was citizenship of the world; and that was no citizenship. Hence, it was said by Plutarch, "Alexander realised the Cynic ideal on its political side by the foundation of his universal empire".[2]

Thus was the city-state sapped, both by the equalitarian assertion, that every man is as good as every other man, whatever his political status, and by the cosmopolitan conception of the wise man sufficient for himself, and in need of no State to train him in ways of righteousness. The rational will of the individual superseded the moral association of citizens as the seat and home of virtue. We seem close to Christianity and the Church Universal; and indeed a continuous line of thought can

[1] Some idea of *αὐτάρκεια* we noticed in the Sophist Hippias, who sought to know all things and to make all things for himself. Heraclitus' "Common" brings us close to the conception of a world-state; and Prodicus in the *Protagoras* is made to regard all men as "by nature" fellow-citizens.

[2] Gomperz, ii., 161. There is a Cynic element in Plato's asceticism: *infra*, pp. 149-50.

be traced from Cynics to Stoics, from Stoics to the early fathers—a line of thought along which the conception of the independence of the individual soul goes together with that of a world-association of souls. The idea of a world-association was certainly present to the Cynics. A number of political treatises are assigned to their founder Antisthenes: he is said to have written *Concerning Law or the State;* and two treatises, a *Menexenus, or Concerning Rule,* and a *Cyrus, or Concerning Monarchy,* are also ascribed to his pen. Apparently he held that the wise man would not live in a State according to its enacted laws, but would live by the law of virtue, which is universal; while he believed that the nearer man approached to "the nature of animals" (a subject on which he also wrote), the better it would be for human life. We shall find Plato borrowing analogies from animal life in the *Republic;* and the Stoics often compare human associations to herds or flocks. As it is used by Antisthenes, the parallel of animal life serves to point the cry—Back to Nature: abandon cities, laws, and artificial institutions for all that is simple and primitive. It is the cry of the Radical Sophists: it is the cry of Rousseau in his youth. When we come to Diogenes, the greatest of the Cynics, we find a greater moderation, and a different atmosphere. In his *Republic* (if the accounts of its views which have been preserved are not coloured by Platonic reminiscences), he taught that the only right State was that of the world (*τὴν ἐν κόσμῳ*). He advocated communism of wives and children: he mocked at the illusions of noble birth and slavery. Advocating the destruction of the family, he must also (though we are not told that he did) have advocated the abolition of private property. But on the other hand he believed in the necessity of law, and he held that law was of no avail without a State. It would seem as if here we were confronted with the idea of a world-state, with a world-law (like the Roman *jus naturæ*)—a world-state in which all were equal, bond and free, Greek and barbarian,[1] and which must have been governed, because it was so wide and universal, by a single autocratic head. When we remember that Diogenes was

[1] Antisthenes was a Thracian: Diogenes came from Sinope. This perhaps suggests one reason of the attack on the Greek city; and it explains the Cynic teaching *omnes homines natura æquales sunt.*

the contemporary of Aristotle (dying the year before him) we cannot but feel that in his teaching (if it is correctly recorded) there is more of a sympathy for the contemporary movement of politics than we find in the pages of Aristotle. While the city-state lay dying, and while Aristotle busied himself with medicines and dietaries, Diogenes lifted up his voice, and cried—the King is dying, is dead: long live the new King of the world.

At the beginning of the *Politics* we find something of an attack on the Cynics: the man who thinks he can exist without a city is either a beast or a God. In truth the Cynics figured alternately as either—sometimes as Gods, creatures of pure reason, untroubled by passion, sufficing to themselves; sometimes as beasts, in the squalor and indecency into which they flung themselves in order to point their protest against the "conventional" character of all clean living and decency. But while Aristotle attacks the Cynics, he borrows from their ideas. His watchword too is *αὐτάρκεια*—self-sufficingness—exactly as that of the Cynics had been. But the Cynics had believed in the *αὐτάρκεια* of an isolated and minimised self: Aristotle believed in that of a social and intensified individuality. Man is only sufficient to himself, in Aristotle's eyes, when he is citizen. Yet, on the other hand, it is in order to attain self-sufficiency that he widens himself out into a citizen. In Plato, as in Aristotle, the influence of the Cynic is not absent. The community of children and wives is a Cynic tenet; and there are many points of contact between the Cynic ideal and the "city of Swine" described in the Second Book of the *Republic*, even if there is no allusion to the Cynics, and Plato does not intend to satirise, or eulogise, their views.

The Cyrenaics

The Cynics made individualism the centre of their system: they believed that the individual was sufficient of himself to do his own duty. The Cyrenaic School, equally descended from Socrates, pursued the same individualistic direction. He who knew, as Socrates had bidden men know, was sufficient in their view for his own salvation; but his salvation lay, according to their tenets, in the pursuit of pleasure.[1] Finding the

[1] Or perhaps one may say that the Cyrenaics followed the utilitarianism of Socrates, while the Cynics followed his intellectualism. But the antithesis is perhaps misleading; intellectualism also characterised the Cyrenaics.

standard of life in the cult of a wise pleasure, the Cyrenaics no longer needed the State to supply any rule of action. Philosophy was good, Aristippus is reported to have said, "to enable the philosopher, supposing all laws were abolished, to go on living as before". Thus the Socratic justification of law as useful, and thereby pleasurable, came ultimately to undo the law which it had served to justify. Because utility was the basis of law, it might serve in lieu of the law. Law was a mere convention, said the Cyrenaics: right and wrong existed by custom and enactment, not by nature. Yet they did not abolish the law to make room for a private pleasure which was its enemy. On the contrary, they conceived that a man might find pleasure in the welfare of his friend or of his country. "The prosperity of our country, equally with our own, is of itself enough to give us joy." The Hedonism of an individual enjoyment thus rose into the Utilitarianism of a general welfare. But the general welfare, in the ordinary Cyrenaic view, was the welfare not of the *πόλις* but of the Cosmopolis. It is with the lover of pleasure as it is with the zealot for duty. Both regard the individual as sufficient, whether to measure his own pleasure, or to discern his own duty. Both regard a wise indifference to externals as necessary for the attainment of the desired end. If a man gives to fortune the hostages of a living interest in anything save the end of life, he may fail to attain it. Both, therefore, deny to the individual an interest in any civic unit; and both leave man with the negative residuum of an interest in the world, and the world alone. A full and active life which realised all possibilities was to Aristotle the result of life in the city: along with citizenship of the world-state went the idea of the calm of a solitude (*ἀπάθεια* or *ἀταραξία*), in which there was none of the struggle and strife, and none of the vigour and life, of the *πόλις*. Such a temper may partly have prepared the decay of the city and the coming of "Alexandrinism": on the other hand, it is also its expression and its result.

CHAPTER II

PLATO AND THE PLATONIC DIALOGUE: THE DEFENCE OF SOCRATES

The Life of Plato

§ 1. PLATO was born about the year 428 B.C. By birth he belonged to a distinguished Athenian family. On his mother's side he could trace his pedigree as far back as Solon, the great law-giver of Athens; and among the men of his own generation he counted as connections two of some note—Critias, who was prominent among the members of the oligarchical clique which ruled for a time in 404, and Antiphon, who had been one of the leaders in the revolution which temporarily subverted Athenian democracy in 411. Belonging to a family of anti-democratic tendencies, he naturally became a member, somewhere about 407, of the circle which had gathered round Socrates. Here too democracy was out of favour. The Socratic principle, that life was an art, and that the proper conduct of life depended on knowledge, found, as we have seen, its political application. Politics was treated as an art: the proper conduct of political affairs was shown to depend on knowledge —a knowledge which neither the democratic assembly itself, nor the officials whom it appointed by the chance of the lot, could be said to possess. The aristocratic prejudices which Plato inherited would here receive a philosophical justification; at the same time they would be modified, in so far as the right of numbers was rejected by Socrates, not in favour of birth, but in favour of wisdom. When democracy took its revenge upon Socrates in 399, and Athens executed her greatest son, Plato might well feel his anti-democratic feelings completely justified. Henceforth he made it his work to defend

Plato and Socrates

the fame, and to continue the teaching, of his dead master. For nearly fifty years his pen was busy with those dialogues whose literary form itself seems reminiscent of the conversations and discussions of the Socratic circle, and whose matter is an expounding, and expanding, of Socratic views. Of these the *Apology* for Socrates is naturally the first, the *Laws* the last; midway between the two, as the summit of Plato's art and thought, stands the *Republic*. Other influences than that of Socrates had gone to the making of Plato's thought before the years in which he wrote the *Republic*, or rather they had united with that of Socrates to produce the peculiar doctrines of Plato.[1] From a passage in the *Metaphysics* of Aristotle[2] we learn that Plato had been conversant from his youth with the doctrine of Heraclitus, that all sensible things are in a state of perpetual flux, and cannot be objects of knowledge. But from the Eleatic school he had also learned that there is a unity behind the phenomena of sense, which is discernible by reason; and he had learned a similar lesson from Socrates. For Socrates, believing that the proper study of mankind was man, and neglecting the physical universe to which the Eleatic school devoted its attention, had conceived that the knowledge which was so greatly to be desired in human affairs might be to some extent attained, if only general definitions of the qualities and actions of men could by some means be formed. In this way would Aristotle explain the genesis of Plato's theory of Ideas, in which the *Republic*, starting primarily from the purely Socratic conception of politics as an art, may be ultimately said to culminate. But—whatever be the advance of Plato's theory upon that of Socrates (if one may speak of a Socratic "theory")—in one cardinal respect Plato always remained entirely true to the mind of his master. He never lost that bent towards a practical reform of man, and of human society, which is the distinguishing mark of Socrates. We have seen that it would be entirely a mistake to regard Socrates as a

Plato a Practical Reformer

[1] Possibly travel may have counted for much in Plato's development. He is said to have visited Egypt and Magna Græcia after Socrates' death. From Egypt he may have learned to value the division of labour among a number of castes, and by his Egyptian experiences we may explain some features of the *Republic*. In Magna Græcia (Lower Italy and Sicily) he would come across Archytas, the philosopher who was also a politician; and this again would suggest another of the features of the *Republic*.

[2] *Metaphysics*, A. 987 a 29-b 10.

mere philosopher; the same is true of Plato. Both master and disciple are prophets and preachers, rather than philosophers—trumpets to summon a wayward people to righteousness, rather than still small voices of solitude. The *Republic* is as much meant to prove, and as earnest in proving, that the eternal laws of morality cannot be shaken by the sceptic, as are the writings of the Hebrew prophets to show that God's arm is not shortened by the disbelief of His people. In life, as well as in thought, Plato showed the same practical bent. Not only did he, like Socrates, gather a circle round him, and publicly teach his views in the *Academy*,[1] but he is also said to have attempted to carry his philosophy into active life (as, according to the *Republic*, every philosopher should), and to have twice visited Sicily with that end in view. On an early visit in 387, we are told, he came into contact with Dionysius, the tyrant of Syracuse, and expounded to him so vividly arguments similar to those of the *Republic* (the composition of which may have been already begun), that Dionysius, annoyed by his denunciation of injustice and condemnation of tyranny, caused him to be sold into slavery. But Plato did not leave Syracuse without having deeply influenced the mind of Dion, the brother of Dionysius' wife; and on the death of Dionysius, and the accession of his son, Dionysius the younger, Dion endeavoured to permeate the mind of his nephew with Platonic ideas. The State of the *Republic* might seem likely to be realised in Syracuse, if Dionysius could once be made philosopher-king instead of tyrant; and Dion invited, and induced his nephew to concur in inviting, the master himself, now long released from his slavery, to visit Syracuse once more. Plato came not only once, but twice (368 and 361); but he failed to make Dionysius a philosopher (having apparently required that he should undergo the severe training sketched in the *Republic*), and only succeeded in bringing about the expulsion of Dion from Syracuse. If all these things happened as they are narrated in Plutarch and the (so-called) letters of Plato, the issue may well have convinced Plato that the *Republic* (which he had written, perhaps,

[1] A gymnasium about three-quarters of a mile from Athens. Gymnasia covered a wide area, and contained open spaces like a modern park. Around the open running-ground were porticoes, furnished with seats, in which philosophers or rhetoricians might discourse.

between 387 and 368, and attempted to realise between 368 and 361) was indeed a pattern laid up in heaven, but hardly to be copied on earth. Disillusionised, it may be, he retired for a time upon the problems of abstract thought discussed in dialogues like the *Sophist*. But the old practical bent was not extinguished: in extreme old age, in a spirit of kindly tolerance and half-humorous sadness (as when he speaks of men as "merely playthings for the gods"), he wrote the *Laws*. In this dialogue (which is almost entirely a monologue, and shows something of the garrulity of age), he sketches the idea, destined to a long history in Greek speculation, of a mixed constitution, and while still adhering firmly to the ideal of the *Republic*, attempts to construct a State on a lower but more attainable level. And so he died, about 347, at the age of eighty-one, still occupied in the service of man, still hoping for new things to come, still striving his best to aid their coming.

The Method of Plato

§ 2. The memory of Socrates seems to live in everything which Plato wrote. Until we come to the *Laws*, there is not a Platonic dialogue in which Socrates is not a character, and indeed a protagonist. Not only so, but the thought of the dialogues, wherever politics and ethics are in question, is Socratic in its principles; and the very form of dialogue which Plato chose for the expression of his philosophy may seem in itself a reminiscence of the Socratic circle. At any rate the purpose, which leads Plato to prefer that form, is the purpose which animated Socrates. Socrates had never attempted to instil knowledge: on the contrary, he had always disclaimed its possession. He desired to awaken thought. He was the gadfly who stung men into a sense of truth; he gave the shock of the torpedo-fish; he practised the art of midwifery, and brought thought to birth. He appealed to what was in man's own mind, and trusted it to respond to the appeal: he called to the moral sense of man, believing that it would reply to the call. And so it was with Plato. He desired to show thought at work, and to avoid the mere exposition of its finished product. He was a lecturer and a teacher as well as a writer; and when he set pen to paper, he would naturally fall into the vein of writing which discussions with his class in the Academy suggested.

The use of the dialogue

Like every genuine teacher, he wished to make men think by his teaching; and, as a writer, he felt that thought would best be awakened in his readers, if they were made to follow the process of the author's own mind. A subject is discussed inside the individual mind in much the same way as it is disputed in a circle of talkers. One view is set up only to be demolished by another, until some final residuum of truth is attained. "One shrewd thought devours another," as Hegel said; and finally truth alone remains on the field as a victor. The dialogue is this process of the individual mind made concrete, with its stages translated into persons. It is a higher, and more artistic expression of the same tendency, which appears even in the concise lecture-notes of Aristotle.

Criticism of common opinion

Dealing with moral problems, Plato naturally started from the *prima facie* views of ordinary opinion.[1] Some character, who with dramatic truth is presented as being in himself, and by his temper and experience, the natural embodiment of one of these views, appears on the stage and gives it utterance. Often such a *prima facie* view will represent one of those lurking principles, which we do not allow to show themselves in our words or in our actions (as we fancy), but to which none the less we pay an unspoken but ready allegiance. "After all—if I dared think it out, which I must not—pleasure *is* everything": or "after all—if things were as they ought to be, which they are not—I *ought* to have what I am strong enough to get". Brought to the light, and pushed to their conclusions, these lurking principles are shown to involve results which their holder cannot accept: when they *are* thought out, they are impossible. And in their place are installed those principles of moral life, to which we pay a spoken but reluctant homage, while nevertheless they are shown to command the assent of our whole being, when they are put before us in their full meaning and bearing. Seen in this light, each of the Platonic dialogues is an education of men, away from the false if cherished views of the "first blench," back again, but on a higher level, to the faith by which they act. But it is not always that popular opinion is presented only to be rejected. Opinion is more than a mere inclination to

[1] *Cf. infra*, p. 94 *sqq.*

error. By a right instinct it also reaches the truth, though it does not really see the truth which it reaches. A popular opinion may serve as a basis of inquiry, and by gradual stages be developed and refined, until it is made into a perception of the genuine truth. It is a true opinion, and worthy of consideration, that the character of a State is determined by the character of its citizens; and from this opinion the *Republic* (after correcting the false opinion that might is right) ultimately takes its start. But the opinion is extended far and wide. Brought into contact with philosophic principles, it is developed and deepened until there results a division of the State corresponding to a division of the human soul which is one of the preconceived principles of Plato's philosophy.

Use of analogy

A particular feature of Plato's method is his use of analogy. We have already seen that the use of analogies from *Nature* marked the first steps from the old Nature-philosophy to the philosophy of man, as when, for instance, the rotation of office in a democracy was justified by the annual revolution of the sun. Analogies from the *arts* were frequent in the method of Socrates: he was perpetually enforcing the need of knowledge and of education by the example of the pilot or the doctor. In Plato analogies of both kinds are frequent. His analogies from Nature are chiefly analogies drawn from the animal world. In the *Republic* the analogy of the dog is more than once made the basis of important arguments. By considering the temper of the watch-dog, Plato arrives at the principle which should dictate the choice of guardians; by a comparison of the male watch-dog with the female, he is able to decide that women ought to be guardians as well as men; and it is by an argument from the breeding of animals that he comes upon his peculiar theory of marriage. The same use of analogies from Nature characterises at least one passage in the *Politics* of Aristotle. It is from the analogy of Nature, and of the relation of animals to men, that Aristotle attempts to justify slavery as a natural institution, and to prove the propriety of the slave's relation to his master.

But it is the Socratic use of analogies drawn from the arts which appears most prominently in Plato. The conception of politics as an art, on which the Sophists had acted when they had professed to make politics, like medicine, a subject of teaching, and which Socrates had made into the basis of his demand for knowledge, penetrates almost everything which Plato has to say on this subject. Conceiving politics as an art, he demanded that in this art, as in others, there should be knowledge. This is perhaps the most prominent feature in the whole of his political thought; and the demand that, on the analogy of all other "artists," the statesman should know what he practised, lies at the root of the Republic. The same conception of politics led Plato still further. Because every artist ought to be unfettered in the practice of his art by any body of rules, he believes that the statesman should ideally be free from the restraint of law; and he advocates in consequence a theory of absolute monarchy. Finally, in the strength of this conception he can prove that every ruler is set to rule *propter commune bonum;* since every artist must necessarily work, if he be a true artist, for the betterment of his art's object.

Dangers of analogy

The use of analogy is difficult, and false analogies are easy. It can hardly be denied that Plato did not always surmount the difficulty, or that he sometimes fell into pitfalls. The analogies from the animal world which he employs can hardly be accepted: the continuation of the human species cannot be regulated by the same considerations which regulate the breeding of animals. A whole world of spiritual motives enters into the one, which is not present in the other; and the whole analogy breaks down for want of recognition of this fact. Nor is the use of analogies drawn from the arts free from criticism. The politician, after all, is not as the physician; and if the one should do his work without the shackles of a text-book, it does not follow that the other should act without the regulation of law. The treatment of the soul involves other considerations than those which guide the treatment of the body, and in many respects, as for instance in his theory of punishment, Plato is not sufficiently alive to their presence. But while we condemn the treatment of political questions according to analogies drawn from physical arts, we must not forget the cardinal position of Plato. Politics is not *like* the arts: it *is* an art. There is identity rather than analogy. Yet criticism is still possible. Politics, if an art itself, must not be simply conformed to the likeness of arts other than itself.

Of the analogy between man and the State which plays such a large part in the *Republic* much the same may be said. Here again there is identity rather than analogy. The virtues of the State are not *like* those of man: the virtues of the State *are* the virtues of the men of whom it is composed. Yet the criticism is possible, and perhaps just, that in the end Plato conforms the State too much to the image of a single man; for though its virtues are the virtues of its component members, it does not follow that its classes must correspond, as by Plato they are made to correspond, to the psychological divisions of its members' minds.

The Lesser Dialogues of Plato

§ 3. The three great dialogues of Plato which deal with problems of political thought are the *Republic*, the *Politicus*, and the *Laws*. But there are few dialogues into which some question which touches politics does not enter. The *Apology* and the *Crito*, in dealing with the life and death of Socrates, raise problems of the relation of the State to the individual. The *Meno*, in discussing knowledge and instruction, necessarily discusses the nature of political knowledge and the possibility of instruction in politics. A similar problem is treated in the *Protagoras*, and the *Gorgias* contains a discussion of the questions raised by the teaching of the Sophists, a teaching which, as we have seen, was almost entirely political in character and intention. Finally, in the *Critias*, Plato begins, but never finishes, a political novel describing the state of the *Republic* in action.

The *Apology*: a defence of resistance

The *Apology* is an attempt to justify Socrates. Suspected by the democrats of being the head of an aristocratic coterie, he had been accused of corrupting the youth, and of disbelieving in the gods of the State. There was a certain truth in this accusation. Feeling the evil of an ignorance which pretended to be knowledge, Socrates had made himself into a missionary for the destruction of shams; and (since what he conceived to be shams were of the essence of the Athenian constitution) he had unsettled the tone and temper of the State in which he lived. The problem which confronted him at his trial was the problem of Antigone, when Creon had issued his edict against the burial of her brother Polynices. Should obedience be paid to the will of the State, or to the sense of justice with which it conflicted? Should Athens be left in her ignorance, because the law would be obeyed by conformity to the wishes and will of her citizens, or should Socrates satisfy his sense of what was right by open warning and denunciation? It is the question which has always confronted the martyr; and in the spirit of a martyr Socrates gives his answer. "This is the command of God. Acquit me or condemn me: I shall never alter my ways."[1] In the name of something higher than the law of the State, he defies the law, as men have done in all ages. But this is only one side of the matter; and another and complementary side is presented in the *Crito*.[2] In this dialogue Plato supposes that Socrates is tempted by Crito to escape from the prison, in which he lies, condemned to death for the answer he has given. If he escapes, he will again disobey the law, which has commanded him to abide in prison until death, and to die there for his first disobedience. Shall he twice sin against the law? No. If he had been forced to defy it once for conscience' sake, he will not defy it again for life's sake. He has already done a grievous thing; he has gone about to overturn the law. He will now by his obedience recognise its claims, and as far as in him lies, he will help to establish its sanctity. In teaching this lesson, Plato imagines a dialogue between the Laws of Athens and Socrates. "So you imagine," the Laws inquire of Socrates, "that a State can subsist in which the decisions of the law must yield to the will of individuals?" "But the decision of the law in my case was unjust." "But the law has none the less a double claim on your obedience." And then Plato expounds the nature of this double claim. In the first place, the law, regulating as it does marriage and the nourishing and education of children (and Socrates admits that he has no objection to urge against this action of law), is in a real sense the parent of every citizen. By law the citizen is legitimately born into his citizenship; by law he is educated into the capacity to use his citizenship. By the grace of the law he is what he is; and as a child owes obedience to his parents, so, and for the same reason, a citizen owes obedi-

The *Crito*: an explanation of obedience

[1] *Apology*, 30 A-C.

[2] The *Crito* is dated as one of Plato's later works by Gomperz, *Greek Thinkers*, iii., 57, and is regarded as Plato's defence of himself from the charge of revolutionary aims, to which the character of the *Republic* might have given rise.

ence to the law. It is the law that has made Socrates, and not he himself: shall he quarrel with his maker? The conception is put in a Greek form, but it is a conception eternally true. We are all the product of a number of influences, which have shaped our character and given us our powers—our School, our Church, our State; and we owe a debt of gratitude for the gifts which we have received. It may be our duty to reject them, in the name of something higher; it is also our duty to respect them. The debt must be all the more keenly felt, and the more carefully repaid, if all these influences are, as they were for the Greek, gathered into one, and if they appeal for recognition, as to him they did, with a single voice. But there is, Plato feels, still another claim of law upon the individual. If he is bound as a child to repay it for its training of his youth, has he not, when he came into man's estate, entered into an *implicit* covenant (ὡμολόγηκεν ἔργῳ) to obey the laws? He has liberty under the law to emigrate: if he prefers to stay, at an age when he realises the obligations which he incurs by staying, he enters into an agreement (συνθήκη), none the less binding because it is not expressed, to discharge those obligations.[1] There is here no idea that the State is based originally on a contract of individuals, and owes its claims to concessions made in that contract: on the contrary, we have just seen that to Plato the relation of the State and the individual is not one between two parties to a contract, but one between father and child. The Sophists were the "contractarians," and Plato was the convinced enemy of their views, teaching rigorously the inevitable nexus which binds man to man in a State, and—as a corollary—the absolute claim of the State upon its members. What Plato means is that every man who regards himself as a member of a State has thereby really and implicitly, though not verbally and explicitly, subscribed to the obligations of membership. He has claimed rights, and has had them recognised: he has acknowledged duties, and is bound to fulfil them. This is implied in membership of the State: it is implied in the membership of any group. No man can belong even to a de-

[1] Compare the argument of modern believers in a social contract, as stated by Hume. "By living under the dominion of a prince, which one might leave, every individual has given a tacit consent to his authority and promised him obedience" (Essay *Of the Original Contract*).

bating society without incurring obligations of subscription and of orderly behaviour, which are the correlatives of his right to make, or to hear, a speech. The fact that he does not resign his membership is a standing proof of his acknowledgment of those obligations. This is Plato's contention; and thus the gist of the *Apology* and *Crito* comes to this: "Obey the law, and obey it cheerfully, where a material interest is at stake: otherwise you are a disobedient son and a faithless partner. Disobey it only, and disobey it even then in anguish, when a supreme spiritual question is at issue." It is the exact opposite of Hobbes' view, that a man should submit in matters of conscience, and only revolt to save his life.

Virtue is knowledge, and therefore teachable

Socrates was a martyr to the cause of knowledge. He had died because he would persist in stinging, "like a gad-fly," until men would recognise their ignorance, and seek after instruction. But are the things and the pursuits of which he demanded knowledge such, that knowledge of them can be got by the way of instruction? The justification of Socrates demands an answer to this question; and in the *Meno* and the *Protagoras* an answer is attempted. Both these dialogues deal with the question—"Is virtue a thing incapable of being communicated or imparted by one man to another?" At the end of the *Meno*[1] political virtue, or the quality of a good statesman, comes under discussion; and Plato admits that experience shows that good statesmen do not transmit their qualities to their sons or successors. Yet they certainly would, if they could; and it would therefore seem that Socrates was preaching the impossible, and that no instruction can make a good statesman. In reality it is not so. The reason why good statesmen cannot transmit a knowledge of statesmanship, is not that it is not transmissible, but that they have no knowledge to transmit. Instead of a reasoned knowledge, connected by a principle, in the light of which it is lucid and teachable, they have only an instinctive tact, a sort of *flair* by which they can travel along the right path, though their eyes are holden from knowledge of the truth. Such an instinctive "right opinion" (ὀρθὴ δόξα), "which is in

The *Meno*

[1] The *Meno* is here discussed first; but in order of time it is placed by Gomperz (ii., 375) "later, not only than the *Protagoras*, but also than the *Gorgias*". It has been treated first here, as containing the greatest justification of instinct which Plato permitted himself, and as therefore *logically* furthest removed from the *Republic*.

politics what divination is in religion," may lead men very far, and "having no understanding," but "being inspired and possessed," they may say and do much that is noble.[1] But right opinion is incommunicable: one cannot teach an instinct; and it has the further defect, that at a crucial moment it may fail. There is no guarantee that it will respond to every fresh problem: under a different set of conditions it may be utterly useless, because it is necessarily connected with mere use and wont. Only a reasoned knowledge illuminated by a principle will meet and master every demand of life; and such a knowledge, so methodised and unified, is a natural subject of instruction. Thus is Socrates justified, and thus the *Republic*, in which a course of instruction for the true statesman is sketched, is already foreshadowed. Much the same may be said of the *Protagoras*. In this dialogue not only Socrates, but the sophist Protagoras himself, appears as a champion of the position indicated in the *Meno;* and while in its course Socrates is made to confute Protagoras, we ultimately find that he only returns to Protagoras' own view on a higher level. Protagoras begins with the assertion, that as a sophist or teacher he teaches political art (πολιτικὴ τέχνη), and that by his instruction men became good citizens, "able to speak and to act for the best in the affairs of the State".[2] Socrates has two objections to urge against the possibility of any instruction in such a subject. In the first place, while on a subject like ship-building nobody commands an audience in the assembly who does not possess a technical knowledge of the subject, in affairs of State tinker and tailor are heard with a readiness, which implies that there is no technical knowledge of political art. In the second place, there is the old difficulty: statesmen are shown by the experience of Athens to be incapable of communicating their wisdom to their sons. In a long speech Protagoras replies to Socrates' difficulties. Underlying his speech is the assumption, which also underlies all the thought of Plato and Aristotle, that political art or the quality of acting rightly in the State, is the same as virtue, or the quality of right action in general.[3] Political art in this wide

The *Protagoras:* the Sophist's view

[1] *Meno*, 99 C-D. [2] *Protagoras*, 319 A.

[3] This depends on the view of the State as an ethical community: *cf.* Introduction, p. 6; and for Plato's view, pp. 101-2; for Aristotle's, pp. 286-7, 322, 337.

sense Protagoras regards as not, like specific arts, the quality of special individuals, but the common endowment of all mankind. This conviction he states in an apologue, which seems to represent the view which he taught of the origin of the State. He believes in a primitive state of Nature, and in the religious origin of political association. In the state of Nature, men, while possessed of the arts of life, were destitute of political art, and though they had religion and language, they were almost destroyed by the beasts for want of the strength of political association.[1] Desire for self-preservation drew them into cities: they contracted, as it were, one with another; but still destitute of political art, they destroyed their own associations by internal dissension, until Zeus came to the rescue, and "sent Hermes to them, bearing reverence and justice to be the ordering principles of cities and the bonds of friendship and conciliation".[2] But while the arts had each been the property of a favoured few, Zeus gave the "political art" of justice to all, since all must share therein, if the cities of men were to exist and prosper. And therefore it is that Athenians listen to tinker and tailor in affairs of State.

A deep truth is stated in this apologue. Mere aggregations of men do not form a State: a contract issuing in an artificial unity maintained by artificial laws would be no sooner formed than broken. What is needed and what is everything, is the life-breath from on high—a common mind to pursue a common purpose of good life. Only in virtue of such a life-breath is a State real and vital: without it, it is but a Frankenstein doomed to destruction. As Protagoras continues his argument, he hits intuitively on further truths. Punishment, he tells his audience, is proof positive that this virtue or political art, which is the life-breath of the State, can be transmitted and taught; for punishment is not the "unreasonable fury of a beast,"[3] or a retaliation for past wrong; it is administered with regard to the future, and to deter the criminal from doing wrong again.[4]

[1] Plato again speaks of early man as almost destroyed by the beasts, *Politicus*, 274 B.

[2] *Protagoras*, 322 C. [3] *Ibid.*, 324 B.

[4] For Plato's theory of punishment, *cf. infra*, p. 204. When Plato puts into the mouth of Protagoras this theory of punishment, we are reminded of the story of an argument between Pericles and Protagoras, which lasted

And not only does a preventive means like punishment imply that virtue can be taught: this is clearly explicit in a positive way in the educational system of a State. For youth, there is all the instruction of great poetry, with its admonitions, and its stories of famous men of old for imitation and emulation: there is music, which by its harmonies and rhythms makes the soul rhythmical and harmonious; and there is gymnastics, which makes the body fit minister of a virtuous mind. For manhood, again, there is the ensample of the laws, which guide men's conduct, as we have already seen, not only by repression, but also by positive direction. Nay, outside all set and formal institutions for the teaching of virtue, Protagoras asks, is there not more? "Are not all men teachers of virtue, each according to his ability?"[1] Is not society one great school of education? Merely by speaking our language to one another, we teach it unconsciously to the young as they listen; and what is true of our words is true of our deeds. Our lives are so many lessons, and some of us good teachers, teaching good, and some of us evil teachers, teaching evil. "All of us have a mutual interest in the justice and virtue of one another, and that is the reason why every one is so ready to teach justice and the laws."[2] And if some of us are good teachers, and yet produce poor results, as Socrates had urged, is it not merely that we have poor material?

Socrates' refutation of Protagoras

Much of the *Republic*—its whole scheme of education, for instance—is an expansion of ideas which Protagoras is here made to express. Where then is he wrong—for Socrates proceeds to confute his speech, in spite of all its acknowledged charm? Briefly, we may answer, in his low conception of "political art". He is perfectly right in holding that virtue can be taught; but it is a more serious thing, and needs a more serious teaching, than Protagoras conceives. True virtue is *not* a thing in which all men can or do participate, one in one way, and one in another. Virtue, as Socrates proves by a long discussion of the unity of all the virtues, is one; and it is one

a whole day. "One of the participators in the game of throwing a spear had unintentionally killed a bystander: who was the guilty party . . . was it the deviser of the game . . . the competitor, or the spear itself?" (Gomperz, *Greek Thinkers*, i., 446).

[1] *Protagoras*, 327 E. [2] *Ibid.*, 327 B.

in knowledge. All virtues are so many aspects of knowledge; and courage, for instance, is simply a proper knowledge of what is really to be feared. Perfect virtue is perfect knowledge, a perfect understanding of the world, and of man's place in the world; and few are those who ever enter into such knowledge. Because it is knowledge, it can be taught, in a far truer sense than Protagoras had ever meant: it can be taught by every means, and can only be fully taught by *all* the means, that give man a perfect understanding of the world. Instead of many phases of virtue, uncorrelated with one another and only dimly understood—instead of the inculcation of these in an empiric fashion by the ordinary, partly irrational ways of punishment and education and social influence, Socrates fixes his eyes on virtue one and indivisible, virtue which is perfect self-knowledge and therefore perfect self-mastery, virtue taught by the "scientific" path of a full education, whose goal is a perfect knowledge of the world and thereby of man's soul. Once more, and here more definitely than ever, Plato's mind is travelling fast to the *Republic*.

The *Euthydemus* on political art

In accordance with this high conception of virtue, the conception of political art assumes in the *Euthydemus* a correspondingly high position. If virtue is the perfect knowledge which controls every human action, the virtue of the statesman, or political art, must equally be a perfect knowledge which controls every action of the State. It is the kingly art, "which may be described, in the language of Æschylus, as alone sitting at the helm of the vessel of State, piloting and governing all things".[1] As this art is knowledge, so its function is the instilling of knowledge. "All the other results of politics—wealth, freedom, tranquillity, are neither good nor evil in themselves: but political science ought to impart knowledge to us; it ought to make men wise and (thereby) good."[2] Since then all who practise political art must have perfect knowledge, it follows that in affairs of State—in matters of political art—only those who have such perfect knowledge have a right to be heard. Wisdom must govern, by right of its wisdom: the tinker and the tailor

[1] *Euthydemus*, 291 D; *cf. Gorgias*, 517 E; *cf. infra*, p. 166, and Aristotle, *Ethics*, *ad initium*.
[2] *Euthydemus*, 292 B.

must be silent, and leave those who know to decide according to their knowledge. This is the logical conclusion of Plato's position, as we find it stated in the *Republic;* and thus Protagoras' justification of the procedure of Athenian democracy, on the ground that all men share in political art, finally disappears. One cannot but regret its disappearance, for it contained a certain truth, which can hardly be said to be recognised by Plato. There are many questions which the many have political art sufficient to decide, and ought to decide, if they are to give a free consent to the action of the State. It is indeed good that the rulers of a State should be wise: it is also good that the ruled should have the education of political action, and the satisfaction of feeling that they are of some moment in the life of the State.

The *Gorgias*: concerning shams

The *Protagoras*, while concerned to justify the Socratic position, that statesmanship and the conduct of life in general is a teachable thing, also contains a criticism of the sophistic conception of statesmanship, and of the nature of sophistic teaching. The criticism is not harsh: there is much in the views of Protagoras with which we can sympathise, and are meant to sympathise. In the *Gorgias*, however, Plato's criticism is more trenchant and destructive: he exposes sophistic teaching as a sham. At the same time he is more hostile to actual statesmen. While in the *Meno* he admits that they have an instinct or tact for affairs, in the *Gorgias* he regards them as mere *prétendants*.[1] The condemnation of both sophist and statesman springs from Plato's conception of art. There is an art of the soul, we are told, which has for its object the soul's health; and this art, which is the art of politics, has two divisions, the one legislative, the other judicial. Similarly there is an art of the body, aiming at the body's health, and divided into gymnastics, which regulates the growth and action of the healthy body, and medicine, which heals its diseases. Legislation is like gymnastics; judicial action is like medicine. These are all real arts;

[1] Gomperz suggests (ii., 355) that the deep resentment excited by Socrates' death had been strengthened, at the date of the composition of the *Gorgias*, (1) by the triumph in Athenian politics of a party to which belonged Anytus, Socrates' accuser; (2) by a pamphlet of Polycrates, directed to the vilification of Socrates and his disciples. Hence the tone of the *Gorgias*, almost Cynic in its bitterness.

they are scientific and based on principles. But there are also sham arts, which are only empiric, and spring from mere experience or routine. The dressing of the body to look healthy is the sham or simulacrum which usurps the place of gymnastics: cookery, pretending to care for the health of the body, is a sham which takes the form of medicine. What dressing is to gymnastics, that is sophistry to legislation: what cookery is to medicine, that is rhetoric to justice. Sophistry gives *false* principles to regulate the growth and action of the soul: rhetoric *pretends* to cure injustice, by making the worse cause appear the better. Thus the art of the great rhetorician Gorgias sinks to the mere pretence of a quack; and thus the oratory which the Sophists generally taught, and esteemed as the essence of political art, is proved to be a mere shadow and simulacrum of the true "judicial" aspect of that art.[1] But underneath this sham of rhetoric there lay a basis of false principles. The orator who valued, and taught others to value, mere eloquence, because it made the worse cause appear the better, was acting on the principle, and was inculcating the principle, that *external* success, howsoever and by whatever means attained, was the aim and endeavour of the soul: he was teaching that the king's daughter should only be dressed in clothing of wrought gold and raiment of needlework, and need not be all glorious within. One of the persons of the dialogue, Callicles, is made to expound this principle in its purest form. Convention, he urges, is one thing: Nature is another. Convention is made by the majority who are weak, "and they make laws and distribute praises and censures with a view to themselves and their own interests".[2] But "Nature herself intimates that it is just for the better to have more than the worse, the more powerful than the weaker". In ordinary life, the strong are under the tyranny of the weak, like young lions charmed with the sound of the voice. But "a man who had sufficient force would trample under foot all formulas and spells and charms, and all the laws which are against Nature; the slave would rise in rebellion and be lord over us, and the

[1] There is something reminiscent of *Sartor Resartus* (the philosophy of "clothes" or quackeries) in the general view and in the very language of Plato. The passage in 523, where "clothes" are regarded as a barrier to a judgment of inner and essential truth, is especially like Carlyle.

[2] *Gorgias*, 483 B.

light of natural justice would shine forth ".[1] Here in its purity is the false principle of sophistry propounded for the regulation of the soul's life and action. And this is not merely a sophistic view: it is the view of an Athenian statesman (for such, Plato tells us, is Callicles), who aspires to be a power in the political life of Athens. This then is the fashion of statesmen, and not merely the teaching of Sophists. Politicians desire only to win power for themselves by hook or by crook; and they act unconsciously on the principle which Callicles has candidly acknowledged, that the trappings of external power, howsoever they are won, are their life's sole aim and object. And how do they generally win such power? Why—by applying to government and the conduct of the State the very principles on which they conduct their own lives. As they dress their own souls into a fair seeming, instead of training them by a spiritual gymnastic to true health, so do they deal with the people. They "treat them with a view to pleasure":[2] they seek to guide them into the paths of mere external satisfaction, instead of training them to spiritual goodness. They use sophistry and not legislation; rhetoric and not justice. They indulge the whims of the people, that the people may indulge *their* appetite for power. Even against Pericles, the greatest figure of Athenian democracy, Plato brings this grave indictment.[3] To get satisfaction for himself, he gave the people their satisfaction. To be the "first man" in Athens, "he gave the people pay, and made them idle and cowardly". He made his citizens worse men instead of better, as was proved in his own person, when at the end of his life they turned round on him in a fury, because affairs were not going as they wished. Not only Pericles, but all the statesmen of Athenian democracy, were equally "sham" statesmen. Serving-men of the State, instead of shepherds, they used their powers of persuasion and force not to improve, but only to please, their fellow-citizens. They were concerned, one may say in a metaphor, with cookery and dressing, cockering men up in mere external welfare. They remembered only—(and Plato here speaks of their "art" from a slightly different, and less condemnatory, point of view)—what should be ministerial and subsidiary arts; they forgot the higher and magisterial art of establishing men in

Sham Statesmanship

[1] *Gorgias*, 484 A. [2] *Cf. ibid.*, 513 D. [3] *Ibid.*, 515, 516.

full health of the soul by that right legislation, that administration of true justice, which are its proper training and healing. "They have filled the city full of harbours and docks and walls and revenues—and have left no room for justice and temperance."[1] Such is the past of Athens: to-day (Plato makes Socrates say) every man who would be a statesman must ask himself—"Am I to be the physician of the State, who will strive and struggle to make the Athenians as good as possible; or am I to be the servant and flatterer of the State?"[2] Such a question Socrates had asked himself: he had answered that he would be a physician, telling the Athenians the things that were for their good; and therefore he is "the only Athenian living, who practises the art of true politics—the only politician of his time".[3] He is the only man who does his public duty, since, going about to preach righteousness, he does the true work of a statesman—he makes his citizens better men.[4] And yet from another point of view Socrates is not, and will not call himself, a politician. He may have the right moral purpose; but he, who always professed that his knowledge was only knowledge of his own ignorance, could never claim the perfect knowledge of the true statesman. He could not show that he had been trained to the art of politics, and had practised it successfully, as a true statesman should. For what is true of the builder is true of the statesman; and as we should examine a man who wished to build us a house, in order to determine whether he knew the art of building, and whether he had ever constructed a house successfully, so and not otherwise must we examine the statesman who would guide the State. From this we may gather that a true statesman has two qualities—a right moral purpose, which demands unselfishness, and makes for the betterment of the citizens; and a full knowledge of political art, which demands

[1] *Gorgias*, 519 A. This judgment of Athenian democracy in the person of its *προστάται* may remind us of Stesimbrotus' pamphlet (*cf. supra*, p. 42), and of Aristotle's *Ἀθηναίων πολιτεία*. The principle followed is *οἷος ὁ προστάτης, τοῖος καὶ ὁ δῆμος*.

[2] *Ibid.*, 521 A. [3] *Ibid.*, 521 D.

[4] It is because he has been a true politician, Socrates tells us in the *Gorgias*, that he will be put to death. Having done nothing to please, but everything to improve the people—having been physician instead of cook or purveyor of dainties—he will be brought to trial by the false politicians he has rebuked, "just as a physician would be tried in a court of little boys at the indictment of a cook" (521 E).

specialisation, and requires regular training. The two qualities meet and are united in the conception of government as an art, if art is rightly conceived in its truth, and not in its mere simulacrum. For every artist, as Socrates taught, and Plato attempted to ensure by the scheme of the *Republic*, must know what he works at, and love what he knows: he must bring knowledge to his subject, and work for his subject's betterment.

So wrote Plato in the *Gorgias*, half as an aristocrat criticising the democratic past of Athens, half as a Socratic, vindicating his master against those who slew him. And so he proves, not only that virtue and political art are teachable (as he had argued in the *Meno* and the *Protagoras*), but also that there is sore need of their teaching. Thus is Socrates finally justified, and thus is the way of the future shown. Sham teaching must be overthrown: *delenda est ignorantia.* Sham statesmen, who exemplify in their practice the principles which underlie such sham teaching, must be banished from the State. Knowledge must come instead—true knowledge taught by a true teaching; and those in whose hearts and minds it is set must guide men's lives in its light. So we turn to the *Republic*, in which all these hints are gathered together and systematised—in which the true knowledge, the true teaching, the true statesmanship of the true State, are all exemplified. The writings of Plato which we have as yet considered have been negative, or preparatory: in the *Republic* comes the positive teaching, and in it arises the building, which these foundations were meant to support. "The artist disposes all things in order, and compels the one part to harmonise and accord with the other part, until he has constructed a regular and systematic whole."[1] In the *Republic* political art does its perfect work of construction.

[1] *Gorgias*, 503 E-504 A.

CHAPTER III

THE *REPUBLIC*, OR *CONCERNING JUSTICE*

THE PLAN AND MOTIVES OF THE *REPUBLIC*

§ 1. THE *Republic*, which was composed in the maturity of Plato's life, between his fortieth and his sixtieth year, and thus, better than any other dialogue, represents the fulness of his thought, has come down to us with a double title—"the State" (in Latin, *respublica;* hence the name by which it generally goes), "*or* concerning Justice". In spite of these two titles, it must not be assumed that it is a treatise either on political science or on jurisprudence. It is both, and it is yet more than both. It is an attempt at a complete philosophy of man. It deals as it were with the physiology and pathology of the human soul in its environment. Primarily, it is concerned with man *in action*, and occupied therefore with the problems of moral and political life. But man is a whole: his action cannot be understood apart from his thinking. Socrates had even thought that right action absolutely depended upon right knowledge. And therefore the *Republic* is also a philosophy of man *in thought*, and of the laws of his thinking. Viewed in this way, as a complete philosophy of man, the *Republic* forms a single and organic whole. Viewed in its divisions, it would almost seem to fall into four treatises, each occupied with its separate subject. There is a treatise on metaphysics, which exhibits the unity of all things in the Idea of the Good. There is a treatise on moral philosophy, which investigates the virtues of the human soul, and shows their union and perfection in justice. There is a treatise on education: "the *Republic*," said Rousseau, "is not a work upon politics, but the finest treatise on education that ever was written". Finally, there is a

Plan of the *Republic*

treatise on political science, which sketches the proper government, and the proper laws (especially in respect of property and marriage), which should regulate an ideal State. But all these treatises are woven into one, because all these subjects as yet were one. There was no rigorous differentiation of knowledge, such as Aristotle afterwards suggested, rather than himself made.[1] The philosophy of man stood as one subject, confronting as equal or superior the other subject of the philosophy of Nature. The question which Plato sets himself to answer is simply this: What is a good man, and how is a good man made? Such a question might seem to belong to moral philosophy, and to moral philosophy alone. But to the Greek it was obvious that a good man must be a member of a State, and could only be made good through membership of a State. Upon the first question, therefore, a second naturally followed: What is the good State, and how is the good State made? Moral philosophy thus ascends into political science; and the two, joined in one, must climb still further. To a follower of Socrates it was plain that a good man must be possessed of knowledge. A third question therefore arose: What is the ultimate knowledge of which a good man must be possessed in order to be good? It is for metaphysics to answer; and when metaphysics has given its answer, a fourth and final question emerges. By what methods will the good State lead its citizens towards the ultimate knowledge which is the condition of virtue? To answer this question, a theory of education is necessary; and indeed, since a readjustment of social conditions seems necessary to Plato, if his scheme of education is to work satisfactorily, a reconstruction of social life must also be attempted, and a new "economics" must reinforce the new "pedagogics".

Such in brief is the content of the *Republic*, and such is its organic unity. It is a "philosophy of mind" in all its manifestations; and the modern work with which it may most easily be compared is that section of Hegel's sketch of philosophy which he entitled the "philosophy of mind," in which he discusses the inner operations of mind as consciousness and as conscience; its external manifestations in law and in social

[1] He wrote two treatises, the *Ethics* and the *Politics;* but political science and moral philosophy are in his eyes one and indivisible.

Division of the *Republic*

morality (the sphere of the State); and its "absolute" activity in art, religion, and philosophy.[1] But German criticism, according to its wont, has set itself to dissect the *Republic* into a number of "lays," written at different times, and afterwards welded together. There is Republic A (to take one instance of such dissection), comprising a discussion of justice, which involves the building of a State and a sketch of its gradual corruption; and there is Republic B, a treatise upon metaphysics.[2] Republic A is practical and political: it is written in the first period of Plato's thought, when in the heat of his young blood he fancied that he could rejuvenate the world, and when the disillusion of failure had not yet driven him from trying to shape living men and actual affairs after a new pattern, to dwell instead with "bloodless categories" in the heavens. Republic B belongs to this latter period of exile and of transcendentalism; while still a third epoch is marked by the time when, weary of the unsubstantial company of ideas, Plato returned, a foiled circuitous wanderer, to men and their cities, and once more, but with a moderation bought by previous failure, attempted to fashion both, if after a less novel manner, in the *Laws*. Such an anatomy of the *Republic* and of Plato has the merit of bringing into relief the practical bent which distinguishes the book and its author; but it is too clear-cut to be true, and too scientific to be correct. A book grows under the writer's hands, through weeks and months and years, and the attitude from which one chapter was written is not as the attitude from which a later chapter was composed. The author is not as the critic: his book has a background in his mind, and this makes compatible in his eyes what may seem inconsistencies to the critic; while even if he leaves inconsistencies, it is only a proof that he is human, and not a piece of precise mechanism. And in any case, an artist like Plato can hardly have pasted together the *magnum opus* of his

[1] To some extent the *Republic* seems to stand half-way between Hegel's *Philosophy of Mind* and Carlyle's *Sartor Resartus*. It combines the philosophic breadth and system of the one, with the ardent hatred of shams and the keen sense of the spiritual foundations of life which distinguish the other.

[2] Rep. A includes i.-v. 471, and viii.-ix.; Rep. B includes v. (471)-vii.; while book x. is A-B, the transition. This is Pfleiderer's division. Nettleship admits that books v.-vii. form a distinct section (possibly inserted), because they are different in tone from the other books, and one can easily read on from iv. to viii.

life from two treatises belonging to different epochs of his life and thought.

The *Republic* and Economics

The *Republic* then is a unity: however manifold its scope may be—whatever varieties of tone and temper may appear in its different parts—it is yet a single treatise of an ethico-political order, treating of man as a member of the State, and of the State as a moral community. It has indeed been suggested [1] that the mainspring of the *Republic* is Plato's aversion to contemporary capitalism—that his aim is the reprobation of the economic man, and the substitution of a socialistic motive. This would make of the *Republic* an economic treatise; and the author of the suggestion enforces his point by attempting to show that in contemporary Greece the struggle between Oligarchy and Democracy represented a struggle of capital and labour,[2] and that in Plato we find a vivid sense of the evils of this struggle and an attempt to deal with those evils by means of socialistic remedies. Hence, he thinks, comes the attack on private property, and the abolition of the use of gold.[3] Aristotle, equally with Plato, is brought into line with this theory; for, though he does not commit himself to the socialistic attack upon property, yet he puts his faith in an agricultural *régime;* he attacks money in the very spirit of Plato; and he even goes beyond Plato, in attacking trade as a species of robbery. The objection which naturally occurs, that such a theory means the importation of modern socialism, which is a revolt against a complex system of production, into the far simpler conditions of Greek economic life, is met by the reply, that those conditions were not simple. Credit was highly developed in the city-state: over-seas trade was abundant in a city like Corinth. Usury was not merely the loan of money to needy farmers, but a vast system running through commerce; and the attacks of philosophers on interest (*Zins*) indicate a socialistic propaganda, such as is to-day connected with attacks upon profits (*Kapital-zins*). The theory is fascinating; but whatever may be the truth of the view of Greek economics which

[1] Pöhlmann, *Geschichte des antiken Kommunismus und Sozialismus.*

[2] πλοῦτος καὶ πενία (421): *cf. infra*, p. 471.

[3] But Plato says that it is the guardians alone who will have neither silver nor gold; from which one may gather that the other classes of the State use the precious metals (417 A).

it postulates, it is difficult to agree with the view of Greek political thought which it suggests, or to admit that the reform of the State proposed by Plato is meant as an economic reform of an economic evil. Plato may touch upon economic questions; but he always regards them as moral questions, affecting the life of man as a member of a moral society. He speaks in praise of the division of labour, for instance; but we soon learn, that division of labour concerns him, not as the best method of economic production, but as a means to the welfare of the soul.

§ 2. But while we see reason to disagree with the application of either political economy or "anatomy" to the *Republic*, we may none the less admit that its *practical* motive is a fact. It is written in the imperative mood. Its author seeks the truth, but he seeks it in order that it shall make men free. The philosophy of mind is written not by way of an analysis, but rather for warning and counsel. In this, indeed, it is true to the general character of the political thought of Greece; but in Plato, more than in Aristotle, the note of warning and of counsel is dominant. Indignation makes the *Republic*. Much of its eloquence and its zeal spring from a spirit of wrath, alike with contemporary teaching and with contemporary practice. First and foremost, the teaching of Sophistic Radicals must be overthrown. Much as he was like them (for was not he too a Radical?)—perhaps because he was like them, Plato waged a long and unrelenting crusade against their tenets. Half professors, and as such thinking their way to new ideas—half journalists, and as such occupied with the dissemination of those ideas—they were still more dangerous as journalists than as professors; for they disseminated their ideas among the young as they made their progresses through Greece, and it was the young who flocked to their lectures, and were trained by them for their future career in politics. The Sophist and not Socrates was the true *corruptor juventutis*; and if Greece was not to follow in the paths they had indicated, their hold on the young must be destroyed, and their teaching exposed. They had preached (so it seemed to Plato) a new ethics, or "justice," of self-satisfaction; and they had revolutionised politics accordingly, by making the authority of the State a means to the self-

The *Republic* directed against the Sophists

satisfaction of its rulers. And so Plato taught *his* conception of justice, according to which the soul, instead of rushing everywhere for its satisfaction, should work out its own appointed function singly and quietly; and he taught a corresponding conception of politics, which made the State and its government no means to the self-satisfaction of its ruler, but the end of his work and the function of his being. No longer should individualism infect the State: a spirit of "collectivism" (for the Platonic reaction runs to its extreme) should permeate the individual. No longer should the ruler use the State for his own ends: the State should demand of the ruler, if it were necessary, the sacrifice of his own ends (if he had indeed ends distinct from those of the State) to the interests of its welfare. But in truth there was no such necessity; there was no such distinction: in a true State the individual would secure his own ends in securing those of his fellows. The old harmony of the interests of the State and the individual, interrupted by the Sophists,[1] was thus restored by Plato, but on a new and higher level, because it was, now and henceforth, conscious and self-justified. In this connection Plato, Radical and reformer as he may elsewhere appear, is Conservative enough. It is his mission to prove that the eternal laws of morality are no mere "conventions," which must be destroyed to make way for a *régime* of Nature; but that they are, on the contrary, rooted beyond all possibility of overthrow in the nature of the human soul and in the system of the universe. That is why a psychology of man and a metaphysics of the world enter into the plan of the *Republic.* Its author has to show that the State is not to be turned into a chance congeries of individuals, exploited by the strongest individuality; it is to be maintained as a communion of souls rationally and inevitably united for the pursuit of a moral end, and rationally and unselfishly guided

[1] The Sophists did indeed reconcile State and individual, by making the State a tyranny working for the satisfaction of one individual. They reconciled it however from the wrong end (if indeed they can be said to have reconciled it at all) when they adjusted the State to one individual, instead of adjusting all individuals to the State. Yet it shows how closely the State and the individual were connected, even by the revolutionaries, that individualism, instead of seeking to destroy the State, should have attempted to recreate it after its own image.

towards that end by the wisdom of those who know the nature of the soul and the purpose of the world.

Attack on contemporary politics

But this, which is the "idea" of the State, and its natural and normal condition, was exactly what in ordinary practice the State was not. The spirit of excessive individualism had infected not only theory, but actual life; and the Sophists were only popular, because they had caught what was in the air. The actual States of Greece seemed to Plato to have lost their true character, and to have forgotten their true aim. And in opposition to the prevalent perversion of the ordinary State, Plato turns as vehemently Radical and subversive, as in opposition to Sophistic teaching he had shown himself Conservative. In either attitude he is consistent with himself. If, like Aristophanes, he attacks the Sophists and rehabilitates justice—if again, like the Sophists themselves, he attacks existing politics and seeks to import a new principle into affairs—it is always in order to enforce a true conception of man's soul, and of the nature of the State, and of the proper relations of both.

What then were the defects from which the States of Greece seemed to Plato to be suffering? Thinking mainly of the Athenian democracy in which he lived (and at the hands of which Socrates had died), he found in contemporary politics two great and serious flaws. One was the ubiquity of ignorance masquerading in the guise of knowledge: the other was a political selfishness which divided every city into two hostile sections, standing "in the state and posture of gladiators" over against one another. There were two classes of men whom Plato's soul hated—the amateur, who dabbled in politics as readily and as inefficiently as he did in every other pursuit on which he could lay his hands; and the self-seeker, who touched politics only to make them pitch, and by his self-seeking made for a permanent state of civil war. To create efficiency—to restore integrity and, with it, harmony—was therefore Plato's concern: "specialisation" and "unification" were therefore his two watchwords. To these two aims the political teaching of the *Republic* is addressed; and as means to these ends its apparent eccentricities, like the communism of wives, acquire meaning and find justification.

Ignorance was to Plato the especial curse of democracy.

Here, instead of the professional, the amateur and the sciolist were predominant. In Athens especially, democracy seemed only to mean the right divine of the ignorant to govern wrong.

Political ignorance

Thanks to the institution of the lot, almost any office,[1] of whatsoever kind, might fall to any man, of whatsoever capacity. But while it is right and proper that everybody should be a member of the government-making organ, because everybody is interested in the character of the government, it is neither right nor proper that every man should have access to the government, because not every man is capable of governing. Yet the tanner of Athens not only elected the government: he swayed the assembly as "demagogue," and might even, by its vote, lead the armies of Athens to meet the first general of the day. Besides the parade of a false equality which it involved, besides the inefficiency which it entailed, such a system was to Plato unjust. Justice meant, in his eyes, that a man should do his work in the station of life to which he was called by his capacities. Everything has its functions: an axe which is used to carve a tree, as well as to cut it down, is an axe misused; and a man who attempts to govern his fellows, when at best he is only fit to be a tolerable craftsman, is a man not only mistaken but unjust—doubly unjust, for not only does he not do his own proper work, but he shoves the better man aside. There was something of a tendency to "pose" in every Greek,[2] a tendency which had been rebuked in the old motto "know thyself". In democracy this tendency was let loose. Hence the picture which Plato draws of the democratic man—drunk one hour, an abstainer the next; veering from violent athletics to no athletics at all, and from both to the study of philosophy; to-day a politician, who jumps to his feet and talks unpremeditated nonsense, and to-morrow a warrior; but, through all his vicissitudes, constant to the one principle of never being constant to one single thing. And so it seemed to Plato that Athens was wrong in entrusting her government itself, as well as the making of her government, to the mercy of the masses; nor can Aristotle, when he assumes the advocacy of the masses against Plato, defend them except as makers and reviewers of government.

[1] *Exceptis excipiendis*, *e.g.* the στρατηγοί.
[2] Nettleship, *Lectures*, p. 106.

It is natural for us to-day to sympathise with the principle, upon which Plato bases much of his ideal State, that every man shall do that which it is his function to do, and shall be trained to its doing. The work of government must be done by a governing class; and if that class is trained to its work, so much the better. The mistake of Plato was, that in his eagerness to deprive the masses of the right of government itself, he wrested from them also the right of making the government, which must, as Aristotle afterwards argued, in the name alike of expediency and justice, be given into their hands.[1]

But nothing impressed Plato more in contemporary politics, and nothing more surely drove him along the path of Radical reform, than that violent spirit of individualism, which engaged in the eager pursuit of its own satisfaction, captured the offices of the State for the better fulfilling of its own selfish purposes, and divided every city into two hostile camps of rich and poor, oppressors and oppressed. If the busy-body was the type of democracy, oligarchy in particular made its people a people of Ishmaelites. The ruling body always tended to dissensions within its own ranks, and it was always in a state of opposition to its subjects. An oligarchical city was a city set in two camps, each spying for an opportunity against the other. And the root of all evil was the love of money. It had been well if this passion had been confined to private life; but it infected politics. The rich who sought to be still richer monopolised office for the sake of the advantage which its corrupt use might give them in their private enterprise: they seized the authority of the State for the sake of the "spoils" which it might bring. The State, whose essence it is that it should be a neutral and impartial arbitrator between the different interests of different classes, became itself the tool of one of these classes. The government, instead of binding class to class, merely accentuated their differences by adding its weight to strengthen one class against

Political selfishness

[1] It is obvious that representative institutions make the way easier for modern democracy. Provided that the people elects its representatives, it may be willing to be governed by the best. It is when there is primary, unrepresentative government, that inefficiency and ignorance emerges. Where there are representative institutions, one can unite the democratic principle of rule by the people with the Socratic and Platonic principle of rule by the Wisest and Best. Accordingly, it may be said that Plato was not criticising democracy in its essence, but in a particular (and perverted) manifestation.

the rest. No wonder the State split into two separate States—that, as Plato says, in every city there were two separate cities. How could the poor feel that they were members of a State, whose influence was cast entirely for their opponents?

But political selfishness was not the fault of oligarchies only, or perhaps principally. It was to Aristotle the feature that distinguished perverted constitutions in general, and marked them off from normal States. The tyranny showed this Greek infirmity in its most glaring form. Modern Cæsarism bases itself upon the *plébiscite*, and finds its mission in the protection of the masses: the Greek tyrant found in his position an opportunity for the accumulation of wealth, and, as many of Aristotle's stories prove, a means to sensual gratification. Nor was Greek democracy itself exempt from this vice. Its supporters indeed viewed it as the true State, where man was equal to man, and an impartial law ruled all—a State which served no particular interest, but did justice to every class. Democracy represented the whole community: oligarchy represented a part. It made room for the rich in finance, the wise in council, the masses in decision.[1] But what struck Plato, and indeed Aristotle, was, that the citizens of a democracy not only paid themselves from the coffers of the State, by their various wages for attending the assembly and sitting upon juries, but also used their authority to pillage the rich, as when they confiscated their estates upon spurious issues, or plundered them more subtly by heavy "liturgies". They made politics into a source of economic gain. It is this confusion of economics and politics that lends to Greek civic strife its fury. Political struggles may be moderate, and the combatants may act by legal form: it is the social war in which passions are as bitter as gall. Greek civic strife (στάσις) meant such a social war; and the constitutional opposition to an oligarchy readily turned into a Jacquerie.[2] And thus it became the mission of political philosophy in the hands of Plato and Aristotle to rehabilitate a strong and impartial authority, which should mean, not the rule

[1] Thuc., vi., 39.

[2] *Cf.* the picture drawn by Thucydides of στάσις at Corcyra: "And the cause of all these things was the pursuit of office for reasons of greed and ambition" (iii., 82).

of the rich over the poor, or of the poor over the rich, but of something either above or at any rate combining both. Whereas "men came to public affairs hungering for their own profit thereby," and, "as a result, struggles for office arose which grew into civil war," [1] there must be unselfish government and civic harmony.

There were, then, two factors—a certain meddlesomeness, which its friends called many-sidedness, characteristic of democracy, and a political selfishness, resulting in constant disunion, characteristic both of oligarchy and of democracy—which suggested to Plato the direction of future reform. It is noticeable that these two factors correspond to the teaching of the Sophists, who had, as was said above, only caught what was in the air. If they had spoken of "self-satisfaction" as the proper motto for the conduct of life; if they had preached that a man should "let himself go" anywhere and everywhere for the satisfaction of his own desires; so too had democracy laid down the rule that a man should "do as he liked"—so too had the democratic man rushed into every channel of action he could find for his own satisfaction. Plato himself notes this affinity, and remarks that the democratic man is the prey of "quack" theories which turn black white and white black, and, dethroning order and measure and temperance from his mind, set on the vacant throne disorder and chaos and excess.[2] And as, again, the Sophists had preached the right of the ruler to rule for his own advantage; as they had elevated political selfishness into the ideal of politics; so had the cities of Greece allowed office to be actually made a source of private advantage —so too had they admitted the principle, that the strongest power in the State should rule the State for its own interests. Sophistic teaching had been but a glorification of common error: in attacking the one, Plato is also attacking the other.

Connection of Sophistic teaching and contemporary politics

It is from the common error of πολυπραγμοσύνη that Plato starts in constructing his State; and in opposition to the gospel of many-sidedness he enunciates that of specialisation—let "the vague universality of a Man" be moulded into "the specific Craftsman".[3] The Sophists had, to some extent, been apostles of "many-sidedness"; and Hippias of Elis had

[1] *Republic,* 521 A. [2] *Ibid.,* 560 B-C. [3] *Sartor Resartus,* ii., c. iv.

given a practical demonstration of its meaning, when he appeared at Olympia in ring, and cloak, and shoes, of his own making. Yet, as has been shown, they had also felt that it was well for a man if he had been trained in the profession he intended to pursue; and they had attempted to reduce professions to rule and method for the purpose of such a training. Socrates had followed in their steps, in his insistence upon knowledge as the basis of action; and the Socratic conception of governing, as an art which needed special knowledge, had especially influenced Plato. Nor were the tendencies of actual life adverse to his teaching: the professional soldier, the professional orator, were differentiating themselves. The victory of the Iphicratean peltast over a Spartan mora had already shown the efficiency which the new tendency could impart; and though a Phocion might, at a still later day, appear as both orator and soldier, he was noted by his contemporaries as an exception. But the teaching of Plato goes far beyond any pre-

Plato's remedy

ceding teaching or tendencies. He divides his ideal State into three classes, the rulers, the fighters, the farmers—the men of gold, the men of silver, and the men of iron and brass. Each of these has its appointed function, and each of these concentrates itself entirely upon the discharge of that function. It is only with the two former classes that Plato is concerned; but these he is careful to train for their work by every means in his power. A professional army and a professional administration—these then are his ends; and what are his means? Primarily he trusts to an education which shall train the governing classes thoroughly for their duties: secondly, not quite content with spiritual, he has recourse to material means. He suggests a system of communism so ordered, that it shall set the time and the minds of these classes free from material cares, and shall enable them to give themselves fully to the acquisition of knowledge and the discharge of their function in the community. By depriving the guardians of any property of their own, he imagined that he would free them from any temptation to desert the work to which they had been trained. Specialisation, he thought, would be safe-guarded by the absence of any reward for diffusion.[1]

[1] There is much in modern conditions that is reminiscent of Plato. One statesman makes "efficiency" his watchword; the favourite phrase of an-

But the way of specialisation was also the way of unification. If a separate class were appointed for the work of government, there would hardly be any room for the old struggle to gain control of the government. If each class abode within its own boundaries, concentrated upon its own work, no class would ever come into conflict with another. Civil dissension had been rendered possible by the want of specialisation. Because there was no proper government ready and able to do its work, there had been the conflict of selfish aspirants for office: because there had been in every State a number of men with no settled function or regular place—men who had more than their own place, or men who had no proper place at all—there had been all the jostling and turbulence which had culminated in civil war. With specialisation these things would cease. Justice would be the present and moving Spirit of the State: each class would work at its appointed function in contentment. But even so, it may be asked, is there guarantee that the ruling class will rule unselfishly? There may be no rush for office and no jostling of classes; but yet all will be lost if the government is selfish. The answer is, we learn from Plato, that those who confine themselves to the discharge of their function cannot be selfish. Selfishness consists in going outside one's own sphere, and trespassing upon that of another (πλεονεξία); and the training to which the rulers have been subjected in their own special work is sufficient security against truancy or trespass. Moreover, they have been trained in an art—the art of government; and that art, like every other (for instance the art of physician or teacher), is designed to promote the welfare of its subjects. If they really know their profession and are not pretenders, they must be unselfishly minded by the very nature of their art. Nor are all who have been trained destined to become governors. To make the assurance of unselfishness doubly and triply sure, Plato reserves office for those, and only those, who have,

other is—"put thought into it". The desire has not been unspoken—"would that our rulers, like those of Plato, might be picked men, and men trained for their work"; and it has been argued that, in view of the complexity of modern conditions, and the consequent need of special gifts and appropriate training, some regular preparation for the work of the State, other than such as comes of itself in the hurly-burly of politics, will be increasingly necessary (*cf.* Sidney Low, *Governance of England*, p. 304 *sqq.*).

under a system of trials and temptations which seems almost Jesuitically subtle, held firm to the belief that the weal of the State is their own weal, and its woe their own woe. But besides all these spiritual means—(besides this training for a special work, this training in an art which as an art must be unselfish, this selection of those whom the special training has shown to be most unselfish)—there is finally the material guarantee of communism. Rulers who have no home, no family, no possessions, have no temptation to selfishness: they have nowhere to carry their gains, nobody upon whom to spend them, no interest in making them.

The conclusion of the whole matter would seem then to be this—let each man do his own appointed work in contentment. But this in Plato's eyes is justice; and therefore the *Republic* is also called "a treatise concerning justice". Its purpose is the substitution of a true conception of justice for the false views which common error and sophistic teaching had contrived to spread; and whether he is combating the Sophists, or reforming society, justice is the hinge of Plato's thought, and the text of his discourse. It remains therefore to inquire, what were the views of justice which Plato found current, and what were the reasons for which he rejected those views: in what way he justified the conception which he advocated, and what were the results to which that conception led. In the course of this inquiry, we shall be expounding in detail what has already been sketched in outline—the polemic of Plato against the Sophistic conception of justice, and his reconstruction of the State with a view to realising his own conception of its nature. We shall see how, beginning as it were dimly with the practical principle of specialisation, Plato throws fresh and fresh lights on its meaning, until finally, in the blaze of the "Idea of the Good," we realise that in specialisation only is justice to be found—for justice, being seen, is nothing more and nothing less than man's performance of the part which the purpose of the world demands that he shall play.

The *Prima Facie* Theory of Justice

§ 3. The first conception of justice which Plato seriously studies is one which is enunciated by Thrasymachus, and which represents what Plato understood to be the view entertained by the Sophists. Thrasymachus takes up two positions, and is successively driven from both. Understanding by justice (what is understood throughout the *Republic*) the standard and rule of action for a man living in a community,[1] he defines it first as "the interest of the stronger". In other words, might is right; a man ought to do what he can do, and deserves what he can get. This is to identify *jus* with *potentia*, after the manner of Spinoza; but while Spinoza somewhat inconsistently limits the *potentia* of each individual by the *imperium* of a State, which enforces a peace consisting in rational virtue, Thrasymachus logically enough argues that the *imperium* of a State merely lays down as the law whatever is to its own interest, and simply makes into justice by its superior power the rights which it claims as the strongest. Accordingly, the standard of action for a man living in a community is, according to Thrasymachus, the will of a ruler who wills his own good; and this, he maintains, is what one must inevitably see, if one looks at the facts with an unblinking eye. For while every man acts for himself, and tries to get what he can, the strongest is surest to get what *he* wants; and as in a State the government is the strongest (or else it would not be the government), it will try to get, and it will get, whatever it wants for itself. Justice thus being whatever is for the ruler's interest, it follows that, for everybody other than the ruler, justice may really and in truth be defined, according to a popular definition, as "another's good". To be

Thrasymachus' definition of Justice

[1] It must be noted that no legal significance attaches to "justice" in Plato's use of the word. We must not suppose for a moment any distinction of private morality and public duty, or restrict justice to the latter. The two are one; and justice is both. Justice is the standard of action to be observed, both by a man acting as a member of a community, and by a number of men acting together as a single community. It is thus the one standard for all human action; for in one of these two ways men must always act. It is the answer to the simplest of questions—What is it that I ought to try to do? There is no question of any difference between what I ought to do as a man upon my conscience, and what I ought to do as a citizen under the law. I always am a citizen, and there is only one "ought". Some distinction there is indeed in Plato, between justice as in one member of a community, and justice as in all the members acting together as a community. But this is a different distinction; and it is not one of principle. Justice whether in the one member (the individual) or all the members (the State), has the same essential nature, and it is only the scope of its action which is different. We must not distinguish politics from ethics (*cf.* Introduction, p. 6).

"just" is to be a means to the satisfaction of another: to be "unjust" is to act for the satisfaction of oneself. But the real standard of action for any sensible man is to satisfy himself; and therefore injustice and not justice is the real virtue and the true prudence. The wise man is he who will be just, and satisfy his ruler's selfish desires, *if he must;* but who, *if he can,* will be unjust, and satisfy his own.

Thus, in Plato's view, do quack theories turn black into white, and make the better argument appear the worse. There is a certain attraction in such theories. The view that the strongest individuality should dominate the rest is after all not unlike modern theories of the Overman, such as one finds in Nietzsche and even in the hero-worship of Carlyle. The whole position represents the revolt of an awakened self-consciousness against the traditional morality, in which it has hitherto passively acquiesced, but which it now brings to the bar of this new sense of self for judgment. The new sense of self is keen and urgent: it finds in traditional morality merely a number of limitations on its play; and in its young vigour it thrusts them aside, and claims room for free expression. With a fresh naïveté it enunciates its new doctrine: "I will do whatever I can, and seek whatever I like". Its cardinal error is the pettiness of its view of self, as an isolated thing to be fed with pleasure and fatted with power; and those who like Plato have to expose this error must answer by urging a true conception of the nature and the "rights" of human individuality. They must show that the self is no isolated unit, but part of an order with a "station" in that order, and that fulness of expression and true consciousness of pleasure are to be found in doing one's duty in the station to which one is called. And this is the ultimate answer which Plato gives, and writes the *Republic* in order to give.

Plato's formal reply

For the present, however, he satisfies himself with a logical refutation. He takes the two positions which are advanced by Thrasymachus—that a government governs for its own advantage, and that injustice is better than justice—and deals with them each in turn. To the former view he opposes the Socratic conception of government as an art. All arts, he argues, are called into existence by defects in the material with which they deal. The physician attempts to remedy the defects of the body; the teacher those of the mind. The aim and object of every art is the perfection of its material: the perfect teacher, for instance, is he who has remedied all the defects, and elicited all the possibilities, of his pupil's mind. And therefore the ruler, so far as he acts as a ruler, and in accordance with his art, is absolutely unselfish: his one aim is the welfare of the citizens who are committed to his care. As a man in need of subsistence—as one who pursues the art of earning a wage—he may indeed seek his own advantage, and earn a wage by the work of his office; but this he does not do as a ruler, or as practising the art of government, but as an earner of wages, and as one practising the art of wage-earning. This is Plato's answer to the first position of Thrasymachus; and to the second he answers by an argument, designed to prove that the just man is a wiser, a stronger, and a happier man than the unjust. He is wiser, because he sees the necessity of acknowledging a limit (πέρας) to his actions—in other words, because he does not blindly rush at every pleasure, but walks steadily along a definite line towards a definite object. Limit is not here used (it never was used by the Greeks) in the sense of a restraint, but in the sense of a guide. It means a principle imposed by reason, which, by narrowing the countless avenues of activity down to a single path, guides man along that path.[1] Wiser, because he acknowledges such a principle, the just man is also stronger. Even if a number of men would fain be unjust, to get the strength for an unjust action they must be just: they must stand shoulder to shoulder, and act justly by one another. Wiser and stronger, in the strength of a principle which binds him to his fellows, the just man is also, last of all, the happier man. The argument by which Plato proves this last attribute of the just man is one of supreme importance. He starts from the position, which has just been proved, that the just man is wiser than the unjust. But because he is the wiser, he is also the better, since the wise man is also the good. Goodness, or excellence (ἀρετή), is therefore to be predicated of the just man. Now ἀρετή is a general quality, which may be defined as the

[1] The conception of limit here enunciated is one which is very prominent in *Aristotle* (*cf. infra*, pp. 229-30, on the end as limit; and pp. 472-73, on the "mean" State).

ideal discharge of function;[1] for each and everything has a function—an end which no other thing can serve, or which no other thing can serve as well. Goodness is a quality which may be shown in the discharge of any function; and the very charioteer who wins a race may be said to have shown ἀρετή. If this quality be present, its possessor will discharge his function well; if it be absent, he cannot possibly do his work as well as it ought to be done. There are thus many ways of excellence, according to differences of function; and the excellence of the just man will be determined by the nature of his function. That function is the function of living; and the just man, who because he is just is possessed of excellence, will discharge this function well. In the full sense of the words he will "live well," and be happy; while the unjust man, destitute of such excellence, must needs live ill, and needs must be unhappy.

In these arguments there are implied deeper conceptions, which Plato ultimately unveils. The theory of justice as the force which gives coherence to any association of men, the theory of a special function for each thing, are theories which are developed to their full consequences in the later books of the *Republic*. But as they stand, these arguments are logical and eristic. They show us Plato playing with the Sophists at their game of words, and beating them at their own game. They are destructive, and not constructive: they tell us why we should not believe in Thrasymachus' view of justice; they do not tell us in what conception of justice we ought to believe. They have not indeed done away with the uneasy feeling, that though the frank brutality of the Sophist may be brushed aside, the fact remains, that justice is something to which human nature does not instinctively take, something as it were unnatural, and only present in man, because it has been put there by convention, and is kept there by force. This is the ordinary feeling of society: this is the tone manifest in

[1] This conception of an ἔργον, of a final cause of action, is to be taken in connection with that of limit: the end of action is the limit. It implies ultimately a teleological conception of the world: if there are ends appointed for all kinds of action, the world must be a kingdom of ends culminating, as they did for Plato, in a single end—the Idea of the Good. The conception of virtue as excellence in the discharge of function, and the teleological view of the universe, are both inherited by Aristotle, and implied (or stated) in the *Politics*.

public opinion. Accordingly Plato turns to the criticism of such public opinion; and, in order to show that justice is grounded in human nature—in order to show what it is, by proving it to be the natural order of the human soul—he leaves his logic for psychology, and deserts his analysis of terms for an analysis of human nature.[1]

Glaucon's Conception of Justice

The new point of view is stated by Glaucon, for the express purpose of being "devoured by the shrewd thought" of Socrates. Without adopting the position of Thrasymachus, that justice is the will of the strongest when directed towards his own interests, he contends, in the same spirit as Thrasymachus, that justice is an artificial thing, the product of convention. Stating practically the position which Hobbes afterwards adopted, he argues that in a state of Nature men do and suffer injustice freely and without restraint. But the weaker, finding that they suffer more injustice than they can inflict, make a contract one with another neither to do injustice, nor to suffer it to be done; and, in pursuance of the contract, they lay down a law, the provisions of which are henceforth the standard of action and the code of justice. Thus human nature abandons its real instinct, which is towards self-satisfaction, and consents to be "perverted" henceforth by the duress of the law. The whole of this theory, which is not only that of Glaucon, but also that of Hobbes[2]—and indeed it is the *prima facie* theory to which our first instincts naturally spring—has been met by modern thinkers point by point. In the first place, there never *was* such a contract: there *is* and always will be a condition of

Objections to Glaucon's conception

[1] Nettleship, *Lectures*, p. 48.

[2] For Hobbes too believes that the sense of right is a thing not inherent in man, but created by a compact, and enforced by a power. "Before the name of just and unjust can have place, there must be some coercive power" (C. xv.): "for in the differences of private men, to declare what is equity, what is justice, and what is moral virtue, and to make them binding, there is need of the ordinances of sovereign power" (C. xxvi.). The fundamentally wrong thing in his position is (exactly what Plato urges against Glaucon's position) the view of human nature which it implies—the *individualistic* view that man is a selfish unit, that "in the nature of man we find three principal causes of quarrel, first competition, secondly diffidence, and thirdly glory". With such a view, justice can only be regarded as an artificial thing, doing violence to the instincts of human nature in the interests of a self-preservation, which the unchecked indulgence of instinct prevents. Accordingly Hobbes has to be met—as Plato meets Glaucon—by a refutation of the view that man is by nature a selfish unit, and by an opposite theory of human nature.

things, which is a condition of tacit and implied contract. For there is always on the one hand a mutual recognition of rights, which has been perverted into a regular contract of each with all: there is always, on the other, a will of the subject that his sovereign should rule, and a recognition by the sovereign of his dependence on that will, which has been formalised into a contract between subject and sovereign. Secondly, law as a whole is nothing conventional or artificial, in any sense of those words which is reasonable. If one means by "conventional" anything created by man, then law is certainly conventional—but so too is everything else, save "rocks and stones and trees". If again one means by conventional the conscious creations of man, opposing such creations to instinctive developments, then many laws will be conventional, and many natural; but there is no great gulf between the two, because man does not consciously create on totally different principles from those along which he instinctively develops. As a matter of fact, law as a rule has first developed, and then been created, if one may speak in a paradox: it has first been a custom, and then a code. At any rate, it is entirely erroneous to oppose the stage of instinctive development to the stage of conscious creation, as the opposite one of the other: man is a unity, and cannot have acted in two entirely opposite ways. In ordinary speech, however, "conventional" means neither *any* creation of man, nor any *conscious* creation of man, but any creation of man, which no longer fulfils the purpose for which it was created, but which still claims a right of existence; and in this sense law as a whole is certainly not conventional, though individual laws may be.[1] Finally, the basis of respect for law, and of the authority of law, is not force, but will. Laws are valid, because they enshrine the will of the members of a community to do what they feel they ought to do. They are strong, not in proportion to the force ready to execute them, but in proportion to the amount of readiness to obey them. What looks like force (as when we speak of the "enforcement" of the law by way of punishment upon an individual) is really the assertion of that individual's right will, even against himself, at the expense of his will to do wrong.

[1] This view of the relation of natural and conventional is based upon Nettleship (*Lectures*, pp. 54-57).

Plato's method of answering Glaucon

But Plato's method of answering Glaucon's position is simpler and more elemental. He sets himself to prove that justice does not depend for its origin upon a chance convention, or for its validity upon external force—that, on the contrary, it is from everlasting to everlasting, and is strong with the majesty of itself—by simply showing that it is the right condition of the human soul, demanded by the very nature of man when seen (as he must be seen) in the fulness of his environment. Justice thus becomes something internal:[1] it is as if Plato's Muse had said—"Look into thine heart, and write". But instead of attempting at once a psychology of the human mind, Plato adopts a method which at first sight seems curious. If we had to read a manuscript, he suggests, of which there were two copies, one in a small minuscule, and the other in uncials, we should certainly attempt to read the copy which was written in uncials. Justice is like such a manuscript: it is one and the same, but it exists in two copies, and one of these is larger than the other. It exists both in the State and in the individual; but it exists on a larger scale and in a more visible fashion in the State. Accordingly Plato proposes to consider first justice as it exists in the State, in its broadest and strongest lines; and not only so, but to consider it as it exists in a *nascent* State,[2] in its simplest and clearest form. And therefore, that justice may be made manifest, he builds an imaginary State from the beginning, and enters definitely upon the ground of political speculation.

Plato's Construction of the State and Discovery of True Justice

§ 4. Here then the purely political thought of Plato may be said to begin, if such a phrase is permissible in speaking of a thinker, who always, like his pupil Aristotle, thought his politics and his ethics together. But before we examine the

[1] Whereas by Thrasymachus and Glaucon it had been regarded as something external, a body of material precepts confronting the soul, and claiming to control it in virtue of a power external to it.

[2] Similarly Aristotle, in the first book of the *Politics*, proposes to consider a *nascent* State, first, in order to explain the difference between the State and the Household. But, as we shall see, it is a logical, and not an historical birth of the State, which Plato really considers.

Parallel of man and the State

"republic" which he proceeds to construct, it is all-important that we should be sure of the meaning of this parallel, or rather identification, of the State and the individual. The use of physical analogies, as we have seen, is characteristic of the *Republic;* but this is no physical analogy. It is not a parallel of the State and the human body, such as Hobbes, for instance, draws in the *Leviathan,* or Spencer in his *Principles of Sociology.* The external and material have been left behind when we reach this part of the *Republic,* and what Plato is concerned to discover is an indwelling *spirit* of justice. The parallel which is here drawn is a spiritual parallel. It is a parallel between the consciousness of man, whether acting as a whole or in its several functions (of desire, for instance, and of reason), and the consciousness of a State, expressed in the whole life of the community and in that of its separate classes. But the word "parallel" is misleading, even with the proviso that it is to be understood spiritually. For it implics that the State and the individual are separate things, which can be conceived apart, and compared together. They are not. One cannot draw a distinction between the consciousness of man, and the consciousness of the State. The consciousness of the State is just the consciousness of its members *when thinking as members.* The courage of the State, to take a particular instance of this consciousness, is simply the courage of individuals thinking and acting as members of the State. Each of these individuals may show an individual courage, when he is met by a ruffian in the street: each of them also (along with his fellows) shows the courage which Plato calls the courage of the State, when he faces its enemies in the field. But the courage of the individual and that of the State are both resident in the *same* consciousness. Why then does Plato first study this consciousness in its social aspect? Simply because, as a consciousness common to a large number of minds, it is a steadier and a larger thing—steadier, because it does not know the varieties and the idiosyncrasies of the individual thinking as an individual; larger, because it issues in outward action of a more visibly imposing kind. In a word, therefore, Plato, attempting a psychology of the human soul, and seeking to discover thereby the essential need of justice for its well-being, sets himself to study the soul as it acts in its social aspect, because he believes that all social phenomena are its products. "States do not come out of an oak or a rock, but from the characters of the men that dwell therein."[1]

All the institutions of man are merely so many expressions of his mind. His institutions are his ideas.[2] Law is part of his thought: justice is a habit of his mind. These things have outward and visible signs—a written code, a judicial bench; but the inward and spiritual thought which makes them and sustains them is the one reality. It is hard to think oneself away from the visible, and to regard it as the mere vesture of thought: it is easier to see justice in maces and parchments, than to see it as a living thought. Yet that we should thus turn inward—that we should leave the conceptions of Glaucon, and follow Socrates in seeing justice in the mind of man—is the great step which we have to make. It is the step which Plato and Aristotle both made;[3] and herein lies their great contribution to political thought for all time. Yet against Plato one may bring the accusation, that he did not carry the truth he had seen to its right conclusion. He saw that the institutions of a community must be its thoughts: he did not sufficiently recognise that they must be thought and willed by the *whole community.* For the Republic which he builds is of the nature of a benevolent despotism: its rulers are those who have thought their way to truth, and who enforce upon subjects who have neither thought it nor willed it the truth which they have realised themselves. And the institutions which he suggests for his rulers—a common property and a common family—are thoughts which ordinary men will never think, "as long as human nature remains the same".

Plato's Psychology

In constructing the State from which he proceeds to illustrate the nature of the soul, Plato presupposes a certain amount of psychology in advance. He makes to some extent a *petitio principii.*[4] The State being a product of the human soul, its

[1] *Republic,* 544 D; *cf.* Sophocles, *Oedipus Tyrannus,* 56-57.

ὡς οὐδέν ἐστιν οὔτε πύργος οὔτε ναῦς
ἔρημος ἀνδρῶν μὴ ξυνοικούντων ἔσω.

[2] Bosanquet, *Philosophical Theory of the State.*

[3] *Cf. infra,* pp. 323-24.

[4] Plato builds a State to illustrate man; but he presupposes a knowledge of man in building it.

construction proceeds along lines suggested by a conception of the human soul as a threefold thing. For, Plato held, there is first of all an element of desire (ἐπιθυμία), in virtue of which the soul hungers, and thirsts, and loves, and longs—the Appetite, as it may be called, a follower in the train of Pleasure and Satisfaction. And then there is an element of reason (λόγος), which has two functions, for by it men both learn to know, and (because they have learned to know) are ready to love. It is an element which must obviously be of great importance in the State; it will be at once a bond of union and a guide of action for its members. Lastly, midway between the two comes an element of spirit (θυμός), an element almost analogous to what we should call the sense of honour, and similarly issuing (for those in whom it is most strongly present) in something of the nature of chivalry. The specific function of this element is that it inspires men for battle; but it is not unlike desire, in that it is also the source of ambition and competition, while it is also a natural auxiliary of the element of reason, inspiring men as it does to hot indignation against injustice and ready submission to justice. It is indeed as an auxiliary of reason that it presents itself chiefly to Plato: "in the battle of the soul it takes its stand by reason's side".

Psychological construction of a State

In the light of this threefold division we may expect to find, and we do find, two features in Plato's political construction. The State which he constructs will grow under his hands in three stages: the constructed State will be marked by the presence of three classes or functions.[1] But the growth of the State will not be determined on historical lines: there will be no attempt, such as is made in the *Laws*, to show the natural steps by which the State has developed. On the contrary, Plato proceeds by a psychological method in the *Republic*. He takes each of the three elements of the human mind, beginning with the lowest and proceeding to the highest, and shows how each of these in its turn contributes its quota to the creation of the State. He gives a logical account of the different elements of

[1] One may add (as is pointed out in Nettleship, *Lectures*, p. 294 note), that there will be three States—the "simple" State of the middle of book ii., the "luxurious" State which follows upon it (to the end of book iv.), and, in books v. to vii., a "nobler" State (543 D)—each marked by the predominance of one of these elements.

mind, which at any time go to make up that creation of man's mind which we call the State. As he takes each in turn, and in an order which proceeds from the lowest to the highest, there is an appearance of historical method in his construction of the State. But it is only an appearance. He does not mean that the State began as economic association based upon the division of labour, although he begins with such an association. He does not mean that there was a progress from a "simple" to a "luxurious" State, though he proceeds from the one to the other himself. He knows that "the features he ascribes to each are taken from the Athens of his day".[1] The same warning, which applies to Plato's sketch of the growth of the State, also applies to his sketch of its corruption. That sketch is no historical *résumé* of the constitutional changes of Greece—though it wears that appearance, because, starting from the ideal State which issues from ideal psychological conditions, it proceeds gradually downwards to the worst form of State, which results from the worst psychological conditions. It is an attempt to show, that while the presence of the sum of right conditions in the human soul means a true State, each diminution of that sum means *pro tanto* a corruption of the State. It is an attempt again to illustrate from the large letters of the injustice of the State the nature of injustice in the individual, in the same way as the justice of the State has already been made to illustrate that of the individual. But in criticising it, as he does, on historical grounds, Aristotle is beside the mark.

Besides an implied psychological basis, there is also an implied conception of the true nature of justice—that each should do his own—present from the first in Plato's construction of the State. The doctrine of specialisation, which Plato so much desires to see realised, for the sake of efficiency, as well as because it means justice, appears even in the lowest psychological stage of the State. Beginning with desire as the primary basis of the State, Plato shows that it involves some form of association. The desires for food and warmth and shelter

Appetitive or economic element

[1] Nettleship, *Lectures*, p. 10. The same may be said of Hobbes' apparently historical construction of the State in the *Leviathan*. That too is logical; and the features presented by Hobbes are those of contemporary England, as they presented themselves to him.

cannot be properly satisfied, except by means of common action. The State first finds its binding force in human *need*. Man cannot dispense with his fellows: each, while able to confer something upon the rest which they need, needs in turn something which they can confer. The result is an inevitable division of labour or specialisation of function, which involves, as its other side, a combination for the reciprocal exchange of the several products. Such specialisation Plato justifies on economic grounds; it means the easier production of a greater number of objects, and those of a better quality. It issues in an association of men united by an economic nexus—an association at first limited to farmer and builder, clothier and cobbler, but subsequently increased by the addition of a class to make instruments for the first four, a class to tend the cattle they require, a third for purposes of foreign, and a fourth for those of domestic trade,[1] until it reaches the measure of an adult State.

The economic moment is not the least in the life of the State. Every State is, in one aspect of its nature, a great economic concern; and wherever a protective system reigns or has reigned, it has made this aspect prominent, by making the State a self-centred and self-sufficient unit in respect of its economic life. To Plato the State, viewed merely as an economic concern, contains features valuable not only in themselves, and from an economic point of view, but also as types and foreshadowings of political truths. It contains the feature of specialisation; and if the cobbler sticks to his last, and thereby produces better work and more work, why should not the statesman stick to his statesmanship, and produce the same result? It contains again the feature of reciprocity; and if the organisation of economics for the satisfaction of physical wants is based upon this plan, why should not the whole organisation of human

[1] In this connection it is important to notice that Plato is kinder than Aristotle to the middleman who conducts the business of trade. When a currency has been introduced, and a medium of exchange has made possible a system of exchange through the middleman, instead of barter between the two producing parties, it would be a waste of time for the farmer to come to market, and wait about in order to sell his goods; and this service (διακονία) is undertaken by the middleman, who thus supplies a need (χρεία). From this one may argue that the middleman, doing a service which supplies a need, in that it saves the time of the producer, deserves his reward; whereas Aristotle recognises no service, and consequently refuses to see the justice of any reward.

life in the State for the satisfaction of every want be based on the same scheme? Why should not reciprocity displace self-seeking, and a mutual exchange of services between ruler and ruled supersede the individualism, which seeks to do and to get everything for itself? "Instead of 'each for himself,' let us write 'each for other'"—here, in a word, is the principle on which the *Republic* proceeds.

But whatever the importance of the economic motive—however valuable the lessons which economic organisation has to teach, it is not the only motive or the sole organisation. Plato, indeed, makes Socrates rhapsodise on the golden age which will ensue in the Arcadian State he has built; but at the same time he makes Glaucon scoff at it for "a city of swine"; and Socrates while laughing at Glaucon's wish for a "luxurious" city, and still asseverating that this is the "healthy" and true type, willingly consents to go further. One suspects some Socratic "irony," some subtle ridicule of the idyllic Nature-State, which the Sophists had painted, and the Cynics still delighted to paint.[1] The logic of the *Republic* demands that Plato should consider two other and higher elements of the human mind, and the part which they play in constituting the State. Accordingly, he proceeds to give its place to the element of "spirit". Men are not content with the supply of the merest "necessaries": they need satisfaction of their desires for refinement (τὰ ἐκ περιουσίας, as Aristotle would say). Pictures and poetry, music and dress, are all "needs" of mankind: a large population is necessary to provide them: a larger territory is necessary to support the larger population. War now enters as one of the functions of the State, which must acquire and defend a sufficient territory; and thus the element of spirit (which inspires men for battle) next appears, and expresses itself in the organisation of the State by constituting a military force. In the logical synthesis of the State from

Spirited or military element

[1] If this be so (and Campbell and Gomperz both think that it is *not* the case), Plato is in opposition to the cry for "reversion to nature," which lay behind the theories that the State and justice were conventional. He would keep the State as it stands developed, in its "luxury," and "purge" it of its mistakes (399 E). At the same time, it must be admitted that there is much reversion in Plato himself—in his theory of art and of medicine and especially perhaps in his communistic principles (*cf. infra*, pp. 151-52); and in view of this the Arcadian State may be seriously meant.

the psychological factors which are its constituents, Plato, having considered the State as an economic community based on "desire," must now regard it as a military organisation based on "spirit".

The first, and the vital question, which arises with regard to the military organisation of the State, is naturally the question of specialisation. Shall a professional and trained army be created, or shall the body of the people act as a general militia in time of need? The answer is already given in what has been said of the division of labour in economics. It would be absurd to set one man on making shoes, and shoes only, that they may be well made, and to leave the art of war, a matter of far more vital necessity to the State, in untrained and unpractised hands. If efficiency is to be gained by specialisation anywhere, it must certainly be gained by specialisation in a matter so arduous and important as war. There must be soldiers whosc business it is to make war, and nothing else but war; and they must be picked for their work in virtue of a special aptitude—of an abundance, that is to say, of the element of spirit—and trained for their work in a way that will develop that aptitude properly. Accordingly, from this point onwards[1] the *Republic* becomes a treatise on the education of the happy warrior,

That every man in arms should wish to be.

Rational or governing element

Postponing, however, for the present Plato's scheme for the education of the ideal soldier, we may conclude the construction of the State from its constituent elements in human nature, by discovering the part which reason plays in its composition. We have already noticed that spirit, in one of its aspects, is the ally of reason, a hater of injustice and a lover of justice; nor are we surprised, therefore, to find that reason is active already, side by side with spirit, in the construction of the military organisation of the State. The natures which are selected for training as soldiers must not be merely quick and spirited. The soldier is a guardian of the State; and like a watch-dog—(here Plato uses one of the analogies which are frequent in his method of exposition)—the human guardian must be mild and gentle to

[1] From ii., 376 E to iii., 412 A.

those who are of the house he guards, though fierce to every stranger. Now the watch-dog is mild and gentle to all whom it knows. Those whom it knows it also loves: according to its knowledge, and by the use of the faculty of knowledge (which is reason), it distinguishes between friend and foe. The faculty of reason must therefore be present in the guardian of the State, that he may distinguish between the citizen whom he defends, and the enemy whom he attacks. In the soldier reason thus appears as a mere empiric knowledge, which is mixed with a dominant quality of spirit, and expresses itself in an instinctive affection for the object of knowledge, because it is known and familiar. But reason expresses itself most (because it expresses itself in its purity, and not as a mere corrective of spirit) in the government of a State. It is perfect, not in the guardian, but in the "perfect guardian," or ruler. Reason, as we have said, is a twofold thing: by it we know, but by it we also love; and there is in it both an intellectual element of apprehension, and an element as it were of affection and attraction. The very watch-dog loves as well as knows, and loves because he knows.[1] Now the quality which Plato originally postulates for the ruler—the element of mind which he originally believes to be expressed in the government of the State—is reason in its aspect of affection (412 D-E). The ruler must be wise; but what impresses Plato most in the earlier part of the *Republic* is that he must be loving (κηδεμὼν τῆς πόλεως). The men who will govern the State best are those who care for it most, and those who care for it most are those who believe[2] that its welfare is their welfare, and its mishap their mishap. If this be the element of mind expressed in the government, the government

[1] This will explain the bearing of the Socratic principle that virtue is knowledge. It is easy to object, that to know that a thing is right is not to do the thing, and that there is *will* besides knowledge. But, in the first place, knowledge here means more than the mere knowledge that A is right and B is wrong: it means an understanding of the world in the light of a principle. Secondly, such understanding is conceived as involving an attraction, and as resulting in a will in accordance with itself. The philosophic element which understands is thereby attracted to whatever it understands—truth, or art, or virtue. To have a liberal education is to love the truth which it teaches: instead of the "will to believe" of which modern writers have spoken, there is belief issuing in will.

[2] The belief is an ὀρθὴ δόξα, a right opinion, without a scientific basis. It may also be said, therefore, that what Plato originally demands of his rulers is a right opinion; while afterwards he demands scientific knowledge.

will obviously be unselfish; and in place of the political selfishness which Thrasymachus had glorified, we shall see realised the conception that government is an art practised for the good of its subjects. In this aspect of its operation, reason is indeed the very bond which unites the State. As a source of affection and attraction it is the factor of the soul which expresses itself in the State by maintaining its unity. Desire may have drawn men together by an economic nexus: it is reason that holds them together by teaching them to understand one another, and, understanding, to love. The ultimate organisation of the State is a rational organisation. Reason has caused the soldier to know, and to like, and therefore to protect, the citizens whom he guards: reason has caused the ruler to comprehend, and out of his comprehension to love and serve, the State which he governs.

Character of the Government

That the rulers, like the soldiers, should be a distinct and specialised class, follows upon this view of the attitude of mind which government expresses. Not in all is there this reason issuing in love; and those in whom it is most to be found are carefully, and by an elaborate system of moral tests, to be selected from the ranks of the soldiers, and set to govern the State. But this specialisation of a ruling class, which shall give itself to ruling, and to ruling alone, becomes still more justified if we regard reason in its intellectual aspect.[1] The real ruler, as Plato ultimately tells us, must be a philosopher; and the philosophic nature is reserved for a few rare souls: "a whole people cannot be a people of philosophers". He must be a philosopher, in the sense of knowing the "Idea" or essence of Justice, and of Beauty, and of Temperance, in order that he may fashion into their likeness the characters of those whom he rules.[2] Ultimately, he must know the Idea of which all these Ideas are but phases, and from which alone comes every perfect work—the Idea of the Good. He must know, that is to

[1] It is not meant that reason exists separately in its aspect of love and its aspect of philosophic insight. On the contrary the one cannot exist without the other. The love for the State, which has just been mentioned, depends on insight: the insight into ultimate truth, which reason gives, postulates and involves an attraction towards truth. All that is meant is that in one passage the one aspect of reason appears more decidedly, in another the other.

[2] *Republic*, 501 A-B.

say, what is the purpose of all doing and of all being—what is the end in the light of which all human action and all existence have a meaning, in order that he may do the work, which is appointed to him in the scheme of things, in such a way as to make it serve the fulfilling of this end. In the ruler, therefore, that final element of mind must express itself, which grapples with the mystery of existence, and arrives at a solution of its meaning. If in him this element is incarnate, then, and then only, has a State come into being, which is the creation (and also the image) of the fulness of man's mind. For if the mind of man is capable of this exaltation of reason, if it can attain to a condition of perfection in which reason guides its operations by the light of a supreme purpose, the State must also be capable of this exaltation, and must equally attain *its* perfection when, and only when, it is guided by the insight of a philosophic reason. This flows inevitably from the premise on which the *Republic* is based, that the State is the product of man's mind, and that each aspect of the State is the product of an element of mind. The synthesis of the State from each of its spiritual factors cannot therefore but culminate in the conception, that it is not only an economic, not only a military, but also a rational organisation, and as such guided by the highest reason which is possible for man. The "philosopher-king" is not a mere addition or insertion: he is the logical result of the whole method on which the construction of the State has proceeded.

From this new conception of the ruler, as a philosopher rather than a lover of the State, a new method of selection naturally flows. Instead of attempting by moral tests to discover those who care most for the State, we must now, by an intellectual test of philosophic power, eliminate those few who can guide it with the profoundest wisdom. But by either path we come upon a specialised class of rulers, to whom their ruling is an art for which they have been selected in view of a special aptitude which they, and they alone, possess. Nor are such special gifts their only distinction. When he considers the ruler as necessarily a philosopher, Plato postulates besides aptitude a special training, above and beyond the training of the soldier, which shall elicit and direct a philosophic nature.

Three-class system

In virtue of this special training, this distinct education, the rulers are, by art as well as by nature, stamped and distinguished as a class apart. Two classes have therefore emerged, a governmental and a military class, each composed of men possessed of special gifts and trained to exercise their gifts, who discharge the one function for which they are fitted, and that alone. It follows logically upon this that there will be a third class in the State, an economic or producing class, composed of men who have not the special gifts of the ruler or soldier, but who, equally with the ruler and the soldier, confine themselves to a single function, which must necessarily be that of satisfying the physical wants of the community. The Platonic State as a whole, therefore, is an association marked by a division of labour between three specialised classes,[1] the rulers (or "perfect guardians"), the soldiers (at first called "guardians," and afterwards "auxiliaries"), and the producing classes (whom Plato calls the "farmers"). There is a *Lehrstand*, a *Wehrstand*, and a *Nährstand:* there are, as in the mediæval conception of "the three estates," *oratores*, *bellatores* and *laboratores*. The three several elements of mind which constitute the State are therefore not only to be logically distinguished as moments in its being (as has hitherto been done); they are actually distinct as classes in its external organisation. This implies that each of the several elements (desire, spirit and reason) is particularly and essentially prominent in particular individuals or bodies of individuals. There is one small body in which reason is prominent: another, and larger, which is dominated by spirit: a third, by far the largest, in which desire is foremost. This is quite another contention than the primary contention, that each element of mind is a moment in constituting the full life of the State; and it is a contention which is far more dubious. The State may be and indeed is a product of mind; but it does not follow that the State is or should be divided into classes which correspond to the different elements of mind. In each individual mind *all* those elements are present; but if in the State each man is limited to an aspect which corresponds to one element only, is he not

[1] *I.e.* it *is* what Aristotle criticises it for not being, a κοινωνία constituted of elements different in kind, each making a different contribution to a common good, and profiting by the contributions of the rest.

forced to live as a citizen with a third of his mind? To take two instances: the ruler must live by reason, and abnegate desire: accordingly, he is subjected to a communistic *régime* which prevents the chance of desire, and thus violence is done by the excision of an integral element of human nature. Again, the farmer must live for the satisfaction of desire: he must be regulated in so doing by the external reason of the perfect guardian; and thus he suffers an atrophy of his rational self.[1]

Criticism of three-class system

This mistake of turning each psychical element into a *separate* social class ultimately springs from a flaw in Plato's psychology. He separates too harshly and too clearly the various elements of mind. He trichotomises the soul "with a hatchet". He conceives of desire as distinct from reason: he even speaks of an eternal war between desire and reason, in which spirit is sometimes reason's ally. He does indeed conceive of a unity of the soul; but it is a unity not of reconciliation but of subjugation. The ideal condition of the soul is one, in which reason has conquered desire, and erected a trophy, and rules as despot over the vanquished. This is (or tends to be) the Platonic conception of Ethics,[2] and by it a rigid separation is combined with a rigid unification. The separatism of this psychology invades the State, and brings separation there. The unification of this system of Ethics also invades the State, and finds its political parallel in the benevolent despotism of the philosophic ruler, to whom the economic and even the military classes are eventually subjected as blindly as are desire and spirit to the rational faculty. Aristotle (thinking of Plato's communism) accused the *Republic* of the vice of "excessive unification": in truth, it can be accused both of excessive separatism, in its caste-like division of classes, and of an excessive unification, not only in respect of the communism, which unifies the rulers by cutting away their desires, but also in respect of the despotism, which unifies the State by subjecting it utterly to the ruler. The fault lies not in Plato's conception of the

[1] The same criticism may indeed be passed on Aristotle. The economic classes, "without which the State cannot exist," but which do not share in its moral life "according to reason," are equally maimed.

[2] Reason is as a charioteer with two steeds to his chariot, Spirit and Desire, driving aloft to the heavenly places, but only too often dragged down again to earth by recalcitrant Desire.

relation of the State to the human mind, but in the separatism of his conception of the human mind, and the application of that separatism to the State—in the despotism of his conception of reason, and the application of despotism to the State. It is his view of human nature which must be criticised, and not his politics, which follow logically on that conception. What must be urged against Plato is, that man's mind is not primarily a war of elements which must be united by the triumph and supremacy of one, but that it is from the first a unity, pervaded throughout by reason. Even in desire itself, it must be contended, there is a rational element. Desire is the *knowledge* of a want; it involves (as Aristotle would say) the *calculation* of the means by which it may be satisfied; and it implies the *conception* of a "good" to be attained by such satisfaction. On such a view of the unity of the human mind will follow a conception of the State, as equally a unity pervaded throughout by reason—as one in virtue of a reason which animates each and every member, and which comes to light not in the minds of a chosen few, but in the will of the whole community. In a society based on a conception of this character, there will indeed be classes—but each class will be a factor in determining the common will: there will be unity—but a unity consistent with the full individual existence of each member.[1]

Advantages of division

Of this "excessive unification" we may treat more properly in dealing with communism. But we must not leave the separatism which we have criticised without noticing that it has its brighter side. The distinction of the three classes is figured by Plato in a myth: all the members of the State are brethren one of another, he tells us, but in fashioning them God wrought gold into the composition of the rulers, silver into that of the soldiers, and iron and brass into that of the farmers and craftsmen. But caste-like as this system appears, it is not a system of caste. God gave the guardians a command, that they should guard nothing more strenuously than the principle, that as is man's composition, so shall his class be. It may be that a

[1] The same line of argument, which has here been based on psychology and ethics, might be based upon metaphysics. The relation of the Idea to particulars as conceived by Plato is parallel to that of the ruler to his people. There is a despotic unity, attained by the annihilation of the full individuality of each of the many particulars, and their subjection to the Idea.

"silver" man is born of "golden" parents; it may be that to "silver" parents is born a "golden" son. Whenever that comes to pass, the rulers must act accordingly; and degrading the "silver" man to the rank of soldier, they must promote the "golden" man to the position of ruler. There is a *carrière ouverte,* and each man finds his appointed level: if there be the light of reason within him, he will have scope for its exercise. Nothing is stifled in the development of man by this differentiation, Plato would fain believe: on the contrary, there is opportunity given, such as without it there could not be, for the fullest use of every power. And again, whatever the criticisms one may pass on Plato's separatism, it must none the less be admitted, that it means specialisation, and spells efficiency. The setting aside to their work of those who are called to be rulers and soldiers is also the banishing of ignorance from politics; and not the least of the defects which Plato traced in contemporary states disappears, with the disappearance of sham statesmanship. Finally, this separation of class from class, which separates especially the governing from the producing classes (liable as it is to the criticism, which Aristotle passes upon it, that it bisects the State into two halves each with its different temper and with its different institutions), may yet be said to make for political unselfishness. On one side stands the economic Society: on the other rises the State in the person of the guardians—a State carefully detached by a system of communism from the economic Society, and likely neither to interfere with it nor to be influenced by it. The distinction between Society and the State, which the Greeks tended to ignore, may here be said to find a full expression.[1]

Justice discovered in the State

But above all, in this separation and specialisation lies the clue to that which the whole argument is intended to discover, the nature of justice. In finally discovering justice, as it exists in the State, Plato pursues a method of residues. Making what he conceived to be a "complete enumeration" of the virtues of the State, justice, wisdom, courage and self-control (the four

[1] "State" is here used in the sense of "government". Hildenbrand, however, argues that even Plato has no true conception of the "idea" of the State, *i.e.*, of an organ representative of the common interest: he makes a *class* sovereign. But that class is viewed by Plato as an organ for the common interest, if not as a "representative" organ.

cardinal virtues of the Greeks), he first assigns to each of the latter three its proper place, and then claims the place that remains for the remaining virtue of justice. Now the "virtues of the State," on the principle laid down before, are the virtues of its members acting *as* members. Wisdom accordingly must be the virtue of the ruling class which directs the State by its reason; courage must be the virtue of the soldiers; and self-control, it might seem, that of the producing classes. But self-control is more than the virtue of any one class. It is a virtue which is attained, when desire submits to rule and regimen; and in the State self-control will accordingly be, on its passive side the recognition by the producing and military classes of the need of submitting to rule, on its active side the enforcement of such rule by the government. As a whole, therefore, it is a harmony between these elements, resulting from the presence of the same conviction in all. What then is justice, and where is the place of its habitation? It is simply the specialisation of which we have spoken before: it is simply the will to concentrate on one's own sphere of duty (*τὸ αὑτοῦ πράττειν*), and not to meddle with the sphere of another; and its habitation therefore is in the heart of *every* citizen who does his duty in his appointed place. The ruler, for instance, must be wise, and if he shows wisdom in his work, and cleaves to wisdom as his true vocation, he is thereby just—or rather (for it is the virtue of the State of which we are speaking) the State is just, because its member, in his appointed place, has done his right work as a member.[1] In this sense justice is the condition of every other virtue of the State: unless a citizen concentrates on his own sphere of duty, he will not show the virtue which that sphere demands. In a word, therefore, justice is the principle of a society, consisting of different types of men (the producing type, the military type, the ruling type), who have combined under the impulse of a mutual need, and by their combination in one

[1] The true ruler will show wisdom, self-control (since that virtue belongs to him in common with his subjects), and, in and through both, justice. Further he must have shown courage (in keeping to his conviction that the welfare of the State is his welfare) in order to become a ruler. Therefore the good ruler, as Aristotle afterwards urged, showing all the four virtues, is the same as the absolutely good man.

society made a whole which is perfect, because it is the product and the image of the whole of human mind. As the principle of such a society, it consists in the full discharge by each of these types of the specific function for which, by its capacities and by the place they have given it in the society, it is naturally meant. The justice of the State is the citizen's sense of duty. It is a conscious sense of the duty of a public position issuing in action: England was just at Trafalgar, because her sons who fought under Nelson's signal showed courage in the battle. Such a conception of justice is the final and ultimate death-blow to the individualism in life and in theory which Plato combated. Its essence lies in a view of the individual as no isolated self, but part of an order,—as not intended to pursue the pleasures of that isolated self, but to fill an appointed place in the order. The individual is not a whole, and cannot be treated as such: the State is, and it must enforce upon the individual the fact that it is, by treating him as a factor and a fraction of itself. The conception of the individual as part of an order, although just, is pushed too far by Plato; and in treating of communism we shall see reason to believe that it led Plato to deny to the individual rights, which are the very conditions of his being a moral person and thereby capable of a sense of duty. But the conception of political justice as the filling by each man of his appointed sphere—as a categorical imperative issuing the mandate (in Goethe's words) *Mache ein Organ aus Dir*, is a conception of supreme value for Greek politics, resulting as it did in a view of public duty, and of public efficiency attained by special training, the very reverse of that political selfishness and political ignorance which to Plato characterised Greece. Nor in this connection should Plato's conception of self-control as a virtue of the State pass unnoticed. Like justice, it is a general virtue; and if justice, by keeping each man to his appointed function, involves as its corollary a harmony (a "fitting together" of the different functions), self-control, in the sense in which it has been defined, supplies that corollary, because it knits to one another the rulers and the ruled.[1]

As a principle of political justice, the rule τὸ αὑτοῦ πράττειν

[1] Self-control is the motive of the whole State in the *Laws*.

Value of Plato's conception of justice

may be criticised from a modern point of view. It may be urged that it is too static, too passive; that, while it bids men keep to their sphere, it does not provide a principle for dealing with the clash of wills and the conflict between one sphere of right and another, which is what we seek in a conception of justice. It may be argued again that it is too subjective: justice is made on an indwelling spirit, but it does not issue in a concrete *jus*, and still less in any law. On the contrary Plato is an enemy of law: he would have the ruler as unfettered by external bonds in his action, as an artist in his creation; and aversion to law is one of the prominent and determining features of his political thought. But such criticism from a modern point of view only shows the difference between Plato's outlook and our own. He does not start from a conception of rights, or conceive justice as the maintenance or correlation of such rights. Thinking of the city-state as an ethical society, he thinks of justice as a quality, or rather *the* quality, of its moral life; and because such an ethical society is a product of mind, and is a mind, he comes by this static or subjective conception of justice. Exactly for this reason he can identify, as he does, the justice of the State with that of the individual. He can argue (and with this argument the theory of justice is concluded) that, justice being what we have seen in the State, and the mind of the State being after this fashion, justice in the individual is no other, and the pattern of *his* mind is the same. As in the State there are three elements, so in man there are the three elements of reason, spirit and desire.[1] As the justice of the State meant that each of its three elements retained its place, so that of the individual means that reason, spirit and desire each keep within their proper bounds. But since the justice of the State is that of the individuals composing it, it follows that each individual has two aspects, and shows justice in either. In one aspect he is a member of a community, and he shows justice by exhibiting

[1] In the text an *explicit* account of these three elements in the individual was first given, and it was then shown how they issued in the three elements of the State. But Plato begins with an *implied* psychology of the individual, constructs a State accordingly, and argues from the State to an explicit psychology. In this way he argues from the uncials of the State to the minuscules of the individual. But in reality the minuscules were there from the first.

the one virtue proper to the peculiar place which the one predominant element in his nature has assigned him—the virtue for instance of courage, if "spirit" is the main mark of his temper. In another aspect he is an individual soul, and as such he shows justice, if he keeps each of all the elements of his soul in its right place, and thereby exhibits all the virtues of wisdom, and courage, and self-control. If as a citizen, therefore, a man may live, as we said, with a third of his mind, as an individual he lives with the whole. For the individual justice is the sum of the virtues:

> In Justice is all virtue's self compact;[1]

and in this conception of justice the "unity of virtue" appears.

Plato's Theory of Education

§ 5. Turning from the justice which is the life-breath of the State to the means by which it is to be realised, we find two great institutions suggested by Plato. One is a system of common education by the State; the other is a system of communism. Both of these are practical proposals, springing from the conditions of contemporary politics, and meant for the remedy of those evils which Plato detected in existing States: both are in reaction against ignorance and selfishness, and both make for knowledge and unselfishness. Both flow again from the new conception of justice, which should sweep like a new spirit of life through a body politic sick almost to death. By the teaching of a new education would be given that training for a special work, and that instinct for keeping unselfishly to its performance, which justice demanded: by the new social order of communism time would be gained for the training, and temptations to selfishness removed, while above all the view of the individual as part of a whole, which is implied in the Platonic conception of justice, would find its fulfilment. Of the two, the new education is greater than the new social order. It is an attempt to touch the evil at its source, and to reform wrong methods of life by altering the whole outlook on life. It is an attempt to cure a mental malady by mental medicine. In this sense Rousseau was right; and the *Republic* is pre-eminently

A new education propounded

[1] Ar., *Eth.*, 1129 b 29.

"the finest treatise on education that ever was written". The new social order is by comparison secondary. It is caution's excess: if spiritual means are not enough—why, then, let us draw upon material reinforcements. Communism is a negative thing. Education means the bringing of the soul into that environment, which in each stage of its growth is best suited for its development: communism means the abstraction of those elements of environment, which may divert the soul from its growth to alien cares.

Contemporary Greek education

Primarily, then, the State which realises justice must be an educational institution. The State is a schoolmaster to bring us to justice. In this conception Plato was definitely and consciously departing from the practice of Athens, and setting his face towards Sparta, as he may also be said to have done in turning to communism. At Athens education was private; and not before the days of the Roman Empire was there any endowment of schools by the State. A law of Solon obliged parents to provide for the education of their boys—(there were no schools, and nothing but domestic education, for girls)—but the keeping of schools was a private venture, which, if we may trust Demosthenes' philippic against Æschines, was not always made by those who were best qualified.[1] Schools may have been controlled and inspected by officials of the State; but even this is not certain. The subjects of education (after reading and writing had been mastered) embraced a literary course in the study and interpretation of the best poets, a gymnastic course in various exercises, and a musical course in lyric poetry with an accompaniment of music. The literary course not only taught taste; but—as the poets were the real religious teachers of Greece, and the priests were sacrificers and not preachers—it also taught religion, and something of ethics. The whole curriculum (which lasted from six to sixteen) would produce a versatile man, who could sing a lyric and accompany himself on the harp, who could quote Homer and Hesiod *à propos*, and was physically as well as mentally developed. If still more than this was desired, there was always the "university" of the Sophists in reserve, where something of a definitely political

[1] *Cf.* Smith's *Dictionary of Greek and Roman Antiquities* (third edition), *s.v.* Ludus Litterarius.

training might be gained from lectures on rhetoric and politics. In this scheme of education Plato missed, first and foremost, any regular organisation. A matter of supreme importance to the State was left to the chance of individual initiative. What could be more vital to the State—a product of mind—than that the mind, of which it was composed, should have been properly developed? Yet at Athens the State shut its eyes to its first task, while cumbering itself about a mass of administrative detail, which might well have been left to individual judgment, if the individual had once been properly trained. In this respect Sparta had a great lesson to teach. The Spartan youth was taken from his parents at the age of seven, and his education was entrusted to officials of the State. Sparta thus recognised that the State must be the schoolmaster of its citizens; and she recognised yet another truth. She recognised that the aim of education was the development of moral fibre. A definite principle lay behind the training she gave: it was calculated to develop that type of character, which the State[1] required in its citizens as the condition of realising its ideal of itself. It aimed at the development of "spirit" towards a true courage, and it did so because success in war was the object pursued by the State. But though in the organisation of an educational system by the State, and in the conception of a principle (and a moral principle) as the necessary basis of that system, Sparta stood for a model, the narrow scope of her principle made for a narrow curriculum, which at the best produced a limited virtue. Developing only the element of spirit, she employed only physical exercises and such music as would stimulate courage, and she altogether neglected the literary side of education. Many were the Spartans who could not read or write, and few indeed were those who knew the literature of Greece. Here Athens had something to give; and it may therefore be said to be Plato's aim to combine the curriculum of Athens with the organisation of Sparta, while informing it with a principle higher and wider than that of Sparta—the principle of justice—and continuing it to a later period of life, and into other and nobler studies, than Athens ever contemplated.

[1] *Cf. infra*, p. 423, for the political aspect of education as also conceived by Aristotle. It involves the view that education is primarily moral, and not intellectual.

From Athens, then, comes the individual aspect of Plato's scheme of education—it must be a development of the whole man: from Sparta its social aspect—it must be controlled *by* the State with a view to fitting the individual for his place *in* the State. It was this Spartan side of his scheme which Plato, as an Athenian, and writing for Athenians, naturally emphasised. The political purpose of education is always prominent: the truth must be brought home, that a scheme of education should fit a man for performing scientifically (if the word may be used), and not empirically, the duties of his station. Only so will the principle of justice (that a man should properly fill his appointed place) find realisation: only so will the sin of political ignorance disappear. But Plato's scheme is none the less meant as a scheme for the education of man. It never loses its Athenian side. Plato may think of himself as primarily educating soldiers and governors; but he knows that he is also speaking quite simply of the ordinary human soul. From our point of view, we have to regard the *Republic* "as a treatise on political and social reform," but we must also admit that it is "the exhibition of an ideal theory of human life, which all may apply to themselves ".[1] We must realise that Plato's theory of education has its foundation not only in practical politics, but also in the psychology of the human soul. Accordingly, the old division of the soul into its component elements appears once more to direct the course of education in stages adapted to the predominance of different elements at different periods of life; and the whole theory of education is dominated by a conception of the attitude of the human soul towards knowledge.

Plato's use of existing materials

This conception represents the human soul as in no sense a passive subject of educational action. It is not a thing which "pedagogics" takes, and, after careful inspection of its carrying powers, and the right way to distribute the burden, thereupon proceeds to load. There is no talk of the "steps" by which an object of knowledge is to be "presented" to the mind. Plato supposes always that the mind is active. Objects are not presented to it: it directs itself to objects. It moves towards every object of its environment because there is in it an attraction towards every object. This active spiritual force the

Psychological basis of his scheme

[1] Nettleship, *Lectures*, p. 217.

teacher never tries to touch—at any rate, directly: he merely believes that it lives, and trusts that it will act. His concern is its environment. That environment he seeks to adjust in such a way that the spirit, as it looks around, and moves in response to the attraction which it feels for what it sees, may look around on things beautiful, and move towards the beauty which it sees. Education, in Plato's metaphor, results in the turning of the "inward eye" towards the light; and it does so, because the teacher sets the light to catch the eye. We may speak of the teacher as "bringing out" the best that is in his pupil: more truly, it comes of itself in response to the right objects, and it is in setting them before his pupils that the true art of the teacher lies. In this there may be something of the theory of "reminiscence" (ἀνάμνησις), which is expounded in the *Meno*: the soul has seen in a former life all things which it learns in this, and learning is a "remembrance" of that life, which flashes to the mind when some facet of an object stirs what we may call an association of ideas. The object only gives a cue: the soul itself repeats the lines. But everything depends on the cue; and the environment makes the soul, in the sense that the soul determines itself by its environment, and assimilates itself to what it sees. From this view of the influence of environment comes the high place which Plato assigns to art as an instrument of education.

Education in its various stages

Education is thus concerned with the reaction of the soul on its environment. The teacher regulates that reaction by adjusting the environment. But this reaction is spiritual life, as much as the reaction of the body on its food is physical life: without it the soul is dead. The soul can no more live without food for its activities, than can the body; and therefore, so long as the soul lives, there is need of education to supply the proper food—to set the right object before the soul for its assimilation—to surround it with its true environment. Education is the matter of a life-time: a man is being educated so long as he is capable of a response to each new stimulus with which he comes in contact, so long as he reacts upon and is refashioned by his experience. Education does not merely seek to induce the best that is in the young soul to reveal itself: it occupies itself with age as well as with youth, and seeks to provide for the development of the whole nature of man at every stage and on every side. Two stages in particular may be distinguished. There is first the stage of youth, lasting to the age of eighteen. In this stage education means principally a moral habituation of the *feelings*[1] (for feeling dominates youth, and by his imagination the young man is captured); and in it the instruments used are such as will sway the feelings towards courage and self-control. Then, after an interval of two years, in which youth serves its apprenticeship to the State by a military training, begins the stage of education designed for the maturer soul, in which the element of *reason* is now fast growing. From the age of twenty to the day of death, step by step and stage by stage, reason is developed by a regular education, until, as life ceases (but not before), education also comes to an end.

Instruments of education

Hitherto we have looked at the human soul, and we have seen that it must be regarded as an active force, and as acting in different ways at different stages of its growth. It remains to consider the environment by which it should be surrounded. The general principle which Plato lays down with regard to environment—his theory, as we should say, of the instruments of education—may be expressed in the proposition, that mind develops through contact with the products of mind. The individual mind grows by assimilating itself to the products, which the mind of man has achieved in many generations,—his art and his literature, his science and his philosophy. But we have already seen that the State is such a product; and it is accordingly Plato's belief, that part of education consists in contact with the State—in other words, that a man is educated by political action. The

[1] In the development of the human soul by means of education, desire and spirit have to be trained, and reason elicited. The training of the two former elements is particularly the work of education when it deals with the young; but the training of these involves an implicit eliciting of the reason. The "spirit" is trained to courage, because the *reason* is imbued with a right, if unexplained, opinion concerning things to be feared. Regarding the human soul in its cognitive aspect, by which it seizes upon, and masters its environment (*i.e.*, regarding this element of reason), we may distinguish two stages: (1) that of *δόξα*, or opinion, which is either mere conjecture (*εἰκασία*), or a feeling of certainty (*πίστις*); and (2) that of *ἐπιστήμη*, or knowledge, which is either understanding (*διάνοια*), the comprehension of mathematical truths, or perfect intelligence (*νόησις*), the comprehension of the world in the light of a principle. The difference between these two stages is the difference between empiric opinion and scientific knowledge; and a certain empiric opinion (and to that extent an eliciting of reason) is involved in the training of youth.

fulness of an education is in proportion to the fulness of experience which it embraces; and no human mind can be said to have developed to its highest, unless it has developed in every way in which mind has developed in the past. In this past development there is included a political development; and through that, therefore, each individual man, whose face is set towards perfection, must go. The evolution of the soul of every man must resume in itself the evolution of the soul of mankind. This is the spiritual counterpart of the material truth which biology has taught us, that the physical evolution of each human being, from the first germ to the perfect body, resumes the whole of the historical evolution of man. There is accordingly no distinction in Plato between mind practical and mind theoretical, and no confining of education to the latter. Since the whole of mind must be developed, all the practical training and experience which we can acquire is a part of our education. The practical and the theoretical are one: they are both products of mind, and mind must be brought into contact with both. From a political point of view, this teaching once more reaffirms the old identity of the State and man. The State is a product of man's mind, as we saw: it is also, we now learn, one of the necessary elements in the development of his mind. But it must be noticed that in this new conception there is something of a new tone. Man appears less as a part of the State, than the State appears as a part of his experience. There is something of an escape from the State, to a self which is greater than its political experience. And in this way Plato easily glides into a view, which he sometimes betrays, that the best life for man is not the political life, but the life of contemplation, which is the ultimate crown of human development. The political life is but a step towards such an ultimate goal; and if those who have attained that goal must sometimes come back to the State, it is with sad reluctant steps, and eyes ever turning backwards—it is for the service of their fellows, and not for the good of themselves.

Education culminates in the Idea of the Good

The fulness of human experience is therefore the instrument of education. But that experience is not meaningless. It is not a chapter of accidents, but a logical sequence, and it must be seen as such. In Plato there is implicit—what in Aristotle is definitely explicit—a teleological conception of the world, based on a teleological conception of mind. In the first place, the human mind as it issues in action moves towards a purpose, an end (or τέλος), because it acts by the reason that is in it, and reason demands a purpose. To say that an action is rational is to say that it has a purpose: to act irrationally is to act aimlessly (μάτην). Nor does the human mind merely move towards *some* purpose in virtue of its reason, but, that reason being a unity, it always moves towards *one* ultimate purpose—the attainment of the Good—whatever proximate purpose it may seek to realise. In the second place, as mind on its practical side is teleologically conceived in virtue of its reason, so is mind also conceived on its cognitive side, and as issuing in knowledge. It understands objects when, and in proportion as, it sees a purpose in them—a purpose, in the sense of adaptation to a place in a scheme. Through purpose mind knows as well as acts; and except through the conception of purpose nothing is known. To know a thing is to see it as part of a scheme (in Plato's terminology, an "Idea"), and to understand it as adapted to the fulfilment of that scheme. Now there cannot be a number of uncorrelated schemes—otherwise, knowledge would be a sum of fragments, each shrouded round by mystery; and mind therefore demands, as the condition of any true knowledge, the correlation of all schemes in a single scheme (*the* "Idea"), corresponding to its own unity. The unity of the world is thus an ultimate postulate of mind, and the unity of the world involves a single purpose. In knowledge as in action, there is *one* ultimate purpose implied. But this postulate of an ultimate purpose as the condition of knowledge really implies (in the third place) that the world is the creation of a mind, which has created it for a purpose. Otherwise the world as represented in knowledge, the world which is a unity with a purpose, would be a fiction of the human mind. To say therefore that a teleological conception of the world is the condition of knowledge, is to say that the world is the creation of a mind: to say that knowledge implies an ultimate purpose is to say that existence implies an ultimate purpose. There is thus an ultimate purpose in the action and the thought of the human mind, and consequently in the existence of the world, which is an act (or thought) of mind. This purpose is one and single, because mind is one and single. Action, knowledge, existence—all therefore imply the Idea of the Good; and true action is action in the light of the knowledge that the Good is the reason of all existence.

Education culminates in the realisation of the Idea of the Good. The soul has only then fully adjusted itself to its environment when it has seen the purpose which animates it all. Nor is it the aim of education simply to understand the world in the light of an end: it is also to gain the master-key of conduct and action, since all right conduct and proper action will be conformed and directed to the end which is the end of all things. This is the real sense in which virtue is knowledge. If this conception be personalised, we may say that the end of education is the realisation of God: it is knowing that all things are one in Him, and doing in the light of that knowledge. But this unity of all things in God must not only be realised by the soul in its education. The conception of the Idea of the Good must permeate all the structure of the State. (i.) The State is one of the schemes in which the idea of the Good expresses itself; and the individual must be understood as having a place in this scheme. He must be understood in the light of a purpose which he serves in the plan of the State. This is what we should call an "organic" conception of the State; for a scheme, in the sense in which it has here been used, is an organism. An organism is a unity, where each member is an instrument (or ὄργανον) in the general plan; where each member has its appointed purpose or function (ἔργον); where each member can only act, and be understood, and indeed exist, through the end and aim of the whole. But such is the unity of the State and such is the relation of the individual to the State: the State is an organism and its citizens are its members.[1] Hence the need of specialisation—each member should serve his purpose in the organism: hence the necessity of justice—for each member should keep to that purpose.[2] (ii.)

The state and its rulers in relation to the Idea of the Good

[1] This contradicts what was said above of the State as only part of man's experience. But the contradiction is there in Plato, and he alternates unconsciously between an organic and an external conception of the State.

[2] It should be noticed that the soul itself is an organism, being a scheme of elements each with its place. And as political justice depends on the conception of the State as an organism, so in the individual justice depends on the same conception of the soul.

But as the individual is part of the State, so the State is part of the world. The organic conception of the State implies a teleological conception of the world. The State as a scheme or organism is part of a *general* unity, since, as was said, there cannot be a number of uncorrelated schemes. As the individual must be understood in its light, it must be understood in the light of the Idea of the Good. Therefore it is that the ruler, whose wisdom lies in understanding and guiding the State, must be a philosopher seeing the State in the light of the Idea, and guiding it thereby. He of all men must be educated to the conception of the Idea; and indeed Plato conceives of education to the height of this conception as reserved for the chosen few who are meant to rule.

Art as an instrument of education

So far we have considered the environment as a whole. We must now consider it in its different parts, as they are presented to the soul at its different stages. We have looked at education as the growth of the soul. We must now look at education as the preparation of the citizen for taking his place in the organism of the State, and the preparation of the ruler for conducting the State as a part of the world, with its own appointed place in the world's scheme. The instruments which Plato suggests for the education of the citizen (and by citizen we must simply understand the soldier),[1] consist in such studies as will lead to the right development of the element of spirit by which he is dominated, and consequently to his discharging rightly the military function to which he is called in the State. These studies are simply the Athenian studies reformed. The three courses of Athens are by Plato made into two, gymnastics and music. But music is made to include a literary course as well as musical study; and indeed in Plato's use of the term it is broadened to include the plastic arts as well. Music is therefore a triad: its general sense is "Art as applied to education"—art as an imitation of life in any of the three media, literature, or music, or form and colour. Both gymnastics and music are to be used for what we should call a moral purpose, and in order to shape character. Gymnastics is a training of the body: it is also meant to elicit certain

[1] The position of the third estate must be left out of consideration for the present.

qualities of endurance and courage, a certain habit of "spirit"; and this is its primary aim. Both in its physical and in its moral results, it prepares the soldier for his place in the State. Music is a training of the soul, primarily in its aspect of reason, which, as we saw, is needed to temper and correct mere spirit, but also, and thereby, in its aspect of spirit. As such a training, it is meant to give, not scientific knowledge, but a right opinion. It is meant, as Aristotle would say, to "habituate" the young soul, which is still in the stage of feeling, to feel as it should about such problems as it has to solve, and in the strength of a feeling ingrained by habit to do as it ought to do, without knowing the why and wherefore of its action. That is why artistic media are used. The rhythm and diction of poetry, the sounds of music, the shapes and colours of statuary, appeal to youth in themselves; and if, when they come to youth with their strong appeal, they carry with them a moral message (such as poetry and music and statuary may all convey), they will insensibly instil into the young mind, which accepts them simply for their artistic appeal, a growing love of righteousness. Since the soul is attracted towards its environment, and assimilates itself to its surroundings, it is inevitable that if *they* are instinct with a moral truth, the soul will be imbued with it also.

Moral reform of Art

But if this be so, it is of all things most important that art should always convey a moral message, and never by any chance lend its attraction to anything which youth should not learn to love. It should always bring suggestions of courage to the spirit; it should always carry to the ears of reason whispers of that ultimate Good, which it will one day hear for itself. Accordingly Plato seeks to reform literature, and music, and sculpture in this light. In reforming literature, he deals both with its content and with its form; and while in speaking of the content he suggests a religious reformation, in discussing the form he lays down the first principles of literary criticism and the foundations of Aristotle's *Poetics*. Such a religious reformation was necessary, because the poets who formed the staple of a literary education were also, as we have seen, the religious teachers of Greece; and Plato seeks to re-edit Homer and the dramatists, wherever they have misrepresented the nature of God, in much the same way as a modern reformer might seek to expurgate the note of revenge or of jealousy from the character of Jehovah as represented in the Old Testament. From a political point of view it is to be noticed, that (since Plato is here speaking as a legislator) he may be said to contemplate an extension of the authority of the State to the regulation of dogma. The powers of the State have already been made to embrace education: through education they are now made to cover religion. Through education, too, they are further extended to the determination of the literary form which the poets and the authors of the *Republic* shall use. As the State must control the pictures of God's nature which poetry draws, because they will affect the character of its citizens, so it must control the forms of poetic expression, because these will equally affect character. This follows on Plato's principle, that the soul assimilates itself to all things with which it comes in contact. Accordingly, if it comes into contact with a dramatic form of expression, it will assimilate itself to the spirit of that form. Throwing itself into different characters, some of them good and some of them bad, in hearing or reading a drama, it will begin to throw itself into different moods in its own actual life. It will begin to pose, now in this attitude, now in that; and it will thus go exactly contrary to the fundamental principle of the State, that a man should do the one thing, and preserve the one attitude, to which he is called. Drama is the literary form for a democracy, where each man in his time plays many parts: it is the form of expression which corresponds to democratic πολυπραγμοσύνη. In a State based on the principle of justice the literary form will be narratival: it will be the epic form, in which the narrator preserves a single attitude, or at the most only occasionally throws himself into one of his characters, and allows Achilles or Odysseus to speak.[1]

[1] As Nettleship points out, Plato's condemnation of the drama must be understood in the light of contemporary Greek history. On the one hand there was the Greek tendency towards posing in many parts: on the other hand, contemporary drama (it would appear from the description of the *Republic*) was losing something of the moral element which had given each play or trilogy its "unity" in the time of Æschylus and Sophocles, and was sinking into a realism (such as apparently Plato detected in Euripides) which sought to represent any and every situation and character—Phædra in love with her stepson, or Medea killing her children in a fit of jealousy.

Like literature, music[1] must also be submitted to the regimen of the State, if the purity of its moral message is to be preserved. The State must act as a universal critic: it must discern between various instruments, choosing the harp and rejecting the flute; it must limit the modes and the times to the simpler varieties. In respect of music, as of literature, a desire for simplicity in the sense of conformity to one single principle, results in a reactionary spirit; and Plato seems willing to reject many of the products of man's mind, in order that the residue may be purely conformable to the purpose by which man's mind should be animated. He is willing to reform mankind even at the cost of not a little surgery; and this readiness ultimately culminates in a system of communism, in which such products of mind as property and the family are cut away in the name of "purification". The surgery from which art suffers may well seem strange in an artist like Plato; and the rejection of the drama by the author of the dialogue cannot but appear inconsistent. A believer in "art for art's sake" may readily object, that a false conception of art as serving a moral purpose is responsible for such eccentricity or inconsistency. He may urge that the free play of the artistic impulse is everything, and that art, cabined and confined by the State to a moral purpose, will lose its "appeal," and fail even in carrying a moral message, because it has lost its moving power. Failing to touch the hearer or reader as art, it will fail to touch him as ethics. There is truth in the objection; but we should misconceive Plato, if we believed that he committed himself to a view of art as didactic, when he committed himself to the State-supervision of art. He never conceived of art as State-messenger, with a budget of moral missives for delivery. Art is not moral to Plato because it tries to convey a lesson external to itself, and only foisted upon it. In itself and as itself it has a lesson which is the essence of its substance. Art is a reflection (μίμησις) of life: in it, as in a glass, man sees the world. But life is informed by a principle, and the world is penetrated by a purpose. What is true of the original must

The morality of Art

[1] The same is true of the plastic arts, though little is said of them expressly.

be true of the copy, if it is a true copy: the substance of any artistic product must be instinct with the "Idea of the Good," if it is the product of genuine art, and a real imitation. Any artistic product, *as an artistic product*, must convey the lesson which is implied in the reality which it imitates. It must convey it still more clearly than the original, we may add, because art is selective as well as imitative, and selects those moments or phases of the original, which will tell most in exhibiting its hidden trend and purpose. That is why[1] youth begins with art, and studies the mirror; and age may rise from the mirror to the original because it has learned to see "as in a glass"—clearly.

Province of the State in respect of Art

The teleological conception of the world must issue, therefore, in the conception of the moral meaning of art: in other words, it must lead us to think that art must be the exhibition of a principle at work. Plato's error lies in this, that he would have the principle exhibited only too clearly; he would have it thrown into prominence by the abolition of everything which does not directly show its operation. Hence he throws upon the State the impossible task of supervising the content and the form of all artistic production. And hence he comes upon a view of the State's province of action which is to a modern mind surprising. No small part of the State's action seems to us judicial; and modern theory, in Hobbes and in Locke, has represented the formation of the State as due to the need of instituting, or at any rate improving, a system of justice. But Plato would sweep away the apparatus of the law, courts and pleaders and pleas, just as he would sweep away the surgery and its drugs. The one is the sign of disease of the soul, as the other is a sign of disease of the body; and his State cannot and will not have its members diseased. It will have prevention and not cure: it will have healthy minds in healthy bodies, secured by sound education in music and gymnastics. If such an education has been given, there will be no need of lawyers or physicians; and where they abound, they abound only for lack of a proper system of education. A true State will diet

[1] And not only because (as it was suggested above) the materials of art—musical sounds, or poetic diction and rhythm—are things which appeal to the feelings.

its citizens, but it will not give them medicine; it will give food to their minds by a right system of education, but not drugs; it will be occupied by problems of physiology, and not by those of pathology. In all this there is embedded the Greek conception, that the function of the State is not preventive, but positive—not the removal of hindrances to a good life which must develop from within, but the application of a stimulus to its development. Accordingly, where we conceive the State as legislating for the removal of hindrances (or in other words in order to guarantee rights), where we regard it as interpreting laws by a judicature, and enforcing them by an executive, Plato thought little of laws and less of a judicature, and viewed the State as an executive only. Even the executive is simple: its great and almost its sole organ is the Board of Education.[1] That is to say, its rulers are principally to act by way of enforcing certain great outlines of education, which the primitive legislator had laid down once and for all. The simple problem for the State is to keep those outlines pure; its one task is to allow no revolutions in music and gymnastics. Plato would have recognised a deep truth in the saying, "Let me write the ballads of a country, and I care not who writes the laws";[2] he would indeed have extended its scope, and made it read, "Let me write the right ballads for a country, and nobody will need to write its laws". A good education in music and gymnastics carries with it everything else: if it has once put the spirit of law in the heart, there is little need for external law which resides in mere "words and letters". Law is a spirit: the lawgiver is not the legislator, but the educator who gives the spirit.[3] And when once that spirit is there, it will solve all things, and bring all things to remembrance. Once more[4] we come upon Plato's aversion to written law: once more we come upon the fundamental lesson which he has to teach, that the State is mind, and its institutions ideas. The lesson is true; but the aversion to law is the pushing of a true principle to an extreme application which is untrue.[5] The spiritual basis of

[1] The same conception underlies Aristotle's ideal State. It is a school—an *Erziehungsanstalt*—principally and primarily; and this is almost the only aspect which Aristotle discusses.

[2] *Cf. Rep.*, 424 C.

[3] *Cf.* Aristotle, *infra*, pp. 323-24.

[4] *Cf. supra*, p. 118, and *infra*, p. 167.

[5] Exactly as his principle that art is moral is a true principle, vitiated by an extreme application when he makes the State enforce the morality of art.

law can never do away with the need of its external expression. Law will sink into subjective caprice, if it does not receive an objective form. This has been the danger which has at all times attended the assertion of the spiritual and subjective basis in the sphere of religion. The reaction against the hard letter of the law provoked in the early Church an antinomianism which covered itself with the plea of the spirit; and when the German Reformation asserted justification by faith, there came with the assertion something of a contempt for the external manifestation of faith in works, which issued in a similar extravagance.

In discussing the great questions which are raised by Plato when he is considering the education of the young—the morality of art, the true province of the State's action, the nature of law—we must not forget to consider, whether this scheme of education realises its political purpose of providing the State with a man, who knows how to fill his due place, and to fill it unselfishly. It is obvious that a training in music and gymnastics, such as Plato proposes, will give the State a capable soldier; and the musical element in his education will have made him unselfish, since it will have cultivated the rational part of his nature, and elicited that mild and gentle temper, which was postulated along with spirit in the original composition of the natural guardian. We have seen, therefore, the education which will make the soldier all that he should be: it remains to consider the education of the ruler. In doing so, we rise from artistic means to scientific. We leave the reform of the ordinary Athenian curriculum for a higher education, which is perfectly new: we add to the school, as it were, the university, and a university of a far different type from that represented by the Sophists. The moral education of the soldier had been one in which the many could share: the philosophic training of the ruler is reserved for the few. The soldier had finished his education by the age of eighteen, like the ordinary Athenian of the day: the ruler is still engaged in the study of the Good, when life comes to its end.

The education of reason

It must not be imagined that there is any cleavage between artistic and scientific education. Plato on the contrary emphasises the nice dovetailing by which they are joined. Already he would have youth trained, during the period of music, in the elements of science. But more important than any external adaptation is the inner and spiritual adaptation of the earlier and artistic to the later and scientific education. Art, we have seen, is the reflection of the purpose of the world to the eyes of conjecture and faith (πίστις); and it naturally prepares the way for science to reveal the pure purpose to understanding and pure intelligence. From the first therefore it was the aim of education to turn the eye towards that Idea of the Good, which it is the ultimate purpose of education to reveal. In the first stage, the soul insensibly grew into harmony and sympathy with the Idea, when embodied under the form of Beauty in artistic reflections: in the last, the soul recognises face to face the friend whose image it has so often seen, and with whose being it has itself become instinct.[1] Both as trained in the elements of science, therefore, and as unconsciously instinct with the Idea of the Good, youth is ready at the age of twenty to begin that life-long education, which lifts it by successive stages to the "contemplation" of the pure Idea—to what the middle ages would have called the Fruitio Dei. We can only look at these stages so far as they bear on the public life of the citizen of the Republic. First of all, between the age of twenty and that of thirty, those who have proved best during the period of artistic education (and those only) have their understanding developed by a course of science, and are practised in war and all other duties, which the service of the State may require. Secondly, from thirty to thirty-five, a training in dialectic (in "thinking things together" in the light of a principle) is given to those (and again those only) who have shown the greatest ability in the study of science. Next, for a period of fifteen years those who have been proved in science, and trained in dialectic, are to give themselves to the service of the State, commanding in war, holding such offices as are not reserved for age, and generally acquiring political experience. All the time of their service they will be tested and tried, and then those who at the age of fifty have come through every test and trial with credit

[1] For the soul assimilated itself to the Idea of the Good, during the period of its artistic education, because the Idea of the Good was made its environment, and the soul accommodates itself to its surroundings.

and distinction,[1] may be allowed to reach the goal, not of rest, but of perfect action. They may spend part of their time in pure philosophy, and in contemplation of the Good: they must still spend part of their time, when their turn comes round, in the service of the State. They must labour and travail for their fellows, perfectly, in the light of a perfect knowledge, not as something noble, but as something necessary, not for themselves, but for posterity, since the purpose of their travail is this, that they should leave the State as they found it, and train the next generation to carry forward their work, in the same faith, to the same end.

Relation of the trained ruler to the State

To the end of life man is a servant to the State. And yet it cannot be denied that there is a change in the view of the relation of man to the State in the later books of the *Republic.* The Idea of the Good works in two ways. On the one hand it involves a teleological conception of the world, which makes the State an organism, and consequently postulates a view of the individual as acting and existing only in and through the State. On the other hand, it results in the conception, that the *summum bonum* lies in contemplation of itself, and that whatever results in an abstraction of man from contemplation

[1] It should be noted that the principle of "distributive justice" implied by Plato—the canon by which office is to be awarded—is here that of ability, as tested and tried by examination, ability of a moral as well as of an intellectual order. In the earlier books of the *Republic* it was less ability than patriotism: the proper ruler was he who identified his interests with those of the State. Two principles are thus implied—reward according to capacity to do the State's work, and reward according to the measure of devotion to the State. The two are not discrepant: the principle of patriotism prepares the way for that of ability, and the man who shows devotion does so because he has the wisdom to know (if only by the light of mere "opinion"), and the courage to act on his knowledge, that the State is indissolubly one with himself, since he is himself an "organ" of the State. Patriotism prepares the way for knowledge, as the moral prepares the way for the philosophic education. The system of examinations is interesting: it is the sanction as it were of the whole system of education, designed to make sure of what the system is intended to produce—that the ruler shall know what he works at, and love what he knows. A system of regular training for political duties, enforced by examination, was thus Plato's cure for contemporary amateurism in politics. To-day, we admit examination, for the permanent civil service (in intellectual qualities only, Plato would remark, and in subjects foreign to the work for which they open the door); but, except for the constant "examination" of a long public career by public opinion, we hardly admit Platonic principles elsewhere. Yet these principles seem as necessary now as they did in the fourth century B.C.; and a special knowledge and ability, proved in practice, is still an ideal to be kept in view.

hinders his attainment of his end. Plato attempts to reconcile the contradiction. The philosophic nature which develops in the ideal State, till it reaches the contemplation of the Good, has grown not of itself, as it must in ordinary life, but under the fostering care of the State; it owes a debt for its fostering, and it must repay the debt by guiding the State which has guided its own growth. In this way the State will gain what of all things it may well pray most to have, a ruler who rules wisely indeed, but yet reluctantly, thinking of his office not as a perquisite, but as a duty and a burden to be borne for the good of his fellows.[1] Such a conception of office will mean the absence of political faction and of selfish politics, for it will mean the end of the struggle for office as a source of profit. This is very true; but it does not really reconcile the philosopher to the State, in any organic sense; it is only an external reconciliation. He has ascended through the State, and by the experience of a life in the State, to a height where he transcends it. There is something mediæval, it has often been remarked, in the atmosphere of the later books of the *Republic;* and this element is conspicuously present, in the idea of a reluctant turning from the vision to mix in secular affairs. It is as if a monk were abstracted from the cell of his contemplation to sit on the Papal chair, protesting, yet consenting. Nor is the whole conception of the Platonic ruler, acting by a higher wisdom in the light of the Good, unlike that of the mediæval Pope, ruling as the Vicar of God, and by the power of the Keys, over the communion of the faithful. For the Platonic State too sometimes appears as a monarchy; it is a State under a king,[2] we are told; though generally it is of rulers, rather than a ruler that we hear, and it is in one passage[3] definitely called an aristocracy.

Communism

§ 6. When we turn from the subject of the new education to that of the new social order, we return once more to the organic view of the State. The communism which is peculiar to this new order is indeed still mediæval; it has its affinities

[1] *Cf.* Aristotle's account of the ancient view of office (*honos*) as an *onus*, p. 310.

[2] *Rep.*, 576 E. [3] *Ibid.*, 544 E.

Relation of Platonic communism to education

with the communism of a monastery. But its theoretical basis is to be found in the philosophic conception of the State as an organism, and of justice as the duty of filling unselfishly and thoroughly an allotted place; and its practical basis lies in a reaction against the selfishness and ignorant inefficiency which marked contemporary Greek politics, as they appeared to Plato. It is a material and economic corollary of the spiritual method, by which Plato has already attempted to enforce his conception of the one, and to mark his reaction against the other. It receives perhaps more emphasis from Plato than these spiritual methods, because he is more conscious of its novelty and its need of justification. On the other hand, in spite of Aristotle's criticism, it cannot be doubted that it was primarily by spiritual means that Plato sought to regenerate man and society; and it must not be forgotten, that the material institutions of a communistic system are only meant to clear the ground and to remove the hindrances in the way of the operation of these spiritual means. This is implied in the fundamental conceptions of the *Republic.* The State is a product of mind, and to reform the State we must reform man's mind. Justice is nothing external, but a habit of mind; and true justice can only be realised when the mind acquires its true habit. Lastly, the realisation of the Idea of the Good is the ultimate condition of a proper State animated by true justice; and it is *education* which is necessary, if that realisation is to be attained. The spiritual motive is thus entirely and indubitably dominant. Herein lies a great and primary difference between Platonic communism and modern socialism. Without denying that socialism has its ultimate spiritual ends, we may assert without injustice, that it starts from materialistic conceptions to achieve a material result. It demands an equal division of material goods, for the sake of an equal diffusion of material happiness. Plato demands an equal abnegation of material goods, for the sake of that ideal happiness, which comes from true fulfilment of function. Where modern socialism is positive, Plato is negative: while in its tenets there is something of hedonism, in his there is only too much asceticism.

We have seen that Plato began the *Republic* with the idea of combating and destroying a false conception of the self as

Communism necessary to the rule of reason

an isolated unit concerned with its own satisfaction. It is his aim to substitute a conception of the self as part of an order, and as finding its satisfaction in filling its place in that order. This conception, we saw, is expressed under the name of Justice, and it means that each man should do one special work truly and thoroughly, and that no man should selfishly and aggressively trespass on the province of his neighbour. Now communism is to Plato the necessary result of this conception of justice. *Two* of the three classes of his ideal State—the rulers and the soldiers—must, if they are to do their work truly, and to keep to it unselfishly, live under a *régime* of communism. They must not work with the part of their soul which is desire, if they are to devote themselves to the perfecting of their proper elements of spirit and reason; and they must therefore abnegate the economic side of life which is the outward expression of desire. If they threw themselves into that life, they would hamper the operation of the proper elements of their soul, both by letting them fall into disuse, and by indulging an element of the soul which is hostile to them. Accordingly, it appears that a communistic life, in the sense of a life divested of the economic motive, is necessarily connected with, and issues from, the supremacy in the State of the proper elements of mind, and particularly of the element of reason. Communism is postulated by the rule of the philosophic nature, in which reason is dominant. Without communism reason would either be dormant (while desire acted, and busied itself with acquisition) or, even when it acted, it would be troubled in its action by desire, which would tend to make it act for selfish ends. Not only is communism necessary to reason, but reason issues in communism. Reason means unselfishness: it means that the man whom it animates abnegates mere self-satisfaction as his aim, and throws himself into the welfare of a larger whole. And it means this because, in virtue of it, the philosophic temper realises the world as a scheme ordered towards the Idea of the Good, and recognises the State as a scheme within that scheme, and the individual, again, as in turn a part of that scheme. Through reason the philosophic ruler sees that he is an "organ" of the State, and that he must put away all the element of desire, since what is required of him as an organ of the State is pure reason.

Communism then *must* come, that reason may be perfect, and that by the perfect working of reason in its appointed place in the State, justice may be realised: while that it *will* come, reason is in itself the guarantee. But just because it is thus connected with reason, which is but one of the elements of the State, and an element represented by a far smaller body of citizens than any other element, communism cannot be a matter of the whole State, but only of the guardians and auxiliaries. Neither the communism in respect of goods, nor that in respect of wives, which are both advocated by Plato, touch the third or economic class. How indeed could a system which means the abnegation of desire touch the class which represents the element of desire? The third class has both property and families. Both, it is true, are under the strict supervision of the government. The government regulates trade and industry (less by law, than by its innate wisdom): true to the main principle of the *Republic*, it assigns to each member of the economic class his special work, in order that, each man practising his own craft, and no man interfering with that of another, there may be no dissensions; and it prevents producers from becoming either too rich or too poor, since both riches and poverty corrupt and destroy the State. But this is a policy of Protection, in its widest sense, and not of Communism: it is a policy, which admits an individualistic management of economics, but regulates it by considerations of the welfare of the State—a policy like that which the Tudors pursued towards the guilds.[1] Unlike

[1] Pöhlmann regards Plato's communism as economic, and as extending to all the classes of the community. This can hardly be right; but the position of the third class in Plato's State is a difficulty, and Aristotle raised the question of its organisation. In truth, the class of producers seems to disappear: Plato is preoccupied with the ruler. It is noteworthy that it has no special virtue assigned to it: the ruler has wisdom, the soldier courage, but the producer can only share self-control with both. Plato, unlike his master Socrates, has little respect for labour: "mean employments and manual arts involve disgrace" (590 C). At the same time, as we saw, Plato has a truer conception of trade than Aristotle; and we must admit that the third estate would share in the benefit of some of his reforms, *e.g.*, the reform of traditional representations of God, and the improvement of music. Both of these would touch the lower classes, which must be supposed to have known myths and music, and would benefit by the purification of the two. But it has been remarked that the third class is practically the serf class: in some ways it corresponds to the serfs whom Aristotle proposes for the tilling of the land of his ideal State; and hence Plato can afford to adopt, as he does, a fairly liberal attitude towards slavery, arguing that no Greek should be a slave (an indication

modern communism in his ideal aim, Plato is therefore unlike it also in his scope; and paradoxically enough, as it may appear to a modern mind, he invents a system of communism which has nothing at all to do with the economic structure of society —which leaves an individualistic system of production still standing, and does not touch a single producer. It must indeed appear a strange communism to any modern communist; for it is a communism in which, limited as are the divisors, the dividend is still less. The guardians to whom the system applies are distinguished from the rest of the State by sharing in a common poverty, like a body of Franciscan friars. Property they have none. Neither individually nor collectively do they own a single acre: the land and its products are in the hands of the third estate of farmers.[1] They have no houses: they live in common barracks, which are always open and public. But on what, then, do they live? On a salary paid in kind by the farming classes according to a regular assessment, a salary paid year by year, and consisting of such necessaries as will suffice for the year. These necessaries are not divided among the guardians for private consumption: they are to be consumed at common tables. Here, as in the idea of a "training" to be given by the State to qualify its citizens for their work, appears the influence of Sparta upon Plato. These common tables are a Spartan institution, somewhat reformed. Instead of contribution being made to the common mess by each citizen individually, as was the case at Sparta, the tables are maintained by the State from the taxes[2] paid by the landed class. The system in general has from one point of view a very modern aspect. Its object may be said to be the substitution of a professional administration supported by a system of regular taxation, in lieu of an unprofessional and unpaid government supporting itself by peculation. It is a political object, such as has been

Communism of property: its scope and character

of pan-Hellenic feeling which does not stand alone in the *Republic*, and is also indicated in the conception of the oracle of Delphi as spiritual centre of Greece).

[1] Aristotle misrepresents Plato, when he discusses common ownership of land as if it were a Platonic idea.

[2] State-provision for the common tables was actually made in Crete. Apart from the common tables, there were some definite traces of communism at Sparta: a Spartan might use the goods of another Spartan with some freedom (*cf.* Ar., *Pol.*, ii., 1263 a 35).

again and again attempted in the course of history,[1] in great things and in small, in wide spheres and in narrow. One may even say that here is the Periclean system of pay (μισθός) for political work,[2] safe-guarded from abuse by being combined with the Spartan system of common tables, and reconciled with an attempt at professional specialisation which Periclean Athens would have repudiated. Regarding the political aim of this system of communism, we can readily differentiate it once more from communism, or socialism, of the modern type. Such schemes have an economic motive. They aim at rectifying the inequalities and injustices of the modern system of distribution. They attempt, if one may be permitted the rudest of generalisation, to give capital and labour their proper places, by nationalising capital and equalising rewards.[3] Yet different as is this economic aim from the political aim of the *Republic*, it may be argued that fundamentally the same object characterises both Plato and the modern socialist. That object is, in a word, solidarity. The socialist aims at destroying the unchecked competition of individual with individual in the economic sphere, exactly as Plato sought to destroy, in the field of politics, the competition for power between one selfish unit and another; he aims at eliminating the gospel of the "economic man," as Plato sought to eliminate the preaching that might was right. Socialism attempts to realise the conception of a social whole, of which each man feels himself a member, and of a common interest, in securing which each man secures his own: Plato attempted to realise the same conception.[4] Against both the same objection is and has been urged—"they destroy individuality": against neither

[1] One may compare the attempt made in England in 1258, by the Provisions of Oxford, to substitute an annual and salaried sheriff, in lieu of the old sheriff, who had made what he could by the use of his official powers.

[2] Plato himself says in the *Timæus*, where he recapitulates the *Republic*, "the guardians were to be like hired troops, receiving pay for keeping guard" (18 B).

[3] I have not distinguished, as it did not seem necessary for my purpose, between modern Communism, as represented, *e.g.*, by Robert Owen, and modern Collectivism, as represented by Karl Marx or Bellamy. The definition in the text is of course a definition of Collectivism.

[4] His rulers, he urges, will be naturally loved by those whom they protect, as guardians, and they will love in turn the producing classes by whose exertions they are supported, as foster-parents (τροφεῖς). Ruler and subject will be knit together by a mutual regard, based on a difference of function, and on the consequent need of the one for the services of the other.

is this objection properly valid, upon any true conception of the meaning of individuality.

But Plato's scheme embraces not only communism of property; it also contemplates communism of wives; and here, it may be said, a vital difference is obvious between modern aims and those of Plato. The difference may be doubted. Communism of wives in the sense in which it was advocated by Plato, may be understood most easily in its negative aspect, and as meaning the abolition of the family. From this point of view it may be doubted whether, if socialism had its day, the zeal of regulation and the passion of unity might not lead men to "reform" the independence of the family out of existence. There is a law which is very true of human affairs, that actions and reforms intended to achieve one result must as a matter of fact involve many and sometimes unexpected results in addition; and this is a law which must be especially true of a great reform like socialism. But whether or no the abolition of the family would be proved by the logic of events to result from the aims of modern socialism, it seemed to Plato to follow logically upon the aim which he proposed to himself. He wished the rulers of his ideal State to be troubled neither by distractions from their work, nor by temptations to self-interest. He had deprived them of property, since its care was a distraction, and the desire to gain it was a temptation. But his aim was only half-achieved with the abolition of property. The family postulates property for its maintenance: it is a distraction from the genuine work of a man's life;[1] it is a temptation to throw oneself into self-seeking, which seems almost something noble, when it is disguised under the garb of a father's anxiety for the "future" of his children.

Communism of wives

To Plato the "home," which is so precious to us, was anathema. "Every Englishman's house is his castle," we say. "Pull down the walls," Plato replies: "they shelter at best a restricted family feeling: they harbour at the worst avarice and ignorance. Pull down the walls, and let the free air of a common life blow over the place where they have been." For the ruler

Plato's dislike of the household

[1] *Cf.* Zola's saying: "On donne sa virilité à son œuvre". The celibacy of the clergy, formally based on the conception that the priest has married his Church, and can have no other wife, is really based on this principle.

and the soldier there is but one home—and that is the State. Had they separate and individual homes, the result would be disunion among themselves, and separation from the subjects whom they should protect and govern. Each of these homes would be a centre of exclusiveness, to which its owner would ever be dragging whatever property he could seize for himself—in which, with the separate life of the family, a separate sentiment with its private joys and private griefs would necessarily reign. Hence, at the worst, spring positive outbreaks of strife between these exclusive centres, one man seizing another man's property, or seducing another man's wife: hence, at the best, comes a frittering of energies that might have been spent upon nobler things—the wife employed as nurse and general drudge, the husband flattering and borrowing, toiling and moiling, to make an income for the upkeep of his house and the education of his children. Cumbered with material cares and the drudgery of serving tables, neither men nor women have time to be what they might be, or to take their place in the State. Occupied with necessities, they cannot heed counsels of perfection; struggling for mere life, they cannot think of the real life, which is the life of the spirit.[1]

The emancipation of women

Plato approaches the reform of the household—with something of a desire for paradox, and a wish to tilt against convention—in the name of the emancipation of woman. Among the Greeks the life of woman approached more to the seclusion of Eastern manners, than to the freedom of the West; and the Greek girl, as we have already noticed, received no other education than what the women's quarter of the house could afford. To Plato it seemed that this meant, not only that the development of woman was stunted, but also that the State lost the service of half of its members. While men had attempted to do all manner of works, and needed to be driven back upon one, women, he thought, had been allowed no single function (except that of child-bearing and child-rearing), and ought to be granted the right of discharging all for which they were fitted by Nature, not excluding the function of serving the State. In judging of their natural aptitudes Plato was guided, as we have seen him

[1] As Aristotle would say, they are too much absorbed by the "necessary" activities of ἀσχολία to enjoy the real (if "supererogatory") activities of σχολή.

guided before, by an analogy. He had compared the guardians to watch-dogs in an earlier passage; and he now suggests that, after all, dogs of either sex can do the work of watching, with the one difference, that the female is somewhat weaker than the male. Against the application of the lesson which this analogy has to teach, it may be urged that there is a vital difference of nature and almost of kind between man and woman. Plato denies the difference: if woman differs from man in sexual function, she is in all the other functions of life a weaker man, possessed of the same capacities but not of the same strength. It is absurd, he argues, to make a distinction in one function the ground for a distinction in all; and he therefore assigns the same training and the same duties to men and to women alike—within the circle of the guardians.[1] Here again, as in the institution of "common tables," the influence of Sparta is obvious. The Spartan girl was trained in gymnastics like the man; and Plato adopts the Spartan practice, while pushing it to its logical conclusion, and insisting that women, since they have been trained like men by the State, shall also serve it like men. For Plato is not a teacher of woman's rights so much as of woman's duties; and if he aims at emancipating women from the bondage of the household, it is only in order to subject them again to the service of the community at large. Yet such service is true freedom; in it woman stands by man's side as his yoke-fellow in the fulness of his life, and by it she attains the fulness of her own; nor must we, in speaking of Plato as the teacher of woman's duties, forget that he is, especially for a Greek, amazingly liberal in his attitude towards women.

But how is this scheme, which devotes woman to the service of the State, to be reconciled with the physical necessity of continuing the species? How can marriage, and the bearing and rearing of children, be dovetailed into a plan, which rejects the family, and (apparently) unsexes the woman? Let us suppose for a moment that monogamy were still to be practised. The men-guardians, living in common and open barracks, have no place to which they can bring a wife: the women-guardians, living the same life and in the same way, can make no home

Plato's scheme of marriage

[1] The producing classes retain home and family, as they retain private property.

for a husband. Under such conditions monogamy could only mean, that the husband saw his wife occasionally[1] (perhaps in his barracks, perhaps in hers), and that neither could attend to their children, absorbed as both were by the State. But monogamy under such conditions, where the husband loses the society of his wife, and both lose the care of their children, loses its *raison d'être.* If therefore for any reason any other system of marriage should commend itself, it will be obviously preferable. A system of communism did commend itself to Plato, and a system of communism he accordingly adopts. He had two reasons for preferring that system. There was first of all a physical reason. The analogy of the animal world suggests, that if you desire to have a good stud of horses, you must put a good sire to as many good dams, and a good dam to as many good sires, as you possibly can. To produce a good stock of citizens, the State must act on the same principle: it must supersede monogamy at will by communism under supervision. The Platonic State, which we have already seen charged with the duties of regulating the forms of literary composition and the methods of literary expression, must undertake to give its subjects in marriage. Quixotic as the idea may seem, it has its parallel in Aristotle: the regulation of marriage in the interest of national physique seemed natural even to the sanest and coolest of Greek thinkers. But it was perhaps the moral advantage of communism which appealed to Plato most. It will eliminate the motive of selfishness, and finally secure the solidarity of the State. Granted communism in the first generation—granted, too, that the State takes means to prevent the identification of children, by removing them from their mothers at birth—then, by the third or fourth generation, every member of the ruling and fighting classes will be generally related to every other, and no member will be (or at any rate no member will know that he is) particularly related to any other. Such a system of relationship will be to the advantage of the State, because it will make for its unity. Unity is secured when all the members of a body can say of the same thing, at the same time, and from the same point of view: "This loss is my loss: this gain is my

[1] The young husband at Sparta only visited his wife by stealth.

gain ".[1] In other words, a body has attained solidarity, when its members have so entirely identified themselves with the whole, that whatever happens to any part of the whole is felt by each member as happening to himself. Now such a perfect solidarity seemed to Plato to characterise a circle of relations.[2] To make the State into a circle of relations will therefore tend to its unity, and so to its good. And thus the State is brought, according to Plato's desire, as near to the unity of the individual man as may be: if it has not become a single individual, it has at any rate become a single family. The political bond which unites citizen to citizen, has been strengthened by the tie of kinship and sentiment, which unites brother to brother: the warmth of domestic affection has reinforced the feeling of political fellowship.[3] The new city, which Plato's imagination has compacted, is the home of its citizens, who know no other; it is their "fatherland," in deed as well as in word. The children who are born within it are all "children of the State," reared as it were in a *crèche,* and under the care of public nurses, until they are ripe for education.

§ 7. By this new regulation of the relations of the sexes, Plato thus hopes to achieve many things—freedom for man and woman to develop their highest capacities, and to exercise them together as true comrades in their proper work; better-

[1] It is from this passage that Aristotle derives his opinion, that Plato aims at "excessive unification". The unity which makes every citizen say the same thing at the same time reminds one of the unity of the educational system, which allowed the minister of education to take his watch out of his pocket and say: "At this minute all the children of this country are saying —X". Plato it is true goes further: they must all say X with the same meaning, and in the same spirit. It is an internal and real, not a formal unity, which he postulates; but it is equally over-driven.

[2] One may argue that this is a singularly optimistic view of the relations of relatives. "Blood may be thicker than water, but the skin of kinship is proverbially thin." But granting that it is true, and assuming that solidarity so perfect characterises a family, surely the family has a *raison d'être*—it attains a "good". Plato is therefore contradicting himself at this point. At any rate he is guilty, as Aristotle remarks, of the logical fallacy of supposing that what is true of a small circle of relations will be true of a large circle of men, if they are related. This is a logical fallacy, because there are two factors, (1) a small circle, and (2) relationship; and Plato leaves out of account the influence of the first of these in producing solidarity.

[3] Thus Herodotus tells us that community of wives is practised among the Agathyrsi in order to make brothers of the tribesmen, and to banish hatred and ill-will (Hdt., iv., 104, quoted in Gomperz, *Greek Thinkers,* ii., 119).

ment of physique; complete and living solidarity. To the first of these results, and to the last, the new regulation of property would also, as we have seen, contribute. It is easy to agree with the aims which Plato proposes to himself, but it is somewhat difficult to accept the means; and here, as elsewhere, one may agree with Plato's principles, and yet reject their over-logical or over-driven application. Take for instance the principle, that a proper field should be given for the exercise of woman's capacities. The principle is perfectly true: the two means for its realisation seem both quixotic and impracticable. It is impossible that a woman should do everything that a man can do. The fact of her sex is not one isolated thing in a woman's nature, in which, and in which alone, she differs from man: it colours her whole being;[1] it makes her able indeed to inspire noble enthusiasms, but not to direct a policy or to drill a regiment, as Plato would require his woman-ruler or woman-soldier to do. Again, it is impossible that men and women should come together merely for sexual intercourse, and instantly depart. They may meet primarily for that purpose, but ultimately, as Aristotle taught, they meet for a life's friendship, for the sake of a permanent interest in a common welfare; and in the "friendship" or permanent interest of true marriage lies one of the greatest influences towards a good life. Not only, however, does Plato make an unreal abstraction of the sexual motive, when he contemplates the regulation of that motive by the State for the sake of producing a good physique; he also makes of the individual a mere means, and that in respect of a side of life on which the individual most naturally claims to be an end to himself. In other words, he denies a fundamental right to personality, in a field where the sense of personality is most vivid,[2] and where the whole man, body and soul, reason and feeling, "all thoughts, all passions, all delights, whatever feeds this mortal flame," cry for their satisfaction. It is indeed one of the most repulsive things in the *Republic*, though it has its affinities on a smaller scale even in Aristotle,

Low view of marriage

[1] Accordingly Aristotle recognises that there is one virtue for men, and another for women. What is courage in a man would be effrontery in a woman: hers must be a softer, tenderer virtue.

[2] Compare Aristotle's criticism, *infra*, pp. 398-99.

the defender of marriage, that Plato should make his State a breeding establishment for the production of fine animals.[1]

Plato's asceticism

Under the whole scheme of communism, whether in property or in wives—underneath the whole attempt to abolish private possession and private life—there lies the assumption, that much can be done to abolish spiritual evils by the abolition of those material conditions in connection with which they are found. Spiritual medicines, it must always be remembered, are the first and primary cure in Plato's therapeutics; but a ruthless surgery of material things is also a necessary condition. Because material conditions are *concomitant* with spiritual evils, they seem to him largely their cause; and since to abolish the cause is to abolish the effect, he sets himself to a thorough reform of the material conditions of life. By compelling men to live under absolutely different conditions in the material and external organisation of their lives, he hoped to produce a totally different spirit and an utterly different attitude of mind. The gist of Aristotle's criticism of this conception is simple: spiritual medicines are all that one needs, or can use, for spiritual diseases. Educate a man to the truth, and by the truth that is in him he will connect the very same material conditions, which were before connected with evil, with everything that is good. Material conditions are concomitants, not causes; occasions, and not reasons; and it is idle to tinker with occasions. It is more than idle: it is corrupting and enfeebling. To free men from drudgery is not necessarily to make them live the free life of the spirit; and one may doubt whether the drudgery in which the lives of nearly all of us are cast is not as much of a moral training as it is of a material necessity, and whether its disappearance would not involve the "life of swine," rather than that of "Olympic victors," as Plato prefers to think. And is it not everywhere true, that to take away occasions of stumbling is to produce a weak-kneed godliness—that to shelter the

[1] At the same time it should be noticed that the conditions of Greek life to some extent explain what has been called the unreal abstraction of the sexual motive in respect of the relations of man and woman. The woman who abode in her quarters all the day, and the man who spent his day in the agora or the palæstra, had little in common; and the Greek vice of παιδεραστία meant that, as between men and women, there was little of what we should call "falling in love".

soul from what may try its endurance is to produce at best a "fugitive" virtue? It is a more robust and virile temper which loves to "welcome each rebuff," and in each, and through each, to strive and to learn. Here again there is something mediæval in Plato—something of a horror of the world and its temptations. He does not, indeed, like a true mediævalist, fly from the world to the cloister: he would rather shatter and remould this sorry scheme of things nearer to his heart's desire. None the less there is a flight from the natural world in Plato; as there is in Aristotle something of the modern spirit, which would cheerfully accept whatever life can offer. Plato's attitude towards the world, like that of the mediæval mind, is based on pessimism: there is something evil in matter, with which the spirit would only contend in vain. Aristotle's acceptance of it, like that of the modern mind, is based on optimism: it is made possible by the belief that

> There is a soul of goodness in things evil
> Could men but knowingly distil it out.

It is in this spirit that Aristotle seeks to vindicate property, as the basis of a moral life, and to justify the family, as a school of conduct and a preparation for the State.[1]

Reactionary spirit of the *Republic*

It is obvious that Plato's attitude involves a certain element of reaction. Institutions, we have said, are a product of mind; yet he rejects many of the institutions of a civilised life. This may well seem inconsistent; and the question naturally occurs, why should the products of mind be rejected by a thinker, who believes that they *are* the products of mind, and can only reject them on the strength of the conceptions of his own intelligence? It is a question which a wise reformer must always ask himself; nor can it but dismay him to reflect that he is opposing his single mind to institutions, which have been created, maintained, and approved by the minds of many generations. Yet in one thought there is consolation. Were these institutions the pro-

[1] It should be noticed that Plato's theory of the mind, as assimilating itself to its surroundings, may be partly responsible for his attempt to recast society, just as it explains his recasting of the ordinary Greek curriculum. And while one speaks of the soul as *distilling* goodness out of evil things, one must not forget that Plato felt keenly the opposite truth, if it may be so called, that evil things *instil* their own evil into the mind. Perhaps he exaggerated the effect of environment: one must also beware of minimising its influence.

ducts of *right* mind, of mind acting in view of a true end and by appropriate means? Error may become inveterate as well as truth; and it has often been seen that the suggestions of some powerful intelligence, when backed by the influence of a strong will and an attractive personality, may enter into the life of a whole people without real examination or discussion. The historian sees that they have entered and established themselves, and he readily believes in their sanctity, and accuses those who aim at their destruction of the want of a proper historical sense, and of forgetting that "the roots of the present lie deep in the past". None the less the philosopher has the right to inquire *how* they came, and to ask by *what* title they exist, and *what* element of mind they express; and if he is dissatisfied with the answer which he receives, he has every right to suggest, what *should* have come instead, what has a *real* title to exist, what element of mind *ought* to be expressed. But history deserves some respect, and Plato pays it little. He rejects the whole of its developments as so many mistakes, and substitutes in their place his own ideas of what ought to be. Aristotle's criticism is shrewd and dry. "We must not forget that we ought to attend to the length of past time and the witness of bygone years, wherein it would not have escaped men's notice, if these things had been right and proper." But, to tell the truth, Plato's ideas of "what ought to be" are not so much the undiscovered novelties of latter days, as the most primitive antiquities of the remote past. We spoke of an element of reaction: we might almost have spoken of atavism, and recurrence to the savage. In music, in medicine, in the reconstruction of society, this trait is prominent. The "luxurious" State is in his eyes suffering from a "fever": it needs a letting of blood, a purification. It must be brought back to simplicity, by which Plato means that the superfluous elements, which are not conformable to the spirit of justice, must be excised in order that the whole may attain to conformity. Back to simplicity it is accordingly brought, but the simplicity which is gained proves in the issue to be the simplicity of the primitive; and Plato falls into the ordinary error of finding the path of progress in the way of retrogression—the error which Bacon rebuked in the saying, "Antiquitas sæculi juventus mundi". It is a case of a true principle twisting round, as it were, in its author's hands, when it comes to be applied; and one begins to wonder if it was not more in earnest than in irony that Socrates found in the primitive "city of Swine" the true and healthy type. Again and again this tendency appears. Music is confined to the simple and direct expression of simple moods by means of simple instruments: the element of reflection and of complexity vanishes, and the pibroch [1] supersedes the sonata. In Plato's theory of medicine the barbarian element is clear; and when one reads of the duty of the physician to leave those who are chronically sick to perish, one is reminded of the savage who helps the aged to die by exposing them to starvation.[2] In the system of communism suggested by Plato it is impossible not to detect the savage once more. It has already been suggested that the study of anthropology was not unknown at Athens in the fifth century; and we have seen reason to believe that the Sophist had sometimes professed to find suggestions for a reconstruction of society in those "nature-peoples," who represented to a modern age the picture of what Greece itself had been of old. Similarly it would seem that Plato was tempted to reconstitute Greece by rejuvenating its infancy. At the bottom of the communism of the *Republic* there is not only something of the "common tables" of Sparta, not only something of the Spartan customs of marriage,[3] but also some knowledge of the supposed communism of wives among peoples, whose marriage customs there were no Greek ethnologists to explain scientifically as the result of exogamy, and some inkling of the communism of property, which appears to characterise the village community. Aristotle, we know, made a collection of "barbarian customs"; but logographers had already recorded these things when Plato wrote, and Sophists had already descanted on their ideal simplicity as the true *régime*

[1] Webster following Jamieson defines the pibroch as "a Highland air, *suited to the particular passion which the musician would either express or assuage*".

[2] Plato's principle in this suggestion is, that there is no "right to life" in the individual as such; there is only a right to life in the individual as a citizen able to serve the State. *Cf.* Green, *Principles of Political Obligation*, p. 157, § 154, for Plato's view, and for its necessary correction.

[3] A Spartan husband might lend his wife to another citizen, that he might produce children for the service of the State. Sparta was indeed in some respects a nature-people in its infancy; and the custom by which a husband visited his wife by stealth at night reminds one of the marriage customs of the early savage.

of "Nature". Here as elsewhere Plato is the debtor, as well as the enemy, of the Sophists; although it must be remembered, that while the Sophist had found in primitive customs the means of dispensing with the State, which lost its *raison d'être* when it was no longer needed for the sanction of marriage and the guarantee of property, Plato used them for the stays and supports of an ideal State still more to be abhorred by every Sophist than the actual, because stronger and more disposed to interfere. Yet in the very conception of the unity of this ideal State there is a latent barbarism: it is a clan, knit together by the bond of blood. It seems easy to accuse Plato of an anachronism, or rather of an inversion of history; and to argue that he begins by tracing the unity of the State to the sense of economic interest, which is its final and conscious bond, and ends by making that unity depend on the sentimental tie of kinship, which is its first rude and unconscious form. And while such an argument would be in so far mistaken, as Plato begins logically, and not historically, with the economic motive, the accusation would at any rate have this truth, that the return to the clan does betray a certain want of historical perspective.[1]

Relation of communism to personality

One final point of view remains to be raised with regard to Plato's communism. Does it, or does it not, destroy individuality? Is it compatible with the preservation of the rights of individuals? Does not Plato deny liberty in the name of fraternity (as he also sacrifices equality in the name of efficiency) when he institutes a philosophic despotism? It is certainly Plato's aim to destroy individuality of the false kind, to abolish individual "rights" as construed in the proposition "might is

[1] This want of historical perspective was natural to a Greek inquirer. Instead of seeing in the present the fruit of the conditions and circumstances of the present, and in the past the fruit of those which reigned in the past; instead, again, of seeing this present linked to that past by the chains of a natural development, he saw, in both present and past, things possible at either time, and in neither any necessary connection with the other. He ignored at once the causation which connects the present with its environment, and that which binds it to the past. He referred the happening of the past in a past age, the being of the present in the present, to the fiat of the State, the will of the legislator. The modern "historic" sense, which corrects this point of view, is less the product of history than of science and the scientific theory of evolution; and Aristotle, who had the idea of development, shows the historic sense in his account of the growth of the State, and in his view of the growth of knowledge.

right," and to deny freedom in the sense of doing as one likes. But on the other hand it is as certainly his aim not only to guarantee but to develop individuality in the true sense of the word, and with it the rights and the freedom it requires. The individual is in reality, as we have seen, part of a scheme, a member of a whole. Such a conception of the individual is implied by a teleological conception of the world. If the world is one, and works towards one end, then the State is a part of the world, with an end subsidiary to its end, and the individual again is a part of the State, with an end subsidiary to the end of the State. Because the whole world is a co-ordinated whole, a single scheme and not a mass of units, the individual cannot stand by himself, but only in his place in the whole, and as playing his part in the scheme. Upon this conception, freedom will mean liberty to play that part freely: the rights of the individual will be those conditions which are necessary to playing that part, and which must be secured to the individual if he is to play it properly. Freedom in that sense, conditions of this kind, Plato certainly tries to secure. The whole system of communism is meant to set the individual "free" from everything which prevents him from taking his right place in the order of the State (and thereby in the order of the world): it is designed to secure those conditions—(in other words, to guarantee those "rights")—which are necessary to the positive discharge of the right function, the function which helps the State to perform its function, and thereby the world to attain its end. But, it may be rejoined, this teleological conception cuts the individual short, and limits him to being and acting merely in the single aspect of a part. On the contrary, we may answer, far from cutting short, it broadens and expands. The self is the sum of its interests;[1] and the individual is narrowest when he stands by himself, with no interests outside himself, and widest when he exists and acts as a part, identifying himself with the interests of the whole body of which he is a part. The wider the whole of which the individual can act as a part, the greater the sum of interests that he has, the greater is his individuality. The motto of life may be said to

[1] *Cf. infra*, p. 269.

be "Live in as wide a fellowship as you may, and have fellowship in as many interests as you can".[1]

Liberty then need not be sacrificed to gain fraternity: on the contrary, through fraternity man comes by the fullest and therefore freest use of his powers. No rights are destroyed when the individual is made part of a community: rights belong to the individual as a member of a community, and are the conditions of his action as a member, secured to him by the community. The teleological conception is "the foundation for all true theory of rights,"[2] because it involves this conception of the individual as a member of the community, acting for its end, and guaranteed the conditions of such action. That no sacrifice of the individual, or of liberty, or of rights, was involved by his philosophy Plato felt sure; and he argued the point under the rubric of happiness. He urged that his guardians were "happy," or enjoyed the sense of free and full play of their individuality which the Greek termed *εὐδαιμονία*, by acting in their appointed place in the State. "In a proper State," he tells us, "the individual will himself expand, and he will secure the common interest along with his own," because he has made it his own (497 A). Where, then, is the error of Plato's communism, in respect of its attitude to the individual? Granted that Plato has a true conception of the meaning of individuality, and a true conception of rights (as the conditions of the free activity of the individual considered as a member of society), is there not some flaw in his reasoning? He starts from right principles: may there not be here as elsewhere defects in their application? There would appear to be two. In the first place, while it is true that the self should grow and spread forth its branches, it is also true that it must have a root. A wide extension of interests may be desirable; but such an extension

Plato destroys the basis of personality

[1] "Forsooth, brothers, fellowship is heaven, and the lack of fellowship is hell: fellowship is life, and the lack of fellowship is death: and the deeds that ye do upon the earth, it is for fellowship's sake that ye do them, and the life that is in it shall live on and on for ever, and each one of you part of it, while many a man's life upon the earth from the earth shall wane" (William Morris, *A Dream of John Ball*). "To be no part of any body is to be nothing: and so I am, and shall so judge myself, unless I could be so incorporated into a part of the world, as by business to contribute some sustentation to the whole" (Donne, in a letter quoted in *Walton's Life*).

[2] Green, *Principles of Political Obligation*, p. 57, § 39; *cf. infra*, p. 225.

is of little avail, unless it has its basis in a strong personality and the conscious sense of an individual self (φιλαυτία). Unless we premise such a sense of self, that which identifies itself with a wide range of interests is—nothing; and the result is nothing. It is obvious that if the expansion of the self is to be a real thing, issuing in action and making for good, there must be a firm and steady basis for its support. It is the error of Plato that he forgot the basis, in contemplating the superstructure—that in aiming at the extension of the self, he forgot that it must have a previous intensity.[1] Too often it is true that it is an ineffective, unindividual type of mind which identifies itself with a wide range of interests; and a strong sense of personality, though combined with a narrow range, will go further and do more for the world, than any watery altruism (ὑδαρὴς φιλία). The diffusion of the one type has to be reconciled with the concentration of the other; and we must first know ourselves as separate individuals, in order to transcend such knowledge, and to know ourselves as part of a wider order, and as serving a wider purpose. It is exactly this power of knowing ourselves as separate individuals which Plato really destroys, when he abolishes property; for property is a necessary basis of any conscious sense of an individual self.[2]

This then is one flaw of Plato's communism, that by abolishing the basis of *any* sense of self, it takes away the possibility of the *true* sense of self which he inculcates. It does deny therefore to the individual a right—a necessary condition of his thinking and acting as a member of society and of expressing a social will; for it denies him that which is a necessary condition of his thinking and acting at all, and of expressing any will. The other flaw which may be traced in his reasoning is this, that he postulates of the individual, that he shall identify himself with no lower scheme nor order than that of the State. Such a postulate is impracticable and impossible. Every individual does and must identify himself with a lower scheme, and a narrower order—that of the family. It is true that the State

[1] As Nettleship puts it, Plato is so much concerned with the virtues of *esprit de corps*, that he forgets "that corporations have no conscience".

[2] This point is worked out in connection with Aristotle's criticism of Plato, *infra*, pp. 393-94, 399.

is a fellowship (*κοινωνία*), "and each one of us part of it"; but it is also true that it is a fellowship of fellowships (*κοινωνία κοινωνιῶν*), and each one of us part of those—which is the great lesson that Aristotle teaches. It is true again that the State is a product of mind—that it is mind concrete in an external organisation: it is not true that the unity of the State is as the unity of a single mind, or that mind must be concrete in a single organisation, the "Republic one and indivisible".

The meaning and the bearing of the line of criticism here indicated may be realised more clearly, if we place ourselves at a point of view suggested by Plato himself, and regard the State as an organism—that is to say, as a whole of which the parts are organs for the attainment of a single end. Of such a whole the human body, whose members are all organs for the purpose of life, has generally been taken as a type. Now the application of the category of organism to the State is necessary and true. It is necessary, because it gives a true idea of the kind of unity which exists in the State: it is necessary, because it is an antidote to a false idea of the unity of the State, as legal in its essence, and contractual in its form. Modern political thought has borrowed from biology an organic conception of the State, which it has opposed to the legal conception of a contract entertained by thinkers like Hobbes and Locke, exactly as Plato drew from his teleology a similar conception, and opposed it to the "conventional" view of the Sophists. The emphasis which is now laid, as it was also laid by Plato, upon the organic character of the State, is just and salutary. A contractual conception degrades the State into a business partnership (*societas*), whose members are linked by a purely voluntary tie of self-interest. They have put as it were their money into a concern which they have called the State, because they thought that it would pay; and if they find that it fails to pay—as the Sophists argued that it failed to pay the "strong" man—they can and will withdraw from the concern.[1] The organic view, on the contrary, substitutes a vital for a voluntary tie.

Organic theory of the State

[1] Compare Burke, *Reflections on the French Revolution*: "The State ought not to be considered as nothing better than a partnership agreement in a trade of pepper or coffee, calico or tobacco, or some such other low concern, to be taken up for a little temporary interest and to be dissolved by the fancy of the parties".

It teaches that the unity of the State is not one made by hands, and by hands to be broken, but an inevitable outcome of human nature and human needs. It teaches that the State can no more be left by its members, than the body by its limbs, and that its dissolution is as much the death of its members, as it is of itself. While in this way it attaches the individual to the State, as the outcome of his nature and the essence of his being, in the same process it also links individual to individual, citizen to citizen. Members of one whole, the citizens are members one of another: as every limb seems to ache when one limb is pained, so the poverty and degradation of one class must impoverish the life of the rest;[1] and the education and assistance of the weaker members is thus inculcated upon the stronger, as the very condition of their own welfare. The conception of a common weal and a vital union supersedes that of self-interest and a casual nexus.

The conception of a common weal is very present to Plato: the quality which he postulates in his guardians is a vivid sense of its existence. Union is very vital in his eyes: "there is no greater good than whatsoever binds the State together into one". But he may be accused of having pushed the organic conception too far, and of having attempted "to unify the State to excess" (λίαν ἑνοῦν). The conception is valuable when it is used negatively: it is dangerous in its positive application. A true organic theory of the State must recognise that, while the category of organism is one which partly covers the State, and, indeed, covers it better than any other category, it does not cover it entirely.[2] In the first place, the State, if an organism, is one whose parts have a will of their own, and

Limitations of that theory

[1] The organic conception, as it presents itself in Plato and Aristotle, has, however, the defect of postulating members who are means to the life of the rest, and who do not share in that life (*cf. infra*, p. 227). And yet Plato argues from his organic conception of the State to the conclusion, that as in an organism part must be proportioned to suit part, and all to suit the whole—as no part must grow unduly, lest every part should suffer, so in a State must class be proportioned to class, and all classes be adjusted to the welfare of the whole (420).

[2] The modern organic theory, borrowed as it is from biology, does not cover or recognise the moral aspect of the State as an entity *consciously* self-directed towards a conception of the Good. Plato's organic theory, based as it was on teleology, does involve such a recognition; and the category of organism, as used by him, covers an aspect of the State, which as used by Herbert Spencer it fails to cover.

with that will the demand for its expression, and with that demand a right to private property, as a necessary subject upon and through which expression can take place. In the second place, the State is an organism whose parts are also members of other organisms. They are members for instance of the family, and the family is an organism whose end may be subsidiary but cannot be sacrificed to that of the State. Any organism which satisfies a vital necessity of human nature, like the family, must be indestructible, however detrimental to the organic unity of the State it may at first sight appear. But the zeal of the State had come upon Plato, and had come as a fire to consume whatever was not of the State.[1] A fire will not stop at exceptions; and these exceptions to the organic unity of the State he could not brook. Nor is this attitude of mind peculiar to Plato or to theory: it has, at different periods of the world's history, played a great part in the actual life of mankind. The conception of the State as the sole organism, to whose majesty all other organisms must be sacrificed, is characteristic of the sixteenth century, and of much of the French Revolution. It may seem eccentric to speak of the Reformation as Platonic; but in one of its aspects the Reformation was part of a general movement for State centralisation, which made for the destruction or utter subjection of all organisations other than that of the State. It is a movement which is expressed in Luther, as well as in Machiavelli, who are both its apostles.[2] In part that movement attacked the organisation of the Church (in a natural attempt to revenge itself upon the Church for its attempt to engulf the State, in the days of Gregory VII., Innocent III. and Boniface VIII.): in part it attacked old mediæval organisations of shire and hundred, as in

[1] In this respect Plato was true to the spirit of Sparta, where "associations intermediate between the State and the individual were either lacking, or had become mere expedients of mechanical subdivision". It was otherwise in Athens; and Aristotle, as we shall see, was true to Athens. Here there was the full life of the deme, and of the household: there were clans and phratries and tribes with common property and common worships. These associations were at once homes of individuality, and the basis of a healthy liberty. For the local opinion of self-governing units is a necessary basis for the general government of the State by public opinion (*cf.* Gomperz, ii., 40).

[2] Treitschke.

England, and superseded them by the nominees of the State. Again, in the French Revolution, the same influence of a movement towards centralisation is seen. The Revolution of 1789 only annihilated the incapable despotism of the *ancien régime* to instal the crushing tyranny of the *Republic;* and the Church, which the monarchy had always attempted to bring into subjection, under the name of "Gallican liberties," was by "the *Republic* one and indivisible" swept into destruction. The argument employed in favour of disendowment is significant: the Church was a corporation, which in virtue of its revenues was dangerous to the unity of the State.

The Republic as an ideal

The line of interpretation which we have followed in dealing with the *Republic* now brings us to our final conclusion. On the one hand, the *Republic* is not a Utopia: it is a practical treatise on politics, written in reaction against contemporary political conditions, and, in its attempt at reconstruction, based upon contemporary facts. It is written to rebuke the intellectual and moral defects, defects of ignorance, defects of selfishness and corruption, which disfigured Athens and other Greek cities; it is written to commend to Athenian imitation the practices and institutions of Sparta. On the other hand the treatise, practical as it may be, has also a theoretical and ideal aim. It attempts to show what politics would be, if they were informed by the highest principle of justice, and what would be the manner of a State, in which the Idea of the Good had found its perfect expression. That politics ever should be after this fashion, that there should ever be a State according to this manner, Plato hardly expects; it must be an ideal to which men may approximate as closely as they can, but not a copy which must be imitated line for line. He well knows that the actual must recede far from the ideal: he also knows that the actual will not go far, unless it has a high ideal set before it, and that, as George Herbert says,

> Who aimeth at the sky
> Shoots higher much than he that means a tree.

Yet there is some variation in his attitude, and while in one passage he speaks of the ideal State (in which justice and the Idea of the Good have been perfectly exemplified) as "laid up in the heavens for an ensample,"[1] elsewhere he thinks that what he has sketched is "no vision, but possible if difficult of accomplishment".[2] And thus, it would appear, there is a certain oscillation between a practical attempt at construction, and the theoretical exhibition of a State based on ideal principles. It would be unjust, on the strength of this oscillation, to criticise Plato as though he had meant the whole of his scheme to be realised. But it is not unjust to criticise the theoretical exhibition of a State based on ideal principles, upon the ground that those principles are in their application pushed to an excess. And this is the line of criticism which we have attempted to take. Plato, as we have seen, had seized upon those principles, which are and always have been the fundamental principles of every State. He saw that the State is a product of mind: he saw that it is an organic unity. But, in the process of application, he pushed these principles to conclusions with which it is impossible to agree. If the State *is* a product of mind, it ought not therefore to be separated into three elements, nor should it be guided towards a purpose higher than it has grasped by the wisdom of one of these. If its unity *is* organic, that does not mean that the family must be abolished, or property destroyed. The tyranny of principles carries Plato too far. He speaks of a stage in the development of reason, when conscious of its powers it uses them as it were in play, for the purpose of contradicting everything, like a young puppy which fleshes its teeth by indiscriminate tearing and rending. It is a stage which one may perhaps detect in the Sophists: they were the wandering "puppies" of dialectic, barking at conventions, and delighting in contradictions. But Plato had himself attained to a stage, when reason is still more masterful, and almost equally destructive. He had risen above contradiction to the eternal verity; and in the strength of his hold upon it he was too eager to enforce it upon the world for its salvation. He did not sufficiently recognise that the eternal verity had been working throughout history, if not consciously realised by man: he was too anxious to make its conscious realisation by the philosopher into a ground for attacking all its past works. Not only so, but with a stern logic he would have enforced truth

Plato and the tyranny of reason

[1] 592 B. [2] 540 D.

to its utmost consequence. If art was moral, it should be made moral, and nothing but moral, in its form, its content, its every phase. This is not the way of truth or of success in practical affairs. In the realm of man's action there is and there must be an absence of utter logic. In the beginning of the *Ethics* Aristotle tells us that the subject with which Political Science deals (and in Political Science he includes the whole field of human action on its practical side), is one which does not admit of absolute exactitude. Political Science must start from principles which are only true "for the most part," and it can only arrive at similar conclusions. To Plato Political Science starts from absolute principles, and arrives at equally absolute conclusions. His principles have their truth: they have also their qualifications. Life ought to be directed by them: it can only be directed by them partially, even if we postulate with Plato an ideal ground for their operation. There is something French in Plato's mind, something of that pushing of a principle to its logical extremes, which distinguished Calvin in theology, and Rousseau in politics. The principle of the sovereignty of *volonté générale* is not more relentlessly preached by Rousseau, than that of the organic unity of the State by Plato.[1] When we turn to Aristotle, it hardly seems fanciful to detect more of an English spirit of compromise.[2] He has his principles—true "for the most part": he seeks exactitude—"as far as the nature of the subject admits". Where Plato turned Radical under the compulsion of the Idea, Aristotle has much sound Conservatism: he respects property; he sees good in the family. He recognises the general "laxity" of actual life, the impossibility of concluding man wholly within the pales of any scheme. He recognises, above all, that a Government can only go so far as a people follows: "the number of those who wish a State to continue must be greater than the number of those who wish the contrary". This is a principle which Plato had not realised: he had forgotten (rather than despised) the people;

[1] Aristotle might have accused Plato of having made Political Science speak in syllogisms, where it should only speak in enthymemes.

[2] Yet it is with an English writer, Thomas Carlyle, that one may best compare Plato. Each, as Pöhlmann says, is the Isaiah of his century: each preached the verity which is beyond shams, and the duty of man to do his function in his place.

but he had left them out of his scheme none the less. His State has some of the features of a despotism; nor would it have been any the less galling in practice, because it was the despotism of an idea. And while we may admit that even Aristotle allows his teleology to justify slavery, and to exclude labour from participation in political life, we must also admit the wide and almost democratic scope of his ideal State.

NOTE.—In the *Timæus* and *Critias* Plato writes, as it were, an Epilogue to the *Republic*. In the former dialogue there is a brief recapitulation of the *Republic*, and a promise to show the State of the *Republic* engaged in action: in the *Critias*—which is a fragment—a beginning of the fulfilment of the promise is made. Apparently Plato wished to justify his ideal State by its fruits; he sought to show how in action its excellence would have issued in great deeds, and—conversely—to prove from those great deeds the greatness of its excellence. Apparently he also wished to justify his ideal State still further, by suggesting that the oldest history of Athens dimly revealed a polity like that of the *Republic*. For before the deluge Athens "performed the noblest deeds and had the fairest constitution of any of which tradition tells": she had a system of specialised classes, and especially a warrior class distinct from the other classes, and devoted purely to war: the castes of Egypt were simply an imitation of Athens. The Athenian warriors dwelt by themselves, with a suitable education, a system of communism, and payments in food from the other citizens. Military pursuits were common to men and women, as the statue of Athene in full armour testified. The ideal of the *Republic* is therefore a looking backward to the "ancestral constitution" of primæval Athens: primæval Athens and the State of the *Republic* are one (*Timæus*, 25 E). In telling the story of ancient Athens engaged in action (as it was when it overthrew the power of Atlantis), Plato thinks, therefore, that he will really be showing the State of the *Republic* in action (26 D). But in the *Critias* he does no more than sketch the scenery. We are shown Athens and its Acropolis; we see the warriors living on the summit of the Acropolis, round the temples, in an enclosure like the garden of a house; we see the husbandmen and artisans living outside the Acropolis and under its sides; we see the State of Atlantis, a sort of primitive Babylon, a vast island, intersected by alternate zones of land and sea, with chariots and horsemen, and "temples covered with silver, and their pinnacles with gold, and their roofs of ivory," and grandeur unspeakable as of Incas or Aztecs. But with these two pictures the story ends. The action never comes.

CHAPTER IV

PLATO'S VIEW OF MONARCHY, AND OF THE MIXED STATE

THE ABSOLUTE MONARCH

§ 1. THE government of the city depicted in the *Republic* represents, it was urged in the last chapter, the despotism of the Idea: it is an ideocracy. That despotism, we have seen, presents itself to Plato in two external aspects—as an aristocracy, and as a monarchy. It seems natural for many reasons to believe that Plato regarded aristocracy as the ideal form of government. He belonged to an aristocratic coterie; and, like the other young aristocrats who gathered round Socrates, he might easily interpret the Socratic doctrine of the necessity of knowledge in the rulers of a State as a philosophic defence of aristocracy. He might learn from the history of Pythagoreanism that a philosophical circle had once governed Croton; and it was easy for him to hope that a "new" aristocracy, composed not of the members of a political club, but of disciples of a philosophical circle like his own, might regenerate Greece. Yet natural as it would appear to regard aristocracy as Plato's ideal, there seems reason to believe that it was monarchy which claimed his allegiance. A famous sentence of the *Republic* tells us, that there will be no rest from their troubles for the cities of Greece or for all mankind, until the days of philosopher kings;[1] and from the *Politicus* we also learn the necessity of ideal and absolute monarchy. Here again, as in

The *Republic* and absolute monarchy

[1] Here we see Socratic intellectualism making for absolute enlightened monarchy, to the neglect of popular *will*. As McKenzie says (*Int. Journ. Ethics*, Jan., 1906, p. 144): "If a real philosopher were made king his first act would probably be to abdicate his office, or at least to secure as rapidly as possible that the real work of government was distributed among the competent members of the State". A true philosophy must recognise the element of will.

other directions, it may be suggested that the Sophists had helped Plato's thought. If they had contributed towards his doctrine of specialisation, by the way in which they had turned subjects into rules and taught them according to those rules—if they had contributed towards the genesis of his communism, by praises of the ideal simplicity of the communistic savage, they also contributed towards a third phase of his thought by their doctrine of the Over-man. True, their Over-man had been the strong man; and justice had meant for them anything which was to his material advantage. But the conception could be moralised: the strong man could be made wise instead of strong; and justice might still consist in the rule of a single man, not because the strongest thereby gained his advantage, but because the wisest was therein discharging his function. To this conclusion the conception of the State as a product of mind must naturally lead. Reason, being one and indivisible, rules the spirit and the multitude of desires in the individual mind: reason, incarnate in one sovereign, must rule all other classes in the State. In such a sovereign the theories of the *Republic* culminate. He will have perfect knowledge because he is perfect reason: he will be perfectly unselfish, both in virtue of his knowledge, and in virtue of that craving to pursue the path of knowledge, which makes him reluctant to face the distractions of office. In him the organic unity of the State will be perfectly represented; and in his single intelligence the Idea of the Good will find its natural habitation. Unchecked by law, and unfettered by rules, he will look upon the Idea, and conform the State to its image as nearly as he may.

The aim of the *Politicus*

The Platonic theory of monarchy is expounded in the *Politicus*.[1] The *Politicus* is intended to be a metaphysical exercise in the art of differentiation, rather than a political treatise (285 D); but politics serves as the sphere of discussion, and a classification of States and a theory of monarchy are both suggested in its course. The statesman is first assigned to his genus; and Plato begins by distinguishing knowledge from practice, and by

[1] The *Politicus* is part of a projected trilogy of dialogues—the *Sophist*, the *Statesman*, and the *Philosopher*, dealing with the theory of human action in an ascending scale. The *Sophist*, however, became in fact a treatise on Being and Not-Being; the *Politicus* or *Statesman* became in large part a treatise on differentiation; and the *Philosopher* never was written.

assigning statesmanship, or "political science," to the sphere of knowledge. The procedure may seem at first sight curious, in view of what has been said above of the practical character of political science among the Greeks. But Plato uses "practice" in a restricted sense, and with reference to arts and crafts; while the sphere of knowledge has a wide bearing, and includes, we are told, two branches, one of the imperative, and the other of the critical order. It is to the former order that political science belongs: it is a science which speaks in the imperative; and upon consideration it would therefore appear, that Plato does conceive of political science, like Aristotle, as one of the practical sciences, and as speaking by way of counsel and command.[1] Delimiting its scope more precisely, Plato tells us that the sphere of its command is all that pertains to the sustenance of man. The word "sustenance" implies (and in the beginning of the dialogue it is definitely stated) that between the management of a household, or economic science, and that of a State, or political science, there is no cleavage. A large house and a small city only differ in degree, and not in kind; and the same is true of the sciences of their management. This view furnishes the starting point of the *Politics;* for Aristotle begins by traversing its truth, and by emphasising the distinction between State and household, politics and economics.

So far we have seen that the statesman acts in the sphere of knowledge, for the sustenance of man. But there is need of further definition. The statesman must be differentiated from those (and they are many) who seem like statesmen, and claim to be statesmen, but are not really such. We must distinguish the one true man from all the Centaurs and Satyrs which flit about his form. The clue which Plato suggests, and which guides the progress of the *Politicus,* is the possession of knowledge. Knowledge is the one criterion of the true statesman. The true statesman is neither he who rules in such a way as to conciliate the good will of his subjects, nor he who rules with respect for law: the true statesman is he who knows how to rule.

Knowledge the criterion of the statesman

[1] The Platonic distinction of imperative and critical sciences is perhaps the basis of Aristotle's distinction of theoretical and practical sciences (*infra*, p. 238). The conception of political science as commanding all the sciences of action, which also appears in the *Politicus* (*cf.* the *Euthydemus*, *supra*, p. 75), is the same conception which appears in the *Ethics*, *ad init.*, 1094 a 27 *sq.*

Such knowledge is too high for the many; and democracy, though it may boast its freedom, does not and cannot know anything of statesmanship. It is only to be found in one or two men. or at the most in a few; and in its perfection it is only to be found in one. The true statesman is the monarch: the ideal government is monarchy, because in monarchy, and in monarchy alone, perfect knowledge is to be found. Provided he have such knowledge, what matter whether he gain his subjects' consent to all that he does, or whether he act according to any form of law? He will always act of himself for the right, because he will always know what ought to be done; and to limit him by the need of consent, or by the forms of law, is only to hamper the free play of his knowledge. From the praise of knowledge Plato accordingly turns to an attack upon law. We have already seen from the *Republic* that, where education has given a living knowledge, law has become unnecessary: we have already seen that Plato viewed an abundance of laws as the sign and token of ignorance and want of education. "If the law be within you, as it should be, it need not be without you." In the *Politicus* law is regarded with an equal contempt, but from another point of view. Plato here considers it more as the imposition of checks and hindrances on the action of a monarch's knowledge, and less as an indication of ignorance in the whole of the State. "Law is an impediment to knowledge, and knowledge is true sovereign," is the thesis which he now prepares to maintain. He begins by referring to the analogy of medicine. A physician who doctored by the book would only limit himself to act by its rules, because he was ignorant or careless of the peculiar complexion of the disease or constitution which he was treating; and in daily life it is obvious that every true physician varies his treatment to suit each individual case. The statesman has an infinite complexity of circumstances, an infinite variety of characters, to handle; and like the physician, he must be left untrammelled by any book of laws, if he is to handle them as he should. The variability of his matter demands a corresponding flexibility in his powers. States which bind their rulers to act according to law lose that flexibility. But Plato admits that laws may be necessary, and that a people may have to bind its rulers, because it fears their cupidity and their

The Statesman and the Law

passions too much to do otherwise. A number of patients who suspected that their physician, if left to his own devices, would poison them to serve his own interests, might very reasonably unite to force him to treat them by the book; and a similar suspicion of their ruler is often natural in subjects, because rulers are only too prone to oppress their subjects for their own ends.[1] In such a case the imposition of a code of laws to guide the ruler's action, if ideally erroneous, is still the best possible course; and the violation or desertion of that code, far from marking an ascent to perfection, would be but an error's crown of error. While therefore ideally reprobating a code, if (and only if) a man can be found who is a law in himself, Plato at the same time strongly insists that in practice, and with actual men, a code is often both necessary and good. The attitude is a little dangerous: it comes too near the sophistic doctrine that law and justice are what the strong man thinks to be law and justice; and we may doubt with Aristotle whether the substitution of the "wise" man for the "strong" really meets this objection. But the attitude is the logical result of following the Socratic conception of Government. Just as in the *Republic* that conception led Plato to insist that every ruler must work unselfishly for the good of the subjects of his art; just as, again, it led him to emphasise the need of a proper training for office; so in the *Politicus* it leads to the conclusion that the monarch who practises the art of government must be as untrammelled as any other artist in his work.

The ideal of Plato would thus appear to be the absolute monarch of a subject people, unfettered by public opinion and unhampered by law. A true physician, neither truckling to his patients nor hampering himself by formulas, he will lead his people along a necessary if unpopular path, and lead them by his own sense of the right end and the proper ways. The antithesis between law and the will of an absolute monarch was one which had often been pointed in Greece; but Plato's exaltation of will above law was none the less a violent con-

[1] Aristotle presses this objection further, in opposition to Plato, *cf. infra*, p. 334. He argues that the analogy of the physician and the ruler, which Plato so often uses (and which underlies his theory of punishment, as well as his theory of absolute monarchy), is a false analogy.

tradiction of cherished opinions and current beliefs. Constitutionalism meant much to the Greeks: they hated the tyrant because he defied it, and because he ruled by his own caprice, boasting, like Richard II., that "the laws were in his own mouth and often in his own breast".[1] The conception of the State as an association of equals was dear to them; and the rule of a single man, tyrant or king, contradicted this conception. But Plato attacks constitutionalism, and thinks but little of equality. To equality he opposed harmony, to constitutionalism flexibility, and in the name of both he advocates absolute monarchy. In a fine passage at the end of the *Politicus* the function of the monarch in binding the State together to the exclusion of selfishness and consequent disunion is emphasised by means of a parallel between statesmanship and weaving. It is the royal art to weave a State of one texture from the warp of courage and the woof of temperance: it is the work of a statesman to bind his State into a unity by the divine bond of a true moral sense, and by the human bond of properly regulated marriage.[2] As a power making for harmony monarchy has still its advocates in German thinkers, and among Positivists. The former discern in a monarch the proper representative of the authority of the "State," who will secure its independence of, and its control over, the various motives and classes of "Society": the latter, struck by the incompetency of the ruling classes, and by the want of political ability which the other classes betray, place their hopes in a dictatorial power, "sufficiently representing the interests of the classes that are growing, and at the same time strong enough to protect the weaker and decaying—a power able to act as a mediator". Such a Cæsarian power "wielding the whole executive power; owning no constitutional check; not the theoretic, but the actual head of the State, securing unity to its policy," would form "the highest function of society, and must not be entrusted to incapable hands". It is, however, only a provisional power, "to satisfy the wants of a transitional state";

The monarch as making for harmony

[1] Euripides speaks of tyranny as a constitution "in which there are no common laws, and one man rules, who has the law in his own keeping" (*Supplices*, 430-32).

[2] Plato refers to the education, and the communisn of wives, which appear in the *Republic*.

and in this respect the Positivist differs from Plato, who contemplated a permanent monarchy.[1]

Monarchy a flexible government

When we turn to the view of absolute monarchy as necessary to flexibility, which is the main ground of Plato's argument in its favour, we enter upon considerations somewhat foreign to modern thought.[2] True to the conception of knowledge as the one thing needful, and regarding a living knowledge as incomparably better than the dead letter of the law, Plato holds absolute monarchy to be preferable to all other constitutions, because in it alone is there the free play of reason, while in the rest there is either the hard rule of an inflexible law, or, still worse, the mere vagaries of caprice and desire. Monarchy is marked by the rule of a principle of reason flexible because it is personal: law-States are equally distinguished by a principle of reason, but it is legal and therefore rigid: caprice-states are marked by the absence of any principle, and by a flexibility which is nothing more than instability. Better, Plato admits, the rule of a principle, even if it be rigid, than no principle at all, even if that means flexibility; but, granted the presence of a principle, better that it should act freely, than that it should act stiffly and by rule. The distinction which Plato thus draws between the flexible and the rigid State is obviously different from that which we now draw between flexible and rigid constitutions. We speak of flexibility where a constitution or a government can be readily altered by the will of the people or its representatives: we speak of rigidity, when the reverse is the case. Our flexibility means the ready response of the State to the will of its members: it seems to us desirable, because without it there is danger of deadlock or revolution. To Plato flexibility meant the ready response of the government to the *nuance* of the case to be treated, or the character to be judged: it seemed to him desirable, because without it there was danger of the hard application of law. In order to make sure of the exact response to such *nuances* he entirely disregards the need of

[1] For this Positivist view, *cf.* Congreve, edition of Aristotle's *Politics*, "Essay on Monarchy," p. 503 *sqq*. Comte himself was in favour of a dictatorship wielded by a triumvirate. There is something Platonic in Comte's belief that "the highest rank is held by the speculative class," and in his assignation to that class of "educational functions, and a regular intervention as moderator in social conflicts".

[2] But *cf. infra*, pp. 330-31.

response to the will of the people: he attains flexibility in *his* sense at the cost of any flexibility in *our* sense.[1] This is one criticism which we may pass: the other is, that he was too much afraid of the rigidity of law. True, there was among the Greeks little of that sense of law as a progressive development which is universally felt to-day. Law was a formed body of precepts rather than a living growth: Greek States valued the law-abiding instinct (εὐνομία) which came from adherence to a fixed code, and they were afraid, just as Aristotle shows himself afraid in the *Politics*, of any innovation.[2] They had something of the mediæval feeling for law as a permanent customary envelopment, in deference to which a reformer like Frederic II. had to explain, that "in nothing do we derogate from the majesty of our ancestors, if we bring forward new laws to suit the needs of new occasions". The modern instinct for progressive legislation, which leads men to expect even a "conservative" government to reform some great department of political life during its tenure of office, is in reality very modern, and in England it can only be said to date from that great epoch of political, administrative, and legislative reconstruction—the reign of William IV.[3] But in any case, we have little reason to fear the rigidity of law (though it may be argued that even to-day there is much rigidity still frost-bound into our law); and possessed as we are of an actively reforming legislature, the like of which even Athens did not know,[4] and of a judicial bench which can modify law to suit new cases even while it seems to preserve ancient law, we can hardly appreciate Plato's position. In the absence, however, of forces such as these, it seems possible that law may become rigid, and that injustice may be done; and to that extent there is in his position an obvious truth. On the other hand, one gathers from Aristotle's criticism that there *was* in

[1] Plato's flexible absolutism, free as it is from any control by the people, is rigid in our sense of the word; his rigid law-state, controlled as it is by law, more nearly approaches our idea of flexibility.

[2] *Cf. infra*, pp. 325-26.

[3] Perhaps it was the belated influence of the French Revolution which led to the passing of a Reform Bill, a New Poor Law, a Municipal Corporations Act, and to the reform of the land-law and the beginning of a system of national education, in the seven years between 1830 and 1837.

[4] *Cf. infra*, p. 456.

equity (ἐπιείκεια) a force which could modify law to suit new cases, without any overt contravention of its form, even among the Greeks; and there is a deep truth in Aristotle's further criticism, that to abolish law because it is rigid is only to open the door for the caprice of a monarch, who may only too readily tend to use his "flexible" powers for interests of his own.[1]

Plato's Classification of States

Value of the *Republic* as an ideal Standard

§ 2. A certain classification of States has already been implied in what we have said of absolute monarchy, and to that problem of classification we may now turn. In doing so we enter upon a new atmosphere. We leave the ideal State and the atmosphere of reform: we enter, for a while, upon the field of existing States, and seek to discover what *is* rather than what *should be.* But the ideal State, and the principles which lie at the root of the ideal State, are still with us; and they now serve us as the criterion by which we may classify, and the standard by which we may judge, the phenomena of actual politics. This is the great function of ideals, such as Plato's *Republic;* if they cannot be realised, they yet enable us to understand the real. By showing us what the State would be if its immanent principles were fully realised, they show us what is the truth, the "idea," of the State as an institution; and in that way they enable us to understand the State. It is only in such an ideal aspect that the State *can* be understood. If the mere phenomena of its actual working were alone considered, we should be able to collect a number of facts about the State, but not to grasp its meaning. In this sense political science must always deal with ideals. It must consider what the State means to be, rather than what it is, in order to understand what it is. It must investigate the healthy and normal specimen, the "right State"; and the right State must be an ideal, because every actual State is to some extent defective, abnormal, perverted. It must abstract the "form" of the State from the matter in which it is involved, exactly as geometrical science abstracts the "form" of a straight line from the matter of the solid in which it is involved. There is no straight line *in rerum natura,* no line in only one dimension: there is no ideal State.

[1] *Cf. infra,* p. 334.

But Euclid postulates the one, and Plato and Aristotle postulate the other, as the condition of sciences, which are none the less sciences because they proceed on the assumption of something "unreal," and indeed are only sciences because they proceed on such an assumption.[1]

Previous attempts at classification

Taking the State sketched in the *Republic* for standard, and its principles for clues, we can see the meaning and the value of existing States. "This State is what it is, because it has not observed the principle of knowledge: this State is better than that, because it comes nearer to the standard of the ideal." We can classify, and not only so, but we can classify in a scale of values. Such classification, based as it is on a principle, differs from most of the previous attempts at classification made in Greece. Herodotus in a famous passage[2] had made the Persian grandees contrast monarchy, aristocracy, and democracy in respect of their value; and he had impartially pronounced that they all suffered from evils, which in each case ultimately involved a tyranny. Democracy at its best, he tells us, means equality before the law, an elective and responsible executive, and the right of the people to exercise deliberative power. But the people do not know, for they have never been taught, what is fitting and proper; they can be more tyrannical than the worst tyrant in their ignorant caprice; and their incapacity permits a public corruption, which provokes ultimately a revolt of the masses led by a champion who becomes a tyrant.[3] Aristocracy means the predominance of good birth and breeding; but the members of an aristocracy are touchy on the point of honour, and quarrels easily arise which develop into civil war, and culminate in tyranny. Monarchy again at its best means due regard to the welfare of the whole State, and capable conduct of foreign policy; but the monarch is liable to the intoxication of power, and falling into insolence and a jealousy of all merit, he becomes a tyrant. While Herodotus thus condemns

[1] Green's *Principles of Political Obligation* goes on the assumption that "the State is based on will, not force". The assumption is "unreal," it may be urged; and Ireland and Russia may be cited. But we can only understand the meaning of the State in the light of this assumption.

[2] III., 80-82.

[3] Compare the revolts, aiming at escape from corruption, and culminating in the Cæsarism of a mayor, which have occurred in American cities of late years.

all constitutions, the orators of Athens praise democracy, and condemn the rest. Democracy is the government of equality, and the home of impersonal law. It gives power to all classes, and favours none; all other constitutions represent the rule of a section, and are based on privilege.[1] This encomium of democracy was answered by the Sophists with the praise of tyranny, as the government most consonant with the natural principle of the rule of the strong. The teaching of Socrates was hostile to the advocates both of democracy and of tyranny. It was his great principle, as we have seen, that government was an art, and, as such, demanded a knowledge which was not to be found in democracy, with its incapable assembly and equally incapable officials, and an unselfish regard to the subject's good, which the tyrant could never feel. This would suggest a classification of States according as their rulers were unselfish and wise, or selfish and unwise. But the Socratic classification, as reported by Xenophon, is not quite so systematic or simple. Taking monarchy, aristocracy and democracy as the three main classes, Socrates, we are told, divided the two former into different and separate kinds. Monarchy he distinguished from tyranny, by the two criteria of its respect for law and the consent of its subjects;[2] aristocracy he distinguished from plutocracy, on the somewhat different ground that it recognised capacity, while the other recognised, and erroneously recognised, mere wealth; and he condemned democracy (of which he only made one type, and found that evil) for the want of knowledge which it showed. Thus we get five constitutions, two of them—monarchy and aristocracy—both good; the other three—tyranny, oligarchy, and democracy—all bad. The Platonic classification, which we find in the *Politicus*, adopts and systematises Socrates' scheme. Plato elevates the principle of knowledge, which Socrates had enforced so strongly in his ethical teaching, and which had led him to condemn democracy, into the supreme

Platonic classification

[1] This line is taken in Athenagoras' speech at Syracuse, reported by Thucydides and mentioned above, (p. 90). One may compare the way in which Liberal speakers and papers attack the Conservative party as fostering privileges, and favouring "sections" like the Established Church, or the landlord classes; while they regard their own principle as one of equality for all, and no favour for any.

[2] Xen., *Mem.*, iv., 6, 12.

and guiding principle of classification; and in the light of the State and the form of government which represent perfect knowledge, he classifies all other States and constitutions. In virtue of this principle he makes three grades of States—the State of perfect knowledge perfectly free to act; the States of imperfect knowledge formalised in a law, which only act where that law can act; and the States of ignorance, which refuse to be guided even by the imperfect and hard "knowledge" of a code of law. Excluding the perfect State, or absolute monarchy, "as if it were a god"—leaving the ideal, which is our standard, and concentrating our attention upon the actual, we have therefore two great divisions of existing States. There are the law-states, and there are the caprice-states—the States which obey the law, under which they are set in lieu of the rule of perfect knowledge, and the States which disobey that law. Either of these may be subdivided according to a principle of number, and as the rulers are one or few or many; and in this way we attain the following scheme.

I

[Outside and above any scheme, the perfect State of perfect knowledge freed from the impediment of law—the ideal State of the *Republic*.]

Law-states, directed by a knowledge expressed in law, by which they faithfully act:—

i. The rule of one, or "constitutional" (as opposed to absolute) monarchy.
ii. The rule of few, or aristocracy.
iii. The rule of many, or democracy of a moderate and "constitutional" kind.

II

Caprice-states, which disobey the law in which the knowledge that should guide them is expressed:—

i. The rule of one, or tyranny.
ii. The rule of few, or oligarchy.
iii. The rule of many, or "extreme" democracy.

Of the six constitutions which thus emerge, Plato places monarchy first, and tyranny last; the rule of a single man is strongest both for good and evil, because authority is placed undivided in his hands. The rule of the many, on the contrary, is weakest for vice, and weakest for virtue, because power is infinitesimally divided among an infinity of authorities; and accordingly, while Plato thinks extreme democracy the first and best of caprice-states, he places constitutional democracy third and worst of law-states.[1] The enmity which he evinces towards division of powers shows once more that tendency towards centralisation in his thought, which brings him into touch with Hobbes, and makes his sovereign, like the sovereign of Hobbes, a mortal god, an undivided and indivisible Leviathan.

Constitutional Change

Plato's sketch of change not historical

§ 3. From considering existing States as they stand in relation to the ideal, we may naturally pass to inquire how they have fallen from the ideal. This is to turn from rest to motion, from statics to dynamics. The ideal State is now no longer the standard by which other States are measured, but the source from which they are traced. It is not, however, any *historical* sequence of corruption from a primary ideal that Plato seeks to trace. He does not imagine that there ever actually was an ideal State in the beginning, or that the order of the stages which he describes represents an historical series. He gives a logical and *a priori* picture of the course corruption would take, supposing that we began with an ideal State, a perfect product of perfect mind, and that the degradation of that State proceeded from within, and not from the accidents of external impulse. The principle which underlies the whole sketch is the old principle, that the State is a product of mind; and the argument is, that successively inferior types of State are the products of successively inferior types of mind. But the "succession" is a logical succession: the priority of the ideal State to the first stage which "succeeds" it, and of that again to the next, is what Aristotle would call priority in "nature" (or idea), not in "time". Just as before we witnessed the logical construction of a State, in which each psychological factor was "successively" introduced, not in order of

[1] It is obvious how much the *Politics* is like the *Politicus* in this point, and in regard to the whole subject of classification.

time, but in order of importance, so we now witness a destruction of the State, in which each psychological factor is "successively" taken away, again in order of importance. As the factor of reason was last added in construction, so in destruction it is the first to be taken away: stage by stage, the State is made to depend on fewer and worse psychological factors, until in tyranny it depends only on desire, and the worst element of desire. But while we repudiate any historical meaning for this sketch, we must not deny its historical bearing. These books have been called the first attempt at a philosophy of history:[1] if they are not history, they explain history, and show *why* history is a record, not of the perfect "idea" of the State, but of its various and successive perversions. They show, that is to say, that history has not been made by the full mind of man, acting in the proper hierarchy of its parts, but created as it were by fragments of mind. And again, it is certainly implied in Plato that the ideal State, considered as existing *in rerum natura*, is subject to laws of historical mutation. It knows a process of growth and of increase;[2] nor, on the other hand, is it exempt from a law of decay, which leads to its final collapse.[3] A law of deterioration, such as is visible in plants, equally affects man; and an inferior progeny will in the course of time produce an inferior State.[4] It is therefore implied by Plato that the ideal State will change, and, if it changes by a logical series of stages, will change in the way which he suggests. Aristotle criticises Plato from a historical point of view, and urges that, as a matter of fact, constitutions do not alter in the sequence Plato describes: oligarchy does not always pass into democracy, and democracy into tyranny; in actual life, a democracy will pass into an oligarchy as readily as into a tyranny. The answer to this criticism is, partly that it is beside the mark, for Plato was not writing history or generalising from history; partly that, even from a historical point of view, Plato's sequence may be vindicated,

[1] Nettleship, *Lectures*, p. 299. [2] *Rep.*, 424 A. [3] *Ibid.*, 546.

[4] Plato implies something like what Horace says:

> "Aetas parentum pejor avis tulit
> Nos nequiores, mox daturos
> Progeniem vitiosiorem".

On the other hand he also believes

> "Fortes creantur fortibus et bonis,"

and in the strength of that belief attempts to regulate marriage.

if we regard not the exception, but the general rule of constitutional change. The actual logic of Greek history, indeed, intercalated the tyranny between oligarchy and democracy, and made tyranny the preparation of democracy, though there are cases in which a democracy passed into a tyranny, as in the instance of Dionysius at Syracuse. But the communes of mediæval Italy exactly followed Plato's sequence: the oligarchical *commune* either succumbed before the democratic *popolo*, or admitted it to a share in the government; and in either case a division of classes still survived, acute enough to divide the State and ultimately introduce a tyranny, open or concealed.[1]

The practical purpose of the sketch

So far of the historical bearing of the sketch of constitutional change given in the *Republic*. But it is a practical, and not an historical purpose, which is served by this sketch. In the first place, Plato intends to classify actual constitutions in the order of their value, by showing them to be deeper and deeper degradations from the ideal. This purpose appears in the jesting condemnation of the tyrant as seven hundred and twenty-nine times worse than the ruler of the ideal State; and to this extent the purpose of these books of the *Republic* is parallel to that of the *Politicus*. There is indeed some difference between the two dialogues. The *Politicus* regards the law-states as good (it is true, in default of something still better, and as a thing ἀγαπητόν rather than αἱρετόν, as Aristotle would say); and it places democracy on a higher level than does the *Republic*.[2] Yet the general trend is much the same, and the *Politicus* only summarises the *Republic*. A second purpose, which this sketch of constitutional change is also intended to serve, is to indicate the true way of reforming degraded States, and of restoring them to the level of the ideal. The corrupt and unjust State does not merely help to show us the corrupt and unjust man, as the ideal and just State did not merely help to show us the ideal and just man. There is more than analogy: there is identity. The corrupt and unjust State *is* simply a society of unjust and corrupt men; it is what it is through the type of character of which it is composed. A State which, like an oligarchy, has gone astray in

[1] It has been pointed out by Lutoslawski that Aristotle uses Plato's theory of constitutional change, in spite of his criticism.

[2] By differentiating two kinds, and pronouncing one of them good.

pursuit of wealth, has only done so, because the money-getting type has become the approved type of character in that State, and has made the "national character" one of avarice. But if constitutions thus originate in, as well as correspond to, national character (the very lesson which Montesquieu afterwards taught), was not the hope of political salvation to be found in an education of character, such as Plato advocated and sketched—and in nothing else? To show, therefore, as Plato showed, the vital connection between corrupt States and corruption of character, was to indicate the one path of any real reform of the actual (and corrupt) state of Greece. In this respect Plato is far more radical than Aristotle in his therapeutics: he prescribes a radical change of the whole scheme of life, whereas Aristotle (in books vi. to viii. of the *Politics*) more cautiously advocates a moderate indulgence in the existing scheme.

From this account of the bearing of Plato's scheme of constitutional change we may now turn to its details. The type of mind which underlies the true State, as we have said, is mind in its fulness, under the control of the sovereign element of reason; and the constitution in which it issues, a constitution similarly marked by the predominance of wisdom over the other elements of the State, is termed by Plato both monarchy and aristocracy, and may be simply called (since the ruler, whoever he may be, is the vehicle of the Idea) an ideocracy. From this ideocracy States sink to a timocracy, when the element of reason loses its due predominance, and gives place to "spirit". Timocracy has in Plato the peculiar meaning of government by the principle of honour (τιμή).[1] The admired type is now the man of high spirit and courageous temper, whose master motive is the point of honour; and the State and the name of the State correspond. It is accordingly a military State, after the manner of Sparta, and it promotes to the highest office those of its members who have won honour in war. It has affinities with ideocracy, because high spirit is allied to wisdom, and thus it retains the common meals and a proper system of common

The successive changes

[1] It generally meant a constitution in which power was given to men possessed of a property-qualification (τίμημα). In this sense of the word, Plato's "oligarchy" would be a "timocracy".

education: it has also its affinities with oligarchy, or the rule of the rich, because high spirit also tends towards desire, and thus it admits private property, and over-emphasises the share of the body in education. In a timocracy justice is already beginning to disappear, and injustice to enter: each element is not in its proper place, or discharging its proper function. The wise man has lost the reins of office: the soldier has taken the place of the ruler; and even the third or producing class loses its right position. Its property is seized, and its members are depressed into serfs by the new rulers. Here the appetitive element of spirit appears; and as it grows, the progress is easy to oligarchy. The type of character now admired is that of the money-making man, in whom desire is uppermost, but in whom all other desires are subordinated to the one passion for wealth. Desire is orderly in the "oligarchic" or money-making man; but the supremacy of desire, however orderly it may be in itself, indicates disorder in the soul, and means injustice in the State. Wealth becomes the passport to office, and a census is instituted: the rule of the State rests neither with the born ruler, nor with the soldier, but with the richest members of the producing class. Oligarchy as a form of government has two great faults. It gives office to wealth, instead of regarding capacity for office; and as the members of an oligarchy farm and fight and rule at one and the same time, their skill disappears for want of specialisation. Again, it splits the State into two: as the wealthy grow wealthier, the poor grow poorer; and a social hatred arises which bodes ill for the State. Oligarchy thus shows the two great evils which Plato deplored in contemporary States—ignorance of the art of government, and political disunion. In the next stage these two evils are intensified. The desire which is the basis of oligarchy is at any rate an orderly desire; but in time, as character deteriorates, there is a revolt of the other desires against the rule of avarice, and a loose mob of passions vindicates for itself the government of the soul. In politics, this deterioration of character issues in the revolt of the poorer classes against the rule of the rich, and the establishment of a democracy. The type of character now admired is that of the man who "does as he likes," and allows the ungoverned mob of his passions to riot in any and every direction. This is freedom—so-called; but it is that false freedom, which is the mere negation of order. It means in reality a refusal to pursue the quiet and orderly path of concentration, which alone makes a man capable of doing his work in the world. Everything by turns and nothing long, the "democratic" man tries everything and does nothing.[1] He, and the State which he makes, are almost absolutely "unjust". In neither is there any concentration upon an appointed function: in both the lowest elements of their composition are let loose in a disorderly array to confound the higher and better. Without any binding principle of justice, democracy loses all unity: it is a State of three classes, demagogues, rich men, and poor, of which the first pillages the second by means of false accusations for the benefit of the third—and of itself. In this respect, as in others, democracy has its great affinities with oligarchy. Both display the same two cardinal faults of ignorance and selfishness; but democracy is more glaringly ignorant and more openly selfish. In both desire is the psychological basis; but in the one the single desire of money controls all other desires, and erects wealth into the end of the State, while in the other a desire for mere enjoyment reigns, and freedom is made a fetish. Both again perish out of their strength's abundance: both collapse as a result of pushing their principles to excess.[2] Oligarchy fell, when the rich gave free reign to their avarice, and impoverished men by heavy usury till the inevitable revolt installed democracy: democracy falls when it allows the demagogue to run into excesses in his advocacy of "freedom". Pillaging the rich until they find the burden intolerable, he at last discovers that he must either become a tyrant, or fall a prey to their vengeance. He chooses the former alternative; and a tyranny arises, animated equally with oligarchy and democracy by the principle of desire, but a desire which is both for gain and for enjoyment, a desire which belongs to a single individual, to whom the rest of the State is sacrificed. Tyranny possesses all the evils of

[1] The danger dreaded by modern thinkers is the opposite. The pressure of a majority, enforcing its own views and clinging to its own practices, may lead to monotony and conservatism.

[2] *Cf.* Aristotle's very similar view, and his advice to those who would preserve either an extreme democracy or an extreme oligarchy, *viz.*, that they should moderate its character (*infra*, pp. 489-90).

oligarchy and democracy, enhanced by their concentration in a single person : it is the worst of constitutions, and the tyrant, who uses his strength to satisfy his lust and his greed, is the worst of men. This is the final rebuke of Plato to the Sophistic position, that justice is the interest of the stronger, and that the ideal of a State is therefore tyranny; and Plato elaborates his rebuke by showing that tyranny is evil squared and cubed, and the tyrant the most miserable of men, who has withdrawn himself into a horror of darkness and isolation from the life and purpose of the world, with which the philosopher—the antithesis of the tyrant—has thoroughly identified his being.

Plato's view of democracy

The whole of Plato's scheme has some analogy with Aristotle's account of perverted States. As Plato discovers corruption in the elevation to a position of supremacy of an element of mind, which ought to be subordinate, so Aristotle discovered perversion in the elevation of something, which should be a subsidiary end of the State, to its final and ultimate good. The attainment of wealth is such a subsidiary end of the State in Aristotle's opinion, just as in Plato's view the desire for wealth is a necessary but subordinate element of mind which goes to make the State. For the one, oligarchy errs in making the attainment of wealth a supreme end; for the other, it errs in making the desire for wealth the ruling element. But in comparison both with Aristotle and with Plato's own scheme in the *Politicus*, it is noticeable that democracy takes a lower place in the *Republic*. In the *Politicus* it was regarded as equally in its good form and in its bad form superior to oligarchy, though in both forms inferior to aristocracy; in the *Republic* only one form of democracy is presented, and that form is treated as inferior to both timocracy and oligarchy. The difference is due to a different point of view. In the *Politicus* Plato is thinking of the greater division of power which marks a democracy, and makes it less powerful for evil (if also for good) than a State governed by the few : in the *Republic* he is regarding the psychological elements which underlie the State, and he finds that these are of a lower order among the masses than they are among the upper classes. But while in the classification of the *Republic* he takes a harsh view of democracy, only recognising the one form of extreme democracy, and judging that harshly, we must also admit that he shows no little appreciation of its difficulties and its real character. It was said above that he forgot the people; and there is some truth in the saying. But while he neglected the many-headed being because it had little brains, he none the less felt that its heart was in the right place. He hates the demagogue rather than the demos. He hates the demagogue with the double fervour of an aristocrat and a *savant*: he has something of the pity of both for the people. Using the old figure of the ship of State, he compares the people to a captain besieged by rival claimants for the helm. The captain is deaf and short-sighted and ignorant of things nautical; but he is a "noble" fellow, drugged by the would-be helmsmen with mandragora (misrepresentations and false doctrines), in order that they may get full control of the ship. Over these *prétendants* Plato pours vials of wrath: quacks and shams and men of fustian, they try to seize the helm though they have never been trained as pilots, and they plead in justification that such training is impossible. From them the people must be saved at all costs—but by their Saviour the people must be led.

The Law-State and the Mixed Constitution

§ 4. A different attitude towards democracy is apparent when we turn to the *Laws*; and here, indeed, a totally new aspect of Plato's whole thought is revealed. As yet we have never left the pure ideal; though we may have been dealing with actual States, it has still been with us, as the standard for their classification, or the source of their derivation. But in the *Laws* it is Plato's aim to construct a half-way house between the actual and the ideal; and here the ideal is not suspended in judgment over actual States, but modified to a degree, which will permit of a counter-modification of actual States sufficient to meet its demands. The State of the *Laws* is a "sub-ideal" State, near enough to actual conditions to be readily incorporated into actual life. From another point of view the change marked by the *Laws* is still more striking. Hitherto, whatever the subject under discussion, there has been one fundamental thought—the conception of politics as an art, and, as an art, demanding a wise practitioner, unfettered by any laws. But

New atmosphere of the *Laws*

the last work of Plato's life is called "the Laws," and the last effort of his imagination is the construction of a State where law is supreme. The change is great; it cleaves Plato's political theory into two distinct halves. On the one side is the "guardian" unfettered by law: on the other the "guardian of the law," who is its "servant" and even its "slave". Yet there is consistency even while there is change. The two ideals are not opposites; they are complements. The man of wisdom, unfettered by law, is always Plato's absolute ideal: in the *Laws* he only states a secondary or relative ideal, secondary, as compared with the State of the *Republic*, relative, as adapted to the exigencies of actual life. Aristotle had equally his two ideals. The ideal State described in his fourth and fifth books corresponds to Plato's *Republic*: the "polity" is very like the State of the *Laws*.

The *Laws* and Aristotle's *Politics*

And here it may be remarked—the point is one of some importance—that in the whole of the *Laws* there is much Aristotelianism. To put the same point in the converse proposition, the *Laws* would appear to have had a great influence upon, and it certainly presents great affinities with, the teaching of Aristotle. Not only does this last treatise of Plato's old age suggest the idea of a second-best constitution to Aristotle; but it also suggests (what it is true was in the air) the mixed form of that constitution. The conception of the sovereignty of law, which Aristotle emphasises in the Third Book of the *Politics*, is nowhere more clearly expressed than in the *Laws*; and Aristotle's definition of law, as "dispassionate reason," is already anticipated there by Plato. The theory of distributive justice, as based upon proportionate equality, and awarding office "according to merit," already occurs in the *Laws*; and it contains an historical sketch of the origin of the State not unlike that which opens the *Politics*, though fuller and more striking. Above all, the spirit which breathes through the *Laws* is that spirit of naturalism, or realism—of practical compromise, and truth to actualities—which distinguishes Aristotle. Aristotle's debt to Plato should not be forgotten. Aristotle wrote the *Politics*, but Plato is the great political thinker of Greece. He had grappled with almost every problem of Greek politics, and suggested some solution which has its vital and fundamental truth, whatever errors or excesses it may contain. Aristotle utilised and systematised the whole of his work. It is easy to overlook this fact in reading the *Politics*: Aristotle only mentions Plato to disagree with his theories. But one must remember that Aristotle was the author of a systematic philosophy, incorporating and ordering previous results, and often only mentioning these results specifically, when they could not be incorporated, or at any rate could not be incorporated as they stood. There is as little absolutely new in the *Politics* as there is in Magna Carta. Neither is meant to be new: both are meant to codify previous development. But Magna Carta remains the great document of English History; and the *Politics* remains the great document of Greek political thought—as Plato remains the great political thinker of Greece.

In considering the *Laws* we have first to determine its relation to the other great political writings of Plato. The law-state, as we have seen, is already foreshadowed in the *Politicus*. In default of the ideal, which is the free action of immanent reason, it is the best course, we are told in the *Politicus*, to institute a State in which the government acts according to an external reason incorporated in law.[1] But the more important question is the relation of the *Laws* to the *Republic*. In what way, and to what extent, is the ideal of the *Republic* modified? Is there any suggestion in the *Republic* of such modification? The *Republic* has justice for its ideal. Justice means differentiation of function; and functions are so rigidly differentiated in the *Republic*, that the political organ, confined to its political function, loses all social rights, while the social or economic organ, confined to its economic function, loses all political rights. There are guardians, who have no property and no family: there are men possessed of property and living in families, who have no vote and no control of any kind over the government. Justice, again, postulating the perfect discharge of their functions by those who guide the State, demands a perfect knowledge; and this demand gives its tone to the

The *Laws* in relation to the *Republic*

[1] *Cf.* also the *Laws*, 875 C: "If a man were born so divinely gifted that he could naturally apprehend the truth, he would have no need of laws to rule over him; for there is no law or order which is above knowledge. But then there is no such mind anywhere, or at least not much; and therefore we must choose law and order, which are second best."

Republic. There is something of a hard and cold atmosphere of intellect: reason shines with a dazzling, but dry light. But besides justice there is also a virtue of self-control mentioned in the *Republic*, which forms a link between the political and the social organs. It is this virtue which, in default of justice, becomes the motive of the *Laws*.[1] This virtue postulates no absolute differentiation of functions. Accordingly in the *Laws* the rulers have both political and social rights; and the same is true of the ruled. The ruler has private property and a family: communism is abandoned, though the "common tables" are retained; and the ruled have a voice and a vote in the election of their rulers. Such a State will not have the perfect unity which springs from the co-operation of elements each contributing its single and special function to the life of the whole; but if it be permeated by self-control, it will have a unity of sympathy none the less. Issuing as it does in sympathy, self-control brings us into a different atmosphere from that of the *Republic*—an atmosphere which is less rare, but more human; less clear, but also less cold. The descent is one from unscaled heights and strange sublimities to the familiar and practicable; and if the light of knowledge still shines, it is mercifully veiled behind the cloud of law. Combining therefore the teaching of the *Politicus* with that of the *Republic*, we may say, that in the *Laws* we have a *law-state* cohering in virtue of a principle of *self-control*, a State in which the sovereign is law, and the ministers and administrators of law are the elected of the people. Two subjects thus emerge for discussion. What is the nature and meaning of law, and what is the character and constitution of a proper administration?

It is natural to find the basis of law, and of the State itself, in *will*. The theory of the Social Contract emphasised this basis, when it made an *act* of will in past time create both. Apart from the criticism of this theory which urges that there is no such creation by an act of will, but a permanent maintenance by a constant determination of will, there is a further and more vital criticism, which urges that the State and its law are not based on mere will, or on any will, but on *right* will. A mere

The State based on will

[1] In this view of the relation of the *Laws* to the *Republic* I follow Hildenbrand, *op. cit.*

basis of will is a shifting quicksand; and only in the right will which is always constant to one purpose, can a real and firm basis of authority be found. Not only so; but we must also realise, that only in the State which is based on this will, only in the individual who acts by this will, is there any true freedom. Freedom, as Montesquieu said, "ne peut consister qu'à pouvoir faire ce que l'on *doit vouloir*, et à n'être point contraint de faire ce que l'on ne doit pas vouloir".[1] In a State, freedom is the right of doing all that the laws permit, and in not being forced to do anything which law does not ordain.[2] That is to say, man is only a free agent when rationally choosing a course which his reason assures him is right, and is never less free than when "he does as he likes," and, obeying the dictates of passion, falls a victim to his own worse self.[3] These are the truths which Plato enforces in the first Book of the *Laws*.

Conception of law as expression of rational will

War is eternal, in man and the State: there is an ancient strife, in the one between the better and the worse self, in the other between the better members and the worse. In both the war is for the sake of peace, a peace gained by the lasting triumph of the better part, and by the subjugation, though not the extirpation, of the worse. The end of the State, therefore, is peace, not indeed the peace of solitude, in which one party has destroyed the other, but the peace of harmony, in which both are reconciled under one leader (631 D). The leader is reason (rational will or right will), and reason is incarnate in law. Since the end of the State is peace, laws like those of Sparta, which look to war, and seek to inspire the one virtue of courage, are awry: the true law looks to peace, and to the sum of virtue; and, as the incarnation of reason the *leader*, it guides at *every* point. It extends over the whole of life: it regulates birth, it arranges marriage, it rules even in death, for the very dead must be buried according to law. Again, it deals with every passion and affection in life: it makes "definitions" (and by the honour and dishonour which it awards it "teaches" men

[1] *Esprit des Lois*, bk. xi., c. 3. [2] *Ibid.*, xxvi., c. 20.

[3] This is what Plato teaches in the *Republic*. Freedom means the free action of the whole man according to the will of the best part of his being; and similarly a State is free, when it acts according to the will of the right ruler (which Plato substitutes for the "law" of which Montesquieu speaks) (bk. ix.). For the similar teaching of Aristotle, *cf. infra*, p. 355.

to follow its definitions) of the right and wrong of every feeling that can arise in human intercourse. Lastly, as it covers the whole span of man's life, as it deals with every spiritual affection of life, so it deals with all its material interests; it regulates property and every nexus between man and man that springs from property. And thus "the sacred and golden cord of reason, called by us the common law of the State" (645 A), works to a perfect harmony. Nor is this law a force acting from without upon the individual: in its spirit he is trained, and education is "the constraining of youth . . . towards that right reason which the law affirms, and which the experience of the best has agreed to be truly right" (659 D)—a constraining which comes from so playing upon his passions, that he rejoices in all things in which the law would have him rejoice, and dislikes all things which the law would have him dislike. In other words, his character is "habituated" into the "spirit of the laws". The very words, as well as the whole tone, suggest Aristotle's teaching in the *Ethics* and in the *Politics*. One may notice especially the insistence upon peace as the aim and only purpose of war, the attitude towards the law as the incarnation of reason, the view of education as a process of habituation, as all Aristotelian; while the emphasis laid in the *Laws* on the part which is to be played in education by music as a maker of character, is very like the emphasis which Aristotle also lays on music in discussing the ideal State.

Law, as yet, has appeared in the guise of order, an order regulating the moral and the material content of the whole span of life, an order not merely external, but wrought through education into the very fibre of the soul. It is a conception very faithful to the ideas of the city-state, and as such it is exactly reproduced by Aristotle. It is a conception wider than ours, in that it makes law regulate the whole of moral life and thereby inculcate a positive morality, besides regulating material life and thereby removing the impediments to free moral action. It is a conception higher than ours in that it demands that law shall be enforced not by punishment and the secular arm, but by education and the appeal of mind to mind. Plato is particularly concerned to make this appeal a reality. He wishes that law shall come as a persuading voice, and enter into the inner soul, rather than as a commanding force, to hale man away in its custody. If there is order, there must also be freedom. This is involved in the conception of self-control; for just as the rulers will not sympathise with the ruled (as that conception demands) unless obedience is paid to order, so, on the other hand, the ruled will not sympathise with the rulers, unless they in their turn respect freedom. Law, therefore, as the supreme ruler, must respect freedom; and Plato proposes a somewhat curious method by which it shall show its respect. The laws must be preceded by proems or prefaces, enunciating the principles on which they are based, and persuading the individual to accept them, by showing that they are the logical result of principles which he accepts. In these prefaces, explaining and justifying the laws they precede, one finds as it were a Greek counterpart of the function, which Parliament and the Press play to-day, in enabling a minister or a party to explain and to excuse the policy of a legislative scheme.

Plato's opinion of contemporary constitutions

We have begun with law: from law we turn to the constitution, and examine in what way the principle of self-control will exhibit itself in the government, and by what means order will there be reconciled with freedom. But before doing so, we must notice that there is an important principle contained in the order which has been followed in beginning with law, and proceeding from law to constitution. The principle is, that the law-state must be the reverse of actual and contemporary States: it must adjust its government to the law, as the servant of the law, and not its law to the government, as the tool of the government. Contemporary States, Plato tells us in the *Laws*, are not really States. They are "aggregations of men dwelling in cities, who are the subjects and servants of a part of their own State, and each of them is named after the dominant power" (712 E-713 A). Democracy, for instance, is not a State: it is an aggregation of men, divided into two bodies, of which the one dominates the other, and deriving its generic name of democracy from the specific name of the dominant body—the demos. There is here no constitution, or order of the whole State, but a clique: there is no polity, but a party; and democracy is merely that party which has vanquished the others. Treating itself as the whole, this party lays down as law everything which it regards as making for its own welfare. "Men say that the law ought not to regard . . . virtue, . . . but only the interest and power and preservation of the established form of government" (714 B). We thus return to the old position, "Justice is the interest of the strongest": law is what the interest of the predominant clique makes it, and varies with the predominance of different cliques. In the law-state it is exactly the opposite. Law comes first, as sole and supreme sovereign: the government is constructed in its interest. But law is one and the same for all, and in the interest of all; and so the government must represent the interest of all, since it represents the interest of law. If we wish, says Plato, to call such a State after the name of the force which predominates in its life, we shall call it God's State, or a theocracy; for ultimately it is reason which predominates, as expressed in law, and reason is God. Here, therefore, the rulers do not make the law: they serve the law which God has made; and here instead of a government which makes the law to suit itself, there is a law which forces the government to conform itself to the interests of all.

What is the government which will best "serve" the law, by consulting the interests of all? An historical sketch is the prelude of Plato's answer, a sketch which, in contrast with the logical construction of the *Republic*, indicates the more realistic temper of the *Laws*. After the Deluge—for Plato "begins at the beginning"—its few survivors lived on the tops of the hills (to which, as a matter of fact, primitive man would naturally cling for safety). They lived in a pastoral State, very like the city of swine of the *Republic*: they were ignorant of much that is good, but also of much that is bad, in civilised life; and, if imperfect, they were nevertheless blessed, in the absence alike of poverty and of wealth, and in the simplicity of their hearts. The dream of a golden "state of nature," and the facts of civilised and political life, seem in this picture to strive for the mastery; and Plato appears uncertain which to prefer. But he admits that men refused to be content in the paradise of the hills. From the hilltops they next descended to the plains at the foot of the hills: from pasture they turned to agriculture. They had been living in patriarchal families on the tops of the hills: the closer society which agricultural life involved brought

Historical sketch of development of State

these families into contact. The customs of one patriarchal family were seen not to be as those of another: a legislator was appointed to select the best customs, and the heads of the families formed themselves into a government to maintain the selection. In the stress here laid upon the patriarchal family, and in the view of law as a codification of custom, Plato hits intuitively upon two truths, the latter of which at any rate was foreign to the Greeks. From the tribal society he next turns to the civic; and a third era is marked by the building of Troy in the plain, away from the hills. The mention of Troy suggests its siege: its siege suggests heroic Greece; and so the progress is made to the fourth and final stage, which is the period of the three Dorian kingdoms, Sparta, Argos and Messene. By an historic consideration of these three Plato attempts to decide "what is well or ill settled, and what laws are the salvation, and what are the destruction of cities, and what changes would make a State happy". The phrase reminds one vividly of the way in which Aristotle speaks in his sixth book: he too will consider what are the ways in which States are saved and destroyed; he too will discuss the manner of making actual constitutions better than they are. But Aristotle bases what he has to say on a full consideration of contemporary States: Plato goes back to early Greek history, or moves eastward to a criticism of Persian monarchy. And there is one great difference between Aristotle and Plato. Aristotle is willing to consider how to preserve the actual State with some modification of its excess: Plato will not for a minute consider the salvation of anything that actually exists except it be recast and remoulded. Aristotle builds an ideal State, and a "polity" which is sub-ideal, and considers even the preservation of the non-ideal, non-moral State: Plato advances to the second stage, but will not enter the third.

Necessity of a mixed constitution

The three Dorian kingdoms had great advantages. They were closely allied with one another;[1] and the stability of each might seem assured by the help of the rest. At the same time there was within each State a free field for the legislator:

[1] The three kings *and peoples* were united by oaths, according to common laws regulating rulers and subjects—the kings swearing not to make their power tyrannical, the peoples, subject to that condition, not to dethrone the kings (684 A). This seems the germ of the idea of a contract between king and people.

there were no vested interests or inherited prejudices to hinder his work. And yet, on the whole, they failed. The alliance proved no alliance; and the cause of its collapse, which was so evident in the Persian wars, was the *unmixed* character of the royal rule, which made each sovereign inclined to act on his own behalf. And thus there appears at any rate one thing that is "ill-settled," one cause of "destruction"; and there is naturally suggested a "change" to a "mixed" government, which will make a State happy. Again, in spite of the free field they enjoyed in internal politics, the legislators failed to secure the pursuit by each government of its proper end of wisdom and understanding. The kings of Argos and Messene fell into ways of ignorance, and in their ignorance they desired to get the better of the laws and to crush the liberty of their subjects. The mistake was that of originally giving all power to one man; it is the mistake of giving disproportionately, as if one should give great sails to a small ship, or excessive food to a little body.[1] Absolute monarchy must, Plato now maintains, necessarily fall into the ignorance which is selfishness. Sparta was saved, where Argos and Messene perished, exactly because her monarchy was not absolute: it was limited on the one hand by the fact that it was dual, on the other by the concurrent powers of Senate and Ephorate. Once more, therefore, in the interests of internal peace, as before for the sake of united action with other States, a "mixed" constitution suggests itself as the natural remedy. And here Sparta, which had served in the *Republic* as a model in respect of her training, appears in a new aspect, as a model in respect of her government. We learn from the *Politics* that this aspect was one on which stress was often laid by Laconising writers, and that Sparta was generally held to be a right mixture of all constitutions, and especially of two, democracy and oligarchy. In dealing with the conception of a mixed constitution, Plato has therefore a background of previous speculation based on Sparta; but, instead of resting upon its results and incorporating its conclusions, as Aristotle would have done, he attempts to find an independent historical and theoretical basis of his own for the conception.

[1] This view that absolute monarchy is contrary to distributive justice, in not respecting the claims of proportionate equality, also occurs in, and is expounded by, Aristotle.

The two forms which naturally suggest themselves for mixture are the two extremes of monarchy and democracy, of which the two types may be said to be Persia and Athens. Pure and unmixed monarchy, already condemned in the experience of ancient Greece, is further condemned in Plato's eyes by the example of Persia. The history of Persia shows the tendency of monarchy to lose all regard for its subjects and all sense of a common weal, and to use its authority for the selfish interests of the monarch at the cost of his subjects' liberty. True distributive justice, we are now told, requires that the honour of office should go not to the strong, not to the wealthy, but to the temperate and unselfish, since these qualities are the bond of society. But pure and unmixed democracy stands equally condemned with absolute monarchy, though for other reasons. "The principle which feels pleasure or pain in the individual is like the mass or the populace in a State." In the individual, desire cannot judge for itself: it listens to the judgments of reason, and follows the dictates of prudence. It is as idle for the mass or the populace to attempt to judge. It goes ill with the drama when a theatrocracy begins, and the mass of the spectators judge the plays, as though they were connoisseurs in matters of art. As in art, so in politics; the rule of intelligence is inevitable. A "mute" theatre, an assembly which only says "yea" and "nay" to the propositions submitted to its decision, seem to be Plato's ideals. Yet he admits that while both monarchy and democracy, considered in themselves, have these defects, either has the qualities of its defects. Liberty is the blessing of democracy, if ignorance is its curse; monarchy suggests, if it does not always supply, a principle of order, though it tends to destroy liberty. Combine the two, and with order maintained by the rulers and liberty secured to their subjects, you will get good feeling between the ruler and the ruled. Now these are the great things for which a State must seek; and if they are found in a combination of monarchy and democracy, that is the ideal State. To the construction of such an ideal State, Plato accordingly turns. Instead of turning kings into philosophers, and utterly rejecting peoples, he tries, as practical men have always tried, to reconcile the principle of order, represented by monarchy, with the freedom of popular sovereignty.

Mixture of monarchy and democracy

In the light of our modern experience, it is easy to suggest that this reconciliation is to be found in constitutional monarchy, limited by a house of representatives. But Plato had neither the modern conception—due to feudalism—of a suzerain king who acts as a principle of order by attracting loyalty, nor that of a representative assembly standing by his side as the organ of freedom. And accordingly in the issue his solution proves to be something like a moderate oligarchy, in which monarchy is diluted by being divided among several officials, and democracy is enfeebled by the limitation of the rights of election and control to a small and "doctored" primary assembly. It is just the solution which we should expect to result from Greek political experience, of which oligarchy and the primary assembly were the predominant factors.

Foundation of a colony

§ 5. It is by the construction of an imaginary colony that Plato gives his solution. This suggests (what has often been remarked) the impulse which must have been furnished by Greek colonisation to the building of Utopias. Modern colonies are apt to carry with them the law and the institutions of the mother country to which they remain attached.[1] Greek colonies, as a rule, began a new and independent life; and what is still more to our point, they were often *mixed*, as Thucydides tells us of some of the Sicilian colonies. They came from no single mother city; and some form of law, some sort of constitution, of a new sort might naturally arise as a result of the mixture of races. Thus the language of Himera was a mixture of the Chalcidic and Doric dialects, though Dorian law, we are told, prevailed. Whether the population of his colony, the site of which is to be in Crete, shall be of one stock or several, Plato does not decide. He sees advantages in colonists of a single stock: he feels, at the same time, that a mixture of several stocks would be more likely to obey a new code of law.

[1] Yet even in modern times colonies have offered a ground for constitutional experiments, and the attempted realisation of the ideal. The fundamental constitutions of the Carolinas (never, it is true, enacted by the colonists, or possessed of legal force in the colonies) were the work of the philosopher Locke. There is something Platonic not only in the scheme, but in its details. "To prevent the multiplication of laws all statutes were to become repealed at the end of one hundred years by efflux of time, and all manner of comment on or exposition of the Fundamental Constitutions was strictly forbidden" (Egerton, *Origin and Growth of English Colonies*, p. 78).

In founding his colony, Plato distinguishes the period during which it gets into working order, from the subsequent period of regular action. The former is abnormal: in it abnormal methods may have to be used. One abnormal method which Plato suggests is tyranny, but this would seem to apply not so much to a new State or colony in process of creation, as to an old State in process of alteration. What impels Plato towards tyranny is a feeling, that it is easy to define what good laws are, and that the difficulty lies rather in getting a motive power behind the laws, which shall impress them on the people. A legislator to define the laws, a tyrant to impress them firmly —these once given, the ideal State may arise. And the way in which the tyrant will impress the law upon his people, we are told, will be the way of example, as well as the way of coercion. He will sketch the outlines in his own actions: he will fill in the sketch by coercing in each case those who have not followed in his steps. It is the old personal ideal of the *Republic* once more, but bipartite and temporary: instead of the philosopher-king, we have philosopher or legislator, *and* tyrant; and both are temporary measures, during the throes of travail. This conception of tyranny as a temporary measure during a great time of stress and reconstruction finds a close parallel in Machiavelli's doctrine of the Prince, and in the Positivist doctrine of a temporary dictator to which reference has already been made. But for the new State in process of erection—for the real colony, from which Plato digresses in his mention of the tyrant—the abnormal measures are different. Instead of legislator and tyrant, we have thirty-seven guardians of the law, and an electoral body of 200 members, who are to be selected by the mother city of the new colony, half from her own members, half from the colonists. When the constitution has attained its normal working, the thirty-seven guardians of the law will still remain; but a new electoral body will be formed to elect both the guardians of the law and a senate. This body has something of the two functions which Aristotle assigns to the masses; it elects, if it does not greatly criticise, the members of the executive. It is a body which, like the burgess-body of Aristotle's "polity," is composed of those who carry arms and have seen service. This body falls into four divisions,

Government of the colony

according to a property qualification. In the election of the senate, which is its most important function, these four divisions each contribute an equal amount of members; but a curious distinction is made. All the four divisions must combine to select ninety members from the first, and ninety from the second, division; the three first divisions *must*, and the fourth *may*, join in selecting ninety from the third division; and the two first divisions *must*, while the third and fourth divisions *may*, help to select ninety from the fourth. The result of this arrangement is that while an equal number will be elected from each class, the first two classes will have a preponderant voice in the election, because the third and fourth classes, not being forced in all cases to join in the election, will tend to stay away.[1] The first two classes, presumably the best, will choose the best men in each class: equality will be saved, and yet the natural superiority of man to man, and thereby order, will be regarded. Such a scheme, Plato urges, leads to the mixed government, which stands midway between democracy and monarchy. It is half democratic, for the electorate embraces, if not all, yet all who have served the State in war: it is half monarchical, for the elections are so regulated, that the wise and able will be elected. It will lead to friendship, therefore, instead of the faction which would result if the State were divided into master and slaves, as in a monarchy, or if all were held in the same honour, good and bad alike, as in a democracy. That all should be held in the same honour does indeed look like equality, and equality, according to an old proverb, is the mother of concord. But there are two equalities—the equality which gives the same to the good and bad, or absolute equality, and the equality which gives more to the better and less to the worse, or proportionate equality.[2]

[1] One may compare the three-class system of Prussia, by which the electorate is divided into three classes, according to the wealth of the electors, and each of these three classes (which are of course numerically unequal) has an equal weight with the others. Such a system consults "proportionate equality," it may be urged; but it also accentuates social differences. Plato's scheme is much more moderate; but the same objection is none the less implied in Aristotle's criticism. The "fancy franchises" proposed in 1867—based partly on education, and partly on thrift—are something of an attempt to secure "proportionate equality," to which this objection cannot so readily be made.

[2] This doctrine of proportionate equality, perhaps derived by Plato from Pythagorean sources, is adopted and systematised by Aristotle.

The latter is God's judgment: it is justice. It cannot indeed be exclusively used: to avoid the people's ill-will the absolute equality of the lot must occasionally be used for some of the offices, but it must be used as seldom as possible. The proportionate equality of an election in which the better have the greater voice is the ideal.

Economic structure of the colony

The division into four classes is based on the economic structure of the State. Communism, we now find, is abandoned. There are three possibilities with regard to property,[1] Plato considers. Communism is one, and it is the ideal; and in sketching any new possibility one must keep as close to that ideal as possible. The second possibility, whatever it may be, is left to future consideration: the third is adopted in the *Laws*. Private possession of inalienable lots, with a limitation of the number of offspring as its safeguard, is this third possibility; but every owner of a lot must feel that it is common to the whole of the State, as well as his own property. Here, as in the law and the government, there must be a reconciling of freedom and order, resulting in self-control. Such a reconciliation is attained when the freedom of private ownership is limited by the sense, that the owner belongs to the order of the State, and that his ownership must be limited by considerations of its good. This must always be the true conception of private property in land; and it is a close approximation to the more famous Aristotelian formula, "private possession, common use". But Plato goes further. The economic man is to be banished: currency is to exist merely for the sake of exchange, and not as a means of storing value: the "wealth of the nation" is to be spiritual and not material. The result of these views is the same tendency to "physiocracy" which Aristotle shared: it is "what husbandry bears and gives" which Plato alone desires. In some ways the *Laws* appears more reactionary than the *Republic*; it harks back still more decidedly to simplicity at the cost of economic development. "The statesman has nothing to do with laws about shipowners and merchants, and retailers and inn-keepers and tax-collectors and mines and money-lending and compound interest: bidding good-bye to these, he gives

[1] 739 B, where according to Hildenbrand the reference is not to three possible constitutions, but three possible ways of dealing with property.

laws to husbandmen and shepherds and bee-keepers" (842 C, D). But while Plato forbids retail trade for the sake of gain, he allows it to be conducted by aliens for necessary purposes at fixed prices and under official regulation. He acknowledges the value of such trade, as intended "to satisfy our needs, and to equalise our possessions," and he admits the use of money in reducing "the inequalities and incommensurabilities of goods to equality and common measure" (918 B, C). In regard to foreign trade he is a convinced Free Trader: "let no one pay any duty either on the importation or exportation of goods" (847 B). And some room is left for private property, over and above the inalienable lot upon which husbandry is to be employed. By gift or by trade a man may acquire property, to the extent of four times his original lot: any further acquisitions escheat to the State. The holder of the indispensable lot forms one extreme; the holder of four times the lot constitutes the other: between both lie two middle classes. And thus are constituted the four divisions or classes of the new State—classes merely separated by monetary distinctions, and not, as in the *Republic*, by separate vocations. Yet the old principle of the *Republic*, "one man, one function," still remains; and it is this which disqualifies for citizenship the artisan (who cannot be citizen as well as artisan), rather than, as in Aristotle, his "base and mechanic nature," subdued to that in which it works. And another approximation to the *Republic*, another "keeping as close as possible" to its ideal of communism, appears in the institution of common tables, both for men and for women. Hence Aristotle's criticism—that while wishing to found a State generally acceptable, Plato veers gradually round to the old unacceptable ideal of the *Republic*, with the two exceptions of common property and common wives. The criticism is somewhat unfair. Plato admits, or rather asserts, that he wishes to follow the ideal of the *Republic*; at the same time he very considerably alters that ideal, at any rate as respects the government. An electoral body of over five thousand is very unlike the irresponsible rule of the philosopher king.

Aristotle's criticism of the state of the *Laws*

But Aristotle's criticisms on the State of the *Laws* go still further.[1] The main criticism concerns the mixed constitution

[1] *Politics*, ii., c. vi.

sketched by Plato. It is liable, Aristotle thinks, to two objections. A mixture of three constitutions, of monarchy, aristocracy, and democracy, is better than one of two; nor has Plato mixed those two which he professed to mix, monarchy and democracy; he has united oligarchy and democracy, with a leaning towards the former. But as far as one can see, Plato meant by monarchy the principle of the rule of intelligence, and by democracy the principle of popular control, which are really the only two principles between which choice can lie, or of which a mixture can be made. He was not thinking of the details or the organisation of either, but of the principles they connoted, and the type of mind they expressed. Both of Aristotle's criticisms break down, if this is the case; and both break down for the same reason, that monarchy is used in so wide a sense, as to include both the rule of one and the rule of a few. In any case, Aristotle's extreme statement—that Plato *professes* that he will mix tyranny and democracy (which are either no constitutions or are the worst of constitutions), while what he *does* is to mix oligarchy and democracy, with a larger proportion of oligarchy than of democracy—cannot be accepted. Plato is careful to profess that it is the good side of monarchy (not tyranny, nor even monarchy, but only the good to be found in monarchy), which he mixes, not with democracy pure and simple, and certainly not with extreme democracy, but with the good side of democracy. In what he does, again, Plato seems painfully concerned to hold the balance fair between the monarchical (or oligarchical) element and the democratic. The same number of members of council is chosen from each division: every member of every division can join in the choice of the members for each division. That the members of the upper divisions must always join—that the members of the lower divisions in certain cases need not join—serves only to lay a duty on the rich, and to take a burden off the poor. But Aristotle's objection, that the scheme inclines to oligarchy, has, nevertheless, some force. It is an oligarchical "trick," according to a view which Aristotle expresses in the *Politics*, to let the people, and the people only, go unpunished for neglecting political duties: it is a trick which aims at concentrating power *de facto*, if not *de jure*, in the hands of a clique. Clubs may be formed: caucuses may "run" candidates for office; and oligarchy may be the practical result of Plato's scheme. Plato might answer that this was what he desired; and that his aim was the rule of an intelligent oligarchy, tempered by the fact that the people had elected, or could elect, all its men of intelligence to office, and could also criticise them, if not during their term of office, at any rate during the time of their final audit. Yet Aristotle might reply, that the people would one day see the trick: they would one day revolt against the tyranny of the clubs; and there would ultimately be a revolution.

Defects of the State of the *Laws*

To tell the truth, Plato's State would seem to incline to oligarchy only too strongly. The old tyranny of intelligence is not banished: it is only modified. The people in the State are like the desires in the individual—to be held under. They have no judgment in art: they are not fit to judge in matters of policy. These are the real ideas of Plato; and if he gives the people the power of electing officers, when he can hardly have consistently imagined that they had sufficient wisdom to detect capacity, such a gift is merely to "avoid the ill will of the people". The mixture is no real organic mixture, in which the elements compounded are all active: a passive people is mixed with an actively intelligent class of rulers. This is a fundamental criticism; and it is one which Aristotle made, not so much in the second book, where he directly attacks the *Laws*, as in the third, where he states his view of the masses. They do not represent a mass of desires, but a collective reason: they can judge in art, and they ought to deliberate in politics for themselves, as well as to elect the executive. Plato, in denying the people the function of deliberating,[1] and practically curtailing that of election, was true to himself, but untrue to his principle of mixture, untrue to his principle that the State is of all, and for all—not of a part, and for a part.[2]

[1] He admits the people, however, to judicial rights: "in the judgment of offences against the State, the people ought to participate" (768 A).

[2] Perhaps this view is too unfavourable. The great need of democracy is a strong executive, able to prevent corruption, and to maintain respect among the people for the law which the people has itself enacted. It may be held that Plato saw this need, and endeavoured to meet it in the *Laws*. "All authority is here derived from the people; but by a wealth of ingenious artifices the people prevents itself from using its own plenary powers" (Gomperz, iii., 250).

In yet another respect may Plato be accused of forgetting his own principle in the course of the *Laws*, and of bringing the law-state back to the *Republic*. We have seen that the very essence of the law-state is a surrender of the idea of flexibility and the free play of the knowledge immanent in the government. The law-state is a State with a sovereign and rigid law, and with a subordinate and ministering executive. For a while Plato remains true to this conception in the *Laws*. He thinks that after a certain time the law will have been perfected; and once perfected, it is to be stereotyped: "from that time there shall be no more change" (772 C). In the same spirit, as part of this fixedness and to defend it, he would have the forms of sculpture and of music as fixed as they are in Egypt. The whole State is to become as it were a political Pyramid, unchanging and unchanged through all the centuries. The men whom it trains will live faithfully in its forms: the government will be its servant and secure its permanence. The guardians of the law, elected by the assembly for twenty years, and including as their president a minister of education, will be the mainstay of the constitution; the senate of 360 members will stand between the guardians and the assembly, counselling the one and guiding the other; a college of elders, annually recruited by a subtle system of indirect election, will keep all from overpassing their appointed bounds. But this excessive rigidity disappears in the later pages of the *Laws*. A Nocturnal Council appears, and in it and in its powers the old ideal of the rule of knowledge and of the philosopher returns. On this council falls the mantle of the departed legislator: it is a sanhedrim and an academy, engaged both in the study of legislation and the amendment of the law. Composed of the ten eldest guardians of the law, of all who have served as directors of education, and of priests, this council must be philosophic enough, Plato tells us, though he does not say how it acquires its philosophy, to acknowledge the relation of particular virtues to virtue in general. Partly in the light of that knowledge, partly in the light of foreign laws and customs, which its members cause to be investigated, it changes and amends the law. Though nothing is said of the relation of the Council to the guardians of the law, it is obvious that it is the real sovereign of the State, since it can control the law, which was before regarded as sovereign; and by its introduction the law-state is really destroyed, though it may be admitted that the conservative composition of the Council would probably mean but little change in the law.

In many respects the character of the State of the *Laws* approaches to Athens, while still retaining some of the Spartan institutions which appeared in the *Republic*. The four great organs of the constitution, assembly, senate, guardians of law, and nocturnal council, are reminiscent of the Athenian Ecclesia, Boule, Archons, and Areopagus. The four classes correspond to the Solonian classification of the Athenian people. It is in the social arrangements that Spartan example tells, in the Minister of Education, the common tables, and the position of women, who are educated along with the men, feed like the men at common tables, and (if they consent) fight on the same field of battle. A mixture of Athenian constitutional forms and Athenian freedom with Spartan training and Spartan order, such is the State of the *Laws*, a practical *via media* between the two extremes of contemporary Greece. This is shown by the very characters of the dialogue—an Athenian, who takes the leading part, a Spartan, and a Cretan, who is naturally linked with the Spartan as living under similar institutions. As is the constitution, so are the laws; for the two, as we have seen, must always harmonise. They too are a mixture of Athenian and Spartan, of the detail of Athens with the principle of Sparta. The law which is the expression of reason and the creation of God proves in practice to contain a selection of what seemed to Plato, after comparison and study, the most valuable parts of ordinary Greek jurisprudence.

Education in the *Laws*

We have now seen the nature of the law, and the character of the government by which it is enforced, in the "secondary" State of the *Laws*. It remains to notice briefly the positive and the negative ways by which the government makes the law a reality among its subjects—to consider education and punishment. The education "in the spirit of the law" is a very different thing from the education of the *Republic*. That led to the final knowledge of the Good; *this* stops short when the citizen has been imbued with the principle of self-control which animates the law and the whole State. Something of philosophic knowledge (however it may be acquired) is indeed demanded in the members of the nocturnal council: for the rest education ceases when it has reached the sciences of arithmetic and geometry, somewhere about the twentieth year. Unlike the education of the *Republic*, therefore, the education of the *Laws* is pitched at a level which makes it possible for all to participate—as Plato enacts that all shall—in the whole of its course. The care of the State for the education of its citizens begins even before birth. Marriage, which in the *Laws* is monogamous, and consistent with the preservation of the family, is still regarded by Plato from a physical point of view: it is still to be regulated by the State with a view to the production of a good physical stock. The child is left with its parents; but a Minister of Education regulates its physical and moral growth, remembering that as the twig is bent, the branch will grow (765 E). There are three sides to education. One is gymnastics, which consists of dancing and wrestling of a military character;[1] another is music; a third is a certain amount of science. To music, in the sense of words set to an accompaniment, Plato would assign a very large scope in the *Laws*, as Aristotle does in his ideal State. It is the great assuager of passion and teacher of self-control; and Plato is anxious that the stability of the law should be reflected in a corresponding system of music. The legislator is to institute types, possessed of a natural truth and correctness, which, after the manner of Egypt, shall remain fresh and true for "ten thousand years". And not only is the stability of law to be enforced in this subtle and more spiritual way, but (*durum sed levius fit patientia*) the young must learn by heart the whole of Plato's treatise itself. The science which is to be studied must be studied in the same practical spirit. Arithmetic, geometry and astronomy must be pursued, with a view to understanding the right distribution of the territory and the citizens of the State. There is here something of that prepossession for the hidden mysteries of number, into which Pythagoreanism had fallen, and which marks the old age of Plato.

[1] The right to share in the assembly, we must remember, is connected with the bearing of arms.

Theory of punishment

Thus does education positively adjust the citizen to Law; but there are also more negative means. In one passage Plato even contemplates a system of espionage, and praises, as "worth many men," the man who not only does no injustice himself, but hinders others from doing any by giving information to the guardians. But the chief of preventive means is to be found in punishment, and the ninth book of the *Laws* contains Plato's attempt at a theory of its action. Starting from the Socratic principle that all sin is the result of ignorance, and in that sense involuntary, Plato asks, On what ground can punishment be inflicted? Not on the ground of *retribution*, he answers: it would be unjust to exact retribution for the involuntary result of ignorance. Only on the ground that it is a *cure* of the disease of ignorance can punishment be justified, if we start from Socratic principles; and this is the theory of punishment which Plato propounds. As education gives knowledge, so punishment, which is closely connected with education, destroys ignorance by means, as it were, of a galvanic shock. It is a drastic method of curing a diseased soul, in which reason, the source of knowledge, is suffering from atrophy, while "spirit" (of the baser sort), and desire, are both swollen as by a dropsy. But to witness the shock of punishment administered to another may cure all diseased minds which witness its administration; and in this sense punishment is also *deterrent*[1]—it is the cleansing of an ailment in the body politic at large. In any case "no penalty which the law inflicts is designed for evil, but always makes him who suffers it either better, or not so much worse as he would have been" (854 D). Modern theory departs from Plato, here as elsewhere, in refusing to regard the State as acting for the positive furtherance of morality. As it believes that the State does not educate men into morality, so it believes that it does not punish them into morality. If it tried to do so, it would defeat its own ends; it would check disinterested

[1] *Cf. Gorgias*, 525 B. "The proper office of punishment is two-fold; he who is rightly punished ought either to become better, and profit by it, or he ought to be made an example to his fellows, that they may see what he suffers, and fear, and become better." In this dialogue Plato even argues that the man who is afflicted by the disease of ignorance "ought by his own accord to go where he will be punished: he will run to the judge, as he would to the physician" (480 A).

moral action and would make goodness at the best automatic, at the worst hypocritical. In modern theory, punishment is primarily *deterrent*. "The State in its capacity as sustainer of rights (and it is in this capacity that it punishes[1]), has nothing to do with the amount of moral depravity in the criminal, and the primary reference in punishment is—not to the effect of the punishment on the person punished, but to its effects on others."[2] It aims at sustaining the scheme of rights in the future by connecting a feeling of fear with its violation in the present, and it does so by means of a striking example. Yet it is true that to deter men from violating this scheme is also to deter the criminal who is punished, and to that extent, and in that way, the criminal is reformed in punishment. Such reformation is however an "incident of the preventive function" of punishment.[3] Plato reversed the order, and made prevention an incident of the reformatory function of punishment.

Epilogue to the *Laws*

At the end of the *Laws* Plato strikes the same note which he struck at the beginning of the *Republic*. He is still a crusader, and the infidel is still the Sophist. Nor is he an infidel only by metaphor. This last work of Plato's life has something of the mystical lore of life's sunset. As he drew towards the shades, he felt more and more the littleness of human things, the greatness of God, and the supreme need of a reverent faith:

> We the brave, the mighty, and the wise,
> We men, who in our morn of growth defied
> The elements,

are after all but "playthings of the gods"; enough

> If, as towards the silent land we go,
> Through love, through hope, and faith's transcendent dower,
> We feel that we are greater than we know.[4]

In this evening spirit Plato returns to the "rationalist," who maintains that all creation is "not by the action of mind or of any God, but by nature and chance only" (889 C). Proceeding from this materialistic hypothesis, he tells us, the rationalist

[1] Whereas to Plato it punishes in the capacity of moral educator of its citizens.

[2] Green, *Principles*, § 193. [3] *Ibid.*, § 204.

[4] Wordsworth's sonnet, "An After-thought".

argues that "art sprang up afterwards, and out of these (*i.e.*, nature and chance), mortal and of mortal birth, and produced certain very partial imitations of the truth". Some of these "imitations," the rationalist argument continues, are merely in play, like music and painting: some have a serious purpose, and co-operate with Nature, like husbandry, for instance, which imitates Nature's process of reproduction, and co-operates with Nature in assisting the process. Of the latter kind is political art; it "co-operates with Nature," but in a less degree than husbandry. In it there is more of art; and "legislature is entirely a work of art, and is based on assumptions that are not true". For the one law of Nature, "red in tooth and claw," is that in the struggle for existence the fittest should survive, or in other words, that might is right. Only law based on such a "true" assumption is right law; only political art which imitates Nature correctly is true art. As it is, the laws of States, "different in different places, according to the agreement of those who make them," make honourable by law that which is not honourable by Nature. Thus according to Plato does a materialistic conception of the world, as without mind and without God, result in a correspondingly material conception of politics. It is such bad metaphysics which make any metaphysics necessary: "if impious discourses were not scattered throughout the world, there would have been no need for any vindication of the existence of the gods" (891 B). But such vindication is necessary; and Plato attempts it. He tells us, as the true rationalist will always tell mankind, that mind is first, and matter last; and that the false rationalist simply inverts the order of the world, when he begins with a mindless matter, and then introduces mind, under the name of Art, as the mere product of matter—and yet its active imitator, and even its perverter. Mind is first, in the sense of the eternal mind, and it is the creator (or, as Plato says, the mover), and not the product of matter; and as the eternal mind of God moves the universe:[1]

Mens agitat molem, et magno se corpore miscet,

[1] Plato cannot get away from his sense of evil as a separate thing, however, and he speaks of two Minds of the Universe, "one the author of Good, and the other of Evil" (896 E).

so a mind moves each of its parts, and "all things are full of gods". And thus we come back upon the old lesson of the *Republic:* the State is a product of mind. "Law and also art . . . are the creations of *mind* in accordance with right reason," and "both alike exist by Nature, and no less than Nature". Here finally disappears the antithesis of "art" and "Nature"; for Nature is not mere mindless being, nor art man's perversion of that being: "Nature" is being which exists through mind, and art is nothing else than that which likewise is through mind.

Two thousand years and more have still left us face to face with the same problems. Nor can the political philosophy of Plato be other than eternally and everlastingly true, because it is wrought into the substance of a philosophy of the world, which can never lose its truth. His philosophy has its time-vesture: it is the philosophy of a limited experience. It is of a city-state he thinks; and it is of a city-state that he states the truth which he has found. Much of its detail has an historical interest: all of its essence is still essential. Much may be criticised; yet the staple of criticism is simply this, that he was too generously eager for the reign of pure truth and the realisation of pure principle.

CHAPTER V

ARISTOTLE—HIS LIFE AND TIMES: THE PLACE OF THE *POLITICS* IN HIS SYSTEM

THE SOURCES OF THE *POLITICS*

§ 1. TO knowledge, as much as to the objects of knowledge, Aristotle applied the idea of development. Truth itself, or facts themselves, compel men to make a beginning of knowledge; and under the same compulsion it is developed, until the object of study is fully realised, and the development of knowledge comes to its "end". Aristotle thus conceived of his own contributions to knowledge, not as breaking fresh ground, but as developing the contributions of his predecessors. Not only so; but he also conceived himself to stand at the end of this process, and regarded his own development of his predecessor's work as marking the final attainment of Greek knowledge. In the field of knowledge of the State, or political science, this eschatology is necessarily connected with a belief that the object of knowledge, which is also progressive like the knowledge itself, has come to *its* "end": the city-state is to Aristotle the goal of perfection, and in politics "almost everything has been discovered". It is easy to regard Aristotelian eschatology as arrogant. But if one confines oneself to Greece, it is true that Aristotle set the final form upon its political thought, and that at a time when the object of that thought, the autonomous city, was coming to its end. The *Politics* is the last word of Greece in political science: the Stoics, when they come, are the reflection and the teachers, not of Greece, but of a world-state created by the Macedonian conquest of the East; and it is to that, and to the Roman Empire which succeeded it, that their philosophy applies. As a matter of fact, his eschatology led Aristotle to

Aristotle's relation to his predecessors

regard himself rather as the systematiser of a given knowledge, than as the creator of an original philosophy. It led him to attach great importance to the results of previous thinkers; and in the *Politics* especially we are conscious of a constant reference, explicit or implied, to the teaching of his precursors in this field of inquiry. It seems at first sight inconsistent with this view, that Aristotle should, wherever he mentions his predecessors, appear to show a spirit of hostility to their views. Especially does his attitude to his own master, Plato, seem open to criticism. If Plato is his friend, truth, and a very candid truth, seems very much more of a friend. The answer to such an objection depends upon an appreciation of Greek habits of quotation and criticism. Where Aristotle agrees with the views of a predecessor, he adopts those views without mention; and it is the fact that he names when he criticises and is silent when he agrees, which makes him appear so critical and so combative. A new charge, that of plagiarism, may indeed emerge from this defence; but plagiarism in days before printing, plagiarism in books which look like the notes of a lecture, whether made in advance by the master, or taken down by pupils from his dictation, is not a serious charge. Pupils who had no libraries would count it for righteousness to a master that he should make them acquainted with views, which were no doubt matters of oral tradition rather than theses maintained in books—which, in that case, without the *litera scripta* to attest their authorship, would be (and were) regarded rather as tenets of this or that school, than as products of this or that thinker's mind. Nor indeed does Aristotle merely adopt; he tests before adoption. He first attempts to discover what amount of truth there is in a previous view, by means of a searching criticism; and then, and only then, as a rule, he assimilates into his system the truth which survives the criticism. And the criticism is on the whole sympathetic: even where he detects error, he often allows that the error is one of stating too generally what ought to be stated with limitation, or, at any rate, he shows "the cause of the error" into which a previous thinker has fallen.[1] On the other hand his criticism is often external

[1] *Cf. Metaphysics*, 989 a 30 *sqq.*, on Anaxagoras: 985 a 4 *sqq.*, on Empedocles.

and defective: he criticises Plato, for instance, in the *Politics*, for saying things which he had never said;[1] or he colours a Platonic view in order that it may be amenable to a criticism which will elicit the right view; or finally, though he states the conception to be criticised fairly, he criticises from some particular point of view, and entirely fails to do justice to the whole conception. But then—is this peculiar to Aristotle? If one knew the Sophists more thoroughly, one might discover that Plato had coloured their views to suit his purpose, or that he had criticised partially, and not sympathetically.

Respect for popular opinion

The respect which, whether by positive adoption or negative criticism, Aristotle thus showed, on the whole, to previous thinkers, was also paid by him, in the realm of practical science—of ethics and politics—to popular opinion and existing practice. In the *Ethics* he speaks of the respect to be paid to the sayings and opinions of the old and the wise;[2] and he even asserts that the *consensus mundi* constitutes ethical truth.[3] In the *Politics*, too, he shows a great respect for the judgment of the many: their collective virtue, their collective capacity, entitle them to rule, and enable them to see how to rule. His aim might be said to be the refining of common sense: he adopts, for instance, popular opinion on the subject of the classification of States, and then proceeds to refine it, by substituting a qualitative and causal for a quantitative and accidental differentia. This respect for popular opinion involves a certain Conservatism, which distinguishes Aristotle from Plato, the Radical innovator, despising popular opinion as the mere verdict of the cave. Aristotle it is true attempted to create an ideal State; but his wings soon flagged in the attempt to imitate the flights of Platonic fancy, and the books which treat of the ideal State are significantly incomplete.[4] The essence of the *Politics* is its justification of existing institutions like the State, slavery, the family; or again its practical discussion of the proper medicines for the diseases of actual States. The "divine right of things as they are" appealed to Aristotle. At the same time, it would be unjust to stop short at such a dictum, and not to admit

[1] It is true that Plato had said things in his lectures which do not occur in his writings.

[2] 1143 b 11-14. [3] 1173 a 1, ἃ . . . πᾶσι δοκεῖ ταῦτ' εἶναί φαμεν.

[4] Von Wilamowitz-Möllendorf, *Aristoteles und Athen*, i., 358.

that "things as they are" only appeal to Aristotle, when they are what they ought to be. The State whose natural character he justifies is no "perverted" State of ordinary life, but a "right" State whose members form an association in good life; and the slavery which he vindicates is one, which, while it sets the master free for a strenuous life, assures the slave of that moral guidance which he cannot find in himself. In a word, Aristotle "does not so much raise new points of view, as conceive given relations in their ideal meaning".[1] The "given" upon which he works, the "data" of his politics, is indeed narrow: he rests upon Greek experience alone, and he does not consider its last phase, the Hellenisation of Asia, any more than he shows traces in his zoological writings of the new store of facts which Alexander's expedition had brought to light. But it could hardly be expected that the Achillean escapade of Alexander should, especially by contemporaries, be regarded as a new datum of science.[2] And the fact that he confined his view to the limits of the Greek world made it possible for Aristotle to arrive at those conceptions of the functions of the State and its various kinds, which are permanently true, but which nevertheless, if he had included a wider area in the mass of details to be generalised, might never have been attained. If he limited himself to the Greek in particular, he generalised the experience of the Greek into laws of universal application.

Extent of his political information

Within the limits of the Greek world, the knowledge he had amassed was singularly full. From Sicily to the Euxine, from Cyrene to Thrace, he knows and can cite the constitutional development and the political vicissitudes of each State. Diogenes Laertius assigns to Aristotle 158 *Polities of States*, "general and particular, democratic, oligarchic, aristocratic, and tyrannical". Some have viewed these *Polities* as compilations intended for a collection—as forming, along with a parallel collection of laws, a sort of dictionary of politics to which reference could be made

[1] Eucken, *Die Methode der Aristotelischen Forschung*, p. 15.

[2] There are many omissions, however, in Aristotle, which cannot be explained in this way. He never alludes to the Athenian empire: he never mentions the federations of which there had been several examples in Greece. He only considers the πόλις, and refuses to look at any of its extensions. Similarly he never considers the subdivision of the πόλις—the Attic deme, for instance; and hence he never discovers the principle of representation, which was to some extent present in the relations of the deme to the Council of 500.

in writing the *Politics*; and some doubt has been thrown upon their Aristotelian authorship. Others again have viewed them, arguing from the extant Ἀθηναίων πολιτεία, as set works in the nature of political pamphlets, written with an attempt, and a very successful attempt, at style, by a writer who was not merely aiming at the collection of facts, but passing judgments on the character of each constitution, and suggesting reform along the lines of those judgments to practical statesmen. This is a view which would make Aristotle physician in general to the States of Greece, and it is, to that extent, consonant with the attitude adopted in the later books of the *Politics*. Whatever view be taken of the character of these *Polities*, they at any rate attest the width of Aristotle's knowledge. And that knowledge is still further attested by other lost works of Aristotle. Three of these, by their practical character, may seem to favour the view which assigns a practical purpose to the *Polities*. These are the treatise *On Monarchy*, the work called *Alexander, or Concerning Colonies*, and the so-called *δικαιώματα of the Greek States*. The former discussed, in the form of a letter to Alexander, the problem of the proper treatment of Greeks and Persians in his new empire; and Aristotle, it would appear, suggested that the two should be treated differently, the former as friends, or constitutionally, the latter like animals and plants, or despotically, on the ground that they were naturally differentiated by their capacities for virtue—a suggestion reminiscent of Aristotle's view of slavery, and of his belief in the natural servitude of barbarians, as men incapable of virtue. The second work, *Concerning Colonies*, had an equally practical purpose; it was written in the form of a dialogue to advise Alexander upon the proper methods of colonising the East. And thus in these two works, if not in the *Polities*, Aristotle does, with the same practical bent which distinguishes his *Ethics* and *Politics*, pay very real heed to the last results of Greek experience. The last of these treatises, the *δικαιώματα of the Greek States*, seems to have discussed cases of law, and to have propounded decisions, according to which, our authorities say, Philip decided the disputes of the Greeks, possibly at the synod of Corinth in 338. A fourth work seems to have differed from these three in the absence of a practical purpose, and to have possessed something of the encyclopædic character which some authorities have assigned to the *Polities.* This is the work, in four books, on *Customs*, probably identical with another work on *Barbarian Customs*, which is also mentioned. The *Customs of the Etruscans*, to which Athenæus refers, would appear to be an excerpt from this work. It is interesting as showing Aristotle's acquaintance with the non-Hellenic world, and as explaining the references which we find in the *Politics* to customs like compurgation and compensation for murder.

The Life of Aristotle

§ 2. To complete this sketch of the background of the *Politics*, some mention must now be made of the facts of Aristotle's own life and the condition of contemporary Greece.[1] Stress has been laid on the fact that Aristotle was the son of an Asclepiad or physician, and that, as such, he was probably trained in anatomy. His practical knowledge of dissection, it has been said, explains the analytic method, by the use of which he begins the *Politics :* it explains the comparison between the State and the human body, which he occasionally draws.[2] But Plato also had spoken in the *Phædrus* of dividing a subject naturally by its joints : Plato also had used the comparison of the State to the body; and the use of analogies from the arts is the commonplace of Greek philosophy. Stress has again been laid, but probably with no more truth, on his birth at Stagira in Chalcidice, whence, it is suggested, he derived a "strong aversion" to Macedonia, which led him to refuse to study its constitution in the *Politics.*[3] From Stagira he came to Athens to study under Plato; but he also studied the writings and the methods of Isocrates, though he did not sit under the great rhetorician himself. The influence of Isocrates explains his interest in rhetoric and poetry : it may also have helped to turn his mind to the study of logic.[4] But the influence of Plato was dominant, and it attracted him from the study of speech to the study of man, to that domain of ethics and politics, which, as the *Republic* and the *Laws* show, was perhaps the greatest interest

Aristotle's early life

[1] *Cf.*, for what follows, Von Wilamowitz-Möllendorf, *op. cit.*, i., c. x.
[2] Oncken, *Die Staatslehre des Aristoteles*, pp. 3-7.
[3] Von Wilamowitz-Möllendorf, *op. cit.*, i., 312. [4] *Ibid.*, p. 320.

of Plato's mind. Before, however, he began to lecture on these subjects himself, he lived for some twelve years, the twelve years which followed Plato's death, away from Athens. Three years (347-345) he stayed with Hermias, tyrant and ex-slave, in Asia Minor; and the problems of a tyrant's rule and the nature of slavery are subjects which would naturally be discussed between the two. He seems to have been a devoted friend of Hermias, and he proved his friendship, when Hermias was ruined and killed, by marrying his adopted daughter. In his friendship for Hermias, as in his still earlier friendship for Eudemus, one detects the basis of that theory of friendship which he preached in the *Ethics*, and which served him in the sphere of politics by helping to explain the unity of the State. In his marriage to a wife, who was by his own testimony "temperate and virtuous," we see the background in his life of that belief in the family as a natural institution, which is stated in the first book of the *Politics;* which leads him in the second to attack Plato's communism; and culminates, in the *Ethics*, in his view of the family as the sphere of a peculiar friendship, and as having, in virtue of that friendship, a great influence for good. In this, as in many other respects, one finds Aristotle acting in the easy, ordinary, natural way of any Greek gentleman: his life, as well as his doctrine, shows a belief in the natural character of the world's existing arrangements, and a respect for the popular opinion which gives such arrangements life. The philosophic livery of long locks and coarse cloak he never assumed: he dressed like an ordinary layman. Nor had he anything of the philosophic contempt for the goods of this world: he was himself a man possessed of comfortable means, and he believed that a man's perfect development demanded a material basis of wealth as its condition. And if the economic views of the *Politics* seem to us idealistic, yet his calm discussion of the acquisition of wealth and the functions of money stamps Aristotle's as an eminently practical intellect.

Aristotle in Macedonia

It accords with his practical genius, that we should find him, for the eight or nine years of his life after he left the court of Hermias, living in the very centre of events and in contact with the greatest figure of his generation, as tutor of Alexander at Pella. He is no lonely professor like Kant, but, like Leibniz, a man of the world, acquainted with the courts of princes. When he writes of education, when he speaks of politics, he is discussing things of which he has been a part. It is not only the knowledge he has amassed, not only his quiet naturalism, not only his respect for popular opinion and the sayings of the elders, which command our respect for his *Politics*: it is, perhaps more than all these, the feeling that he knew from the inside the meaning of politics. There is evidence that he had some influence with Philip: the refounding of Stagira is attributed to his suggestion; and his δικαιώματα, as we saw, are said to have been Philip's guide in the solution of Greek disputes. His advice to Alexander on the treatment of the conquered Asiatics and on the settlement of colonies suggests something more than academical exercises after the Isocratic fashion. But the most important part of Aristotle's life is not that which he spent at Pella; and his relations to Philip and Alexander are perhaps not the most influential of his political relations. His life at Athens as the head of a school from 335 almost until his death in 322, and his connection with Antipater—these are the things which touch the *Politics* most closely.

During this period Antipater was regent of Macedonia, while Alexander was absent in the East. In that capacity he had the general superintendence of Greek affairs. Aristotle was his intimate friend; and remembering this fact, one feels that Aristotle's suggested emendations of actual States, and his proposal—as the practical ideal for Greece—of the "polity" or rule of the middle class in all her States, possess (or must to hearers who knew his relations to Antipater have seemed to possess) a very important contemporary meaning. For why should not Antipater use the *Politics* to solve constitutional difficulties, as Philip had used the δικαιώματα to settle judicial disputes? Yet it is not as meant for Greece at large, but as speaking to Athens, that the *Politics* is most eloquent; and some account of that Athens, in which Aristotle lectured on politics, seems indispensable, for it cannot but be that he spoke most directly to the city which he had learnt to know better than any other in Greece, the city in which he taught, the city whose constitutional history was the most instructive of any in Greece, the city which had in her day been the mistress of the

Aristotle and Athens

Ægæan. During his stay in Athens as a pupil of Plato, Aristotle had seen Eubulus quietly repairing the finances and maintaining a policy of peace: he had seen the Radicals, on the other hand, advocating an imperial policy, coupled by the ruck of that party with pay for the citizens, though patriots like Demosthenes would gladly have used the pay to serve the imperial policy. But there were some, who, like the party which ruled Athens in 411, wished to sink the dream of a greater Athens in the strengthening of the real Athens, and, in order to do so, were willing to abolish or to limit the pay. But inasmuch as many of the citizens could only act as citizens because the pay furnished them with leisure, any limitation of the pay must diminish the number of citizens, and modify the constitution in the direction of that "polity," or government of the middle class, which Aristotle afterwards came to applaud. And here this party of "little Athenians" covered itself with the mantle of archaism, explaining the progress which it sought to achieve as retrogression to the old times of Solon or the Areopagus. While however, in its propaganda, it carried its archaism back to Solon, it really sought to recreate, what it really knew, the constitution established in 411, with its limited body of 5,000 citizens. With this party Aristotle would seem to have identified himself; and in the light of its principles the "polity of Athens" may have been written in his later days. But new features had arisen to mark the Athens of the time when Aristotle taught there as a master. Archaism had applied itself to practice; and the revival which resulted was of a distinctly religious character, while its leader, Lycurgus, was a man of priestly descent and pious temper. The temples of the gods were restored, as in the Augustan age of revival: what is still more interesting is the treatment by the State of the Attic youth. That moral education of the individual, combined with the formation of a citizen army, which distinguished Plato's *Republic*, now appeared, and in the same connection, in actual Athens. The Attic youth, between the age of eighteen and twenty, were to be drilled in barracks: their initiation into this life was through a religious service. They fed together at common tables managed by "masters of discipline": a "moderator" presided over the whole system. The approximation to Platonic ideas, perhaps those of the *Laws* still more than those of the *Republic*, is striking. It is clear that the State was thrown into the melting-pot: this actual innovation, and the archaising tendencies of earlier years, are both significant proofs. But these are the conditions, in which the sketch of an ideal State is absolutely practical; and under these conditions Aristotle's ideal State, equally with his practical suggestions to diseased constitutions, acquires a contemporary meaning. Nor, living as he did in an Athens animated by a religious revival, an Athens supervising its youth by moral officials, whose very names represented moral qualities like self-discipline and moderation, could Aristotle do otherwise than insist on one of his cardinal lessons, the moral purpose of the State.

"Indeed, these are giant times, and in them Aristotle stands like a giant. In distant Susa the young lord of the world solemnises his marriage to Rhoxana, a symbol of peace and reconciliation in that ancient feud of the nations, which Homer and Herodotus had painted. It is the new-born Achilles' wedding to Polyxena; and yet again it is the dawn of Hellenism, for the child of the marriage of the nations is Christianity. In distant Athens rises undismayed the voice of the old man, wise, and yet of little faith for all his wisdom, denying the possibility of the union, and asserting relentlessly the superiority of the Hellenic race against the barbarians and the King of Macedon. In Athens herself, and in all Hellas, it lies like a mountain of lead upon all patriotic hearts, that the tiny States of their birth, which they love so well, should cease to mean the world. With redoubled ardour they cherish the sanctity of their domestic gods and customs and institutions, calling to remembrance the great deeds, which with these, and through these, their fathers had done before them."[1]

These then are the times in which Aristotle lived, and this is his attitude to the past and its thinkers. But to have considered these does not yet entitle us to say that we have sketched the background of the *Politics*. The *Politics* and the *Ethics* form practically one treatise: what then are the exact relations of the one part of this treatise to the other? Many terms from Aristotle's philosophic terminology are applied to

[1] Von Wilamowitz-Möllendorf, *Aristoteles und Athen*, i., 370, 371.

express political conceptions, words like "nature," "association," "compound": must we not study these terms, if we are to understand the political conceptions which they are used to express? In a word, the *Politics* is by no means a detached treatise, but part of a system, a link of a chain: other parts throw light upon it, other links supplement it; and it must therefore be considered in the light of Aristotle's general method and as supplemented by his general philosophic attitude, but most of all as closely connected with his ethical views, if we are to understand its full meaning.

The Teleology of Aristotle

Aristotle's conception of Form

§ 3. Science,[1] according to Aristotle, deals with "forms": matter, as matter, is unknowable, because it is in a constant flux. Form, on the contrary, is permanent, and knowable because it is permanent. Here he was following Heraclitus and Plato; and in the *Politics* there occurs what seems a definite reference to the former. What is the identity, he asks, and what constitutes the permanence of a State? Not its matter, not, in other words, its citizens: true, you *might* "step twice into the same river,"[2] so long as its particles consisted of water, and you *might* meet twice the same citizen-body, so long as its members were of one stock; but what makes the State's identity and constitutes its permanence, is not its particles or members but its form, that is to say its constitution, for the constitution is the form of the State. Science, then, is a science of forms: political science is a science of political forms, or constitutions. But while form is the subject of science, and not matter, yet, with the exception of the Divine Mind, form cannot exist apart from matter, as Plato had thought: on the contrary, the two are indissolubly connected. Therefore science, or knowledge of forms, demands sense-perception of matter for its basis; and the process of human inquiry is an ascent from the individual of matter to the general of form, or, in other words, induction. Investigation being thus directed towards facts will, Aristotle

[1] In this section I follow Eucken, *Die Methode der Aristotelischen Forschung*.

[2] A contradiction of Heraclitus' saying that there is no stepping twice into the same river.

holds at the beginning of the *Politics*, attain the best results, if it follows the facts most closely, and if, when they develop, it follows their development from the beginning. It will attain a true conception of form most certainly, if it observes matter in its growth towards form.

The word development brings us to a new conception, that of "end," which is universal in Aristotle's philosophy, and is closely connected with the allied conception of "form". The conception of end is applied by Aristotle to the whole of Nature. His view of the world is teleological:[1] everywhere things are regarded as determined towards an end. If we ask why we should regard the world teleologically, we are only told that "if the products of art are determined to an end, obviously the products of Nature are also".[2] This anthropomorphic argument in its bare statement is not very conclusive; but perhaps Aristotle's teleology rested, not on any such argument, but on his whole conception of matter and form, and of their relation one to another. Form is an end towards which matter is determined; matter is the primary material necessary for the realisation of some end; and this primary material develops until the end is realised. There is thus a constant movement from matter to form, or from the "Potential," which is matter, to the "Actual," which is matter informed by form. This great general conception, of "movement" towards an "end," is applied by Aristotle, as we have already said, to knowledge or science itself: it is applied to poetry; it is applied to politics. In a science like astronomy there is a certain primary material consisting of obvious empirical generalisations about the stars made by the shepherd or sailor, which "moves" towards an "end" of scientific knowledge: in poetry, there is the primary material of impromptu imitations, which has "increased" until

Teleological view of the world

[1] *Cf.* what was before said of Plato, pp. 126, 154. Aristotle differs from Plato in not believing in a single end of all being, an Idea of the Good: each form is to him the end of whatsoever it shapes, but there is no single end of all existence. On the other hand, as we shall see, Aristotle believes in a single end of human action, the human good, which must be postulated, unless we are to fall into a *progressio ad infinitum*. *I.e.*, if it be said, Callias did *this*, in order to get at *that*, then we may ask, Why did he want to get *that*? and this process would continue *ad infinitum* unless it could be stopped, as Aristotle supposes that it is, by the final answer—"To attain the human Good".

[2] *Physics*, 199 a 17-18.

it reached "its own nature" in perfect tragedy: in politics there is the primary material of family association, which developed until it reached its "bound" in the State whose constitution is its final "form". This dynamic conception of the relation of matter and form is not indeed quite the same as the static. Dynamically, the matter of the State is the family association, while statically it is the individual citizen: dynamically the matter of tragedy is impromptu imitations, while statically it is the individual words, rhythms, and musical notes.

Conception of nature

In considering the dynamic conception of the relation of matter and form, we naturally inquire whether "the necessary" matter is always such as to develop into its form, and is always subordinate to its end; or whether, on the other hand, matter may not sometimes be incongruous with form, and possess an independent existence. Generally, it may be answered, Aristotle does assume congruity: the end for the sake of which "movement" arises finds a necessary material suited to itself and to movement towards itself. But it is not always so: a matter may exist which is not congruous with form, and that matter may limit the extent to which movement attains its form. In politics the primary matter may be so rude, that the movement from it never reaches a constitution, but stops at a tribal State; or again, it may be less rude, but yet so imperfect, that the movement, while attaining a constitution, attains a "perverted" constitution. Again, a second inquiry naturally arises, partly springing from this last. Does matter move towards form *sua sponte*, or are external agencies at work, which may, along with a rude or imperfect matter, explain occasional failures to reach a final form? A distinction has to be made. As regards "things possessing in themselves a source of movement," the movement does take place *sua sponte*. That is to say, Aristotle speaks of "Nature" as its cause; and "though Aristotle in countless passages speaks of Nature as a person, we soon learn to seek its agency rather in things themselves".[1] It might seem as if there were here two conceptions of Nature, which cannot be reconciled, one regarding it as an external thing, the other as an immanent force. But perhaps there is more consistency than at first sight appears. In one of the passages where Nature is treated as a

[1] Newman, *Politics*, i., 19.

person, it seems to be parallel with God: "God and Nature do nothing in vain".[1] Now God, we are also told, "causes movement as an object of love";[2] that is to say, He does not cause movement actively, or as acting of Himself, but passively, and as being the cause of matter's acting. He is not an active, but an attractive force. But if He be an attractive force, He is not external, but immanent in things in the attraction which He inspires. Similarly Nature if it be parallel with God, is not an active, but an attractive force: it does not act on matter, but attracts matter, so that matter moves *sua sponte* towards Nature in response to its attraction. But, indeed, when pushed to its ultimate meaning, Nature is not merely parallel with God, but *is* God; and the "nature" of each thing is its immanent impulse to become as like God as possible. This being so, Nature is present as an agency in things, in the sense that the attraction towards itself which it inspires is present as the mainspring of movement. And it is present throughout, both in the primary material, and in its movement, and in the form in which that movement ends. Aristotle therefore applies the term "Nature" in the *Physics* to each of these three stages. Nature is "the primary material which is the substratum of all things possessing in themselves an impulse towards movement":[3] secondly, "Nature, when the name is applied in the sense of development, is the path towards Nature" in the sense of form:[4] thirdly, "Nature is form,"[5] or "end". Each of these three is called "Nature," because it is what it is "by nature," or, in other words, by the agency of Nature as immanent in it. But it is obvious that form or end is, as Aristotle says, Nature in a peculiar sense, because it means the final identification with Nature, attraction towards which is the root of the whole matter, and because in it the agency of Nature is therefore most vivid and close. The instance of human association, as the sphere of a movement of matter culminating in the form of the State, may serve to illustrate this view. Such association belongs to the class of things possessing in themselves a source of motion. It is therefore in the sphere of Nature's action, or

[1] *De Caelo*, 271 a 33. [2] *Metaphysics*, 1072 b 2.
[3] *Physics*, 193 a 28. [4] *Ibid.*, 193 b 12.
[5] *Ibid.*, 193 a 30; *Politics*, 1252 b 32.

rather, attraction. Its primary material, the family association, is "Nature," because it is "by nature," and it is by nature, because it is what it is through the agency of Nature,[1] attraction towards which determines in the first place its primary character, just as that same attraction causes, in the second place, its movement from that primary character towards ultimate form. But the State, the final goal or form of such movement, is most of all Nature, most of all by nature. And this brings us to one of the most fundamental things in Aristotle's political philosophy. While he holds primitive society to be natural (like Hobbes), he also holds the final State to be natural, and still more natural (whereas Hobbes would regard it as artificial). Nay, he would hold that primitive society was only by nature because it was an approximation to the State, and through the State to Nature itself.

Relation of Nature and Art

But movement may also take place by art as well as by Nature, by external agencies as well as by an immanent force. Things not possessing in themselves a source of movement are changed by human agency: the marble becomes a statue by the hand of the sculptor. But human agency acts not only within this province: it also acts in the province of things which have in themselves a source of movement. It may act to thwart Nature: it may also act to realise Nature. Human agency may, like rude or imperfect material, be a reason for the failure of the movement of human association to find its proper haven, and may account for that movement's stopping short at an imperfect form, or going awry into a perverted constitution. But human agency is rather conceived by Aristotle as a force co-operative with Nature. Art, we may say, loves Nature, and Nature too loves art: man is animated in his action by that same attraction towards Nature, which inspires movement in the sphere of things which have in themselves a source of movement. Art, in Aristotle's words, partly finishes what Nature fails to finish, and partly imitates what she actually does.[2] There is no necessary distinction between the artificial and the natural, such as the Sophists had made.[3] Poetry naturally

[1] In the sense of God, or the purpose of all movement.
[2] *Physics*, 199 a 15.
[3] *Cf.* Plato, *Laws*, 709 B: "God governs all things, and chance and opportunity co-operate with Him in the government of human affairs: and art should be there also". (*Cf. supra*, p. 207.)

grew—as men carried it forward;[1] and again the impulse towards a State existed by Nature—but the man who compounded the State was the greatest of benefactors.[2] That there should be this room for human co-operation obviously implies that there may be a certain defect in Nature. And Aristotle admits that this is the case.[3] Nature is indeed like "a prudent man," or "a wise steward": it does nothing in vain; "its product is perfection". It gives the proper tool along with the capacity for its use: to each capacity it gives its separate tool. Yet "where it is not possible to do otherwise, it uses the same tool for several purposes"; and it may fail of perfection; it may wish one thing, and the opposite may often happen.[4] And the reason is that matter, as we said, is not always congruous with form; and Nature, as the force impelling matter to form, may therefore, and indeed must therefore, sometimes fall short of its aim. But Nature's defects are man's opportunities: it is through them that art gets a new sphere of operation. It is because Nature does not always succeed in its political creations that "political art" can arise to offer its suggestions and apply its remedies. For Political Science, to Aristotle as much as to Plato, is an art as well as a science: it acts as well as analyses.

The end as the cause of development

In what ways did this conception of teleological development, realising itself, or realised by man, determine the political theory of Aristotle? It helped him, as we have already incidentally seen, to an evolutionary view of the State: it saved him from any mechanical view of political origins. Believing in development, he naturally turned to an historical method: he traced the historical growth of the State from its first origin: he criticised Plato's theory of revolutions on the ground that it was unhistorical, and attempted an historical account himself. It is this evolutionary and historical character of his work which makes it appeal to modern minds. But it must always be remembered that his view of development *is* teleological, and as such, both free from defects that beset modern views of evolution when applied to politics, and liable, on the other hand, to errors of its own. Because his view is teleological, Aristotle

[1] *Poetics*, 1449 a 13.

[2] *Politics*, 1253 a 30; *cf.* Plato's *Cratylus* (434-35), where Socrates says that language is both natural and artificial.

[3] *De Part. Animal.*, 683 a 22. [4] *Politics*, 1254 b 27-34.

emphasises, not the process of development, but the end. "Animals are not constructed as they are, because they have developed as they have: they have developed as they have in order to attain the construction which they show."[1] The end explains the development, and not the development the end. Asserted against Empedocles, and in another field than that of politics, this might still be asserted against Spencer, in the sphere of human "conduct". Because it explains the development, the end is in a sense prior to it, while yet, because it comes before the end in order of time, the development is also prior to the end. Thus Aristotle can both say in the *Politics* that the State is prior to the household and the individual, and assert in the *Ethics* that the household is prior to the State. The end, then, explains the development: the development does not explain the end. The immediate reasons which move a thing as it develops will not explain the reasons which underlie the thing as it stands completed. Mere life is the immediate reason of the development of the State: good life explains its existence. Similarly, "the lips are soft, fleshy, and able to part, both for protection of the teeth . . . and *still more* for the Good; for they are a means to the use of speech".[2] They developed, we may say, for protection: they exist for the sake of speech.[3]

The end as giving an organic conception of the state

In both of these ways, in insisting on the priority of the end, and in asserting that what animates development is not what animates completed result, Aristotle supplies the corrective of

[1] *De Gen. Animal.*, 778 b 1-5. [2] *De Part. Animal.*, ii., 659 b 30.

[3] The thing as it develops is the "necessary" matter, which is moved immediately by necessity, as is the family association by the need of life, or the tissues which develop into the lips by the need of protection; but the thing as it stands developed has also an element "of supererogation," and matter of supererogation is moved by a final end, or a *good*. *E.g.*, the developed State has an element of supererogation in its moral institutions, the reason for which is the final end of man, the human good; the lips, as a developed organ, have an element of supererogation in their power of speech, the reason of which is once more the human good; for speech, as we learn in the *Politics*, is the basis of justice. So too the human seed, "superfluous matter" remaining after the needs of nutrition (which led to its growth) have been properly satisfied, serves man for the final end of "partaking in the eternal and divine"; since the continuation of the race by the propagation of the species represents a certain attainment of immortality. True of Nature, this principle is also true of man: he may, for an immediate reason of necessity, do something which ultimately serves a final purpose of good; he may find a kingdom, when he is only seeking his father's asses.

any view, based on modern theories of evolution, which would treat natural man as explaining political man. His teleology gives him the idea of development, but of development determined and coloured by a final cause. And it gives him further, and above all, an organic conception of the relations of the individual to the State. Since membership of a proper State is the end of human development, and since its end is the real nature or meaning of anything, it follows that man has his real meaning as a member of a State. In the State, and as a member of a State, he lives and has his being: without the State, and apart from the State, he has no meaning. This is the meaning of the famous phrase, "man is by nature a political being". His real "nature" or meaning consists in that citizenship of a πόλις, which is the end of his development. Until he has attained this citizenship, he has not attained his nature, and he is not man in the full meaning of man. Complete *humanitas* implies *civitas*; and every proper man, as a man, is a citizen. As the end of his development is citizenship, so the end of all his action is "the political good". He *is*, only as a member of the State: he *acts*, only as a member of the State, and to promote its aim. The one proposition follows inevitably upon the other. It may seem at first sight as if the being and the action of the individual were limited by this way of thinking to a single aspect, and as if the right of the individual to a free and full development were consequently destroyed. But as we have seen in treating of Plato, such a *prima facie* view is quite unjustified. Teleology comes not to destroy, but to justify. "It was because Plato and Aristotle conceived the life of the πόλις so clearly as the τέλος of the individual, that they laid the foundation of all true theory of rights." For Aristotle "regards the State as a society of which the life is maintained by what its members do for the sake of maintaining it, by functions consciously fulfilled with reference to that *end*, and which in that sense imposes duties; and at the same time as a society from which its members derive the ability through education and protection to fulfil their several functions, and which in that sense confers rights".[1]

[1] Green, *Principles*, § 39. At the same time, it is obvious from this passage that the teleological method leads to the emphasising of duties

Criticism of Aristotle's teleological method

But while through his teleology Aristotle comes upon these two great conceptions—while it enables him to regard the State as a development and as an organism, it is nevertheless true that there are defects in his teleology, and that a defective teleology involves defects of political thought. Teleology taught him that there had been a development of the State: it did not teach him that there was a development still to come. On the contrary, it led him to see in the city-state the final goal and completion of all political progress, and to shut his eyes to the universal empire, which even in his own days was already beginning, and which was destined to endure as long as the name of the Roman Empire was used among men. Yet "the city-state, as he depicts it, without a Church, without fully developed professions, with an imperfectly organised industrial and agricultural system, and a merely parochial extent of territory, cannot be considered 'self-complete,' as he asserts it to be: perhaps, indeed, no single State can be held to be so".[1] While teleology thus appears as an enemy of progress, from another point of view it introduces a despotic and illiberal element into Aristotle's conception of politics. As it failed to give a *full* idea of development, so it fell short of supplying a *really* organic view of the State. The origin of this latter defect is not far to seek. A true teleology regards the State as a scheme, and each individual as having a function in that scheme. It does not seek to differentiate degrees of value in those functions, or to distinguish between subsidiary and primary functions; nor does it therefore regard one function as a means to another, or one performer of function as the "instrument" of a higher performer. But it is easy to fall into a false teleology. A simple and crude form of false teleology is that which regards everything as meant for the service of man, and man as the final end to which everything else is a means. This is an *external* and unreal teleology, which makes objects subserve an end outside and foreign to themselves, and which splits asunder, instead of organically uniting, the scheme which it postulates. A true

rather than rights; and a political science based on a teleological method begins from duties, as naturally as a political science which, like that of Spinoza, denies the doctrine of Final Cause, begins from rights (or rather powers).

[1] Newman.

teleology must be *internal ;* it must involve an immanent end, in working towards which the members of a scheme are united to one another in a common participation. Now it can hardly be denied that an external teleology creeps into Aristotle's conception of the State. He may regard the full citizens as united to one another in a common participation: he also regards a large class of non-citizens as subsidiary to them, and as means to an end external to themselves. A degradation of those who are not concerned in actively and immediately realising the end is a feature of his political philosophy. So far as the end is an object of active realisation by man, Aristotle tells us that it is a "function". Activity, or "energy," in the direct realisation of the State's function makes a man "part" of the State, or citizen; and those who do not actively aid such a direct realisation are not parts, but necessary material—not citizens, but drudges. Who then are those who actively contribute to that realisation, and who are those who do not? The end or function of the State is moral life: those who have the material wealth and the proper leisure to help forward that moral life are therefore citizens; and the artisan or labourer, who has neither the one nor the other, and cannot therefore contribute to an end demanding both, can never aspire to citizenship. Insistence on a teleological conception thus disfranchises all but the men of means and leisure. This conception is not peculiar to politics. The distinction between the "parts" which actively energise, and the necessary elements which passively contribute, is true of the human body. The anhomœomerous parts, or organs, like hand and foot, actively work, and are citizens, in the polity of the body: the homœomerous parts or tissues, like blood and sinews and bone, passively contribute, and are accordingly disfranchised.[1]

The kingdom of ends

We have not yet exhausted the importance of the teleological conception in the field of politics. We have to notice a further development of that conception. To Aristotle the world is not an uncorrelated mass of separate movements towards separate ends: Nature is not episodic, not a number of disconnected scenes, like a bad tragedy. There is to some extent a

[1] The parallel does not work properly, and there is an important difference, *cf. infra*, p. 280.

kingdom of ends: that which is the end of one activity may be itself the means to a still higher end. This view is stated of creation, in a somewhat external form, in the first book of the *Politics:* plants exist for animals, and animals for man. It is stated of the arts in the beginning of the *Ethics:* the art of bridle-making is subordinate to that of riding, that in its turn to the art of war, and that in its turn to political art. It helps Aristotle to a view of the State which makes it, not the one association and the sole end of man, as it had tended to become in Plato's hands, but the supreme association and the dominant end. The State is an association embracing other associations, like the family: its end of good life involves in itself other and subordinate ends, like that of mere life, or that of a common life of friendship. It is this conception of the State as embracing, not negating, other associations,[1] which gives to Aristotle's views much of their sanity and wholesome truth. The zeal of the State has not eaten him up, as it had Plato. Yet, on the other hand, while the teleological conception, in this form, helps Aristotle to save the household, it also helps him to preserve slavery. If the household is saved, as having an end subsidiary to that of the State, the slave is preserved, as having a means to the household's end. Teleology as a philosophical principle helps the practical principle of respect for the given to justify slavery as a natural institution. The slave is one who is necessary to the household's realisation of its end, and is also intended by his moral nature merely to serve as a means.

The end as criterion of classification and standard of distribution

The conceptien of end has a still further use. It serves to classify States, and to classify them in order of merit. The "essence" of a thing lies in its end; and therefore in defining we must always give the end. Everything is defined by its function, we read in the *Politics:* definitions, we are told elsewhere, must not only state the facts, but also their cause.[2] An axe is defined by its function of chopping: we must not only say that it is made of iron, in a certain shape, but that it is made to chop. What is true of definition is applicable to classification; and as the State in general is defined by its function, as an association for good life, so will individual States be classified

[1] *Cf. Ethics*, 1160 a 9-30. [2] *De Anima*, 413 a 13-15.

according to the exact kind of function they discharge. We shall have one class of States engaged in the pursuit of wealth; another aiming at liberty; a third with virtue for their goal. Nor does the end only give classification: it gives classification in order of merit. States are valued as they approximate to, or recede from, the normal end of virtue. The danger of this method of proceeding, this measuring of the lower by the higher, is, that in assuming the normal to be the natural and real, as he does, Aristotle falls, or seems to fall, into a confusion of the actual and the ideal which is apt to perplex the reader. That he does not also fall into a contempt for the actual, or despise the perverted States of his classification, is due to his knowledge of their working and his respect for existing institutions, which lead him, not to attempt to force perversions into the image of the ideal, but to reform them according to their own principles. But the conception of end is not only useful to the theorist in classification: it is not only the *criterion* used in the study. It serves the practical politician as a *standard* in actual life for the distribution of rewards: exactly as a citizen has actively contributed to the realisation of the function of the State, requital is measured back to him again for his contribution. Such reward or requital is made by the gift of office; and hence the end of the State determines the holders of its offices. As a criterion of classification, and as a standard of distribution, theoretically as well as practically, the conception of end is thus all-important for Political Science.

The conception of end has come before us in many names, and from many aspects. As "form," it represents the shape into which amorphous matter is moulded: as "Nature," it represents identification with that ideal, towards which all movement is directed. As "function," it is that full height of action, to participate in which constitutes partnership in the body politic; while the degree of participation in the function of the State is also the "standard" by which office is distributed. As "essence," the end has already presented itself as the content of definition and the criterion of classification: as "limit," we have still to notice, it determines the character of its means. Limit, a conception so dear to the Greeks in itself, that the infinite and illimitable were to them the synonym of evil,

The end as limit

received a philosophical basis in the conception of end. The end must limit and define whatever serves as its means: a boat cannot be either a span or two furlongs in length, for in either case it will fail to discharge its end of sailing properly. A play must be neither too long nor too short to exhibit the change of the hero's fortunes, which it is the aim of tragedy to delineate. The same ideas are applied in the *Politics* to wealth, and even to the State itself. Wealth must be limited, because wealth is a "mass of instruments," a complex of means, "necessary for life, and useful for the association of the State or family". The State is equally limited in size by the necessity of discharging its functions: it must definitely stand between a minimum, constituted by the lowest number of citizens sufficient for the end of good life in a political community, and a maximum constituted by the greatest number of citizens whose faces it is possible to carry in mind, as the ruler must do in order to discharge his functions of command and judgment. And thus it is the conception of end, as issuing in limit, which involves Aristotle in these parts of his political philosophy which a modern most readily criticises—his reactionary economics, and his unprogressive politics; his belief in barter, his leaning to parochialism. Yet from another point of view one can readily sympathise with the doctrine of limit. The conception of limit readily passes into that of the "mean". The boat is limited by its end of sailing to a mean size: wealth is similarly limited to moderate possessions by the end of a virtuous life. Because it is best calculated to aid the realisation of some end, the mean comes to be viewed as in itself the best. Moral excellence lies in the cultivation of the mean of passion which lies between the two extremes—foolhardiness and cowardice, indulgence and asceticism—to which each passion is prone. And Aristotle's political aim, while ideally an "extreme" State where all are virtuous, tends to become in practice a "middle" State, in which neither rich nor poor, but the middle classes, are vested with ultimate power. In this way the conception of limit, if it makes for rigidity, makes also for moderation.

The mean

Here we may close our sketch of the bearing of a teleological method upon Aristotle's political thought. We should be mistaken in holding that this method had determined or originated all the views which we have attempted to bring under its scope. It is actual Greek practice, and contemporary Greek opinion, which form Aristotle's starting-point. It is they which give him his ideas of the proper size and constitution of the State; it is they which supply him with a classification of States; it is they which give him a distinction between subsidiary and disfranchised members of the State, and primary and enfranchised sharers in its life. What he does is to generalise and to rationalise all these data in the light of a doctrine of Final Causes; and in the light of that doctrine he occasionally corrects or modifies the opinions and practices on which his theory is based. But, as it stands, his whole system of thought is informed by a teleological conception of the world; and to that conception, as we have seen, objection may be taken on some of its sides. That is why a revolt against Final Causes marks the beginnings of modern philosophy, a revolt whose champion is Bacon in the sphere of science, and Spinoza in the province of human life. Yet science and politics have returned, and must return, to teleology. Science deals in the conception of organism, and organism, as we have seen, is a conception based on teleology: it is the conception of a whole whose parts can be seen to be "organs" to a common and single end. Nor can the ultimate conception of the State be other than the conception of a whole working for a single end, from which "all the body fitly framed and knit together through that which every joint supplieth, according to the working in due measure of each several part, maketh the increase of the body".

Aristotle's Conception of the Unity of the State

§ 4. So far, we have discussed the influence of Aristotle's teleology upon his conception of the State, and incidentally we have been led to speak of the conception of the State's unity, to which teleology leads. We may now consider more fully his views of the nature of unity, as further determining his conception of the State. We have to speak both of the formal character of the State's unity, as an "association" or "compound," and of its inward and spiritual meaning, as a friendship and society. Aristotle's theory of its formal character comes to light in the beginning of the second book of the

Aristotle's conception of Unity

Politics, when, in combating Plato's conception of political unity, he suggests his own. To Plato's favourite "oneness" he opposes his more moderate conception of "association". A city is not one in the identity of exactly similar members; it is one in the co-operation of dissimilar units. Here we touch the general question of the relation of universal to particular. Shall the one be destructive of the individual existence of the many, or shall the many retain that existence, while yet sharing in a common existence which "blends, transcends, them all"? In politics, as in metaphysics, the answer of Aristotle is cast in favour of the latter alternative. In metaphysics, he holds, the one does not exist above and beyond the many: it is in and among, in the sense that it is predicable of, all its individual constituents. In politics, the State does not tower above the individual to the negation of his individual self: it is an association of individuals bound by spiritual chains about a common life of virtue, while yet retaining the individuality of separate properties and separate families. In that life it is one body, "knit together through that which every joint supplieth"; but, though it is of the very essence of man that he should be a member of that body, its claims upon him are not unto the last surrender of every vestige of self.

The nature of an association

The elucidation of Aristotle's view depends upon an understanding of the full doctrine of "association". An association must be composed of men diverse indeed in kind[1] (and this, we shall see, is of the essence of association), but yet so far alike as to be fairly equal; for master and slave cannot form an association. Each of these diverse, yet like and equal elements possesses his own specific advantage; and each naturally exchanges his own advantage, which his neighbour needs, for his neighbour's, which he needs himself. Differentiation, and a consequent exchange, are therefore of the essence of association. And thus it issues in a common action, which, in the sphere of ordinary labour, is the production of material wealth, but in that of political activity is the realisation of virtue. So far therefore the State, as an association, is a union of members of different aptitudes, mutually benefiting by the products of

[1] *Ethics*, 1133 a 17.

those aptitudes in the realisation of a common aim.[1] Of such associations there are various kinds. Each has its justice, regulating the mutual exchange of services: each its friendship, knitting the association together. All kinds of association are parts of the supreme association, which is the State. Other associations than this are directed towards some partial good, or temporary advantage: this aims at the whole good of man, for the whole of his life. Like other associations the State has its justice: it has also its friendship—a friendship which it is the great concern of the legislator to preserve, for it is the bond which knits the State in harmony.

Criticism of Plato

But before we turn to justice and friendship, there is more to be said of the character of the formal unity of the State. In speaking of it as an association, we have not accounted for the presence of ruling and subject elements, which characterises the State, but is not involved in the conception of association. Yet we have already gone far enough to understand something of the criticism which Aristotle levels against Plato's conception of the unity of the State. Diversity, he argues, is as essential as unity; or rather, it is essential *to* unity. And therefore Plato's procedure in the *Republic* was self-destructive: he was so fixed upon his end, that he swept away the means. Pure unity, such as he desired, is best attained where there is but a single unit: as Plato himself dwarfs his State into a family or clan, so in strict logic, for perfection's sake, it should be dwarfed from a family into a single individual. And from yet another point of view the defect of conceiving the unity of the State as undifferentiated is equally apparent. One of the aims of political society, indeed *the* aim of political society, is "independence,"[2] in the sense of satisfaction by that society itself of its own wants, material and moral. The greater the number of agents possessed of diverse capacities, the more likely are those wants to be satisfied, and independence to be attained; while a society of members all alike can only result in a single contribution and an imper-

[1] As was noticed before, p. 112, n. 1, this conception is not so far removed from that of Plato as Aristotle would lead us to believe: on the contrary, it is implied in the second book of the *Republic*. But Aristotle insists, as Plato hardly does, that an association is composed of equal members; and his conception of association has thus a democratic flavour which the Platonic conception does not possess.

[2] *αὐτάρκεια*.

fect independence. As against Plato, the criticism is not absolutely fair, for Plato had not said, as he is assumed to have said, that the State is constituted of like elements: on the contrary, he had insisted primarily on the differentiation of classes. Yet Aristotle is not entirely unjust in his criticism. If the classes of the State are differentiated, the members of the two ruling classes are indeed "unified" at the cost of all diversity.

The State as a compound

But the full conception of the State's unity is not properly expressed by the term association. To express the State's unity adequately, we have seen that an additional category must be employed, which will do justice to the presence of authority and subordination in the State. The State is therefore classed as a "compound" (σύνθετον), or more precisely as an organic compound, or "whole" (ὅλον), in which the composition of the parts results not in their mere aggregation, but in a new identity.[1] As a "whole," it is viewed as composed of parts different in kind, which are subordinated one to another; for in all compounds which form a whole, there may be traced a ruling element and a ruled.[2] It is not, however, a whole in which the separate existence of the parts is lost: it is on the contrary a union of elements which still continue to subsist as parts of the new whole which they form. It is neither a mere compound of parts placed in juxtaposition and retaining their integrity, nor a whole constituted by the fusion of elements which lose themselves in the process: if, like the latter, it forms a new identity, like the former it is consistent with the continued existence of its separate parts. These parts are generally regarded as being the individual citizens, though Aristotle uses the word in a variety of senses, and sometimes means by it classes, sometimes households and villages. The whole conception is important as the basis of many conclusions. Because the State is a compound whole, Aristotle begins the first book of the *Politics* by an application of the analytic method. In the third book the problem of the State's identity is solved by considerations based upon this view. By it, again, the priority of the State to the individual is proved in the first book. For the whole is prior to the part, in the sense that the part cannot exist, unless

[1] *Pol.*, 1274 b 39-40. [2] *Ibid.*, 1254 a 28-31.

the whole be presupposed; nor can the individual exist as a moral being apart from the presupposition of a State in which he is a part, and which is therefore "prior to him".

Hitherto the unity of the State has been regarded from a formal and external point of view. The *inner* unity of the State, like that of all associations, is to be found in the justice and friendship which unite its members. They give and receive, it may be according to the dictates of a justice which means even-handed requital, it may be in a spirit of generous friendship. In the *Ethics* justice and friendship are closely connected; but while justice is regarded as needing friendship in addition, friendship is viewed as of itself sufficient for the State in which it is found. *Ubi justitia, ibi amicitia; et potior amicitia.* But the true spirit of a political association, in Aristotle's general view, is nevertheless justice. Justice is "the political good": defined as a "reciprocal rendering of equal amounts," it is termed the "saviour of the State" (1261 a 30). The life-breath of the State, we may say, is a justice which assures to each his rights, enforces on all their duties,[1] and so gives to each and all their own. Somewhat similarly in the *Republic* Plato had found in justice the harmonising quality, whereby, each "doing his own," the State was kept in equilibrium. Similarly again, in modern times, we find in the State a scheme of rights and duties resting upon justice—that habit of mind which leads us to respect rights and acknowledge duties. Yet behind justice, Aristotle tells us, there always stands friendship. Friendship follows on the feet of justice—and varies as it varies. There is little justice in a perverted State; and accordingly there is little friendship. There are different forms of justice in different constitutions; and accordingly there are different forms of friendship. In a State where justice gives much to a small body of rulers, because they deserve much, there is a corresponding friendship as between inferior and superior. Where justice awards equally, there is a friendship of equals. Men do not merely live in a cold region of reasonable acknowledgment of the principle of requital. The relation to their fellows, which such acknowledgment means,

Inner unity of the State: justice and friendship

[1] *I.e.* by giving A a right, and also imposing on him the duty of recognising B's right, and *vice versa*, it enforces "a reciprocal rendering of equal amounts".

involves a further and a warmer connection by ties of feeling and affection; and Aristotle can even speak of friendship in the *Ethics* as the bond of the State. The friendship which thus results within the association of the State expresses itself in various ways. (i.) The "energy" of friendship is social intercourse. Its active expression involves more than a mere feeling; it means the sharing of a common life. One of the aims of the State, as an association of friends, is therefore social intercourse, such as is to be found in sacrifices and various ways of passing the time pleasantly together; and the State aims at securing not only life and good life for its members, but also social life (not only τὸ ζῆν and τὸ εὖ ζῆν, but also τὸ συζῆν). (ii.) Again, where justice is even-handed, friendship will be generous. Justice may secure to each a private property: friendship will throw that property open. Thus, and thus alone, will the true rule of property—private possession, common use—be duly satisfied. (iii.) But in still another way, friendship is a yet more vital factor of the State. The State is based on a common good, a good which is the same for each man, a good which each man can only attain for himself by promoting it in his fellows. Now friendship means that a man regards his friend as "another self," for whom, exactly as if he *were* himself, he wishes and does all that is good for his own sake—with whom, again, he shares the same preferences, the same pleasures, the same pains. The conception of a common good, the conception that the good of another is one's own good, these things are thus the essence of friendship, as they are of the State. If the State is to have political fellowship, it must possess the virtue of friendship. (iv.) Finally, friendship is an essential part of happiness, of *εὐδαιμονία,* which is the good of the State. One must have friends for society's sake, if one is to have pleasure; and pleasure is part of happiness. Or, it is argued more esoterically, happiness is an energy, or more strictly the consciousness of an energy; and while energy is more possible to a man when working in company with friends, the consciousness of energy, which is true happiness, comes most easily when the energy is seen as active in the person of "another self," where it is most readily perceived. In all these ways, then, friendship is of the essence of political association—both as leading to social intercourse and the right use of property, and as making for political fellowship and full happiness.

The State has already been described as an association of associations. Each of the subordinate and subsumed associations has its justice and its friendship. Aristotle means, by the subordinate associations of which he speaks, the connections of husband and wife, of father and child, of brother and brother. In each of these connections there is a justice and a friendship. Husband and wife, for instance, mutually respect rights and acknowledge duties; and besides this justice, there is between husband and wife a friendship expressed in a common social life. But the family being included in the State, the justice of the family has become a part of the justice of the State: the rights and duties of the members of the family towards one another are guaranteed and enforced by the law of the State. Just because the family is a natural association, with its own justice, which the State has incorporated not to destroy but to confirm and guarantee, making that association part of itself, and that justice part of its own,—just for that reason is the integrity of the family preserved by Aristotle from the destruction with which it was menaced by Plato. Aristotle, indeed, could regard the various family relations as microcosms of the different kinds of States. The relation of husband and wife suggests to him an aristocracy; the husband rules by virtue of his merit, and assigns to the wife her due share, as the rulers in an aristocracy rule by the same title, and act together towards their subjects on the same principle. The relation of father and child suggests a monarchy: that of brother and brother a timocracy, as it is termed in the *Ethics*, or, as it would be called in the *Politics*, a "polity".

Ethics and Politics

Division of sciences

§ 5. It now remains to discuss the ethical conceptions which colour, and which dominate, the *Politics*. The *Ethics* and the *Politics* form a single treatise in Aristotle's conception, and the subject of that treatise is political science. We must therefore understand, first, what is the relation of political science to science in general; secondly, and particularly, how it stands related to ethics. The first book of the *Ethics* begins with a horizontal and a vertical arrangement of sciences. Horizontally, they are divided into theoretical sciences, which deal with objects unalterable by man, and therefore aim at understanding, and not at altering, those objects; and practical and productive sciences, which deal with objects alterable by man, and therefore aim not only at understanding, but also at altering, their objects. Theoretical science seeks to bring man into conformity with the immutable and eternal; and the name of that conformity is truth. Practical science attempts to bring external things into conformity with some principle in man disclosed by its investigations. Theoretical science therefore *analyses* its given material, until the mind absorbs that material in all its bearings—in its causes, its construction, its results—and is thus brought into that full conformity with the object of study, which is truth. Practical science *calculates* the means by which the external object shall be brought into conformity with the principle in man which it has elicited. The two thus employ different faculties. Of the two parts of the rational soul, theoretical science employs the scientific, practical faculty the calculative. The calculative faculty in the sphere of moral action is called moral prudence, or political faculty; the former term regards the individual and his welfare, the latter regards that of the State.

Before turning to the vertical division of sciences, one should notice the importance of this classification of political science among the practical sciences, and its divorce from the theoretical sciences of metaphysics, mathematics, and physics. It means that instead of analysing the facts of political life, and seeking, like physics, to classify and to explain, political science first discovers a principle—happiness, or the supreme good—and attempts to calculate the means by which human life may through the State be brought into conformity with this principle. This is the point at which Greek political science seems to part company so decidedly with that of modern times, as expounded for instance by Seeley, who would make political science an analysis and classification of the facts of history. But it must be admitted that this scientific method of dealing with political science is not alien to Aristotle himself. We have seen that he based his *Politics* on the facts of history, so far as to collect a record of

Aristotle's conception of political science

a great number of Greek constitutions. The *Politics* itself is full of references to Greek history; and three of the books, at any rate, which deal with ordinary constitutions, have, along with their practical therapeutics, much that is of the nature of scientific analysis and classification. And, indeed, Aristotle refuses to acknowledge any strict separation of theoretic from practical science.[1] He says, indeed, that practical science aims not at knowledge, but at action; but this is an emphasis of his real point by means of a paradox. And his real point is, that practical science, through knowledge, influences practice, while theoretical science stops at knowledge. But both seek knowledge (1253 b 16-18). Knowledge is the prior end even of practical science: that action flows from the knowledge acquired is a great thing—so great, that he sometimes makes it everything—but yet it is in a sense secondary. Hence in the *Politics* he contrasts the philosophic treatment of a practical science, aiming primarily at knowledge, with the merely utilitarian (1279 b 13): the latter treatment hardly beseems the magnanimous and liberal soul (1338 b 2).

Political science the master science

To understand the full scope of political science, we must now turn to the vertical division, that is to say, to Aristotle's classification of sciences in a hierarchy, one subordinate to another, and all to a common end. Science differs from science in the dignity of the end it serves: political science is the greatest and most dignified of all practical sciences, because its end is the ultimate end to which all others are subservient, the end of man's life. For in man's action, as we saw implied in Aristotle's teleological conception of the world, there is always an end pursued: each action has its purpose (like each growth of Nature), and each purpose is subordinate to the one final and ultimate aim of all action, which is happiness. To act for this end, to act teleologically, is to act rationally: to act rationally, as we shall see, is to act morally. This end behind all ends thus makes morality possible. And as all other ends are subservient to this end, so are all other sciences to its science. Political science is a master-science, "architectonic" in its character, from which all other practical sciences take their cue. Are we then to conclude that ethics, which also discusses the Good, is

[1] *Cf.* Introduction, p. 6.

one of these other sciences, and shall we say that ethics is a separate and subordinate science, treating of the end of the individual, while politics treats of the end of a whole society? Such is not Aristotle's view. He does not know ethics as a separate science: he has no word for ethics, as a branch of study distinct from politics. Politics *is* ethics: to treat the end of a society is to treat the end of an individual, for both have the same end. There is one end of man's action, happiness: there is one science of that end, politics. Whether man is considered as living a life in himself, or as living with the life of the State to which he belongs, he lives the same life, for the same purpose, in the same way; and there can be no distinct science, which treats him as living a life by himself, distinct from his life in the State. True, this one and indivisible life can be considered in two aspects: it can be considered as a condition of mind present in the individual, or as a political fact to be realised by the State; and corresponding to these two aspects, we get the two treatises, which we call the *Ethics* and the *Politics*. But the *Ethics* opens by telling us that its subject is politics: it is concerned with a man as the member of a πόλις, or ethical society. To such a man the State is everything. It tells him his good, and it employs the means which habituate him to its pursuit. And therefore the *Ethics*, as a treatise discussing the moral life of a πολίτης, must ultimately culminate in the *Politics*, as surely as the State is the great, the single means of the realisation of man's good. Conversely the *Politics* is indissolubly united with the *Ethics*. As the State was all in all to individual morality, so was its moral mission the whole duty of the State. It was through and through a moralising agent. Yet this belief in the identity of ethics and politics, this conception of the State's subordination to a moral purpose, is afterwards modified by Aristotle. Political science vindicates its independence of ethics in three books of the *Politics:* setting aside moral considerations, it discusses perverted constitutions, and the methods of their preservation. It seems to lose all ethical connection, though not its practical purpose, and to become a study of the character and the method of preservation of non-moral States.[1] But the close connection of ethics and

[1] Thus there would appear to be two kinds of political science—a science of the Ultimate Good, as pursued by the πόλις; and a science of the πόλις, even

politics is normal; and in this respect again the course of modern political science has generally been contrary to Aristotle. Machiavelli, as he is the parent of the modern view of political science as a scientific induction from history, is still more eminently the author of the divorce of politics and ethics. "It is frequently necessary for the upholding of the State to go to work against faith, against charity, against humanity, against religion." That is to say, the divorce appears in the shape of a liberation of the State from any ethical control, and this divorce appears to be confirmed to-day by German, if not by English, political thought. It appears again, in regard to the individual, in the distinction which we make between private and public obligations, between obedience to the dictates of conscience, and obedience to the commands of the State expressed in law. But it must always be remembered that such a distinction is foreign to Aristotle. It is *not* implied in the separation of a treatise on the *Ethics* from the treatise on *Politics:* the same word justice serves Aristotle, as it served Plato, for goodness and law-abidingness, for the virtue of man and the virtue of citizen.

Stages of moral growth

We are now ready to discuss the exact way in which political science, as a practical science with an ethical purpose, works towards the realisation of the end of human life. There are three stages in morality—natural disposition, habitual temperament, and rational action, according as natural instinct, or an external and habituating force, or the internal conviction of reason, dictates and controls our behaviour. We are born good, or we have goodness thrust upon us, or we achieve goodness. But generally we are in the second stage, of an habitual temperament determined by the pressure of external forces, such as the opinion of our family or country, which may indeed have become so inveterate, owing to repeated action in obedience to their dictates, as to be of the nature of internal forces. But even if they be internal, they are not assimilated. We have absorbed them because we must, not because we willed to do so

when it is *not* pursuing the Ultimate Good. Even in its higher sense, as the science of the Ultimate Good, political science may be said to have two aspects; and while at the beginning of the *Ethics* it regards the Good as social, and looks to the welfare of the State (in whose welfare the individual will share), at the end of the *Ethics* it seems rather to regard the Good as individual, and the State as a means to its realisation in the individual.

out of a clear knowledge and a voluntary acceptance of their reason and purpose. And as they are unassimilated, so they are unconnected. The commanding forces within us are a chance congeries, united by the fact of their co-existence within a single personality, but not by any causal tie of reason. Political science in its widest sense teaches us to assimilate, because it teaches us to unify, these commanding forces, as all issuing from the single compulsion of the one end of human striving—happiness, or the Good. And because such a union gives for the first time a clue for *self*-guidance—because it enables a man to determine himself rationally in the light of a principle—it lifts him to a higher stage of moral life. Progress in political science is not so much to know more as to be better—not an increase of knowledge, but of goodness through knowledge. It means self-knowledge, and with that self-control: to be without that knowledge is not indeed to be uncontrolled, but to be controlled from without. But it is not to all that it is given to attain self-direction in the light of a principle. It is only to a few men morally gifted by Nature, or carefully trained by man. The majority must always remain in the state of creatures of habits which they do not understand. But even for them political science is still necessary. It does not minister to them directly an inward light, but none the less it guides them indirectly. They receive a guidance from without: they are led by those in whom that light is burning. The rulers of the State guide them towards their end by punishments and by rewards, by pain and by pleasure, acting upon their instincts because they cannot appeal to their reason, and supervising alike the education of the young and the habits of adult life. In this sense political science "lays down the laws of what is to be done, and what is not to be done".

It remains to inquire into the end, which whether it is present to us, or only to the statesmen who guide us, is always the clue of life. Aristotle discovers man's end by investigating

The end of life

his function.[1] That function is not life—for that is the function of all things that live, of plants and animals as well as men—but life of a peculiar sort, corresponding to the specific difference of man from other living things. Aristotle conceived, and was

[1] *Ethics*, 1097 b 24 *sqq*.

the first to conceive, that life was identical throughout organic Nature. But life has its different kinds.[1] There is the life of nutrition and of growth, with which the reproduction of the species is connected; and this, and this alone, is the life in which plants share. There is the life of sensation, involving the power of having images presented and consequently of feeling desire; and this, as well as the life of nutrition, is the life of animals. Lastly, there is the life of reasoning, peculiar to man, but combined in man with the preceding stages of nutrition and sensation, each higher stage always presupposing and containing the lower. But the lower life, when united with the higher, to some extent alters its character under the influence of the higher. Sensation in man is modified by the presence of reason; and the desire which springs from sensation is equally modified by the same influence. And thus, while the function of man is broadly and generally a life in which his complex powers of nutrition, sensation, and reason all come into play, it is specifically and properly a life of reason—not indeed pure reason (that is for higher beings than man), but reason permeating and controlling the physical elements to which it is tied. This is the function of man: this is happiness. Herein is virtue; for virtue consists, as Plato had said, in the proper discharge of function; and therefore the virtue of man lies in a life duly lived in accordance with reason. And so we come to a closer understanding of the work of the State in encouraging virtue. In individual men the reason which should control their being is involved in other elements of appetite and passion. These elements are not, indeed, entirely dissevered from or antagonistic to reason: reason modifies that with which it is combined, and the appetite of man is not the utter appetite of the beast. It partakes in reason: it hearkens to reason as a son to a father.[2] None the less, in any human soul reason is always adulterated: it is always mixed with passion. But the State in its ideal form is the vehicle of *pure* reason: the law of the State is reason without passion. Out of its purity the State is strong: in his complexity the individual is weak.

As the science of the Ultimate Good, political science would

[1] *De Anima*, ii., c. 2. [2] *Ethics*, 1102 b 30-33.

Scope of political science

thus appear to be concerned with the direction of men towards a rational life. Such direction it gives in two ways. Some men it teaches to realise for themselves the end of life; and such realisation both unifies their character, and lifts their moral action to the plane of self-conscious direction by the light of an inner reason. But most men it aids indirectly and by means of the few it has taught; for the legislator and the statesman (of whom the former is the greater to Aristotle, as laying down the main principles, which the latter only applies in detail) determine for most men the end to be realised, and the means for its realisation. By political science they have learned to know both the end and the means: by political science they impart their knowledge to others. Political science, therefore, must needs be the master science, declaring what other sciences are to be studied, and by whom, and to what extent: it must needs have subject to itself the sciences which men most value, like economics, strategy and rhetoric. Hence domestic economy and the theory of education are both treated in the *Politics* as vitally connected with political science. It is by the State that the material outfit and the spiritual equipment necessary to the good citizen must both be regulated. Particularly is the education of its citizens the State's concern: as the end is one, so, it is argued, the education and the educational authority must also be one. Since education is *ethical*, a making of character (or ἦθος) rather than of intellect, the great ethical influence of the State must here if anywhere be omnipotent, and here if anywhere find its great mission. And so Aristotle argues at the end of the *Ethics* that paternal authority is insufficient for the moral training of youth. It has not force or power of compulsion, such as is vested in the law of the State; and while the young may hate the hand that chastens them for their own good, so long as it is the hand of a definite person, they cannot hate the impersonal State. To the State therefore, and to political science, which is the science of the State's action, must be assigned above all things the province of education, and the function of leading man towards the rational life which is his Ultimate Good. A treatise on political science must ideally be a treatise on the objects and methods of the education of man.

Connection of politics and ethics

It has been suggested above that in modern times ethics and politics have been divorced, and that the sphere of ethics has been conceived as the separate sphere of the individual. None the less, we still conceive of the State as inculcating moral laws, and as entering to that extent upon the sphere of ethics. "We differ from Aristotle not in our view of what is fundamentally important to the community, but in the line we draw between things which the State can touch with advantage, and things which it should leave alone."[1] The essential mission of the State is still ethical: whatever else it may do, it is pre-eminently and particularly a moral force. It is the expression of our will, as the doctors of the school of contract taught; but it is further the expression of our moral will, as only one of those doctors, Rousseau, was wise enough to teach. That the State is thus concerned not merely with the life, but also with the good life, of its subjects, is already writ large in the statute book, and would be written larger still, if reformers had their way. It can only be anticipated that the sphere of the State's action will be widened. The old theory which confined the action of the State to the protection of life and property was due to a revulsion of feeling directed, not against the State itself, but against monarchical authority. Whig and Liberal theorists, from Locke downwards, sought to save liberty, not only by trying to liberalise the government, but also by trying to emancipate the individual. In our days the government is liberalised, or at any rate popularised; and as a result there is no distrust, but rather a demand for its action. The emancipation of the individual seems an almost forgotten creed; and our modern danger is rather the opposite excess of collectivism. It seems to be expected of the State that it shall clothe and feed, as well as teach its citizens, and that it shall not only punish drunkenness, but also create temperance. We seem to be returning to the old Greek conception of the State as a positive maker of goodness; and in our collectivism, as elsewhere, we appear to be harking "back to Aristotle".

If the State is, and seems likely to be still more largely, a moral force, political science must always be closely connected with ethics. It is a science, which lacking a terminology of its

[1] Nettleship, *Lectures*, p. 144.

own, has always had to borrow from other sciences, and to be interpreted in alien terms. It has borrowed from law, in the days of the theory of a social contract: it has borrowed in our own times from biology—though the metaphor of the body politic is very old and from psychology—though, again, in Aristotle we already get some attempt at a "psychology of the crowd". But the only safe creditor of political science is Ethics. Law can only explain the external: biology can only afford a simile. The real explanation of the inner life of a group of men in action must be accommodated to the explanation given of the inner life of individual men in action. As Plato said, the letters are the same: they are only written larger in the State. Ethics, with psychology as its handmaid, must be our basis in any philosophical explanation of the State.

Extent to which politics and ethics can be connected

None the less, ethics hardly figures in our political science in the same way as in that of Aristotle. The State cannot be said to habituate its citizen actively in the ways of virtue. Once the State attempted the task in England, under the Commonwealth; and it raised up in one generation a crop of imitative hypocrites, and in the next a crew of reactionary debauchees. Ethical life, we feel, is nothing without spontaneity. Automatism has no moral value; and the end of legislation is to get rid of itself. The modern State sets itself therefore[1] to the removal of obstacles to a moral life. It enforces education, not so much to compel the father to perform a moral duty, as to remove from the son's path the obstacle to a moral life which ignorance involves. It seeks to make no man good by act of Parliament; but it does by act of Parliament see to it that every man shall have the chance of being good. Aristotle went further. He did believe in the direct enforcement of outward conduct, in forcing men to act habitually along certain lines. It was not that he was satisfied with the act alone: no man taught more than he that true morality is in the spirit; but he believed that to become habituated to a certain line of action *might* ultimately bring the corresponding spirit, and with it spontaneity of action. Habituation was, as it were, a ploughing and harrowing of the land for the

[1] According to modern theory; but in practice, as we have just seen, men clamour for more.

seed, which it should afterwards receive and nourish.[1] It was similarly the aim of Laud, who acknowledged Aristotle as his master *in humanis*, to habituate men in conformity to a certain ritual as an avenue to the religious spirit.[2] But it must be admitted that self-direction by an indwelling spirit was, in Aristotle's opinion, reserved for the chosen few, *paucis quos . . . ardens evexit ad æthera virtus*. His State is one of men taught by an external force to follow a higher code than they could ever themselves conceive. It is the height of the ideal that is at fault: the means are inevitable if once the ideal is accepted.

Relation of Aristotle's *Politics* to his *Ethics*

In conclusion of this study of the relations of ethical and political science, it remains to inquire into the relation between the two treatises of Aristotle which deal with these sciences—the *Ethics* and the *Politics*. In a sense these two works are parts of a single treatise, whose subject is political science in the higher meaning of that word. But the fact remains, that we have two separate works, distinguished by many differences, and that while Plato contented himself with treating politics and ethics in a single treatise, Aristotle preferred to make a division for the purpose of his study of human action. How shall we explain the difference between Plato and Aristotle? How shall we account for the division which Aristotle makes? Plato, as we have seen, felt strongly the connection between

[1] *Ethics*, 1179 b 24-26.

[2] There is much in the theory of religion which lies behind Laudianism that is parallel to Aristotle. i. It postulates the need of habituation by means of a ritual which is charged with the beauty of holiness; and similarly Aristotle desired the habituation of youth by means of artistic influences. ii. In accordance with this postulate, it conceives man as necessarily a part of an ecclesiastical "association," and a member of a Church; and this conception of man as essentially bound to a group is peculiarly Aristotelian. iii. It believes in the *continuous* life of the Church, as a living development from the days of its Founder; and with this belief the Aristotelian view of the natural and unbroken development of the State may naturally be compared. As Laudianism is akin to Aristotelianism, so is Puritanism to the Cynicism which Aristotle rebuked. Puritanism believed in a personal religion, attained by direct contact of the soul with its God, as Cynicism in a personal morality, achieved by the wise man for himself by his own reason. And as Cynicism was a force hostile to "association," and disbelieving in the necessity of the State, so was Puritanism hostile to the conception of a "Church" in the sense of an indispensable and living group with a continuous history. Puritanism, indeed, believed in a congregation; but its conception of a congregation was individualistic. The congregation was somewhat mechanical, "made by hands" for the edification of its units.

moral character and political environment. States, he believed, did not spring "from an oak or a rock," but depended vitally on the characters of their members. Writing a single treatise, he emphasised this interrelation as the vital truth of the science of man. And again, the nature of his philosophic principles impelled him in the same direction. Particular could not for him be separated from universal: the particular only existed so far as it "imitated" or "participated in" the universal. To study it separately was to study nothing. But man is the particular and the State is the universal in which he participates; nor can man be studied except in relation to the whole which gives him meaning and existence. To Aristotle the relation between particular and universal appeared in a different light: the individual had emphatically a real existence, and the universal was no divine "Abstraction" separate from the individual, but a concrete being immanent in the thing which it informed. The study of the individual came naturally to Aristotle. He believes, indeed, in the vital connection between man and the State of which he is a part; and no writer has emphasised more vividly the necessity of the State for man's development. But none the less the individual comes by his own in Aristotle's teaching; and one may cite, as a simple instance, the vindication of the right of private property which appears in the second book of the *Politics*. The individual self was to him a precious thing: φιλαυτία, the due respect of a man for his own true self, was not the least of the moral virtues. It was inevitable that the ethical aspect of the individual self should receive a separate treatment at Aristotle's hands, although he well knows, and often emphasises, the necessity of a political environment for the ethical life of the individual. And thus he writes a work on *Ethics*, as a separate inquiry, but one so vitally connected with the inquiry of politics, that the two must always be "thought together," if we wish to arrive at the truth of either. In the *Ethics*, morality is treated in connection with psychology, as a state of the soul: it is viewed as a composition of the parts of the soul into a habit of deliberate action, in which the supremacy of the rational part is recognised. In the *Politics*, morality is regarded in connection with its environment: it is seen, in its *creation* by the educative influence of a political authority, and in its *action* in the proper field of its exercise. In a word, the *Ethics* are static in comparison with the *Politics*, the *Politics* dynamic in comparison with the *Ethics*; but both are fundamentally ethical treatises, concerned with the theory of the moral life of man, ἡ περὶ τὰ ἀνθρώπεια φιλοσοφία.

Ethics static: *Politics* dynamic

In this account of their relations, however, we are rather sketching the ideal which may have hovered before Aristotle, than the actual result which he has achieved. It is tempting to call the *Politics* the dynamics of morality, and to find in its teaching the complement of the statical treatment of the *Ethics*; but it is by no means entirely true. We do indeed find in the *Ethics* something of a progress towards a work on dynamics. Virtue, we soon find, is not achieved without a training in habits: to preach the truth of ethics is a thing of little avail, save for a fine character which Nature has endowed with a love for the "beauty of holiness". All must be trained in their youth: the majority must be coerced into goodness throughout life; fear is their motive, and punishment their spur. It is the training of the young that occupies Aristotle most at the end of the tenth book; and for its perfection he desires the State. Education is best when it proceeds from the State, both because it proceeds from rulers chosen for their goodness, and because it is nothing empirical, but the expression by a legislator, who has grasped the end of life, of the means which conduce to that end. The problem, which the last pages of the *Ethics* raise, is how to produce such a legislator. In words which recall his master Plato, Aristotle complains that the practical politician is an empiric, who cannot train another in his knowledge; and that the political theorist, like Isocrates, is not only unacquainted with practical politics, but also ignorant of what political science is, or with what it deals. The want of any proper treatment of "legislation" (in the sense of determination of the training which makes for a moral life), makes it incumbent upon Aristotle to attempt an inquiry, which shall complete the "philosophy of men". The statics have thus brought us to the door of dynamics. But the dynamics are by no means what we should expect.

In the first place, there is no neat suture of politics and

Difficulties and discrepancies

ethics. We close the *Ethics* with the feeling, that a State is necessary for the education and habituation of the individual: we open the *Politics* to find that the individual is a part of the State, for which he was meant, in which alone he comes by himself, to which he is "posterior". It follows naturally upon this difference of tone, that while we leave the *Ethics* with the feeling that in the speculative life of each man lies the height and depth and breadth of his being, we begin the *Politics* with the sense, that, the individual being essentially a citizen, his essential life is that of civic action. This difference of spirit suggests of itself that the two courses of lectures were distinct in composition as well as in delivery. In a consecutive course there would have been some adjustment: it was natural not to trouble to tie the ends of thought together, when the two "inquiries" were separate. But the same difference of tone is apparent, not only in this want of adjustment of the beginning of the *Politics* to the end of the *Ethics*, but also in the body of either work. On the one hand, there are some questions which are treated in the *Ethics* in a different way from that in which the same questions are treated in the *Politics*. Particularly is the scheme of constitutions expounded in the *Ethics* different from the classification in the *Politics*. The perverted forms are more unreservedly condemned in the *Ethics:* a constitution called a "timocracy," which is regarded as based upon a property qualification, and as a near neighbour to democracy, apparently takes the place of the later "polity"; and the cycle of constitutional change suggested in the *Ethics* is distinct from any suggested in the *Politics*. Even the vital teaching of the *Politics*, that the State is a natural growth, seems contradicted by the language of the *Ethics*, which assigns to political societies an origin in compact, or more strictly, regards them as "appearing to be by contract". On the other hand, there are some questions treated in the *Politics*, which, judging by the *Ethics*, we should not expect to find treated there, or which, at any rate, we should expect to find treated differently. The marked attention paid in the *Politics* to perverted and non-moral forms of the State is not what we should expect, if the State is to be viewed as a moral institution; and it is perhaps still more striking, that some of the forms, which a perversion like democracy may assume, should be selected for praise. But, as we have already noticed, Political Science comes to mean something else in the *Politics* than it does at the beginning of the *Ethics*: it becomes a technical practical science, dealing with what is given and with all that is given (normal or abnormal); it loses its character of an ideal moral science, concerned with the nature and production of the highest type of character. Yet whatever the differences between the two, the *Ethics* are indispensable to the full understanding of the *Politics*. However much the argument may assume in its course a practical aspect, it still remains the fundamental characteristic of the *Politics*, that its author treats his subject ideally, from a moral point of view, in terms of ethics. If later generations were to approach that subject through Roman Law, he approached it as decidedly through the moral philosophy of Greece; and our approach to the study of Aristotle's *Politics* must similarly be made through the avenue of Aristotle's *Ethics*.

Form and Text of the *Politics*

§ 6. To a modern reader, one of the striking things about the *Politics* is perhaps its form. Equally with the Platonic dialogue the Aristotelian monologue represents thought at work, and not the finished product of thought. The author has not thought out his chapters and his sections: he has not determined exactly what he is going to say in each: still less has he made sure, that the view enunciated in one passage is consistent with the view suggested in another. He is working his way to conclusions in the treatise itself. The labour which should precede composition seems to be done in the very article of composition. A subject is dropped, because something said in the course of its discussion suggests a digression, and that another digression; and then it is resumed (if it is resumed at all) from some other point of view, without any attempt to link the second discussion to the first. Each view taken in its contexts, may seem convincing; but to attempt to co-ordinate two views on the same subject, enunciated in two different contexts, may involve violence to the one or the other. And then there are times when no view seems to be reached. Possible or probable solutions are suggested to some question; but each, it is found, has its difficulty, and none may be finally

Aristotle's method

adopted. "He disputes subtilely to and fro of many points, and judiciously of many errors, but concludes nothing himself." [1] The reader of the *Politics* must determine not to expect consistency, still less certainty, but to content himself with being stimulated to think. He must take a view in its context: he must beware of quoting as Aristotle's view what is perhaps only a tentative solution, or what, again, may be some previous thinker's view, which is ultimately combated or modified.

The explanation of these characteristics of Aristotle's work seems most naturally to be found in the view, that it represents rather a lecture than a set work, and a lecture more by way of discussion, than of set enunciation. Postponing for the present this question, we may first of all notice the form which Aristotelian discussion takes. It is Aristotle's first object to collect the received views on the subject which he is discussing, whether they are the ordinary and accepted popular views, or those of previous thinkers. This is a procedure followed in theoretical works like the *De Anima,* but still more in practical treatises like the *Ethics* or *Politics.* Here it is popular opinion which is the fundamental basis of inquiry. For in subjects like these popular opinion is not simply what most people think about the subject of discussion, as it is in biology: popular opinion is itself the subject of discussion. Ethics deals with the types of character generally approved by men's opinion: universal opinion is the test of ethical truth. Similarly, the subject of politics is no subject simply given, like the bones of an animal, to be treated in itself by the inquirer, without any necessary reference to what any man ever thought of it before: its subject is political institutions moulded, worked and directed by men's minds—alterable by human thinking, and by human thinking made what they are. And thus while a theoretical science like physics, dealing with things eternal, need not so much be treated—though by Aristotle it *is* treated—with reference to previous research or opinions, a practical science like politics must always be discussed with regard to opinions, because it is constituted by them. The opinions of the many or the wise are therefore the basis of discussion; but opinion needs correction or amplification, if not, as with

A constant discussion of current opinion

[1] Filmer, *Patriarcha,* ii., c. 10.

the opinions of some thinkers, entire rejection. To examine opinion is to see difficulties or inconsistencies, statements that err by excess or defect, or statements that contradict one another. This is the stage of *ἀπορία*, in which thought is involved in an apparent *cul de sac*, from which some escape must be found. And here the second, or *a priori*, element of discussion enters. For Aristotle applies to opinion metaphysical principles of his own, principles elsewhere established, to elicit the deeper meaning of opinion, or to correct its errors. Seldom, if ever, is opinion rejected in the sphere of practical science. It is developed by criticism: its excesses or defects are qualified: its inconsistencies are reconciled by some proof, that either of the two contradictories represents one aspect of truth. The presence of these two elements—received opinion and metaphysical principle—has various results. It makes Aristotle's method of science neither inductive nor deductive, but "a continual and living play between both". It makes his style assume almost the form of a dialogue, in which popular opinion states its case, or previous thinkers urge their views, on the one side, and on the other Aristotle the metaphysician answers. There is a constant dialectic for the eliciting of truth. This is no eristic—no chopping of logic for the sake of confutation; on the contrary, Aristotle seeks to absorb what he can from previous opinion, and, even if he rejects it, to appreciate its better side by showing that its error is half a truth. It is an honest facing and weighing of all possibilities for truth's sake. But dialectic such as this, dialectic which almost leads to dialogue, reminds us naturally of Plato; and the suggestion comes readily, that enough of the spirit of Platonic dialogue had been imbibed, during those years of study under the master, to inspire, not only the exoteric discourses of Aristotle, but also his lectures in the inner school. Nor is the dialectic reminiscent only of Plato; it suggests the very process of the human mind in its normal working. Do we not all bring to the facts we are considering certain general conceptions, to which our experience and temper have brought us, and which we always tend to use as clues to the truth? These conceptions are our principles (*ἀρχαί*): conformity to them means for us the mental satisfaction which we call truth. Nor is the process by which these principles meet their material in the mind at all unlike dialogue. It is often a one-sided dialogue, in which the side that suits our principles says everything; but so is the Platonic dialogue too. Indeed, compared with Aristotle, Plato himself may sometimes seem, for instance in the *Laws*, less dialectician than preacher; and the peripatetic monologue, which has been contrasted with the Platonic dialogue, may appear the true dialogue.

It is this play of dialectic which leads to the constant use of the aporetic method—a tentative method of propounding a thesis, stating its difficulties, and working towards a solution of those difficulties before attempting to prove the thesis. Take, for instance, the thesis that the virtue of the good man is the same as the virtue of the good citizen. Aristotle, proceeding as he himself says by the aporetic method, suggests various difficulties in the way of this thesis. The State as an association is composed of dissimilar members: citizen differs from citizen. Different citizens have different virtues; but the good man has always the same kind of virtue, and the virtue of the good citizen is therefore *not* the same as that of the good man. But Aristotle suggests, in the form of a question, a tentative escape from this *impasse*. May it not be the case, that though *all* good citizens are not as good men, yet *some* citizens have the same virtues as they? Logically this is possible; and Aristotle proceeds to prove that it is in fact the case. The citizen who rules has political faculty: the good men moral prudence. But these virtues are really identical; and therefore the good citizen, *if he be a ruler*, is the same as the good man. The thesis is finally established, but only under limitations and with a qualification, which the use of an aporetic method has discovered.

Analysis

We may finally notice the part played by analysis in Aristotle's procedure. This has been referred to his medical training; but, as we have seen, the Socratic tradition was *divide et intellige*, and analysis was a method inherited by Aristotle from his master. He speaks of it as his guiding method in the *Politics*; and his first procedure in the very first book is to employ the method of analysis for the understanding of the State. As a compound the State is analysed into its constituent units of family and villages, in order to attain a proper comprehension of its character, just as life is elsewhere considered in its divisions—nutritive, sensitive, rational—in order to attain an understanding of the principle of life in general. In other passages in the *Politics*, analysis is used to distinguish the several attributes of a subject, with the aim of eliminating its essential attribute, and thereby attaining a proper definition. Such an essential attribute is one which is true in every instance of a subject, and true of nothing but that subject. Hence in the third book, in discussing the essential attribute of the State, he dismisses successively the various attributes which his analysis gives—necessary aid to life, alliance, commercial union (c. ix.); habitation in a common city, intermarriage (c. iii.) —because all these are attributes of other things than the State. They are not true of the State specifically; and they are not essential attributes of the State. But the sixth and final attribute, a common interest in a good life, does characterise a State specifically: it is the essential attribute of the State; nor can a State be otherwise defined, than as an association, whose members are united by a common interest in a good life.

Dialectical, aporetic, analytic—such are the characteristics of Aristotle's method. And now it follows, in the light which these considerations furnish, to inquire into the text of the *Politics*, and the proper order of the eight books of which it is composed.[1] A treatise in which terms are carefully analysed, and in which difficulties are raised and considered, but not necessarily solved, suggests of itself the lecturer rather than the author. And such a suggestion receives confirmation from what we know, or can readily guess, of the philosophic schools, which arose at Athens in the fourth century. They depended simply on oral teaching, transmitted orally. A master relied on the living word, and sought to quicken men's minds rather than to leave written monuments. A pupil, who had heard and imbibed the teaching of his master, arose in his own day, to propound the same doctrine with more or less modification, as his greater or less originality suggested. Where the master had been an Aristotle, the divergence of his pupils would be but slight. This oral tradition, transmitted inside the school, would have one fixed and central point, which would preserve continuity

Politics lecture-notes

[1] For the history of the text I follow Shute, *History of the Aristotelian Writings*.

and a certain stability. The original master must have made notes for his lecture: it is impossible that a teacher like Aristotle, covering such a wide range of subjects, and referring to so many facts as his political lectures, for instance, embrace, should ever have done otherwise. Such notes, whether in the master's own hand, or, as Shute prefers to think, in a good copy, would be treasured in the school: they would be treasured with the more veneration, the more scrupulous adherence to every word and syllable, as the school grew older and the prestige of the master became greater. It is likely that our text of Aristotle represents notes of this kind, thus carefully preserved. It is more likely than the view that it represents the notes of pupils. That view involves the difficulty of explaining how one pupil's notes became the *textus receptus*, when there would be numbers of versions: it involves the graver difficulty of accounting for the unity of style which pervades all the Aristotelian treatises—for though that unity may be explained by the assumption, that our text of all these treatises represents the notes of a single pupil, such an hypothesis is very improbable.

It has thus been assumed, on general grounds, that the Aristotelian works which we possess are not set compositions intended for publication and given to the world by Aristotle himself, as the Platonic dialogues had been by Plato; they are not writings for the world, but notes for a school. The assumption is supported by a variety of particular reasons. In the first place, we cannot explain the ignorance of the *Politics* which the world showed for some centuries after Aristotle's death, if we assume that it had been already published by Aristotle himself. Polybius would not have shown knowledge of the *Polities*, and ignorance of the *Politics*, if the latter had been accessible to him in the form of a book. This ignorance is however explicable if we assume, that the *Politics* was preserved esoterically in the school for some centuries, before it was given finally to the world. Secondly, the difference in style between Aristotle's set writings, and treatises like the *Politics*, is so great, that one cannot hold the two to be in any way parallel. It is true that we have very little of Aristotle's set compositions by which to judge. The dialogues, and the set discourses like the *Protrepticus*, are lost. There is, indeed, the *Αθηναίων πολιτεία*; and possibly the two

Reasons for this view

books of the *Politics* which deal with the ideal State, forming as they do a decided exception to the rest in point of style, were published by Aristotle himself. A German critic speaks of the "masterly style" of the former;[1] and Shute points to the set avoidance of hiatus in the latter. No one would speak of the masterly style of treatises like the other six books of the *Politics*, or notice in them any particular avoidance of defects of style. But, apart from any judgment on this ground, we can use two other and perhaps more cogent reasons for regarding the Aristotelian works which we possess as no set compositions. The first is the high opinion entertained by antiquity of Aristotle as a writer, if that opinion may be taken to be represented by Cicero, who again and again praises the "eloquence," the "golden flow," of his style. The second[2] lies in the fact that Aristotle was at any rate versed in the theory of style. He had lived in an Athens where style was cultivated—where Isocrates taught and practised eloquence, and Plato chiselled his sentences to perfection; and he had put contemporary practice into theory in the *Rhetoric*. But the theory of the *Rhetoric* is not followed—it is consistently violated—by the practice of the *Ethics* and *Politics*. It would seem to follow, therefore, that we must regard the Aristotelian treatises as sets of notes—notes made by Aristotle himself for use in his lectures. As such, they were meant for an audience, which could be assumed, as it is constantly in so many words assumed by Aristotle, to know previously something of the main Aristotelian doctrines. The hearer of the opening lectures on ethics is required to know something of Aristotle's metaphysics, in order to understand his teleological point of view; of his logic, in order to appreciate his criticism of the "Idea of the Good"; and of his psychology, in order to follow his theory of man's highest Good. The same is true of the *Politics*: the political lectures imply a previous knowledge of the Aristotelian system, in the light of which they acquire a deeper meaning; while in every way they would naturally be vivified by a fuller, richer, and more explicit treatment in class.

Publication of *Politics*

[1] The Aristotelian authorship of the Ἀθηναίων πολιτεία is, however, dubious.

[2] Used by Oncken, *Staatslehre*.

It remains to determine the date of the publication of these sets of notes. It is possible, *a priori,* that it may have been some centuries after the lectures were delivered by Aristotle, when they were first given to the world as a published work. During those centuries the notes, in a form modified by the working of oral tradition, would be continuously delivered and expounded in the Peripatetic school at Athens, where they might be heard by all who cared to join the course. Among the Peripatetics there would be no oblivion of Aristotelian doctrines; but for want of publication they would be unknown to a wider public. It is possible, however, that the lectures on politics may have fallen into desuetude: the city-state was dead, and men's minds were more set on the problem of individual happiness, as Stoic and Epicurean philosophy shows. Copies of some of the notes may have been procured for the Alexandrian library, and the notes of the *Politics* may have been among those which were copied. But according to the tradition of antiquity there was no real publication until shortly after 100 B.C., or almost two centuries and a half after Aristotle's death. Anxious for Greek authors with the anxiety of the modern Renaissance, the Roman Renaissance, which had developed under the patronage of the Scipios, now won for itself a published Aristotle through the instrumentality of Sulla,[1] who brought the Aristotelian books to Rome, to be edited there by two Romanised Greeks. "From this time forward . . . Rome is the centre of Aristotelian culture, as Athens is of Platonic."[2] And at Rome a *published* Aristotle is the basis of this culture; while previously at Athens it had been an *oral* Aristotle, modified in the process of oral transmission, which had formed the basis of Peripatetic philosophy.

Several questions arise out of this theory. Does the text which we possess represent Aristotle's own notes, word for word, or have we a text modified in the course of tradition? Are the books, as we have them, of Aristotle's dividing? Did he leave them in our present order? Leaving, for the moment, the question of the absolute authenticity of our text, we may suggest that it is very unlikely that lecture-notes would be divided

Division into books

[1] Apellicon had already begun a published Aristotle at Athens, before Sulla carried away his library to Rome. [2] Shute.

into books. They might be divided according to the terms in which they were delivered, or according to the main subjects they treated, but not according to books. The division into books would be made by editors, after the lecture-notes had been published in the form of a book, a form which would naturally suggest such a scheme of division. But if the later editors charged themselves with this function, may they not have ventured on more? May they not have altered the text itself? It is true that the Sullan editors had before them, if not Aristotle's autograph, at any rate the copy belonging to Theophrastus, his immediate successor, which, after having lain in oblivion for some time, had been lately recovered. On the other hand, they would also have the modified version of the Peripatetic school at Athens. It seems possible that if there were any lacunæ or obscurities in the former text, they may have been supplied, or elucidated, from the text of the Peripatetic version. It may be doubted if the respect of modern textual criticism for *ipsissima verba* would then be felt. At any rate the references in our present text, which allude to a past or promise a future treatment of some subject, would certainly appear to have been added by later editors. In the light of these considerations, the problem of the proper order of the books becomes easy. In discussing that problem, we must first ask, what was the order left by Aristotle, and secondly, what was the order adopted by the editors. Now if the *Politics* formed a single body of lectures, it might be expected that there would be a single natural order left by Aristotle himself. But the *Politics* does not seem to form such a single body. There are three sets of lectures, on distinct subjects, in distinct styles. It is important, not only as regards the order of the books, but also for the general understanding of the *Politics*, to realise this division. There is, first, a set of lectures, general and introductory, which lays down the principles of political science and of "economy" as one of its branches (books i. and iii.), and criticises the suggestions of Aristotle's predecessors and the construction of the most generally admired of existing States (book ii.). There is, secondly, a set of lectures practical and detailed (books iv.-vi. in the old order), discussing and classifying the actual constitutions of contemporary Greece; showing where they are wrong or likely to go wrong, and in what way they may be corrected; and suggesting in conclusion that a mixture of oligarchy and democracy is—for practical purposes, and as an average best—the proper aim of the statesman. The first of these sets is to the second, as a treatise on the principles of physiology to a manual of pathology. Lastly, there is a set of lectures on the ideal State (books vii.-viii. in the old order), discussing the best methods of realising the conclusions attained in the first set of lectures with regard to the purpose and aim of the State, and forming the positive or constructive side to the negative criticism which, in that set, Aristotle had passed on Platonic ideals and Spartan institutions.

Now it seems most likely that Aristotle left these three sets separate and distinct, and in no definite order relatively to one another. In our traditional text they stand to one another in the order in which they have just been mentioned. But that is not, apparently, the order in which they were placed by the editors who supplied the references. The references are inserted on the supposition that the lectures on the ideal State immediately follow the set of introductory lectures. Now as we have no original Aristotelian order, it seems best to follow the order which best suits the internal development of ideas. That order is the order which the editors who inserted the references had adopted. The lectures on the ideal State follow most naturally on the introductory lectures, which alike in their constructive principles and their destructive criticisms lay the foundations for the building of such a State. Thus the plan of the work would be (i.) a beginning of preliminary principles and criticism (the first three books); (ii.) a middle in which those principles and that criticism are used in the construction of an ideal State (the fourth and fifth books, traditionally arranged as the seventh and eighth books); (iii.) lastly, an end, peculiarly Aristotelian in character, analysing and classifying the actual facts of Greek politics—accepting those facts as given, while yet seeking to modify them into something better; and applying to politics the favourite doctrine of a golden mean, in the suggestion of a State midway between democracy and oligarchy. This end would form books six, seven and eight—the traditional fourth, fifth and sixth. The further and less important question of

Order of the books

order (whether a further rearrangement of the traditional order should be made in the three books which would now form the end, so that the old fourth should become the sixth, the old sixth the seventh, and the old fifth the eighth book) is perhaps too slight, and too dubious, to be discussed here. It is on the strength of the references that the change has been made; but they cut both ways. Hildenbrand argues that internal logic postulates the old order; and Newman preserves that order, while suggesting that the fourth and sixth books (of the traditional order—the sixth and eighth of the new) formed one treatise, into which the other book was intercalated.

But it cannot be said that even with this re-arrangement the *Politics* forms a complete and logically ordered treatise. It is obvious that the books on the ideal State are by no means finished. Something is said of its foundation: something, but not all that was intended, of its education; but there is little or nothing said of its constitution or of its laws. It may be, as has been suggested, that Aristotle, sober and practical by nature, soon tired of constructing an imaginary Utopia; or the composition may have been interrupted by other causes. In any case there is a lacuna. There is again a lacuna at the end of the set of lectures on practical politics—at the end of the last book of the *Politics*, in the revised order. One would have expected the discussion of the executive to be followed by a discussion of the judicature and the deliberative: the very words with which the book ends show that it is interrupted, and not finished. Besides these lacunæ at the end of two sets, there is also a large omission in the middle of one. In dealing with practical politics, it might seem that not only the constitution, but also the laws, would naturally have been discussed. In the *Laws* (the work of Plato which in many respects corresponds to this section of the *Politics*) they bulk largely. Aristotle himself had the greatest faith in laws: law, which is reason itself, is to him the only true sovereign. Indeed he practically promises to discuss legislation at the beginning of the three books on practical politics: it is part of political science, and the whole of political science must be fully discussed. There are thus three decided gaps in the *Politics;* and the plan of the whole work, had it ever been completed, would have been somewhat as follows.

Politics unfinished

First Set of Lectures

Prolegomena of Politics, or the theory of the State in general, including:—

Plan of the *Politics*

Book i.—the State in its relation to the household and household management; and books ii. and iii.—the data for the construction of an ideal State. Of these two books the former discusses the best constitutions already suggested in theory or existing in fact, in order that, when they have been sifted, the residue may be absorbed into Aristotle's projected construction; the latter, the fundamental book of the *Politics*, discusses the definition and classification of States. Incidentally to this definition, the meaning of citizenship is elucidated; while in treating of classification, Aristotle discusses the standard for the distribution of office, which is the same as the criterion of classification. In both respects he lays down principles of great importance to a builder of States.

The second and third sets of lectures both deal with particular States, the second with a suggested ideal State, the third with actual States.

Second Set of Lectures

Suggested ideal State. The first of the two books which deal with an ideal State begins with a short preface, on the nature of the best life which that State is to realise. It proceeds to postulate the elements of an ideal State, for which the founder must trust to fortune, *e.g.* the nature of the soil and the character of its people; and Aristotle then begins to discuss those elements, which it is within the province of human art to supply—discipline and instruction. He lays down the rules of discipline, beginning with the discipline of the body in tender years, and proceeding in the second book to deal with the discipline of the body of the young by gymnastics, and of their instincts by proper music—a subject which engages his attention for some chapters, and in the middle of which he suddenly breaks off this last set of lectures. The body and instincts have received their *discipline;* but nothing has been said of the *instruction* of the intellect by reason. And not only is the subject of education unfinished; but practically nothing is said of the constitutional arrangements of the ideal State, and nothing at all of its laws. The ideal State is altogether imperfect; and some account of the further stages of education, and of the State's legal and constitutional structure, would naturally have followed.

Third Set of Lectures

Actual States. The three books relating to these deal only with their constitutional arrangements; and it has been suggested that there is a gap of as many more books, which should have discussed their laws.

(*a*) The first of the three books which discuss the constitutional arrangements of actual States analyses the existing governments of Greece, and suggests in the light of that analysis what is the best average constitution under actual conditions. It further indicates, in a brief passage, to what sort of populace each of the existing governments is suitable; and then proceeds to prepare the way for discussing the method of constructing these governments, by distinguishing the three powers of government, executive, judicature, and deliberative.

(*b*) The second of these three books continues the preparation for construction, by discussing what are the causes which ruin or preserve the State in general, and existing States in particular. It is obvious that before one proceeds to construction (by putting the three powers together in various combinations), such a knowledge of preservative and destructive forces is necessary: one must know, for instance, before constructing a democracy, that to combine a democratic form of the executive power with a democratic form of the deliberative power ruins a State, since it makes it too extreme to survive.

(*c*) The third of these books, naturally, after these preparations, proceeds to the construction to which they were preliminary. It does not, however, construct by suggesting combinations of the three powers, but gives broad principles, both for oligarchy and democracy, based on the conclusions gained in the preceding book, the main principle being, that in forming either constitution, men should be careful of pushing its characteristics to excess. There would naturally have followed next a detailed examination of laws from the same practical and mediatorial point of view; but the examination was never made.

CHAPTER VI

[*Politics*, I., c. i.-ii.; IV. (VI.), c. i.-iii.; c. xiii.; III., c. iv.]

THE TELEOLOGICAL VIEW OF THE STATE

The Origin of the State

§ 1. IN Plato's writings we have seen various theories of the origin of the State propounded. We have seen it logically explained in the *Republic*: we have seen it sketched in the *Laws* according to a scheme of historical development. Even before Plato, and in the days of the Sophists, we have seen that political origins were discussed, and the beginnings of the State referred to a convention or contract. It is almost by an accident that Aristotle comes to lay down his own views.

Beginning of the *Politics*

The *Politics* opens by a reference to the *Politicus* of Plato, and to the view there upheld, that the authority of the master over his household is the same as that exercised by the ruler over his State. To make such an identification is to deny, at any rate by implication, the possibility of a separate science of the State. Aristotle therefore, at the beginning of a course of lectures devoted to that science, naturally attempts to disprove this assumed identity. In doing so he has recourse to his "guiding" method of analysis. He begins by dividing the State, as a compound, into its component parts, in order to discover the real nature of the State, and to differentiate it correctly from the household, which is one of those elements. But this analytic method at once turns genetic; for, it is suggested, we shall come to understand the real nature of the State best, if we trace the development of its parts—from individual to household, from household to village, from village to city or State. But to trace this development, as Aristotle does, is to come inevitably to a conclusion, alien indeed from the original question, but germane to the process of the argument, that the State is not made, but develops naturally—that men are not unsociable beings artificially aggregated in a State, but associative creatures naturally meant for political life. In this conclusion the original question disappears, nor is any set solution given to the original difficulty.[1] The whole process of argument affords an instance of the truth, that Aristotle's *Politics* represents, not the finished results of thought, but thought itself at work.

This half-accidental sketch of the origin of the State has to be co-ordinated with brief suggestions made elsewhere, in other contexts, and from other points of view. Any interpretation must therefore be a little tentative; but it may be laid down that Aristotle is convinced, that the origin of the State is not of purpose aforethought, but of "necessity, or, in other words, nature," and that the State is thus natural and necessary, because man is not sufficient to meet his wants by himself. To attain this sufficiency, to satisfy all his wants, material and moral, an inevitable instinct drives man to take unto himself helpmates, first wife and servants, then fellow-villagers, and last of all fellow-citizens, until in the last and widest circle of associates he finds sufficiency, satisfies his wants, and realises himself. His wants have been his salvation: they have been the sting towards progress.[2] He has been blessed in his discontent: he is finally blessed in the contentment of a rounded life in a civic community. Satisfaction cannot come to man by himself, and in a solitary life: for its attainment he needs and has sought the company of "parents and children and wife, and indeed of friends and fellow-citizens".[3] Perfect happiness is not for the solitary;[4] man is meant for the State, and intended by nature for social life.

Natural origin of the State in human wants

What is it, then, that man wants? Like all things, he has a desire towards his end; for all things move towards their final

[1] Filmer laid his finger on this inconclusiveness (*Patriarcha*, ii., c. 3, where he is trying to prove that the State is a great patriarchal family, and attempting, in consequence, to refute Aristotle). "From this argument," he wrote, "nothing doth follow but only this, that conjugal and despotic communities do differ"—the one having generation, the other preservation, for its end.

[2] Exactly in the same way want (χρεία) is conceived to lead men inevitably to form an association (κοινωνία) in the *Republic*.

[3] *Ethics*, 1097 b 9. [4] *Ibid.*, 1169 b 17.

form, their limit, end and satisfaction. The question thus becomes one of the end of man, or (from another point of view) of his potentialities, of the material within him ready for development, and marked for development towards a destined end. Man's want is towards his end, an end indicated by his potentialities; and because he is not sufficient to attain what he wants of himself, he is instinctively impelled to seek its attainment along with others, and by the aid of others, in an association.

The potentiality of man, that which man has it in him to be, must be determined by a consideration of human nature. We have already seen that man is complex—partly plant and animal, a creature of nutrition and sensation, and as such destined to perform the processes of life; but partly also a being endowed with reason, and destined, in virtue of his reason and its power of controlling the appetites of sense, to discharge the function of a moral being, and not only to live, but to act, and to act nobly. Man, therefore, has it in him both to live, and to live a good life. These are his potentialities; this is his end: it is his impulse towards this which gives him his wants. But he cannot satisfy those wants by himself. He cannot even live alone; far less can he live well.

Growth of household

He cannot live alone. Necessity—which is here "Nature in disguise," Nature as the force formative of the primary elements in a process of development—necessity joins man and woman together for the propagation of life, as she joins master and slave for its preservation. Out of these two unions springs the primary association of the household. The household not only satisfies imperious instincts: it enables the recurring wants of existence to be met from day to day, by providing food and clothes and shelter. Nor is the household merely meant for life. Man acts altogether if he acts at all: he acts as a rational and therefore moral being, even when he seems merely to act as an animal. The household may be primarily meant for mere life, but it also secures good life. It has a moral use. The father has a moral influence over his children ("for every household has its father for king"), and the master over his slaves. Husband and wife may unite to produce children, and to secure a livelihood by division of labour: they are also united in a moral friendship, each rejoicing in, and helped by, the other's goodness.[1] But in addition to the satisfaction which it gives to man's desire for life and his craving for good life, the household satisfies his longing for what Aristotle calls "common life". Man has a simple instinctive liking for society and companionship, quite apart from their serving economic or moral ends. His faculty of speech, it would seem, is not only the basis of justice; it is also an impulse towards good fellowship and sociability. And there is this pleasure of "common life" in the household, in the companionship of husband and wife, of parent and child. But with all the various facets which it presents, the household is not sufficient for man. It is absolutely necessary to him, Aristotle confesses: it must not be rejected, as it was by Plato, in favour of the larger association of the State; it must be retained—but as part of a larger whole. Neither materially nor morally can it altogether satisfy man's wants. He needs a greater supply of the things of this world than it can give; nor is the moral influence of the household sufficient; there is needed greater impartiality, and greater force, than can be found in paternal rule. The household must thus broaden into a village, for the greater satisfaction of man's wants (chiefly, one feels, of his material wants); but for their ultimate satisfaction, the circle must widen once more into the final association of the State, in which man finds his moral needs, as well as his material wants, completely realised.

The village arose by a natural extension of the household. The village
It was an association of several households, oftenest formed by the natural growth of a single one, and by the despatch of several colonies (as it were) from the parent hearth. The rule of the parent hearth would be exercised over the colonies: the village was a little monarchy, and when the city arose by a federation (συνοικισμός) of different villages, its government was monarchical, by a natural imitation of that of the villages. As a wider association, the village was naturally able to supply new needs—not merely those of insistent daily recurrence, but also those of a more occasional character, like festivals or sacrifices. As it satisfies material needs more fully, so it also affords a wider society; while the authority of the parent hearth will be exercised with greater impartiality, and backed by a greater

[1] *Ethics*, viii., 12, § 7 (1162 a 25-27).

force, than that of the father of the single household. But the village is not important in itself. It is only a half-way house on the road of "development"; it makes possible the transition from the household to the State. Yet the State begins on the same plane as the household. It arises as a union of households formed for mere life: it secures, one may suggest, a greater division of labour, and a perfect supply of material things. Man as a member of the State is materially self-sufficing (αὐταρκής); within that association he finds every material want supplied; nor is he dependent on any external person or body of persons for any satisfaction of such wants. But if the State began in life, it exists to serve good life—a life of noble actions; and if it was once only an economic association, is now also a moral community. Necessity taught man to make a State for life's sake: the State once created, the elements of supererogation—elements not absolutely necessary, but making for the beauty that lies beyond utility—naturally developed.[1] Man makes an association to satisfy his material wants, the wants of the nutritive and merely sentient part of his soul: he makes a "city" with a wide supply of all material things, and with an acropolis or citadel that gives material protection. But that association develops moral institutions: it becomes a school and a church to its members: it educates and refines their inmost being. It satisfies their moral wants: it satisfies the human part of man—that part which differentiates him from the beasts that perish—his rational or moral self. It gives complete satisfaction: it is the terminus *ad quem* of man's whole development. In the city he stands complete and four-square, not yet "wrought without blame," but gradually fashioned into shape and symmetry. Life's struggle has reached its term:[2] in the State he stands approved:

Development of the State

> A man, for aye removed
> From the developed brute; a God, though in the germ.

[1] It is a simple fact, which must strike every student of institutions, that any institution formed for a single purpose inevitably, in the course of time, comes to serve a number of purposes. It is a nucleus, a magnet: new uses gather round it. In the case of an association so wide and so powerful as the State this is obvious; but even a mediæval craft guild formed for the regulation of industry naturally became a social centre (τοῦ συζῆν ἕνεκα), and a religious society (τοῦ εὖ ζῆν ἕνεκα).

[2] Not in the sense that man reposes quiescent at the goal; but in the sense that he has reached the field in which he can exercise his powers most fully.

One might put Aristotle's teaching in a single phrase: in the State man has gained his full self. It is easy to think of self as a solitary something inside four walls, with all its interests, thoughts and aims equally isolated. But it is essentially false. A man's self is the complex of his interests. He makes a part of himself anything with which he "identifies himself". A political club, a literary society, or a cricket eleven may be essential parts of a man's self. To cultivate as many interests as possible, to present as many facets to life as possible, is to attain the fullest possible self. Now a man who has "identified himself" with a State, so that his inmost self is pained with its pain (like the younger Pitt), has broadened that self to an extension which, in Aristotle's conception, is the ultimate. To Aristotle, indeed, the process appears not so much a *broadening* of human *interests*, as a *supplementing* of human *defects*; but fundamentally his conception is the same—man finds his full self in the State. In the developed city he attains all things—life; society (or common life); morality (or good life). But what he particularly finds—and what is the real truth of the State and its essential purpose—is moral life. The State does not exist for life, as a species of military alliance for common protection, or as an economic union (though it is incidentally such an alliance or union); it does not exist for the sake of society, or as an association of friends (though again, as is shown by the connections of kinsmen and neighbours, and the religious and social gatherings, which are to be found in the State, it is incidentally such an association): it is specifically and essentially a communion of households and villages in a moral life—in a completed and entirely self-sufficing existence.

The State a wider self

On all that has been said the natural character of the State inevitably follows. (i.) It is natural because it is the conclusion of a process of human development, in which each step is necessary and natural, the outcome not of human purpose but of human instinct (ὁρμή) struggling towards its goal, while the whole is marked by unbroken continuity from beginning to end. As the conclusion of such a process, the State is still more natural than any preceding step in the process. The end of a process is more particularly "by nature," as the nearest ap-

The State natural

proach to Nature herself: "what anything is, when the process of its development is ended, is called (not only its end, but) its nature"; and the State, as the end of man's process of development and his nearest approximation to Nature herself, is his nature. It is that for which he has been destined by Nature: "the State is natural to him, and he is by nature a member of a State". (ii.) Again, "Nature always works for the best"; and one may convert the proposition, and say, that what is best is the product of Nature. The self-sufficiency which man attains in the State is his *summum bonum;* the State is, therefore, the best form of life to which he can aspire; and because it is the best, it is a product of Nature. (iii.) Finally, "Nature makes nothing in vain". But Nature has endowed men with a faculty of speech which points to social and ultimately to political life. It follows that Nature destined man for the State, and that the State is natural. In these different ways, and from these different points of view, the natural character of the State is fully vindicated. It is natural as the result of a process of development, wrought by the agency of Nature (though with the co-operation of man): it is natural, because it is the best possible: it is natural, because Nature, who works by purpose, and not idly, gave man speech, and thereby destined him for political life.

The argument from speech is notable for the light which it throws on Aristotle's conception of the State. By speech the associations of men are distinguished from the flocks or packs in which animals unite. In the *Politicus*, Plato had used the simile of a herd of cattle in speaking of the State; and the Stoics afterwards compared the life of their ideal cosmopolis to that of a herd feeding together on a common pasture. In the *Politics* Aristotle alludes to the most wonderful of all instinctive associations, the polity of the bees:

> Solæ communes natos, consortia tecta
> Urbis habent, magnisque agitant sub legibus ævum.

But animals have a communion only in place, and in sensations communicated by cries: man has a communion in moral ideas, communicated by speech.[1] By speech men indicate to one

[1] Speech (λόγος) is the voice of reason, and to make speech the bond of the State is to make the State cohere in virtue of a principle of reason. Animals may be united by a common basis of sensation: men can only be

another the expedient and inexpedient, the just and the unjust. From speech comes justice, and justice is the basis of the State. "Justice is bound up with the State; and adjudication, which is the determination of justice, forms an institution of political society." In other words, the due administration of justice requires the impartial authority of a civic tribunal, as Locke afterwards argued that the need of an impartial judicature, administering a uniform law with the aid of a strong executive, dictates the creation of the State. In this passage Aristotle would appear to regard the negative or punitive aspect of the moralising influence of the State, rather than its positive and educative work. For, he urges, without a restraining force man would only use the faculties which give him his superiority over the beasts to be still worse than they. He is born with faculties like speech, which prudence and virtue should employ, but which vice may wrest from their grasp to use for opposite ends. And in that case the superior faculties of man give him a superiority even in vice. Not only therefore do man's faculties for good need a State to elicit their powers; his capacities for evil make a State indispensable to prevent their consequences. The view of human nature here suggested reminds one of Machiavelli or Hobbes: man appears to be utterly bad, and the State seems meant to bit and bridle his passions. But this is not really the Aristotelian conception of human nature or the province of the State. Man is naturally born with a disposition to virtue: the work of the State is to train the disposition in a habit of regular action. The function of the State is positive: it exists not so much to repress evil as to encourage good. It is a school rather than a court of law: it is an association of friends mutually provoking one another to virtue, rather than a union of repressive rulers and rebellious ruled.

The State based on reason

From all of this, and particularly from these last considerations, it results that the State is absolutely necessary to man, and that without it he can do nothing. Without the supply of his material wants which it affords, he sinks back towards the beast

Answer to Cynics and Sophists

truly united in a life of reason. The State, based as it is on reason, is the expression of the highest part of man; while the household, based more particularly on the senses, is a lower and more animal stage, at which man cannot rest, because he is a reasoning being.

into a precarious existence: without its moral encouragemen he is still worse than the beasts. It is idle to deprecate the existence of the State, as the Cynics had done; idle to assert that the wise man is sufficient by himself for his own moral salvation. If the wise man were thus self-sufficient, the necessity for the State would indeed disappear: Diogenes might indulge in the boast that he was a citizen of the world alone; and his followers might take for their motto the lines:

> No city, home, or country I profess,
> But trust each day to bring its daily bread,
> Vagrant and beggar.

But there is little material independence in such a life, and human nature itself confutes the view that man can save his own soul. So long as man is a creature of appetites and passions, so long will he need some guidance; and it could only be in the event of his losing every appetite, and becoming a creature of pure reason, that he could be trusted to his own moral devices. But that would mean that he ceased to be a man, and became a god. And every man who professes independence of the State must be either a god, and above it, or a beast, and below it.[1]

Destructive, consciously or unconsciously, of these minor Socratics, Aristotle is also rebutting, again it may be unconsciously, the teaching of the Radical Sophists. The State is no artificial construction, whereby the weak have defrauded the strong of the right of their might, and defeated Nature's intentions; it is the natural supplement of the weakness of us all, which has grown inevitably out of our needs and instincts. Its laws are no covenant securing for men their natural and pre-social rights against one another, as Lycophron had taught; nor are they the maxims of deceit by which the weak juggle the strong into submission, as Plato had made Callicles argue in the *Gorgias*: they are the expression of the reason that is in man,

[1] It is perhaps fanciful to interpret this to mean that the would-be outlaw and ἄπολις is either a Cynic or a Cyrenaic. But the cap fits. The Cynics aspired to be as gods, knowing good and evil; the Cyrenaics, preaching the cult of "moments of pleasure," might well be regarded by an opponent as content with the life of beasts. Their leader Aristippus had said, much like Diogenes the Cynic: "I shut myself inside the gates of no city: I am but a sojourner in all". No State was necessary to suggest to the Cyrenaic the moment of his pleasure.

enforced, as against the passion that is also within him, by the association into which he has grown. Its government does not represent a privileged section, using its powers to the promotion of its own selfish interests; it consists of those whose merits have justly been rewarded by the right to use a power, which they exercise for the advantage of the whole community —a power which has been awarded to them for their virtue, and which they employ to further the ends of virtue, and thereby the ends of the State. In all this one sees a rehabilitation of the majesty of the State, undermined by the individualism of the Sophists, the hedonism of the Cyrenaics, and what may be called the Stoicism of the self-sufficing Cynic. Nor had it only been undermined in theory. Professional armies had superseded the city militia: Demosthenes is ceaselessly rebuking the Athenian's want of patriotism for Athens: civic virtue seemed to be dead. New life must be poured into the city: a "revival" must begin, which should rejuvenate Greece. Athens had her reformers busy with this task, at the time when Aristotle was writing the *Politics;* and his rehabilitation of the theory of the State went side by side with their attempts at a practical renovation of the old glories of the fifth century or of Solon. It was natural that he should warn the Greeks of his time not to be carried away by false philosophies, nor to grow slack in their devotion to the city whereof they were citizens. That city was indispensable to their independence: it had grown up around them because it was. Fashionable philosophies might decry its claims; politics might be uninteresting and even sordid. None the less the State, which had given all, claimed from every man the use of his best faculties in its cause: it could permit no man to retire into the solitude of a Cynic's tub. What was bad in actual States might be bettered: a new government by the middle classes might here and there arise to remedy social discontent; somewhere across the seas, a colony might be born, where the ideal itself should be realised.

Not only was Aristotle, in the opening of the *Politics*, speaking words charged with a meaning for the Greece of his time; he was also, in the sketch which he gives of the development of the State, generalising from the Greek history

Aristotle's sketch and Greek History

of the past. In Greece there had been a development from village-communities to city-states, which were formed by the grouping of villages together, "for the sake of life," around some central citadel. The change from life in scattered villages to life in a central city was often promoted by kings, who induced the various villages over which they had naturally come to rule, either by conquest, or as a result of expansion from an original nucleus, to gather round the royal fortress. In Attica particularly we find at an early date unions of villages, not indeed directly into the larger unity of Athens, but into subsidiary groups, which were in their turn united in the "city" of Athens. Thus Marathon and three other villages united themselves into a tetrapolis: the Four Villages of which Peiræus was the chief united at an early date in the common cult of Heracles. At a later date the city which had been formed around the acropolis of Athens conquered these subsidiary groups, and gave their members full franchise in Athens. Henceforth the city-state of Athens extended over the whole of Attica, a country as large as an average English shire. Of the action of kings in forming cities, of the influence of religion as a bond between villages, we hear little or nothing in Aristotle. He knows that early cities were under kings, and he mentions sacrifices as one of the elements of the social life of a State. It is perhaps something of an omission that he should not have stopped to consider the influence of religion in the genesis of the State. To have shown that even that act of man in which he is most individual, his worship of his God, is an act which he is naturally impelled to do in company with others, would only have strengthened his case. And religion was one of the most essential elements which went to form a city: the units which made a city "always lit a sacred fire and gave themselves a common religion".[1] The unity of the city was religious as well as political: Athens had Athene as the sign and symbol of herself.

Patriarchal theory

In conclusion we may notice that the view of the origin of society propounded by Aristotle is a patriarchal view.[2] It is true that he does not speak very definitely of a *potestas*; but the father of a household (as we learn partly from the *Politics*

[1] De Coulanges, *La Cité Antique*, p. 143.

[2] *Cf.* the patriarchal view suggested in the *Laws*, *supra*, pp. 190-91.

and partly from the *Ethics*) rules with a despotic rule over his slaves, and with a constitutional rule over his wife and children. His authority over his wife is aristocratical; his authority over his children monarchical. As the number of descendants grows, the sphere of monarchical authority widens, until there arises a village under the control of a patriarch or king. The coalescence of villages monarchically governed begets a State after the same pattern: the cities of ancient Greece were under patriarchal kings, as the tribes, which had never developed a civic constitution, still were in Aristotle's time. We have here the germs of a patriarchal theory. Yet the *Politics* opens with an attack upon the patriarchal theory, in the sense in which it was afterwards conceived. Supporters of that theory, like Filmer, in arguing for the divine right of monarchy, made the monarch's power over the State exactly the same as Adam's power over his household. Both were granted by God: both were appurtenant to their owners by divine right. Such an identification naturally follows on the attempt to justify the divine right of monarchy by tracing its descent from the divine right of *patria potestas*. But this identification of royal with paternal authority is exactly what Aristotle at the beginning of the *Politics* impugns. He quarrels with his master, "the divine Plato," who had concluded "a commonwealth to be nothing else but a large family".[1] He denies the identity of the family and the State. That Aristotle should at once hold a patriarchal view of the origin of the State, and deny the identity of the State with the household, may at first sight seem a contradiction. But a reconciliation is readily made. Aristotle regarded the State as *beginning* in one thing, but as *existing* for another. It began, we may say, in monarchy: it exists as an association, where office alternates among the citizens, and is awarded to many at each new allocation. Men have altered: in place of the one pre-eminent hero of early times, with a body of clannish subjects quick to obey, we have a society of equals, claiming to rule and be ruled. In the beginnings of political life, there was little difference between the State and rule over the State, and the household and rule over the household; but as things now are, Aristotle would say,

[1] Filmer, *Patriarcha*, ii., c. 1.

there is a great gulf fixed. Domestic rule is monarchical: political rule is the rule of an equal over his equals. The household exists primarily for life: the State exists for good life.

The Organic Character of the State

§ 2. We have seen how a teleological method leads to the conception of a natural development of the State: we have seen man grow, as all things grow, towards his destined end of a political being. But the same method also leads to the conception of the organic character of the State. The words "organ" and "organic" are fairly frequent in the *Politics*, in the sense of "instrument" and "instrumental". They are words which imply the conception of an end, to which the thing they denote is subservient. Wealth is an "organ" for moral life: slaves, as part of a householder's wealth, are "animate organs". Every organ is limited in size by the end for which it is used: a boat, as an instrument for sailing, must be neither too large nor too small to sail. In this respect an organ is like animals and plants, which have equally a certain limited size, suited to the end for which they are designed; and the State is like an organ, as it is also like an animal or a plant, in being subject to a necessary limitation of size.

Use of term "organic" in Aristotle

If the State is here said to be in the same class with "organs" in respect of its limited size, it cannot be termed itself an organ. Though like an organ, it is not an organ; it is not an instrument for a purpose beyond itself. But, though it is not organic in the sense of instrumental, may it not be organic in the sense of being a whole composed of a number of organs or instruments?[1] Though not organic in the sense of being part of a system, and instrumental to the realisation of a purpose, may it not be organic in the higher sense of being itself a system, composed of parts which are instrumental to the realisation of its own purpose? A conception of the State as organic in this latter sense certainly follows upon the teleological view which is everywhere present in the *Politics*.[2] If the State

[1] This is the modern sense of the word "organic". Whereas to Aristotle organic is the adjective of ὄργανον, to us it is the adjective of organism (*i.e.* a scheme whose parts are ὄργανα for the fulfilment of a single purpose).

[2] *Cf.* what was said of Plato, *supra*, p. 127. To Plato the State *was* an organ in a higher and universal scheme. That view does not occur in Aris-

is the end of its citizens' activities, as Aristotle everywhere assumes, it must be a system of which they are the organs or instruments. Its function must be the function to which their separate functions are all so many contributions; its life must be the life in which they all partake, and by partaking in which they have any life of their own.

The State organic as an association

In such an organic unity it is necessary, first, that there should be a differentiation of organs, each performing a separate function; and, secondly, that each organ should be absolutely dependent upon the whole to which it belongs for its life. Now the conception of the State as an association contains both of these features. As an association, it is composed of dissimilar parts, mutually supplying each the deficiencies of the other, and all combining to realise the end of a full and self-complete existence. As an association, therefore, it is also indispensable to its members, who absolutely depend upon it for the full and self-complete existence which they can only attain by participation in its life. Putting these two propositions together, we may say that as an association, the State is a system of different organs, which by their membership of the system attain a fulness of life otherwise impossible. So far, the individual is dependent upon the State for his *fulness* of life; but Aristotle goes further, and lays it down that he is dependent upon the State for his *very life.* This he does in a comparison, or rather an absolute assimilation, of the State to the human body, and of its citizens to the bodily organs. Because the individual is not full and complete (αὐταρκής) without the State, Aristotle assumes that he stands to it in the relation of an organ to the body, the bodily organ and the citizen being *equally and in the same degree* insufficient without the body to which they belong.[1] The individual is not only dependent upon the State; he is dependent upon it as absolutely as a

totle, for he rejects the Platonic Idea of the Good, and regards the scheme of human life, directed towards the human good, as self-subsistent and ultimate. (At the same time the idea of God as the Final Cause, if pushed to its consequences, would involve the Platonic conception: the State would become an "organ" to God.)

[1] As Newman points out, the degree of dependence of the individual upon the State is by no means necessarily the same as that of the member upon the body. The *equality* of the two dependencies (ὁμοίως ἕξει, 1253 a 27) is simply assumed.

hand or foot is dependent upon the body. He exists only in its life, and has no meaning or existence except as sharing in its life.

State prior to individual because organic

This conclusion Aristotle states in the proposition, that "the State is prior to the individual". One thing is prior to another when it has first to be present to the consciousness in making a definition of that thing. A right angle is in this sense prior to an acute angle, and a circle to a semi-circle: they are the wholes which must be present for a definition of their parts. And so in every case; you cannot define a finger or a foot, except by the whole body of which it is a part. To define man therefore involves, as precedent, the idea of the State, to which he is related as part to whole. Nor must the whole only be prior if the part is to be *defined*: it must be present as a prior condition if the part is to *exist* at all.[1] A hand which is not the hand of a body is not a hand at all: it bears the same name, indeed, but that is by an accident of nomenclature, such as gives a key and a collarbone the same Greek word (κλείς). And the reason why a hand cannot exist apart from the body is that everything is what it is, because, and so long as, it discharges its due function.[2] The due function of the hand being to minister to the body, a hand cannot be a hand except when it is part of the body, and able to discharge its work. From all of which it follows, as regards man and his relation to the State, that he can only properly be defined as πολίτης (for man *as man* is a citizen [3]); that he can only exist so long as he discharges a function which consists in contributing to the State; and that, finally, for both of these two reasons, the State is prior to the individual. This "priority" is, of course, consistent with posteriority in time: in time the individual comes before the State, [4] though philosophically the State is to-day a prior and presupposed condition of his definition and very existence.

Other instance of an organic conception

This conception of the State as an organism like the body reappears elsewhere in Aristotle. We are told, for instance,[5] that the exaggeration of any feature of a constitution (for in-

[1] *οὐδὲ γὰρ εἶναι δύναται (sc. τὰ μόρια) χωριζόμενα (sc. τοῦ συνόλου)* (*Met.*, 1035 b 23).

[2] *Pol.*, 1253 a 22-24.

[3] *I.e.*, *humanitas* = *civitas*: see before, p. 225.

[4] See before, p. 224.

[5] *Pol.*, 1309 b 21-31.

stance, the exaggeration of liberty in a democracy), is as great a defect as the exaggeration of any feature of the body. In an organism each organ must always have its appointed and limited size. To exaggerate any part of the body will result in its losing its due proportion as a part, and finally even in its losing its own character, as a result of the excess to which it has been pushed and the deficiency in all the counterbalancing parts. Nor is it otherwise in a democracy: liberty pushed to an excess will be degraded into licence, for the lack of any counter-balancing order. We can only agree with the lesson which this analogy points: it is less easy to agree with another Aristotelian view, which the analogy of the human body seems to suggest. In regard to the human body, Aristotle distinguishes between integral and contributory parts—between parts which share in the *full* life of the whole, and parts which are the *conditions*, and indeed the indispensable conditions, of that life, but do not themselves share in its activity. Integral parts are organs like the hand or foot: contributory or conditional parts are elements or constituents like blood, bones, or sinews. Much the same distinction is made within the State. In classifying its parts, Aristotle distinguishes the parts or classes which are integral, and share in its full life and activity, from those which are contributory, and only serve as conditions of that activity. The former are the military, judicial, sacerdotal, and deliberative classes; the latter the cultivators, artisans, labourers, and traders. In the life of the State, which is a moral life, the former have the time and the capacity to share; and because they can share in the life, they are the only citizens known to the constitution. The latter classes, however, have neither time nor capacity to participate in the moral life, or, consequently, to become citizens. Their function is the provision of wealth, of means to that moral life which is the destined end of the State; but between means and end there can be no community, nor can there be any real union between the providers of means and the achievers of the end. The distinction which is thus made within the State is compared by Aristotle himself to the distinction which reigns in all natural wholes;[1] but the comparison with the human body in par-

[1] See before, p. 234, on "wholes"; and for the particular conception, pp. 227, 407, 418.

ticular, though not made by Aristotle himself, naturally suggests itself. At the same time, it should be noticed that the comparison with the human body is not exact. The contributory parts of the body are really the same as the integral: the blood, bones, and sinews *are* the hand or foot of which they are the conditions; and the distinction between the two is more logical than real. The contributory parts of the State are *not* the same as the integral parts: the traders, artisans and labourers are distinct from the citizens of whose life they are the conditions. The distinction is real; and it means the sacrifice of one man as a means to the welfare of another, in whose welfare he does not partake.

Limitations of an organic theory

In this last instance a crude teleology may be said to push the organic view of the State to a false extreme, by attempting to differentiate a scale of values in the various functions of its members, and by making one set of functions "instrumental" to another. But apart from this particular and extreme application, it is possible to criticise the general view of the relation of the individual to the State, which makes him a member, and nothing but a member, of the body politic. As we saw in treating of Plato, the State can only be regarded as an organism with certain limitations and qualifications. Of these limitations and qualifications Aristotle was quite well aware; and he is himself the best critic of the organic view of the State which he propounds at the beginning of the *Politics*. He knows that there is in the individual a *φιλαυτία*, a self-love, which demands an expression and needs property for its expression: he knows that the individual is a member of other groups than the State, and a part of other "organisms" than the political. And if man can only be defined and can only exist as a citizen, it seems difficult to understand how any question can arise of the difference between a good man and that of a good citizen, such as appears in the third book of the *Politics*. In truth, it would appear as if we had, in this organic doctrine, an extreme instance of that rehabilitation of the State which characterises the opening of the *Politics*. Aristotle is teaching that "men ought not to believe that they belong to themselves, but that they all belong to the State of which they are parts" (1337 a 27). Like every teacher of a truth that needs to be emphasised he lays almost an excess of emphasis on the truth which is needed to counteract current errors. But the normal and regular Aristotelian doctrine stops short of being fully organic: it does not lose the individual's life in that of the State, though it fully recognises the necessity of the State to the individual's life. Man, as having his nature supplemented by the State, rather than the State as controlling man's every faculty, is the pivot of his thought. The State is an organic growth[1]—but man co-operated in the growth, and man can modify its character: man is inevitably knit to man, and to the whole society in which he lives—but it is for the achieving of his own "independence" that he becomes dependent on others.

The End of the State

§ 3. It naturally follows upon what has been said of the teleological method of Aristotle, to discuss more fully than has hitherto been done the end of the State, and to inquire more closely into its relation to the end of the individual. We have seen that the end of the State is good life. In a wider sense, indeed (it is admitted in the third book), mere life, which has a certain goodness of itself besides its natural pleasure, and social life, with all its attractions, are also ends towards which man is drawn; and those who contribute towards these ends are competitors for the rewards which the State has to offer—the rewards of office and dignity and honour, which in justice the State must confer upon those who have done most to realise the ends of its own life and action. But in a more exclusive and specific sense, good life alone is the end of the State: the State is a spiritual association in a moral life. No union

The State's end a moral life

[1] The term organism is generally used to-day, not merely as meaning a system of ὄργανα (in which sense it has here been used), but as also meaning a *living* system, which has grown, and has a principle of life in itself. In this fuller sense the State is "organic" to Aristotle, because it is natural. Things natural, as we have seen, are things possessing in themselves a source of motion—things which develop from within, as the result of an immanent force. As such a natural thing, the State has its own life, and it has grown. At the same time, Aristotle does not push this view, as Burke did, into a conservative antipathy to human interference: his whole conception of political science, as a practical and remedial thing, postulates human action. Yet on the other hand Aristotle could justify slavery, as Burke could defend rotten boroughs: the sense of the State as a living system due to development tends to over-conservatism, as the sense of the State as a mechanism created by contract leads to excessive innovation.

that is specifically and solely directed to mere life can be a State: if it were so, a gang of slaves (destitute, it must be remembered, as every slave in Aristotle's conception is, of moral capacities), or a drove of animals, might form a State. Nor, upon a slightly higher plane, can an association formed for mutual protection and exchange of products ever constitute a State: if it were so, any two States which have formed an alliance for either purpose would have to be regarded as a single State. But they could not be so regarded, in the absence of a common government of the alliance, and (what is still more indispensable) of a moral care for the character of the members of the alliance. The true State aims, not at preventing its citizens from doing evil to one another, but at preventing them from being evil or in any way disposed to evil: its law is no guarantor of men's rights as against one another, but a maker of goodness and righteousness among men. Any city which is worth the name has virtue for its object and its care. This is the essential and specific attribute which makes a State: and, without this, habitation in the same territory, relations of intermarriage, and laws regulating the exchange of products, will not make ten thousand men into a State. They are indeed indispensable: a moral purpose is still more indispensable. They are the conditions: it is the essence. Political association, it must therefore be insisted, is association not in material production, but in moral action; and as, in the sphere of material production, those who have produced, and can offer to the economic association, the maximum of objects, receive in return the maximum of reward, so in this sphere of moral action, those who have done, and can contribute to the spiritual association, the maximum of noble actions, receive the maximum of honours in requital of their work. In this view of the State as a spiritual association, expecting good works and requiting them with honours, we touch the most fundamental part of the *Politics*.

But certain questions arise, in the first of the two books on the Ideal State, with regard to the exact nature of the good life which the State aims at living, and its relation to the good life of the individual; while, in the third book of the *Politics*, the cognate question of the identity of the virtue of the good citizen and that of the good man comes under discussion. We have now to ask what Aristotle's answers to these questions were. In beginning his account of the ideal State which shall realise for men the best possible life, Aristotle first inquires, what that best possible life may be, or, in other words, what is happiness. The answer is found in a reference, not to the course of lectures upon ethics, where the nature of happiness had been already discussed, but to certain less scientific inquiries, possibly a *published* dialogue[1] in which the end of life had been considered.[2] From these inquiries is borrowed a distinction of the good things, which together constitute happiness, into three kinds—external, physical, and spiritual. All three are necessary to happiness, but spiritual good things are supremely necessary; and a man may be said to have as much of happiness as he has of virtue and moral wisdom. The definition of happiness will therefore be a life of virtue, but (since external and physical good things are necessary if subordinate) a life of virtue equipped with external advantages of wealth and health and the like, sufficient to make virtuous action possible.[3] The highest virtue will be the fullest play of such activity, and for its fullest play there is needed complete freedom of action. There must be no limitations placed upon the action of a good man: otherwise he will only attain the highest activity possible under those limitations. His activity will not be *absolute* and perfect in itself, but limited and *conditional* upon those limitations; and his happiness will accordingly not be absolute, but only conditional.[4] It is an act of virtue to punish vice; but it is an act conditional upon the existence of vice, and it is not therefore an act of absolute virtue. Absolute virtue is positive and creative, not negative or destructive. It is virtue to bear up nobly under sickness or poverty; but it is virtue conditional on these limitations, and not absolute virtue. It is virtue negatively employed, in trying to rise above these limitations: it is not positive virtue.

The nature of happiness

[1] See before, p. 257, for the view that these two books were themselves a published work.

[2] It is perhaps an argument for the view that the two books of the *Politics* on the ideal State differ from the rest, in being a set work for publication and not notes of a lecture, that in these two books Aristotle refers not to his lectures, but to his published works. He would naturally do so, if he were writing for publication with an audience in view that only knew these works. At the same time, reference to non-scientific inquiries also occur in *lectures*.

[3] *Cf. Ethics*, 1178 b 35. [4] *Pol.*, 1337 a 7-21: *cf. Eth.*, 1100 b 28-30.

Need of material good things for happiness

The necessity of a proper equipment or furniture for the moral life is one of Aristotle's strongest convictions. He disagreed with the Cynic view that virtue is self-sufficient for happiness. Virtue is a spiritual activity, or a set of spiritual activities, arduously and strenuously pursued: sickness limits, or even maims, these activities. Chronic poverty deprives men of leisure and liberal impulse: a man upon whom the task of earning life's "necessary" bread weighs heavily, can have little time and less inclination, for listening to "councils of perfection".[1] The full play of virtue, the full expansion of spiritual energy, involves the display of qualities like generosity, which are impossible without means. But though happiness is impossible without external advantages, it must not be thought that the advantages which are necessary are either many or considerable. Virtue and happiness are possible with moderate resources. There is a natural "measure" fixed for wealth; it must be neither less nor more than is necessary as an instrument for virtue. The corollary of the doctrine that wealth is necessary to virtue thus comes to be, that wealth is an instrument for virtue, and limited, like every instrument,[2] by considerations of the end it serves. If the former proposition seems below the level of modern ideas, the latter is above the level of modern practice. If our theology professes belief in the blessedness of the poor, our political economy tends to go upon the assumption of wealth for wealth's sake. Aristotle's two conceptions (which are not really distinct, but the different sides of a single conception) are indissolubly connected; and the one explains the other. If virtue required means, it was because the conception of virtue, as the full unfolding of human possibilities in active life on every side, in intellectual energy as well as in moral, demanded (as it still demands) a certain leisure and a certain detachment from the cares of mere existence. Plato had sought to secure this leisure and detachment for his guardians by a system of communism, a system by which the guardians could count upon being "furnished" by their subjects with material necessities which they enjoyed in common. But the outcome of the need for leisure and detachment, which meets

[1] The antithesis of *τὰ ἀναγκαῖα* and *τὰ ἐκ περιουσίας*.
[2] See before, pp. 230, 276.

us prominently in Aristotle's pages, is slavery. The slave is a necessary instrument, like other kinds of wealth, for the moral life. It must be remembered that he is an instrument, after all, for a high purpose, and that, by being used as an instrument in such a service, he receives a moral benefit himself. Yet though one may seek to be fair to the whole conception of life indicated by this philosophy, one cannot but admit, that it is the conception entertained by an intellectual aristocracy (which would fain be also a political aristocracy) of itself, and of its possibilities and its necessities. Its flower would have been a fine manhood fully open; but many a life must have gone before, like autumn leaves, to fertilise the ground. It was natural that philosophers should set before the youth of Greece who came to their lectures such an ideal: these young men had the instruments—the wealth, the slaves, the leisure—and it was much to tell them that these things were to be used as instruments in a high work. But a wider thinking was necessary, which should propound an ideal that needed no instruments upon which all men could not count, and which above all made no man a mere instrument to the welfare, even if it were the moral welfare, of another.

This being, then, the conception of man's happiness—a life of virtue furnished with the conditions of virtuous action—it remains to ask whether the best life of a political society, "the happiness of the State," was after the same pattern. The answer is (i.) that a State like any individual must show virtue, and the same virtues as those which a man must show; it must show courage, and self-control, and justice; (ii.) that inasmuch as man's happiness springs from and is proportionate to his virtue, it follows that the State, having the same virtues as those of the individual, will, provided that its happiness springs from and is proportionate to its virtues, be happy or attain the best life, in the same way as the individual. But the happiness of a State does spring from its virtue: "the more virtuous State *is* the more happy". The conclusion which we attained in regard to the individual is therefore true of the State: its happiness, or best life, is a life of virtue properly furnished.

(i.) The identification here made of the virtue of the individual with that of the State, and consequently of the happiness

Moral life of State same as that of individual, but with a distinction

of the individual with that of the State, is the same as the teaching of Plato in the *Republic.* But it is not always observed by Aristotle. The conception of the unity of virtue, which had been the Socratic creed, is attacked by him in the *Ethics;* and in the third book of the *Politics* the identity of the virtue of the individual with that of the State is also impugned. The general proposition, indeed, that a State has a moral life and that its welfare depends upon the strength of its moral life, is perfectly Aristotelian. But that general proposition has been elsewhere explained to mean, that the authorities of the State, consisting of men who have attained the stage of conscious morality, enforce upon the individual by education (and by adjudication) a *habit* of moral action. It follows from this explanation that the authorities, as having attained that stage, are possessed of "moral wisdom,"[1] of a faculty of directing themselves and others in the light of a principle; while the ordinary citizen or subject is still in the stage of habitual obedience to an external command. Now while habitual obedience to an external command constitutes the virtue of a good citizen, the virtue of a good man resides in a faculty of conscious self-guidance. It follows therefore that the virtue of a good man differs from the virtue of the good citizen, but is identical with the virtue of a ruler, since the good man and the ruler are both distinguished by the possession of moral wisdom. Consequently, as regards the identification of the virtue of the individual with that of the State, the virtue of the good man will be the same as that of the State, if the virtue of the State is that of its rulers, and will be different from that of the State, if the virtue of the State is that of its citizens. Now it seems easy to identify the State with its rulers;[2] but the State means to Aristotle the association of all the citizens.[3] The virtue of the State is therefore the virtue of *all* its citizens; and since the virtue of the ordinary citizen is different from that of the good man, we may conclude that the virtue of the

[1] φρόνησις—which is also termed, when it is displayed by the ruler, "political faculty," but which is the same thing, whether it is displayed by the ruler or the individual.

[2] See below, p. 307.

[3] "State" means both "political society," and the "government" of that society. The Aristotelian word πόλις (or State) means the "political society": πολίτευμα indicates the government.

State is different from that of the individual. Of one State, however, this conclusion is untrue. In the ideal State *every* citizen is ultimately a full ruler; in it, therefore, every citizen must ultimately show the quality of moral wisdom, which is the essence of a good man; and in it, accordingly, the virtue of the State is exactly the same as that of the individual. Of any other State than the ideal, however, the conclusion remains true, that the virtue of the State is distinct from that of the good man. But such a conclusion, though logical, is perhaps too precise. After all, the virtues of the good man, virtues of courage and self-restraint and justice, are the same in kind as those of the ordinary good citizen, though the good man has the additional quality of moral prudence directing his acts of self-restraint and justice. Further, though the truly good man has moral wisdom, we may speak of a "good man," meaning only a person habitually acting in obedience to the moral enactment of the State. A good man in this lower sense is exactly the same as a good citizen: the virtue of the individual is the same as that of the State. Thus a rough identification may be retained between the virtue of the individual and the virtue of the State; though strictly and properly, a truly good man is not good in exactly the same way as the ordinary good citizen, or, therefore, as the association of citizens, the State. Yet even such a rough identification becomes impossible in a State which does not pursue a moral purpose, but has made wealth its aim and goal. In such a State, to be a good citizen is simply to seek and to accumulate wealth; and, consequently, in such a State, the good citizen would be a bad man, and the good man a bad citizen. One feels about the whole discussion that it is a little unreal, after the teaching of the first book, that man is not self-complete without the State, and still more after the suggestion of that book, that man only exists and is man, in so far as he is a citizen. But Cynic teaching had made familiar the contrast between man, as an independent moral agent, and the State of which he was a member; and Aristotle, after having combated, unconsciously reverts to that antithesis.

Happiness of State same as that of an individual

(ii.) From the virtue we now turn to the happiness of the State and the individual. It is the same, Aristotle says in the *Ethics*, as he also says in the *Politics;* but there is a wider and more perfect happiness, a happiness of finer and diviner quality in membership of a State. Participation in a general happiness is higher than any individual happiness; and with the latter we may perforce be content—we cannot be really satisfied.[1] A question, however, arises, which concerns both the State and the individual. Should an active and militant "happiness" be the goal, or should a quiet development of the inner life be made the aim? Strictly speaking, these questions cannot be answered in the same way for the individual and the State. The choice which lies before the individual is one between the life practical and the life philosophic, between action and contemplation: the alternative presented to the State is vigorous expansion or internal consolidation, imperialism or liberalism. It introduces some confusion into Aristotle's argument, that the case is argued as if it were the same for both; and it may be perhaps best to separate the case of the individual from that of the State.

Should a State seek happiness in a life of action or one of peace?

The customs and laws of many States, both Greek and barbarian, proved to Aristotle that they had made rule over other States their goal. Of such States Sparta was a most striking instance; and in arguing against imperialism Aristotle has probably in view writers on the Spartan constitution like Thibron. He rejects their political teaching on various grounds. A State which has acquired empire illegally cannot legally rule an empire; and imperialism must often mean illegal acquisition. But here (one may answer to Aristotle in Aristotle's own manner) a difficulty arises. Can the word illegal be applied to the action of a State? Is a State in its relations with other States under the law, which it enforces upon its subjects? It would hardly seem to be under any legal liability, save such as it has itself acknowledged, as for instance the rules of the Amphictyonic League (the international law of Greece), which regulated the conditions of war; while in the wide sphere in which there is no such acknowledgment, the only limitation upon a State must be consideration of its own welfare, in the highest sense of that word. Another objection raised by Aristotle carries more weight. A State which is constitutionally ruled itself, he argues, is illogical when it seeks to rule other

[1] This is a very mild statement, in the light of the doctrine of the early part of the *Politics*—that no existence at all is possible apart from the State.

States imperially. Whether it be illogical or no, it is perhaps impolitic: it is hard for *imperium et libertas* to be yoke-fellows, and empire abroad may involve a strong hand at home, in the place of constitutional liberty (1333 b 33). There are, indeed, Aristotle suggests, countries meant to be ruled by the stronger: and it would indeed appear as if countries like India or Egypt were meant for the foreign direction, by which they have for so many centuries been guided. But though an empire may occasionally be natural, Aristotle holds that empire is by no means necessary to the welfare of a State; and he therefore inclines to the "philosophic" life, the life of internal development in the paths of virtue. If the apostles of the militant life object to such a State that it is inactive and stagnant, there is an answer ready. As Pericles said, it is possible to have a philosophic life without falling into slackness. Though the whole may not "act" in reference to other wholes, the parts of the State may "act" with reference to one another. God Himself is not active: if He moves the world, it is by attraction, and not by action; yet God is supremely happy in His life of contemplation of Himself, and His own thought. If this be the happiness of God, it follows *a fortiori* that a self-centred State may be happy.

The practical and the philosophic life for the individual

But should an individual be practical and political, as Gorgias had taught, or should he, like Anaxagoras, withdraw himself behind the veil, and live for thought? It is certainly the supreme aim of man to live according to reason, which is the highest and most peculiar part of his nature. But reason is twofold. It is practical, in so far as it is its work to direct action in accordance with what is right; it is theoretical, in so far as it is its function to bring thought into conformity with truth.[1] To which side of his reason shall a man give preponderance? Upon Gorgias' view, it would follow that every man, since his conception of happiness was the practical life of politics, should eagerly contend for office. But, as a matter of fact, office is for those to whom it is due: it goes to the man whose merit demands reward, and whose capacity invites trust; and there must be many who are not chosen. A practical life of politics cannot therefore be the general ideal; and Aristotle comes to the conclusion, that the ideal life is one

[1] *Pol.*, 1333 a 24 *sqq.*; *cf. supra*, p. 238.

of activity, indeed, but of intellectual activity.[1] It is an activity that does not express itself in external action, or involve relation to others: it is the activity of processes of thought and reflection, pursued not for any ulterior satisfaction, but for their own immediate gratification. And Aristotle indulges in the apparent paradox that thought never resulting in overt action by the thinker is in itself the highest form of action; for, even in the sphere of overt action, is not the mere thought of an architect more truly active than the hands which build, and may we not go further and urge, that pure thought, even when never translated into overt action, is always the higher form of action? From all of which one gathers, that man may either find his happiness in a political life, in exercising constitutional authority over his fellows (and so becoming like those States which exercise a just authority over other States); or, if his capacities are not for such a life, he may look for happiness to a philosophical life of active thought. Not indeed that the two are mutually exclusive alternatives: on the contrary, active thought on the deepest of moral questions is necessary to the political life, and the statesman is a philosopher as well as a politician. Nevertheless, in this emergence of the individual as finding his happiness in contemplation, one seems to see a divergence from the moral and political atmosphere of the first book. Man as a political animal somewhat recedes: man as a thinking being comes more prominently forward. There is no necessary contradiction: at all times Aristotle contemplates the activity of thought as the specific goal of man, in virtue of that reason which differentiates him from the beasts. Nor is anything said in the discussion of the ideal State, which indicates that any man can dispense with the State, as the Cynics, who pushed the conception of man as an essentially rational being to its furthest extreme, were disposed to think. Aristotle only says that it is not every man who can be, or need be, a politician; he does not say that any man can dispense with the

[1] *Cf.* for this answer the tenth book of the *Ethics*, c. vii. The pleasure of "contemplation" is there argued to be most intense and continuous; to possess most αὐτάρκεια; to be alone loved for itself; and to be the only pure employment of leisure. Contemplation (c. viii.) is the happiness of gods; and men are happy, in so far as they have something of the divine energy.

necessity of being "a political animal". None the less there is a slightly different atmosphere, as of a separate treatise,[1] not rigidly co-ordinated with the rest of Aristotle's political deliverances. It is easy to believe that here there is an unconscious gliding into Hellenism; and that something of that withdrawal upon the inner life, which followed upon the death of the city-state, already casts its shadows on the pages of Aristotle. But the same wavering between an active and strenuous life in the State, and the life of the philosopher who by contemplation identifies himself with the whole world, is already apparent, as we have seen, in Plato. The philosopher, looking at the world, can readily see that the State is one of its schemes, and each of us part of it; but he feels that to look at the world is in itself a thing transcending all other things, and he easily forgets *what* he has seen, when he thinks of the bliss of the *seeing*. In that feeling, and that forgetting, the organic relation of the individual to the State may readily disappear.

Identification of State and individual

On the whole, we may say in summary, there is in Aristotle an identification of the State and the individual. As a self-contained ethical society, the State lives the same life as the individual: like him, it acknowledges a moral law, and like him it forces itself (its members) to conform to that law. It has the same end, and it attains the same happiness in pursuing that end. Man, acting as a member of a group, is no other than man acting as a separate unit: he and his fellows who together form the State have the same virtues and aims and satisfactions as a group of beings, which they have as separate beings. It is the old thesis of Plato, that the virtues of the State are the virtues of the individual writ large. The thesis is somewhat modified by Aristotle, but it is modified in a direction, which is not inconsistent with Plato's thought, and is, indeed, implied in the *Republic*.[2] We learn that in acting as members of groups, men are conditioned by the place they occupy in the group, and by the character of the group to which they belong; and conditioned in this way, their virtue must fall short of the "absolute" virtue of full and free self-direction towards an ideal end, which belongs to the good man who acts simply and absolutely without such limitations. Only in one case will the

[1] *Cf. supra*, p. 257. [2] *Cf. supra*, p. 116, n. 1, and p. 118.

virtue of a member of a group acting in that capacity attain to the height of the virtue of a good man. When the member of a group occupies the place of ruler, he has the opportunity of exercising full and free self-direction; and if the character of that group is distinguished by perfect virtue, he will be able to exercise his powers for an ideal end. Short of this, men acting as members of a group must fall short of men acting without the limitations of such membership. Aristotle's thought is clear and simple: the only difficulty is to understand how, having laid it down that man can only act and be understood as a member of a group, he can postulate a virtue which belongs to a man acting as it were *in vacuo*, and apart from membership of a group.

The whole conception of the State as a moral being, living the same life as the individual and moving towards the same end, is a conception like and yet unlike modern conceptions of the State. To us, too, the State is a communion of men united to one another because they have a common interest in the same object: to us, too, that object must ultimately be nothing else than the best object that men can attain. However men may talk of the defence of life and property as the object of the State they will inevitably act in common for the highest object which they can individually conceive, whether consciously or unconsciously. Men cannot limit themselves to acting in a group, especially in a group like the State, in only one way: they must necessarily act there in as many ways as they can act at all. On the other hand, while Aristotle expected a political group to be righteous, and to make its members righteous as the conditions of its own righteousness, we only expect it to *make for* righteousness, to the extent to which group-action can do so; and that extent seems to us determined by the limits which the need of moral spontaneity sets to the automatism involved in State-action.

CHAPTER VII

[*Politics*, III., c. i.-viii.; VI. (IV.), c. iii.-iv.]

THE STATE AS A COMPOUND

THE UNITS OF THE COMPOUND

State as a compound

§ 1. THE teleological method must necessarily enter into any definition of the nature of the State. We have already seen that every true definition must be teleological: an axe must be defined by its function of chopping, and in the same way the State must be primarily defined, as an "association of households and villages sharing in a life of virtue, and aiming at an end which consists in perfect and self-complete existence". Such a definition has been implied, and practically stated, in the discussion of the origin and aim of the State with which we were occupied in the last chapter. But the definition of the State may also be approached from another point of view. We may regard the State as a compound, and attempt to define its nature by determining the character of its component parts, and the scheme of composition by which they are united in a single whole. Instead of the teleological we may use the analytic method, resolving the State into its elements; and we may then employ a method of synthesis for reuniting the elements which we have previously distinguished and defined. The use of the analytic method, as we have seen, already appears at the beginning of the First Book of the *Politics*. There, however, Aristotle regards the village and the household as the constituent elements which go to form the State. In the Third Book, in which a definition of the State is attempted, it is the individual citizens who appear as its component parts; and the definition of the State is therefore preceded by a definition of the nature of a citizen. Beginning with this definition of citizenship, we may then rise to some conception of the scheme of composition by which the individual citizens are united in a single body: in other words, we may arrive at a theory of the nature of a constitution. Possessed of a view of the meaning of citizenship, and of a conception of the nature of a constitution, we shall understand the State sufficiently, to define its essence, and to classify its kinds.

In defining the term citizen, Aristotle pursues the aporetic method of suggesting, and then rejecting, a number of possible definitions, in order to arrive at a residuum of truth. Analysing the conception of citizenship into its constituent attributes or elements, he weighs each to determine which is the essential. Residence is an element of citizenship, but it is not an element essential to citizenship. The essential element of citizenship must be something, which every citizen possesses, and which no one else than a citizen can show; but foreigners may be residents as well as citizens. Participation in legal privilege is also an element; but this, again, is not peculiar, for foreigners may sue and be sued in the courts as well as citizens. What constitutes citizenship is neither residence nor privilege, but function: by that a citizen must be defined, and by that accordingly he is defined, as one who participates in the rights of judging and governing. This definition may be somewhat simplified, if we consider a distinction which may be drawn between two kinds of office. Some offices are held for a determinate period; and when that period has elapsed, they can only be held again (if they can be held again at all) after a fixed interval of time. Other offices, again, are held for an indeterminate period, like that of the judge (Aristotle is thinking of the Athenian "dicast," whose "office" was practically permanent), and that of the member of a deliberative assembly, such as the Athenian Ecclesia, which consisted of all genuine Athenians over twenty years of age. In the light of this distinction, a citizen may be defined as one who participates in those offices which are held for an indeterminate time; and this definition appears to Aristotle to be the one, which is applicable to the greatest number of citizens. But based as it is upon Athenian institutions, the definition is obviously democratic; and Aristotle confesses that it really applies to democracies alone.

Nature of citizenship

Though democratic in its scope, it was still true of Greece as a whole in Aristotle's time: "the size of the modern State," he says elsewhere, "would seem to make any other than a democratic State almost impossible". And hence it is not without justice that Aristotle bases his general view of citizenship upon the practice of democracy. There are, however, States of which this view is not true. Such States have assemblies consisting not of the whole people, but only of certain summoned members; and in these the judicature is not popular, but consists of small sectional bodies. These States, of which Sparta is an example, are of an oligarchical character, and for them a separate definition of citizenship is necessary. It is still true that in them any man is a citizen who shares in deliberative or judicial office, but it must be added that such office is not open to all, or held for an indeterminate time: it is confined to a few, and limited in duration. Having thus defined the citizen, we may now define, to a certain extent, the State. A State, we may say, is a body of men, sharing in deliberative and judicial office, and sufficient in number for a self-sufficient existence. That a share in the exercise of deliberative and judicial powers should be made the touchstone of the citizen is natural; for Aristotle regards these two functions as the essential functions of the State. Accordingly those who discharge them are the essential or integral parts of the State, and, as such, the only full and true citizens. Particularly is a share in the discharge of the deliberative function necessary to a citizen. The deliberative is "supreme over the constitution"; in it resides the sovereign authority, and in that authority the full citizen must share.

To Aristotle, therefore, citizenship means direct participation in the exercise of sovereignty. It does not mean, as it means to-day, the right to share in the election of the sovereign. Every citizen will, indeed, in Aristotle's conception, have a right to join in the election of the executive; but then the executive is not the sovereign; it is the servant of law, and its election is no great matter. To be a citizen is to be a direct part of the active sovereign; it is not merely, as it is with us, to be a part of the sovereign behind the scenes, who determines and controls the visible sovereign. The difference is due to the small extent of the city-state, which involved, as its inevitable

Citizenship primary

corollary, a system of primary government. The size of the modern State involves the presence of representative institutions; it involves a system of secondary government, in which the citizen shares in the deliberative indirectly, through the medium of his representative.[1] Nor is it only in the government of the State that the representative principle is applied to-day: it exists in our towns, and in still smaller units. In some of the Swiss cantons alone is a primary assembly to be found; and even here the *Landsgemeinde* merely votes on prepared resolutions at rare intervals, while the Athenian Ecclesia met almost every week, and could if necessary take the initiative itself. It may indeed be urged, that where the Referendum exists, as it does all over Switzerland, there is a direct participation of all the citizens in the deliberative function; but the difference between the submission to the body of the citizens of a measure which has already gone through the legislative, and origination by that body of its own measures, is very considerable. Much the same is true even of the Swiss Initiative; for though the people would here seem to originate their own measures, the body of representatives can generally thwart their proposals, and proposals are generally only started by cliques. The direct sovereignty of the body of the citizens still remains peculiarly Greek.

It is obvious that the number of citizens must tend to vary inversely with the extent of the rights (or duties) of citizenship. The wide extent which Greek conceptions gave to those rights involved a correspondingly narrow body of citizens. Where much is given, few can receive: where the power conferred is small, it can be lavished on many; and the history of Rome shows that the number of citizens only increased, as the rights of citizenship diminished. Democratic therefore as is Aristotle's conception of citizenship in appearance, it is, in reality, aristocratic. To participate in deliberative and judicial office requires both ability and leisure; and these are the gifts of some, but not of all. They are gifts, Aristotle believes, denied to the mechanic and the labourer, who, tied to life's bare necessities, have no leisure for counsels of perfection. Nor are these classes

Narrow circle of citizens

[1] The jury system may be said to be the representative principle applied to the judicature, corresponding to Parliament in the deliberative sphere.

merely disqualified by want of leisure: they are in a sense servile. They stand to the community, which they provide with its necessities, as the slave stands to his master. They are as it were the Sudra caste, on which the Brahmin must depend, but over which he must rule. In ancient times, Aristotle adds, the labourer and the mechanic were actually slaves or aliens; and most of them were still in that position in his own day. Their disfranchisement was therefore an historical fact[1] which he accepted with his usual conservatism, as he accepted slavery itself, and for which he found a philosophical justification, as he did for slavery. Accordingly the working classes sink, in his philosophy, into the "conditions" of a State of which they cannot be "parts". The view is repellent: it lowers the workers of a community into the community's slaves. But it was the general view of the Greeks, a view against which the only revolters were the Radicals, who revolted against everything—against slavery, against the social position of women, and against social conventions in general—and taught in opposition the natural equality of man. Of these Euripides is the exponent, and a famous passage of the *Orestes* introduces the yeoman, who tills his farm with his own hands and without slaves, as the only salvation of the land—shrewd, and ready to come to close quarters in discourse; pure, and of blameless life. But this half-English figure is contrary to Greek ideas: the Sudra rather than the yeoman is the true parallel for Greece.

Modern citizenship less intense, though more extensive

So far, Greek citizenship has been contrasted with modern as wider in the privileges it conferred, and consequently narrower in the number it admitted to those privileges. We have seen that it was connected with primary government, and that representative institutions and secondary government form the differentia of the modern State. To the Greek, citizenship was thus already a higher thing than it can be to-day; and what is true of the Greek is here also true of the Roman of Republican times. But the absence of any religious organisation, co-extensive with (or wider than) the State, still further

[1] But in a democracy labourers (θῆτες) were often citizens; and Aristotle's definition of citizenship, however democratic, is therefore more exclusive than the ordinary definition of democratic practice.

intensified the meaning and the width of citizenship. We are all nowadays Churchmen as well as citizens; and the claims of the Church may at times run counter to those of the State, and involve the Churchman in "passive resistance" to the State, while at all times a large province which belonged to the ancient State is now assigned to the Church. In that province is included the teaching of a positive morality, as well as that maintenance of religious observances (or "sacrifices") which Aristotle made part of the State's action; and man to-day looks to his Church for much, which the Greek received from the all-containing, all-sufficing State. Not only has our citizenship less content: even in the sphere which remains for it, it is liable to have its claims over-ridden by what claims to be a higher authority.

It would thus appear that Greek citizenship meant far more than membership of a modern State; but that, on the other hand, it had the defect of its quality. Citizenship which meant participation in sovereignty was confined to a leisured and capable class, which owed its leisure to the possession of slaves; and the producers of the wealth of the community were necessarily excluded from a share in its action, as deficient alike in leisure and political capacity. The decrease in the connotation of modern citizenship involves a corresponding increase in denotation: because it means less, it can be shared by many more. And on the principle, which Aristotle himself lays down, that the number of those who wish a State to continue must exceed the number of those who do not, it may be argued that the modern State is more stable than the Greek. Above all, it has a capacity for expansion which the Greek State never showed. Athenian citizenship could not be extended beyond Attica: a regular residence in or near Athens was indispensable for the discharge of civic duty. The judicial and deliberative functions of an Athenian citizen were never extended either to the colonies, which started a separate and independent political life of their own, with its own citizenship,[1] or to the subject cities, which continued a separate but dependent life, under

[1] The cleruchies must be excepted: they were garrisons of Athenian citizens in a subject State. The citizenship of a κληροῦχος was dormant; but it would become active on his return to Athens.

Citizen and "subject"

control of the mistress city—a life separate enough to give them a sense of individuality, and yet dependent enough to make them resent the suppression of that individuality. It was this want of any principle of cohesion for larger units than the city, which, as much as anything, proved the ruin of the Greek State. Federalism might have proved such a principle; but though there had been instances of federation before the time of Aristotle, they had been of a loose kind, and the "Federal Revival" first begins many years after his death, in the reconstitution upon a new basis of the Achæan League. Except through federation, which Aristotle never discusses, the expansion of the Greek city was thus impossible; and Aristotle could consequently regard the city as the final form of association. The modern State has no exacting conception of citizenship to bar its expansion; but even in the modern State expansion has come not through the extension of citizen rights to a wider sphere, but through the widening of the sphere of *allegiance* to a sovereign.[1] The idea of a personal tie to a personal monarch has served to bind, not only conquered populations to their conqueror, but also distant colonists to their mother country.[2] It is an idea essentially feudal, as the word allegiance of itself indicates: it is the idea which underlies the British Empire today. Common allegiance to the Crown, not common citizenship issuing in the election of a common parliament, is the basis on which it rests. This conception of allegiance, over and above citizenship, is still, in most countries, a differentia of the modern from the ancient State. It supplies a new political motive, that of loyalty, which is for many, even in a constitutional monarchy, the one motive of political action. It is the motive of sentiment; and in a monarchy, "the sentiment of honour in the subject often takes the place of the political virtue of the citizen as the inspirer of the noblest actions".[3] In summary,

[1] Rome was able to expand, even with the Greek conception of citizenship; but her expansion ultimately involved the person of an emperor for its expression.

[2] Allegiance, defined by Coke as "a true and faithful obedience of the subject due to his sovereign," was held by the judges in Calvin's case (1608) to be limited to no spot—*nullis finibus premitur*. Unlimited in space, it was also held to be indefeasible in point of time—*nemo potest exuere patriam*. But this doctrine has been modified by recent legislation, especially the Naturalisation Act of 1870.

[3] Montesquieu, *Esprit des Lois*, book iii., c. vi.

therefore, it may be said that the idea of citizenship has been altered since the time of Aristotle, not only by the development of representative institutions and the growth of a separate religious organisation, but also by the gift which feudalism gave (but which the Roman Empire had already anticipated) of a personal loyalty to the head of the State.[1]

We must now return from this contrast of modern conceptions of citizenship with those of Aristotle, to Aristotle's own further development of the subject of citizenship. We have as yet seen citizenship defined by function: he is a citizen, we have been told, who does civic work. There is, however, a rival definition, which leaves function and defines by birth, following the ordinary practice of actual politics. But to define a citizenship as a man born of citizen parents is not to define, but only to push the *definiendum* a stage further back. What made the parents citizens? Gorgias had answered this question by a pun. Greek magistrates were in many places called "makers," δημιουργοί; and, taking advantage of this name, he had said, that as mortar-makers made mortar, so the Larissæan "makers" made citizens of Larissa. But to explain who made a citizen is not to explain what a citizen is, any more than one explains mortar by saying that it is what the mortar-maker makes. Definition must always be by final cause: "all things are defined by their function and capacity". An interesting question does indeed arise with regard to the making of citizens: are the citizens newly admitted after a revolution to be regarded as true citizens? But in discussing such a question we enter upon new ground. We leave the problem of defining what a citizen is, to determine whether certain men (who, as discharging the functions of citizens, should certainly, in Aristotle's opinion, be called citizens) have or have not properly acquired that title. When Cleisthenes, after the revolution which expelled the tyrant Hippias, enrolled in the tribes,

Creation of citizens

[1] It may be added that under the Roman Empire the idea of a citizen as a member of a free self-governing community gave way to the conception that citizenship meant: (1) a personal status and private rights guaranteed by law; (2) membership of a local *municipium* and its government. This conception has largely entered into modern citizenship, which means a personal status and a local membership; but an English citizen has political rights, like the franchise, which bring him nearer to the Greek πολίτης than to the *civis Romanus* of the empire. *Cf.* Matheson, *Intern. Journ. Eth.*, viii., 22.

as full citizens, both aliens and slaves, was his action altogether valid? Aristotle assumes that if the action of Cleisthenes was the action of the State, it was valid: the only doubt touches the point, whether it *was* the action of the State, or merely that of a faction. Had the Athenian State lost its *identity* and disappeared, and was its place taken by a mere party? No doubt Cleisthenes' opponents would in this particular case have answered in the affirmative. But Aristotle will only be satisfied by a discussion of the general question—What constitutes the identity of the State? In virtue of what feature can a State be pronounced the same to-day as it was a year ago, whatever other feature may have altered?

The Scheme of Composition

§ 2. We have seen the State defined as a compound of parts, a union of citizens participating in judicial and deliberative office. In what ways are these parts united together? Which of the ways in which they are united is essential to the identity of the compound? Here again, as in the determination of the nature of the citizen, or the discovery of the end of the State, Aristotle proceeds aporetically, and analysing the unity of the State into its several elements considers each in turn. One element in the union of the citizens who form a State is space; another is race. But it is not continued residence within the same walls which constitutes the identity of a State: indeed, there may be residence within the same walls, and yet no city at all. The Peloponnese might be surrounded by a single wall: Babylon actually was; but neither of them could ever be a State in the Greek sense. They were both far too large for that primary government which was essential to the city-state. Nor again, is permanence of race necessary to the State's identity. The same stock may continue to reside within the same walls, and yet the State may not be the same State. For it is really a third[1] factor altogether, the permanence of which means the permanence of the State. The nature of this factor at once appears, if we consider other things, which like the State are compounds

The identity of State resides in the constitution

[1] Aristotle omits to consider other factors which may constitute the unity of the State—*e.g.* unity of religion, as in a Theocracy. But such a factor would hardly occur to a Greek.

—if we consider, for instance, a chorus or a piece of music. Retain the same individual members of a chorus, the same separate notes of a musical composition, but alter the scheme by which they are joined—and the identity of the chorus or composition will utterly disappear. The "form" is everything. Any compound varies with the scheme in which its parts are arranged: every compound remains the same, as long as the scheme of its composition remains the same. Accordingly the State, as a compound, varies as its *constitution* varies. For that is its scheme: that is the way in which the citizens, who form the parts of the State, are arranged in relation one to another. And since every citizen is, as we have seen, possessed of office, the constitution may be defined as an arrangement of the offices of the State, determining which of its members shall hold the different offices, and especially which of them shall hold the highest office.

The conclusion to which we have thus come is most important. It is not, indeed, a very clear solution of the questions which it was meant to solve—when and under which circumstances the acts of a revolutionary government are to be counted valid. One may perhaps argue, that Cleisthenes had made Athens a new State, by rearranging the offices and giving her a new constitution, and that accordingly the new citizens he made were properly citizens of *that* State, so long as it endured. To those who urged that it was not the State of Athens, but the democratical party, which had made this charge, Aristotle might answer—"No: the State of Athens has altered its identity by altering its constitution, and acting as a new democratical State it has made this new body of citizens". He might, that is to say, deny the antithesis between the State and a party, and identify the State with the party whose ascendency determines the constitution. But the practical application of his views of the identity of the State is, as he says himself, another matter. The essential fact is the general conception, that the identity of a State depends on the identity of its constitution. For it follows as a logical conclusion, that every member of an oligarchy will regard his State, when a democratical revolution has taken place, as a new and alien State; and that he will, if necessary, for the sake of the old State which is gone, bear arms against the new.

It will not be treason to do so: he may very possibly have no other alternative, if he wishes to live in the State of his birth. For the revolution will probably have sent him into exile in some other State, oligarchically governed, and as such more nearly akin to his own true State than the new State which has arisen within its walls. He will consequently aid that other State in any war against the new State, whose usurpation has sent him into exile. It might even be said—paradoxically, it is true—that the real treachery of the member of an oligarchy would be loyally to accept the government of a democracy. This is the political morality of Greece, as it was the political morality of Florence and the other city-states of mediæval Italy.

Nature of constitution a vital thing

This identification of the State with the constitution is one which naturally follows upon Aristotle's views of the meaning of citizenship. If the State consists of citizens, and citizens only, and if every citizen is an office-holder, then the constitution, which determines the holding of office, must determine the State. For it determines the character of the citizen body, which is the State; it makes that body democratically large, or oligarchically small; and within the body (of whatsoever size it may be) it determines the position which each member is to take. The nature of the constitution must therefore be the vital thing to men whose leisure has set them free for a life entirely devoted to politics, and whose position in that life, higher or lower, is determined by the constitution. Around the constitution a battle must rage—a battle for life or death. According as the constitution is decided, so is it decided for each man whether or no he shall share in the political life which is the one life he cares to live, or at the very least, whether he shall share fully and deeply, or unsatisfactorily and incompletely. The party life of modern times has far less zest than struggles such as these. Our parties are divided by principles, half real, half imaginary, in which some of us are interested, and many of us are not. The struggle between the two is to decide whether the leaders of one party or the other—in either case an infinitesimally small proportion of the whole party—shall have the offices through which those principles may be realised. The division of parties does not coincide with any division of classes. All classes are gathered on both sides, and the leaders of both are generally men of the same high birth, the same wealth, the same social and intellectual interests. Greek political life is different at every point. There the division between the oligarchs and the democrats who fought round the constitution was a division of classes: the venom of a social war entered into political contests, and sometimes inflamed them to an almost incredible frenzy.[1] There was no lukewarm difference about principles, no mere struggle to determine which of the rival leaders should lead: there was bitter war to determine the constitution, and the issue at stake was whether the rank and file should participate in its offices, or a few should monopolise them all. Only too often there was a still further issue; should the poor, if they had won office in the strife, use its powers to pillage the rich, or should the rich, if the victory had been theirs, grind the faces of the poor by the authority which they had won? To the Greek, therefore, the constitution is itself the battle-ground: on that battle-ground two classes meet in social war: victory for either is a means of pursuing its own social interests by the oppression of the other. With us, the constitution is lifted above strife: two parties, each of the same social standing, contend for the power of working the constitution through their leaders in the interest of certain principles; and because these different principles only represent different views of the general welfare, one may be confident that the victory of either party will result in nothing, but an honest attempt to pursue the good of both—as that good is conceived by the victor.[2]

The constitution thus discussed in its relation to the State, the way seems clear for a classification of States according to their constitutions. But something more must first be said of the meaning of the term constitution. It has been described as the plan on which the city is arranged; and the "arrangement" of the offices has been particularly discussed. But the

[1] As at Argos or Corcyra, in Thucydides' description (iii., 80-82).

[2] The view here suggested, that modern parties are not sectional but national, not horizontal according to the stratification of classes, but vertical according to a cleavage of principles which bisects each class, is perhaps only true of England, and even there not entirely true. Abroad, Clericals or Social Democrats seem intent on a sectional interest; and while it is profoundly to be hoped that the English Labour party will not prove "horizontal" in practice, the language of some of its leaders points in that direction.

scheme of composition of the units of a State goes far beyond determining their hierarchy. That scheme determines, or perhaps more correctly it *is*, the end in the pursuit of which the units are bound together as a composite whole. Similarly, it may be suggested, the scheme of composition of a piece of music is not the mere arrangement of notes, but the motive of the whole composition. The constitution may therefore be more fully defined as an arrangement of the offices of a State, determining their distribution, the residence of sovereignty, *and the end of political association* (1289 a 15). That end is really the primary concern of the constitution: it is the end, or the degree of contribution to that end, which determines the distribution of office. A constitution is essentially a determination or conception of the end at which a political community aims. It is the expression of the kind of life which that community sets before itself as its ideal; and it is accordingly described as the manner of life of a State (1295 a 40). Different constitutions involve different manners of life: "pursuing their ideals in different ways, and by different means, States arrive at different manners of life and different constitutions" (1328 a 41). Every constitution involves a corresponding type of character in its citizens. In a democracy, said Plato, the slaves are less obedient, and the very dogs less in hand. Pericles more kindly told the Athenians that as their political life was informed by the spirit of liberty, so their social life was distinguished by a freedom which suspicion or scandal never attacked. The later books of the *Republic* sketch the different types of character which correspond to different constitutions, describing, for instance, as we have seen, how democracy issues in a type of man to whom all desires are of *equal* strength, and who turns his hand equally to all manner of occupations. Aristotle tells us that an oligarchy, which makes wealth the qualification for office, and in this way enables the most sacred of trusts to be bought as it were with money, tends to encourage a materialistic and money-loving spirit in the whole State (1273 a 38 *sq.*). This conception is one not peculiar to the philosophers, but common among all Greeks. Greek States were, as a matter of fact, divided from one another by broad differences of character; the Stoical Spartan, the versatile Athenian, the "piggish" Bœotian, the

The constitution as determining the end of the State

mercantile Corinthian, were all recognised types. Pericles contrasted, at the opening of the Peloponnesian war, the Athenian with the Spartan ; and differences of dress itself brought home this contrast to every eye. It was partly because the Greek communities were so small, that they could develop such distinct idiosyncrasies, and impress that idiosyncrasy so firmly upon each individual member. A local opinion might easily arise, in one of those small groups, to define the etiquette of behaviour and the proper " tone " of action. An approved type of character would naturally come to be imagined, to which all would instinctively conform themselves. In a small society, where the authorities were expected, as Aristotle says, to know every man personally, and men met one another every day, the constant supervision of rulers possessed of such personal knowledge would enforce what instinct had already suggested ; and a distinct dress, a distinct method of behaviour, a distinct line of action would become the rule. This rule was expressed in law, not only in written law, but, as Thucydides says, in that unwritten law whose contravention yet brings with it disgrace. These distinct types of character, therefore, depended for their permanence upon the magistrates and upon the law—in a word, upon the constitution, which determined the magistrates, and which also, as we shall see, determined the laws; for laws are relative to the constitution, and different constitutions have their corresponding laws. Spartan character is not the outcome of Spartan blood, in the way in which, we generally feel, English character is the outcome of English blood: it is due to the Spartan constitution. Should that constitution alter, Spartan character will alter, although Spartan blood is still the same; while the English constitution might alter again and again, and yet the English character remain unchanged. Once more we see that the constitution was far more vitally important to the Greek than it is to us. Not only did it decide whether or no he should share in the direct sovereignty of his State: it determined the daily life he should live; it gave him his manners and morals. One can understand that an aristocrat would not willingly see his whole scheme of life shaken to the ground by a democratic revolution, and that, if such a revolution came, he would feel strange and isolated in the new democratic State.

From this consideration of the meaning of the term constitution we have gained our final definition of the State, and much besides that will be of service in the classification of States. The State may now be defined as a compound of citizens sharing in judicial and deliberative office, and united by a constitution which both determines their places in the compound and supplies the motive of all their action. Before, however, we proceed to the classification of States, one more consideration remains; and that concerns the relation of the constitution to the Government. We have seen that the identity of a State resides in its constitution: we have yet to see that the constitution is identical with the Government.[1] This is twice affirmed by Aristotle in the third book of the *Politics.* A constitution is an arrangement of offices, and especially of the supreme office, or government; and the government, whether it be that of the few or the many, is the constitution. In other words, the constitution being *par excellence* a determination of the residence of the supreme authority, one may say, *convertendo,* that the residence of the supreme authority determines the nature of the constitution. In a democracy the people is the supreme authority or government: in an oligarchy the rich form the government. The supreme authorities are different; and *therefore* we regard the constitutions as different—which shows that we believe the constitution to vary with the government.

Constitution and government

The Classification of States

§ 3. We may now proceed to the classification of States according to their different constitutions or governments. Two standards suggest themselves as a result of what has been said. The constitution being a determination of the end of a political community, and the end or final cause being the essence of definition and classification, we shall naturally classify States by the end at which they aim. Again, the constitution being a determination of the government, with which indeed it is identical, we shall also classify States by the differences which appear in the spirit of their governments. These are the two standards which Aristotle uses, and by the use of which he arrives at a classification almost exactly similar to that of Plato

Standards of classification—end of State, and spirit of government

[1] πόλις = πολιτεία = πολίτευμα : State = constitution = government.

in the *Politicus*. It must, however, be admitted in justice to Aristotle, that if his results are the same, his method is different from that of Plato. Plato's standard of classification is respect for law; and Aristotle is original in his use of a teleological standard, and of the criterion furnished by the differences between governments in the spirit of their rule, though the hint for this last criterion is certainly to be found in the *Republic*.[1]

Of the standard which is furnished by considerations of the end of the State little need here be said. There is one true end, which, and which alone, the State as a moral community can pursue; and that is a life of virtue. Every State that walks by this end is a *normal* and proper State: every State that pursues other aims is a *perversion* from the normal State. A good constitution differs from a bad constitution, we are told in the *Ethics* (1103 b 6), because the legislator of the one endeavours by habituation to make his fellow-citizens virtuous, and the legislator of the other fails to accomplish this end. From the *Politics* it would appear that the bad constitution fails even to attempt its accomplishment. Democracies pursue only freedom: oligarchies pursue only wealth; and both of these would appear to be utter perversions. It must, however, be admitted, that such perversions are not absolute. Perverted constitutions do not erect into their end something which has no concern whatsoever with the true end of the State. What they do is to make something which is *subsidiary* to the true end into their sole and *principal* aim. We have seen that mere life is one of the subordinate aims of the State, and that one of its endeavours is therefore the accumulation of wealth, which, however, is only meant to serve as an instrument for moral ends. But it is easy to do what an oligarchy does, and to stop short at the accumulation of wealth, without advancing to the moral life for which it is meant. An oligarchy is therefore a falling-short, rather than a backsliding.[2] It is an imperfect development rather than a thing degraded from perfection. The soul of goodness which lives in evil things is so far present in oligarchy that it aims at

[1] Plato implies a distinction between States which have for their rulers true artists, ruling in a spirit of unselfishness for their subjects' betterment, and States which are selfishly governed by "wolfish" rulers.

[2] An ἔλλειψις rather than a παρέκβασις, though it goes by the latter name.

something at which every true State aims, though it certainly fails to aim at everything at which a true State ought to aim. And hence it is never wholly rejected by Aristotle: on the contrary, he suggests means by which it may be improved and preserved; and he contemplates, as almost an ideal constitution, something which is really a mixture of two perversions.

The same distinction between normal and perverted States may also be drawn, if we consider the different tempers in which governments may act; but from this point of view the distinction is more profound, and reconciliation is less possible. States naturally fall into two kinds, according as governments act for their own interests, or for those of the community. In every normal State the government must necessarily be directed to the common welfare. It is of the very nature of the State as an association of equals that this should be so. And the analogy of the arts, which Plato (true to Socrates' views of the art of government) had already employed in the *Republic*, equally proves that governors should govern in the interest of the subjects of their government. Every doctor, and every trainer, makes the bodily health of his patient the aim and object of his skill; nor should it be otherwise with the ruler. His wisdom should also be directed to the welfare of his subjects, though there is this difference between him and the trainer, that as a member of the community, he must always consider his own welfare, along with that of the rest, while the trainer will only very occasionally merge himself with his class, and regard his own health. Ideally, therefore, those who practise the art of government must needs be unselfish, and the normal State must necessarily be one which is unselfishly governed; nor can that State be other than perverted, in which this is not the case. Whether this new standard coincides in its results with the previous standard of end, Aristotle does not inquire. But it is possible to imagine a State which is perverted in its end, and yet normal and correct in the sense that its government works disinterestedly for the whole community. A government given over to the mercantile system, and pursuing wealth as the end of the State, may yet be acting with entire unselfishness. Aristotle seems to assume that there will never be such a cross-division; that where wealth is pursued, there selfishness reigns;

that a society which is a moral society is linked together in the pursuit of a common good of which its rulers are the unselfish servants, while a society which is an economic society is split asunder by the selfish endeavour of its rulers to secure for themselves the good things of this life. Whatever may be the truth in respect of modern politics, it would seem as if, in the Greek city, the neutral and selfless character which should distinguish a government was so imperfectly attained, and so easily abandoned, that, upon any other than a purely moral basis of the State, selfishness was inevitable. There is safety in size; and the very minuteness of the city-state, while it gave politics their intensity, also made possible their corruption, when the saving principle of an ethical aim was once abandoned. Aristotle, indeed, regards the tendency to corruption less as an inherent vice, and more as a fall from original purity. Once upon a time, he thinks, the ruler, as by nature he was intended to do, ruled for the benefit of all his subjects. He regarded his office as a duty, from which he would be relieved at the end of his term, and which others would then take upon themselves in their order. But Greece had fallen upon degenerate days; and in Aristotle's time the profit to be made from public property and from the use of official powers [1] led every ruler to desire perpetual rule. The process which Aristotle here describes was probably the natural result of an increased economic activity, which had enriched the State, and added new spheres of influence to its control; and, both from the new riches and from the new spheres of control, new opportunities were offered to the selfishness of a ruler, who was willing either to peculate or, still better, to be bribed into using his official powers in a particular interest. The city fell into corruption; the aggrandisement of the ruler was answered by the hatred of the ruled; and the horrors of social war threatened the end of Greece.

Constitutions, we therefore find, fall into two main divisions

[1] Aristotle's meaning may perhaps be illustrated from the municipal life of the United States. "Profit from public property" is "boodle"—"the sale of public rights and privileges to financiers": the "use of official powers" is "graft"—"the abuse of the police system in levying blackmail on the saloons". The system of boodle, one is told, has been a profitable business for the politician. "A new member going to the city hall in a street car gave the conductor his last nickel. The next day he was able to deposit 5,000 dollars in a savings bank" (Sidney Low, in the *Standard*, 6th Jan., 1905).

—the "normal" kind in which the government is unselfish, because it pursues a moral purpose, and the "perversion," in which the government is corrupt, because it fails to pursue such an aim. These two divisions differ with a difference of kind: they differ with a difference so great, that the first group of constitutions may be described as prior, and the second as posterior. As the whole is prior to its parts, because the understanding of the parts presupposes the whole, so is the normal prior to the abnormal, because the understanding of the abnormal presupposes the normal as a standard. Within each of these two divisions—the normal and prior, the abnormal and posterior—Aristotle next proceeds to make a triple subdivision. The constitution, we have seen, is identical with the government; and in subdividing the two great types of constitutions, Aristotle naturally starts from the government. In all constitutions of the normal type, the governments agree in unselfishness: in what respect then do they differ, and where can we find a ground of subdivision? The principle of number naturally offers itself: the governments differ in the number of their members, and according as the one, the few, or the many compose the ruling body. The normal type of constitutions thus contains within itself three species—Monarchy, Aristocracy, and Polity. Monarchy and aristocracy explain themselves: the term Polity (πολιτεία or constitution) is the generic term applied particularly to one species, because that species has no name of its own. Polity accordingly means that subdivision of the normal type of constitution which is characterised by the rule of the many: it is the rule of the many for the common good: it is democracy turned unselfish, and translated, in consequence, to a higher sphere. The same subdivision according to number also applies to the abnormal and perverted type of constitution. That type equally contains within itself three species, according as the selfish government consists of one, or few, or many members. These three species are tyranny, oligarchy, and democracy. The first aims at the selfish interest of a single individual; the second at that of the wealthier classes; the third at that of the poor.[1]

Two main types of constitutions: their subdivision

[1] Democracy, it would thus appear, does not mean for Aristotle the government of the people by the people for the people: it means the government of a people by the poor and for the poor. *Cf. infra*, pp. 460-61.

But this numerical subdivision is no sooner established than it is overturned. It had been adopted by Aristotle from ordinary usage: with that respect for the *consensus mundi*, which distinguishes his practical philosophy, he had made it a basis of his own classification of States. But, according to his regular method, he now applies to the data of popular opinion both the solvent of "difficulties" which arise from that opinion, and the test of his own metaphysical principles, in order to elicit the meaning, or correct the errors, which it contains. The very definition of oligarchy and democracy, which has just been given, suggests of itself a difficulty. It is *not* the number, but the social class of the governing body, which has been made to constitute the differentia of these constitutions: the rule of the *wealthy*, the rule of the *poor*, have been the phrases used. And the difficulty which arises is consequently this—shall numbers, or social class, serve for criterion? It is true that the wealthy are generally few, and the poor are many—that the number and the class generally coincide; but it is possible that such may not be the case. The wealthy may be many, or the poor few; and shall we, in such a case as the rule of the many wealthy presents, prefer to speak of democracy in view of the numbers, or of oligarchy in view of the class? Aristotle answers in favour of the use of class as the criterion of classification. It is the rule of the wealthy which makes an oligarchy. Class distinctions are the *cause* of political distinctions, while numerical distinctions are merely symptoms, or, at best, secondary attributes following upon the primary and vital distinction of class. This teaching is not, however, extended beyond democracy and oligarchy: the previous use of number is not systematically replaced by the new criterion of class. But from hints elsewhere given we may learn, that what makes aristocracy is the rule of a class distinguished by inherited excellence, and that the polity is constituted by the rule of the middle class.

Standard of subdivision—social class

There are times when this classification according to the ruling class is abandoned for what is really the same classification from another point of view. Occasionally one State is regarded as differing from another according to the principle by which it awards its offices. To one State that principle is wealth; to another it is virtue; to another it is merely free birth; and hence, we are told, spring oligarchy, aristocracy and democracy. But it is obvious, that as is the principle of award, so is the ruling class to which office is awarded; and if the principle be wealth, the ruling class will be the wealthy, while, if it be free birth, the ruling class will be the poor who form the majority of the free-born. We therefore attain the same classification; but we have pushed our standard a remove further back, and classified rather by the principle which distributes, than by the class which receives, the offices of the State. We have borrowed in fact the principle of distributive justice as the standard of classification. By the use of this principle of distributive justice we are able, not only to classify constitutions, but also to classify them in order of merit. Two main kinds have, indeed, already been differentiated, of which one is the higher, and the other the lower; but we can go further. We can discover which is the highest of the high, and the lowest of the low, in virtue of the different principles which different forms exhibit. In this way we discover monarchy to be the first of constitutions, because its principle of distribution is not merely virtue (*that* is the principle of all good constitutions), but the supreme virtue which can only be found in one solitary individual. Aristocracy follows next, taking as it does a high type of virtue for its principle; and polity comes last, with its more mediocre and simply military virtue—for the virtue to which many men can attain will never be the whole of virtue, or even a fine side of virtue, but at best the virtue which is shown in the steadfast courage of a civic militia under arms. Turning to perverted constitutions, we find tyranny set lowest of the low, on the maxim "*corruptio optimi pessima*"; for tyranny is a corruption of monarchy, and monarchy is the best of constitutions. Oligarchy, as it is the corruption of the second best, is also the second worst; while democracy, the corruption of the least good, must needs also be the least bad. The same conclusion appears, if we regard these constitutions in a less negative light, and as exhibiting positive principles of their own. The principle of oligarchy is wealth: the principle of democracy free birth. As free birth is a wider and better principle than wealth, and wealth in its turn is wider and higher than mere force and fraud (which alone constitute the tyrant's claim to authority), so must democracy excel oligarchy, and oligarchy excel tyranny. And thus we finally come on the following classification.

Normal constitutions, where the right end is pursued, and the government is unselfish.	Monarchy: principle, supreme virtue. Aristocracy: principle, culture and high virtue; social class, the cultured and virtuous. Polity: principle, a military and mediocre virtue; social class, the middle.
Perverted constitutions, which pursue wrong ends, and are all distinguished by the selfishness of the government.	Democracy: principle, free birth; social class, the poor. Oligarchy: principle, wealth; social class, the wealthy. Tyranny: principle, force and deceit.

Classification in later books of *Politics*

In another part of the *Politics*[1] the differentiation of constitutions according to the ruling class recurs, from a somewhat different point of view. Aristotle is here concerned to prove, that the political reformer must by no means limit his attention to an ideal constitution, if he wishes to succeed: he must be alive to the existence of the various constitutions of actual life, whose diversity will condition his work; and he must beware of thinking that oligarchy and democracy are the only actual forms which his reforming activity will find ready to hand. They are by no means the only actual forms of constitution. Constitutions vary, according as the part of the State which is predominant varies; and there may be as many various forms in actual existence as there are parts, or, in other words, classes of the State. Indeed there may be still more; for the different classes may be combined in different ways, and every different combination of classes makes a new form of constitution. The different classes which form a State are the upper classes (*οἱ γνώριμοι*), the middle classes, and the poor. Of these the upper and the lower classes fall into various groups: among the latter there are farmers, tradesmen, and craftsmen (not to mention labourers), while the former is divided naturally into three sections, distinguished respectively by the marks of birth, wealth and virtue. If we consider these various classes, and their groups, and the number of possible combinations of *both*, it is obvious

[1] *Pol.*, vi. (iv.), c. iii.-iv. This passage is probably not co-ordinated with its context, and it contains two uncorrelated accounts of the same thing—the different parts of the State, and their influence on differences of constitution—but it seems genuine.

that we must assume a number of constitutions. This in itself is an argument against the view (which seems to have been current in Aristotle's time), that there were two main constitutions, one in which the upper classes predominated, and one in which the poor were supreme—a view which made oligarchy and democracy the only two constitutions, subsuming aristocracy under the former, and the "polity" under the latter.[1] But not only does such a view neglect the number of constitutions which actual life presents: considered as a division of constitutions into two great types, and as that only, it seems to Aristotle superficial, and inferior to the distinction of normal and perverted States which he himself had made. For when oligarchy is made wide enough to include aristocracy, and democracy to include polity, this is only done by making mere number the determinant (and number was a principle which was rejected before), and by neglecting those fundamental qualitative differences between polity and democracy, oligarchy and aristocracy, which appear in the end they pursue, and the spirit of their pursuit.

An alternative treatment of this same question still survives in the *Politics*, side by side with the treatment which has just been sketched. Constitutions vary, we are again told, according to the predominance of different parts, or of different combinations of parts; but a new account of the parts is given, which differs considerably from the previous account. Instead of emphasising the different *social* groups, as distinguished by different *social characteristics*, Aristotle now considers the different *political* parts of the State, as distinguished by different *political functions*. Instead of two main groups, each with its subdivisions, there emerge some nine parts of the State: the farmer, the craftsman, the tradesman, the day-labourer (the three first of which before formed subdivisions of the poorer classes); the soldier, the judge, the man of means, who contributes with his wealth to the working of the State, and the members of the executive and the deliberative organs. There

[1] Kingship and tyranny are here disregarded, partly because Aristotle had himself discussed them before, partly perhaps because the supporters of the view here enunciated left them out of account, as not entering into the practical politics of their day.

seems to be here a certain confusion of the organs of government with the classes of society; and when this classification apparently comes to be used (c. xiv.), it is only the difference of the organs of government which is regarded as creating differences of constitution. Starting from the principle that there are three parts of the State to be regarded, the judicial, the deliberative, and the executive organs (in the latter of which the military is perhaps included), Aristotle lays it down that constitutions vary according as these organs vary in their structure and relation. But this obviously introduces a new principle: instead of asking what class governs, irrespective of the structure and allocation of the functions of government, Aristotle now concentrates his attention upon these functions. The functions of government are not, however, discussed without regard to the different classes of the State: on the contrary, their allocation inevitably raises the question of the classes to which they are to be assigned. None the less, new considerations do emerge: the functions differ (and with them the constitutions) not merely in their allocation to different classes, but also in themselves, according as they cover more or less ground, and are more or less subdivided. Different deliberative organs may have very different provinces; while the executive may be either united or subdivided. But it is the deliberative which is the key: it is the sovereign determinant of the constitution, as its powers of auditing and electing the magistrates are the highest powers in the State. Accordingly it is the extent of the powers of the deliberative, the allocation of those powers, their concentration in one body or dispersion in several, which, from the new point of view here raised by Aristotle, must form the criterion of every constitution. No new classification upon this basis is attempted; and we are not told whether any modification of the old classification by social class would be introduced if it were. It would obviously have supplied a new line of division, which might have cut across the old line: for instance, a democracy like Athens, where the province of the deliberative was large, and the executive was weak, would have had to be contrasted with any type of democracy similar to that of modern Switzerland, which left power to its executive, and limited the scope of the deliberative. Just in the same way England and

Classification according to distribution of functions

the United States, while commonly classed together as democracies, must nevertheless be distinguished when we look to the functions of government. In the former all functions are concentrated in the Cabinet; in the latter they are divided between President and Congress. Yet, in spite of this distinction, we should probably say that the two constitutions were fundamentally of the same order, because in both the ultimate sovereignty rests with the people, or, as Aristotle would say, the sovereign function of deliberation (which includes the election of the government) is allotted to the poorer classes. We should find the ultimate criterion in the class to which political power is given; and in this we should agree with Aristotle. Other points of view may suggest other lines of classification; but this is the ultimate classification. Tell me the class which is predominant, one might say, and I will tell you the constitution.

We shall find still further points of view suggested, when we come to discuss Aristotle's detailed treatment of oligarchy and democracy. Respect for law there becomes a criterion; and democracy is distinguished from democracy, oligarchy from oligarchy, according as it does, or does not, exhibit this respect. Differences in the character of the population, we learn, have a great effect in determining constitutions: a farmer democracy is not like a democracy of sailors. But we have now sufficiently discussed the main lines of Aristotle's treatment of the problem of classification; and we may ask ourselves what is its value, how far it is valid to-day, and to what extent it was new in Aristotle's own time. Whatever defects the Aristotelian classification may have, it cannot be said to be merely numerical. "That very obvious classification," which makes "States differ . . . according to the number of persons which compose the government," does *not* "come down to us from Aristotle".[1] On the contrary Aristotle definitely rejected a merely numerical classification, because it made a merely external feature its criterion. Instead of dividing States by the number of their rulers, Aristotle divides them on a moral basis, according to their ends and the spirit of their governments, and then subdivides them according to the social class which holds office, or the principle on which office is awarded. We do not distinguish States to-day on moral grounds,

Modern value of Aristotle's scheme

[1] Seeley, *Introduction to Political Science*, p. 45.

because the moral meaning of the State is not so clear to us as it was to Aristotle. Yet the category of end is still employed to classify States, though without Aristotle's clear distinction between moral and non-moral ends, whenever States are classed as war-states or culture-states, law-states or commerce-states. And we distinguish between free countries, where the common weal is pursued by the government, and despotically governed countries, where the interest of the ruler predominates, in a way somewhat analogous to Aristotle's distinction between "constitutional" government, which rules in an unselfish spirit for the good of its subjects, and "despotic" government, which consults in a selfish spirit the good of the ruler. Nor when it comes to subdivision according to social class, does our practice disagree with that of Aristotle. We generally speak of the English constitution as an aristocracy in the eighteenth century, because the landed interest controlled the House of Commons, and through the House of Commons the country: we date the beginning of a moderate democracy from the admission of the middle classes to the franchise in 1832, and of a more Radical democracy from the admission of the poorer classes towards the end of the nineteenth century. On the other hand, Aristotle's classification is certainly in some respects defective, even as applied to his own day, and still more as applied to ours. His formal scheme leaves little room for the mixed constitution which, nevertheless, he himself afterwards discusses. Federations existed in his own day, but he has no place for federation. The effect which the structure of the government may have in differentiating constitutions is suggested rather than explained. And if we attempt to apply his scheme to modern politics, we are confronted by factors which make our task difficult. One is the disappearance of the city and the appearance of the nation. This involves a new differentia between States which had not occurred to Aristotle. In a nation there is local as well as central government: in the city there was only one government. Nation differs from nation in the demarcation of the spheres of local and central government: England has much local government; France has by comparison little. Aristotle's suggested differentiation of States according to the structure of their government has to be applied, and extended, in order to meet this new fact. Again, in a nation there are generally representative institutions; and we have to distinguish States in which the representative body controls the government, and the executive is responsible, from States in which this is not the case. Another and perhaps equally serious factor is the amount of unreality and convention which exists in the modern State. The English convention assigns all authority to the Crown: it used to be said that facts assigned real authority to Parliament. But it seems to-day[1] that even this is a convention, and that the real authority resides with the Cabinet. And yet behind the Cabinet there is the electorate. But by which shall we classify—Crown, Parliament, Cabinet, or electorate? Here there is such simple issue as confronted Aristotle; and the answer is not easy. It has just been suggested, that the electorate is the determinant of the constitution. But what if the electorate only chooses within a charmed oligarchical circle, as in England it seems (or till of late seemed) to do? Is the government democratical, because the electorate is large, or is it oligarchical, because the eligible are few? One is almost driven to say that there is no absolute standard of classification; and that England can only be classified according to several standards as a State with a large measure of local government, and with a central government conventionally composed of King and Parliament, but really of an oligarchical Cabinet constituted by a democratic electorate; while, from still another point of view, this constitution must be regarded as unwritten and flexible, in contrast with written and rigid constitutions. But then, England is not really England: she is part of a State called the United Kingdom, which as contrasted with federal governments we must call a unitary State. And yet again the United Kingdom is a member of a system often called an Empire, which is neither a federation nor a unitary State. There are thus, it would appear, far too many factors to be reduced to any one scheme. But it is this very complexity which, while it makes Aristotle's classification inapplicable, also makes it valuable. The simplicity of his material made a scientific attempt at classification possible; and that attempt must always remain an example and a model, though not an authority.

It remains to ask how far Aristotle was indebted to Plato

[1] This was written in 1905.

for the scheme of classification which appears in the *Politics*.[1]

Aristotle and Plato

Excluding the constitution, which stands by itself, "as it were a god," we saw that Plato distinguished two main types of constitution in the *Politicus*, by the criterion of observance or non-observance of the law; and within each of these types we saw three subdivisions made by the principle of number. Further, the classified States were arranged in an order of merit, according to which monarchy was the best of the good States, and tyranny the worst of the bad; while good democracy was the worst of the good, and bad democracy the best of the bad. Aristotle is obviously indebted to Plato for this scheme; and yet his own scheme is very different. His two main types are distinguished not by the degree of the observance of the law which they exhibit, but by the ends they pursue and by the spirit of their government; and his subdivision is made, not by the principle of number, which he rejects, but by the criterion of social class. And Aristotle himself points to another difference between himself and Plato. Plato had not used the term polity for unselfish government by the masses: he had classed it as a good kind of democracy. To Aristotle all democracy is of the nature of perversion. But here, as so often elsewhere, one finds Aristotle building by means of reconstructing Plato's material. Not only the classification of States, but other vital elements of his theory, are Platonic in their origin.

We have now finished the study of the State as a compound. We have seen the nature of its units; the scheme of its composition; the variety of those schemes. We have next to turn to the inward and spiritual unity of the State: we have to consider the permanent expression of its moral life which appears in its law, and the regular operation of that moral life which appears in its justice.

[1] The same scheme appears in the *Ethics* (viii., 10), except that the term timocracy is used instead of polity; and a property qualification is thus suggested as the essence of this form. *Cf.* also the *Rhetoric*, i., c. viii., where four constitutions are distinguished—democracy, oligarchy, aristocracy, and monarchy—according to the residence of sovereignty. In democracy, it rests with the nominees of the lot; in oligarchy with those who satisfy a property qualification; in aristocracy with such as are possessed of culture. Monarchy with indeterminate powers is here classified as tyranny; but there is no mention of the Polity.

CHAPTER VIII

[*Ethics*, V.: *Politics*, II., viii.; III., ix.-xviii.]

ARISTOTLE'S CONCEPTIONS OF LAW AND JUSTICE

THE NATURE AND SCOPE OF LAW

§ 1. THE laws of Alfred contain, in addition to their legal and secular matter, a number of religious enactments and the whole of the Decalogue. Law is here attempting to be universal: it would fain embrace every species of control or inhibition, to which instinctive impulse should subordinate itself. **Law catholic and positive** To Aristotle law is equally catholic: it is equally the sum of all the spiritual limits, under which man's action must proceed. The great spiritual limitation upon man, as we have already seen, is reason. It is the duty of man to bring his passions under the control and the limitation of reason. Law, as the sum of all spiritual limits, is therefore identified with reason: it is defined as "dispassionate reason". In man reason is close neighbour of many passions and can hardly be heard for their clamour: in law it emerges pure, a clear and solitary voice, which calls aloud through a silence in which all passion is hushed. But morality consists in a life according to reason: the words of reason are the moral code. The law, which is one with reason, must therefore also be one with the moral code.[1] The law enjoins courage, and continence, and consideration: it speaks about every virtue and vice, commanding and forbidding.[2] Its rules are laid down by political science, as the standard of what men should do, and what they should forbear to do.[3] As the moral code of a community, law sets forth the end, the Final Good, which that community pursues.

[1] Law=reason; reason=the moral obligation: ergo law=the moral obligation.

[2] *Ethics*, 1129 b 14-25. [3] *Ibid.*, 1094 b 5-60.

The content of the law being thus identical with that of morality, it follows that action in accordance with that content, or justice, is equivalent to action in accordance with the content of morality, or virtue. Justice is one and the same with virtue. There is, however a difference. In a sense justice is higher than virtue: it is virtue in action. It is more than an internal spirit: it is the active fulfilment of an internal spirit in the conduct of a member of society towards other members.[1] To be considerate is virtue: to act considerately *towards another* is justice. As law is the moral code of a community, so therefore is justice (which is action in conformity to the law) the quality of its members. Justice means that each member of a community should so act in regard to his fellows, as to fulfil every moral obligation, because every moral obligation is enacted in the law, and to realise the Final Good, as the aim of the State expressed in its law. Conduct is just, in Aristotle's words, when it creates and preserves happiness (the Final Good), with every part and member of happiness, for a whole political society. We shall presently see that Aristotle distinguishes another conception of justice from that which has just been explained, a conception in which it is connected with the preservation of equality. As contrasted with this other conception, justice, in the sense in which it is connected with observance of the law, acquires the name of "complete" as opposed to "particular" justice. Here we are only concerned with this "complete justice," which is primarily law-abidingness, but ultimately and in consequence (because the law by which it abides is the moral law), virtue itself in action, virtue as shown by one member of a community in his dealings with others, virtue as the life-breath of a moral community acting in obedience to law.

Law and the legislator

What is the source of law, and by whom is it made? Does Aristotle define it, as a modern thinker would, as the expressed will of a community? It is true that in the Greek city the whole body of the citizens sometimes enacted the law, either of its own unaided initiative, or with the aid of a committee which draughted the law, and submitted its draught to the assembly

[1] Hence the *Ethics*, as a treatise on virtue, discusses goodness as a psychological condition in the individual; while the *Politics*, a treatise on justice, discusses goodness as the quality of a member of a community.

for confirmation. But the general Greek conception was that of the sole legislator, the Solon or Lycurgus who was responsible for the laws of his State. The ordinary amendment of law might proceed from the people: its original creation was assigned to some almost superhuman wisdom, which shaped the law in one great operation. The conception is unhistorical: it was none the less universal; and it appears in both Plato and Aristotle, who indeed themselves pose as nothing else than "legislators" in constructing their ideal States. To Aristotle the legislator is greater than the statesman, because he lays down the great lines on which the State is to move, while the statesman is an administrator of detail. He is responsible, we learn, alike for written and unwritten laws; for he may initiate customs, which are never set down in writing. To these latter Aristotle assigns a very large province. Valuable as are written laws, laws resting on unwritten customs are still higher than they, and concerned with higher things.[1] And further, above and beyond written law and unwritten custom, the legislator must also produce a right habit and spirit in those who are going to live according to both:

> Quid leges sine moribus
> Vanae proficiunt?

"There is no profit of the best laws, passed with the consent of every member of the community, if those members be not habituated and educated therein."[2] To lay down the principles of an education, which will make obedience to the laws come naturally to every citizen, is the prime work of the legislator. Greater than the writing of excellent laws on paper, is the writing of them into the spiritual fibre of a people: law-abidingness is more than law. Law, after all, *is* the expressed will of a community;[3] for the essence of law is the will of the citizen to abide by the law.

Law as a spiritual force

Over the lesson here implied it is worth while to linger. One of the great lessons which Aristotle, like Plato, teaches, is that institutions and laws, taken concretely and in themselves,

[1] *Pol.*, 1287 b 5. [2] *Ibid.*, 1310 a 14.

[3] But while a modern thinker would regard law as originally created by the will of a community, Aristotle regards it as originally created by a legislator, who *then* makes it the will of the community, by training its members to will the law.

are mere stocks and stones; and that everything depends on the far deeper question, whether they live and are rooted in the mind of the members of the community in which they exist. Their true reality is not objective, but subjective. A law exists so far as it is a spiritual motive, apprehended and acted upon by a mind. The formal language is a mere external and visible sign of this inward and invisible spirit; and if this spirit does not exist, the law ceases to exist. What is true of law is true of all institutions, and of the whole of government. No utterly external force, no stimulus that is not met by an answering reaction, can permanently exist. Government is powerful not in the stimulus which it gives, but in the answering reaction which it finds. Government exists and has its power in the minds of its subjects. The remembrance of this truth is the beginning of political wisdom. It teaches that the way of political progress is the education of a people in new ideas, and not the creation of new institutions to which there are no answering ideas, and which are therefore nothing. It teaches that any change of laws or institutions must be slow, because the ideas in which they are rooted can only be eradicated with difficulty; and must be along the lines of the past, for a people will never come by a wholly new set of ideas. It is in the strength of his hold on the subjective side of law and of institutions, that Aristotle reaches some of his greatest conclusions. He can answer Plato's communism with the rejoinder, that it is a cleansing of the heart, and not of garments, that the world requires.[1] Communistic institutions will not create unselfishness; but a mind trained to unselfishness by education will treat even private property in a spirit of communism. He can tell all founders of States, that the one guarantee for the preservation of the government which they institute is a training of the people in its likeness: he can even insist, that the spirit of the constitution, living in a people, not only preserves the constitution, but gave it originally whatever vitality it has.[2] He knows well enough that government must be based on consent, that "more must be the number of those

[1] The criticism of Plato is unfair: the point urged in the criticism is very true.

[2] *Pol.*, 1337 a 15.

who wish a State to continue, than of those who do not"; but he also knows that the consent is no mere passive acceptance, but a spiritual habit in conformity with the State "creating and preserving" its institutions. He knows that the primary work of every "legislator" who aims at political progress is to educate a people into the ways of thought and action, which make possible and will alone make permanent his legislation. This is why education bulks largely in Aristotle, and why, in the fragment on the ideal State, a sketch of the education of its citizens is his first, and indeed his only, concern. Finally, as he had answered Plato in the strength of his feeling for the subjective basis of laws and institutions, so, in the same strength, he answered Hippodamus. Hippodamus had proposed rewards for those who found out inventions which were for the advantage of the State. It is specious, says Aristotle;[1] but a premium upon inventions of new things is an incitement to political instability. And the suggestion raises, he adds, another question: is it good to change traditional laws, if newer and better laws be discovered? It may be argued in favour of change, that political science is an art, and should, like other arts, alter and improve its product—which is law—as knowledge alters and advances. Primitive man was a rude and witless being, and his laws were simple and uncouth things, which are not worth cherishing; nor, in any case, is it the aim of men to be true to tradition, but rather to pursue the ideal. This is an argument which applies particularly to unwritten tradition; but even written laws of a more modern type have their defects. They are couched in general terms: the actions which they seek to control are concerned with particulars; and an accumulation of greater experience may show that the one is not properly adjusted to the other. To these considerations Aristotle answers, that while some laws should sometimes be altered (and here he is probably thinking of primitive customs), yet on the whole change is to be mistrusted. It is an ill thing to fall into the spirit of change, even if it be the result of a series of changes for the better: the advantage of change will be less than the disadvantage of instability and disobedience to authority. In this Aristotle speaks as a Greek, dreading the Greek vice of

Stability of Law

[1] *Politics*, ii., c. 8.

"loving always some new thing"; but he has also a more fundamental reply. The strength of the law is in the habit of obedience to the law, which only comes with years. Better, we may say, are bad laws with a spirit of law-abidingness, than good laws without any root. Once more Aristotle appears as a conservative, pleading for the right of existence of the existing, as elsewhere he pleads for slavery. If we cannot follow him to-day—if we feel that in modern England no greater or better work can be done by a statesman than to overhaul our laws, it is because we can count on a basis of law-abidingness in the temper of the English people, which Aristotle could not have assumed among the Greeks, except perhaps at Sparta.

We have seen to what extent the legislator is, in Aristotle's opinion, responsible for law. He makes the written law and the unwritten custom; above all, he educates his citizens in the spirit of both. But a question now arises, which had often been discussed before Aristotle's day, and of which Aristotle has something to say. Is law conventional, or natural, in its origin? The conventional character of law had been asserted by the sophist Lycophron, who had spoken of law as a covenant, which guaranteed to men their rights against one another (1280 b 10). That law represents a set of conventions directed to an end so low as the mere protection of life and property, which is the implication of Lycophron, Aristotle instantly denies. The State is no mere society for mutual assurance against assault or robbery, but a moral community, formed for the ends of virtue. The rules by which that community lives are not negative prohibitions of offences, but positive counsels of moral perfection. But if this be the purpose of law, it cannot be a set of conventions; it is identical with the eternal and immutable laws of morality, and must be therefore natural. In a word, law is natural because it is moral; as slavery is held to be natural for the same reason, and as private property is proved to be natural by its moral uses. The natural character of the law precludes any distinction between what is legally just, and what is naturally just: to Aristotle, as to Socrates, the Legal and the Just are one. The law being natural, there is only one species of the Just, which is both legally and naturally just. That the law is natural does not, however, preclude the agency of man in creat-

Law natural

ing law. Aristotle, as we saw, refuses to make an antithesis between Nature and art: the State is by Nature, and yet man's art contributed to its structure, imitating or perfecting Nature; and similarly law is by Nature, and yet the legislator is responsible for its enacting.

Thus the law of the State and the law of Nature are one: as Hobbes says (though from quite another point of view), "they contain one another, and are of mutual extent". But this identity, while ideally true, must be modified when we come to deal with actual States and existing laws. In the first place we must, after all, distinguish between natural and positive law, between the naturally and the legally just, not however as antithetical, but as supplementary one to another. Natural law has everywhere the same validity, and does not depend upon enactment for that validity: it deals with the eternal and universal duties of man. Positive law varies from State to State, according to the enactments which each State makes; it determines a particular rule as henceforth alone admissible, in a case where, before the enactment, any line of action was possible. It determines for instance that a ransom shall consist of two minæ, or that a goat and no other animal shall be sacrificed on a given occasion. This positive law Aristotle describes as the fruit of convention and convenience; and he speaks of the law, which makes prisoners in war the slaves of their captors, as due to such a convention. But not only does positive law vary from State to State; natural law may also vary. Nature lays down a rule everywhere valid, but man may change that rule to a greater or less extent; just as Nature has made men right-handed, and yet they can make themselves ambidextrous. It is this variability even of that which should be invariable, which leads to the view that law, appearing as it does to vary from State to State, not in any part but in its whole substance, is everywhere and always conventional. It is easy to exaggerate the sphere of convention, and to call everything conventional: it is easy to minimise the province of Nature, and to find nothing natural Pascal gives expression to this tendency, when he remarks that to kill a man may be murder on one side of a river, and nothing wrong on the other. But Nature and convention coexist; hidden as it may be, there is always side by side with the con-

Conventional element in law

ventional or positive law a natural law to be found. It is merely the variety of States, with their various systems of positive law, and their various interpretations of natural law, which obscures its existence.

But this variety of States may modify the identification of the law of the State with the law of Nature still more fundamentally. As yet, we have seen that the variety of different States involves a variety of interpretations of natural law, as well as a number of different systems of conventional law. But it is possible, and we must consider the possibility, that a State may pervert, rather than interpret, the principles of natural law. To understand this possibility, we must stop to consider the relation of law to the constitution. The constitution, as we have seen, determines the end of the State, and the magistrates who realise that end. Law consists of the rules, by which the magistrates and the other members of the State act in view of that end. Law accordingly must be adjusted to the end determined by the constitution, and therefore to the constitution; it must vary as the constitution varies. Where the constitution is good, the laws are just, or in other words, they correspond to the law of Nature which is the same as the moral law: where the constitution is bad, the laws are unjust, and therefore unnatural and unmoral. As the ideal State is natural, so are the laws of that State natural: as other States represent perversions of Nature's ideal, so are the laws of those States perversions of Nature's law. In a perverted State the whole of the law must be artificial and conventional: the law of the State must be absolutely discrepant from the law of Nature.

We may now turn to discuss in conclusion the proper sphere and province of law in the government of the State.

Law and the "god among men"

Law there must be in every State. Where law is present in a State, we are told, the State has a constitution: the absence of law means the absence of a constitution. The absence of law, in other words, means the presence of incalculable caprice; and a constitution, as we have seen, implies a *definite* order of the government, and a *definite* aim for its action. Accordingly tyranny, extreme democracy, and that form of oligarchy which is called dynasty, as they are all characterised by the absence of law or at any rate of respect for law, are properly speaking not constitutions at all. But while there must be law, to determine the channels of the action of the government, a difficult question at once arises, if we seek to determine the extent to which the law should control the government. On general principles, indeed, Aristotle comes rapidly to the conclusion that the true relation between law and government is secured by making the law sovereign and the government its servant. Whether power be given to the few or the many, it is argued, there is every probability that the government will tend of itself to selfishness. The few will oppress the many, or the many the few. To preserve unselfishness, law must be constituted sovereign, and the government left sovereign only over those particular details which law cannot touch because of its generality. But this consideration only touches oligarchy and democracy, and what applies to the few or the many will not necessarily apply to the one. If we suppose the existence in a State of a man ideally gifted in character and political capacity, of a "god among men," it cannot but appear ridiculous to impose laws on his actions, for his own wisdom is a still higher law. It would be absurd to consider him as a part of the State, when his supreme gifts make him as it were the whole, and when the rest of the civic body, less richly endowed, sinks by comparison into a mere part.[1] Two courses are open—either to banish him from a society of which he is too great to be a member, or to make him its absolute ruler. The former plan, which is that of ostracism, cannot be lightly dismissed as the mere "trick" of a tyranny or a democracy, intended to preserve a government which feels itself threatened: it is a practice known to good constitutions as well as to bad, and to barbarians as well as to Greeks. The excision of a too prominent feature from his work is necessary even to the artist, if he does not wish to spoil the unity of his composition. But ostracism can hardly be the right policy of a State, which makes virtue its aim, towards a member who is distinguished by a supreme degree of virtue. It would be too glaringly illogical. It remains therefore that the citizens

[1] That is to say, he possesses of himself everything which it is the aim of the State to secure, a perfect *αὐτάρκεια*; while the other members, even in their totality, are without him insufficient, and fall short of *αὐτάρκεια*.

of such a State should put themselves entirely in their hero's hands, and make his words their law.

Prerogative *versus* constitutionalism

But here we embark upon an old Greek speculation, whether it be better to be ruled by man or by law. It was a question which the natural growth of population in the Greek cities (making inevitable democracy, which was identified with the rule of law) had long been answering against monarchy. But the Socratic theory of politics as an art came to give a new turn to the discussion. No artist, it was maintained, could do good work, if he were limited by rules and regulations; and the statesman must be as free as the artist, if his work is to be well done. This, as we have seen, had been the teaching of Plato; and therefore Aristotle, when he came to discuss the question, found the voice of authority raised against law. As it presented itself to Aristotle, the question was somewhat academic: if democracy was inevitable, why discuss monarchy? Yet, if we may be allowed to translate the antithesis of man versus the law into the antithesis of Cæsarism and Constitutionalism, we shall find that much of what Aristotle says is still of value. On the one side we have to place the flexible power of a single intelligence, quick to grapple with circumstance; on the other the quiet, if somewhat rigid impartiality of an impersonal law.

Of this antithesis there would seem to be two separate treatments in Aristotle, which are not so much supplementary as alternative to one another.[1] Both present the point of view of the opponents of monarchy; while Aristotle himself finally propounds a mediatory solution, which holds the balance between law and absolute monarchy. The first, and less fundamental treatment, suggests in favour of monarchy both the negative argument, that law speaks in general terms and cannot meet the play of circumstance, and the more positive consideration, that the monarch will deliberate more readily on particular issues. On the other hand, it is argued, there is still more to be said in favour of law. Every man should always be ruled in his actions by reason, and not by passion: he should seek the general good which reason indicates, and not the particular and selfish aims which his passions may suggest.

[1] *Politics*, iii., c. 16 and 17.

But if reason is to rule every man, it must rule the ruler himself; and the ultimate sovereign of the State will be dispassionate reason. But dispassionate reason is nothing else than law; and it is therefore necessary, if a State is to be normal and directed by unselfish rulers towards the general good, that it should have law for its ultimate sovereign. If a single man is to rule at all, he must be a man who has tied his hands by law; though it may be conceded that his hands should be unbound for a free course of action, in cases where the law stands in need of correction, or has nothing to say. This conclusion would involve a monarchy of the Stuart pattern, as defined by James I., where the monarch is the source of a law to which he conforms, but where he also possesses a large prerogative which can override or act outside the law. And indeed the issue here suggested is not unlike the issue debated between the early Stuarts and their Parliaments. The Stuarts claimed a flexible authority, which could meet the vicissitudes of foreign policy promptly and effectively, and could desert the normal course of parliamentary taxation for prerogatival levies where circumstances demanded. They spoke in the name of "efficiency," which is still, as it was to Plato, a name with which to conjure. On the other hand the popular party was afraid that a policy of extending monarchical authority lurked behind the veil. It demanded that regal action should "run in certain and known channels,"[1] or according to law; and it even argued, that if delay and inconvenience resulted from the necessity of observing forms and rules, it was "more tolerable to suffer an hurt . . . for a short time, than to give way to the breach and violation of the right".[2]

But the conclusion in favour of a monarch, acting by law of his own free will except where the law is silent or in need of correction, is not by any means final in Aristotle. He is inclined to doubt whether, when law fails to decide a question at all, or at any rate to decide it fully, one man is a better supplement of the law than are the many or the few. Much may be said in favour of the many: their collective wisdom and their incorruptibility are perhaps their greatest recommendations, when

[1] St. John in Hampden's case.
[2] Whitelocke in the debate on Impositions.

one contrasts the inferior judgment, and the greater facility in yielding to passion, of a single individual. But whatever may be said of these qualities of the many (and they will have to be discussed hereafter), there is everything to be said in favour of the few, if they are men of private and public virtue. They are few enough to meet emergencies as quickly as the monarch: they are less liable to corruption than he. An aristocracy, administering and supplementing the law, is a more ideal government than monarchy. Monarchy means heredity; but what guarantee can be given for the capacity of the monarch's issue? It means the nucleus of a standing army for the protection of the monarch's person; and there is no security that this will not be abused.

Here ends the first discussion of the subject. But it will be noticed that it has hardly been a discussion of absolute monarchy unfettered by any law, and meeting each new stimulus with a spontaneous adjustment. It has been a discussion of the value of monarchy as a force supplementary to law. We have still to discuss it simply as a force acting in lieu of law, and without any limitation: we have still to grapple with the Platonic conception of monarchy. And this Aristotle next proceeds to attempt. In doing so, he suppresses his own personality, and puts himself into the position of the critics, who had already attacked the Platonic conception. It may be argued, he tells us, that the absolute sovereignty of an individual is altogether contrary to the fundamental idea of the State. The State is an association, and every association is composed of units, different indeed in kind, but like in worth and standing. In such an association, every individual has the right to rule in his turn; and the rotation of office is imperatively demanded by justice. But once introduce rotation of office, and you introduce law, to regulate, for instance, the terms for which office shall be held.[1] You institute the rule of law; and if by the side of law there must be an executive, it is in the nature of a guardian and servant of the law. It will not be the office of the executive authorities to correct or even to supplement the law from their own wisdom. It is their work to fulfil the law, in the wisdom

Discussion of Platonic monarchy

[1] Not to determine the principle on which office shall be given: that is the affair of the constitution.

which the law has given, for law itself has educated them for their work, by informing them with its own lofty spirit. It is law itself which will correct or supplement the laws. Law is not set rigidly against all alteration: on the contrary, it always concedes and admits an alteration of itself in the light of a wider experience. Even without any formal amendment of the law, it is always possible to adapt the law to cases where it may seem inapplicable. Besides the law there is equity; or rather there is equity *in* the law. That is to say, when the letter of the written law may be harsh, it is always possible to apply its spirit, which can never be harsh. Equity is no other than justice, or conformity to the law; but while justice would interpret the law as it stands written, equity interprets it according to the intention of its creator.[1] The legislator has spoken in general terms, denouncing a penalty against some offence. That offence has been committed; but the guilt of its commission disappears before a number of modifying circumstances, which the legislator never contemplated, and which the law cannot therefore itself envisage. It is here that equity appears, and taking cognisance of these circumstances, pronounces as the legislator would have pronounced himself in a similar case. In a sense, equity is a correction of the law, where it fails on account of its generality: in another sense it is a fulfilling of the real law. In either sense it gives the law that flexibility in which it has been accused of failing: through equity, law is alive to the play of circumstance; through equity, it can meet each new stimulus with an answering reaction.

We thus come upon the conception of the State as an association, in which justice is done to the practical equality of its members by rotation of office. In this association law rules as the sovereign; but that law readily admits of the modifications, which a wider experience of facts combined with the teaching of its own spirit may suggest. The Platonic conception regards the State not as an association, but rather as a workshop, in which the rulers are so many craftsmen busy at work, shaping the rude material of human character into form. On the walls of that workshop there shall be hung no rules

The parallel from the arts

[1] *Ethics*, 1137 a 31 *sqq*.

dictating the models to be followed, or the tools to be used in the shaping. The fresh creative spirit shall have no let or hindrance: the craftsman shall deal with his material freely according to his own deft craftsmanship. But the parallel between political office and the mastership of a craft seems to Aristotle dubious. The instance of the physicians, which Plato had employed, may be turned against Plato. It is not good, Plato had urged, to bind the physician by the letter of medical rules. No —for the physician, in attending his patient, is never liable to be swayed by personal motives: he has no private interest which can induce him to betray the trust of his office. There is no reason to impose rules, precisely because his discretion can be trusted. A ruler has personal motives: an antithesis is inevitable between his private interest and his public duty; and there can be no permanent security that public duty will prevail, unless the letter of the law restrains the ruler to that single line of action which public duty demands. A physician who thought that he might be biassed in his treatment of a case, as he might if the patient were himself, would have recourse to a neutral authority. Because a ruler is certain to be biassed in *some* cases, and one cannot tell what they will be, one must make sure that he will have recourse to the neutral authority of the law in *all* cases. The argument seems convincing; and yet it may be suggested there is some little difficulty in subscribing to it unreservedly.[1] There is no guarantee that the law itself will be impartial. On the contrary, as Aristotle himself holds, laws are adjusted to constitutions, and constitutions tend to be adjusted to the interests of a class. What shall deliver us from the tyranny of selfish interests, which may invade even the sanctuary of the law? May we not be driven back upon a Cæsar, who, in virtue of his exalted position, will be untouched by the economic motives which urge the poor to legislate against the rich, and the rich against the poor? Certainly it is one of the great merits of monarchy, that its occupant is set in a serener air, above the dust of social warfare, or the din of party struggles, and that he can see events more clearly, and hear the voice of reason more distinctly. The one doubt (and it is a very great doubt) is whether he will have eyes to see,

[1] Aristotle himself hints at this difficulty (iii., 10 *ad fin.*) (1281 a 36-38).

and ears to hear. The difficulty is not his possible selfishness: it is his probable ignorance. And if elective monarchy might secure a wise ruler, it might on the other hand fail in detachment, and in elevation above contentious issues. Yet, as we have seen, it has been advocated in modern times as the cure of political evils, "during the present State of transition" to a "new industrial society," and as the one hope for that neutrality and mediation, which Aristotle, or the party for which Aristotle is here speaking, expected to find in law.

Law sovereign; but who shall supplement Law?

We have not yet concluded the case of those who opposed monarchy in the name of law. We have yet to see that behind the defence of an impersonal law there lurked the defence of the more personal and more vital cause of popular government. Assuming that it is now proven (the advocates of law will tell us) that law is sovereign in the whole of the sphere which it can cover, it remains to determine the authority which shall control the residuary sphere of what may be called deliberation on particular issues. That authority, it is suggested at the end of this second discussion, must be the masses. Two pairs of eyes are better than one, and many pairs of eyes are better than two: deliberation belongs by right to the collective insight of a popular assembly. Does not even a monarch take unto himself the eyes and ears of his friends, and are not friends the equals of their friend? A monarchy, in which the monarch governs with and through his equals, is a virtual democracy; but why not begin with an acknowledged democracy? It would be easy to meet these considerations. One might urge that the "many-headed beast" is not so much a many-brained being, possessed of collective insight, as a many-passioned thing, liable to a collective brutality tempered by a collective fickleness, as had been argued by Plato, and as had been shown by the conduct of the Athenians to the revolted Mitylenæans, whom they first condemned to death, and then in a revulsion of feeling allowed to live. Nor is monarchy, which is a virtual democracy, the same as democracy: constitutional monarchy, which is somewhat after this pattern, has peculiarities and qualities of its own.

Here end, however, the two discussions, in which Aristotle, this way and that dividing his mind, discusses the pros and cons of absolute monarchy and the rule of law. The final verdict of Aristotle himself, when he comes, at the end of the third book, to sit in judgment on the controversy, is based upon a new and characteristically practical suggestion. There is no absolute and single principle. We cannot decide unreservedly, either for the monarchical or the democratical principle, either for man or for law. It is not a question of principles to be imposed on peoples: it is a question of the character of the people, and the principle which that character demands. Constitutions are based on the character of the people who live under their sway; and differences of constitutions depend on differences of character. Plato, as we have seen, connected constitutions with character, but Plato had meant a type of moral character: he had meant that the political licence of a democracy corresponded to a similar licence of private life. Aristotle is referring to the political genius of a people: he is distinguishing the character of a people of equals, cherishing equality and suited for democracy, from that of a people to whom reverence for authority and the instinct of loyalty to a superior is natural. He is anticipating Montesquieu; though Montesquieu goes still further, and bases character on climate. If then there be a people such that one of its members stands supreme,

Final verdict of Aristotle

οἶος πέπνυται, τοὶ δὲ σκίαι ἀΐσσουσι,

such a people is meant for monarchy, and this one man for monarch. Justice demands that he should be king: the only alternative, that of ostracism, is illogical and impossible. But where the people is composed of members equal and similar to one another, it would be as inexpedient as it would be unjust for one man to rule them altogether, whether absolutely and as a law in himself, or constitutionally and under the limitation of the law. On the whole, therefore, since the conception of the State as an association involves the equality of its members, and since this is the conception which Aristotle holds, it may be said that his verdict is given against monarchy, and in favour of law and the rotation of office. The absolute king is an academic speculation *in nubibus*. It would be a mistake to imagine that Alexander is anywhere contemplated in the discussion of absolute monarchy. It is an old scholastic question, revived by Plato, which occupies Aristotle; it is not the epiphany of a hero-king, posing as in very deed a "god among men".

The problem of Alexander's position never occurs to Aristotle's mind. If he had attempted to define the authority which Alexander held over the Greek world he would have classed it, quite soberly, as belonging to that kind of monarchy which he calls a military command for life, and to the elective species of that kind. He would simply have thought of Alexander as having, like his father, been elected by the Congress of Corinth "plenipotentiary general of Greece".

Justice

(i.) Justice as complete virtue

§ 2. In speaking of law, we were led to speak of a conception of justice, which was characterised as "complete" justice, and which meant the fulfilling of the law. As law was found to be one with moral obligation, so was justice found to be one with virtue, if not, indeed, higher than virtue. It was seen to be the quality of a member of a moral community, acting in accordance with the whole of the moral law, because that law was the law of the community. Such a conception of justice is essentially connected with the Greek view of the State as an ethical society. To hold that view of the State was to be committed to this conception of justice; and Aristotle shares it accordingly both with Plato, who made justice the sum of the virtues, and with the proverbial philosophy which held that "to be just is to have all the virtues in one". When the State ceases to be an ethical society, the identity of justice and virtue also ceases: the citizen of a perverted State may still be just, in so far as he obeys the law of that State, but while he is just, he is not virtuous, for the law which he obeys is an aberration. To be a good citizen of a moral State is to be just, and, in such a State, to be just is to be virtuous: to be a good citizen of a perverted State is also to be just, but to be just is not to be virtuous. From this point of view we again come to see (what has already appeared to us from another point of view) that the good citizen of an ideal State, but only the good citizen of an ideal State, is also a good man.

The conception of justice as "complete virtue" is foreign to modern thought, just because the Greek conception of the State is also foreign. Justice is to our eyes a particular virtue: it is *one* of the ornaments of virtue: we count

> the king-becoming virtues
> As justice, verity, temperance, stableness.

But Aristotle has also the conception of justice as a particular virtue, and as a branch rather than the whole of virtue. There are, he believes, *two* kinds of justice. There is the justice which is observance of the law; and here that which is just is that which is legal, and he who is just is he who is law-abiding; while again the legal is the moral, and the law-abiding man is the virtuous, because the law is identical with the moral code. But there is also the justice which consists in observing the rule of equality; and here the just is the equal, and he who is just is he who takes no more for himself than he allows his fellows to take for themselves. We have now to see what is the meaning of this new conception, and how far *it* agrees with modern conceptions of justice.

(ii.) Particular justice

The conception of the State with which complete justice is connected, is that of a moral community of men striving after righteousness, and therefore regulated by a law which expresses their aim. The conception of the State on which particular justice rests is that of an association of equals, which, because its members are equal, is preserved by a principle of equality. Considered in the light of this latter conception, justice means that each individual has his due, and that he is so treated, and so treats others, as to preserve the proper proportion between the members of the association. But what is the due of the individual? It may be regarded as two-fold. On the one hand, he has his rights in regard to the whole: on the other hand, he has also his rights as against every other individual. (i.) In respect of the whole, he must be regarded as a contributor to the association, bringing to the common stock some one or other of those objects, which are necessary to the aim of the association. That aim is to pursue a moral life; and therefore every good man must be regarded as contributing his virtue to the common stock, while further every wealthy man must also be regarded as a contributor, inasmuch as wealth is a necessary condition for the realisation of a moral life. But the association, to which contribution has been made, has in its turn something to distribute. It has tangible things like office and (it may be) money at its disposal: it can also assign honours and distinctions. The individual has a right to receive his share of these things from the association. The association will only be just if it distributes them in such a way, as to give each individual his due, and to proportion its awards to the contributions of its members. If all have contributed equally, it will distribute equally to all: if some have given more and some less, to some more will be given, and to some less, exactly in proportion to the differences of their gifts. It may seem, *prima facie*, that the State violates the principle of equality, when it distributes unequally; but as we shall presently see, a superficial inequality is here the sole way to a real equality. Such equality of distribution it is the work of distributive justice to secure; and distributive justice is one of the two branches of particular justice. (ii.) But secondly, and as regards the rights of the individual in respect of other individuals, it may be laid down that every member of the association has a right, as against all other members, to emerge from all transactions and relations without giving more than he gets, or suffering a loss where another makes a gain. Yet it is always happening that one member inflicts a wrong and gains, while another suffers a wrong and loses; and equality is thus continually violated, whenever one man gets more than he should have, and another loses what he ought to possess. If the association is to remain true to its principle of equality, it must restore the lost balance: it must take from the aggressor his improper gain, and restore to the sufferer what he ought never to have lost; it must reinstate both in the equal position of having everything that either ought to possess, but nothing more or less. This restoration of a lost equality it is the work of corrective justice to secure; and corrective justice is thus the second branch of particular justice. Particular justice may therefore be defined as the quality of an association of equals, which, on the one hand, awards to its members, according to the amount of their contribution, the offices and other rewards it has to bestow; and, on the other hand, prevents encroachment by one member upon the sphere of another. In a word, it both guarantees the province of each individual against every other, and secures to each individual his proper position as a part of the whole.

Aristotle's conception of particular justice as a whole is

Peculiarities of Aristotle's conception of particular justice

analogous to our modern conceptions,[1] except perhaps in one point. While we might define justice as the principle which delimits and guarantees the sphere of every member of a political community in regard to other members and to the whole, we should hardly include the right to office as part of the sphere so delimited and guaranteed. We should indeed probably regard the franchise as included within the complex of rights possessed by each individual and guaranteed by the State. But we should not be regarding even the franchise in the light of distributive justice, or as awarded on a principle of justice which bound *the State* to award it; we should rather be considering it in the light of corrective justice, and as a private right guaranteed to each citizen by the State (when it has, on whatever principle, been once conceded) against invasion by others. We may indeed speak of a distributive justice which regulates the relations between the individual and the State. But we do not mean a principle which determines the right of the former to political influence: we mean rather a principle which decides the right of the latter to financial contributions. We mean that the State ought so to distribute its taxes, that their incidence will bear equally on every contributory member. The conception of a justice which distributes offices according to the worth of the recipients is peculiarly Greek. It is connected with the political structure of the city-state. "The citizen was a

[1] It should be also noticed how analogous it is to the Platonic conception of justice. But while Plato's formula is that each individual should *do* his own, Aristotle's formula is that each individual should *have* his own. Plato thinks of the individual as bound to do the *duty* to which he is called as an organ of the State: Aristotle thinks of the individual as deserving the right which he *ought* to enjoy in a society based on (proportionate) equality. Thinking of grades of duty, Plato regards justice as issuing in a *hierarchy* of classes: thinking of each as deserving his rights, Aristotle emphasises the equality between the different members of the State. Further, and finally, the two conceptions of justice are differentiated by Aristotle's distinction of justice into two kinds, complete and particular. Plato makes no such distinction; and his justice is both Aristotle's particular justice (in the sense and to the extent here indicated), and his complete justice (since justice means for Plato the discharge by the individual of the whole duty to which he is called by his place as a member of a moral community). We may say that Aristotle adds to Plato's moral conception of justice an additional and legal conception, while borrowing from Plato's principle of moral justice ("each to his sphere") the formal principle of that legal conception. At the same time, as we have seen (*supra*, pp. 192, 196), the principle of proportionate equality already appears in the *Laws*.

shareholder, not a tax-payer."[1] Every one of its five or ten thousand citizens might expect some office or other to be given into his hands; and it was vital that they should be given upon some principle, which would secure that the office, when it came, should properly represent his place in the community. For these offices were chiefly of the nature of honours: they were not heavy responsibilities, which demanded discretion and capacity. They were the honours of a civic body, demanding indeed discretion in their exercise, but awarded far more for considerations of worth and public spirit than of capacity.[2] Just because they were honours, they had to be distributed with a nice adjustment and an exact propriety: nothing can more easily raise disputes and disturb a society, than the award of dignities and the settlement of precedences. But where the Greeks had honours and titles to distribute in their various grades among all the members of a small and sensitive society of equals, we have trusts and responsibilities to give to a chosen few. We have not to deal with an association of equals, but with an association of which the extremes are poles asunder. We have not to give honours, but duties, though the highest duty is still with us the highest honour. Justice determined the grant of various degrees of dignity to the citizens of a Greek State: expediency rather determines our action to-day. It is expediency which determines a nation to entrust its destinies to the hands of that one among the candidates for supreme office who seems the most able to guide its destinies. It is still our effort to get the right man in the right place; but the right man is the ablest rather than the worthiest. He is not the man who has contributed most virtue, or most wealth, to the common

[1] Burnet, *Ethics*, p. 202.

[2] In book vii. (v.), c. ix., Aristotle raises the problem—Of three conditions, friendliness to the existing constitution, capacity, and moral worth, which is most necessary to a ruler? It depends partly on the office, he answers: few have the capacity of a general, while many have moral worth, and we must therefore take the man of capacity; while in an office like that of treasurer, few have the moral worth to withstand temptation, while all have the requisite knowledge, and we must therefore take the worthy citizen. After this solution Aristotle raises a further question—Is there any need of virtue, if capacity and friendliness to the constitution are both present? Yes, he is inclined to answer: without self-control the two other qualities may prove of no avail, just as in private life moral insight without self-control is useless. Aristotle here leaves room for capacity, but on the whole clings to virtue as the touchstone.

stock—(though it is indeed necessary that a statesman should behave with decency, and it is good that he should be endowed with riches as well as with virtues)—he is the man who has come out best from the competition of intellects in practical life. Particularly in our civil service, where the conception of office as a pure duty reigns, and where this conception is emphasised by the payment of officials—particularly here is the qualification of capacity apparent in the system of competitive examination. Capacity, it is true, can hardly be said to be the principle on which we award the "office" of the franchise. On the contrary, it is sometimes said that the franchise is given not because its recipients have capacity, but because by using the franchise they will come to have capacity, through the political education which its use involves, or may involve. But if capacity is not the immediate determinant, the ultimate motive is still at any rate expediency. The franchise was extended in 1832 because those who opposed its extension came to see that it would be worse to say No than it would be to say Aye, and that if the extension might mean a dangerous novelty, a veto upon it would certainly mean a revolution. And it may be argued that it is always expediency which dictates the widening of the franchise. Votes are given to wider numbers, in order to give the State as wide as possible a basis of active consent, and to interest as many as may be in its welfare. It is true that "the *right* to a vote" is a common phrase, and that such a phrase seems to postulate the conception of a distributive *justice*. But the *right* to vote involves, as its logical corollary, that one should have done something to create a claim for the vote. Otherwise, there can be no right, and no injustice. And as those who use the phrase do not stop to consider its corollary, they can hardly be said to be animated by the conception of a distributive justice. We may lay it down, therefore, that modern practise does not award office on principles of justice according to the worth of the recipients, but rather on grounds of expediency and for the welfare of the State, giving the higher office to those who can best consult the interests of that welfare, and the office of the franchise to as many as can be induced to consider them at all. And we differ in this way from Greek practice and ideas, because we have to deal not with a small community of equals, but with a vast association which admits of many differences and inequalities, and must therefore, alike by reason of its size and of its discrepancies, be compelled to aim at efficiency and to consider expediency. Some qualification may indeed be made in this distinction between ancient and modern ideas. Aristotle, as we shall see, speaks not merely of the worth or merit, but also of the capacity of the recipient of office as constituting his claim. An office is an instrument for action: it is but right that the instrument shall be given to the man who can use it properly. If this be justice, then we, who award office on the same principle, are actuated by the motive of justice. But the discussion of this difficulty may be reserved for the present, until we come to the more detailed exposition of the theory of distributive justice.

(i.) Corrective justice

We may now leave the general consideration of particular justice, and turn most especially to its two kinds. Of corrective justice, indeed, little or nothing is said in the *Politics;* and the absence of any proper treatment of the laws, which direct the procedure of such justice, has already been noticed as one of its lacunæ. From the *Ethics*, however, we learn that corrective justice covers the whole sphere of what we should call civil and criminal law: it extends both to voluntary dealings and involuntary sufferings. What it does in either case is to restore a violated and interrupted equality. The buyer who fails to pay his mina for a purchase, the robber who has stolen a talent, have both made a gain: the seller and the owner of the talent have both suffered a loss. Justice takes away his gain from the one, and makes up to the other his loss: the buyer is mulcted in his mina, the robber in his talent, and equality is restored. To every one his sphere; and he who has removed the land-mark of his neighbour's sphere shall lose the addition he has improperly made to his own, while the neighbour shall recover what he has improperly lost. Such a statement appears, at first sight, rather to supply a formula for the method of the State's action, than an explanation and justification of that action. What the State is really concerned to do, it may be argued, is to guarantee to the injured man the *right* to the sphere in which he has been invaded, and to enforce upon the aggressor the *duty* of respecting the sphere which he has attacked. The right of the injured man to the sphere which he controls is based upon personality: it depends upon the fact that he has a self which it is his aim to express, and which requires, for its expression and development, a certain sphere subject to its own immediate control. The duty of the aggressor to respect that sphere is based upon the fact, that he is a member of a community, whose members, in claiming each for himself the recognition of his right to such a sphere, have *ipso facto* recognised the right of every other member to such a sphere, and have therefore imposed upon themselves the duty of respecting all those rights. The interference of the community flows from the recognition by all its members of the right of the injured member, a recognition which it puts into action by compelling the aggressor to recognise it also. Nor does the community merely enforce upon the aggressor the recognition of the right of the injured man by process of civil justice: it forces him also (when it is a question of what Aristotle calls involuntary sufferings) to recognise the whole scheme of rights and duties which he has disturbed, by the punishment which it exacts as a matter of criminal justice, and measures accordingly, not by the amount of injury done to the sufferer, but by the amount of disturbance of the scheme on which it is based.[1] We thus reach the conception of (1) a community of persons possessed as persons of rights which have duties for their corollary; and (2) of that community as enforcing (through a specialised organ called the government) recognition both of the rights of individual persons, in civil justice, and of the whole scheme of rights and duties, in criminal justice. Aristotle's conception is different. He thinks of a community of equals, and of that community as enforcing through the government a principle of equality. But granted this conception of the State, it may be suggested that equality supplies more than a formula for the method of judicial action: it supplies something of a justification and a basis for its existence, at any rate on the civil side. Even on this side however Aristotle does not attain to the full conception of a right:[2]

[1] It not only enforces a *bot*, but also exacts a *wite*, because he has broken the *frith*. A doctrine of this kind *may* perhaps be detected in the *Ethics*, 1132 a 4: see Prof. Burnet *ad locum*.

[2] As Green suggests, a conception of "rights" *can* be elicited from his teleological method; and a conception of a right to property based on personality seems to be suggested in his criticism of the *Republic*. But there is no explicit conception of rights in Aristotle.

he does not explain *why* equality *ought* to be maintained. And though, on the criminal side, he speaks of punishment as inflicted by virtue, and again of penalties as the rudders by which rulers steer their subjects into goodness, he can hardly be said to have any real theory of the basis of punishment.

(ii.) Theory of distributive justice

The conception of distributive justice is very prominent in the *Politics*. This conception, as we have seen, involves a view of the State as an association, which on the one hand receives "contributions" from its members, and, on the other, distributes offices or honours. Different kinds of contributions may be made. Many contribute wealth; some virtue; some merely freedom of birth. Every State has to determine which of these it will take as its "standard" in distributing offices: it has to decide whether it will regard the contribution of wealth as the essential contribution, and award its offices to the wealthy, or whether it will rather find its standard in virtue, and its magistrates in the virtuous. That there must be a standard, and that distribution must proceed according to that standard—in other words, that there must be a distributive justice—every State admits: where States disagree is in respect of the particular standard they adopt. All are just, in so far as all attempt to distribute according to a standard; yet such of them as distribute according to a wrong standard are also unjust. They are just, relatively to the standard they have adopted: they are unjust, relatively to the standard they ought to have adopted. It is therefore of the greatest moment to choose the proper standard: otherwise a strenuous but merely relative justice becomes the worst of injustice.

Difference of democratic and oligarchic standards of distributive justice

Democracy emphasises the conception of the State as an association of equals. It accordingly takes freedom of birth, in which each citizen may be supposed to be equal to every other, for its standard of distribution. It regards no other contribution but freedom of birth; and it refuses to admit any differences of degree in that contribution. Accordingly, all the recipients of its offices being *ex hypothesi* equal, democracy has to consider not persons or personal differences, but merely the things, the offices, which it awards. In awarding these offices, it will be just, according to its standard, if it distributes them in exactly equal amounts, and if it secures a simple equation between the amounts received by each and every citizen. But when we come to oligarchy, the case is more complicated. Oligarchy emphasises the conception of the State as an association of contributors of wealth. It accordingly takes wealth for its standard. It admits, as it obviously must, the presence of differences in the amounts contributed. First and foremost, there is the great difference, which is practically a difference of kind, between those who contribute something, and those who contribute nothing; and the latter class oligarchy altogether omits to consider in its distribution of offices. Secondly, among those who do contribute something, there are differences of degree. It might seem, therefore, as if oligarchy would naturally put itself at the opposite pole from democracy, by making inequality its aim; and indeed Aristotle does, in one passage, speak of its justice as identical with inequality. But, more fundamentally considered, the aim of an oligarchy is still equality. It is a proportionate equality—an equality of ratios. Oligarchy may not aim at distributing equal amounts; it may be resolved on the contrary to distribute unequal amounts; but it does aim at distributing to (let us suppose) Alcibiades and Nicias in such a way, that what Alcibiades receives stands in the same relation to what he has contributed, as the amount received by Nicias stands to the amount contributed by Nicias. The ratio between the office which Alcibiades receives and the wealth which he has contributed is exactly equal to the ratio between the office and the wealth of Nicias.[1] Oligarchy does *not* forget the principle of equality: what it does is to rise from its standard of wealth to the higher conception of proportionate equality, while democracy cannot rise from its standard of free birth to anything higher than mere equality. Oligarchy regards the persons receiving, as well as the amounts distributed, and it proportions its reward to the desert of the recipient; while democracy considers merely the things distributed, and awards them in equal portions. There is a subtler and truer conception of equality in an oligarchy; and yet it has its defect. The defect of the oligarchical conception

[1] If Nicias has contributed 30, and Alcibiades 14, Nicias receives 15 and Alcibiades 7: and 30: 15 = 14: 7. Oligarchy thus reckons in 4 factors, *viz:* 2 persons, and 2 things: democracy only in 2, both things—the office of x, and the office of y.

of distributive justice resides in a narrow view of the meaning of desert, and in the belief that a man's worth is his wealth. But in justice one must judge a man's worth by that aspect which truly represents the real man; one must judge by moral character. And so we rise to the higher and truer conception of distributive justice to be found in aristocracy, which, taking moral worth for its standard, distributes in an equality proportioned to that standard. The conception of the State as a moral community must be the determining factor in the proper distribution of office. The end pursued by such a community constitutes the standard by which its offices are distributed; and as that end is virtue, so the standard by which office is assigned is the degree of contribution to virtue. Everywhere, indeed, the end of the State and the standard of distributive justice are one and the same; and it is just because perverted States have taken to themselves false ends that they adopt false standards of distribution. The end is everything; and a teleological conception of the State is made to determine the award of office, as it determines so much of the teaching of the *Politics*.

We have hitherto regarded the State as giving offices by way of reward, and in return for contributions made towards the end which it pursues. But if we make a slight change in our point of view, and regard the end as a function, we may regard the State as giving offices, not as rewards for contributions already made to its end, but as instruments towards contributions to be made towards its function. We may regard the holder of an office as discharging, by means of his office, a subsidiary function which is necessary to the State's discharge of its function. But from this point of view we shall make capacity our standard: we shall obviously award the better instruments to those who are best at the work for which these instruments are intended. If we were distributing musical instruments to the members of a musical society, we should give them to the best musicians: they are instruments for playing, and they ought to go to those who play best. Some of the members might be wealthier than the rest, and others of better birth; but we should regard these as totally extraneous considerations, and if the best musician were the poorest and the basest born, he would none the less receive the best of the flutes, while the wealthiest subscriber, or

Distributive justice as rewarding capacity

the noblest patron, would not be considered at all. The superiority which entitles to a superior function must be a superiority in respect of the gifts which make for the discharge of the function. In politics, the greater right to office will rest, not with the man of superior wealth or superior birth, but with the man of superior political gifts and superior "political capacity" (πολιτική δύναμις). Here, it appears, we come upon a new qualification for office. Political capacity seems different from virtue, though it is more than once mentioned along with virtue by Aristotle. It is "capacity for the function of office". But the distinction between the two must not be pushed too far. After all, in a moral association, the supreme function of office is to make the citizens good men; and one who is himself a good man will alone have the proper capacity for such work. The good ruler, as we have seen, is particularly and pre-eminently identified with the good man: virtue of the highest type is his characteristic and his qualification. He must have "moral wisdom"; he must have attained to self-direction in the light of principle, in order to guide the feet of others into the ways of habitual morality, as it is his function to do. Capacity for the function of office *is* identical with virtue, and with the highest form of virtue. If this conclusion be correct, then the difficulty raised before—whether Aristotle did not agree with modern practice in making capacity the standard of the distribution of office—may be solved by the answer, that the capacity of which we speak, and the capacity which Aristotle meant, are different things. We mean the capacity of a keen intellect: he meant the capacity of a moral character.

Various qualifications for office

It would appear that virtue, whether viewed as a contribution to the end of the State, or as equivalent to a capacity for directing the State, is the real qualification for office. But it would be a mistake to assume that it is the only qualification. Virtue, as we have seen, requires an "equipment" of wealth. The State, as a moral community, must accordingly have its due complement of wealth; and they who contribute that wealth contribute to the end of the State, and deserve their due reward. Nor need we stop at wealth. We can lay down a more general proposition. Though the end of the State is peculiarly and specifically virtue, and though virtue is therefore its standard of distribution, and the virtuous its rulers, yet, fully considered and as a whole, the end embraces every proper human aim, and every man who contributes anything of moment to this vast end must be regarded as worthy of his share. Accordingly Aristotle admits that everything which goes to constitute the State deserves consideration, wealth, free birth, nobility, justice, military prowess—though the former three are only necessary to the life of the State, while the two latter are necessary to its good life. If we pay regard only to good life, justice and military prowess (or, in a word, virtue in its widest sense) will monopolise office: if we remember that the State has to live, as well as to live a good life, the justice of the claims of wealth and birth will be obvious. The rich have a greater stake in the country, and can be more readily trusted in commercial dealings; while good birth and a clean pedigree is always honoured in its own country for itself, and may be presumed to bring character and capacity in its train—*Fortes creantur fortibus et bonis.* But to have introduced these new candidates for office complicates any solution. There are now three possible authorities—virtue, wealth, and birth. Nor have we merely to compare these three several qualities; we have also to weigh the quantity of these qualities. That is to say, we have to measure the sum of virtue, or of riches, possessed by those few individuals who are pre-eminently endowed with these qualities, against the sum of either possessed by the many, who, if each is only moderately endowed, can collectively show perhaps the greatest sum. Not only therefore have virtue, riches and freedom to be set over against one another; but the sum of the virtue and riches of the few has to be contrasted with the sum of those of the many. Finally, still a new problem is raised by the intensity of a quality like virtue which a single man may possess, an intensity which may be such as to outweigh any considerations of the quality resident in the few, or the quantity possessed by the many.

The various questions thus propounded may be brought together for solution, if we ask, whether the greatest contribution towards the general aims of the State is to be expected from the few, or whether the claims of the few are liable to be defeated either by the collective claims of the many, or by the individual claim of the One. By this method, which Aristotle follows, the government of the few is adopted as a basis for discussion, and then attacked from two sides. It is adopted as a basis, because the presumption would appear to be in its favour: it would seem proper to distribute office to the few, who are likely to be superior not only in wealth and in birth, but also in virtue. In an aporetic passage, it is true, doubt is cast on the right of the few to govern, even where they are superior in virtue: if they are vested with office, it is suggested, the greater part of the citizens will be deprived of political rights and dignities; and this, it may be argued, is not only unfair, but also dangerous, because it will produce a discontented majority. But (Aristotle replies) the paucity of numbers of the virtuous is no bar to their title to office, provided that they are numerous enough to do the work of administration. The real unfairness would be to exclude them from the office which they have deserved; and the danger of discontent with the unselfish rule of an enlightened government is no real danger at all. It is less from the side of their being too few, than from that of their being too many, that the rulers in an aristocracy may be attacked: if their superiority in quality is to tell against other claimants, then, by the same argument, the supremacy in quality of the One should tell against them in turn. An ideal and absolute kingship may be thus more consonant with the principles of distributive justice than the rule of a few; though against even such a kingship, as we have seen, the advocates of law have many objections to urge, and among them its violation of the rule of equality. But, neglecting these objections, we may say, that distributive justice would seem *prima facie* to decide for aristocracy, or (in the rare case of an heroic virtue) for monarchy, as the ideal constitution.

Qualifications of the Few

We must not, however, decide too quickly for the few or the One, without considering carefully and dispassionately the claims of the many. Individually, the few are always superior: the greatest riches, the noblest qualities, must always be the possession of a small minority. But if one measures the qualities of the many by a collective standard, the gulf which seemed to separate them from the few begins to disappear. Their collective riches begin to bulk heavily: their collective virtue begins to count for much. Each unit of the mass has its particle of

Claims of the Many

virtue and of moral wisdom; and the meeting of the mass is not merely the union of many bodies in one place, but also the confluence of many characters and intellects in a single stream. Each intellect acts as complement to its fellow, until ultimately there is no defect. Every facet of a problem has some intelligence directed upon it, until finally the whole problem is surveyed by a whole intelligence, which may well judge securely, because it judges with every faculty, on every point. The best critic of music and of poetry is the *vox populi*.[1] It might seem as if this teaching altogether exalted the many above the few. But the few have still their prerogative. Their members possess, compacted in a single person, the qualities which in the masses are scattered and dispersed among many. Nor can it be said of every collective body that it has an eminent faculty of judgment: there are peoples who are no better than brutes, and whose judgment is worse than useless. There can be no uniform rule of distributive justice, which will always assign to the collective merit or capacity of the many the sovereignty of the State. It is a question of national character, it would appear, as absolute monarchy was also seen to be. But nevertheless distributive justice can lay down certain rules to determine the *share* in political office which the many should always possess. Something they must have: excluded from all offices, they will be hostile to the constitution under which they live, and their hostility will be fatal. On the other hand, it would be unsafe to entrust them with the higher offices: folly might lead them into error, and injustice into crime—a phrase in which Aristotle puts strongly the opposite possibility to that which he had himself emphasised, turning round, as he so often does, and listening to, or rather speaking for, the other side. A middle way remains, suggested by the peculiar faculty which Aristotle detects in a collective body—the faculty of judgment. That way consists in bestowing upon the many the rights of judging and deliberating,[2] or more particularly the right of

[1] This is almost the exact antithesis of the views of Plato, who objected to the "theatrocracy" of the vulgar as much as to democracy. Indeed the whole of this argument (1281 b 1 *sqq.*) is anti-Platonic.

[2] Aristotle seems to forget that he has elsewhere spoken of the deliberative as sovereign—a position which he does not here intend to give to the many. But possibly he here means little more by deliberation than election of the magistrates.

Aristotle's recognition of the claims of the Many

electing the magistrates (which may come under the head of deliberation), and that of examining their conduct at the end of their term of office. In discharging these functions the many will be mixed with the few: the two will mutually qualify one another, and their interaction may produce a better result than the separate action of either. Reasons may indeed be suggested why the people should not be allowed either to elect or control the executive. The analogy of the arts is unfavourable to the people. The choice of a geometer is best left to a geometrician; and the best judgment on a physician's treatment of his case may be expected from another physician. On this analogy the election and audit of the executive should rest with those who have served in executive office. But the analogy may be rebutted by an appeal to the collective wisdom of a collective body; and the plea may be urged, that those who are to use the services of any person are best qualified to decide upon the person they will have, and, when they have used his services, to determine what they have been worth. The proof of the pudding lies in the eating: the wearer of the shoe knows best where it pinches. It is for the eater to choose his cook, and for the wearer of the shoe to criticise its maker.

In speaking of the qualities necessary for such criticism, Aristotle makes a suggestive distinction. In an art like painting, there may be distinguished the painter who practises the art, the professor of fine arts who lays down the theory, and the layman of artistic culture, who may be, after all, not the worst judge of the actual result. In Aristotle's phrase, there is the practitioner, the man of directing skill, and the man who is merely "cultivated" in the art. In this distinction, and in this vindication of the cultured layman, lies the philosophy of much of our own practice to-day. We expect a lay House of Commons to criticise the special and complicated actions of different branches of government; and we get a criticism which is more fundamental because it is not specialist (for the specialist will rather quarrel with details), and all the more thorough and outspoken, because it is not swayed by professional bias. Every general election, again, is both an election and an audit in one —an audit of the outgoing, as well as an election of the incoming, ministry; and these great duties we entrust to a highly lay electorate, trusting dimly in the "common sense" of the people for good results. There are dangers in our confidence, as there were dangers in Aristotle's confidence. The people may cast its decision for the thing which is immediately pleasant, rather than for the ultimate advantage of the State: it may be ready to listen to the demagogue who persuades it to advance along the path to which it only too readily inclines of itself. It may decide in favour of its own interests, at the expense of the other elements of the State: it may indulge in wasteful expenditure on vast enterprises, because it is careful to put their burden on the shoulders of others. All these things it may do, and all these things in Greek democracies it had done, as Aristotle knew and tells us. And yet Aristotle could still trust the many: he was not like Plato driven by their failings to rely on the one hope of an ideal aristocracy. Aristocracy is indeed to him as to Plato always the ideal; but he can see the soul of goodness in everything, and he finds a soul of goodness in the people. Once more he is justifying the given and actual fact (for democracy, as he says, was a fact, and a necessary fact, in the populous States of his time) by conceiving the actual in its ideal meaning, and by lifting what is to the plane of what might be. It is in this trait that Aristotle reminds one of Burke: the two stand together as conservative reformers. It is a trait which he owes to his philosophic procedure. Instead of leaping beyond facts to an ideal, which they must reflect, and by which, if they do not faithfully reflect its perfection, they are rejected as false and erroneous, Aristotle patiently studies the facts, in order to arrive at their meaning and estimate their value. And here the "dynamic" quality of his philosophy enters, to help his patient respect for the real in dealing tenderly with all beings and all institutions. The idea of development is gracious in its influences. Things must be judged not only as what they are, but as what they may come to be. Their meaning and value cannot be appreciated apart from their possibilities.

In pursuing the study of distributive justice we have started from a presumption in favour of aristocracy, tempered by a preference for monarchy in those rare States where one of Nature's monarchs is born, and we have ended in a vindication of a certain degree of political power for the Many—a power which would apparently be allowed in all constitutions except that of the ideal State, where, all the citizens belonging to the class of the Best, there would not exist any separate class of the Many.

Liberty in Aristotle

Before leaving distributive justice, it may be worth while to turn back again to two conceptions, with which we have already been concerned, and to look a little more closely into the meaning of Liberty and Equality, as these terms are used in Aristotle.[1] Liberty, to a modern mind, often conveys the sense of freedom from the interference of the State—a sense which implies that no man is free, in so far as he is a member of a State, and abides by its rules. Often, again, it appears as synonymous with self-government; and while in this sense it means freedom from any authority which is obviously external, it also means subjection to such authority as is constituted by the subject himself. In Aristotle the word liberty is used primarily in the sense of free birth. It denotes one of those qualifications on the strength of which office is claimed; and its possessor is contrasted with the slave. To enjoy liberty is to be "one who exists for his own sake, and not (like the slave) for that of another".[2] In a wider and fuller sense, liberty involves a certain political status and a certain legal position. (i.) The political status differs in different constitutions. In a democracy (and democracies boast that they are the homes of liberty), to enjoy liberty is to possess a right to participate in office, a right secured, by the alternation of ruling and being ruled, to every man who is neither slave nor alien.[3] On this conception of its meaning, it follows, that liberty involves the sovereignty of the majority, or, in other words, of the poor, who are always in a majority. But elsewhere than in a democracy, political liberty has another meaning. It means subjection to authorities who govern in the interest of the governed: it means submission to a "constitutional" government.[4] In the sense of a political status, therefore, liberty was interpreted by the Greek democrat in much the same sense as it is to-day by those who identify it with self-government;

[1] The conception of Fraternity has already been discussed under the name of Friendship.

[2] *Met.*, 982 b 25. [3] *Pol.*, 1317 b 2. [4] *Ibid.*, i., c. 12 (1259 a 39-41).

while elsewhere it was understood as subjection to an authority working for the interests of the subject, and agreeable to his wishes, if not constituted by his will. (ii.) On what may be called its legal side liberty had equally different senses. In a democracy, " to be free was to live as one liked " (1317 b 12). Liberty had the negative sense of freedom from interference. The democrat argued—" Liberty is, what slavery is not: slavery means *not* to live as one likes; ergo, liberty means to live as one likes ". Liberty in this sense of laxity or licence was regarded by Plato as the curse of democracy; to Pericles, on the contrary, it was one of its blessings. Aristotle agrees with Plato in censuring this democratic conception: to live as one likes, and for what one desires, is a bad definition of liberty (1310 a 34). And one would gather, though he does not in so many words say, that liberty, on its legal side, is " obedience to rightly constituted laws ". While, therefore, like many modern thinkers, the Greek democrats found liberty in a somewhat incongruous mixture of the government of the majority and the release of the individual from governmental restriction, the true classical theory, as represented by Aristotle, viewed it as subjection to unselfish and constitutional authority and obedience to right and proper law. Hobbes' strictures on Aristotle, as one of the fathers of false ideas of liberty, were altogether mistaken. Aristotle taught the same doctrine which Montesquieu afterwards taught, that " liberty is the right to do as one ought to do, and not to do what one ought not to do ". " One ought not to believe that it is slavery to conform one's life to the constitution: one ought to believe that it is salvation " (1310 a 35). It is a doctrine from which the natural man revolts; he is instinctively of the school of the democrats, and wishes to find liberty in some assertion of his own will, rather than in conforming his will, as the other conception would seem to involve, to something outside himself. But if liberty is self-determination towards an approved object, and if authority and law represent approved objects, it follows that liberty consists in determining oneself by their commands.

Equality in Aristotle

In regard to equality the teaching of Aristotle is equally just. True equality does not consist, as democracy believes, in every man's counting for one and no more than one. Equality does not mean the levelling of distinctions, or the dragging of the wealthy from their pedestals : it means the preservation of distinctions. For equality is not numerical, but proportional: it is not the equality of unit to unit, but of ratio to ratio. Equality means, not that the recognition of the better man is equal to the recognition of the worse, but that the ratio between the recognition and merit in the one case is equal to the ratio in the other. Equality recognises the higher as higher: it preserves distinctions. And thus we may say, in a paradox, that a liberty which is subjection, an equality which consists in inequality, are the guiding conceptions of Aristotle.

From this account of the moral unity of the State, as that moral unity is conceived by Aristotle, we may now turn to discuss the degree of material unity in economic life which that unity permits or postulates. We have seen that moral life requires its equipment and furniture of things material. We have seen that economics is one of the sciences subordinate to political science. We have now to sketch the "principles of economics" to which these conceptions lead.

CHAPTER IX

[*Politics* I., c. ii.-xiii.; II., c. i.-vii.: *Ethics*, V. v.]

ARISTOTLE'S PRINCIPLES OF ECONOMICS

THE SPHERE OF ECONOMICS

§ 1. THE subject of the first book of the *Politics* is defined by Aristotle himself as household management (οἰκονομία) and the method of dealing with slaves (δεσποτεία); and it is contrasted with the rest of the *Politics*, whose subject is the State and questions of politics. In dealing with the household before the State, Aristotle is following Nature: he is taking first that which comes first, and dealing with the part before he describes the whole. The end of the household is something necessary, but subsidiary, to the supreme end pursued by the State; it is equally necessary (if also a subsidiary matter) to begin a book on politics by an account of the methods and purpose of economics. But in postulating the necessity of a discussion on economics, we must be careful to define the term we use. In the first place, economics means the art of managing the affairs of a household, as politics the art of managing the affairs of a State. "Political economy" would therefore be, to a Greek, a contradiction in terms. One of the aims of Aristotle in the first book of the *Politics* is to distinguish carefully economics and politics, domestic management and political government; they had been, in his view, improperly confused by Plato in the *Politicus*. The sphere of economics is for Aristotle the family: for us it is the State. A second difference appears, when we reflect that the art of managing a household implies much more than we understand by the word "economy". It implies a faculty of dealing not only with the material necessities of life, but also with the

Meaning of οἰκονομική

moral problems which the control of a family involves. It determines the relations of the householder to wife and child and slave. Accordingly we read that the province of economics is human beings, rather than the acquisition of material things: its aim is the excellence of these human beings, rather than excellence in acquisition—virtue rather than wealth. As we have found politics so closely involved with ethics, as to be really one and the same science, so too we find economics determined by moral considerations. Economics does not abstract an "economic" man for its hypothesis: it does not postulate wealth as its sole object and aim. It considers man in his entirety when engaged in managing his household: it discusses wealth as a means to the ultimate aim of that household, or, in other words, as the necessary instrument of a life of virtue. Economics is less extensive than political economy, for it only considers the household: it is more intensive, for it considers the *whole* activity of man in the household. It denotes less: it connotes more. The moral side of its connotation appears most decidedly from the division of economics which Aristotle makes. There are three divisions, we learn: one deals with the householder as master, one treats him as father, a third considers him as husband; while each of the three regards him as a moral influence. But if this be an exhaustive division of economics, what (one asks) has become of the acquisition of the wealth? Is it no part of economics? We learn in answer to such a question, that in the true sense of the word the acquisition of wealth is *not* a part of economics. It is a condition which must be satisfied if economics is to do its work; but it is not an integral part or function of economics. The full meaning of this view will appear later; but from what we have seen of Aristotle's philosophy of the State its general trend is apparent. As the producing classes are not parts but conditions of the State, whose full life they help to make but cannot share, so production and acquisition are only the conditions of economics, whose pure action (which is a moral action) they make possible, but do not concern. And thus, so far as this conception is present to Aristotle, his economics altogether parts company with modern economics, and becomes a treatise "on the ethics of family life".

Divisions of Economics

It may be convenient to divide economics (including acquisition, which if not an integral part is nevertheless a part of the subject for the purposes of theoretical discussion) into some three main divisions. One of these will be concerned with slavery; a second will be occupied by the theory of property, and its proper production, exchange, and distribution; a third will regard the family. Strictly speaking, indeed, there is but one subject—the family, of which slaves are a part, and property is an adjunct; but the division here suggested is one which seems to represent the actual process of Aristotle's argument.

The Theory of Slavery

§ 2. The Aristotelian theory of slavery possesses a peculiar interest. It is a reasoned defence for an institution, which the civilised world has now long conspired to reject; it is an attempt to justify what has often been called the blot on Greek civilisation; it is an effort to show that what was necessary for the full flower of Greek life was not only necessary as a condition, but also just in itself. In defending the natural character of slavery, Aristotle starts from the same sophistic view, and uses the same arguments to controvert that view, as in defending the State. Slavery was conventional, the sophists had maintained: on the contrary, he answers, it is natural, and natural because it is moral.

Aristotle defends the natural origin of slavery

The doctrine of the natural equality of man lay at the basis of the sophistic attack on slavery. Many of the sophists, it is true, argued for the natural *inequality* of man, and defended the right of the strong to use their strength. But sophistic doctrine was a Protean thing; and there were apparently others who held that slavery was a thing of pure convention, and that, as a later rhetorician said, "God had left all men free, and Nature had made man a slave". The institution of slavery had, however, been shaken less by theoretical attacks than by the logic of events. When the great disaster at Syracuse involved hundreds of Athenians in slavery; when again the overthrow of Sparta by the Thebans led to the liberation of the long-enslaved Messenians, these things could not but produce a feeling that the slavery which could suddenly engulf an Athenian, and from which the Helot could as suddenly emerge after three centuries of bondage, was a fortuitous, accidental thing, based not on the foundations of natural law, but at best on the fiat, just or unjust, of man. Aristotle himself had been the guest at Atarneus of a man who had risen from a slave to be a tyrant: must not a case so striking give him pause before he could pronounce slavery to be justified by Nature's own indications? Nevertheless, he ventured on that pronouncement. Taking slavery as a given fact, and conceiving the fact, according to his usual method, in its ideal meaning and full possibilities, he holds that some are born natural masters and others natural slaves; and that the moral possibilities of the subjection of the one to the other are sufficient to justify an institution, which is indeed already justified in itself by the mere fact of its existence as a part of the natural scheme of things. Slavery is natural, that is to say, both because it is suggested by the potentialities of master and slave, and because it is the highest and best condition possible for the slave. Nature, alike as meaning potentiality and as meaning completion and end, has set her seal upon this institution.

Character of Greek slavery

We may first inquire what was the manner of Greek slavery, with which Aristotle is concerned. In many respects it was not unlike what has been seen in modern times. There was a slave trade which imported into Greece men of alien race and lower civilisation from the countries of Asia Minor, in much the same way as Hawkins and his successors carried negroes from Africa to the new world. In Attica almost the whole body of slaves—and the slaves outnumbered the citizens in the proportion of two to one—consisted of such imported aliens. In Sparta, on the contrary, the Helots were indigenous Greeks enslaved by the Dorian conquest; and there were few purchased slaves. But the Helots were exceptional: they were prædial serfs rather than slaves; they were vassals of the State, who could not be emancipated or sold by their masters. The Attic slave is more typical of Greece; and it is the Attic slave whom Aristotle has in mind. The slaves in Attica were almost without exception recent importations; few had been born of slave parents in the country, and there was nothing like the problem of a class of hereditary slaves which the United States had to face, and with the results of which it is still confronted. Their lot was comfortable; there were no features of dress to distinguish them from the ordinary citizen; "in their owner's household they were treated as members of the family".[1] Legally as well as socially, they were not degraded: they were protected from ill-usage by the State; and they could not be punished with death except by its tribunals. There were slaves who lived by themselves and only paid their masters an annual rent; and it seems like a *métayer* system applied to industry instead of land, when we find gangs of slaves working under slave overseers in a factory, and dividing among themselves the profits which remained when their master had been paid his annual rent. The Athenian policeman was a slave; and slaves also filled the lower posts in the civil service. Emancipation was not difficult; the slave might even purchase his own freedom. With this state of affairs, one can readily understand why Athenian slaves are described as impudent and shameless, and why Plato regards it as characteristic of democracy, that its slaves share the prevalent laxity. One feels, too, the difference between this domestic slavery, in which the slave is not separated by a gulf from his master, and the slavery of the modern plantation, with its deep lines of demarcation, and its exploitation of the slave to the uttermost farthing.

Aristotle's definition of the slave

What then is Aristotle's philosophy of this system? He begins by asking—What is a slave? (i.) Every art, he answers, requires its proper instrument (*ὄργανον*). The art of economics requires the instruments which are necessary for managing a household. The generic name for the instruments which it requires is property; and "property is a collection of instruments". Instruments may be either inanimate or animate. The art of piloting a ship, for instance, requires the two instruments of a rudder, which is inanimate, and a man on the look-out in the bows, who may be called the animate instrument of the pilot. Similarly the art of managing a household needs for its object (which may be for the present defined as the sustenance of life[2]) both inanimate instruments, like dress

[1] Gilbert, *Constitutional Antiquities*, Eng. Trans., p. 171. The author of the treatise *De Republica Atheniensium* remarks: "If it were permissible to strike an unknown slave, metic, or freedman, there would be great danger of assaulting a free citizen unawares"—so much were citizen and slave alike in dress (Gomperz, *Greek Thinkers*, ii., 16).

[2] But this definition is imperfect, since the household is concerned with virtue rather than with property, and with producing goodness rather than with fostering life.

or furniture, and animate instruments, or servants. But, as an instrument, the servant is a piece of property of an animate kind; and as a piece of property he is a slave. Such a conclusion is inevitable, if one admits the identification of instrument and property: human instruments are obviously and as a matter of fact required by the householder, and if instruments are regarded as property, it follows that human instruments are human chattels, or slaves. But is not this identification merely the assumption of a too thorough teleology? And does not the analogy of the man on the look-out show that one man may be instrumental to the activity of another, without becoming his property? (ii.) Assuming, however, this identification, Aristotle proceeds to define the slave more closely. Instruments, we learn, may be classified, not only as animate and inanimate, but also, and according to another standard, as productive of commodities (*ποιητικά*), or productive of services (*πρακτικά*). The use of a shuttle is to produce a piece of cloth: the use of dress and furniture is to be serviceable. What is true of dress and furniture is true of all other instruments for the sustenance of life—of all the property, that is to say, which a householder possesses. The householder does not use his property as capital for the production of commodities: he consumes, as it were, the services which it can render to the sustenance of life. It follows that the slave must not be regarded as a labourer employed in producing commodities, like the slave of our modern plantations, but as a servant engaged in performing services within the house. By slavery Aristotle means what we mean by domestic service; and the definition of the slave, it now appears, is "a piece of property of an inanimate kind engaged in rendering services". (iii.) As the property, the slave is a part of his master. The conception of property, and the conception of part, agree in this, that either loses itself and is absorbed in the owner or the whole to which it belongs. Either is nothing in itself; both are entirely what they are, through that to which they belong. The whole being of the slave is in his master; you exhaust his meaning when you say that he is his master's slave. There is no life, activity, or existence for the slave, save as a slave, though there is much that the master is and does otherwise than as a master. The view seems parallel to the theory which Aristotle holds of the relation of the citizen to the State: the citizen, similarly, has no life or meaning but that of citizen. In either case Aristotle departs from his original position; and as he contemplates the citizen as a man and not only a citizen, so too he ultimately regards the slave as not only a slave, but a man.

Slavery justified by the analogy of Nature

So far, the slave has been simply defined; though incidentally he has been proved to be so far natural that he is necessary as an instrument to the life of a household. But the definition of the slave naturally raises the serious problem: *Is* there such a being as the idea of the slave demands for its realisation? Are there such natural lines of demarcation between man and man as is here implied? That there is such a being, and that there are such lines, both reason and facts seem to Aristotle to prove. Slavery is part of the teleological scheme of the universe. Reason proves that a principle of rule and subordination runs through the world. It is as true of inanimate as it is of animate Nature. Even in music there is a "dominant" tone. Wherever, in fact, there is a union of elements in a single compound—(whether these elements be musical notes or human beings)—there is a scheme co-ordinating those elements in the pursuit of a single end; and wherever there is a scheme, there must be a supremacy of one element, and a subordination of others. The union of master and slave forms a household, and the scheme of the household demands the subordination of the one and the rule of the other. Universal as is this principle of rule and subordination, reason shows that it is not uniform. There are different degrees of rule and subordination. If the thing ruled is good in its kind, the thing ruling will exercise a nobler kind of authority, and the two together will produce a finer result, than if it be poor. The rule of the master over the slave is one of these degrees; it is a rule nobler in kind than that of the shepherd over his flock, but less noble than that of the statesman over his citizens.[1] Nature supplies us with parallels.[2] The soul rules the body with the "despotic" rule of a master over his slaves; reason controls the desires with the "political"

[1] This is in opposition to the doctrine of the *Politicus*, and in proof of the contention that the political art, by which the rule of the statesman is directed, is a thing *sui generis*. [2] *Cf. supra*, p. 26.

and by the character of the slave

rule of a statesman over his fellows. But this parallel is not a mere parallel; it goes deeper. It is a case of identity. The slave stands to his master, exactly as body stands to soul: the slave is a mere body, meant to be ruled by the soul of his master, as much as the master's own body is meant to be ruled by his soul. He is, as it were, an extension of his master's body, and therefore, just because soul is meant to rule body, the master (who is soul) is meant to rule the slave (who is body) with the full and absolute rule of soul over body. The reason why the slave must be subject to the exact degree of rule to which he is subject is to be found in the very fact which at first sight seems only a parallel.

So far, the process of the argument has led us to two conclusions, the one irrefragable, that in the world there is a scheme, and schemes involve rule and subordination; the other more disputable, that there are degrees of rule and subordination according to the quality of the object ruled, and that the quality of some men being merely that of bodily strength, they are to be subordinated to their rulers as utterly as body is subjected to soul. This last conclusion involves the corollary that there are men whose sole use is their bodily strength, and whose best and highest activity is merely that of the body. Aristotle, in assuming that there are such men, rests apparently on the fact that the body of the natural slave is obviously marked for slavery by its sturdy strength and capacity for work, while that of the natural freeman is as obviously marked for freedom by its upright carriage and unfitness for menial labour. He admits, however, that the fact is really no fact at all; and that though Nature wishes to make this physical distinction she often fails.[1] She gives to a freeman the frame of a slave, to a slave the carriage of a freeman. But if she fails in the body, she does not fail in the soul. There are men who have the souls of slaves, though they may be hard to discover, since the quality of the soul is not to be seen with the eyes. What then is the soul of the slave? It is the purely irrational or animal part of the soul—

Criticism of Aristotle's theory

[1] Nature, as we have seen, may fail to achieve the best, which is always its aim, because the necessary matter in which it works is imperfect. In that case its action may seem idle or purposeless, as it produces something not suited for its object.

and that only, if strict logic be observed. If the slave is a mere body, he must indeed have enough of soul to perceive objects and to move his body; but he cannot have more.[1] He cannot have reason; or he will be more than a mere body, and something of a spirit. Now it seems somewhat strange that a man should exist, in whom reason, which is the differentia of man, and the very essence of his individuality, should be entirely absent. Such a being will be a man who has none of the marks of a man: he will be an animal in human form. Nor does Aristotle ever really suppose that he exists. He always regards the slave as being possessed of the *semi-rational* part of the soul, and as so far enjoying reason that he can listen to its voice. The slave is therefore a creature possessed of desire—of will, and spirit, and appetite. He is a being in a state of perpetual youth (since youth is the age of desire), and therefore of perpetual tutelage. But tutelage is not slavery. The rule of reason over desire is only the *political* rule of a statesman over his fellows: it is the rule exercised by the rulers of the ideal State over the young whose appetites they are training. Slavery is *not* justified by the fact that the slave has only a minor reason: that will only justify a certain guardianship. Nor can this guardianship be really perpetual. For it is as impossible to imagine a class of beings who always *must be* perpetual children, as it is to imagine a class of beings who are animals in human form (though there may be isolated specimens of both, and particularly of the former). That reason should be present even in an imperfect form means a potentiality of reason in its fulness. And that the slave can attain reason in its fulness, and with reason the freedom of self-control, is admitted by Aristotle. He provides for the emancipation of slaves: in speaking of the ideal State, he lays it down as an axiom, that *all* slaves should have the prize of an ultimate freedom set before their eyes—though he does not explain, as he promises to do, why this should be so.[2] But if the slave can one day come by his freedom, it follows that he was always capable of attaining that ultimate freedom, and that he should always have been treated as a man, in whom the potentialities

[1] It is argued in the *De Anima*, 1413 b 24, that perception involves appetite; but nothing is said of spirit or will. [2] *Politics*, 1330 a 33.

of full manhood resided. There can be no gulf between the day before emancipation and the day after, in respect of the man's own nature: if slavery was justified by the man's nature the day before, it was justified the day after, just as, conversely, if freedom was justified by his capacities the day after, it was justified also the day before. To admit emancipation for all slaves is to admit that there is no man naturally intended for slavery and nothing else but slavery. But Aristotle goes still further. Not only does he admit the slave to an ultimate freedom, which implies that he ultimately becomes fully possessed of reason, and enters into the full inheritance of man: he practically admits that the slave, *while a slave,* is really on a level with his master, and therefore already possessed of reason. We learn from the *Ethics*,[1] that though the slave, as a slave, cannot enjoy the friendship of his master, yet, as a man, he is able to do so. There is a right and a wrong in the conduct of any man towards any man who can share in law or be a partner in a contract: there is, in other words, a justice which regulates their relations. Now as a man (it is implied), the slave *can* share in law and be a partner to a contract; and justice must therefore regulate his relations to his masters. But where there is justice, there is also friendship; and thus, because there is a possibility of justice, there is a possibility of friendship between master and slave. Two things are here asserted—that a slave has rights; and that he can be a partner with his master, even in friendship. But if he has any right, he must have that most elementary right of freedom: if he is a friend, he must have a purpose common to him and his master; and if he is a partner or associate (κοινωνός) with his master in a common purpose, he must be an equal in virtue of this association. It is true that all these conclusions only regard the slave as a man, and not as a slave; but the distinction is impossible. If the slave can be treated as a man in any respect, he ought to be treated as a man in all; and the admission that he can be regarded as a man destroys that conception of his wholly slavish and non-rational (one might say non-human) character, which was the one justification of his being treated as a slave.

Thus Aristotle's theory of a natural slavery would seem to

[1] *Ethics*, VIII., c. xi.

be vitiated by the facts that the slave is a *man:* that, as a man, he is possessed of reason; that, as possessed of reason, he is capable of self-direction; and that, as capable of self-direction, he requires freedom for its condition. These are the reasons which must always condemn slavery. No man can properly be a slave, just because he is a man, a person possessed of a rational will. "Prevent him (if it were possible) from using his body to express a will, and the will itself could not become a reality: he would not really be a person." The primary basis of liberty is thus *personality*—as personality is the basis of all rights. At the same time mere personality (or the person viewed as an isolated individuality) does not of itself involve the right to liberty; nor does the mere capacity for expressing a will demand freedom for its realisation. Only a social personality and a social will can claim freedom.[1] Freedom demands "capacity on the part of the subject for membership of a society, for determination of the will, and through it of the bodily organisation, by the conception of a well-being as common to self with others".[2] For freedom, like all rights, has a double aspect: on one side it is individual, as rooted in a person; on the other side it is social, as meaning the recognition of that person by a society. And that recognition will not be given except to a person who recognises on his side the same aims and purposes as the society in which he lives. If a slave were an enemy to the aims and purposes of society, he would have no right to liberty.[3] But Aristotle himself admits that he is not an enemy: he speaks of him as "able to share in law and covenant," just as he admits (by allowing emancipation) that he is capable of self-direction by his own will. And in making these admissions he really states the case for freedom, and destroys the basis of slavery.

The right to liberty

So far, we have attempted to show that Aristotle's theory of a natural slave and natural slavery is, as all false theories tend to be, refuted by its own author in the course of its statement. For a false theory must always fall into inconsistency,

[1] A rational will must however always be social; and a rational will was postulated above for the slave.

[2] Green, *Principles of Political Obligation*, p. 156.

[3] Society imprisons such enemies.

if it deals with all the facts and data of its subject; and some of these facts must contradict the assumptions on which it goes. Hobbes, for instance, in basing a false theory of Contract on the supposed unsociability of natural man (who has "no pleasure, but, on the contrary, a great deal of grief in keeping company"), contradicts himself when he casually admits the fact of "men's aptness to society". But if this theory of slavery is thus defeated by its own inconsistencies, one must at any rate admit that Aristotle himself supplies his own refutation, and by his own full admission of the facts shows his width of view even in a false conclusion. Nor can the theory of natural slavery be simply dismissed as inconsistent and mistaken. To understand and appreciate it fully, there are three things which we must still notice. In the first place, while justifying natural slavery, Aristotle rejects *legal* slavery. Secondly, even if he admits natural slavery, he admits it because he believes that it is morally justified, and that it gives the slave a moral excellence which he could not otherwise attain. Lastly, it still remains true that the higher products of civilisation depend upon a basis of manual work which alone makes them possible, and that the only way to justify this fact is by assuming that some men are "meant" to produce the higher things, and others to do the lower work.

Defence of Aristotle

Aristotle rejects as wrong the slavery of Greeks

(i.) Aristotle had intended, by his doctrine of natural slavery, to rebut the sophistic doctrine that slavery was conventional and artificial. There was a kind of slavery, he maintained, which was neither. But he admits that there is a kind of slavery which is both—the slavery which depends upon the convention generally admitted in war, that the vanquished are the spoils of the victor. In regard to this admittedly "conventional" kind of slavery there was, Aristotle tells us, a difference of opinion. Some, regarding victory as the product of superior force, believed this slavery to be merely based on force, and therefore wrong. Others, regarding victory as the reward of superior "excellence" (ἀρετή), thought that conventional slavery was justified by the moral superiority of the victor. Both schools of opinion seemed to Aristotle to rest on one underlying principle, that slavery may be justified by "force which is not without virtue". But the former school interpreted this principle to mean, that besides mere force there must always be virtue as well, to conciliate the goodwill of the vanquished, and to justify their slavery by a basis of consent. The latter school interpreted the same principle as meaning that force of itself always involved virtue for its corollary, and of itself justified slavery. Either school really gave its adhesion, it seemed to Aristotle, to his own view, that only a natural superiority in character was a proper foundation for slavery. Some there were indeed who, contenting themselves with the mere letter of the law, held that every man who was legally a slave was rightly a slave. But inasmuch as they also admitted that no Greek could ever be rightly a slave, they contradicted their own position, and testified once more to the view that only those whom Nature has meant for slaves can rightly be treated as slaves. They admitted in fact that not law, but Nature, determined freeman and slave; and that the differences of moral endowment which Nature had given were the ultimate arbiters of liberty and subjection. And in admitting this they limited, as Aristotle intended his doctrine to limit, the scope of slavery. If only the natural master, endowed with moral capacity, had a right to his position, and the merely legal master, or the master who rested merely on force, were disqualified: if, again, only the natural slave, whom Nature had left morally imperfect, could properly be a slave, and the Greek was exempt from slavery—then, it is easy to see, the number of masters and slaves would be seriously diminished; and the doctrine of "natural slaves," far from condoning, would seem to challenge existing slavery.[1]

(ii.) From the postulate of moral superiority in the master, and moral inferiority in the slave, it follows that slavery is a moral institution. The slave is supplemented, and becomes a moral being through being supplemented, by the moral faculty of his master. The slave attains through his slavery not only the virtue of being a good servant, but also, to the extent of which he is capable, the virtue of being a good man. The former is a little thing in comparison; and it comes to the slave, not necessarily from his master, but (it may be) from his overseer. The latter is everything. The essence of the

Aristotle only defends slavery when it is morally justifiable

[1] Aristotle's doctrine may seem to us to defend slavery: it is quite possible that it struck his contemporaries as also an attack.

relation of master and slave lies in its moral meaning. The slave is a partner in his master's life, and the admonition and correction of his master is the great benefit which he receives from the partnership. It is clear from this conception that the slavery which Aristotle contemplates is one which has lost half its sting. It is a slavery in which the slave is admitted into the life of the family, and in which he becomes imbued with the tone and character of the family in which he lives. Within the circle of the family the slave is a person. He is a member of this lesser association, sharing in its full moral life, as a real "part" (at any rate in the sense in which the child is a part), and not as a mere "condition". Through his membership he attains the virtues, in the peculiar "ministerial" form which befits his position. He attains self-control; but it is the self-control of a servant subordinating himself to his superior. Not only for the slave, however, have the virtues their peculiar form, but also for the wife and the child. The self-control of the wife is not as that of the husband: hers is the quiet and modest self-control which issues in a discreet silence. For the slave, accordingly, slavery means that he, like the other members of the household, shares in its moral life according to his place and in his degree. For the master it means a detachment from material cares, which sets him free for higher things. It is not merely negative in its results, setting him free from work: it is positive, since it leaves him at leisure for noble activities, for a life of politics and of philosophy. Modern slavery has too often involved a contempt for labour: ancient slavery ultimately involved, in Aristotle's theory, the highest possible activity for both master and slave.

Higher activities involve a basis of lower labour

(iii.) The higher activities of man must always involve a basis of lower labour. We may still make a division something like that which Aristotle made, between those activities which are in themselves an end and a pleasure, and those which are pursued in pain as the means of earning daily bread. To the former class we may assign the work of the scholar, the artist, the musician, the thinker: to the latter the work of weaver and miner and farmer. It is true that in modern times the division is obscured by the fact that all alike are paid; and indeed it is possible to conceive of the higher activities as pursued in pain for the sake of their ultimate reward, and of the lower activities as sources of pleasure and satisfaction in themselves. There is nothing in modern times quite corresponding to the clean cleavage of work into its "liberal" and "mechanical" kinds, which was made by the Greeks. They might have classed *all* the work done in modern society as "mechanical," because it is generally done "for the sake of another," and paid; while we, on the contrary, tend to think of all work as liberal, believing in the "dignity of labour," and holding, with St. Benedict, *laborare est orare.* And yet the distinction remains, between those whose day's work it is to do that which they love to do, and the doing of which means the happy energy of every power, and those whose appointed portion it is to till the ground with their hands in weariness, and to use but the powers of the body. A passage in the book of Ecclesiasticus[1] runs: "The wisdom of a learned man cometh by opportunity of leisure: and he that hath little business shall become wise. How can he get wisdom that holdeth the plough, and that glorieth in the goad; that driveth oxen, and is occupied in their labours, and whose talk is of bullocks?" And then, having spoken of these latter, the author continues: "without these cannot a city be inhabited: . . . they shall not be sought for in publick counsel, nor sit high in the congregation: . . . but they will maintain the state of the world". "They will maintain the state of the world," for it cannot be denied, that the work of the "learned man" is only rendered possible by that of him "that holdeth the plough". The thinker is set free for his thinking, because he is maintained by the work of toiler upon toiler beneath. Not only has his household its servants: the whole economic community is, almost literally, the handmaid of his "leisure". It is obvious that, if the ministering of these agents stayed for a week, the building of thought would cease. We cannot get away from the fact that, whether we will or no, we employ countless servants, "whose use is that of their body". They are not indeed tied to us by a domestic slavery: so much the worse, Aristotle would tell us, for they are removed from the humanising and refining influence of adoption into a higher life. Yet on the other hand they do not give without receiving. Thinker

[1] C. xxxviii.

and artist give back to them their thought and their art for the material things which they have received. In truth, there is no relation of means and end between the lower and the higher workers: they are both parts of one whole, and they do according to their place in the whole, each giving, each receiving, and all contributing to the common life by that which they supply. Yet it is still true, that one has a higher place, and one a lower: it is still true, that we cannot justify this allocation, except in the manner of Aristotle. We must still hold, if we believe that there is any justice in society, that some are born for a low place, and some for a high place. But one can only hold this view with diffidence. How long would the man, who seems born for menial work, continue to be fitted only for menial work, if he found the right environment and proper training? Is a man's place Nature's intention, or the product of poor environment and defective education? These are knotty questions; and one can only hope, that with the perfecting of society each man may come to find what is really the true place for his true self, and that the man who is born among silver men may rise to the golden, if he is golden within. But whatever the perfecting of society, one cannot but think that there must still be men of copper and silver as well as of gold, since there is work for men of copper and silver, as well as for men of gold. To hold fast to this belief is not to justify slavery: it is merely to assert that there is a plan in the world, and that "Nature does not act at random".[1]

How far we have risen above Aristotle's position

This truth, then, there would seem to be in Aristotle's theory of slavery. Lofty work needs a basis of lower work; and there are men who are born to do the lower work. The falsehood of his theory is, that he believes these men to be lower than men, mere bodies, or at best half-rational beings. They are men as fully as the men who do the higher work; and they have every right that attaches to man, and especially the primary right of freedom. Modern practice recognises the right of every man to life and liberty. Socially, it refuses to tolerate slavery; politically, it refuses to exclude the labourer

[1] But it may be argued that division of labour is as "conventional" as the distribution of talents. It does not follow that, because one man ought to do one thing, he ought therefore to do *only* that thing the whole of his time.

from a vote, as Aristotle would have excluded him from the assembly. One thing it does not do. While recognising the right of every man to life and liberty, it does not make it real. There is a positive implication in the recognition of a right to liberty. We give freedom to all, because all *can* help to realise the common aim of society by discharging some function which contributes to its realisation. But we do not attempt to see to it that each man *shall* have the function, the work, which is the positive side of his freedom. "While we say that he shall not be used as a means, we often leave him without the chance of using himself for any social end at all."[1] One of the saddest things in our modern life is the man who has no place, and who has yet full capacity and every desire to fill a place. The sadness is deeper than starvation: it is the sadness of loneliness in a crowded world. Nor can we boast that we have risen superior to slavery, unless we make our freedom no bare liberty to live somehow, but a concrete liberty to do a definite work, and to take a definite place in the world.[2]

Aristotle's Theory of Wealth and Its Production

§ 3. We now turn to the "economics" of Aristotle in the modern sense of the word—to his theory of wealth, and its production, exchange, and distribution. We saw that the slave was an "instrument" of the householder, and that the same was true of property—of dress and food and furniture. But the slave, we also saw, is a real part of the household, because he shares in its moral life; and the treatment of the slave is a real part of the art of the householder, because it involves the inculcation of virtue. With property it is obviously otherwise. Property, we have already learned, is external to the good life: it is a condition, but not a part. Accordingly the science of acquiring property (κτητική) is no part of "economics," in the strict sense of the word; though it must be treated under that head, as a necessary condition of the "economist's" activity.

Definition of wealth

Such being the place of the science of acquisition, we have now to inquire into the nature of wealth, and the means of its

[1] Green, *Principles of Political Obligation*, p. 159.

[2] I do not mean this to imply *le droit de travail*, or that the State ought to employ its unemployed members in production on its own account.

acquisition. For the family, as for the individual, wealth can only be a "furnishing" of material things, sufficient for the purposes of a moral life. Accordingly, wealth is defined as "a store of things which are necessary or useful for life in the associations of city or household"; or again, it is termed "a collection of instruments for the use of a household or State". It is interesting to compare this definition, which makes of wealth a sum of objects possessing use and value only in so far as they can serve the moral life, with that of J. S. Mill. Here a utilitarian philosophy enters; and wealth is defined as "all useful or agreeable things, which possess exchangeable value". Mill, indeed, expressly refers to the definition of wealth "as signifying 'instruments': meaning . . . the whole accumulation possessed by individuals or communities as means for the attainments of their ends"; and he remarks that "this view of the subject is philosophically correct," though "it departs too widely from the custom of language". None the less, his own definition departs from Aristotle in two essential points. He conceives of wealth as meaning things "useful" in the sense of giving sensations of comfort or pleasure: Aristotle meant by things "useful" the things which were serviceable to a Final Good. He conceived of wealth, as consisting only of objects possessed of value in exchange: Aristotle deprecated exchange, and it was far from entering into his conception of wealth.

Wealth limited in amount

Wealth which is a means or instrument to a moral life will as such be limited in amount, just as wealth which consists of things useful and agreeable will be by its nature unlimited. We have already learned to conceive of the end as imposing a limit; and it is not surprising to read that the amount of property which is necessary for the supreme end of a good life is a limited and definite amount. There is no *processus ad infinitum* in wealth, any more than in other things: here too there must be a mean, and an appointed term. Every art has a definite number of tools, and those of a definite size; nor is it otherwise with the instruments of economic art. In this conception of wealth as necessarily limited Aristotle parts company with modern thought. When we think of the little there is to distribute, and the many there are to receive, we feel that only an infinite wealth will satisfy an infinity of need. Aristotle, thinking of the earth as yielding her abundance readily, and of men as only too prone to put out her gifts at usury, felt on the contrary that the moral purpose of life might be choked in riches, if riches exceeded the measure which the fulfilling of that purpose demanded.

Of the acquisition of wealth Aristotle has much to say; but the fundamental characteristic of his theory of production, if it may be so called, is a reactionary archaism, which abolishes all the economic machinery of civilisation in favour of the self-supporting farm and a modicum of barter. The acquisition of wealth, we are told, is the subject of the art of profit-making (χρηματιστική).[1] This art is related to "economics" (of which we have already seen that it is not really a part), as provider is related to user. It may provide in two ways; and there may consequently be said to be two divisions of the art of profit-making. It may make its profit *from the soil* (ἀπὸ γῆς); entrusting to the ground its seed-corn, it may reap from Nature, who pays liberal interest on what is lent to her, a hundredfold in return. Or again, the man who pursues this art may make his profit *from his fellows* (ἀπ' ἀλλήλων): selling commodities, he may sell at a large profit; lending moneys, he may lend at a heavy interest. Here the return is not given by Nature; it is wrung from man. The two methods may almost be called the vegetarian and the cannibal: the one enables man to live by the fruits of the earth; the other makes him a Shylock, living by the pounds of flesh which he exacts from customer or debtor. To the latter method in particular the term chrematistic may be applied; and thus the art of profit-making is often to be understood, as including only the practice of traffic and usury. But we must first discuss that branch of acquisition which is concerned with the making of profits from the soil, before we turn to its "perversion".

Two methods of acquiring wealth

In his discussion of economics, the antithesis of "natural" and "conventional," on which he is not elsewhere inclined to lay

Reactionary character of Aristotle's economics

[1] The generic science of the acquisition of wealth (κτητική) falls into two branches, according as it is exercised peaceably, and by agriculture or trade (χρηματιστική), or violently, and by slave-hunting or piracy (θηρευτική). Chrematistic seems, however, to be also used as the general term.

great stress, grips Aristotle hard. Instead of refusing to recognise the antithesis, instead of insisting that Nature and art are really one (as he does, for instance, in speaking of the State and its origin), he contrasts the natural modes of acquisition sharply with the unnatural and conventional. In addition, he seems to commit the error of identifying Nature altogether with the primitive and undeveloped rudiments, oblivious of his general teaching, that the supremely natural is the absolutely complete and developed end. In this way, he comes to be as reactionary in economics as was Plato in his theory of the family, and to make his motto, like Plato, "Back to the simple and primitive".[1] It seems curious that he should have adopted a tone so much unlike that of the rest of the *Politics* in discussing economics. It may be partly the result of his preference for an agricultural democracy; partly, and still more, the effect of social prejudice against the "mechanical" money-maker; partly, and perhaps most of all, the consequence of a teleological system somewhat naïvely interpreted. Nature makes nothing in vain, and since she has made the earth and all its creatures for the service of man, it would be a mere flying in the face of Nature if man attempted to provide for his necessities otherwise than by accepting her bounty. Nature, who provided for man the milk in his mother's breasts at the beginning of life, provides for him in his maturity the plants of the field and the beasts of the wood. Thus does the *scala naturæ* of Aristotle—plants, animals, and man—work itself out in a naïve and external teleology,[2] which confuses his outlook on economics. But it was only natural that early thought should indulge in such *naïveté;* and Socrates himself is very like Aristotle, when he argues that "the movements of the sun in summer and winter are arranged with a view to the advantage of man". None the less, however we may excuse or explain the fact, it remains true that the ideal economic society of Aristotle comes perilously near the "golden" age—

The acquisition of wealth from Nature

[1] This is the confusion of simplicity, in the sense of conformity to a principle, with simplicity, in the sense of primitive archaism, which also appears in Plato, and drags him, as we noticed, back to the clan.

[2] But Aristotle has also a fine and internal conception of teleology, in which man is the end of other things, not as their "destined eater" (Hegel said of food at a dinner, "Bring it, that we may fulfil its destiny"), but as the final aim towards the production of which Nature moves.

When wild in woods the noble savage ran.

Yet even through this *naïveté* a fruitful conception emerges; and there is much truth in the hint that the social life of men is determined by the manner in which they get their food from Nature. It may seem a truism, and even a tautology, to remark, that a people which lives on corn will form an agricultural community, and that a people which feeds on cattle will be a pastoral people. Yet the remark has a wider application. In a deeper sense than Aristotle intended, the food of a people determines its history. A change of diet, it has been said, is often more important than a change of dynasty. The life of a primitive people would certainly seem to vary with the manner in which it satisfies its wants. When men turned from hunting to pasturing cattle in grassy spaces, society began to change accordingly. The value of steady labour became obvious: there were cattle to be tended; and the demand for labour probably produced both permanent marriage (resulting in a patriarchal system) and the institution of slavery. Social life had altered profoundly with the alteration of the method of acquiring food from Nature.

The rise of unnatural acquisition

But the art of profit-making, in the stricter sense of the word, is confined to that unnatural method of acquisition, which makes a profit not from Nature, but from men's necessities. Such an unnatural method comes to be pursued in the following way. Every commodity has a double use: it may be employed for immediate consumption; or it may be used for the purposes of exchange. In either case the commodity is used as a commodity; but while in the former case it is put to its proper use, by being made to serve the end for which it was destined, in the latter case it is less naturally used, by being made to serve an end outside itself. Within its limits, however, the use of commodities for purposes of exchange is necessary and natural. It serves to correct that "inequality" which results when one man has too much of one thing, and another too much of another; and its proper function is to "equalise" by giving to both of the men a sufficiency of both commodities. So long as equality is thus secured, so long is justice safe—so long is exchange natural. Either man gives to the other his surplus, and either receives in the same proportion in which he gives; and thus the sufficiency which it is the aim and object of exchange to produce is attained by both. But if a man aims at getting *more* than a sufficiency, if he gives in a *less* proportion than that in which he receives —then equality disappears, and injustice enters. The day of profit-making begins; and unnatural acquisition at the expense of other men succeeds to the natural exploitation of the soil. How does this transition from legitimate barter to unnatural exchange arise? The bridge by which man passes from the one to the other is, Aristotle tells us, money. The primitive exchange of the village (for there exchange first began) was a simple bartering of one commodity naturally acquired from the soil against another similarly acquired. If Callias, seeking sufficiency and not superfluity, sells a sheep to Callicles, his fellow-villager, for a bushel of corn—equal value for equal value, one bounty of Nature for another—the result is practically the same as if Callias had himself produced the corn which he consumes. He makes no profit which is not of Nature's giving: the exchange is natural, equal, and just. Let us suppose, however, that instead of one villager exchanging with another, we have a man who belongs to one country exporting to another —for instance, a Byzantine exporting corn to Attica. He may not desire to barter his corn for Attic olives or Attic marble: he may not desire the burden and cost of importing any heavy commodity at all. He will, in such a case, desire something containing great value in small bulk, provided that this thing possesses enough utility to be readily used in exchange again. Now there are things which possess such qualities; and these things are the precious metals. A natural agreement has therefore made these the medium of exchange. At first used in the bulk, and weighed in each transaction, they finally came to be stamped with an indication of their weight, which was at the same time a guarantee of their intrinsic value, and in this way a "currency" was finally established. The Byzantine merchant of our instance returns home with money for his corn; and he has consented to sell his commodity because, and only because, he was offered money in exchange.

The introduction of money

This is the origin of money traced back to its function as a medium of exchange. In the *Ethics* another and complementary view is presented, by which the origin of money is principally referred to the necessity of a measure of value. The essence of exchange is proportionate requital; Callicles must return to Callias, in quantity and quality, what he has received.[1] The difficulty is, that exchange is necessarily of two *different* objects, the one of which has to be weighed against the other. If this is to be done, a *tertium quid* must be taken, which will serve as a common measure for these (and for all other) objects. Fundamentally, this *tertium quid* is demand; and objects are measured against one another in terms of the amount of demand which they excite. But demand being in itself intangible, money has been introduced as its representative by a general agreement.[2] In these remarks we seem to have a theory of value, as *determined* by demand, and *measured* by money, to which modern economists would have little to object, save that the seller's cost of production must also be taken into account, as well as the buyer's demand.

Value of money—conventional or natural?

Both in the *Ethics* and the *Politics* Aristotle regards money as a thing depending upon convention (νόμος) rather than Nature: its very etymology (and Aristotle sets store by etymologies) attests its artificial character.[3] But we learn from

[1] In an association of exchange (ἀλλακτικὴ κοινωνία), justice, in the sense of proportionate requital, must be the principle followed (*Eth.*, 1132 b 32). "It is this reciprocal rendering of an equivalent amount of dissimilar things . . . that holds the State together" as an economic association (*Pol.*, 1261 a 30, and Newman's note *ad locum*). Thus the theory of justice leads to a false theory of value (because it leads to the belief in a *justum pretium*, *infra*, p. 384).

[2] To Aristotle demand, or need (χρεία), holds men together in an association of exchange, inducing them to exchange their goods, just as, in Plato's view, it brought men together into the primary form of society. Holding men together as a *single* principle, it is the one *common measure* by which the goods they exchange are valued. The nexus is also the standard. In a state of barter demand serves by itself as the measure of value, and makes couches commensurable with house, producing the equation 5 couches = 1 house. Except for demand, there is no commensurability and therefore no possibility of equation. But where men have passed from an economy in kind to a monetary economy, by agreeing upon a "currency," that currency may be said to form the concrete and objective form of the subjective standard formed by demand. It makes objects commensurable, and renders an equation possible—not in itself (for only demand can do that), but as the representative of demand. As an objective standard, money also forms an objective nexus: it holds the association of exchange together, being as it were a demand held in reserve by its holders, and giving them a guarantee that, though they may not demand at present, yet they can at any time demand effectively.

[3] Currency (νομισμα) is from the same root as convention (νόμος). *Cf.* p. 386.

the *Politics* that there were two opposite views among the Greeks with regard to money. There were some who identified wealth with money, as the mercantilist school is supposed to have done in modern times, and made money something *sui generis*, something above and beyond all other commodities. Such a view was natural. After all, money unlocks the door to all other commodities; and it was little wonder if men regarded the "open sesame" to all other things as itself a thing apart. On the other hand there were some, like the Cynics, who went to the other extreme, and regarded money as less than all other commodities. Not money, they argued, but the knowledge how to use things rightly, is true wealth. They felt that though money may procure things worth possessing, it is in itself of no value: it cannot satisfy a single human desire. Midas among all his gold was hungry and thirsty.[1] Hence, argued these thinkers, whatever value money may possess is an imported, conventional, and artificial value, due to the fiat of men. If men were to declare that silver was of no value, then it would be of no value. Here are two extremes; and one naturally expects Aristotle, as usual, to adopt a middle line, subscribing to neither view, but absorbing the truth of both. But he appears, contrary to expectation, to give his allegiance to the extreme view of money as a mere convention. More than once he speaks of it as introduced by an agreement: in the *Ethics* he tells us definitely that money is not natural but conventional, since it is in man's power to change it or even to make it entirely useless. On the other hand there are traces, both in the *Politics* and the *Ethics*, of the middle view which we should expect—that money is neither more nor less than other commodities, but "a commodity like other commodities, with its value determined in the same way as that of other commodities".[2] In the *Politics* he remarks that "men agreed to take and receive in their dealings something which was *itself possessed of use*, such as silver".[3] But if silver is possessed of use, it is a commodity; and its value must be

[1] But, as Newman pertinently remarks, his plight was not due to his being confined to gold, but to his being limited to a single commodity. He would have starved in the midst of corn, if he had had only corn. Madame de Sevigné wrote: "Seated on a heap of corn, I shriek, 'I am starving'".

[2] Mill, *Political Economy*, ii., vii., § 3 *ad finem*.

[3] *Pol.*, 1257 a 36.

determined, like that of other commodities, by demand and supply. In that case money will have a natural, and not a conventional value.[1] It is a natural corollary of this view of money, that it must fluctuate in value, like other commodities, with the fluctuations of demand; and the *Ethics* tells us, that this is the case. "Money has not always the same value, though it always tends to remain steady."[2] And thus it would appear that here, as in regard to slavery, Aristotle is the best critic of himself: he recognises, after all, that money is a commodity, possessing a use, with a value determined by the demand, which it "represents," and fluctuating according to the fluctuations of that demand.

The middleman condemned

From this digression on money we must now return to profit-making of the baser sort, to which, as we have already seen, money forms the bridge of transition. A cumbrous exchange by barter is pursued only by those who *need:* an easy exchange by money attracts those who *covet.* As a medium of exchange, money facilitates the rise of the dealer who stands midway between the two producers: itself a "middle" thing, it naturally begets the middleman. And with the middleman comes evil. He is a channel through which goods pass from A to B, and from B to A; but he is a channel which intercepts in their transmission no inconsiderable share of the goods transmitted. He grows at the expense of A and B alike. He is the parasite of the working world: instead of finding his own sustenance, he lives by abstracting from others part of the sustenance which they have acquired for themselves. To a modern mind even parasitism may seem a part of Nature: to Aristotle the parasite of exchange is unnatural and immoral. The evil of parasitism is not only to be found in the loss of the workers who suffer: it also appears in the degradation of the parasite itself.[3] The dealer who acquires his sustenance at the expense of his fellows is not content with mere sustenance, or

[1] The intrinsic utility of the precious metals lies in their appeal to the desire for ornament, which is primitive and universal, and almost as deep as the desire for food. In that they thus appeal to a fundamental element of human nature, they have certainly a "natural" value.

[2] *Eth.*, 1133 b 13.

[3] Similarly biology tells us that the parasite in nature is also degraded, in the sense that it suffers an atrophy of the higher organs, by which it might have found its own sustenance for itself.

sufficiency: he does not aim at acquiring wealth as a means and instrument to his true life. He desires a superfluity. He elevates wealth into an end; and, since men always desire whatever they regard as an end in the fullest measure possible and without any limit or bound, it follows that he desires an unlimited and unbounded wealth.[1] This is the greatest moral error which a man can commit, since it involves a misconception of the whole purpose of life; and it is an error which directly flows from the influence of money. Easily stored, without detriment to its value, the very quality of money is its defect: it lends itself so naturally to accumulation, that prone as men are to take the easy path, they readily make its accumulation the purpose of their lives. It is true that this cardinal error is not peculiar to the dealer. The practitioner of an art like medicine may fall into the same mistake. As the dealer pursues the art of acquisition not for the sake of its true end, but for the false end of accumulating money, the physician may similarly practise his art, not with a view to its true end of producing health, but merely to augment his own wealth. In either case money-getting dethrones well-doing: in either case, since different ends involve different means, the whole colour and complexion of life is altered. Aristotle would never have conceived of a man as showing self-control or courage in the pursuit of wealth. Self-control and courage are the means to the attainment of life's proper end; and if a wholly different end be sought, the means used, though they may resemble the means used by a good man for *his* purpose, are nevertheless entirely different things. Yet while he condemns money-getting, Aristotle would not be Aristotle if he did not allow for the half-truth which it contains, and did not attempt to discover "the cause of the error". He will not condemn without understanding. And accordingly he suggests, that the error of misconceiving the purpose of life has two natural sources. Acquisition is necessary for a moral life; but men have confused its necessity as a means with absolute necessity, and so given themselves over simply to its pursuit. And again pleasure *is* necessary to happiness; but men, dimly feeling this necessity of pleasure,

[1] And thus, forgetting the moral life, he suffers an atrophy of his moral faculties.

have once more surrendered themselves to treating as the whole what is only a part or ingredient. They have sought pleasure, and nothing but pleasure, and pleasure *ad infinitum ;* and for the sake of unlimited pleasure they have sought unlimited wealth[1].

The middleman performs an economic service

What shall we say of this condemnation of the middleman, which makes him first a parasite, and then a moral enormity, who by the very nature of his position has gone awry from virtue? That the middleman is not necessarily a parasite a very brief consideration of his function will show. If he is not a producer of commodities, he certainly renders a service. He gives his time to the economic community, and he gives it for the discharge of a function which is necessary to the community. He does a service to A when he takes his commodities off his hands; he does a service to B, when he provides him with what he requires.[2] Those who contribute their services are not the least members of an association of exchange: on the contrary, it is easier to produce most commodities than it is to render services, like that of the middleman, which require no inconsiderable powers of mind. That it is easy to shut our eyes to an intangible service does not justify us in defrauding it of its reward. A must pay X for taking the goods he desires to sell: B must pay X for providing the goods he desires to buy. In reality, X is an agent in production, who must be paid like other agents. One cannot say that the production of an article has ceased, until it has reached the consumer. Exchange is the last of the stages of production: it is as much a stage of production as transport; it is no less a stage of production, than manufacture, or than agriculture itself.[3] As the last link in the

[1] The man who makes money his aim does not really desire the mere satisfaction of possessing a number of counters. The money is a symbol of something which is his real aim. To many that aim is the sense of success and capacity which the visible symbol inspires: they have pitted their calculations in a game with chance and their fellows, and they like to feel that they have beaten both. Aristotle, however, only contemplates a more vulgar class, who have made pleasure their aim, and who, seeking unlimited pleasure, desire unlimited wealth as a means to its attainment. In thus considering wealth as a means, he somewhat contradicts his previous view of the nature of the profit-maker, who, we were told, made wealth an end.

[2] Plato had recognised this service; *cf. supra*, p. 106, n. 1.

[3] We use "produce" in English as meaning not only "to create" but also "to bring forward when required," as when we speak of producing a witness or a document. Economic production embraces both meanings; and the middleman is an agent of production more especially in the latter sense.

long chain of production, the middleman has his appointed place and his proper reward. And not only does a proper theory of production (as including services, and embracing exchange) justify the existence of the dealer. A true theory of value, and consequently of price, is equally destructive of the idea of his parasitic nature. As Aristotle himself tells us, value depends on demand, on felt utility; it is not determined simply by cost of production. If it were, there might be a *justum pretium* which alone could be asked and taken; and if that just price were not observed by the middleman, then he might be regarded as living parasitically on his fellows, in giving less and taking more. Even so, this could only be done by disregarding two things—the part played by the dealer in production, and the fact that there are several costs of production, according to the amount of articles produced, or the producer's skill. But since the element of demand enters into value, it is plain that X may buy the same commodity for a low price from A, who is more eager to sell than he to buy, and sell it for a high price to B, who is more eager to buy than he to sell, without either falling short of, or going beyond, the "just" price.

The ethics of commerce

Thus the middleman would appear to be justified from the charge of parasitism. Does not this justification purge him also from the charge of moral obliquity? If the dealer discharge a service, like the doctor, there is no more need for every dealer to make wealth his sole object in life, than there is for every doctor. Some dealers may go astray, just as some doctors may; and there is a greater temptation for the dealer to do so, than for the doctor. Dealing as he does in money every day, he may easily find that

> his nature is subdued
> To what it works in, like the dyer's hand.

He may make money his aim; and in petty commerce he may do what the dealer in great commerce cannot do—he may make his profit out of his fellows, by preying upon their "need". It is of such commerce, perhaps, that Aristotle is thinking most in his condemnation of the middleman. Adulterated goods sold for genuine, and "hire systems" of the worse sort—into these modern terms Aristotle's meaning may be translated; and if we understand him in those terms we shall see that he was condemning what we should still condemn. The very term which he uses for the commerce which he condemns, "huckstering," seems of itself to point to such a conclusion. At the same time it must be admitted that no exception is made in favour of the merchant or commerce from the strictures which he passes on the middleman ; and the impression which Aristotle leaves is one of hostility to trade in general, as mechanical, parasitic, and immoral.[1]

Interest condemned by Aristotle

In coming to the subject of interest, we must again remember that it is petty interest (ὀβολοστατική), and not great finance, which concerns Aristotle. He is not thinking of heavy loans on the security of a whole cargo, such as Athens knew, but of petty lendings to the necessitous poor at heavy interest.[2] Accordingly, classing usury under the head of profit-making of the unnatural sort, he condemns it even more decidedly than commerce. It is a means by which men make profit, even more obviously than in commerce, from the necessities of their fellows. When a creditor lends £100, and requires £120 at the end of the year, he is guilty of a more flagrant theft than if he had acquired £20 by a series of petty thefts from many customers. He makes his profit at a single stroke; he makes it without stirring a finger. But there is another sense in which the craft of the usurer is unnatural. Not only does he make his profit from his fellows rather than from Nature: he makes barren metal breed an issue. A portentous birth, an unnatural abortion—such is the interest which springs from a principal, which by the very nature of its being must be sterile. *Nummus nummum parere non potest;* yet the usurer flies in the face of Nature, and makes the impossibility a fact. The argument is based on a single word. The Greeks

[1] Perhaps we shall be right in thinking that Aristotle is attacking the conception of a system of "business ethics," which condones harshness, and connives at meanness—which exacts the last ounce of interest from the creditor, and allows any subterfuge or strategy to outstrip a rival.

[2] Pöhlmann, however, believes that Aristotle was condemning a great credit system in attacking usury, and a system of developed commerce in attacking the middleman. He believes that, like Plato, Aristotle is enunciating a gospel of Socialism, of which the last word is "Back to the Land". But, like Plato, Aristotle is in reality speaking throughout from a moral and not from an economic point of view ; and it seems to me certain that Aristotle was lecturing *ex cathedra*, as a moral philosopher, "on certain aspects of the morality of business".

spoke of interest as the child (τόκος) of the "parent" principal; and Aristotle, it would seem at first sight, confuses word with thing, metaphor with fact, and concludes that to make money produce a (metaphorical) child is wrong, because money cannot (literally) have a child. But he is not quite so confused as might appear—and for this reason. While a modern thinker, knowing several languages, would never think of any word as indissolubly wedded to the thing which in a particular language it expressed, the Greek, who was confined to a single speech, might readily believe that each word of that speech was divinely adjusted to the corresponding thing. Men have often been haunted by the problem of the relation of word to thing. Sometimes they have tried, as the Egyptian king and Frederic II. are reported to have tried, by means of experiments on new-born children, to discover the inevitable language which knits the right word to the right thing. More often they have simply assumed that their own was the one true tongue which was spoken in Paradise. To the Greek this attitude was natural. To him the barbarian was, what Cassandra seemed to Clytæmnestra, "one who chattered in an unknown tongue like a swallow". His own tongue was the one vehicle of truth. And therefore Aristotle often appeals to etymology in support of his doctrine: it is the voice of "facts themselves" when the word speaks for him, for the word is the fact.[1] The same feeling is the basis of the argument about interest: "facts themselves" proved it unnatural, since the word by which it went was one which could not be naturally applied.

How far Aristotle's condemnation of interest was justified

It is easy to show that Aristotle has not understood the theory of interest. The lender does a service to the borrower, which has to be repaid. He loses control of his money for a season; and he demands a recompense for the lost time, during which it might have been employed. It is not barren money which he lends. The money which he lends is exchanged for

[1] One may cite by way of illustration Reuchlin (quoted in Ranke's *History of the German Reformation*, Eng. Trans., i., 299): "The names which God has given to Himself are an echo of Eternity; in them is the deep abyss of His mysterious working expressed; the God-man called Himself the Word" (*De Verbo Mirifico*). Plato argues in the *Cratylus*, 434 A, τὸ ὄνομα ὅμοιον τῷ πράγματι: *cf.* 435 D, ὅς ἂν τὰ ὀνόματα ἐπίστηται, ἐπίστασθαι καὶ τὰ πράγματα.

"tools": the tools breed increase from the earth over and above the outlay: out of his superfluity the borrower, well content, can pay a quota to his creditor. All this is true of interest—among "economic men". But Aristotle was not thinking of this—although the impression which he leaves here, as in regard to commerce (and in both cases for want of defining and limiting his scope), is an impression of general hostility to the practice which he discusses. He was thinking of loans to the indigent, spent not in providing a capital for work, but in necessary consumption for the sustenance of life, and therefore incapable of repayment with interest, if capable of any repayment at all. He was thinking of what may be called agricultural, in contrast with industrial, interest—of loans advanced to a farmer who has suffered from inclement seasons, and has mortgaged his land to get food for the winter, and seed for the spring. These things had brought Attica to an evil pass in the days of Solon, and their results had been swept away by his Seisachtheia: these things still led in Aristotle's own day to the revolutionary clamour for an abolition of debts. It was because they were familiar with this species of usury that the Middle Ages clung to the teaching of Aristotle, finding it consonant with their own experience and with the teaching of Christ in the Gospels—"Lend, hoping for nothing again".

Influence of Aristotle's theory of commerce and interest in the Middle Ages

The economic theory of the *Politics* is perhaps that part of Aristotle's work which during the Middle Ages exercised the greatest influence. Fathers and Churchmen readily adopted Aristotle's ideas, the more because the conception of Nature which had come to them from Roman law, as well as the teaching of the Gospels, accorded with those ideas. "To seek to enrich one's self was not simply, they could argue, to incur spiritual risk to one's own soul (as the Gospels taught); it was in itself unjust, since it aimed at appropriating an unfair share of what God had intended (according to natural law) for the common use of men."[1] The affinity between these ideas and those of Aristotle is obvious. Ultimately, in the triple sanction of the Gospel, natural law, and Aristotle, they became enshrined in canon law. On two doctrines especially did this law insist—"that wares should be sold at a just price; and

[1] Ashley, *Economic History*, i., i., 128.

that the taking of interest was sinful ".[1] The conception of a just price, unaffected by demand and corresponding to the permanent cost of production, passed from the Church to the guild and to the State: the ordinances of both attempt to regulate the just price of commodities, and the State in particular concerned itself in fixing the rate at which staple commodities like bread and beer should be sold. The view that the taking of interest was sinful similarly passed into general acceptance on the same triple warrant. The prohibition of interest was indeed an easy corollary from the attempt to enforce a just price; regarding moneys lent as really sold, the canonists naturally held that only an exact equivalent should be repaid. In regard to both trade and interest, it should be noticed that actual economic conditions of the Middle Ages were such as to foster these theories. They were by no means mere academic theories, but the natural results of practical experience, as we have suggested that the similar theories of Aristotle also were. Mediæval trade was a direct dealing of craftsman and consumer, in which the question was naturally put—What did this cost you to make, and what is a fair price for your work? Mediæval borrowing was usually meant " to meet some sudden stress of misfortune, or for unproductive expenditure ": [2] " there was such an absence of opportunities for productive investment as relatively to justify this strong prejudice against interest ".[3] The survival of Aristotelian theory, and its absorption into the teaching of canonists, is only explicable, when we remember that it was firmly rooted in fact.

Nicholas Oresme

One writer there was, in the later Middle Ages, who used the economic theory of the first book of the *Politics* as a basis for speculations which have been pronounced " thoroughly correct according to the views of the nineteenth century ".[4] This was Nicholas Oresme, who lived in the fourteenth century, and wrote a *Tractatus de Mutatione monetarum.* Nicholas was an Aristotelian scholar, and one of the first, if not the first, to translate Aristotelian writings into a modern tongue. The

[1] Ashley, *Economic History*, i., i., 132.
[2] *Ibid.*, p. 155. [3] *Ibid.*, p. 156.
[4] Cunningham, *Growth of English Industry and Commerce*, i., 355-59 (third edition).

Tractatus, written thirty or forty years after the *Defensor Pacis*, is very like Marsilio's work, in its attempt to handle a modern problem in terms of Aristotelian philosophy. It is concerned with the problem of a debased coinage which then occupied France, whose monarchs had already been branded as *falsarii publici* before Nicholas wrote. In settling this problem he starts from the Aristotelian distinction of the tyrant who rules for his own welfare, and the monarch who rules for the good of his people.[1] From this he argues that the money of a country belongs to the community and not to the prince, and that the prince has no right to make a gain from the coinage. Incidentally, he discusses many matters of economic interest on Aristotelian lines. He distinguishes, for instance, those who supply the commonwealth with natural riches from those who enrich themselves by transactions in artificial riches—the exchangers and usurers, whose riches are often obtained by the impoverishment of others. For one thing only he can find no basis in Aristotle; and that is the action of the prince, who makes money by issuing a false coinage, and is worse than the worst Aristotle had known, since the usurer gives good money to creditors who desire it, while the prince forces bad money on his subjects in lieu of good, and that against their will.

False "asceticism" of Aristotle's economics

In his whole theory of the production and exchange of wealth, Aristotle may seem altogether reactionary. His ideal is a State of natural simplicity, in which men raise their crops and breed their cattle, bartering one with another when necessity impels, and using money only in foreign exchanges. It is a State which approaches the condition of Sparta before the days of her corruption, when she knew but an iron currency, and strangers were few in her gates. But Sparta was a survival of primitive times; and to imitate Sparta was to return, consciously or unconsciously, to primitive barbarism. It was to reject and abandon all the gains of civilisation. True, they are rejected on the ground that they involve new possibilities of evil. Exchange, Aristotle feels, opens the door for a parasitic class of society, and for a false conception of the purpose of life. But it is unlike Aristotle to reject an institution because

[1] This distinction seems greatly to have influenced thought in the Middle Ages; see Epilogue, § 2.

it may be perverted. It is the very fault which he objects to Plato. When Plato rejected private property, because it conduced to selfishness, he had forgotten, Aristotle tells us, that it is human nature and not property which is to blame for selfishness, and that property may serve on the contrary to elicit the finest moral qualities. Is not the same true of exchange conducted through the medium of money? Is not human nature the real culprit, if evil results from monetary exchange, and may not exchange be made to serve so high a purpose as the "self-sufficiency" of a State? Self-sufficiency seems indeed to be forgotten, when exchange is condemned. It is obvious that the material self-sufficiency of the State involves, in the first place division of labour, by which, each producing his best, the maximum is attained; and, in the second place, as a corollary of division of labour, the exchange of the different products of the labourers. Aristotle admits the need of self-sufficiency, and yet rejects exchange; nor has his economics anything of the Platonic appreciation for the advantages of division of labour. It is indeed somewhat curious that Aristotle, who criticised Plato for forgetting that an association must be composed of dissimilar members, practically makes his own economic association one of similar members, all engaged in the same pursuits.[1]

Aristotle's Theory of Distribution

§ 4. But if one may criticise Aristotle's theory of production and exchange, his theory of distribution is still one of the truest and most admirable things which he wrote. There are

[1] Aristotle's economic theory is very like that of the French Physiocrats of the eighteenth century. They too "confined the epithet 'productive' to *agricultural* labour, and denied it to every other class of labour". They too felt that it is agriculture, and similar extractive occupations, "that furnish the materials for all wealth; and that all other labour is merely engaged in the working of these materials" (Gide, *Political Economy*, E. T., p. 113). They forgot, like Aristotle, that production is a process which does not stop till the article reaches the consumer; and they failed to realise that every stage in this process is equally valuable, and equally "productive". Hence "they attempted to show that exchange was profitable to no one. For, said they, all exchange, if it is equitable, presupposes *the equivalence of the two values exchanged*, and consequently implies that there is neither gain nor loss on either side" (*ibid.*, p. 171). It may be remarked that the Physiocrats, with these views, were not Socialists; nor need we therefore make Aristotle, with the same views, into a Socialist.

three possibilities in respect of distribution, we are told. There may be common possession and common use: there may be private possession and common use: there may be, as among barbarians (in the "mark"), common possession and private use. The problem of deciding between these is discussed by Aristotle only with reference to land; and it is discussed as part of his polemic against the communism of the *Republic*. He assumes that Plato had given his adhesion to the system of common possession. The assumption is quite erroneous: Plato advocates in the *Republic* not common possession, but the common use by the guardians of a part of the produce paid them by an agricultural class, which owns, *as private and individual property*, the soil from which the produce comes. But, assuming that Plato is committed to communism, Aristotle proceeds to criticise, under the name of Plato, any communistic distribution of property.

Aristotle objects to common ownership of land

He was not criticising what Plato had meant; nor was he criticising anything quite parallel to modern socialism. Modern socialism thinks in terms of capital and labour, and would fain prevent capital from gaining too much, and labour too little, of the profits of production, by some new system of distribution affecting the whole sphere of economic action. Aristotle is simply thinking of the soil of a city-state, and asking himself, whether it will be better, for material and moral reasons, in the interests alike of good crops and of civic virtues, that it should be owned in common by the citizen body, or individually by the citizens. But different as are the two points of view, they have their affinities in certain simple elements. Both involve social ownership: both seem to limit the individual. And consequently, in criticising these simple elements, which lie at the root of any communism or socialism of any kind, Aristotle is criticising modern socialism. He is criticising that more than he is criticising Plato; for Plato did not advocate any social ownership such as Aristotle condemns.[1]

Aristotle's objections to limitation of the individual by social ownership may be said to be both economic and moral. Economically, he objects to a system of common ownership, because it means common neglect. The magic of property is a

Grounds of his objection

[1] In the *Laws*, however (739 C), Plato speaks of κοινὰ χρήματα ξύμπαντα as the "better way".

necessary stimulus to the maximum of production. But it is on moral grounds that ownership must be judged: it is by its moral value that it stands or falls. Since economics is part of politics, and politics is the science of the Ultimate Good, the problem of property must be primarily a problem of ethics. The fundamental questions which a communal distribution of property suggests are accordingly two: will such a scheme ensure the virtue of common-mindedness (which is what it professes to ensure); and may it not, even if it does, destroy still more than it fosters the growth of the moral life? That it ensures any unity of sentiment Aristotle denies. It does *not* attain the end for which it is devised. Easy as it is to fall into disputes about the proper distribution of private property, it is no less easy to drift into quarrels about the proper allocation of the produce of a common soil. If an equal partition is attempted, some will feel that they have received less than their work deserves; if proportional division is sought, it will be condemned as unequal and unfair by those whose share is small. And in the mere management of any common concern difficulties are sure to arise. It is just when we rub against people most closely and most constantly, that we find it least easy to keep an even temper; and a scheme of common ownership must mean an intimate and daily contact. Men live most quietly with their neighbours when they do not touch them at too many points; and a system of communism brings men into touch with one another at exactly those points where friction is most likely to arise. While it is thus unlikely that common-mindedness will be secured by common ownership, it is certain that those sides of the moral life which are connected with a system of private property will suffer or even disappear. For as we have already seen, private property is an instrument for righteousness, and conversely righteousness demands a certain furnishing of private property. Without such an equipment it must be lame and halt. It is thus from his high sense of the meaning of property, as a thing held in trust for virtue, that Aristotle comes upon the supreme defence of private ownership. It is right and natural, because it is a necessary factor in a good life. It is exactly the same reasoning, by which the State itself was proved to be a natural and necessary thing, because it is the condition of moral growth.

In developing this line of defence, which is indeed the ultimate and only defence of any fact or institution of human life, Aristotle appeals to two virtues in particular. Liberality is impossible, he argues, without private possessions. One cannot have the virtue of giving, if one has nothing to give. It is easy to answer that what makes charity is not the thing given, but the spirit of giving; and that such a spirit depends upon no external conditions. It is easy to say, again, that if private property is to be justified by the fact that it is sometimes connected with liberality, persecution may be justified, because it is sometimes connected with faith. But Aristotle was thinking of the active virtue of a civic life, of which public munificence was a part; and he meant that the fulness of civic virtue would be lost to the citizens, if they had nothing to give to the State. But far more important, in any case, is his appeal to the sense of personality and its concomitant virtue of self-respect (φιλαυτία), as the ultimate foundation of property. After all, each of us must have *his own*, just because he is *himself*. Our growth and expansion is conditional upon the annexation, of each new sphere as it were, in our progress. To such annexation we have a right, just because we have left the mark of ourselves impressed on the sphere of our growth. Not only the growth, but the very sense of self, the feeling of a personality, is conditional upon possessing something which makes its expression possible. I cannot know myself, unless I can express my will (which is myself) in action; I cannot express it in action, unless I have a medium for such expression. I come to know myself, through what I have made my own: my property is a mirror, which reflects myself to me. In this way property is "realised will"; and it stands justified as such —provided always that such will is a right will. It is the reflection of the self, and it is thereby justified—provided always that the self reflected is the moral self. Unless these conditions be satisfied, there can be no right to property. Every right postulates a recognition by society, and society will never recognise any casual will, or any chance determination of the self. It will only recognise a will that is set towards its own

Moral justification of private property

aim, a determination of the self in the direction which it is itself pursuing.[1]

Something of this seems implied in Aristotle's argument, that it is not idly, and not without Nature's ordinance, that each one of us feels a love towards himself; that such a feeling is perfectly natural, provided that it is not in excess; and that to consider a thing one's own is everything for the satisfaction of this feeling (1263 a 40). This self-love is not selfishness: it is self-respect. It is the sense of a self, which must come by its fulness, and claims private property as the condition of that fulness. More exactly, it is the sense of the rational self, and a desire to satisfy that self.[2] It is a quality, therefore, which we can only predicate of the virtuous man, who lives by the light of his reason, and in order to satisfy his rational self, covets for that self all forms of virtuous action. And since it is to the satisfaction of this manner of self-love that, as Aristotle tells us, private property is "of unspeakable moment," one can truly say, that in his view, private property is rooted in personality, and is necessary to the realisation of the moral will.

True communism spiritual, not material

Here therefore as elsewhere Aristotle is a Conservative, who justifies the given, but only justifies it because he conceives it in its ideal meaning. Private property is not simply pronounced right by Aristotle: it is pronounced right when, and in so far as, it subserves the moral end. It is not to be simply retained: it is to be retained when it has been "improved and perfected by proper customs and proper legislation regulating its use". Such customs and legislation, making, as all customs and legislation do, for virtue, will provide that private property shall be used as an instrument for moral purposes. And thus in practice it will come to pass that property, being used as such an instrument, and as a means to charity and munificence, in a generous and liberal spirit, will become public as well as private, and common as well as individual. There will be, in Aristotle's formula, *private possession with common use*. The benefits of both individualism and communism will be secured. Private

[1] Private property, especially in land, must be made consistent with social service: along with private possession must go common use. Aristotle's defence of private property, like his defence of slavery, is also an attack—*on actual practice*. [2] *Ethics*, ix., 8.

possession will bring its economic and moral advantages: common use, not merely dictated by law, but flowing from a proper spirit, will issue in that unanimity which Plato so greatly desired. But it is to be noticed that Aristotle conceives of this communism which he suggests as very different from that of Plato, not only in its external working, but also in its inner meaning. Whereas (so it seems to him) Plato has attempted to reform humanity by readjusting its material environment, he will rather seek to reform mankind by improving the spiritual condition of the soul within, and trusting it to adapt itself to its environment. It is the preaching of the Gospels: "Mend your hearts, and not your governments"; "the kingdom of Heaven is within you". If society is awry, as Plato felt and said, it is because its members are themselves awry. It is not property or anything external which causes disunion, but a spirit of disunion; and if you abolish property to-day, that spirit, which has hitherto issued in disputes about private property, will at once issue in disputes about the distribution of the common fund. It is a well for ever springing from beneath, whose flow one cannot check by putting a finger over the vent at which it issues: it will only burst a new opening for itself. No material cure will heal a spiritual evil: only spiritual means will produce a spiritual result. To heal disunion and division of spirit, one must employ a common education, which will put all men on the same spiritual level, and initiate them into the same spiritual community. Then, but then only, will they be a single and indivisible community, when they are a community in the spirit; and without communion in the spirit a material communion *will not* abolish, and *may* intensify, the spirit of disunion.

Justice of Aristotle's criticism of Plato

This is very true, but not a fair criticism of Plato. Plato had never thought that material means would of themselves reform humanity: he had not even thought that they ought to be the first means employed for that end. Spiritual means—a common education—had been his primary object; and a scheme of education is the subject which engages his attention most closely and most constantly. It is merely from an excess of caution that he has recourse to material means, and it is merely as a reinforcement of the scheme of education that they are first suggested. Plato was attempting, in this proposal of a communistic life, to give an economic basis to what was primarily a spiritual structure. He felt that his scheme of education would make good citizens: he determined, by his economic scheme, to take away from them the chance of lapsing into badness. In the light of these considerations it is plain that Aristotle's criticism is harsh and one-sided. He forgets the greater half of Plato's mind, and speaks of the residue as if it were the whole. Plato would have agreed with almost every word of his criticism; he would have rejoined: "Exactly; that is what I am attempting to say". The true line of criticism upon Plato, which Aristotle does adopt, and ought to have adopted exclusively, would have been to criticise him, not for forgetting spiritual means, but for an ascetic distrust of human nature. There are some aspects of Plato's teaching in which, as we saw, he seems mediæval; and one of these is the ascetic tendency, which would pass a Root and Branch Bill against natural instincts, like that of imitation or that of appropriation. In attacking the former, he practically annihilates the drama: in attacking the latter, he would abolish property. The theory which Aristotle implies is both higher and truer. Use your instincts, but use them properly. Use them, because they are there, and Nature gives nothing in vain: use them rightly, because you are a man, endowed with reason, and discerning between good and evil. It is at least as great to meet temptations as to fly them; and to indulge one's instincts within measure demands as strenuous a virtue, as to root them out altogether. Plato insults his own scheme of education, when he so far distrusts its efficacy as to leave it nothing to do; for this, after all, is the practical result of taking property and the sexual relations away from the control of the citizens whom he has educated. On the other hand, Plato was not altogether mistaken in believing that education was not in itself sufficient, and that some economic basis was necessary. A common education may give us the highest type of socialism; but a starving man is not ready to receive his education. Some form of material readjustment is after all necessary, not so much to reinforce, as to prepare, the ultimate adjustment of the soul.

Aristotle's Theory of the Family

§ 5. From Aristotle's theory of property[1] we turn in conclusion to what naturally follows upon property—to what in Aristotle's sense of the word is peculiarly and particularly a matter of economics—the family (*οἰκία*). As we have already seen, it is Aristotle's view that the family is the chief concern of economic art, and that the true activity of this art is apparent, when a father is seen inspiring his children and slaves towards a life of virtue. But the whole of this conception disappears, if Plato's theory of the inutility and positive disadvantage of the family be accepted, and the family be in

Aristotle defends the family against Plato

[1] There are two suggestions about property in the *Politics* which perhaps ought to be considered. (i.) Ideally, if private property be postulated, as it is by Aristotle, the land of a State ought (apart from what the State retains for its own uses) to be divided into equal lots. This is the scheme of Plato's *Laws:* it was also the scheme of Phaleas. A system of equal lots is adopted by Aristotle himself in his ideal State; but he points out that it involves some regulation of the population of the State. Here there emerges a certain Malthusian element in his theory: population must be regulated (not so much lest it should outrun subsistence, as) lest its growth should interfere with the system of property, and ultimately produce poverty and dissension. Aristotle mentions Pheidon of Corinth as having attempted to regulate the population of Corinth by the despatch of its superfluous members to colonies; but he believes himself not in this positive, but in a preventive, check. The example of the French peasantry seems to show that this preventive check operates naturally of itself.

In speaking of Phaleas, Aristotle raises a further objection to mere equalisation, above and beyond the question of population. Admitting that equalisation has some political value, and that it has been partly attempted in several States, he urges against it the same objection that he urges against communism: *it is the desires of the mind which ought to be equalised by means of the education of the law, rather than estates.* It is true that Phaleas would have equalised education as well as property; but what is wanted is not an equal education for all, but an education which equalises the desires of all. Finally Aristotle urges against Phaleas the objection that to equalise property (and Phaleas did not equalise even all property, but merely property in land) is not sufficient to stop dissension: men will fight as much for honours and distinctions and offices, intangible though they be, as for visible property; and indeed, the instinct to fight for the former affects men of education most. In fact, there are many causes which lead to dissension; and equalisation of property is the least of the cures, because it fails to touch the greatest of these causes. There is needed a moral training in addition: there is needed, in addition to that (if one would cure *every* cause), the cure of philosophy, which alone will give men a right appreciation of values, and of the garlands really to be coveted and "run for".

(ii.) From a practical point of view, in speaking about Sparta, Aristotle suggests as a cure for its social evils, a system of inalienable lots, with little or no power of bequest or dowry. This would prevent the concentration of the land in a few hands; and one may notice that J. S. Mill suggests somewhat similar remedies for the same difficulty (*cf. supra*, p. 44).

consequence abolished. Accordingly Aristotle is forced, by the principles which he has laid down in his first book, to investigate and to criticise in his second Plato's scheme for the regulation of sexual relations. That scheme attempted to abolish all individuality or privacy in family relations, and made every wife the wife, and every child the child, of the whole community. In this way Plato imagined that he would not only destroy the exclusiveness of family life, and the disputes which it produces; but that he would also extend the warmth of family feeling over the whole State, making it one family, and reinforcing the political bond by an additional nexus of sentiment. To these conceptions Aristotle answers much as he answered to the scheme of communism. It is unlikely that anything will be gained: it is certain that much will be lost. No greater unity will be gained. Affection varies inversely with the circle which it embraces; and a limitation of the number of associates is a necessary condition of a strong sentiment of common interest. In Plato's scheme the circle is so large, the number of associates so many, that only the shallowest sentiment of a common interest can be possible. In this sense the scheme destroys what unity there was in the State: it abolishes the former groups, because, though each possessed a real unity, none was sufficiently large to embrace the whole of the State; and it substitutes a larger group in their place, which is so large that it has scarcely any unity at all. While nothing is gained, there is much that is lost. We have already seen that the family is an institution intended by Nature, which man and woman naturally combined to form. Since it is natural, it has, like all Nature's products, an appointed end. (i.) It is meant to further the moral growth of the children, and to prepare the way for the State, which in due time will take over from the father this duty, and will educate them for itself. There are times when Aristotle seems almost ready to think that the father may suffice for the moral instruction of his children. (ii.) Again, we are told in the *Ethics* that man is more naturally a husband than he is a citizen; we learn, that there is a division of functions, and that man and wife mutually help one another, by contributing each a different gift to the common store. Nor is their association merely natural in the sense that it is based on a

Moral justification of the family

natural instinct; it may be a moral association, based on virtue, in which either helps the other by example to pursue and to realise the Good. (iii.) But much as the children and their parents owe to their association in the family, the slave owes still more. He is more than an animate instrument, only because he has a place in the family, and a share in its inspiration; and with the disappearance of the family, his guide and friend is gone. To abolish the family is to abolish all these things. It is to sweep away as capable of perversion an instrument which is capable of producing a wise and loving father and mother, disciplined and educated children, trained and obedient servants. It is to deny a primary instinct its due satisfaction, which Nature herself had intended to give. Deep as the instinct of self-love, in which property is rooted, comes the instinct of loving and caring for others, in which the family is rooted. In truth, this instinct of loving and caring for others is but one aspect of the true self-love of which Aristotle speaks. For if, as has been said, the self is as wide as the sum of its interests—if it *is* all that it loves, then a man may be said to have made part of himself the whole of his family; and that family has thus become, as much as his property, an extension of himself. Through it he realises his will for righteousness: his family bears the impress of that will, and is a "realised will" in the same sense as property, with this difference, that its members have themselves a will of their own. To abolish the family is therefore to truncate the self, and to limit the will.

It may be objected, that Plato was fully aware that self is the sum of a man's interests, and that far from wishing to limit or truncate it, he desired to widen and fulfil it, by increasing the sum of its interests. And this is true. And so is Aristotle's objection true—that to widen is to make shallow, it may be indeed to drain away altogether, the interests of the ordinary man. Some there are indeed, but they are few, to whom a great cause is more than a group of persons, and who can give wife and child and much that men care for to identify themselves with this wider and fuller being. Ordinary humanity seeks its fulfilment in a narrower sphere; and of the vast majority it is true, that the love of their family (along with an interest in their profession and its circle) is, and is quite rightly, the sum of their life. Man hungers and thirsts for the tangible and visible; and causes cannot be seen with eyes. The prophet who sees the "Idea" cannot legislate that men shall act as if *they* saw what he sees.

The State as an association of families

But (it may be again objected), if this be true, what becomes of Aristotle's conception of the State, as constituting the essence of its citizens' life? Was not the Greek State small enough to be visible and tangible? Certainly it was; and it is just this size which helps to explain Plato's theory that a man should make the State his family, and Aristotle's conception of the State as a body of which each citizen must feel himself but a member. And it is true that while to the modern, on the ordinary plane of life, the State remains in the background, only coming to the front in times of crisis, to the Greek his city stood always in the foreground of his thoughts and interests. What has just been said is thus perhaps truer of modern, than it is of Greek life; and the Athenian at any rate, living much out of doors, and much in the agora, would naturally feel himself more of a citizen, and less of a householder, than an Englishman to-day, who can only act as a citizen very occasionally, and often forgets to think of himself as a citizen at all. Yet it is equally true that the State is not a compound of individual units, but "an association of associations," in Aristotle's conception; and that it is his aim to preserve the subordinate association, even while he admits the sovereign and architectonic character of the supreme association. Concurrently with the activity of the politician must run that of the householder. Not the only, but the supreme, association of men—such is his conception of the State: necessary, because it is based in human nature, but in itself insufficient—such is his conception of the family. Nor is there to him any antithesis between the one and the other. By his citizenship of the family the child is prepared for citizenship of the State; and by his rule over the household the father is prepared to rule the State.[1]

[1] "We begin our public affections in our families. No cold relation is a zealous citizen. We pass on to our neighbourhoods and our provincial connections. These are our inns and resting places. . . . The love to the whole is not extinguished by this subordinate partiality. Perhaps it is a sort of elemental training to those higher and more large regards, by which men come to be affected, as with their own concerns, in the prosperity of the kingdom" (Burke, *Reflections; Works*, v., 352).

Aristotle's criticism of Platonic striving for Unity

§ 6. And thus we come to Aristotle's general criticism of Plato's whole position. In his eyes, Plato had exaggerated the element of community, or fellowship, which a State should possess. Of the two possible alternatives,—that a State should mean the communion of its members in everything, or that it should only mean their communion in certain things, and should leave the rest to the individual—he had preferred the former. By increasing the sphere of communion he had imagined that he would increase the sense of community, which Aristotle thinks he had thus made the be-all and end-all of the State. Assuming that Plato had made this unity the end and endeavour of the State, Aristotle criticises this conception of the end of the State on three grounds. First, the end or good of any object must, as Plato had himself argued, be something which serves and preserves that object. And an end, again, is something of which one cannot have too much: it is only a means that is limited, and the more one has of an end, the better one is. But unity is an end such, that if it be pursued thoroughly, it will destroy, and not preserve, the State of which it is the end. It is an end of which one *may* have too much. An absolutely unitarian city will be a city of one man—and even that will not be unitarian, since as the myth of the Phædrus tells us, there is a constant division between the two parts of the human soul. But this is a *reductio ad absurdum;* for the State must obviously be composed of more men than one. Secondly, Aristotle argues, if the State is a communion, its very character postulates that it is composed, not only of several, but also of unlike members. We have already seen that every communion or association (κοινωνία) is necessarily constituted of dissimilar members, whose dissimilarity makes possible that mutual exchange of different services for which all associations exist. Men who were like one another would never associate together: it is just the hope of finding a complement to themselves in the different capacities of their fellows that draws men together in societies. Differentiation is therefore the necessary basis of any communion; and homogeneity implies a stage too low to be called one of association. In a city, which is the highest form of association, we get the completest differentiation. Ideally, there is a permanent differentiation of rulers and ruled, each with his several and distinct capacity; and where this is impossible, as it is in a community of equals, men make as near an approach to it as they can, by differentiating temporarily between this year's rulers and this year's ruled. Everywhere again there is differentiation between ruler and ruler; and, as we learn from the later books of the *Politics*, States differ from one another in the degree of this differentiation. But, if unity be made the end of the State, and unity be attempted by the enforcement of a uniform type, the differentiation which is essential to political association must necessarily disappear. That Plato was attempting to enforce such a uniform type, Aristotle assumed to be true; and he probably based his assumption on Plato's suppression of such institutions as property and the family, which make individuality and distinction possible. Lastly, and by way of a more positive criticism, Aristotle suggests that as the end cannot be unity, the true and proper end of the State may be found in the full satisfaction of all his wants which it secures for each of its members (*αὐτάρκεια*). Such a suggestion flows naturally from his conception of an association, as formed for the purpose of supplementing the defects of unassociated man. But self-sufficiency and full satisfaction is incompatible with unity; the less *one*, and the more *manifold*, anything is, the more likely it is to attain its completion.

Validity of Aristotle's criticism

It is possible to criticise the critic; and Aristotle may be accused of misunderstanding Plato. Plato had recognised—as he had indeed been the first to show—that the State is an association based upon divergence of capacity. He had laid down the doctrine of division of labour; and he had shown that "need," or in other words the craving for satisfaction and self-sufficiency, had impelled men to join in an association in which the division of functions was an essential feature. Nay, specialisation had been, as we saw, one of his dearest aims; and specialisation means differentiation. He had even attempted what Aristotle terms the ideal arrangement; he had proposed a specialised class of rulers, dissimilar and distinct from the ruled. The metaphor in the *Politicus*, by which the State is compared to a web, and the art of politics is said to consist in assigning to each his fair share in its making, attests, as does the whole of the *Republic*, Plato's feeling for the necessity of dissimilar parts and complementary functions. May we therefore say, that true as were Aristotle's propositions in themselves, they do not form a valid criticism of Plato, because Plato had realised, and had shown that he had realised, every consideration which Aristotle accuses him of having forgotten? Hardly; for though Plato does see the need of differentiation, and though he attempts to secure it by distinguishing three classes for three separate functions, the fact remains, that the zeal for unity nevertheless consumed him. The third estate disappears from view early in the *Republic*; and the other two, treated as one, seem to lose all differentiation in a uniform system of common life. Emptied of themselves, they are conformed to the type of the one and indivisible Idea which the State is to realise: the oneness of that Idea annihilates the individual to assimilate him to itself. It is some feeling of this which Aristotle had, and which may be said to be natural and just. It was the general quarrel of Aristotle with Plato that he misconceived the relation of the universal to the particular: that he postulated a One "outside" and annihilating the Many, whereas the truth is that the One is inside and "predicable of" the Many, which retain their individuality while they are united through a common predicable. This quarrel appears with regard to ethics: for Aristotle there is no such unity of virtue as Plato had held to exist. It appears again here in this attack upon Plato's conception of the unity of the State; for that unity, it seems to Aristotle, is made into a One outside and annihilating the many citizens, whereas it should be a communion including them all, and depending upon the fact that they are manifold, and, as manifold, mutually complementary.[1]

True nature of the State's unity

Difference with regard to the nature of the State's unity is one of the fundamental differences between political thinkers. Thinkers of the school of the social contract have conceived of the State as legally united in a *societas*; and Aristotle criticises

[1] Aristotle emphasises only his opposition to Plato; but Plato is none the less the fountain of his political theory, as has been again and again suggested in previous chapters. The teleological conception of the State in general; the theory of the mixed constitution and the principles of the classification of States in particular—these, and much more, descended to Aristotle from his master.

that conception, as we have seen, on the ground that such a legal unity may mark an alliance, but does not constitute a State, which possesses a moral unity, and coheres through a common moral purpose. The conception of the State as forming a moral unity had been seized by Plato, and, Aristotle thinks, exaggerated. Not content with moral unity, he had attempted unity in all things, in order to make the moral unity absolutely firm and compact. Not content with the unity which reconciles, but does not annihilate differences, he had sought to make unity a destroying fire. It is Aristotle's aim to insist, first of all, that the State *does* indeed cohere through a moral purpose, and in a moral life—but in that way and that sense only. Its unity is spiritual, and only spiritual; and if you wish to draw the bonds of unity tighter, you must use the spiritual means of a common education. It is his aim, again, to insist (and this he does with equal vigour and truth) that the universal which denies and abolishes its particulars is a false universal, bare of any meaning, abstract and unreal. In logic and in politics alike, only a concrete universal, which recognises and gives their full meaning to its individual members, can ever possibly be true. And if we recognise the individual in his full meaning and value, as a personality, we shall also recognise the truth of Aristotle's contention, that the only unity in which individual can be united with individual is that of the spirit.

If we realise such a conception of unity, as consistent with differentiation, we see that Aristotle's attack upon unity as the end of the State is not final. He was not really attacking unity as the end of the State, but a false unity. In fact it may be urged, though it seems paradoxical, that he sought to substitute a higher for a lower form of unity. Undifferentiated unity belongs to a lower scale of evolution: it is the lowest type of animal which is composed of like and similar parts. Heterogeneous unity belongs to the highest; and it is man who is composed of unlike and dissimilar organs. The parallel between the State and man, properly conceived, involves the maximum of differentiation in the State; and the State which is most one, "most like to a single man," may also be the State which is most manifold. In upholding the doctrine of differentiation, in comparing the relation of the citizen to the State with that of the limb to the body, Aristotle was really suggesting the highest unity as the aim of the State. With unity thus conceived, self-sufficiency does not quarrel: on the contrary, such unity is the only true avenue to it. Yet it is but an avenue; and the true end of the State must be, not to make its members one, but to raise them to the fulness of their being, by encouraging the highest activities of a good life.

CHAPTER X

[*Politics*, IV.-V. (VII.-VIII.)]

THE IDEAL STATE AND ITS SCHEME OF EDUCATION

THE State which is one with its ideal may be under the rule of one man, or of a few: its constitution may be either an absolute kingship, or a genuine aristocracy. In any case its essence is, that it actually lives a life of complete virtue (and is therefore *a fortiori* equipped with all the material conditions of such a life), and that it entrusts with the direction of its life a man (or men) also distinguished by complete virtue and by a supply of those material things which are requisite for its exercise. We have already discussed the nature of a life of complete virtue: we have already seen what are the conditions which sometimes make it imperative that a monarch should be entrusted with its direction. It remains to ask: (1) What are the material conditions of the ideal life? (2) Under what circumstances will its direction properly rest with an aristocracy? (3) In what ways will the activity of the government be most properly employed for the realisation of the ideal life?

THE EXTERNAL FEATURES OF THE IDEAL STATE

§ 1. The material conditions of the ideal life are discussed by Aristotle with some fulness. He considers, with a certain *naïveté* and an apparent relish, the geography and climate of the ideal soil, the ethnology of the ideal people, and the architecture of the ideal city. He has something of the zeal of the founder of a colony, looking with a speculative eye for the land of promise, and methodically tabulating beforehand the qualities which it must possess. First of all, people and soil must both be ideal; and they must be ideal in respect both of quantity and quality.

The population: its quantity

The quantity of the population is determined by a teleological standard. Mere quantity is nothing to be desired:

a great population only means difficulties of government.[1] What is necessary is the maximum of quantity necessary and useful for the proper discharge of the functions of the State. Whether we regard the rulers, and their function of sitting in judgment, or the ruled, and their function of awarding honours in proportion to desert, we see in either case that the population must be limited in size. The rulers cannot afford to be ignorant of the character of those whom they judge, or the people unacquainted with the merits of those whom they honour. Ideally, the population must be small enough for every citizen to know something of all the rest; otherwise the rulers will "judge crooked judgments," and the people will delight to honour the undeserving. These considerations impose a maximum size on the State: a minimum is to be found in that function of the State which Aristotle terms the achievement of self-sufficingness. A small population cannot be sufficient unto itself: it is necessarily dependent on others. Teleology and the doctrine of the mean thus combine to prove, that the ideal State is one not too populous for citizens and magistrates to be mutually acquainted, and yet populous enough to be self-sufficient. The former of these conditions holds good of municipal life to-day, in so far as it would seem that municipal offices are better filled in smaller towns: the latter is a condition with which only a nation, and not all nations, can nowadays comply. And this well shows the character of the Greek city-state—as intimate and as intense in its life as a city, as wide and as all-embracing in its aims as a State.

The limited size of Aristotle's ideal State and its reasons

But we must remember, as peculiarly Greek and as necessarily resulting from Aristotle's teleology, that this estimate of population has regard only to the integral parts of the State—to those who participate fully in its privileges and its life and its end. "It is perhaps necessary," Aristotle adds, "that there should be a large number of slaves, and numbers of resident aliens and foreigners;" but these are not of the essence of the State, and their number may be left to chance. It matters little or nothing that the magistrates or people should know who or what they are; though another canon of size which

[1] "Who could command such a population in war? What herald, who was not a Stentor, could make his voice heard through its ranks?" (1326 b 5).

Aristotle also suggests[1] (that the population should not be so large as to destroy a law-abiding and orderly spirit), would perhaps serve to limit the number of non-citizens and of citizens alike. It would appear, then, that the teleological method supplies a limit of size which makes the State no larger than a municipality, and a line of cleavage which divides its members into effective participants and necessary but not integral contributors. It stretches its mantle to cover the great defects of Hellenic politics: it condones parochialism, and encourages slavery. It is blind to the great State, which, founded in a feeling of nationality, acquires from that feeling a vitality which cannot be killed, and, in virtue of its very size, crushes and obliterates into a general equality those distinctions into which small communities are liable to fall, and upon which they are prone to insist. Such criticism has its truth; but the defects to which it points are not so much the defects of the method of final causes in itself, as of the character of the final cause postulated by Aristotle. If the final cause be—not, as we should say to-day, the maintenance of the necessary conditions of the moral life, or rights, but the very formation and direction of the moral life, then a State which knows all its members, and their habits and character, is postulated by the character of that final cause. The State, which is to make Callias and Charicles into good men and true, must know who Callias and Charicles are, and whether Callias has a merit and desert which require greater recognition than that of Charicles. It must keep its attention fixed on Callias and Charicles and their like, who have possibilities of goodness, and whose one aim is to realise those possibilities, while it turns aside from slave and craftsman and trader, who are cumbered with this world's gear, and with all its cares and duties. The State which has only to secure Callias and Charicles the conditions of attaining virtue for themselves, conditions which are the same for both (and for craftsman and trader as well), may leave them undistinguished ciphers in the millions of its members. The teleological method is, therefore, not of itself the theoretical ground of Aristotle's failure to recognise the great State; while on the other hand it is the

[1] And which results from a conception of the State's function as being the maintenance of law and order.

ground of his success in recognising (what is eternally true) that the great State is not great because it trusts in the multitude of its subjects, but because it is strong in the number of its sons who are able and willing to do the work which it sets them to do.

The quality of the population

From the quantity Aristotle turns to discuss the quality of the ideal population of an ideal State. In doing so, he is led to generalise on the different characteristics of European and Asiatic races. European races, like all races which live in cold climates, are distinguished by abundance of vigour and fire, and by a certain want of quickness and skill.[1] They have the spirit and the dash, the simplicity and the slow wits, of an uncorrupted but primitive stock; and while they can always vindicate their freedom, they can seldom combine it with political organisation. In thus emphasising the effect of climate, Aristotle approaches Montesquieu: one is reminded of the fourteenth book of the *Esprit des Lois*, and particularly of that chapter in which the merits of the English constitution are derived from the demerits of the English climate, and our freedom is assigned to that distaste for all things, even for life, which springs from an inclement sky, and makes us impatient of all restraints. To the peoples of Asia Aristotle assigns qualities exactly the opposite of those of the European races.[2] They lack the vigour and spirit which these possess: they possess the quickness and skill which these lack. This difference is not explicitly assigned by Aristotle to the effects of climate; but it would seem to follow logically, that if a cold climate explains the qualities of European races, the exactly opposite qualities of Asiatic peoples are to be explained by the heat of their climate. It has often been remarked that a hot climate is destructive of an independent spirit, partly because the terrors of lightning and tempest are more awful, partly because the earth yields her increase in fuller measure for less labour, and the habit of self-reliance is not enforced by a constant struggle with Nature. And again, looking not to climate but to physical conformation, we may add, that

[1] Possessed of *θυμός*, they are deficient in *λόγος*.

[2] By Europe, Aristotle seems to mean the lands that lay to the north of Greece, and to be referring *e.g.* to Thracians and Celts: by Asia, he seems to mean Asia Minor, for the Persians could hardly be said to be deficient in fire of spirit.

if liberty rejoices in the chosen music of sea and mountains, it has not loved the flat plains that lie along the great rivers of Asia. But Greece was for Aristotle distinct from both Europe and Asia. As it stood geographically mid-way between the two, so it nourished a people which formed the mean between the races of either—a people which mixed in a just measure the spirit of the one with the skill of the other, and combined freedom with order in the constitution of its cities. There were indeed diversities in Greece: there were Greeks who inclined more to the European type, and Greeks who inclined more to the Asiatic, as well as Greeks who followed the golden mean. But the ideal population of an ideal State may be roughly defined as a population of Grèeks, characterised by quickness of wits and vigour of spirit. Of these two qualities Aristotle is inclined, in opposition to Plato, to emphasise the latter. From spirit, he thinks, there comes not only the love of freedom, but also the spirit of authority and the impulse to friendship; and freedom, authority and friendship are very vital principles of every State.

Agricultural class one of slaves

Just as Aristotle's estimate of the quantity of the population had only regard to the integral and essential members of the State, so with this definition of its quality. It is only the full citizen who must be a Greek; and the ideal State has need of many members besides the full citizen. It needs an agricultural population, for instance; and who will be the tillers of its soil? They will be slaves, we are told, but slaves who are not all members of the same stock, nor possessed of a spirit too lofty for their position. They will be a congeries of non-Hellenic races, united in nothing except an obedient temper and a want of that spirit which every Greek possessed: they will be a body whose own disunion, as well as the temper of its members, fits it for nothing but subjection. If slaves cannot be had, the ideal State may content itself with a class of cultivators in the condition of serfs; but they too must be non-Hellenic in race and temper. This was a condition which it would have been hard to fulfil: serfs were generally conquered Greeks, who had been masters of the soil before conquest came. This was the case with the Helots of Sparta; and homogeneous in race and spirited in temper, the Helots were always as a great ambush, lying in wait for an opportunity to fall upon their masters. Probably because he feels that there is this difficulty with a population of serfs, Aristotle prefers to people his ideal State with slaves, the sweepings of Asia, speaking a Babel of tongues, but all ready to cringe to their masters. It might not be an ideal thing; but it was a better thing than serfdom at Sparta, where the serf would gladly have "eaten his master raw," and the masters made it one of the first duties of their sons that they should go on "the secret mission," which slew the serf by stealth in the night, if he promised to be dangerous.

The territory of the ideal State

A population neither too large nor too small, comprised of Greeks in whom neither spirit nor intellect predominates, is therefore Aristotle's postulate for the ideal State, regarded personally and as a body of men. But a State is also a certain territory; and the proper amount and nature of that territory are questions next in order of importance to that of the population. It must be large enough to enable all the citizens to live at leisure, and in a manner not only temperate, as Plato had said in the *Laws*, but also liberal. In other words, it must be large enough for the moral purpose of the State: it must provide at once the detachment from material cares, and the necessary furnishing of external goods, which the realisation of that purpose requires. The quality of the soil, again, must be determined with due regard to that self-sufficiency, which it is one of the aims of the State to secure; and the territory must be such as produces crops of all kinds, and makes its inhabitants independent of foreign supply. If the territory is at once sufficient for the moral purpose of the State and for its material independence of other States—if it be large enough for the latter, and not too large for the former, it will meet the great purposes of the State (purposes which before decided the population, as they are here made to determine the territory), and it only remains to regulate its distribution. Two problems here arise: one concerns the relation of the city to the rest of the territory; the other the division of the territory among the citizens of the State.

The city

It is of great moment, in Aristotle's eyes, to determine the position and the construction of the city. The city is the brain of the State: the adjacent territory is merely the body which ministers to and is moved by the brain. The life of the State is altogether centred there: there is its worship, there its politics, and there the home of its members.[1] The State and the city are one: the Greeks know only one word for both. The country, as opposed to the city, is merely a place of farms belonging to the citizens. There is little of the local life of the Attic demes to be traced in Aristotle's sketch of the ideal State. In the country there are guard-houses in which the young citizens are cantoned during their military training, and in which the wood-wards or stewards of the country mess together; and there are temples of gods and of heroes. But it was from the city that every man came, and to the city that every man returned: it was upon the site of the city, the disposition of its buildings, the activity of its magistrates, that the health of the whole State depended. Aristotle does not mention (what in the ordinary feeling of the Greeks counted for much) that in the city dwelt the gods of the State, whose presence, symbolised it might be by the flourishing of sacred olives or the presence of the sacred snake, gave the State its genuine centre and its deepest principle of vitality. If the gods said one to another, "Let us go hence," and so saying arose and deserted their city, the State died: if the gods abode within the city when every citizen deserted his place (as, Herodotus tells us, happened at Athens in the days of Salamis), the State lived unimpaired. But this religious sentiment, of which Aristotle appears almost everywhere unconscious in his handling of politics, only reinforces with a deeper sanction his lesson, that the city is the soul of the State.

Should the city be situated by the sea?

The site of the city is determined by Aristotle with an eye to the advantages which it may draw from land and sea. It must be the strategic centre of its appendant territory: it must be so situated as to facilitate the march of its citizens to any and every part that may be threatened. It must also be an economic centre: the corn, the timber, and the other products of the country must naturally converge by easy routes upon its granaries and warehouses. Both in order to protect its territory, and in

[1] This would not be true of a State like Athens; but it seems to be intended by Aristotle for the ideal State. One may compare the Italian town, set on a height above the reach of malaria, to which every man retires at night from the surrounding country, leaving the farms on the lower ground to the care of dogs.

order to draw readily upon its resources, the city should lie by the sea, and enjoy the advantages of a ready transit by water of its troops and its commodities. This, however, raises a question, which had been much discussed in Greece, and to which Aristotle consequently devotes some attention. Does the stability and order of a State suffer or gain from the proximity of the sea? An unfavourable view of the influence of the sea is maintained in the *Laws;* and Plato argues that it means the risk of an alien immigration, which may make for the corruption of the State. But that view had been far more ardently championed, it would appear, by thinkers of oligarchical tenets, who hated the sea because they hated democracy, and because they regarded sea-power as tending to promote democracy. The sea, they argued, not only brought aliens, who had been bred in alien habits and under alien laws, and were therefore a hindrance to good government: it also encouraged the risk of large populations, which, as Aristotle himself acknowledges, brought with them democratic aspirations. In any case, they might have added, a navy like that of Athens, manned by the lower classes, is a force which of itself tends to promote democracy. On the other hand, Aristotle pleads, these things, though they may result from the proximity of the sea, are not in themselves inevitable results. Laws can be made to regulate the influx of foreigners, and to determine when, and under what conditions, they may have dealings with the members of the State. A navy can be manned in such a way as to avoid that mass of oarsmen, which formed a large part of the Athenian people, and served as the basis of Athenian democracy. The citizens can serve as marines: oarsmen can be recruited from the ranks of the serfs who cultivate the territory of the ideal State; and with citizens in the higher and more vital branch of naval service, the balance of the State will be secured. If the noxious results of contiguity to the sea can thus be avoided, there are positive advantages which it brings. The safety of a State will be more certainly assured, if it can meet and deliver attacks by sea as well as by land. The prosperity of a State depends upon its being able to export its own superfluities freely, in order to acquire sufficient commodities in return for the satisfaction of its wants. It was easy to exceed this limit, as Athens had done: a State might aim at a great revenue rather than satisfaction of its wants, and might by making itself the market of the world profit from the duties which it imposed on commercial transactions. But any limit may be exceeded; nor is a thing bad, because it can be abused. It is really a false logic, Aristotle implies, which condemns the sea as a source of evil. Nothing is evil in itself: evil is an element of human importation. Everything is in itself indeterminate: man determines each thing by his action, when he makes it contribute to some purpose or other of his own. He may make it contribute to an evil purpose, as, for instance, he may make the sea contributory to an aim of wealth; but what is wrong is his aim, his purpose, his use of the thing, and what must be attacked and amended is that aim and purpose and use. If the purpose for which man takes the sea into the realm of his activity be the preservation of the "independence" (*αὐτάρκεια*) of a State (in the full sense of that word), the sea is justified of its users. Nor can one lay down any uniform law of the effects of the sea upon the history of States which have a sea-board: the effects are as various as the purposes to which it has been put. It is indeed inevitable that a people which lives by the sea should use the sea for the purpose of trade; and trade may in its turn have various results. But these again depend on the purposes to which that trade is put. A Venetian oligarchy may be the issue in one case; an Athenian democracy in another.

The construction of the city

We have not yet done with the determination of the site of the ideal city. Apart from its relation to the territory in which it stands, and to the sea to which it should be contiguous, the city must satisfy certain conditions when considered by and in itself. It must be planted in a healthy site, facing east or at any rate north, and provided with an abundance of water, which, in a city where it is not all of equal quality, should be carefully distinguished into water for drinking and water for other purposes. Again, it must be planted in a site which not only commands a ready access to the whole territory in time of war, but is also in itself defensible. It need, indeed, not have a central citadel: monarchy and oligarchy both affect a citadel, but democracy is content with a plain which cannot be dominated, and aristocracy prefers a number of strong places, like the Seven Hills of Rome. On the other hand, it should be provided with walls: the Spartan boast, that the best walls of a city were the bodies of her citizens, was to Aristotle an antiquated conception, only suited to the days in which engineering was in its infancy. A city should make its walls at once a thing of beauty and of terror; and it will find that the best security of peace is to be prepared for war. Finally, streets ought to be driven through the city in a manner which shall form a mean between the straggling old alley of the past and the new fashion, which Hippodamus had introduced, of scientific lines and avenues. The former were easily defended in spite of their inconvenience: the latter are indeed convenient, but as convenient for the attack of the enemy as for the business of the citizen. The mean between the two will be taken, if the streets are arranged, like the rows of vines in a vineyard, in the pattern of a quincunx.[1]

And where shall the public places of the city be set? The temples must occupy some far-seen height, which is at once a natural throne, and a place of vantage where images and offerings may safely repose. In these temples the chief magistrates take their common meals: the far-seen height contains, in one, cathedral and *hôtel de ville*.[2] At the foot of the hill, but still on high ground, lies the great square (ἀγορά), in which the citizens from time to time meet for political business, but which normally serves as a place for the enjoyment of leisure. It will be a place of beauty, a place of running water and whispering trees, a fit abode for the leisure of the free, for whom it is jealously guarded by the law from mechanics and farmers and all base and vulgar souls. By its side will stand the gymnasium of the elders, to which they may turn when talk or siesta is done; and meanwhile the young men, on whom devolves the whole burden of war, have their station, and take their common meals, in guard-rooms and towers along the circuit of the walls,

[1] *I.e.*:

The streets will run transversely, and an enemy who wishes to get to the centre of the town will have to zig-zag slowly to his objective.

[2] Cathedrals served as *hôtels de ville* for some of the French communes of the twelfth century.

or practice themselves in a gymnasium of their own, distinct from that of their elders, under the supervision of the State. Besides the great "place" of the city, there is still another square, where the market is held, a square on the level ground, to which the roads from the country and from the sea converge. Near this square are naturally to be found the quarters of the magistrates who are concerned with judicial matters like cases of contract, or are responsible for the order of the city and its public places. Distinct from the city, which lies a little inland, is its port, with its own walls and defences, and its great road leading from the sea to the market-place. Around the city stretches to the frontier a territory clothed with corn and vines and olives, and studded here and there with the guard-houses of the young citizens, and the temples of gods and heroes.

Division of territory

How is this territory divided? It must not be common property, though it may be *used* by its owners in such a friendly spirit that a certain communism reigns. On the other hand it must not be so entirely abandoned to private possession, that any of the citizens are reduced to beggary. A certain happy mean must be taken between common ownership and private property. Two considerations suggest the way in which this is to be done. In the first place, the Spartan system of common tables is one which the ideal State will adopt, not indeed on the Spartan plan, by which each individual contributes his own share (for that, as we shall see, has evil results), but rather on the Cretan plan, by which the State makes itself responsible for the maintenance of the tables. Secondly, the expenses of religious ceremonial, of sacrifice and procession, must be met by the community from its corporate resources. For both of these reasons it will be necessary that one part of the territory of the State should be reserved as public property, and should be used to meet the expenses of the common tables and of religious ceremonial, while the rest of the land is surrendered to private possession.[1] A further division suggested by Aristotle, and already suggested by Plato in the *Laws*, would dis-

[1] The Attic demes had communal property, landed estates which they let to tenants, and from which they defrayed communal expenses such as sacrifices; and Athens itself owned not only the silver mines at Laurium, but also houses and land (including the estates of temples).

tinguish the private property of each citizen into two parts, one contiguous to the city, the other close to the frontier. Such an arrangement will secure an equality which would otherwise be lost: land near the city must always be most valuable because of its position, and it would be an injustice to allow a few citizens to enjoy a monopoly of the most valuable land. Similar considerations dictated the system of strips, by which, in the middle ages, the land of a village was divided among its inhabitants, in such a way as to give each a portion of every quality of land. Nor will this arrangement merely produce equality: it will also produce unanimity. It had been found at Athens during the Peloponnesian War, that the citizens of the frontier hated a war which the citizens of the city cheerfully faced because they were not likely to suffer from the enemy's ravages. And one of the causes which had produced the tyranny of Peisistratus was the division of Attica into parties based upon diversities of local sentiment, a division which Cleisthenes, on the fall of the Peisistratidæ, tried to counteract, by making each of the ten tribes which he instituted consist of demes from different quarters of Attica.[1]

The Organisation of the Ideal State

§ 2. These are the material aspects of the ideal State. We may now turn to discuss its social and constitutional organisation. The functions which have to be discharged in the State may be said to be six: they embrace the provision of food, the practice of arts, the profession of arms, the acquisition of wealth, the cult of the gods, and the determination of what is right and expedient for the whole society. The discharge of all these functions is the attainment of complete "independence". But a great distinction has to be drawn. The farmer who is occupied with the provision of food, the artisan who practises the arts, and the trader who deals with the products of both, are all discharging functions which are subsidiary to the rest, and (a man being what his function makes him) they them-

The parts of the State

[1] One may compare with Cleisthenes' scattering of the demes the supposed "policy" of William the Conqueror (which was partly the accidental result of a gradual conquest, partly a survival of Anglo-Saxon conditions) of scattering the manors. In either case the scattering would, *de facto*, check the tendency to localism.

27

selves are merely subsidiary to the rest of the community. This means that they are not part of the community: the end and means, the subsidiary and the final, cannot form one whole. Because they are the means, and it is the end, the tools which build a house (and workmen may be included among the latter as "animate" tools) have nothing in common with the house which they build; and similarly "property," which is a tool for the building of the State, and includes (in the slaves who till the soil or practice an art) "animate" varieties, has nothing in common with the State. But why, it may be asked, can there be no community between the end and the means? For two reasons. Any whole, any association, depends on the fact that its members share in some single, common and identical purpose; but since the purpose of a means is to serve the end, and the purpose of the end is something different and higher, there can be no such identical purpose common to the means and the end. And, secondly, any community or association is composed of equals (since to share in the same purpose both presupposes and involves equality); but the means cannot be equal to the end. Thus, somewhat technically, the teleological method enforces its stern results—results which follow with a logical inevitability if the premisses be conceded, that there is a political end too lofty for all to pursue, and that those who cannot pursue that end themselves are naturally meant to be its means. To challenge these results, therefore, one must deny both premisses: one must believe, as we have seen reason to believe, that every man, as a man, is a person with an end of his own, and can never be a means to the ends of others: one must maintain, that each man thus being a person with an end of his own, every man has rights, the maintenance of which is the political end—from which it follows that the political end is the same for one and all, and constitutes all men equal, since all are possessed of rights.

The two functions of the provision of food and the practice of arts being eliminated, and those who discharge these functions being shown to be no part of the political community, it remains to ask how the community will regulate the discharge of the four functions with which alone it is concerned. Will

The allocation of the functions of government

it follow the Platonic principle of specialisation, and assign separate persons to the separate functions? That is Nature's own plan, as Aristotle tells us: she is no maker of Delphic knives which will serve more purposes than one. But the practice of man varies. In some constitutions all men share in every function, as is the case in a democracy—the constitution of the "versatile" man, or the "busybody," as Plato had preferred to say. In others the theory of the right man in the right place is followed; and oligarchies profess to be based on this principle. In deciding the practice of the ideal State, Aristotle naturally begins with the two great functions of war and government. Was it the wisest plan to give the province of military affairs into the hands of a special class, as the increased professionalism of the times, especially visible in this province, seemed naturally to demand; or was this only to court the danger of subversion of the constitution by that class, and were the citizens who governed the State to be also its defenders? The solution which Aristotle gives is meant to reconcile both possibilities, and to give the advantages while avoiding the dangers of a trained military class. Different qualities are obviously necessary for war and for government; and he suggests that the quality needed for war is exactly that which characterises youth, and the quality required for government that which belongs to age. War needs the spirit and vigour of youth: government needs the experience and reflection of age. Let the same men therefore be soldiers in youth, and rulers in age, and the State will gain the advantage of specialisation, without running the risk of division into two opposing interests.[1] The soldier will not be hostile to the government, of which he will one day be a member; and a prudent government will restrain the fire of youth, which will be willing to tolerate its interference. The rule of the aged will thus prevent the ideal State from declining into a war-state on the model of Sparta, and from preferring a practical life of con-

[1] This plan will have the advantage which Plato sought to gain by the scheme of the *Republic*, without the defect which Aristotle traces in that scheme. But Plato had said much the same as Aristotle here says himself; his rulers were the aged, his soldiers the young. The one difference is that only a few of Plato's soldiers could ever hope to be rulers, while all Aristotle's soldiers will one day be rulers.

quest to the development of the true life within. It will bring more than negative blessings: it will mean that the State is guided by those to whom age has brought the faculty of self-conscious direction by an indwelling principle, and who are therefore qualified to lead men by the paths of habit towards the moral life: it will mean that the supremacy of law (which is reason that has put away all passion) is realised so far as it can be by any rule of men. In this praise of the aged, Aristotle follows the track of the *Laws*, in which Plato, writing in his own old age, had made length of years the condition of the higher offices; and Hegel in turn has followed both, when in the system of Social Ethics, he discovers the voice of "intelligence free and entire" (or, in a lower form of speech, of true public opinion) in the words of the Aged and the Priests. "The real voice of experience is elicited through those who have attained indifference to the disturbing influence of human parties, and who see life steadily and whole."[1]

In this scheme of giving the duties of war to the young, and the cares of peace to the old, Aristotle claims that he is true to Nature. Like her, he has given separate functions to separate persons; but he has done this upon a plan which is of Nature's own devising—he has used the different stages of men's lives for the different purposes, which their different aptitudes naturally suggest. It is natural, that he should next propose to devote the last stages of a long life to the service of the gods, and should recruit his priesthood from the ranks of those whose shoulders time has wearied, and who have well deserved the "relaxation" of serving the gods before they go to their long rest. Thus shall one and the same man in his time play many parts—gallant warrior, sage ruler, and grey-bearded priest;[2] and all the great functions of the State will always be open, when his due time comes, to each and all of the citizens. As the citizens play all parts, so they possess all things: all property is concentrated in their hands, whether they hold it collectively to the use of common tables or religious ceremonies, or possess it in full private ownership;

[1] Wallace, *Hegel's Philosophy of Mind*, clxxxiii.

[2] Nothing is said of the acquisition of wealth by a particular class, or at a particular time, though it is one of the integral functions of the State.

while their leisure is safe in the multitude of slaves to whom all work is committed.

In the State which he has here constructed Aristotle has been careful to avoid the faults which he detects in the *Republic.* Like Plato he aims at specialisation, but in such a way that every man moves with advancing years from one sphere to another, and no man is stamped for life as gold or silver. Like Plato he aims at unity; but he seeks to achieve that unity by avoiding any division of the citizens other than by the natural difference of years, and by providing (as we shall see) a common education by the State for all alike.[1] He does not demand of the individual any surrender of his rights in the name of unity. On the contrary the Aristotelian citizen owns his property, and rules his family, even if his rights in respect of the latter are limited by the claim of the State to regulate marriage and to educate its offspring. The hard pressure of the Platonic ideal upon actual life is thus mitigated. There is no tyranny of a supreme Good, issuing in the benevolent despotism of a philosopher king on the one hand, and the surrender of wife and child, house and lands, on the other; there is a quiet sense that if the end of life be *one* for all, yet *all* must combine in its realisation, and by its realisation *each* must fulfil, not lose, himself.[2] The insistence on the combination of *all* in the direction of the State may indeed be said to approximate the Aristotelian ideal to a democracy, though it is always termed an aristocracy.[3] In the ideal State, we are told, every citizen shares in the rights of the constitution. If there had been men towering over the rest, as gods and heroes tower above humanity in mind and

Moderate and almost democratic character of Aristotle's ideal State

[1] Whereas Plato had divided the ruler and the guardian by a difference of interests and class, and had given them different degrees of education; while he had also rigidly distinguished between the governmental class of rulers and guardians and the rest of the State.

[2] Aristotle's ideal State is not the logical result of a single principle (like the Platonic principle of justice) pushed to its full conclusions and enforced in every detail. It is rather the result of a number of sound suggestions about property, about government, about education, which are systematically arranged, but do not form a system. Both in social and in political matters Aristotle, in comparison with Plato, pays more attention to the individual, and less to the principle.

[3] But it is a democracy in which the farmers and artisans are slaves; and it must not be imagined that the ideal State of Aristotle is one which can be *technically* called a democracy (even of the moderate kind). (*Cf. infra*, p. 473.)

body, then all power and authority might, as in those Indian communities which travellers describe, have been placed in the hands of a king who was king by right divine. But "in our State it is necessary that all should share alike in turn in the exercise of power: all are equals, and deserve equal rights; nor will a constitution which contravenes this equality readily endure".[1] That all should share, and all share equally, in the rights of government, may well seem an adoption of democratic principles; and one is tempted to speak of the Aristotelian ideal State as an idealised democracy, in which there is an equal distribution of property, and all are equal in material things—in which there is the same education for every member, and all are equal in culture—in which, finally, the direction of the common life of the State falls equally to all, because all are thus socially, and intellectually, and morally, on the same level of attainment. It is a democracy which has made its supreme end peace, but is yet prepared for war, whether to protect its independence, or to acquire an hegemony in Greece and to subdue the barbarian to his proper slavery—a democracy which is not afraid to stand on the high-way of the world, to send out ships and to receive merchandise, but yet refuses to surrender itself to merchandising, because it covets the higher things of the spirit. But democratic as the ideal State may appear, much as it may remind us of Athens as Pericles conceived Athens, it cannot be called in Aristotle's terminology anything but an aristocracy. For it has set virtue before its eyes for the aim and purpose of its life: it has made virtue the measure by which its citizens receive the honours it has to bestow. It is in a word a State where "the best" rule, though all are "the best". It has the width and the equality of a democracy, but it has the intensity and high purpose of an aristocracy; and since by their purposes shall all things be judged, it must be judged an aristocracy. And indeed if one remembers that, though in the long run every man enters upon the government, yet at any given time authority is vested in the natural aristocracy of years and experience, the name aristocracy will seem to be deserved not only by the purpose of the State, but also by the character of the sovereign class.

[1] *Pol.*, 1332 b 25 *sqq.*

Aristotle's Theory of Education

§ 3. The ideal State has now been equipped with all the material conditions which it depends upon Fortune to give. We have supposed Fortune to have endowed it liberally in every way; and we have constructed a government, which will be ideally fitted for using human art to second Fortune's gifts. On human art—on knowledge and purpose aforethought—it now depends to make the State as good spiritually as it already is materially. By what means, and in what ways, will the government best attempt to promote the realisation of the ideal life? It is a wide question, and its full solution would involve a theory of legislation and of punishment, as well as of education. But the ideal State is only sketched by Aristotle in the rough. The account of its constitution, which has just been discussed, is a bare outline of the most general principles: nothing is said of their application. We are not told, for instance, how the deliberative assembly will be organised, or what it will discuss: we hear nothing of the offices of the executive or their powers: nothing is said of the judicature. And so it is with Aristotle's account of the action of the government in promoting the ideal life. We have only a treatment of the subject of education, fuller indeed and more detailed than the treatment of any other subject connected with the ideal State, but yet incomplete.[1]

Aristotle's general view of education

To appreciate the educational theory which Aristotle propounds, one must notice, that he starts from a different point of view from that of the modern theorist. In the first place, it is obvious that he primarily aims at providing an education which will adapt its subject to membership of a State. Education is part of politics: it has a political aim. This does not mean that Aristotle wishes the young to be instructed in the past history of their State, its present politics, the aims of its parties, and the duty of some day using a vote in the assembly carefully and judiciously. It means that he wishes the young

[1] But the subject of education must necessarily demand most consideration in an ideal State, in which (ideal citizens being postulated) the repressive or judicial aspect of the State disappears, as Plato had urged, and its suggestive or educational aspect comes to the front. A theory of punishment is, therefore, after all, hardly required by Aristotle's plan.

to be trained in a certain type of character, which corresponds to the demands of the State upon the individual, and is therefore, because it means a harmony between the two, calculated to preserve the integrity and stability of the State. It is in this sense that the education of a State must be adapted to the constitution, or in other words to the manner of life, which the State has chosen to adopt. In the ideal State, and indeed in any proper State, the citizens have set their faces towards a moral life; and hence, because education is political, it is also moral—it is a training of the moral faculties calculated to produce a proper type of character. This constitutes a second difference, flowing from the first, between the aims of Aristotle and those of modern educationalists. Not only does he regard the State, rather than the individual, as the primary object of attention; but he also regards character rather than knowledge as the end to be sought, and will rather than intelligence as the subject to be trained and developed. This being the aim of education in Aristotle's conception, there will result certain differences between the means of education which he prefers to use, and those which we employ. Working on the intelligence, we use the means that influence the development of intelligence, the subtleties of grammar, the abstractions of mathematics: working on the will, he lays stress upon those influences which are calculated to mould the will insensibly, such as the fascination of noble music or the attraction of great literature. The artistic element has a large place in Aristotle's scheme of education, not because he wishes to develop an artistic taste (though he allows some room for that object in his theory of music), but because he hopes through art to reach the moral sense.

Contrast with modern views

These then are the peculiarities of Aristotle's general conception of education: first, that education means to him something which prepares a future citizen for taking his place in the community to which he belongs; secondly, that it does so by acting upon his will in such a way as to produce a moral tone in harmony with that of the community; and thirdly, that it uses by preference artistic agencies to attain that end. It is political: it is moral: it is artistic. The distinction which has been drawn between this conception of education and modern conceptions is of course rough, and liable to qualification in every point. Any true education aims to-day, as much as it could two thousand years ago, at making a man capable of doing his duty in the state of life to which he has been called within the community to which he belongs. Any true education affects the character. Merely to have learned the grammar of a language faithfully means a habit of accuracy and application; and every mental discipline is also something of a moral training. Nor again can the whole educative influence of a great school (apart from direct instruction and conscious effort) fail to result in a certain tone and type of character. None the less, there is a decided difference between the aims of Aristotle and our own, if it is only a difference of emphasis. The adjustment of the individual to the community, the moral aim of instruction, are much more simply and directly present to his mind; and the use of artistic means to produce a direct effect is peculiarly Greek.[1] Aristotle aims at producing by direct methods and conscious efforts a result, which we either leave to indirect methods (as when we put our trust in the moral effect of games or of steady intellectual work), or to quiet insensible influences like the public opinion of a school. He leaves less play for the action of the family, though, one gathers from the *Ethics*, he is alive to its importance; nor can he find in Greek religion, a matter of sacrifice and ceremony, that teaching and sanction of morality which modern life finds in Christianity. And thus he may be said to attempt, by direct means and by public agencies to achieve results, which are now supposed to be properly attained by indirect methods, and through private (or at any rate non-political) agencies. He feels that morality must be *made*, because it is a matter of such vital importance to the State that it cannot be left to chance: we feel that morality must *grow*, and grow without the coercion of the State, because the "kingdom of Heaven must be taken" by every man for himself.

The foundation of any educational system must be found in psychology; and having spoken of these political conceptions

[1] Aristotle would never have given a prize for the best copy of Phrygian verses, or the best essay on the financial system of ancient Babylon, but for the best piece of solemn music expressive of a brave man doing a brave deed.

Psychological basis of Aristotle's scheme of education

which determine Aristotle's views on education, we must next examine their psychological basis. Education is a development of the soul. There are three stages, we are told, in the development of the soul—that of natural disposition (φύσις), that of habitual temperament (ἔθος), and that of rational self-determination (λόγος). Natural disposition is of course beyond the reach of education; but Aristotle does his best to secure an ideal disposition, in the first place by postulating a population of Greeks for his ideal State, and secondly by regulating marriage with a view to the improvement of its offspring. The stage of habitual temperament is that which is peculiarly amenable to education: it belongs to the age of desire, which is the age of youth. Desire is composed of appetite and spirit and will:[1] it is the normal state or condition of the irrational half of the human soul—of feeling and sentiment, as opposed to reason and deliberation. Reason and deliberation should control desire; and youth, which is all desire, and in which reason and deliberation are undeveloped, must be trained and controlled by age, in which reason is most nearly pure. Nor does youth resent such control. The "irrational soul" of youth is not entirely irrational: "appetite and indeed desire in general have a certain element of reason, in so far as they are disposed to hear and obey its voice".[2] The soul of youth is pliable, its feelings quick and responsive; habits may be inculcated which will never be lost, though they may develop in later life into methods of rational self-direction. It is here that the main problem of education is to be found; and that problem is accordingly the discovery of those influences, which will most readily and most deeply imprint a lasting mark on the young soul—those forces of suggestion, to which it will most readily respond, and which it will most easily absorb into the habits of its being. Now the habitual modes of action to be created are those, in which the different virtues express themselves; and therefore the young must be drilled into acting habitually in the ways which are required by the conceptions of courage, self-control, and each of the other virtues. They themselves have

[1] ὄρεξις is composed of ἐπιθυμία, θυμός, and βούλησις.

[2] *Cf. Eth.*, 1102 b. 31. This conception corresponds to the Platonic conception of θυμός (as disposed to take the side of reason).

not attained, nor are they to be taught those conceptions: they are merely to learn, from those who know, the laws of action which they involve. Theirs will be an empiric knowledge (which is not merely knowledge, but must translate itself inevitably into action) of attributes without subject, of effects without cause. But in process of time, when man at last comes by his heritage of reason, a further education will appear. It will no longer appeal to the feelings, or endeavour to set them so absolutely in tune with moral modes of action, that those modes will become inevitable habits. It will appeal to the reason, and use the instruments which appeal to the reason—mathematics, logic, philosophy. Through it men will learn to appreciate the conceptions according to which they have been acting (though they have not been acting in their light), and they will thus gain the stage of rational self-direction. The training of desire must culminate in an education of reason, for which it was always intended to prepare the way; and the development of the human soul, which was begun in the cradle (one might almost say before the cradle), and has been continued till middle age, reaches its final limit, when reason, the highest element of the soul and the peculiar differentia of man, has become conscious of itself and has learned to use its powers. Now at last may man take over the direction of his own life, which has been before in the hands of others; and in this way the supreme goal of education may be said to be a perfect freedom. But reason is not only practical: it is also theoretical. Through the education of reason man learns not only to guide his actions for himself, but also to contemplate the truth. He arrives at conceptions which he values not only as clues to conduct, but also as sources of intellectual pleasure. For their sum is the full conception of God; and beyond that there is nothing.

And so, as the State itself is the result of a development, so is the perfection of man. As the State has gone through its stages of family and village, so has the perfection of man through its stages of natural disposition and habitual temperament. The State has grown: man has been made. But he has been made along lines which were inevitable, and which his own nature from the first dictated. There is nothing arbitrary in education:

it is the development of human capacities along a path which they indicate to an end which they demand. Yet it is a sphere for human action: it lies in the province of art, and not of Nature;[1] it is less the growth of an inner impulse, than the action of an external force, resting upon internal assent and eliciting internal powers. Since, then, it lies in the province of art, who, it may be asked, is the proper artist, and with what tools will he work?

The State as the one educational authority

The one true educational authority is the State. Education cannot, in Aristotle's view, be left, as it was at Athens, to private enterprise. The end pursued by the community which is bound together in the State is one and the same for every member: the education, which its members need in order to attain that end, must be one and the same for all; and in order that the education may be uniform, it must be committed to the care of the State. The theory of a final cause thus postulates State education; so, too, does the organic conception of the State, which flows from that theory. If man is a "member" of the State, the State to which he belongs must so regulate the training of its member, that he will fill the place for which he is meant in its economy. Nor can it afford, even if the matter be put on grounds of pure utility, to neglect to imbue its citizens with the tone and temper peculiar to its constitution—that tone and temper which may be said to have originally made every constitution what it is, and which certainly maintains every constitution in its present life and vigour. It is the glory of Sparta to Aristotle, as to Plato, that she should have realised the necessity of a common training of her citizens for the end which she chose to pursue.

As there is to be one educational authority, so, it would seem to follow, there ought to be one sole system of education. In the ideal State this is the case. In it there is no distinction of classes, each with its separate mission, and each with its separate training. There is no class of rulers, distinct from the ruled, and needing to be trained in the virtues of authority, as the ruled in those of obedience. There is indeed a difference, but it is a difference of years, and not of classes; and there are accordingly

Aim of education the supremacy of reason

[1] But here as elsewhere art only tries to fill out what Nature has left deficient (1337 a 1). *Cf. supra*, p. 222.

no separate schemes of education for different classes, but different stages in a single scheme for different ages. For youth, the stress will fall upon the duty of obedience to the wisdom of age; for age, it will fall upon the need of moral prudence to guide the young. But the education will be fundamentally one and the same for every citizen; and since in the ideal State the good citizen is the same as the good man, the education which makes a good citizen will be the same as that which makes a good man. And therefore the true training of a citizen will be one which, like that of the good man, has the supremacy of reason for its final aim. It will adjust everything else to this final triumph of reason; and if it trains the irrational element in man it will train it with a view to the rule of the rational. Reason means leisure spent in high contemplation: reason means peace: reason means the choice of things beautiful and good. But a State has to inculcate action: it has to train its sons for war: it has to choose what is necessary and expedient for its interests. Nevertheless the ideal State will so inculcate action, as always to remember that action is for the sake of leisure: it will train its sons for war, without forgetting that war is for the sake of peace: it will choose things necessary and useful, as means towards things beautiful and good. It will do the things which are not themselves the things of reason for the sake of the things which are. It has been the mistake of Spartan training that it has reversed this order. Sparta has taken things necessary and useful as in themselves beautiful and good: she has used her leisure as a means for action, and peace as a preparation for war. She has not looked to the final supremacy of reason: she has not indeed sought to train the rational element at all. She has made her aim the training of the irrational in man—the training of desire, of will and spirit and appetite; and she has trained even these with a view to their own ultimate gratification. She has trained, for instance, the spirit of the Spartan youth to war, that in war it might be satisfied. And because she has misconceived virtue, she, who alone of Greek cities has trained her citizens to virtue, has profited nothing of all her training. She has fallen none the less, because she knew not how to use leisure, or to live at peace. And the lesson which her fall teaches is that *all* the cardinal virtues must be enforced by a State in *all* their forms. Sparta had taught but two of the four which the Greeks recognised, self-control and courage, the virtues of the irrational side of man; and she had only taught these partially, to the extent, and in the ways, necessary for martial success. She should have taught these and taught them fully, that the citizens might have had self-control in the use of their leisure, and courage to face the temptations of peace; and she should also have taught the other two virtues of justice and wisdom, and by teaching them have trained reason as well as appetite, thereby acting as nobly in peace, as she had fought gallantly in war. She should have made her citizen not the half (or the quarter) but the whole of a good man, possessing all the virtues, possessing them all in their fulness, possessing them in that proper hierarchy, in which the virtues of the rational element are enthroned as sovereign.

Regulation of marriage

The only perfect education, therefore, which State-training can give to make a good citizen, is exactly the same education as that which makes a good man. Now the State may go very far back in the making of a good man. A good man needs, as we have seen, external goods, like health; and the State can provide that he shall be born with a sound constitution, by regulating the conditions of marriage, and that he shall maintain it sound throughout youth and age, by enforcing a system of gymnastics. The regulation of marriage, "in order that the bodies of the children may be fit for the purposes of the legislator," may seem to a modern mind something of an unwarrantable interference with that liberty of the individual which Aristotle had himself vindicated against Plato in this very sphere. Men and women, we feel, cannot be made to fall in love by act of parliament; and to determine the right age for marriage, and the proper number of children, is only to court disaster. This is true; but it is at the same time true that the State cannot afford to neglect the physique of its citizens. The State has interfered, during the last century, in various ways calculated to prevent the degradation of its population. It has sought, for instance, to modify "the influence of the factory system on the women who would be the mothers of the next generation".[1] While not posi-

[1] Cunningham, *English Industry and Commerce*, ii., 622 (third edition).

tively regulating marriage, it has by negative means sought to prevent the perpetuation of a poor physique. And it is possible that it may even actually interfere with marriage in the future, upon moral rather than physical grounds, and may, by regulating the conditions under which the feeble-minded can marry, attempt to limit the growth of a population, which cannot help, but seriously hinders, its life. It would therefore seem that we acknowledge the aim of Aristotle (a proper national physique), though we do not use the means which he advocates for attaining that aim; and that, again, we may yet use that means (the regulation of marriage), though for a moral rather than a physical purpose.[1]

The first seven years of a child's life, between birth and the age at which training in a system of gymnastics enforced by the State begins, are to be spent at home. Aristotle is not without many wise hints about the problems which occupy a mother's mind, the proper feeding of children and the right ways to introduce a child to the knowledge of good and evil. Till the age of five he would impose no lessons and no tasks upon a child: it is a time of games which should be mimicries of future earnest, a time of tales and stories, which should be foreshadowings of future knowledge. These things will be in the hands of officials of the State, "inspectors of children," who will always bear in mind the truth, that first impressions are freshest and longest lived—

Early years

> Quo semel est imbuta recens, servabit odorem
> Testa diu—

and they will accordingly keep young eyes and ears from seeing or hearing any unclean thing, lest it sink into the soul, and poison life at its source. The last two years of early childhood, from five to seven, will be spent by children as spectators of the training which they are themselves shortly to receive, particularly perhaps of gymnastics.

Education runs in cycles of seven years; and as seven years have been devoted to life at home, so within the period during which the young are trained by the State, there are two epochs

[1] At the same time, the aim of Aristotle in regulating marriage is ultimately moral: he wishes for a good physique, as the proper habitation of a good moral disposition.

each of seven years. From the age of seven to puberty the body is being trained ; from puberty to the age of twenty-one the mind is being cultivated ; at twenty-one the young man brings to the service of the State the trained vigour of both body and mind. What is he to be taught during those fourteen years?

Contemporary curriculum

Aristotle begins his account of the proper curriculum by considering, like Plato, the usual subjects of general instruction in contemporary Greece—music, gymnastics and letters. By gymnastics was meant a whole system of physical training: it consisted of anything and everything which trained and inured the physique, but principally of running and jumping, wrestling and boxing, and hurling the javelin or discus. Music, in the sense in which it was used by the Greeks, meant more than our music ; and it may be defined as poetry wedded to the music, whether of voice or instrument, required for its proper presentation.[1] By "letters" we must understand reading and writing, and the study of the poets ; while as a fourth subject of general study Aristotle adds "drawing," in which he would seem to include painting. Gymnastics, music, letters, and drawing represent therefore the curriculum, which Aristotle had ready to his hand for the training of the fourteen critical years from seven to twenty-one. Of these four, he would have gymnastics taught from the age of seven to that of fourteen : at fourteen he suggests that letters should first be taught, and the study of drawing and of music begun.

Aristotle's theory of gymnastics

The period of physical development seems long protracted, and the training of the mind long delayed. But Aristotle is insisting on a principle, which he has very much at heart, that the natural development of the human being should be recognised, and that each stage of that development should only receive what is appropriate to it. We have already seen that, in view of this principle, he so arranges the constitution of his State, as to give military affairs to the young, who have an instinct and capacity for war, and political control to the men of mature years, who have the wisdom and capacity for government. The same principle which determines the constitution must also determine education. Education must be a develop-

[1] For music in the narrower sense in which we use the word the Greek term is "harmonic".

ment, in which each stage duly corresponds to the growth of the human being who is its subject. Body is prior to soul in growth: the irrational element is prior to the rational. The development of education must accordingly begin with the training of the body, proceed to the training of appetite, and culminate in the training of reason. At the age of the body, of desire, or reason, must come the training of the body, of desire, or reason. Were the appetite trained during the age of the body, the training would be wasted, because the untrained body would reject lessons of self-control, to which it had not already been physically inured. For it must not be forgotten that the training of each stage prior to reason, if an end in itself, is also a means to the next. In the period of the growth of the body the body must be trained; but it must be trained in such a way as to subserve and to prepare the training of the desires which is next to come. From this it follows that gymnastics is not mere gymnastics: it is already something of a moral training from the first, and the light of a moral purpose will grow plainer and plainer, as gymnastics draws nearer to the dawn of a definitely moral education.

Cultivation of the Mean in gymnastics

This teaching that gymnastics is no end in itself, but a means to a further end, and that it must be informed by the spirit of that further end, leads to conclusions which are still of value. A means is always limited by the end which it serves; and there must be a limit to gymnastics. This is a rule which Aristotle accuses the Greeks of having forgotten. On the one hand, gymnastics tended to pass into athletics. Athletics was the art of those who had made gymnastic performances their profession, and to whom gymnastics had become an end in itself. This was doubly mischievous. It made the soul base and mechanical, diverted from the use of reason and the pursuit of virtue to things material. It spoiled the body for the purpose of the legislator: "the athletic habit of body is of little good either for the kind of bodily fitness which a citizen needs, or for health, or for fertility". On the other hand, gymnastics as pursued at Sparta, while directed towards the attainment of a civic virtue, were made so severe as to be brutalising, in the belief that such severity would produce courage. But brute courage, Aristotle feels, is no true courage: true courage means the quiet temper, which restrains itself from foolhardiness, and seeks not all, but only noble, dangers. It means self-control and a seeing eye: it needs qualities of the mind; and no training of the body will produce it, least of all an excessive and mistaken training. Once more is Sparta judged by Aristotle for her deficiencies: she has taught but gymnastics, and she has taught them ill; she has not even produced true courage, and yet she has subordinated everything else to its attainment. From this criticism of her defects, and of the defects of Greek gymnastics in general, we may learn what is the nature of the training in gymnastics which the ideal State will give. Till puberty there will be such light exercises as will not hinder, but only direct, the growth of the body. There will be no Spartan system of scanty food and violent efforts till the age of seventeen, when, after three years' study, some hard training may be imposed, as a preparation for military service. These suggestions have still their value. It is true that all modern education must be, to some extent, differentiated from Aristotle's scheme by the fact, that every subject of education must be supposed to have ultimately the duty of making his own living. It is not, indeed, incumbent on the educationist to train men for that purpose—far from it; but his opportunities of training them for the purpose he *has* in view are greatly curtailed by its presence. Yet, since his purpose is to turn out men, some degree of physical training must be counted necessary for its realisation. Physical conditions play a large part, and have a wide bearing, in the life of every man; and the State, whose mission is concerned with the life of man, must necessarily be interested in the welfare of his body. It cannot, for mere want of time and of leisure, give anything like the physical training which Aristotle suggests; but it can do more to improve the physical condition of its members than it does. It can do more than the merely preventive and negative work of sanitation; and some system of compulsory physical training, which shall not interfere with economic activity, seems one of the needs of the future. Such a training, if compulsory (like most of the action of the State), would not therefore interfere with true liberty. On the contrary, it would promote true freedom of action, by

Physical training to-day

removing impediments from its path; and it would set free a natural instinct of self-development, which is more universally felt in physical things than in moral.

The period of education in which the liberal arts of music, letters, and drawing are studied is only partially discussed by Aristotle. Two questions, the one general, the other more particular, can alone be said to receive any solution. The first concerns the aim and purpose towards which education in the arts generally should be directed: the second touches the value of music in particular as an instrument of education. In the light of what has already been said, there can be little doubt about the purpose which Aristotle would assign to instruction in the liberal arts. It can only be the promotion of virtue. But a consideration of contemporary methods does not, he confesses, leave so simple an impression. Some may seem designed to the promotion of virtue: others profess to teach what will be of use in after life. And Aristotle admits, seeking as ever to absorb the element of truth which any theory or practice may contain, that there are some studies which must be pursued with a view to their utility, and because they are absolutely necessary. Such studies are reading, writing, and a certain amount of arithmetic and geometry. They embrace part of "letters" and part of "drawing"; they form the "technical" element of education. They are needed for the management of a household, and for many branches of political administration; they are the necessary means for the acquisition of a species of knowledge, which is valuable in itself. Pursued for their use, these studies must not be pursued to an excess. There is a limit beyond which the pursuit of a liberal art becomes illiberal. Excessive attention to any one part disturbs the proportion and balance of the whole mind, and results in that "professionalism," if it may be so termed, which a freeman should avoid.[1]

Purpose of education in the arts

But if it be admitted that the non-artistic side of education is within the sphere of utility, there still remains the artistic; and what are we to say of that? In other words, what will be

The value of musical instruction

[1] To write *e.g.* a copper-plate hand is βάναυσον: it belongs to the slave-copyist, not to the freeman.

our view of the purpose and aim of a training in music?[1] The majority still answer "utility": music is desirable for the pleasure which it brings. That this answer contains part of the truth, Aristotle is willing to admit; but he denies that it by any means contains the whole. Musical instruction has also two other aims in view: it seeks to promote virtue, by habituating the young to find pleasure in the right sources of pleasure, and by forming the character as gymnastics forms the body; and it affords a proper and a pleasant means for the employment of leisure.

(a) Music as a means of relaxation

As a thing useful for daily life, music must be studied in connection with the theory of relaxation. To appreciate that theory we must distinguish between the two provinces of "leisure" (σχολή) and "work" (ἀσχολία). Leisure is an end in itself, and has a pleasure of itself: "work" aims at something beyond itself, and is always accompanied by effort. Leisure is the negative, not of action, but of effort devoted towards an external end: far from being opposed to action, it is a condition of the highest spiritual activity, such as contemplation. It is indeed just because it is such a condition of activity that it is pleasant; for pleasure at its best is nothing but a sense of the activity of the soul. "Work," on the other hand (in the sense of effort directed towards an external end), attended as it is by pain, involves the importation of a *foreign* pleasure to cure the pain which it has caused.[2] "Toil causes pain, and pain is cured by its opposite:" pleasure is necessary by way of relaxation after work. This is the basis of amusements. Like sleep and conviviality they are means of relaxation.[3] Metaphorically speaking they are drugs to cure the pains of action; and like drugs, they should be used only when they are needed. Of all pleasures music is one of the greatest,

[1] The artistic side of drawing is not considered.

[2] The distinction between activities pleasant *per se*, and activities painful *per se* and therefore needing the compensation of a subsequent pleasure, is one which some economists have sought to obscure. It has been thought that action in the sense of effort directed towards an external end might become, under a socialistic *régime*, a source of pleasure. This is the doctrine of "attractive labour," expounded by Fourier (*cf.* Gide, *Political Economy*, ii., ii., § 4, "On Pain as a Factor of Labour").

[3] "Relaxation" (ἀνάπαυσις) is necessary after work: the means of "relaxation" are sleep, conviviality, and above all "amusements" (παιδιά). Under the head of amusements comes music (from this point of view).

and for that reason it is also the highest amusement, the best means of relaxation. It possesses therefore a natural "utility" within the sphere of work, forming as it does an antidote to the pain with which all work is attended. The danger of its use is a danger which it has in common with all amusements. Men are prone to find in amusement the end of life. They feel, that the end of life is something pursued for the pleasure which it brings in itself, and not for the sake of any further result: they feel, that the same is true of amusement; and they readily identify the two. And thus they take a drug meant for the healing of pain, when they have no pain: they become, as it were, opium-eaters. A man who turns to music in this spirit is one who, as Plato says, surrenders his soul to be flooded through his ears with sound, until it loses its proper balance and adjustment. His soul becomes unstrung: he has missed the end of life, which means the stringing of the soul to action at its highest pitch.

(*b*) Music as an employment of leisure

On the other hand, music has also its meaning in the sphere of leisure, as well as in that of work; and, in so far as it has, it *is*, to some extent, identical with the end of life. For leisure, as we have already seen, is greater than work, so much greater indeed that it is the very end of life, to which all work is but a means. But it is not a bare leisure of which this can be predicated: it is a full and concrete leisure, which must have a content of proper action. And therefore Aristotle asks the apparently paradoxical question—In what work must leisure be spent? First and foremost, the answer runs, in a "contemplation" which sees all things in the light of a final purpose towards which they are always moving; but next to that (for contemplation belongs to rare moments of life), in hearing, or it may be playing, noble music. Accordingly, while men must certainly be taught those sciences which are the steps towards such contemplation (a theme fully handled in the *Republic*, but not touched by Aristotle), they must also, and equally with a view to the right use of leisure, be instructed in music. For it is of vast importance that men should know what use to make of leisure. In this respect, as we have already seen, the defects of Spartan education are apparent. Sparta had taught her citizens how to work for external ends like glory and dominion: she had never taught them how to use their leisure. There was ancient and honourable authority, which she might have followed if she had chosen, for the use of music as a means of spending leisure. The testimony of Homer shows to Aristotle that music originally came into vogue in this way. The witness of the ancients to his views was precious in his eyes; and if that witness showed, as he thought it did, that the primitive and *natural* use of music was connected with the enjoyment of leisure, he might well regard his conception of the purpose of music as proven.

(c) Music as an agent of moral instruction

The kinds of music used in time of leisure must be such as not only to afford pleasure, but also to carry something of a high message in themselves. It is not mere music, but good music, which will be a delight to leisured ears; and good music will be music which mirrors in itself the goodness of the world. This is what links the hearing of music to contemplation of the world's purpose. By the one we see, by the other we hear, that the world is good, because we see or hear it moving by an orderly progress towards an appointed goal. And if this be so, if there is a soul of goodness in music, and if its harmony be the image of the harmony of an ordered world, then the question arises, whether music may not serve as an instrument of moral education, as well as a means of relaxation or of spending leisure. Will not music affect character and soul, and ought it not to be used in order to affect character and soul in youth? That character *is* affected by music is for Aristotle evidenced by facts: the melodies of Olympus possess and inspire his hearers, and such possession and inspiration is certainly an affection of the character. But a basis may also be found for this contention in abstract argument. Virtue involves a certain adjustment of the emotions: it means that one feels an emotion of pleasure, and an emotion of pain, at the right time and with regard to the proper object. An education in virtue must aim at producing this adjustment of the emotions; it must endeavour to produce a temperament, which feels pleasure when and as it should, and, in a word, identifies pleasure with duty. But to listen to a piece of music means an emotion of pleasure; and if the content and meaning of that music is a moral content and meaning, to listen to it means an emotion of pleasure felt with regard to something, which is a proper object of pleasure. In that case to listen to music will be a moral education; and its result will be that identification of pleasure and duty in the human soul which we call virtue. But *is* the content and meaning of music moral? Can the content of a piece of music be something brave, something just, something generous? Obviously it cannot be the brave, or just, or generous thing itself; but it can be, and is, its semblance or image. We should never feel brave after hearing a piece of music (and yet we admittedly do), unless courage, or rather the image of courage, were in the music. Music shares with other arts this power of presenting images of things virtuous; but it possesses this power in a peculiar degree. And therefore to be pleased in listening to the peculiarly true likeness of things virtuous, which music can present, is little short of being pleased with virtuous things themselves. The adjustment of the emotions which fine music produces is only a little lower than the equipoise of virtue itself; but while it may be difficult to find pleasure in the actual object in which we ought to find it, because the pleasure which it brings is not at first sight obvious, it is easy to find pleasure in its semblance, because it comes to the senses through a medium of pleasure. For youth especially an instruction in music is fitting and proper. Youth will bear nothing that is painful—and yet it needs to be habituated not only to bear but to love the commands of virtue and justice: music is pleasant—and yet it carries in its strains their message and command.

Music produces the clearest image of virtue

But why, of all the five senses, should hearing be the greatest? Why should not sight, for instance, present images of virtue with equal fidelity? That sight can also present such images, Aristotle allows. But the images produced by the painter or sculptor are not copies, they are only symbols,[1] of the thing they signify: they signify character, indeed, but only in so far as character is revealed in the body under stress of emotion. It is otherwise with music. One may go to see a picture, and yet come away much as one went: one cannot listen to "a solemn music" without some feeling of solemnity, or to a quick allegro without some stirring of the blood. The message of

[1] *I.e.*, they have "no essential resemblance, no natural connection, with the thing signified" (Newman, iii., 546).

modern music is vague and complex; and not one feeling, but a blend of many, forms the response with which it meets. It is true that Greek music was also tending in the same direction by the time of Plato; and one of the reforms suggested in the *Republic* is a reduction of music to its ancient simplicity. But Plato and Aristotle nevertheless discover a simple message and a direct moral appeal in the different keys (*ἁρμονίαι*) and the various times (*ῥυθμοί*) of contemporary music. Plato rejects the "slack" Lydian and Ionian keys as soft and voluptuous, the "tense" Lydian and Mixolydian as plaintive and exciting; and he retains only the Dorian and Phrygian keys as expressive, the one of calm endeavour, the other of sober enjoyment. Aristotle criticises this retention of the Phrygian key, on the ground that it too is exciting; but he agrees with Plato in thinking that the Dorian key is a mean between the extremes of "slack" and "tense," and that it is most expressive of true courage. And so too with regard to times: some, says Aristotle, have a grave character as of rest, some a light character as of motion; some are vulgar in movement, and some noble.[1] What is true of the elements of music is also true of their union; and the same distinction of character holds good with regard to melodies, or musical compositions. Ancient theorists made a triple distinction of melodies, according as they expressed "a magnanimous and heroic, or low and effeminate, or calm and refined character of mind". The distinction drawn by Aristotle is of a somewhat wider scope. To him melodies are either ethical, or practical, or passionate and inspiring, according as they influence character, or stimulate action, or affect the passions. Each has its appropriate key: the Dorian key will be used in ethical melodies, for instance, and the Phrygian for melodies which excite and inspire the passions. Each kind of melody, with its appropriate key, will have its proper use. Ethical melodies in the Dorian key will serve for the moral habituation of the young: practical melodies (apparently in the hypo-Phrygian key) will serve to play troops into battle.

What will be the use of passionate melodies? Here we

[1] "Time" or rhythm, and its science, apply to dancing and spoken language, as well as to music. The word "motion" almost seems to suggest dancing to music.

(d) Music as a means of purification

come upon a new and interesting side of Aristotle's theory of music, and indeed of his general theory of art.[1] He regards music (as he also regards tragedy) as a means for the "purification" of the feelings. It has already been said that music, as an instrument of moral education, makes for virtue by producing a certain adjustment of emotion, by which pleasurable emotions are excited by things good, and painful emotions by things evil. But adjustment of emotion may be made in another way, and for a different reason. Men who are especially prone to moods of exalted excitement, or to an excess of strong feelings of pity or fear—who, in a word, are of an emotional disposition, need as it were a purging and purification of their accumulated emotion. They are like patients in a fever; and they must be dosed with some cooling medicine, which will clear the system of disorders. To present to a person who is labouring under suppressed emotion some object, which will attract and draw away his emotion, is to provide a medicine for this fever of the spirit: it is to purge away the excess of passion, and to leave the patient as it were with a quiet pulse and normal temperature. Tragedy achieves such a purification of the passions of pity and fear, by presenting objects of misery or terror:[2] music, it would seem, has a still wider scope. Moods of exalted excitement can be relieved by the music of sacred melodies; and these same melodies will also cure an excess of pity, or fear, or emotion of any kind. At the bottom of the doctrine of the purificatory effect of music there would seem to be the same conception which underlies Aristotle's theory of its moral effect. Music presents images which affect the soul; and as a musical image of courage or temperance affects the soul with a love for these virtues, so a musical image of misery or terror affects the soul with pity or fear. It is easier for youth to love virtue in its musical image: it is better for the soul to feel emotion at the musical counter-

[1] For Aristotle's theory of κάθαρσις, see Professor Butcher's work, *Aristotle's Theory of Poetry and Fine Art*, c. vi.

[2] *Cf.* Plato, *Rep.*, 606 A. "The passion which is forcibly restrained, and which hungers for a proper outlet and satisfaction in tears and lamentation, finds its fulfilment and pleasure in poetry." But Plato fears that to indulge this passion over feigned sorrows is not to draw it away, but to encourage it.

feit of the true object of emotion, because the emotion will be under greater control. The whole theory of purification, one feels, is a Greek theory—the theory of an emotional people, afraid of losing self-control, and anxious to preserve a spiritual sanity. It was easy for a Greek to "get out of himself" (ἐκστῆναι): he could readily pretend to be something which he was not (whence Plato's hatred of the "lie in the soul"); he could readily be carried into a state of emotion, which made him feel that he had lost himself. It is this temper which explains the Socratic and Platonic teaching: "Be yourself, and nothing but yourself, and above all things understand yourself"; and this, again, explains the Aristotelian preaching: "Save yourself: do not let your passions make you other than yourself; and therefore go to music for an outlet of superfluous passion, as you would go to a doctor for blood-letting, if you were afraid of losing control of your body in the height of a fever".

These are the aims of a musical education. Several problems of method emerge; but they are solved by the use of principles which we have already come to know. Boys must be taught to play music after they have reached the age of fourteen; otherwise, they will not understand it sufficiently to derive pleasure or edification from listening when they are older. On the other hand they must not spend so much time on music that the development of their bodies is neglected; nor must they study it with so much application as to make its study into a technical and mechanical thing. A boy must no more become a trained musician than he must become a professional athlete: he must no more practice the *tours de force* of the one than he would the feats of the other. Such considerations as these will banish the use of the flute from musical instruction; it is too "technical". And besides it has little moral value; it interferes with the use of words, which ought always to accompany music, since they contribute to its moral effect.

Aristotle's scheme of education and that of Plato

Here ends what Aristotle has to say on education. It goes no further than the stage of youth and of training in habits; and it is not a full sketch of that stage. Something, for instance, might have been said of "letters": Plato, at any rate, has much to say of the proper literature for the study of the young. More might have been said about "drawing". We are told that it makes men capable of perceiving beauty of form, and we may guess that Aristotle, like Plato, regarded a sense of beauty as akin to the moral sense; but we are not told in what way, and with what object, drawing would be taught in the ideal State. Nothing again is said of the last and highest stage, in which reason is elicited by a study of science, and set free to control the passions for itself, and to contemplate freely the meaning of itself and the world. Much as he resembles Plato in his views on education, Aristotle is at once less complete and less systematic than Plato. He gives scattered hints, rather than an ordered whole; and the system of philosophy into which they fit is but briefly mentioned. We are left to fill out the scheme, and to fit in the details for ourselves. But apart from this, there is little difference between Aristotle and Plato. Both have the same fundamental view of education as a training of character: both have the same high conception of art as influencing character. The main difference between the two arises from Aristotle's principle of "following Nature" and giving to each stage of growth its appropriate instruction—a principle which induces him to prolong gymnastics, and to defer letters and music to a later age than Plato had contemplated. With this respect for Nature there goes a certain respect for facts, such as we should naturally expect. Not only does Aristotle build his theory of education more in the light of Spartan experience and the contemporary practice of Greece; but he has, for instance, a wider and more catholic view than appears in Plato of the uses which music actually serves. He fits music less into his theory, and considers it more by itself, and in its own full possibilities, as a means of relaxation, or of purification, or of spending leisure, as well as of moral instruction.

CHAPTER XI

[*Politics*, IV.-VI. (VI.-VIII.)]

ACTUAL STATES AND THE LINES OF THEIR REFORM

THE SCOPE OF ARISTOTLE'S PLAN

§ 1. ON the analogy of other arts, such as gymnastics, we must, Aristotle suggests, discuss various possibilities in dealing with the art of politics.[1] We must inquire into the ideal State, as we should inquire into the ideal course of training: we must suppose ideal conditions, and attempt to discover the best State possible under such conditions. Secondly, we must suppose actual and given conditions, and inquire into the form of State which in each case suits these conditions best. Thirdly, we must ask whether there is any type of State which can be generally accepted, as an average best, under various conditions, and in a number of cases. Finally, we must discover how to create, and how to preserve, a given type of State. In the first two cases, we shall start from given conditions, and adapt a proper constitution to them; in the latter two, we shall start from a given constitution. A width of inquiry is here supposed, which seems to Aristotle not to have been attempted by previous thinkers. *They* have generally concentrated their attention upon the quest of the ideal; *he* will be more impartial, and take heed of the actual. For it is as hard to change an existing, as to make a new constitution; and change only becomes possible, when one has set oneself to understand the thing which is to be changed. Thus does Aristotle mark the new sense which he is attaching to the term Political Science: it is to be a study of existing constitutions, and of the methods by which they may be improved or preserved. The moral meaning of Political Science disappears: the science acquires a technical and practical aspect.[2]

Scope of Political Science

[1] *Pol.*, vi. (iv.), c. 1.

[2] *Cf. supra*, p. 240, n. 1.

It is henceforth to discuss perversions (for the actual, in the sphere of politics, is only too often the perverted); it is to inquire into the setting right of what is out of joint. We turn from physiology to pathology and therapeutics. And here we must first enquire: What were the data which Aristotle studied? What had been the history of the Greek State which he sought to reform, and what were its prevalent forms and prominent features in his own day and generation?

Constitutional changes

The cycle of political affairs in Greece had brought many changes. We have already seen the psychological scheme of change sketched by Plato. Aristotle has more than one scheme to suggest. In an aporetic passage in the third book[1] he suggests that monarchy came first, because it was difficult to find several men of distinguished merit in the small States of early Greece, and because the rudeness of the times enabled single individuals to emerge as distinguished benefactors of their fellows. In the progress of time, distinguished merit could be pleaded by several of the members of the State: the days of heroes were numbered, and a constitution arose in which office was shared among the few. These were the times of aristocracy; but the magistrates yielded to temptation, and began to make their private profit from public affairs. Wealth became the end and standard of political life, and oligarchies arose. Tyranny followed, and, in the wake of tyranny, democracy. Democracy was the inevitable reaction against the exclusiveness of oligarchies, and democracy seemed to Aristotle, in view of the increased population of States in his own days, to have almost become the only possible constitution. This sketch is meant principally to explain the decay of monarchy, and its impossibility in Aristotle's time. Another sketch of constitutional change, in the sixth book,[2] follows on the suggestion that the "polity" should make the possession of armour the qualification of its citizens. From this point of view Aristotle connects changes in the constitution with military changes. Cavalry was the arm in which States put their trust in the days after the fall of monarchy: men had not as yet the knowledge of tactics which the proper use of infantry requires; and cavalry implied an oligarchy. As infantry came into vogue, the con-

[1] *Pol.*, iii., c. xv. (1286 b 7-22).
[2] *Ibid.*, vi. (iv.), c. xiii. (1297 b 16-28).

stitution was widened; and there arose "what would now be called polities, but were then called democracies". Finally (if we may conclude this cycle by a hint borrowed from another passage) when sea-powers arose, and the day of great navies came, constitutions altered accordingly, and "extreme democracies" became the rule.

Of the constitutions which these cycles suggest for study, two especially must engage our attention, as the two alternatives into one or other of which Greek States generally fell. These two are oligarchy and democracy. If any study of the diseases and of the cures of contemporary States was to be attempted, oligarchy and democracy, the two ordinary forms of contemporary States, must be the subjects of that study. There were some, indeed, who thought that these were the only two constitutions, as there were only two winds, north and south, and that all the others were varieties of these. But this view seems to Aristotle mistaken. It is true that the line which divides the few from the many is both deep and broad; but deeper and broader still is the line which divides good from evil. We must therefore conceive of constitutions as falling into two kinds according to this line: we must place the good constitution or constitutions on the one side, and on the other the perverted varieties of these. But though oligarchy and democracy are not the only constitutions, with all others for their varieties, they are yet the most important, and either of them *has* varieties. This is one of the lessons which Aristotle is most anxious to inculcate as an absolutely necessary presupposition of all reform. There is not one democracy, but several—not one oligarchy, but many; and the reformer who would remodel either an oligarchy or a democracy must first discover the exact variety of its kind to which it belongs, or his labour will be in vain.

Oligarchy and democracy the two main types

Greek Democracy and Greek Oligarchy[1]

§ 2. The varieties of democracy are due to two causes—to the different character of the peoples of different States, and to the extent to which the institutions characteristic of democratic government are adopted—whether wholly, or only in part. The people may be an agricultural people: it may be composed of

Causes of different species of democracies

[1] For democracy, see vi. (iv.), iii.-iv.; viii. (vi.), ii.-iv.: for oligarchy, vi., v.-vi.; viii., vi.

craftsmen: it may be engaged in trade; or it may be occupied on the sea, whether in the navy or in commerce, in transport or in fishing. It may consist of labourers, or of persons who are not citizens by both parents; and according as it consists predominantly of any one of these classes, so will the democracy in which it is sovereign vary in character. Again, the institutions characteristic of democracy, which may or may not be adopted, and with the adoption or rejection of which the character of democracy varies, are numerous enough to account for a number of varieties. The fundamental postulate of democracy, which colours its ethical character as a peculiar constitution, and which its institutions attempt to realise, is liberty. Liberty, as we have seen, is interpreted in a democracy as meaning, on the one hand, that all shall rule and be ruled in their turn, and, on the other, that each shall live as he likes. This being the postulate, the fundamental aim, of democracy, its institutions are marked by corresponding features. The democratic executive is distinguished by the eligibility of all the citizens to office: each is ruled by all, and in his turn each rules over all. The Athenian citizen might reflect with pride that he was at all times the forty-thousandth part of a sovereign in the assembly, and that in his time he would also be the five-hundredth part of the government. To secure this share in the government for each and all various regulations were necessary. Offices must rotate quickly, and accordingly the term of office was made as brief as possible: the same office was only allowed to be held once—the same individual only to hold a few offices, except in military affairs. Nor were any barriers to be erected before the gates of office: there was to be a small qualification, or none at all; and the use of the lot instead of election, for all offices where skill was not required, was made universal. In regard to the judicature, the whole people, or committees of the whole people, decided either every matter, or at any rate matters of the greatest moment and most frequent recurrence. But it was in the deliberative—the assembly—that the strength of democracy lay: the assembly controlled practically every matter of any moment, and to its greed for power was sacrificed the strength of the executive. Even the council, which prepared the business of the assembly, and was the most democratic of all the executive organs, saw itself stripped of power in those States, where the receipt of pay enabled the assembly to meet frequently enough to despatch all business of itself. Pay was indeed the characteristic of a democracy: its citizens were in truth "political beings," since politics furnished their weekly business and their weekly wages. The executive, the judicature and the deliberative might all be paid, though in some States only those boards of magistrates which had a common table, and those meetings of the assembly which were stated and regular, would receive a salary. It would therefore appear that the characteristics of democracy are, socially, the predominance of the poorer classes and the relaxation of any moral discipline (since numbers are everything, and each "lives as he likes"); and, politically, the sacrifice of a divided executive to an overgrown deliberative.

Main varieties of democracy. (*a*) Democracy of farmers

We are now in a position to discuss the varieties of democracy, and to explain their differences, in the light of these considerations; and we shall then be able to arrive at some comprehensive view of the meaning of Greek democracy in general. Four main varieties of democracy may be traced. The first of these is marked by a genuine equality, in the sense that the law assigns as much weight to the rich as it does to the poor. Both share alike in political power; but the poor form an inevitable majority, and may therefore be termed the ultimate sovereign. The class which forms the majority in such a democracy is the agricultural class. The institutions by which it is marked flow from this fact. The farmer has little property and little leisure: he cannot attend an assembly frequently, even if he would. But he has no wish to do so: he prefers his business to politics. Politics, in the stage of which Aristotle is speaking,[1] means honour only: business means profits; and the sober farmer prefers profits to honour. A people, Aristotle adds, will voluntarily suffer an oligarchy or a tyranny, if it is left to the uninterrupted pursuit of its own affairs (the more readily if, like the Tudor *τυραννίς*, such governments actively encourage the prosperity of their subjects). The farmer, then, will have no desire for office: he will make the law sovereign, and confine himself to attending the minimum

[1] He seems to be speaking of a time and a thing that is past.

of meetings, such as those in which the government is elected or subjected to audit. Such a democracy is almost more than a democracy: it is in a sense an aristocracy.[1] These farmers will elect to office the men of leisure and culture, the men who have deserved well of the State in the past, or who promise to guide its destinies skilfully in the future. But the constitution may still be termed a democracy, because there is no narrow limitation of the number of citizens: the franchise is open to all who can show the necessary qualification, and that is not high. It is a State of peasant proprietors; but Aristotle does not love the peasant proprietor, like modern thinkers, because he has a sound physique for the national army, or a sound mind for the national business, free from the fever and the fret engendered by town life: the secret of *his* admiration lies in the fact, that the farmer will be too busy to govern, and will have the sense to leave it to his betters. But just for this reason Aristotle is as anxious to preserve this class as any modern thinker, and he suggests, in order to prevent the rise of great estates, that the farms shall be restricted to a certain size, and that they shall be made inalienable.

Farmer-democracy and the ancestral constitution

It is perhaps worth while to discuss this form of democracy a little more closely. The sketch which Aristotle gives may have a definite allusion to historical conditions. Lysander imposed on Athens, at the end of the Peloponnesian War, the condition that henceforth her citizens should live by their "ancestral constitution" (*πάτριος πολιτεία*). But it seems to have been as difficult to define what that ancestral constitution was, as it was found in England after 1066 to define exactly the laws of Edward the Confessor, which had been granted by the Conqueror to his subjects. Was the constitution of Periclean Athens ancestral, or a modern innovation? Was that of Cleisthenean Athens ancestral, or also decadent? Must one hark back as far as the days of Solon? Theramenes was apparently the champion of the latter view: an extreme view, of which Critias may have been the exponent, declared even

[1] Strictly speaking, as a constitution which it is difficult to classify under either head, and which respects virtue as well as numbers, it ought to be called a "polity," or more exactly an "aristocracy" (mixed States in which virtue is respected being properly called aristocracies, *cf. infra*, p. 478).

Solon to be a revolutionist and a demagogue, and found the "ancestral constitution" in the days of Eupatrid domination; while the democrats who believed in Periclean Athens endeavoured to save their cause by finding in pre-historic Theseus the author and inventor of democracy. In this controversy Aristotle, it would appear from the *'Αθηναίων πολιτεία*, followed Theramenes. He believed in an "ancestral constitution" which had first been realised under Solon (or, by his own account, under Draco), and to which the nearest approach in modern times had been made in 411, when affairs were entrusted to a limited assembly of 5,000, and payment for political work was abolished. This is the tone which inspires the *'Αθηναίων πολιτεία*; and something of the same tone may be traced in the account of democracy in the *Politics*. Here the phrase "ancestral democracy" is used; and the first and best species of democracy is marked by those rights of election and audit of the magistrates which Solon had given to the people. The State of peasant proprietors would seem to be the Solonian State, when the Seisachtheia had freed farmers of their mortgages, and Solon had given them political privileges. But it is perhaps in his account of the "polity" that Aristotle's agreement with Theramenes most appears, and that the echoes of the old controversy are best heard. At the same time, one must not push to extremes the historical interpretation of the *Politics*. Athens must indeed lie behind what Aristotle says of democracy, however seldom Athens be mentioned. But it would be a mistake to suppose that all which Aristotle has to say relates to Athens, and that the four types of democracy represent four stages in Athenian development from the "ancestral" to the "ultimate" democracy. These four types represent rather philosophic generalisations of possible forms, than any historic grouping of stages; and what concerns Aristotle most is to distinguish moderate democracy, founded on a solid social basis, from the extreme type which is founded on poverty (wherever and whenever either is found), because any successful construction of the one, or reform of the other, depends on a sense of this distinction.

Between these two opposite poles of democracy, which must be the main objects of study, there lie two intermediate (*b*) and (*c*)—middle forms of democracy

forms, in some respects akin to moderate, in others approximating to extreme democracy. As law is sovereign in moderate democracy, so it is in both of these forms: as all participate in the privileges of extreme democracy, so there is a tendency in these two forms for all to share in political rights. In the one citizenship is conferred upon all, who can show a clean pedigree —upon all, who are children of citizens by both parents, and the offspring of a legal marriage: in the other, it falls to all who can prove that they are free from any taint of servile origin. The latter is obviously the wider and more democratic form; but it is none the less distinct from extreme democracy. There is here no revenue which can be assigned to the citizens as pay for judicial or deliberative work, and the majority therefore abstain from claiming functions which they cannot afford to discharge; nor is there a sovereign assembly, with its regular meetings and greed for power, to over-ride the law by popular decrees. Law is therefore the ultimate sovereign in this form —as it is in all the three forms of democracy which have been hitherto discussed; and this is the cardinal fact which distinguishes them from the fourth and final form, which is marked by the sovereignty of the caprice of a popular assembly, and the subordination of the laws to that caprice. It will thus be seen that the standard, according to which democracies are classified, turns out in practice to be partly the old standard of social class, by which constitutions themselves were classified in the third book, partly a standard not suggested there, consisting in the degree of respect for law which marks each constitution. It is to this latter that Aristotle narrows down the second criterion which he originally suggests for determining varieties of democracy—the extent to which the institutions, commonly accounted characteristic of democracy, are present or absent. But it is to be noticed that these two standards are not systematically applied, nor are they necessarily compatible. They are not systematically applied; for while the social classification which Aristotle puts forward is one based on occupation or profession, and while the first democracy is accordingly characterised as a democracy of farmers, the second and third democracies are not distinguished by the occupation common to the majority of the members, but by their descent from parents, who are either citizens or freemen.[1] Logically, one might have expected a pastoral or maritime democracy to succeed the agricultural, and in one passage a pastoral democracy is mentioned, as especially adapted for war; but a completely logical scheme is hardly ever to be expected from Aristotle. Nor again are the two standards ever proved to be compatible. It is conceivable that a democracy may be composed of citizens who are born of citizen parents on both sides, and may therefore belong to the second type of democracy, while nevertheless such a citizen body rules in a sovereign assembly, and with that absence of respect for law which is characteristic of the fourth and extreme type of democracy. Indeed, this was actually the case at Athens during the fourth century: the old decree of Pericles, which required descent from citizen parents on both sides, had been re-enacted in 403, but nevertheless the burgess body received pay for attending the assembly, and was able to rule as sovereign in that assembly, even in the teeth of law.

(*d*) Extreme democracy—its origin and character

We now come to extreme democracy—"modern" democracy, as it is sometimes termed by Aristotle. Here the citizenship is thrown indiscriminately open, and law is subordinated to the will of the citizens as expressed in the shape of decrees. The accounts of the origin of this form which Aristotle gives vary in different contexts. Speaking with an eye to the class which is dominant, he assigns its origin to the preponderance of artisans and day labourers; while from a military point of view and in a context where Athens is specifically in question, he assigns it to the supremacy of the sea-faring classes after their victories in the Persian wars. But when he is rather thinking of the attitude of the citizens towards the law, he speaks more particularly of the action of demagogues and the introduction of pay. Cities became populous, and all their members claimed a share in political power: their revenues became abundant, and the distribution of pay to the masses gave them the leisure for politics. In this leisure the people had henceforth that qualification, to which the rich had before exclusively pretended; and it abounded still more for them than it did for the rich, whose time

[1] It is true that the original classification of "peoples" mentions, side by side with agricultural, trading, and martial "peoples," a people composed of persons who are not citizens by both parents.

was partly absorbed by the cares of their own possessions. Now that the people had leisure for affairs, the demagogues were quick to provide affairs for their leisure. They referred every decision to the people: it was to their interest to do so, because they could influence the decision of the people. The law was thus disregarded in order that popular decrees might rule; and the magistrates were similarly dethroned. The people were told that they were the best judges: they gladly received the invitation to judge; and the powers of the executive slipped from its hands. Supreme over the laws and over the magistrates, the people thus became, as it were, a composite sovereign—a sovereign not unlike the tyrant in its disrespect for law, and like the tyrant attracting a crowd of flatterers to its court—the so-called demagogues. Parallel to tyranny in its disregard for law, parallel also, for the same reason, to the "dynasty" (or hereditary oligarchy ruling in contempt of law), extreme democracy, like both of these, may be denied the name of a constitution. There is no constitution, where there is no law; and here there are no laws, enacting general principles to be applied in detail by the executive: there are only decrees themselves dealing with detail. There is nothing fixed or determined: life is a chaos in which anything may happen, but nothing can be foreseen. The essence of a State is that men should live by known rules, which will enable them to recognise in advance the results of their action: the very savage clothes himself in a saving garb of custom. But here all goes by hazard: it is the motto of such a State, that

'Tis best to live at random, as one may.

Particularly upon the upper classes fell this horror of darkness and uncertainty. In the old days, when they had ruled themselves, they had loved discipline and order: the young had been enjoined to show modesty before the old, the slave to go quietly about his work, the women to stay within their quarters. With extreme democracy descended the hubbub of a "life at random": the quiet fixity of the old life yielded to confusion, and discipline slipped from the shoulders of wife and child and slave. In the old days, again, each had known his place, and the upper classes had been united in exclusive associations of clan and phratry, with their religious rites and consecration. With democracy came the deluge, sweeping away old landmarks, mixing all classes together, and at all costs weakening old and exclusive associations. Upon the rich in particular this new order pressed hard. The *sansculottes* had their hour; and the rich man lay down at night uncertain whether the morrow would not sweep away all his garnered wealth. It was an easy thing for an informer to accuse him of disaffection to the sovereign people; and an information before the assembly must mean condemnation and confiscation, for it was in the interest of the people to swell the revenue from which it was paid. But there were many burdens short of the *ultima ratio* of confiscation. While the people paid itself from the revenues, the charges which the revenues might otherwise have borne had to be met from other sources; and the rich had heavy liturgies put upon their backs—ships to furnish, choruses to provide, and fellow-tribesmen to feast.

It might seem as if a State based on these foundations were too much divided against itself to stand. The classes who could swear in their clubs to be enemies of the people, and to injure it to the best of their power—who could erect to one of their members a monument, in memory of the deposition for a space of "the cursed People from its mischievous rule," were not likely to leave democracy standing for any long time. And yet democracy was tolerably safe in the breadth of its basis: there were more who wished the constitution to continue, than there were who desired its subversion. It was indeed the rule of a section in the interest of a section: it was no true State, rising above the conflict of interests, and harmonising without abolishing their living play. But it was the rule of a section which formed a large majority; and provided that this section recognised that "half was greater than all," its permanence was secured. The more modestly the predominance of the people was urged, the more generously the claims of the rich and the educated classes were recognised, the safer was the supremacy of the people. Accordingly Aristotle urges that extreme democracy is most likely to be preserved (for he is willing to consider, as we have seen, the preservation of perversions themselves) if the property of the rich is either spared, or is confiscated,

Means of preserving extreme democracy

at least, to the service of religion and not in a political interest, and if the pay of the citizens is curtailed—(abolished it cannot be, so long as this form of democracy remains the same)—by the diminution of the number of meetings of the assembly. The less pay is needed, the less spoliation of the rich is necessary. In a final suggestion, Aristotle goes to the very root of the matter. What is radically wrong is the pauperism of the masses: what will set it permanently right is their elevation to some degree of lasting prosperity. This may be done, if a funded sum saved from the revenues be applied to purchasing small farms or finding some sort of business for the poorest of the poor. The suggestion recalls the agrarian policy of the Gracchi. Its results, according to Aristotle, are likely to be the ending of popular tyranny (for the assembly will not meet so frequently when its poorest members have their own affairs to engage their attention), and the mending of the oppression of the upper classes. Quit of the danger of confiscation and released from the idler liturgies, like that of providing a chorus, the rich man might even be willing to take charge of some section of the poor, and to start its members in life. Oratorical tradition attributed such sense and good feeling to the rich Athenians of earlier times, and in the archaizing days in which he lived Aristotle might hope that the present would, here as elsewhere, attempt to repeat the past.

Extreme democracy at Athens

To what extent did the historical democracies of Greece, so far as we know anything of their character, conform to the picture drawn by Aristotle? We must turn to Athens; and for a description of Athens we must turn to the *'Αθηναίων πολιτεία*, where we find stored the very facts on which Aristotle must have largely drawn for the generalisations of the *Politics*. At Athens sovereignty resided in the assembly. Every citizen had the right to sit in the assembly, and there were, about 430 B.C., from 40,000 to 47,000 citizens resident in Athens. The official year was divided into ten prytanies, and in each prytany there were four ordinary assemblies. About 400 B.C. the citizens attending the assembly had been granted pay, which in Aristotle's time was at the rate of ninepence (a drachm) for each meeting.[1]

[1] One of the four ordinary meetings of the prytany was paid at the rate of 1½ drachms (or about 1s. 2d.).

A paid primary assembly of 40,000 citizens meeting forty times a year was thus the sovereign at Athens.[1] This assembly could debate and decide any matter, subject to two conditions. Every matter brought before the assembly must have been introduced by the Council, an annual body of five hundred members appointed by lot; but, on the other hand, a member of the assembly could always get the council to introduce a question which he wished to discuss. Secondly, any decree of the assembly might be challenged by an "indictment of illegality"; and the mover of the decree would be tried in a popular court, where, if the plaintiff won his case, the decree would be set aside. Of the laws which thus limited its decrees the people was not in itself the author. The popular assembly was not a law-making body: "it shared in the proceedings preliminary to legislation, but not in legislation itself". It decided, at a stated meeting in each year, whether the laws stood in need of revision; and if it decided in the affirmative, any private citizen could give notice of amendments, which were then tried by a judicial process before a court specially appointed *ad hoc*, and, if approved by that court, became law. It would thus appear as if "the sovereignty of the Athenian people, which finds expression in the psephism of the Ecclesia, was limited by law".[2] But it was only a popular court which guaranteed this limitation; and cases were not infrequent, "in which the decrees of the Ecclesia were regarded as superior to the laws".[3] The *'Αθηναίων πολιτεία* uses language which implies that this was the general rule: "the people has made itself sovereign in every respect, and determines every issue by its decrees or by courts in which it is itself supreme".[4] Before the supreme deliberative the executive sank into insignificance. The offices were only annual: there was a multiplication of many departments, which diminished the power of each; and every office was put in commission, and held as a rule by a board of ten members. For the most part they were elected by lot, in order to secure an equal chance to every citizen. Some were paid, some were not: all

[1] In theory; but in practice an assembly of 6,000 citizens would have been considered large.

[2] Gilbert, *Constitutional Antiquities* (Eng. Trans.), p. 299.

[3] *Ibid.*, p. 310.

[4] 'Αθ. πολ, c. xli., 24-26 (Sandy's edition).

were subjected to a stringent responsibility. Month by month their accounts were audited by a committee of the council: month by month the assembly must renew each magistrate's tenure of office. At any moment an "information" might be laid before the council by any private citizen against any of the officials. At the end of their year of office a final audit of accounts had to be undergone; and a board of audit (εὔθυνοι) sat to hear accusations against them with regard to any of their acts during the past year. On the other hand, the Board of Generals must, at any rate in the fifth century, have exercised *de facto* a considerable power. Its members were not only supreme in military matters; they had the functions of a treasury as well as those of a war-office, and were concerned in raising the funds which they required. They had charge of foreign affairs; and they must even have exercised some sort of discretionary power, in order to discharge their duties of preventing and punishing treason, and protecting the democratic constitution. They were appointed by election, and not by lot: on them depended much of the security of the Athenian democracy; and they supplied along with the Council something of that executive strength which a democracy particularly needs. Defective as was the executive, the judicature was perhaps more defective. It was thoroughly democratic: as in Teutonic antiquity, so at Athens, a distinction was drawn between the judge, who presided and conducted the legal proceedings, and the "judgment-finders," a body of some hundreds of members, who found the verdict. The whole body of judgment-finders constituted the Heliæa, which consisted during the fourth century of all who applied for a place on the list, and which "as representing the community, formed the supreme court of justice".[1] It might sit as a body, or in larger or smaller sections, containing from 201 to 2,501 members. The verdict of historians upon this popular judicature was one of condemnation. The judges were ignorant of the law: their decisions were biassed either by a sentimental impulse or an actual bribe. To few was an even-handed justice measured out according to the law, and least of all to the rich, whom sycophants were only too eager to accuse before a court which was only too ready to condemn. A

[1] Gilbert, p. 393.

"general uncertainty in the administration of justice" is one of the greatest defects of Athens.

Since the time of Pericles the dicasts had been paid; and indeed the system of payment to the citizens for civic work generally was one of the most striking characteristics of Athens. Aristides, we learn from the *'Αθηναίων πολιτεία*, had introduced payment for military service: Pericles had instituted pay for the jurymen and members of council; and before the Peloponnesian War, it is calculated in the treatise, 20,000 citizens were maintained by the State.[1] About 400 B.C. attendance at the Ecclesia also began to receive its reward; and by that time the system of payment for civic work had already been extended to one of doles. Cleophon had introduced the method of giving money to the citizens by way of poor relief; and in time money came to be distributed at all the more important festivals, while largesses of corn were also given occasionally by the State, and money was paid to the Athenian for the purchase of his seat at the theatre. As the poor were fed, the rich were bled. There were the ordinary liturgies of equipping a chorus, of defraying the expenses of competitors in the torch-races, and of giving a banquet to a tribe: there were the extraordinary burdens of furnishing a ship to the State, of contributing to the income tax raised for purposes of war, and of paying what may be called "benevolences" or voluntary contributions invited by decree of the people. In all these financial arrangements there appears one of the worst tendencies of democracy—the tendency of the people to shift burdens to the shoulders of the rich, and to find for itself a source of gain in the use of political power.

Several thinkers had passed judgment on this type of extreme democracy before Aristotle. Not to mention the sarcasms of the treatise *De Republica Atheniensium*, falsely attributed to Xenophon, and written by some oligarch towards the end of the fifth century,[2] there are the pronouncements of Thucydides,

[1] But this is a dubious passage; and the treatise is probably referring by an anachronism the practice of the fourth century back to the fifth.

[2] The author believes that every feature of extreme democracy at Athens is the logical consequence of the democratic principles of freedom and popular sovereignty, and of the position of Athens as a sea-power. He praises Athens and her demagogues, because they have logically followed out their principles to their full conclusions; but his real purpose is, by showing that every feature, including the worst, is logically essential, to induce his brother oligarchs to destroy the whole system. (*Cf. supra*, p. 42.)

of Socrates, and of Plato. The high music of Pericles' speech in the second book of Thucydides celebrates Athens as the model and type for the imitation of Greece. In her the unfolding of human capacity in every direction was best attained: in her were the sisters, Equality and Liberty, to be found together. All her citizens were equal before the law in their private differences; all had an equal chance of public distinction. Personal merit was the one qualification of office; birth counted for no more than character, and poverty was not allowed to obscure any man, who could be of service to his country. So were her citizens all free, alike in their relations to the State, and in the conduct of their social life. In the same spirit Thucydides makes Athenagoras defend democracy at Syracuse: it is the rule of all, and not, like oligarchy, of a section; and while the rich are the best guardians of property, the wise the cleverest in council, and the people the best judges of a case which has been discussed in their presence, all these classes and all these claims have an equality of rights in a democracy. But Thucydides' own judgment, like that of Aristotle, is in favour of a very moderate form of democracy: the temporary constitution of 411, which gave affairs into the hands of a limited assembly, and which Thucydides defines as a mixture of democracy and oligarchy, wins from him the measured praise, that this was the occasion in his own days when the Athenians seemed most to have had a good government. Socrates, as we have already seen, condemned democracy, because it trusted to the lot, and encouraged the ignorant to pretend to an art of which they knew nothing; because its sovereign assembly consisted of men, whose one thought was to buy in the cheapest and sell in the dearest market,[1] and who knew nothing of the art of the statesman; because, in a word, his creed was the value of knowledge, and democracy disdained knowledge. Plato could not love Athenian democracy, which his master had condemned, and which had condemned his master; and we have seen that in the *Republic* he sets democracy below oligarchy, on the ground of its lack of political knowledge and excess of political selfishness. Its psychological basis is to him desire—the mere desire for en-

Views of democracy entertained by Thucydides, Plato, and Aristotle

[1] *Mem.*, iii., 7, 6.

joyment at any cost: its motto is "Do as you like": its standard-bearer is the demagogue whom the logic of his situation turns into a tyrant.[1] Unlike Plato, Aristotle brings neither philosophical prepossessions nor personal prejudices to his judgment of democracy. He knew Athens thoroughly, and had written, or studied, a treatise on its history: he had started, as always, from "the facts themselves". He took democracy at its best, as well as its worst; and he found the best good. Indeed, the best practical State which he can suggest, short of the ideal itself, is a "limited democracy"—for this, as we shall see, is the true meaning of the "polity". He feels that democracy in general is true to some conception of justice: it attempts to realise a principle of equality, though it makes the mistake of interpreting that equality as merely numerical. He feels, again, that it is animated by an ideal of liberty; yet he sees that it misconceives liberty as the right to do what one wants to do. Its theory is thus a misinterpretation of truth, and its practice suffers from corresponding defects. Its standard of numerical equality comes to mean the supremacy of the poor, who are always in a numerical majority; and hence Aristotle defines democracy as essentially the government of the poor. Its cult of liberty sinks into a negative thing: it comes to mean the absence of that moral discipline, which it is the aim of the State to provide. Democracy, therefore, in the practice of its ultimate form, is no true State: it is not the rule of the whole for the benefit of the whole, but that of a section for the benefit of a section: it is not a society directing itself by a body of known rules towards a common life of virtue, but a confused congeries of men, living by caprice and not by law, living for pleasure and not for virtue.

Comparison of Aristotle's views of democracy with modern views

This is what democracy claimed to be, and what it actually was, in Aristotle's view. It claimed to be government of the people by the people for the people: it actually was government of the people by the poor for the poor.[2] In attempting to com-

[1] In the *Politicus*, it was noticed, two types of democracy appear, one observing and one disregarding law—the very clue which Aristotle also uses; and the illegal democracy is there classed as the best of the bad constitutions, and preferred to oligarchy.

[2] Compare a recent definition of American democracy as "government of the people by the machine for the trust".

pare his conception of democracy with modern conceptions[1] we must not forget, that while modern thought tends to regard democracy in its ideal meaning, Aristotle, while aware of that meaning, looks rather to its actual results. To him it is a perversion of the present: to us, it would appear, it is the goal of the future. To him, therefore, it was the rule of a section, a selfish rule: to us it is the rule of the whole, assumed rather than proved to be for the weal of the whole. Ideally, indeed, it may be admitted, or rather contended, democracy is the only perfect government. All government is based on will; and a perfect government involves a perfectly full and free expression of will. But all government is really based, we must add, on a *moral* will; and a perfect government really involves that the will which is fully and freely expressed shall be a moral will. Here lies the danger of democracy. In practice democracy may very well come to mean for us much the same as it did for Aristotle. The people may put burdens heavy to be borne upon the rich, and will a selfish will, when it becomes conscious of its power: it may vote for the things that are pleasant, and refuse the things that are good, if these good things be presented, as they generally are, with an unpalatable harsh outer rind. Like Henry VIII., the people requires ever to be told what it ought to do, but never what it is able to do; "for if a lion knew his own strength, hard were it for any man to rule him".[2] Even if, like Rousseau, we trust the people to will its true good, it will still require, as Rousseau admitted, to be told what its true good is: there must reside somewhere in the State an exegetic authority.

But it must be admitted that, with the nation-state as the unit of politics, democracy can never be what it was in the days of the city-state. Ancient democracy was that of the primary assembly, in which the people spoke with an immediate voice: the size of the modern State involves representative institutions. There must be as it were a filtering of the *vox populi*, and from

Modern democracy combined with representative institutions

[1] For such a comparison see a paper by Professor Mackenzie, *Int. Journ. Eth.*, Jan., 1906. He points out that Plato and Aristotle, like Ruskin and Carlyle in modern times, condemn not democracy as a principle, but particular instances of democracies.

[2] This seems harsh; but I have attempted to bring into prominence the truth contained in the Aristotelian point of view.

the filtering may come a purification. A representative body must always be more of a filter than a phonograph: however much its members may approach to the character of mere delegates, the assembly as a whole must have a mind of its own, a sense of its own dignity and of the demands of that dignity: it must tend to think not only of what the people wishes, but also of what it ought to wish. Rousseau and even Kant disliked parliaments as the graves of freedom: in truth they are or should be homes of that freedom which is obedience to rightly constituted law. So long as a parliament retains that independence of judgment, which Burke strenuously vindicated, but which Rousseau believed to defeat the supremacy of the people,[1] so long may the true good of a country come to consciousness in the minds of its chosen exponents. It is indeed necessary that a parliament should have, what it can only have by deserving, the honour of the people's trust; and only so long as it has that trust is it effective.[2] It is true too that in a State, in which that trust has not been given, and whose size has rendered possible some approximation to Greek conditions, modern democracy has been found not incompatible with something like a primary assembly. The popular initiation of alterations both in the laws and in the constitution, and the popular decision upon alterations in either which have been passed by the body of the representatives—institutions which are characteristic of modern Switzerland—would seem to suggest that primary democracy is still possible. But it is dubious whether these institutions could flourish elsewhere than in their native soil; and it is still more dubious whether, if they could, they would not, by diminishing the sense of responsibility in the representative body, be inimical to the true interests of the people.

Similarly, modern conditions involve a capable and strong

[1] Though on Aristotle's principle, that what is most democratic is what makes most for the permanence of democracy, *i.e.* for its real welfare, it may be urged that a parliament, which is not a mere body of delegates, will alone realise the supremacy of the people. "A real democracy must be aristocratic—it must aim at government by the best; and there can be no practical realisation of aristocracy except through the cultivation of the democratic spirit—the spirit that is ready to recognise that to be governed by its best is to be governed by itself" (Mackenzie, *ut supra*, p. 139).

[2] It may be argued, that the true policy of democracy is to realise those conditions under which that trust will be most readily given, because most thoroughly deserved.

executive, which the conditions of the city-state did not secure. There is no question in modern times of the award of offices for worth: they go to capacity of some kind or other. Nor is there a primary assembly, eager to assert its sense of its own importance at the expense of the executive. It is true that in the seventeenth century the progress of popular principles in England seemed likely to cut short the executive in order to broaden the hem of the legislature; but the growth of democracy has of late coincided with the growth of the executive, and would seem to have culminated in the sovereignty of the Cabinet. The complexity of the manifold relations which need to be adjusted within the State, the problems raised by the relations between State and State, may help to explain why this should be so. And provided that the executive should be, either through the medium of parliament, or, as the tendency would now seem to be, directly and immediately in touch with the people from whom it comes, its strength is of good omen for democracy. Montesquieu held that the principle of democracy was *vertu*, because it issued in a sense of obedience to the laws, and because, without that sense, democracy would be untrue to laws which simply rest on its own consent. This sense of obedience to the laws involves as its corollary the strength of the organ which executes the laws; and where that sense and that organ are both strong, there democracy has a safe basis. The house of liberty cannot be built without the foundations of order.

Need of a strong executive in modern democracies

Modern democracy, then, cannot be as extreme as Greek democracy tended to become, because the greater size of the modern State, involving representative institutions and a stronger executive, must always mean a difference between the two. It is a commonplace to point to the more exclusive character of Greek democracy, and to urge that, resting as it did on a basis of slavery, it was really in comparison with its modern equivalent of the nature of an aristocracy. There is this truth in the commonplace, that, while the citizens of Athens, for instance, numbered about 50,000,[1] the slaves have been calculated at about 100,000. But it must not be thought that each of the 50,000 was the owner of one or two slaves, whose possession

Ancient democracy *not* aristocratic

[1] There were, in addition to the 40,000 and upwards who were resident in Athens, about 10,000 absent in Athenian cleruchies, but retaining citizenship.

made him a gentleman at leisure. Almost the last sentence in the *Politics* tells us that the poor use wife or child in lieu of slaves; and the poor constituted a majority of the citizens in almost all democracies. The slaves were public servants, hands in factories or mines, or lackeys in great houses: "the maintenance of a slave, to say nothing of the purchase of one, would be too heavy a burden for a poor man's purse".[1] There was in reality very little of an aristocratic flavour in Greek democracy, as it munched its sweetmeats in the theatre, or listened to the voice of the Tanner in the assembly: there was much more, one may conjecture, in the Italian communes of the Middle Ages. Many of the citizens of Greek democracies were of semi-alien or semi-servile origin;[2] and those who were not, were "fullers and cobblers, carpenters and blacksmiths, farmers or traders".[3]

Real differentia of ancient democracy: centralisation of all power in one primary assembly

The fundamental antithesis between ancient and modern democracy is less social than political. It rests in the distinction between the primary assembly and representative institutions. The characteristic of ancient democracy was omnipotent sovereignty of that assembly. Primarily deliberative, it turned itself also into an executive, at the expense of the council and magistrates; and it acted as a court of justice in great cases, while the Heliæa (which was only the assembly transformed) did the great bulk of judicial work. There was no supreme judicature, as there is to-day in America, to check the action of the assembly. All the functions of government were fused together under the sole control of the people; nor was there, it is generally said, any distinction between central and local government. "The State was ruled from one centre: in modern democracies it is ruled from many, which check and balance each other," and there "are a number of widely scattered constituencies, no one of which is dominant over the rest."[4] But, as a matter of fact, there was in the Attic deme a local unit possessed of considerable vitality. The deme was a community possessed of estates and governing itself by its demarch and assembly. Though it was not in any sense a constituency, the

[1] Newman, iv., 568.

[2] This was the case even at Athens, in spite of the Periclean law to the contrary.

[3] *Mem.*, iii., 7, 6. [4] Newman, *Politics*, iv., lix.

members of a deme who happened to attend the assembly together might very well cluster together, and form a separate body of local opinion. The interests of one deme were not always as those of another: the metropolitan demes, for instance, might easily differ from the country demes, as they did during the Peloponnesian War. Nevertheless, the main fact remains, that there was not, in Greek democracy, that distinction between the various functions of government, or between the central and the local powers, which is generally characteristic of the modern State, whatever form it may assume. Modern democracy can never be so whole-hearted, because the inevitable checks and balances of the modern State must necessarily abate its fervour. Yet while the medium in which modern democracy must move is necessarily different from that of Greek democracy, the spirit is the same, because the attitude of mind from which it springs is eternally the same. Liberty, in the sense of being left to do as one pleases, has been extremely strong in the United States:[1] equality is one of its fetishes, and Bryce traces "a tendency, particularly in the West, to dislike, possibly to resent, any outward manifestation of social superiority".[2] Rotation of office is secured by the "spoils" system:[3] the same man seldom holds any office twice. The sovereignty of the people is affirmed by the doctrine that the people makes the constitution, and its representatives the laws (subject to that constitution); while the weakening of the executive is one of the aims of the American system, and is secured by various means, such as the division of authority in many hands, and the shortness of the tenure of office. In Switzerland, on the other hand, democracy has been more marked by jealousy of the legislature; and the peculiar Swiss institutions of Initiative and Referendum are calculated to weaken the power of the representative body. It is in this respect that a State, which otherwise perhaps offers the nearest approach in modern times to Athenian democracy, departs from its ancient prototype.

§ 3. There is no ancient oligarchy which possesses the fas-

[1] Bryce, quoted by Newman, iv., 496.

[2] *Ibid.*, iii., 245.

[3] That is to say, when a new President belonging to a different party comes into office, he changes the administrative staff, and gives offices to his adherents.

cination of Athens, or even the attraction of Venice—unless the name oligarchy be given to the constitution of Sparta. But in the Greece of Aristotle's day the conception of oligarchy was always present as a rival by the side of that of democracy; and Aristotle, who was naturally impelled to its closer study for that reason, had also the additional motive for an examination of its various forms, that he hoped to realise the best practical State by fusing oligarchy with democracy in what we may call a mixed constitution. In determining the varieties of oligarchy, Aristotle uses the same clues which served him for distinguishing the varieties of democracy—the social character of the predominant authority, and the degree of its respect for law. Once more he discovers four main varieties. In the first or moderate form, the predominant authority is composed of a class determined by a property qualification sufficiently high to exclude the multitude of the poor, but elastic enough to admit to full rights all those who may come to satisfy its requirements. In such a State there is no exclusive class fenced by iron barriers: there is a regular ladder of ascent, which any man may climb if he can. In an oligarchy of this character, which is closely related to the "polity," Aristotle suggests [1] that a double qualification should be established, the higher of which must be satisfied in order to attain the higher offices, the lower alone for the less important. Such a scheme, while excluding the poor, will yet broaden the basis of the constitution by admitting successive relays of the people to office. It will make the privileged class stronger, if less numerous, than the unprivileged; while the possibility of one day rising into the ranks of the privileged will of itself render the unprivileged class content. In such a constitution power will thus rest with men possessed of moderate incomes, who are neither so wealthy that they will naturally have leisure for political aggrandisement, nor so poor that they have to be maintained by the State in an artificial leisure, which they abuse in the same way as the excessively rich. The constitution will accordingly be distinguished, like the better democracies, by the sovereignty of law: the deliberative, composed (one would imagine) of the whole of the privileged class, though Aristotle seems to imply that it only consists

Varieties of oligarchy

[1] Book viii. (vi.), c. vi.

of members elected from that class (1298 a 36), will not attempt to introduce innovations in the teeth of the law. A constitution of this kind has many advantages: on the other hand, in the cleavage it makes between the unprivileged class and the privileged, and between the two sections of the privileged, it has its defects. But such a cleavage is inevitable in oligarchy, and there is a *carrière ouverte:* a man may "thrive" (as it were) "to thegn-right". In the second variety of oligarchy this feature disappears: not only is the qualification for admission into the privileged class higher, but such admission does not follow instantly upon the possession of that qualification, and election by the members of the privileged class is also necessary. The privileged class has strengthened and stereotyped itself, and it expresses its strength by this provision; but it is not strong enough to override the law, although it thus adapts the law to its own altered position. In the third variety the process of stereotyping the privileged class is complete: there has been a *serrata del maggior consiglio,* as there was at Venice; and the son succeeds to the privilege of his father. Even yet the law remains; but in the fourth variety it disappears. A close hereditary caste marks this variety, as it does the third; but this caste has flung away the restraint of law, and strong in its wealth and its connections, it rules like the assembly of an extreme democracy, according to its own caprice. To this variety Aristotle gives the name of "dynasty": in his view, it is of all governments, save tyranny, the most unstable; and only a strict observance of good order can preserve it from ruin.

This sketch of the varieties of oligarchy wears the appearance of an *a priori* history of the genesis of extreme oligarchy, rather than of an analysis of actual varieties. It would be difficult, and indeed impossible, to fit into this scheme the oligarchies which Aristotle himself mentions in the *Politics.* For this the practical purpose, which underlies the whole of Aristotle's analysis, is responsible. It is not his aim to analyse for the sake of analysis, but to analyse for the aid and instruction of the practical reformer. Such a scheme of oligarchies as has just been sketched may be of service to the reformer, by enabling him to take the bearings of the constitution with which he has to deal: it is hardly intended to be anything more.

There were more varieties of oligarchy in Greece than are set down in this philosophy: there were more varieties of democracy than those which Aristotle depicts. There were also, as Aristotle himself suggests, elusive constitutions, which might formally, and with regard to their laws, be counted among oligarchies, but must really, and with regard to the spirit which inspired their customs and directed the training of their youth, be reckoned as democracies. Such a phenomenon Aristotle ascribes to some great constitutional change, which, while it has left the law standing, has swept away the old spirit of the constitution. Such an elusive constitution, and for much the same reason, is that of England to-day: in the formulas of its law it is still a monarchy in which the king is the source of law, the fountain of justice, the head of the executive; in reality and in spirit, a constitutional change has gradually made it a sort of moderate democracy, which entrusts supreme power to men of its own choosing, who have leisure and capacity for their work.

Two main forms of oligarchy

Taking the Aristotelian classification of oligarchies as it stands, we may perhaps reduce them to two main forms. The first of these is that form, which is based on a property qualification or *census*, and in which the governing body consists of those who possess this *census*: it may be called an oligarchy of wealth, or a plutocracy. The second is that form, in which the governing body consists of a close hereditary corporation; and this may be called an oligarchy of birth, or, where respect for law is wanting, a dynasty. In the first of these forms there is evidently a certain flexibility: in the second there is a certain rigidity, as of a system of caste. Of the former, Corinth may perhaps serve as an example. It was the form characteristic of the commercial State, which tends as naturally to plutocracy, as does the industrial State to democracy. The government rested in the hands of merchant princes, whose assessed property (personal, it would seem, as well as real) was the basis of their authority. The latter form need not necessarily be based on a qualification of birth: any narrow clique, provided that its personal ascendency or connections allowed it to despise the law, might properly be called a dynasty; and the Ἀθηναίων πολιτεία assigns the name to the rule of the Thirty at Athens. Neither form could be regarded as stable. A plutocratic form was liable to be radically transformed, if a general increase in wealth turned a property qualification, which had once been high, into something relatively low and easily attained. An oligarchy might thus insensibly slide into a democracy as social conditions altered. A dynastic form of oligarchy, again, could only last so long as the solidarity of the ruling class was preserved. But solidarity was very difficult to maintain. Narrow as was the government, it narrowed itself still further: some small section within the ruling class made itself too powerful, and challenged by the other members, who might even ally themselves with the unprivileged classes in order to strengthen their hands, it fell, and with it fell the dynasty itself. The example of Crete is particularly interesting. It was a country in which there were great families, each with its *comitatus* or retinue of young warriors, and all contending with one another for the powers of government. Sometimes, indeed, a clique of families would abolish the government for the time being, and thus dissolve the State itself. These facts prove to Aristotle the dynastic character of Cretan government, and the insecurity of dynastic government: they show to us that Crete was in a feudal, one might almost say mediæval, state of society, in which the feuds of the great barons, and their attempts to override the government, were, as in Lancastrian England, the predominant motive in politics.[1] But the vital difficulty of Greek oligarchies was neither the regulation of the *census* nor the prevention of feuds: it was by the people that they were generally brought to ruin. If they injured and oppressed the people, as they only too often did, a popular rising was the result: if they took the people into partnership and gave them arms, the victory of the people was equally assured. "In the populous States of to-day," wrote Aristotle, "it is hard for any other constitution than democracy to exist."

Yet the members of an oligarchy could put forward various titles to the pre-eminence which they claimed. Economically,

[1] One might almost say that the baronial policy, from the days of Magna Carta and Simon de Montfort to the end of the Wars of the Roses, was directed towards the erection of a "dynasty" in England.

they had a greater stake in the country: they were more to be trusted in the observance of contracts than were the poor; and they could urge that as they contributed most to the exchequer, they had the right to receive most in return. From a military point of view, they were by far the strongest arm of the service in the days of cavalry; and even when cavalry gave way to infantry, they must have been the best and most fully trained soldiers. They could urge that justice was on their side, and that like the democrats they pursued equality—not a numerical equality, but a true proportionate equality, which gave to each his desert. And there was some truth, Aristotle allows, in their contention; but it was vitiated by a false interpretation of desert, as constituted only and entirely by wealth. Wealth is indeed the necessary equipment for a life of virtue: wealth secures that detachment and leisure for political affairs, which the poor cannot enjoy (unless maintained by the State); but wealth is not the whole man, and a true interpretation of desert must have regard to the whole. Adhering however to its partial interpretation, oligarchy makes wealth the standard of distribution and the aim of action: it constitutes a State in which the wealthy govern for the increase of wealth. It is hard for a government based on such a foundation to escape selfishness, and oligarchy is therefore regarded by Aristotle as a form of constitution, in which the government not only pursues wealth, but pursues it for its own advantage, and the holders of office seek profit as well as honour. Perverted to the interests of a class both in its aim and in its spirit, it can only produce a warfare of classes—an enmity of rich and poor, such as characterises also, if in an opposite way, the temper of democracy; and indeed an oligarchy may be called, in view of its essentially selfish character, a democracy "writ small".

Estimate of the meaning of Greek oligarchy

That oligarchy was the rule of a section, in the interest of a section, was perhaps true of Aristotle's day and generation. It had been in place in early Greece,[1] and it had done much for early Greece. But a change had come over its character, as a result perhaps of the Peloponnesian War, or at any rate of the rivalry of Sparta and Athens, which had preceded, as it survived, the actual war. Democracy, almost of itself secure in

Deterioration of oligarchy in the fourth century

[1] *Cf. supra*, p. **445**.

the breadth of its basis, was still further secured by the example and protection of Athens: oligarchy, naturally insecure, had to find its shield and buckler in the support of Sparta. It might seem a denationalised, unpatriotic thing (though, as we have seen, patriotism was loyalty to a form of constitution, according to Aristotle's doctrine, and in that sense the members of an oligarchical clique were thoroughly patriotic); and it tended, feeling its want of native root and its half-alien character, to throw itself, as tyranny in a similar position did, into a policy of terrorism. Something of an economic motive may have entered into this policy: the propertied classes may have had pauperism and socialism to face. The cry for "abolition of debts and redistribution of the land" was not unknown, as the oath of the Athenian dicast shows; and Plato, in the sketch of constitutional change which he gives in the *Republic*, strongly emphasises the force of economic considerations. And thus, from the consideration of oligarchy and democracy alike, the same fundamental result emerges—that Greek politics were setting fast towards a warfare of classes. Political selfishness was leading to political disruption. Democracy used its powers in practice to confiscate the property of the rich by judicial processes: it had sometimes a theoretical programme which spoke of things like the abolition of capital and the nationalisation of land. Capital and the landed interest, on the other hand, sought to defend themselves against the people and "the people's friend" (προστάτης), by acquiring political power for themselves, and using it in their own interests.

THE MIXED CONSTITUTION[1]

§ 4. Against all these tendencies Plato and Aristotle preached. They taught a political theory of the unity and solidarity of the State, and of the unselfishness of the State's authority. Plato emphasised only too strongly, in Aristotle's judgment, the need of unity: he attempted, by means which were only too drastic, to provide for the exercise of "political art" in the unselfish spirit which should attend the exercise of all arts. But to Aristotle himself, as much as to Plato, the State is an association in a *common* life directed to a *common* good: to him too the ulti- **The need of a non-sectional government**

[1] See vi. (iv.), c. vii.-ix.; xi.-xii.; and *cf.* iii., c. vii., and ii., c. ix., xi.

mate distinction between constitutions is formed by the selfishness or unselfishness of the government. There is the same fundamental theory: the difference is one of stress and accent. And the States, which both philosophers would in practice construct, are only different ways to a common goal. Plato's ultimate ideal in the *Republic* seems to be an enlightened monarchy: Aristotle, too, in a striking passage, speaks of the king as by nature "a guardian, preventing the propertied classes from suffering injustice, and the people from suffering insult". But (not to speak here of the ideal State sketched by Aristotle) the practical "guardian" which he proposes is not monarchy, but the middle class. The cure for the evils of oligarchy and democracy is to be found in a mixture of the two. Thus arises the conception of the polity, a middle constitution, in which the middle class rules—a constitution which is by no means ideal, since it does not require ideal conditions, but which can be generally accepted as an average best under the actual conditions in which Greek oligarchies and democracies stood.

Doctrine of the Mean

Aristotle's own philosophic temper impelled him in this direction. We have already spoken of the weight which he was always inclined to attach to received opinion in the field of practical science. Now an essential article of received opinion was "nothing in excess". The ethical temper of the Greeks was in conformity with this maxim: its ideal was a steady balance, an equilibrium, a life lived as it were in the half-way house. It was perhaps the natural ideal of a people conscious of an emotional temper and a capacity for extremes; but it was connected with the intellect as much as with the emotions: it became the ideal of the philosophers as well as of the people. The Greek mind desired order, a system of definite lines with nothing vague or fluid, as the ideal condition of itself; and it imported into Nature its own demand. Physically, therefore, the early philosophers conceived a state of chaos (corresponding to the indeterminate ignorance in which the mind begins) upon which there had supervened a principle of order and definition. "All things were in confusion: reason came, and set them in order." The order of Nature is here identified with the reason of man, and both are supposed to represent a system of definite lines, an enclosing limit or πέρας, set to ancient chaos. Only things so defined, enclosed and limited by the ordering of reason are intelligible—only the limited is knowable; the illimitable is unintelligible. Now it was an easy step to transfer this physical teaching to ethical things; and that step, as Aristotle tells us, the Pythagoreans took. The finite became the concept of virtue: the infinite and unlimited became the symbol of vice. Morality was regarded as the attainment of a definite order: it was viewed as the setting of limits, within which they should always move, to the "infinity" of human passions. This is a central thought in Aristotle's *Ethics*: virtue is *in its essence* a definite mean, constituting a limit to the disorderliness of passion, which tends of itself to excess or defect. It was a natural teaching for Aristotle: not only did it agree with the thought of previous philosophers, but it also harmonised with the received opinion of "nothing in excess"; and besides it flowed, as we have seen,[1] from his own teleological method.

The idea of the mean thus sprang, partly from the ethical temper of the ordinary Greek world, partly from the philosophic demand for order—a demand which in physical things required a limit set by reason, and, in the moral world, equally required a similar limit, and found it in this conception. It is an idea not only cardinal to the *Ethics*, but also constant throughout the *Politics*. It defines the size of the State: it limits the amount of wealth: it determines the theory of the "polity". For the problem which is to be solved by the polity is that of discovering a neutral, mediating, and arbitrating authority, which shall form a principle of order to limit the clash of wills and the chaos of party strife; and the solution is found to lie in taking a mean between the extremes of parties, because this mean will make for order and good government. But the "mean" constitution is *not* the ideal, for all that. It is indeed good, in so far as the government rules for the common weal; its very *raison d'être* is that the government should rule in this spirit, and not for any private interest. But the ideal State has for its aim the blessedness of a complete and active virtue, the achievement of a common good for the State which is also the supreme good of men. It is not so with the polity. The polity is modest and middling: it is content with a military

The mean State *not* the ideal State

[1] *Cf. supra*, pp. 229-30, also p. 97.

form of virtue, such as a number of men can be reasonably expected to attain. Because its aim is lower, the standard of distributive justice on which a polity acts will also be lower than that of the ideal State: office will go to those who can show military virtue, and good work done for the common weal, but it will not go, as in the ideal State it must, to men who have a complete virtue, completely equipped for its work with a store of this world's goods. The polity, in which the burgess militia rules according to its lights, will live the humdrum life of a quiet *bourgeoisie:* the ideal State is by comparison a communion of saints.

Rule of the middle class

In describing the polity, Aristotle starts from the definition of virtue given in the *Ethics.* Virtue is a mean, both for the individual and the State (since the virtue of both is the same); and a life directed to the pursuit of the mean will therefore be the normal life of the State, and determine its true constitution (a constitution being the "manner of life" pursued by a State). What constitution, then, will suit a life directed to the pursuit of the mean? A constitution in which the middle classes [1] are supreme; for, since constitutions vary with the social class which predominates, a mean or middle constitution must be marked by the predominance of a middle class. There is much to be pleaded in favour of such a middle class. It is the natural arbiter of strife between rich and poor; the mean is always arbiter and judge between extremes, because it comes into contact with both.[2] And the middle class is more ready to listen to reason than either the rich or the poor. Riches breed insolence; poverty tends to petty vice. Again, the members of the middle class are less inclined than the rich to waste their money upon costly and ruinous liturgies, which only corrupt the giver and the receiver, the rich man and the poor, and, with them, the State of which they are members. But there are still weightier considerations in their favour. The spirit of equality and the stability of the State are both maintained by their predominance. The rich only know how to rule: an instinct for domination is the natural result of the

[1] The middle class embraces all the citizens of a State who are not distinguished by πλοῦτος or by πενία—men whose interest did not lie in the rule of an oligarchy (and the pursuit of πλοῦτος), nor in the supremacy of a democracy (and the exaltation of πενία). [2] *De Anima,* 424 a 6-7.

condition of their domestic life, and it overflows into their political action. On the other hand, social conditions make it natural for the poor to obey a master; and therefore a State composed of rich men and poor is composed of masters and slaves, whom the arrogance of the master and the envy of the slave keep irretrievably divided. There is here none of the equality, and therefore none of the friendship and but little of the justice, which should animate and pervade a political association. It is essential to such an association that its members should be "like and equal". Where a large middle class has its proper recognition, these conditions are most likely to be fulfilled. But an association of like and equal members, held together in justice and welded together by friendship, will be stable and secure; while a union of warring opposites which know no friendship, and too often forget, if they know, the dictates of justice, can only be doomed to early destruction. The middle classes are thus the best government; they neither seek to rob others, nor do others seek to rob them; they neither plot against others, nor are they plotted against themselves.[1] A State which desires freedom from civil war, can only pray that its middle class may be numerous enough to outweigh one, or if possible both, of the others. A large and populous State may congratulate itself on its very size, which must always mean a large middle class; while a small State may easily fall into two extremes, unbalanced by any counterpoising mean.

Why the middle class was ineffective in Greek politics

There were writers who had seen in the middle classes the saviours of society long before Aristotle. He himself cites Phocylides, who had prayed to be of a middle condition in his city; and Euripides had said that the middle order saved the State, maintaining the discipline appointed by law. But the predominance of the middle classes had been rare in Greece. Thucydides tells us that they had been the victims rather than the physicians of political disorders, and had been destroyed in times of civil war by both of the contending parties. Aristotle

[1] It might seem from this that the middle constitution, realising virtue considered as a mean, were the ideal. But Aristotle expressly says that he is considering the manner of life which the majority can attain—the constitution which *most* States can imitate; and the virtue considered as a mean, of which he here speaks, must also be an *average* virtue.

recognises and seeks to explain the inconsiderable part which they had played in Greek politics. The small size of the middle classes seems to him to explain something. The heated atmosphere of political life, he admits, is only favourable to the flourishing of extremes; and when one of the two extremes has crushed the other, it naturally demands predominance in the State as the prize of victory.[1] With the Greek belief in the power of the legislator, he urges that those who have won supremacy in Greece (he is thinking of Athens and Sparta) have made it their policy to foster democracy or oligarchy, because it was to their own interest to do so: they have never had regard to the interest of the State whose destinies they controlled. One statesman of importance and one alone, he concludes, had ever attempted to call a polity into existence. This would seem to have been Theramenes, whom the *Ἀθηναίων πολιτεία* praises as a genuine statesman. It had been his professed creed, that the best constitution was one in which power rested with those who could help the State with horse or with shield: he had championed the solid and respectable middle classes who, as Aristotle says, could plead their military virtue as their title to political power. It was he who had really been to a large extent responsible for the eventual form of the constitution of 411, in which power had rested with the Five Thousand who possessed heavy arms, and the system of pay had been abolished; and he had thus helped to institute the one "polity" which had ever been deliberately made. But though seldom if ever realised, the polity still remains for Aristotle the ideal to which both oligarchy and democracy should in practice approximate; while he also suggests that it may serve in theory as a standard to measure the qualities and the defects of any species of either.[2] Accordingly the best oligarchy or democracy will be that which stands most remote from oligarchic or democratic extremes, and nearest to the mean of polity. The best oligarchy is the least rich: the best democracy

[1] *Cf.* Thucydides, iii., 82. "Either party had a specious programme: the one alleged equality before the law as its aim, the other a moderate government by the best heads; but while they nominally were concerned to advance the common weal, they really made it the prize of victory."

[2] This introduces a new element into the classification of States propounded in the third book.

the least poor. And thus the polity serves Aristotle, as the ideal State had served his master Plato, for a standard by which to judge States other than itself.

If we regard the polity as a fact already in existence, it will appear to us, as it has hitherto appeared, in the light of a moderate constitution characterised by the rule of the moderates. But if we look at its construction, and at the elements from which it has to be built, it may be viewed as a mixed constitution, the result of blending together oligarchy and democracy. Regarded in this way, the polity acquires a new justification. It is a constitution which recognises the claims not of some one quality, and that alone, but of several. It remembers wealth, and does not forget free birth; and in it both the rich and the poor come by their own. This will explain how the blending of two bad constitutions makes a third which is good. It is in their one-sidedness that oligarchy and democracy are defective, and it is from this one-sidedness that all their evils spring. Just because it reconciles both sides, the polity escapes these evils, and is free to become a positive influence for good. Such a reconciliation may take place in various ways. We may simply take an oligarchic institution and a democratic institution, and fuse the two together; or, by a slight modification, we may take *part* of the one, and *part* of the other, and unite the two parts in a new institution. In an oligarchy, for instance, offices are elective, and there is a property qualification: in a democracy there is the lot instead of election, and there is no property qualification. The two can be reconciled, if the elective part of the oligarchical system is adopted, and the absence of a property qualification is borrowed from democracy. But there is a third and separate species of "mixture," which consists in taking a mean between the two extremes. One can mix 15 with 9 in 12, which is the mean between 15 and 9; and a constitution which has a high qualification for office may be mixed with one in which the qualification is low, by the same arithmetical method. If, for instance, one constitution demands of those who would attend the assembly a qualification of 100 medimni, and another demands only 5 or even none, the two may be reconciled by fixing the qualification at 50 or thereabouts. Thus the "mean" constitution and the "mixed" con-

Polity a mixed constitution

stitution are definitely proved to be identical. The mean participates in the nature of either extreme: it is a mixture ready to hand; and the constitution which pursues it must necessarily be a mixed constitution. But it is not the only kind of mixed constitution. The mixed constitution is a wider thing than the mean constitution. The mean constitution is only a species: the mixed constitution is of the nature of a genus. The mean constitution is one, in which the only two things mixed are wealth and free birth, while the mixture is achieved by taking a mean between these two extremes, and entrusting power to moderate incomes. It is possible to conceive of mixtures, in which there are either three elements, or, if there be only two, those two are not necessarily wealth and free birth; or in which, again, the mixture is achieved by simple composition of the various elements, and not by taking a mean between the two extremes. Such mixtures Aristotle describes. A mixture in which the three elements of virtue, wealth, and free birth are all regarded, he terms an aristocracy. The same name will apply to a mixture of two elements only, if one of these is virtue; and it is even given in common speech to mixtures of wealth and free birth, where these incline towards oligarchy.[1] There are thus three varieties of mixed constitutions which bear the name of aristocracy (though they are all distinct from genuine aristocracy, in which the single element of virtue predominates); while the name of polity is reserved for a mixture of wealth and free birth which inclines towards democracy, and gives sovereign power to a large middle class.[2]

Instances of mixed constitutions

Illustrations of various forms of mixed constitutions are to be found in the *Politics*. Carthage is an example of that variety of aristocracy which unites respect for virtue and wealth with regard for numbers: Sparta is an aristocracy which unites numbers with virtue. At Carthaget he assembly (whose rights

[1] The reason is, that culture and high birth seem natural concomitants of wealth; and indeed common parlance designated the wealthy, merely as wealthy, by the name of καλοὶ κἀγαθοί, which was proper to the members of an aristocracy.

[2] In the *Ethics* the term timocracy is given to this form of constitution, because it is based on a moderate census (τίμημα). This census is defined in the *Politics* as one low enough to put those who enjoy the franchise in a majority (1297 b 5); but it may be more closely defined as the sum necessary to provide a suit of armour.

represented the weight attached to numbers) had power, in certain cases, to decide what subjects should be introduced; and it had always the right of discussing whatever was actually introduced, and of giving the final decision. There were also oligarchical features: wealth was a qualification for certain offices; and the fact that an important office like the Board of Five was filled by co-optation, and that this board nominated the Hundred, almost approximated Carthage to a "dynasty". But virtue was also a qualification for office at Carthage: offices were unpaid, and they went by election, not by lot; and these facts attested the presence of aristocratic elements in the constitution. Carthage had, however, some defects as a mixture: the democratic and the oligarchic elements were both pushed to an excess. The powers assigned both to the assembly and to the Board of Five were too extensive; and in the actual working of the constitution, the oligarchical element played far too great a part. Offices were as a matter of fact bought by their holders; and this made wealth the aim both of politicians and of the people, who always tend to imitate their rulers. This criticism might with equal weight have been passed upon Sparta; but in the Sixth book Aristotle extols Sparta as an excellent example of a proper mixture. It is the test of a State which attempts to mix democratic and oligarchic institutions, that it should be able to be called both a democracy and an oligarchy, according as attention is paid to this or that feature of the constitution. Sparta satisfies this test.[1] It may be called a democracy, if regard is paid to the equality of social life maintained in the training and at the common tables, or to the general equality of access to the great office of the Ephorate; but it may equally be called an oligarchy, in view of the fact that the offices are elective, and the highest judicial powers are restricted to a few officials. The attitude adopted towards the Spartan constitution in the Second book is far more critical. Aristotle indeed admits, that on the principle that it is well with the State which has the support of all its citizens, Sparta may be

[1] It is to be noticed that Aristotle here speaks of Sparta as a mixture of oligarchy and democracy. Respecting as it does the claims of virtue, it should be called a mixture of aristocracy and democracy; but the term oligarchy would seem to be loosely used.

regarded as prosperous. Her kings are content with their honours: the aristocratic element finds its place in the Gerusia; the democratic in the Ephorate.[1] Birth, merit, and numbers all find their recognition. But there are defects in the recognition. The virtue which is recognised is only one side of virtue: it is only the military side, which, if it makes a State strenuous in war, fails to bring it stability in peace. And another principle has crept into the Spartan constitution, besides respect for virtue or numbers; and that is respect for wealth. This has infected the whole of social life and the whole polity: it has narrowed the franchise, which depends on contribution to the common tables, and is therefore forfeited by the poorer Spartans. Sparta has ceased to be a mixture so well balanced that no element can be exalted above the rest: one can lay a finger on the oligarchical element, and call Sparta pre-eminently an oligarchy. Her land is in the hands of a few owners: a love of wealth characterises all her citizens.[2]

These are the types of mixed constitutions which are illustrated in the *Politics*—the mixture of virtue, wealth and numbers, and the mixture of numbers and virtue. The third type of aristocracy, and the Polity itself, are not illustrated; but of the Polity the constitution of 411, which is fully discussed in the *Ἀθηναίων πολιτεία*, was the natural example. It remains, after this statement of the theory and practice of the mixed constitution as conceived and illustrated by Aristotle, to examine briefly the history of the conception, and to compare its meaning with that of the mixed constitution of to-day.

Previous history of the conception of a mixed constitution

The conception is one which Aristotle inherited, like so many others, from Plato: in the *Laws*, as we have seen, a mixture had been advocated of monarchy and democracy, of "authoritative hereditary government and the temper-

[1] This implies that Sparta is a mixture of monarchy, aristocracy and democracy. In the sixth book, where only the claims of the few and the many were in question, monarchy was naturally omitted.

[2] This criticism of Sparta (which is frequent in the *Politics*, especially with regard to Spartan training) is explained by the Spartan collapse at Leuctra and Mantinea. Since the composition of the *Republic*, Sparta was a pricked bubble. Hence Aristotle could naturally look with some coolness on the old romantic conception of Sparta; though Oncken regards his view of Sparta as showing, like his criticism of ideals, a "sane realism". But the romantic conception of Sparta persisted, in spite of Aristotle (*infra*, p. 482).

ing element of freedom". Aristotle complains that Plato proposes to mix two of the worst constitutions, tyranny and extreme democracy (which is an utter misrepresentation of Plato); that he actually mixes with democracy not tyranny but oligarchy, and in doing so gives too great a share to oligarchy, by concentrating offices in the hands of the rich; and finally, that he should have mixed three elements rather than two, if he wished to form a constitution as near as possible to the ideal. One gathers from his criticism that the idea of a mixed constitution was not new even in the pages of Plato: Sparta had already been regarded as a mixed constitution by various thinkers, some of whom had seen in it a compound of oligarchy, monarchy and democracy, and some a mixture of the tyranny of the ephors with the democracy of the common tables.[1] Aristotle could therefore draw upon Platonic theory and Spartan practice for the theory of the mixed constitution. In his hands, however, the conception assumes a peculiar form, which can only be understood with reference to his theory of distributive justice. A mixed constitution is one which does justice to all or several of the claims—wealth, virtue, and numbers—which distributive justice should recognise in the award of political power. These claims being the claims of different social classes, a mixed constitution may be further defined as one which either distributes political power among several classes, or awards it entirely to the middle class, which in itself is a combination of rich and poor. The mixed constitution of Aristotle is therefore one which recognises several claims, and accordingly awards some share of political authority to several classes. It is primarily a combination of social elements. Ultimately, it must also be a combination of constitutions; for a constitution is the recognition of a claim advanced by a class, and a constitution which recognises several claims advanced by several classes is therefore a combination of constitutions. But the difference between Aristotle and those writers, who before and after him lauded Sparta as the type of a mixed constitution, is that he looked primarily to a combination of social elements (whether two or three), while they looked primarily to a com-

[1] While Aristotle himself regards it as a mixture of kingship, aristocracy, and the people (ii., c. ix.), or of virtue and numbers (vi. (iv.), c. vii.).

bination of constitutions, and generally of all the three constitutions which they recognised, kingship, aristocracy and democracy. The typical mixed constitution of Aristotle was a polity which mixed the two elements of wealth and numbers, the two classes of rich and poor; *their* mixed constitution was a combination of monarchy, oligarchy, and democracy. While Aristotle fused two constitutions representing two social classes, and dominated by two social classes, into a new and distinct constitution, these thinkers seem rather to have aimed at a juxtaposition of three constitutions, which left each still separate, though all were united.

The mixed constitution in later Greek theory

Later Greek theory was much concerned with the mixed constitution, viewed rather as a combination of constitutions than as a union of classes, and with Sparta as its type. There was always indeed another side of Sparta which also attracted attention. The training of the Spartan citizens which enforced on them a moral code, may help to explain the preoccupation of philosophers with Sparta. She was twice over the model of Greece: her constitution, whether regarded as "an arrangement of offices," or as expressing "the moral life of the State," might well engage the mind of any thinker.[1] But the purely political side of Sparta seems to have been discussed both by Aristotle's own school, the Peripatetics, and by the Stoics. Dicæarchus the Peripatetic wrote a work called the *Tripoliticus*, dealing, one would suppose, with the three constitutions and their mixture. Athenæus quotes from the work a passage which describes the common tables of Sparta; and it has been conjectured that Dicæarchus developed in it the theory of a mixed constitution on the Spartan model. The work must have had some vogue: a lexicographer gives the name of γένος Δικαιαρχικόν to the mixed constitution, much as we might term it to-day *le genre de Montesquieu.*[2] Another and more famous Peripatetic, Demetrius Phalereus, wrote a work on the polity; and, indeed, being a politician as well as a reformer, he not only wrote, but also reformed the Athenian democracy.

[1] The common tables, and the supposed original equality of estates, made Sparta figure in later writers as also an economic paradise.

[2] While, to continue the parallel, England takes the place of Sparta as the type of a mixed constitution.

He seems to have been true to many of Aristotle's conceptions, and to have done much to give them life during his *régime* at Athens. Of the Stoics generally we are told, that they regarded the mixed constitution as the best. Their ideal, however, as expressed by Zeno, was a cosmopolitan ideal leading to the destruction of all constitutions and all States: "men should not live in cities and in demes, distinguished by different codes, but should regard all men as fellow-citizens and demesmen: there should be one life, one order, like that of a single flock feeding on a common pasture". The Stoic thus rose above the conception of "the city of Cecrops" to that of the City of God. But the City of God was an ideal only realised in full conformity to Nature; and failing, it would seem, that ideal—granting that separate States were still to exist, the mixed constitution had still its place. Two of the Stoics are recorded as having written about Sparta—Persæus, and Sphærus the friend and counsellor of the Spartan King Cleomenes. But the latter, at any rate, was more concerned with the moral code of Sparta than with the constitution: Stoic asceticism readily turned to the praise of Spartan self-sacrifice.

Like other tenets of Stoicism, that of the mixed constitution became the belief of Rome, and was expounded by Cicero. The bridge between the two may be found in Polybius. No unmixed constitution can endure, we are told by Polybius: the blast of change sweeps away each in its turn,

> Each changing place with that which went before.

Only in a mixed government, combining kingship, aristocracy and democracy, is there stability; for a mixed government, though liable to be overthrown from without, is not liable to be destroyed from within by the hostility of an unprivileged class. The king is checked by the people, the people by the few; and in the play of these checks and balances the constitution reposes secure. Rome is the great example of Polybius: Sparta is now beginning to be abandoned by the votaries of the mixed constitution; and Roman writers naturally adopted a theory which glorified the constitution of their own country. The *De Republica* of Cicero simply adopts the theory of Polybius. "He is dissatisfied with all the three simple forms of government, both on account of their inherent character and because they all have a dangerous tendency to perversion. . . . He is therefore in favour of a form of government, compounded of the three simple elements, possessing some of the virtues of each, and possessing in greater degree the quality of stability."[1]

Montesquieu's theory of a division of powers

Ancient theory had thus in its last phase completely parted from Aristotle. Whereas mixed constitutions, in his view, aimed at equity and the social solidarity which springs from equity, and whereas they secured their aim by recognising every social claim that deserved recognition, the mixed constitution of Polybius and Cicero aims at stability, and secures its purpose by a system of checks and balances derived from a juxtaposition of all constitutions.[2] If we turn to the theory of a mixed constitution expounded by Montesquieu, with England for a model,[3] we find something more akin to Polybius than to Aristotle. To Montesquieu the aim is now liberty, the means a division of powers, so arranged, that while the executive power rests with the monarch, the legislative is entrusted both to a body of nobles and to a body of popular representatives, and the judicature (which is independent of both) is vested in the hands of a professional body. A division of the functions of government is thus characteristic of Montesquieu: it is only a secondary consideration that the division is a division among different classes. The essence is division in itself, which secures liberty by hampering authority. To Aristotle union is the essence—a union of classes.[4] He is thinking of a reconciliation of the claims of the different classes of society to a share in the government, and not of a limitation of the government's freedom. Montesquieu like a modern looked to the State: Aristotle like an ancient looked to society.[5] But he too speaks of functions and their combinations, in a way almost reminiscent of Montesquieu, at the beginning of the Eighth book. The legislative function, we are told, may be assigned to the Few in the same State which assigns judicial functions to the Best. It is such combinations, where some function is assigned to

[1] Carlyle, *Mediæval Political Theory in the West*, i., 16.

[2] *Cf.* Henkel, *Studien*, p. 101 *sqq*.

[3] *Esprit des Lois*, xi., vi.

[4] One may say that Aristotle desires a union of classes for the sake of equity; Polybius a union of constitutions for the sake of stability; and Montesquieu a division of powers for the sake of liberty.

[5] *Cf.* Introduction, pp. 11-13.

another element than the one preponderant in the constitution, which makes an aristocracy (for instance) oligarchical in character, or a polity democratic. But this division, or rather (in Aristotle's language) combination of powers is only incidentally mentioned; and it is not connected with the theory of mixed government. So far as one can see, in a properly mixed government each separate function would, in Aristotle's conception, bear the impress of the same mixed character: in a polity the legislative, executive and judicature would each be entrusted to the mixed or middle class; but mixture would *not* be attempted on the plan of making one part black, another white, and trusting the whole to come out grey. It follows from this that for Aristotle there is no idea of a check exercised by one department (or even class) on another: the different departments will work harmoniously together, because each is permeated by the same spirit as the rest. Montesquieu, on the other hand, agreeing apparently with Polybius,[1] does trust to the action and reaction of black and white to make a grey. He would encourage antithesis, to produce the political result of liberty: Aristotle desires a synthesis, which will achieve the social result of solidarity. The one feared the tyranny of the concentration of political power: the other dreaded that warfare of classes, which the annexation of power by a single class would tend to produce.

The mixed constitution in regard to the classification of States

In conclusion, it must be noticed that the consideration of the mixed constitution introduces a certain amount of change into the Aristotelian system of classification of States. It has already been observed that the polity is regarded by Aristotle as the standard by which degrees of oligarchy and democracy may be measured. And this suggests a further step. The mixed constitution in general may be regarded as a class by itself, distinct, on the one hand, from all actual constitutions (or perversions) of which it is the norm and standard, and, on the other, from the ideal State, which is almost as far removed from the mixed constitution, as it is from the perversion. Constitutions may therefore be regarded as falling into three grades or stages. There is the stage of the actual, which is also the stage of the

[1] Polybius agrees with Montesquieu and disagrees with Aristotle in believing in a system of checks, just because he combines constitutions, and does not like Aristotle unite classes.

perverted, a stage containing democracy, oligarchy and tyranny. There is the stage of the reformed actual, a stage filled by mixed constitutions of different kinds, which combine, and by combining purify, the elements of the actual, while, so far as they recognise the claims of virtue, they even contain some elements of the ideal. Finally, there is the stage of the ideal, in which the ground of the actual is left, and a State is constructed such as *might* arise under ideal conditions. In one passage (vi., c. 8) these three stages are connected: the first is regarded as a perversion of the second, the second as a perversion of the third. The scheme is natural, but it is somewhat alien to the rest of the *Politics;* and we may simply leave these three stages as they stand, without determining their exact relation to one another. In any case the old classification of constitutions into two great kinds, the normal and the perverted, has been disturbed by the elevation of the Polity (reinforced by the varieties of so-called aristocracy, and viewed as a mixed constitution) from the rank of a species to that of a kind.

The Theory of Sedition and its Cures

§ 5. Not only did Aristotle suggest a cure of the evils of actual States, which consisted in the adoption of a new and moderate constitution: he also proposed another cure, which consisted simply in the adoption and improvement of existing constitutions themselves. Here he advances altogether beyond Plato; for Plato, while he was willing to sketch a sub-ideal constitution in the *Laws*, had never attempted to study the therapeutics of actual and imperfect States. Here too he finally allows Political Science to abandon its ethical connection, and permits his respect for "things as they are" to lead him to study perversions themselves with a view to their preservation. Such a study, so definitely medicinal in its aims, naturally involves a consideration of the causes of disease as well as of their cures. Accordingly the seventh book of the *Politics* is devoted first to a discussion of the causes of revolutions, and then to a sketch of the methods of securing political stability.

Causes of στάσις

In practice the discussion of revolutions (*μεταβολαί*) turns out to be a discussion of seditions (*στάσεις*), whether they are ultimately followed by a revolution and a change in the constitution, or involve no such result. What interests Aristotle is not so much change in the body politic, as disturbances. What he is considering are those sharp fevers, which unsettle the spirit of a constitution, and undermine political security.[1] He is studying the great Rebellion, and not the Reform Bill. Whether or no a great rebellion involves a revolution and a new scheme of government, is a matter of comparatively slight importance: what is of moment is that something has happened which unsettles the "tone" and disturbs the "law-abidingness" of a city. What are the causes of these disturbances? Fundamentally, there is one cause; and that one cause is a sense of injustice. Some person or persons, some class or classes, feel that the distributive justice of the State is for them a system of injustice, giving them the same as others when they ought in justice to have more, or giving them less than others when they ought in justice to have the same. Such a sense of the injustice of existing order must indeed always be the ultimate motive of all rebellion; and as it underlies all political revolt, so it has inspired social revolts like the peasant rising of 1381 in England, and that of 1525 in Germany. In either case an appeal was made in arms from man's poor justice to God's Justice: in either case a sense of the terrible unevenness of distribution drove men to attempt to restore equality. In the *Politics* Aristotle is only concerned with the inequalities of a political distribution of offices and honours; but in pointing to these as the real authors of all sedition and rebellion, he was stating what, for a society like the city-state, with its primary government and jealous sense of distinctions,[2] was the fundamental truth. Great movements never arise on petty issues, though they may spring immediately from some trifling occasion; and whatever the spark which sets fire to the train, there has always been a train laid before the flare of rebellion comes. Granted such a preparation, almost anything may serve to bring the crisis. Men have always

[1] In this respect the seventh book of the *Politics* differs from the eighth and ninth books of the *Republic*. Plato is concerned not with disturbances, but with changes—not with shock to the ἦθος of a State, but with changes in that ἦθος.

[2] As was said above, it was round the constitution that the battle raged in Greece. A new set of men would attempt either to introduce a new or to capture the old constitution; or at any rate they would attempt to alter a part (*Politics*, 1301 b 6 *sqq.*).

something to gain by rebellion: to set injustice right is to win for themselves, as Aristotle tells us, profit or honour; and for men possessed by a sense of injustice, and looking forward to the advantages to be gained, the excuse of any occasion will suffice. To see the magistrates making money from individual citizens or the common purse—to see oneself dishonoured, and others improperly honoured—a sudden passion of revenge—a violent access of fear—all these may prove occasions, though they are not causes, of civil disturbance. In a word, then, three things generally coincide to produce a *στάσις*, inequality and injustice in the political system, an expectation of future advantages, the seizing of some occasion; but of these the greatest is the first.

Economics and politics

It is important to notice that the economic motive does not appear prominently in Aristotle's philosophy of seditions. He does not suggest that revolts are due to the impoverishment of the poor, nor does he mention the cry for abolition of debts and redistribution of estates. It is a sense of political injustice which seems to him responsible for sedition. The economic interpretation of Greek *στάσις*, whatever its truth, finds little support in his pages. It is often tempting to explain revolutions by economic causes, and to find in the power of the purse the *causa causans* of history. Aristotle's philosophy is less materialistic: the purse is not the maker of history. Speaking of Phaleas' proposal to stop disturbances by an equalisation of property, he tells us that men fall into sedition not only through inequality of possessions, but also through inequality of honours (1266 b 38). The many may be moved by the former, but it is by the latter that the finest spirits are touched to the greatest issues. Men do not become tyrants in order to be warmly clad; nor do they kill tyrants for money, even though tyrannicide has its reward. Yet Aristotle admits that inequality of possessions *is* a cause of a sedition; and he allows that the desire of profit as well as of honour may be the final end which men have set before themselves in a revolution. Indeed, he postulates *some* desire of private advantage in every leader of revolt. He does not contemplate a Mazzini, fighting for a " cause " in which self has been lost. The city was not the home of abstract causes: it was the abode of a concrete constitution, in which a man sought his proper place. To get his proper place, with its profit or honour, he would readily rise in arms; and in his rising there would always necessarily be a note of self-assertion. He would indeed be fighting for a cause, in so far as he was attempting to set injustice right; but the injustice was one by which he suffered himself.

To vindicate a proper place in the constitution, or to punish those who used their place in the constitution wrongfully—these, then, were the aims of sedition and rebellion. Such movements were more likely to occur in an oligarchy than in a democracy; for in an oligarchy there was more exclusiveness and more abuse of power. Accordingly, having discussed the causes, Aristotle next proceeds to sketch the cures of civil disturbances, beginning with oligarchy, but quickly advancing to cures which are applicable in all constitutions. The cures follow the causes closely, in true scientific fashion; and each of the methods of preservation suggested may be shown to be connected with some cause of disturbance already discussed.[1] Fundamentally, the one method of preservation is to prevent the operation of the one great cause of dissolution—a sense of the injustice of the constitution. From this principle there flow many results. In the first place, the constitution must be based on the consent of all the members of the State. The one elementary principle of paramount importance is that the number of those who are in favour of the constitution should be greater than the number of those who are not (1309 b 16-18). Such consent and acceptance must be honestly won: it must not be purchased by sham concessions, which will certainly be detected, and only tend to aggravate the evil they profess to cure. In the second place, and consequent upon this principle of the need of consent, comes the principle, which appears most prominently in Aristotle, of the need of moderation. The best means of preserving either democracy or oligarchy is to pursue democratic or oligarchic aims with moderation. Everything which glitters is not gold; and what seems most democratic at first sight is in the long run most calculated to destroy a democracy.[2]

Methods of preserving constitutions

[1] See Newman, iv., Appendix A, pp. 568, 569.

[2] Newman (Introd., 538) contrasts the teaching of the treatise on the Athenian constitution once ascribed to Xenophon. It is argued there that all the excesses of democracy are inevitable results of its principle, and necessary to its salvation.

The oath of an oligarchical body ought not to be one of eternal hostility to the people: it ought to be a vow not to injure the people. *Sanguis martyrum semen ecclesiæ;* and a wise party will never give its opponent the stimulus of oppression and the prestige of martyrdom. On the contrary, in a democracy the people will spare and even honour the rich: in an oligarchy the few will spare the feelings and the purses of the poor. They will limit their own power of accumulating estates, and voluntarily give the representatives of the people equality or precedence in unessential offices. Every government, indeed, should go out of its way to conciliate every interest and every section, which may possibly feel a sense of injustice; and the mixed government itself should be careful to conciliate every citizen, and to introduce new citizens continually from the most promising members of the State who are excluded from the franchise. Thus is the golden rule of moderation and pursuit of the mean enjoined upon all governments. Even the mixed constitution, which is already a mean between two extremes, must choose counsels of moderation; and governments like democracy and oligarchy, which are by their nature extremes, must seek their salvation in a course of moderation still more strenuously pursued. The teaching is such as we should expect from the general tenor of Aristotle's philosophy: the difficulty which it raises—that if you concede an inch, you are in danger of having an ell taken—is one which he does not seem to have noticed.

There is still a third rule which should be observed, if the preservation of a State is to be attained. The offices should be arranged in such a way as to preclude any possibility of their being used as a source of profit. Such political selfishness and corruption was, as we have already seen, the curse of Greece; and nothing could provoke a more poignant sense of the injustice of a constitution. "The masses are not so much aggrieved at exclusion from office (such exclusion may even be to their taste, if it gives them leisure for business), as they are at the thought of public peculation by their officials. *Then* they feel a double grievance: they have no share in office, and they have no share in its profits" (1308 b 34-38). But if, by publicity of accounts and rewards for incorruptibility, office be prevented from becoming a source of profit, a number of objects are instantly secured. The masses will no longer covet office, but will attend to their private affairs and grow prosperous: the rich will hold the offices, for which they alone have the time and the capacity, and they will be satisfied by a pre-eminence of honour.[1] Whether these results will necessarily flow from a system of honorary offices may be doubted; but it is certain that a suspicion of governmental corruption is a peculiarly keen incentive to opposition, as has often been seen in modern history. It is a "very great thing" therefore to avoid the least breath of this suspicion; but "greater than all else" for the preservation of a constitution is Aristotle's final principle, that all the citizens of a State should be bred and trained in the spirit of its constitution. For a constitution is a "manner of life," and its permanence can only be really secured, when by discipline and habituation that manner of life has become second nature to every citizen. But to train a people in the spirit of a democracy is not to train men to do what men in democracies like to do, or what seems at first sight democratical: it is to train men to do what will enable them to be comfortably governed under a democracy for the longest time. The member of an oligarchy must not be educated to live in luxury and pride, nor the member of democracy to spend his days in wanton licence: the one must be educated in caution and capacity for business and politics; the other must be educated in the self-control which a democracy particularly needs, and in the right use of his voice in the conduct of affairs. Nor must the government of a State be content merely to habituate its citizens: it must watch carefully all slight and gradual changes of tone and temper, and it must prevent that constant dropping which in time will wear the State away. It must not only lift men up: it must see that they do not slip back. The only fundamental guarantee against the rise of that sense of injustice which is the mother of sedition and revolution is an educating and establishing of men's minds in a right moral habit—a habit so much at

[1] Thus there will be an equal distribution of comfort and content through the State. Such an equal distribution is of the greatest importance, Aristotle believes. A statesman must not give to one class all prosperity and all political power into the bargain: an attempt must be made to give to one class political power, to another private prosperity, in order that the one may counterbalance the other (*Politics*, 1308 b 24-31).

one with the structure of the constitution, that no question can arise of any discrepancy between the political system and the rights of the individual.

Here ends Aristotle's account of the causes and the remedies of revolutions in general. But the latter half of the sixth book is devoted to a particular study of the dangers which beset the monarch and especially the tyrant, and of the proper course for either to take. Of the king and kingship Aristotle has little to say in the *Politics*. He discusses absolute monarchy in comparison with the sovereignty of law in the third book of the *Politics;* and in the same book he classifies the various kinds of monarchy, of which he enumerates five. But there is no attempt at any theory of Macedonian monarchy, though one fine saying, that the king is set as a guard between the rich and the poor, might well have been expanded.[1] With tyranny on the contrary Aristotle deals in some fulness: partly perhaps because he was anxious to study the worst of Greek governments, partly, it may be, because he wished to hint at the dangers to which Macedonian monarchy was liable. Yet, whatever his condemnation of tyranny, he is willing to consider the means of its preservation, and nowhere does he show more fully the realism of his political science, or the extent of his departure from Plato's idealism, than in his attitude to tyranny.

Tyranny—its rise and character

Tyranny,[2] we have already seen, is a perversion of monarchy, and the worst of all perverted constitutions. Perverted constitutions are constitutions selfishly governed, and directed towards a false end: tyranny therefore means the selfish rule of a single man, who has made mere wealth his aim (1311 a 10), because by means of a treasure he is able to gratify his appetites and protect himself in his position. A further feature of tyranny, by which Socrates had already distinguished it from monarchy, is that the tyrant rules without any limitation by the law, and without the consent or good will of his subjects. This was a feature on which the Greeks generally seized, as we learn from the *Supplices* of Euripides; but it was a feature which many

[1] It may be noticed that in Aristotle kingship is conceived: (1) not to be necessarily hereditary or for life: it may be elective and for a fixed period; (2) to be limited by law; (3) to rest on desert. It is a great office, which may fall to one man: it is not something *sui generis*, distinct from all other offices.

[2] See vi. (iv.), c. x.; vii. (v.), c. x.-xi.

tyrannies, like that of the Peisistratidæ at Athens, did not exhibit. To Aristotle this feature is characteristic of one particular species of tyranny; for tyranny has its varieties. There are two species,[1] for instance, which closely approximate to monarchy: they are limited by law, and receive the consent of their subjects; and they are only tyrannical in the wide scope of prerogatival action which is reserved for the ruler. But there is also a third kind, which is termed by Aristotle extreme tyranny. It is the opposite of absolute monarchy, equally absolute and free from legal restraint, but directed to the selfish advantage of the ruler, and without the justification that the ruler is a better man than his subjects (vi. (iv.) c. 10). Thus is tyranny subdivided, exactly as we have seen oligarchy and democracy subdivided; and the criterion of subdivision is here, as it was there, the presence or absence of respect for law. In its utter want of respect for any law, extreme tyranny is exactly parallel to extreme democracy or extreme oligarchy, and indeed Aristotle speaks of it as a compound of the two, plundering the rich equally with democracy, and oppressing the poor equally with oligarchy.

The origin of this form Aristotle ascribes to the pressure of an oligarchy. While monarchy is instituted by the better class as a protection against the people, and the monarch himself is a member of this class, distinguished for some pre-eminence in virtue, a tyrant is instituted by the people to check the rich and to prevent their aggression (1310 b 9-14). In a word king and tyrant are both the products of a social cleavage: both are arbitrators, with the difference that the king is nominated by one side, and the tyrant by the other. It was thus the social dissensions springing from political selfishness that led to the actual institution of a tyrant, as they led Plato to advocate the theory of enlightened despotism. We must not forget that the tyrant could plead this justification for his position; and in this respect we may compare the tyrant of Greece with the tyrants of mediæval Italy who sprang from a similar cleavage between an aristocratic *commune* and a democratic *popolo*. But while the Greek tyrant might plead some justification for his origin, he could not plead such a justification for his subsequent

[1] Absolute hereditary monarchy, among barbarians, and dictatorship (αἰσυμνητεία).

career. Once in power, he surrounded himself by a standing army, often composed of aliens like the Scotch guards of Louis XI. A standing army necessitated a system of regular taxation, such as the ordinary Greek constitution never possessed; nor was the tyrant merely content with regular taxes—he aimed at the acquisition of a hoard (or reserve in bullion) for use in emergencies. Here, as in the maintenance of a standing army, there are features in Greek tyranny which remind us of the New Monarchy which followed on the Wars of the Roses; and one may define Henry VII. as a tyrant, instituted by the people of the towns to check "the notables," and supporting himself by regular taxation and the formation of a hoard. Other features of the development of Greek tyranny also find their modern parallels. To divert his subjects from their loss of liberty the tyrant often became a maker of war (*πολεμοποιός ὁ τύραννος*). One reflects on the Visconti turning Milan into the hammer of Italy. To keep his subjects from conspiracy, the tyrant discouraged or forbade all social gatherings. One remembers the putting down of ale-houses and the prohibition of race-meetings in the most suspicious years of Cromwell's protectorate.

Preservation of tyranny

In many ways the tyrant is the modern figure in the history of the Greek *πόλις*—the figure which it is easiest to understand, and with which it is easiest to sympathise. Many of the Greek tyrants would have been Protestant heroes if they had lived in the sixteenth century: many would have been munificent patrons of the scholars and painters of the Renaissance, if they had lived in the fifteenth. Often, like Augustus, they found their cities brick, and left them marble: seldom, we may conjecture, could they fail to offer the substantial boon of material prosperity. But the city-state, an association of equals, managed on a system of primary government, had no room for a generation of men like Henry VIII. or Louis XI.; and the seat of the tyrant was always instable, because it could never be fixed in a solid and permanent consent. We hardly need inquire into the reasons of movements for the overthrow of tyrannies: it is obvious that in the face of a tyrant the sense of injustice, which is Aristotle's fundamental reason for all revolutions, must have been especially quick. It is more pertinent to ask—How could a tyranny possibly be saved? There are two ways suggested by Aristotle. One is the old way indicated by Periander, when he took the envoy of a fellow-tyrant into a corn-field, and quietly decapitated the tallest ears. It is the aim of this method to make the subjects *unable* to revolt: it is the aim of another, and—Aristotle is inclined to think—a better method, to make them *unwilling* to do so. The old traditional way of the school of Periander was calculated to produce a city, in which all were crushed into a level uniformity of subjection, and each was isolated from his neighbour: a city in which spies were always peering about, and men were set to toil at great buildings: a city in whose streets were often seen the banners of alien troops, and in whose centre rose a palace with its gates haunted by loafers, and its courts full of flatterers and slaves. Three things, says Aristotle, does a tyrant of this school seek—that his subjects should turn to mean thoughts and material things, that they should distrust one another, and that they should become powerless for political action. Far other are the aims of the better way which Isocrates had preached before Aristotle, and which Machiavelli was to preach centuries afterwards.[1] These aims exactly correspond to the general principles for the preservation of constitutions which we have already studied. The tyrant indeed can hardly educate the citizens in the spirit of the polity; but he can—and Aristotle desires that he shall—attempt to conciliate the good-will of his subjects. He can use his giant's strength, not like a giant, but in moderation and within limits: he can refrain from using his power and his office as a source of gain. A wise tyrant will accordingly maintain himself in the position of arbitrator of social strife, in which he originally began: he will stand, like Solon, "with his shield held aloft over rich and poor alike," preventing either from doing or suffering injustice: he will, at the very least, win either the poor or the rich to his side, taking care to attract the stronger of the two. In every way he will aim at moderation. He will control his passions into the show of morality: he will appease the religious as well as the moral sentiment of his people. He will not raise up a Grand Vizier to his side, but will use a number of ministers: he will reward

[1] *Cf. infra*, Epilogue, § 2, *ad finem*.

the good citizens himself, and the bad he will punish by means of his agents. He will adorn the city as if he were its guardian rather than its tyrant: he will act as if he were steward of the city's interests, and not a seeker of his own advantages. He will tax lightly and spend rightly: he will give a public account of his incomings and outgoings; and playing the part of servant and guardian and steward, he will hide his private authority under the cloak of official duty. He will speak of "reasons of State" and the "Commonwealth": he will speak of the "Crown" rather than the king, the "State" rather than the government. So shall his days be prolonged, and he himself shall become, if not a good man, yet at any rate not a bad man, and die the half of an honest man, if also the half of a knave.

EPILOGUE

THE HISTORY OF THE *POLITICS*[1]

§ 1. IN the autumn of 336 B.C. Alexander asked and obtained from the deputies of the Greek cities assembled at Corinth, what his father had obtained two years before, the position of generalissimo of Greece with full powers for the prosecution of the war against Persia. At the same time he sanctioned a convention, which his father had also made before, which "recognised Hellas as a confederacy under the Macedonian prince as imperator".[2] By this convention existing constitutions were guaranteed: no city was to attack, or to aid political refugees in attacking, any other city; and every city was bound to discourage confiscations and spoliations, re-division of estates and abolition of debts. Without and within, stability was thus secured; but it was secured by the institution of a federal authority with a power of federal execution. One of the provisions of the convention ran: "The council (*οἱ συνεδρεύοντες*) and those appointed for the common protection shall see that in the contracting cities there are no confiscations or outlawries in contravention of existing laws". This, then, was the end of political selfishness and civil strife. Neither the enlightened monarchy which Plato had suggested, nor the mediating middle class on which Aristotle set his hopes, could avail to save the city-state; and to be rescued from itself it had to lose its cherished independence.

The death of the city-state

Henceforth the political thought of the Greeks was destined to run in other channels. The Macedonian Empire, which had superseded the city as the real and effective unit of politics, did not, indeed, develop any political theory of empire to take the

[1] For the history of the *Republic*, see Appendix B.
[2] Grote, xi., 340.

Stoic cosmopolitanism

place of the old theory of the city. It acted rather as a bridge, by which thought passed from the narrow unit of the city to the whole world; and the political theory which it helped to produce was that of cosmopolitanism. This theory is prominent in Stoicism. Zeno, the great Stoic, taught, as we have seen, that men should not live scattered in separate demes and cities, with separate laws; the whole world should form one city, with one order and one law. "The poet hath said, Dear City of Cecrops," wrote a later Stoic; "wilt thou not also say, Dear City of God?" Here, as with the Cynics, cosmopolitanism is connected with individualism. The wise man will determine his life for himself—according to the law of the world. He will not be instructed or habituated by a city: he will of himself make it his aim to live "conformably to Nature". To live conformably to Nature was to live by a law which no man had enacted, and which was the same for all: it was to live in a city of God which no man had made, and which included all who had wisdom enough to enter—bond as well as free. A spiritual city, with a spiritual law, thus superseded for the Stoic the city visible, and its enacted and written law. He retired from things visible upon things unseen:[1] he became a subject of the kingdom of Heaven, ruled by a spiritual law; and he entered into that kingdom by his own spiritual insight. It is obvious that we are here in the circle of ideas of Christianity. We are moving from the πόλις to the Universal Church, whose law is of God, and its citizenship by faith. It was natural that the Fathers of the Church should borrow, as they did, the political theory of the Stoics—its conceptions of a universal communion, a natural law, and the equality of all men before that law.[2]

Yet the Stoics had not departed utterly from the πόλις or from statutory law. Though the wise man was sufficient without any city, and though his true State was the world, he would not abandon the city of his birth. *Noblesse oblige*, and the

[1] "The service of the gods needed no temple, education (which was only disgraced by popular methods) no schools, justice no courts, commerce no coinage, sexual intercourse no restriction by the ties of marriage" (Henkel, *Studien*, p. 99).

[2] Stoicism thus departs from Aristotle in two ways. It deserts the πόλις for the cosmopolis; and it abandons slavery (which was the basis of the πόλις), asserting the equality of all men in the "city of God".

wise man will legislate for his citizens; he will join in the social life of his city by marriage; he will even meet danger and death for its sake.[1] Stoic philosophers even indulged in the construction of ideal States. What engaged the attention of the Stoics most was the theory of the mixed constitution. Using Sparta as their model, they advocated, as we have seen, a mixture of monarchy, oligarchy, and democracy as the ideal form of constitution. Retaining in this way, and even seeking to improve, the city and its government, they also left room for its laws. They distinguished between φύσις and θέσις, Nature and Convention; but they did not include all enacted law in the sphere of convention. On the contrary, in the manner of Heraclitus, they regarded enacted law as an emanation from natural law; and they were able to keep together, and in harmony, the conception of a *jus naturale* and a *jus civile*. In the conception of a mixed constitution, and in that of a natural law which does not destroy, but may inform and improve the law of the State, the Stoics greatly influenced the Romans.[2]

Political theory of the Church

But while the conception of a city might thus be retained by the Stoics, the march of history inevitably destroyed its meaning. The world-empire of Alexander, succeeded by centuries of universal domination by Rome, made the world the one actual unit of politics; and the teaching of the Christian Church, which recognised one body of all the faithful, strengthened by a spiritual sanction the trend of secular affairs. Political philosophy became the philosophy of universal empire: in 1300 the *De Monarchia* of Dante still shows this width of view. But at the same time that the unit of political thought gained in extension, it lost in intensity of meaning. Membership of a universal empire in any case means but little; but membership of any secular organisation, however great or small, could mean little indeed to minds imbued with Christianity, and counting things spiritual the only things of price. The State came to be

[1] Ritter and Preller (8th ed.), § 523.

[2] The political teaching of the Epicureans was not so immediately fruitful; but its central tenet of a social contract was destined to exercise a great influence in modern Europe. The Epicurean definition of the State regarded it as based on "a covenant neither to injure nor to be injured". The State was thus based on mere utility; and law was identified with the terms of a contract. For what is practically the Epicurean position, *cf. supra*, p. 99.

despised. By its side there rose, overshadowing its dignity and claims, the spiritual organisation of the Church. The divorce between the spiritual world and its organisation, and the secular world and its institutions, had already appeared in Stoicism, in the antithesis of the Civitas Dei and the "city of Cecrops": it appeared still more definitely when a Church organised under the Pope confronted a State subject to the emperor. Since the Church, the city of God, was the one real and vital organisation, the State necessarily sank to a secondary position. It was a result of original sin: it would never have existed but for Adam's fall.[1] Its mission was preventive: it existed merely to do the sordid work of executioner. It was inferior to the Church: it was set to defend and exalt her authority.[2] The old Greek conception of the State, as an ethical community, engaged in actively furthering a life of virtue, perished. Divested of its ethical meaning, the State assumed a purely judicial and legal character: it became, as the Stoic Cleanthes had said, an "erection to which men might have recourse for getting or giving justice".

Adoption of Aristotle by the Mediæval Church

§ 2. It might seem, *a priori*, as if the coming of the Reformation and the emergence of the nation-state in the sixteenth century would be the signal for a return—the first return—to Aristotle's conception of the State. The Reformation meant a liberation of the State from subjection to the Church: the nation-state was a unit narrower than the world-empire, and nearer to the old city-state. The one seems to involve a higher view of the State's province: the other makes possible a closer relation of the individual to the State in a vital "association". But the result of the Reformation in the sphere of political thought was, if anything, hostile to the old Aristotelian view of the State. And the reason was that in the thirteenth century the Mediæval Church had adopted Aristotle; and the Reformation rejected Aristotle as one of the mediæval superstitions. The *Politics* did not come to the Middle Ages, as many treatises

[1] The view is enunciated by St. Augustine (*De Civ. Dei*, xix., 15); and to Gregory VII. kingship is "the invention of those who in ignorance of God, and by the instigation of the Devil, have presumed to tyrannise over their equals" (*Epp.*, viii., 21).

[2] This is the view enshrined in the English coronation oath, by which the king swears to defend the Church, and to repress *rapinas et iniquitates*.

of Aristotle did, through the Arabs. It had not attracted the scholars of Cordova, who confined their Aristotelian studies to his logical and metaphysical writings. Averroes wrote on politics; but he only wrote a paraphrase of the *Republic* of Plato—a paraphrase of no originality, which stolidly accepts, and amplifies or illustrates, Plato's most novel suggestions, proving, for instance, that women are suited for war by the example of certain African tribes. There was no basis in Arabic politics and civilisation for the building of an Aristotelian system of politics. It was quite otherwise in the Christian West. The growth of political theory in the Church had prepared the way for the "reception" of some of the main Aristotelian ideas: the struggle of empire and papacy, since 1076, had produced a shower of pamphlets, *libelli de lite imperatorum et pontificum*, and given a new impulse to political thought; while the vigorous political life of the thirteenth century, especially visible in England, formed a natural soil for the new seed.

Preparation for Aristotle

The distinction between king and tyrant is one very old in the Fathers.[1] The Gospels spoke of obedience to the powers that be; but a distinction had to be drawn between the powers that be and the powers that ought not to be,[2] and here the Old Testament, with its story of the rejection of Saul, was a natural fountain of inspiration. Chrysostom already suggests the distinction; and it appears in the *Etymology* of St. Isidore of Seville, a work which formed one of the great repertories of the Middle Ages.[3] The true king is distinguished from the tyrant by one great feature: he rules under the limitation of law. St. Augustine, the chief source of political thought before the reception of Aristotle, was understood in the ninth century as teaching that the king is bound by the law; and Hincmar of Reims sustains the theory of limited monarchy, quoting the dictum of St. Augustine, "that men judge the laws when they

[1] I have endeavoured to show, in the next two paragraphs, that, while the *essence* of the ecclesiastical theory of the State was anti-Aristotelian, there were elements in that theory which might be harmonised with Aristotle.

[2] This is the problem attacked by St. Thomas in his commentary on the *Sentences*, *super* Distinct. xlv. (quoted by Janet, *Hist. de la Sci. Polit.*, i., 418-19).

[3] Carlyle, *Mediæval Political Theory*, i., 222, n. 2; Isidore distinguishes *rex* and *tyrannus*.

make them, but when they are once made, the judge cannot judge them, but must act in accordance with them ".[1] Two texts from Roman Law offered some difficulties: if it be true that *rex legibus solutus est*, and if *quod principi placuit legis habet vigorem* be a good definition of law, what shall we say of the king's subordination to law? [2] But men rose superior to legal texts; and they continued to think, in spite of them, that the true king was distinguished from the tyrant by his respect for the law. In the *Polycraticus*, John of Salisbury is even willing to accept the *reductio ad extremum* of the doctrine, and to preach that tyrannicide is justifiable, even when it is accomplished by perfidy. A theory of monarchy as limited by law, with its corollary of the subject's right to resist, if the monarch tyrannically violated the law, was thus, at the end of the twelfth century, accepted by the keenest intellect of his age. In the thirteenth century the theory reappears in the pages of the great lawyer Bracton. In a passage (perhaps interpolated) in the *De Legibus*, he declares that the king has for his superior God, his court, *and the law;* while elsewhere he declares that if the king does wrong, the *universitas regni* and the baronage may be regarded as having the duty and power of correcting and amending the wrong.

Along with this theory (which finds its practical expression in Magna Carta) there went the idea that the king was "ordained for the common good". In almost every thinker of the time, law is defined "as a rule of action regarding the common good". If this be the definition of law, and if the monarch is limited by the law, it follows that the monarch is limited to the pursuit of the common good of his subjects. From this again, the further conclusions may be drawn, that the monarch is instituted by the people whose good he seeks, and that he should consult them with regard to the measures which their common good demands. The whole of this position is expressed most piquantly in the *Song of Lewes*, a Latin poem written by some Franciscan friar in 1264 in support of Simon de Montfort. The "root of perturbation," he argues, is the principle maintained

[1] Carlyle, *ut supra*, p. 234; *cf.* St. Augustine, *De Ver. Relig.*, 31 (quoted on p. 164, n. 1).

[2] This difficulty is solved by St. Thomas, *Summa*, *Prima Secundæ*, *qu.* xc.

by Henry III., that the will of the prince has the force of law:

> quod imperaret
> Suomet arbitrio singulos ligaret.[1]

To this principle he replies by a direct negative:

> Legem quoque dicimus regis dignitatem
> Regere, nam credimus esse legem lucem,
> Sine qua concludimus deviare ducem.[2]

The writer "has never heard that *rex* is *lex*; but he holds it most common and true that *lex* is *rex*":

> Ista lex sic loquitur: per me regnant reges,
> Per me jus ostenditur hijs qui condunt leges.
> Istam legem stabilem nullus rex mutabit,
> Set se variabilem per istam firmabit.[3]

If the king be thus under the law, he must rule for the common weal, since law is the ordinance of those things which tend thereunto:

> Et rex nichil proprium preferat communi,
> Quia salus omnium sibi cessit uni;
> Non enim preponitur sibimet victurus,
> Sed ut hic qui subditur populus securus.[4]

Further, the friar contends (in an argument which shows a very true conception of the real meaning of liberty), in limitation by the law lies true liberty; and "to force a king to be free," a people may have to resist him when he becomes a slave to passion and tyranny.

> Non omnis artacio privat libertatem,
> Non omnis districtio tollit potestatem. . . .
> Qui regem custodiunt ne peccet temptatus,
> Ipsi regi serviunt, quibus esse gratus
> Sit, quod ipsum liberant ne sit servus factus,
> Quod ipsum non superant a quibus est tractus.[5]

But this corollary of lawful resistance is only drawn *in extremis*: in normal times a milder result follows from the limitation of the king to the pursuit of his people's good, and that is the need of parliamentary institutions:

> Igitur *communitas regni* consulatur,
> Et quid universitas sentiat sciatur.[6]

[1] Lines 503-4. [2] Lines 848-50. [3] Lines 865-68.
[4] Lines 893-96. [5] Lines 667-68; 688-92. [6] Lines 765-66.

It was on a soil thus prepared that the *Politics* of Aristotle fell in the latter half of the thirteenth century. Aristotle had never been forgotten in the West: on the contrary his logic had, in Latin translations and in commentaries like those of Boethius, been studied assiduously for centuries. But the physical and metaphysical, ethical and political treatises of Aristotle had been on the whole unknown; and it was these which the Christian West recovered, step by step, during the thirteenth century. Much came from the Arabs, in translations, often made by Jews, of the paraphrases of Avicenna or the commentaries of Averroes. But the *Ethics* and the *Politics* came directly in translations from the original Greek. St. Thomas was using before 1262 a Latin translation of the *Ethics*: by about 1270 William Moerbecke, "the Fleming" of Brabant, who was translating Aristotle at the instance of St. Thomas, had produced the first Latin translation of the *Politics*.[1] This translation, the *Vetus Versio*, as it is called, if so literal as to be almost unintelligible, is nevertheless a faithful translation of a better Greek text than any we now possess. In the next hundred years this translation had served as the basis for works, many of which are still known and quoted, and some of which are among the books that do not die. A commentary on the *Politics* (not, as is usual with the universal doctor, a *paraphrase* in the manner of Avicenna) is ascribed to the pen of Albert the Great. In four of the many works of St. Thomas the influence of Aristotle appears—in the commentary on the *Sentences* of Peter the Lombard, in the *Summa Theologiæ*, in the *De Regimine Principum*, and in the *Expositio* (or Commentary) *in octo libros Politicorum Aristotelis*. The *De Regimine Principum* of Ægidius Romanus is merely a systematisation of the *Politics*: the *Defensor Pacis* of Marsilio of Padua is an adaptation of the *Politics* to modern conditions. Dante refers again and again to the *Politics* in the *De Monarchia*: Nicholas Oresme translated it into French, and made it the basis of a treatise on political economy. In the beginning of the fourteenth century Burley wrote a commentary upon it at Oxford, and Buridan wrote *Quæstiones* at Paris: a little earlier Siger of Brabant is reported (like several other doctors) "to have expounded the *Politics* in a revolutionary spirit".[2]

Reception of Aristotle

[1] See Sandys, *History of Classical Scholarship*, pp. 562-63. [2] *Ibid.*, p. 565.

It is obvious that the quasi-democratic theory of the *Song of Lewes* was one which was well calculated to serve the interests of the Church. The Papacy, engaged in its struggle with the Empire, could find no better weapon with which to confound emperors than the rights of the people. Manegold, one of the early pamphleteers in the interminable strife, had made great play with this weapon. "The People exalts one man that he may govern and rule men justly. If he breaks the contract (*pactum*) under which he was chosen, the people are free from the duty of submission, since he has first failed to keep faith." [1] It was natural that St. Thomas, the great champion of the Church, should adopt this line of thought, and allow his Aristotelianism to run along these channels; and accordingly his work may be said to be the harmonisation of the political theory of the Church (proceeding ultimately from St. Augustine) with the forms of Aristotle's *Politics*. Starting from the same teleological point of view which runs through the thought of "the Philosopher" (as Aristotle is generally termed in the Middle Ages), St. Thomas lays down, first and foremost, a theory of law.[2] "Law is a rule and standard of action: the rule and standard of human action is reason; for it is the function of reason to order things to *an end*, which is the first beginning in action, according to the Philosopher." To Aquinas, then, as to Aristotle, law is identical with reason.[3] Now the end towards which reason orders all actions is happiness; and law contains the rules which make for happiness. But "since the part is always adjusted to the whole, and man is a part of a community, the happiness which the law regards must be a common happiness". Law must create and preserve happiness for a whole political society (*supra*, p. 322). And granted that law contains the rules for the common good, it follows that "to make ordinances for the *common* good belongs either to a whole *commonalty*, or to some man who carries the person of a whole commonalty; and therefore the making of law appertains either to the whole

St. Thomas Aquinas

[1] Quoted in Kingsford's edition of the *Song of Lewes*, p. 130. The idea of the social contract thus springs from the conception of the king as limited by law.

[2] *Summa Theologiæ, Prima Secundæ, qu.* xc.

[3] *Cf. supra*, p. 321; and for the conception of reason as acting towards an end, pp. 126, 239.

commonalty, or to some public person who has the care of the whole commonalty". Accordingly, when he comes to treat of government in another passage[1] of the *Summa*, St. Thomas can postulate, *quod omnes aliquam partem habent in principatu*, since such participation means a universal consent to the government. Further, he can borrow from Aristotle the principle, that the best governments are monarchy and aristocracy, in which the One or the Few rule according to virtue. And thus, combining the postulate of universal participation with the principle of the excellence of monarchy and aristocracy, St. Thomas concludes in favour of a *mixed government*, or, in other words, constitutional monarchy. *Unde optima ordinatio principum est in aliqua civitate vel regno, in qua unus preficitur secundum virtutem qui omnibus præsit, et sub ipso sunt aliqui principantes secundum virtutem; et tamen talis principatus ad omnes pertinet, tum quia ex omnibus eligi possunt, tum quia etiam ab omnibus eliguntur.*

This is the theory of the *Summa*.[2] The theory of the *De Regimine Principum* seems somewhat different; but the principles are really the same. In the beginning of the *De Regimine* St. Thomas seems to argue simply for monarchy, and that on Platonic principles: "the good and the safety of an associated commonalty lies in the preservation of its unity . . . whereunto the government of one is most efficacious".[3] But we soon find that this monarchy is constitutional monarchy, and that the mixed government is still the ideal of St. Thomas. The monarch is both instituted and limited by the commonalty. "If it pertains to the right of a commonalty to institute a king, the king whom it has instituted may without injustice be destroyed, or his power may be limited, by the community, if he use his royal power tyrannically."[4] And St. Thomas even asserts, like Manegold, that a king turned tyrant "does not deserve that the *pact* should be kept by his subjects". In much the same spirit he argues, in the *Summa* itself, that it is not sedition to overthrow a tyrannical government. Here is the

[1] *Summa, Prima Secundæ, qu.* cv.

[2] The *Summa* is said to have been written by St. Thomas before he was acquainted with the *Politics*. It seems to me that the doctrines here quoted rest on the *Politics*; but in any case St. Thomas used the political teaching of the *Ethics*.

[3] *De Reg. Princ.*, i., c. ii.

[4] *Ibid.*, i., c. vi.

doctrine of the *Song of Lewes;* and the parallel is still more striking when we read in the *De Regimine* that liberty consists in obedience to a government which governs in the common interest. But while, in this way, St. Thomas interprets Aristotle into conformity with the democratic principles which suited the interests of the Church, it must also be admitted that he gives his adhesion to Aristotelian doctrines which the Church can hardly have welcomed with such readiness. From the first there had been in the Church a tendency to theoretic belief in communism, and St. Augustine had taught that according to natural law all things were common; yet St. Thomas defends private property. From very early days the Church had professed an equally theoretic belief in the natural equality of all men; yet St. Thomas argues in favour of slavery. In regard to property, it is true, the Aristotelian formula was elastic enough to be reconciled readily with St. Augustine; and by following the distinction between κτῆσις and χρῆσις—between *potestas procurandi et dispensandi,* which demands private property, and *usus,* which demands that men should have their goods in common, St. Thomas was able to effect the reconciliation.[1] In the matter of slavery Aristotle was less pliable; but St. Thomas, while refusing to accept Aristotle's position that there was any reason *in nature* for slavery (and thereby preserving the opinion of the Fathers), was able to justify slavery, not only on the Aristotelian ground of its utility to master and slave, but also by the more Christian argument of the results of original sin.[2] On the whole, therefore, we may say that St. Thomas makes Aristotle's politics, like Aristotle's logic, the faithful handmaid of the Church. Nowhere, perhaps, does this appear more strikingly than in St. Thomas's one great departure from Aristotle's teleology. To Aristotle man had one final cause, and he found its attainment in the πόλις: to St. Thomas man has two ends, one temporal, one spiritual, and he needs two societies,

[1] *Summa, Secunda Secundæ, qu.* lxvi.

[2] Like Aristotle, St. Thomas rejects legal or conventional slavery. It is therefore surprising to find such slavery admitted and justified in the second book of the *De Regimine.* But this only goes to prove (what the distinction maintained in the second book between royal power and ἀρχὴ πολιτική also helps to show) that the later books of the *De Regimine* are not by St. Thomas. St. Thomas's share extends to somewhere about book ii., chapter viii.: the later books are generally assigned to Ptolemy of Lucca.

the Church and the State. And of these the end to be found in the Church is the greater end, and the Church itself is the greater society.[1]

It is impossible here to attempt to trace the influence of St. Thomas's Aristotelianism. Three thinkers may, however, be noticed, the one because he is so greatly indebted to Aristotle, the others because they are great names in English political thought. The *De Regimine Principum* of Ægidius Romanus, addressed to Philippe le Bel, is a recasting of the *Politics* for the edification of the prince.[2] Ægidius follows Aristotle closely and obediently: his great merit lies in his neat systematisation of material drawn from the *Ethics* and the *Politics*. He devotes his first book to a theory of self-government, or ethics; his second to domestic government, or economics; his third to the government of the State, or politics. One new and interesting feature is the addition which he makes to the sketch of political development which comes at the beginning of the *Politics*. Besides the family, the village, and the city, there is the kingdom, "a confederation of territories and cities under a single prince or king, of service in making war against the enemy, and averting the dangers which threaten family, village and city".[3] The guiding thread of Ægidius' treatise is the old distinction, reinforced from Aristotle, between the king and the tyrant, between unselfish and selfish government. The same distinction reappears in the fifteenth century, in the pages of the English lawyer Fortescue. Following Aquinas and the mediæval publicists, he divides governments into two main classes—*dominium regale*, established by the aggression of individuals, and *dominium politicum*, established by the institution of the nations. The King of England, he thinks, is a *rex politicus*.

The School of Aquinas

[1] Is it not true that the mediæval schoolmen, in adopting the *Politics* into their system, were adopting something in large part alien both to the facts of their time, with its Universal Church and Universal Empire, and to current ecclesiastical ideas of the State, as due to original sin, and confined in its function to the punishment of crime? It would seem that there is a contradiction at the core of mediæval Aristotelianism. Men quietly taught the philosophy of the πόλις under the shadow of the Civitas Dei. They spoke of kings as furthering the *Good* of mankind, where the Church had regarded them as executioners.

[2] I follow the account of this treatise given by Janet, *Hist. de la Sci. Polit.*, i., 439 *sqq*.

[3] *De Reg. Princ.*, ii., i., iv. (quoted in Janet, *op. cit.*, p. 442).

He exists for the sake of the kingdom (or, as Aristotle would say, his rule is in the interest of the governed); and his institution is meant to secure the safety of his subjects' laws, their persons, and their goods. Law is not his will: *quod principi placuit legis habet vigorem* means nothing in England.[1] Like Fortescue in the fifteenth century, Hooker at the end of the sixteenth is still under the influence of scholastic Aristotelianism. In his political theory Hooker may almost be termed a belated mediævalist. Following St. Thomas, he postulates in the first book of the *Ecclesiastical Polity,* that "the lawful power of making laws to command whole politic societies of men belongeth properly unto the same entire societies".[2] Like St. Thomas and Aristotle, he believes that "we are naturally induced to seek communion and fellowship with others . . . forasmuch as we are not by ourselves sufficient to furnish ourselves with competent store of things needful for such a life as our nature doth desire".[3] He speaks of men, it is true, as "growing unto *composition and agreement* amongst themselves by ordaining some kind of government public,"[4] and it is from the *Ecclesiastical Polity* that Locke quotes in justification of his theory of the social contract; but St. Thomas had spoken of a *pactum,* and Aristotle had regarded the State as originally "constructed"[5] by man. Yet Hooker remains a Janus-like figure, and while he looks backward to Aquinas and Aristotle, he looks forward to Locke and Rousseau. Through him the Aristotelianism of the Middle Ages helped to found a theory of original contract, utterly different from itself, and bitterly hostile to its own teaching.

When we turn from St. Thomas and his school to Dante, we enter upon a new atmosphere. St. Thomas was a Churchman and a Guelf: Dante was a layman and a Ghibelline. St. Dante Thomas wrote to defend Holy Church: Dante, like Marsilio of Padua after him, wrote to defend the Holy Roman Empire. St. Thomas, again, had erected upon Aristotelian foundations a

[1] Stubbs, *Constit. Hist.*, iii., 247. Fortescue however makes the English constitution, strictly speaking, a *dominium regale et politicum,* because, while the government is conducted by an administration in which the many participate, the authority of the king is required for making law.

[2] *Eccl. Polit.*, i., x., 8.

[3] *Ibid.*, i., x., 1.

[4] *Ibid.*, i., x., 4.

[5] *Pol.*, 1253 a 30.

regular system: Dante starts from a theory of the unity of the world which is almost Platonic, and a conception of the continuity of the empire which is certainly non-Aristotelian, and supports both by scattered citations and references from all the Aristotelian writings, physical or metaphysical, ethical or political. In the *De Monarchia*—a waste of learning shot through by a historic imagination—Dante, appealing to the "venerable authority of the Philosopher," starts from the principle that it is the end of man *actuare semper totam potentiam intellectus possibilis;* whereunto he needs "the tranquillity of peace".[1] Such peace is best secured by the rule of a single man,[2] or monarchy; but of monarchies there are two kinds. There is true monarchy, and there is false monarchy, or tyranny, which prevails in perverted polities. The true monarch rules for his subjects' good: *non enim cives propter Consules, nec gens propter Regem; sed e converso Consules propter cives, et Rex propter gentem.*[3] In such a right polity, therefore, and in such a right polity only, is true liberty to be found: *et hujusmodi politiæ rectæ libertatem intendunt, scilicet ut homines propter se sint.*[4] So far, the argument would have received St. Thomas' assent: it is when Dante pushes his principle of unity to the conclusion that the world forms a single society, whose peace needs a single Emperor, that he departs definitely from canonical opinion. The use of an historical method to support this thesis is also new and striking; while the conclusion to which Dante ultimately comes, that there is no basis for the temporal power of the papacy, is in direct contradiction to the doctrine of St. Thomas—*papa . . . utriusque potestatis apicem tenet*[5]—and in close agreement with the views of Marsilio of Padua.

Marsilio of Padua

It is, perhaps, in Marsilio of Padua that Aristotelian influence is most remarkable.[6] It has been said that whereas

[1] *De Monarch.*, i., iv.

[2] *Cf.* St. Thomas, *De Reg. Princ.*, i., c. ii., quoted above.

[3] *Cf.* (Ptolemy of Lucca) *De Reg. Princ.*, iii., ii., *regnum non est propter regem, sed rex propter regnum.*

[4] *De Mon.*, i. c. xii.

[5] *Commentary on the Sentences*, Distinct. xlv., q. lxvii. (quoted in Janet, *op. cit.*, p. 423). But, like St. Thomas, Dante admits that man has two ends, two societies, two guides; while, in opposition to the ecclesiastical view, he contends that both are equally ordained of God. See the last chapter of the *De Monarchia*.

[6] Because, unlike St. Thomas, he does not simply comment on or borrow from the *Politics*, but works through their teaching systematically; while,

Wycliffe built a somewhat unreal and detached political theory upon feudal law and scholastic logic—a theory which imagined man as holding of God by tenure of grace, Marsilio, his predecessor, founded a real and practical philosophy upon the civic life of the Italian commune and Aristotle's *Politics*. Marsilio was happy in the agreement of his two bases. Nothing in modern history corresponds better to the *πόλις* of Aristotle than the Italian cities of the Middle Ages. Machiavelli, as we shall see, drew upon Aristotle, and particularly upon the three books of practical politics, for the express purpose of elucidating the agencies destructive or preservative of the constitutions of those cities. It is from these same books, and from their theory of the agencies destructive of the State, that Marsilio also starts. But he also uses the whole general theory of the State laid down in Aristotle's first three books; and he writes with a purpose quite his own—to demolish the grounds alleged for the interference of the papacy with the affairs of the State, and particularly with those of the empire, whose ruler, Lewis IV., he defended with his pen against Pope John XXII. in the last great struggle of empire and papacy. Aristotle, says the opening chapter of the *Defensor Pacis*, omitted one cause of revolution, or *intranquillitas*—a cause springing from an agency produced long after Aristotle's time by the Supreme Cause beyond all the probabilities of ordinary nature—to wit, papal interference. In the second chapter Marsilio borrows the Aristotelian analogy of the State and the body (quoting the relevant passages in the *Politics*) to prove that as health is the proper state of the body, so is *tranquillitas* the best disposition of a State, by which each part will be able to discharge its proper function. The third chapter discusses the origin of the State—for Marsilio has to trace the origin and analyse the composition of the State in order to get full and satisfactory grounds for rejecting papal interference. The discussion follows Aristotle: the growth is traced through household and village to the State; but Aristotle's views are expanded with some original power. It is argued that law first arose in the village; for within the household the father might forgive his

unlike Aegidius Romanus (who has the same feature of a regular system), he not only adopts, but also adapts, that teaching.

son, but unless an equal law is administered and all wrongdoers punished within the village, dissensions and struggles will arise. In words which anticipate the modern category of evolution, Marsilio suggests that the early State had no articulation of parts, and that the progress of men meant increasing differentiation within the State. But before explaining the rise of different organs within the State he first discusses, as a necessary preliminary, the end or aim of the State. The end of the State is *vivere et bene vivere,* as Aristotle had said; and without the State these ends cannot be secured. Life may be used in two senses—physical and moral. In both the State is necessary. It is necessary for physical life, to protect man from the dissolution of his body by giving him food, and from the outer elements by giving him clothing and furniture. The adequate supply of these things involves arts, which cannot be exercised except by a plurality, nor their products had except by exchange. But exchange implies already a need of justice; and thus the physical side of man entails an economic association with its regulative justice—or, in other words, a State. But the State is supremely necessary for *moral* life. Within the moral life of man come actions and passions; and these need regulation to prevent excess, or stimulus to produce a due measure. The giving of such regulation or stimulus is the work of the State. These considerations of the end of the State suggest its division into parts. Following Aristotle, Marsilio makes six parts—an agricultural part, a manufacturing part, and a *pars thesaurizans* for physical life; and a judicial, a military or executive, and a sacerdotal part for both physical and moral life. For Marsilio's own purpose, the point of importance is the position to be assigned to the sacerdotal part. It is treated as only one part of the State (and not an *imperium in imperio*), instituted for the same reason as the rest (*vitæ sufficientia*), and under the control both of the people, who instituted it along with other parts, and of the sovereign part (*pars principans*), which, itself created and controlled by the people, creates and controls the other parts. To the student of political philosophy, however, it is most interesting to notice how Marsilio follows or expands Aristotle in discussing the institution of the ruling part of the State and its relation to its subjects. In the opinion of Marsilio, as the apostle of *tranquillitas*, the ruling part or power is the judicial: it is first instituted, and by it are instituted the other powers. The sovereign is therefore principally and essentially a judicature. Of sovereigns there are two kinds, the constitutional (*temperatus*) and the perverted (*vitiatus*): the former is directed to the common advantage, the latter to the monarch's private interest. The former therefore rules willing, the latter unwilling, subjects. Here in Marsilio reappears the Aristotelian distinction of constitutions, which we have seen used by St. Thomas and Dante and Fortescue. That the will of the subjects of a constitutional sovereign accepts the rule of the monarch readily suggests, by a natural extension, that the institution of a sovereign is by the election of his people. Marsilio proves that it must be so by an elaborate Aristotelian argument. The prince should regulate all civil acts by rule, that is, according to law. Now the same authority which creates law should also, Marsilio holds, create the sovereign. What then is law?—for this must first be decided in order that its proper author may be discovered, since the true nature of law will decide its right author. Marsilio analyses the conception of law into different species—law in the scientific sense, like physiological laws; law in the sense of rules of construction in the arts; divine law; and lastly civil law, which is the particular law discussed by political theory.[1] In this last sense law is a universal judgment defining what is just and expedient in a State, enforced by a temporal sanction. The necessity of such a law is proved on Aristotelian principles: without an inflexibly general law the sovereign might be swayed by a particular bias; nor has the sovereign the knowledge which is embodied in law, where the experience of time is crystallised. Who then is the true maker of law thus defined? The answer is, that such a universal judgment is properly made by the universal body of the citizens or a major part thereof (*universitas civium aut ejus valentior pars*). And for this view Marsilio quotes the *Politics*, referring to the passage in the third

[1] This analysis of the conception of law is remarkable. St. Thomas, however, has also a division of law into four kinds—eternal, natural, human, and divine; and one may compare with St. Thomas' teaching Marsilio's conception of law as originating in the people.

book, where Aristotle discusses the claims of the people, and speaks of their power of collective judgment and their right of electing the executive. Marsilio supports his view of the people's right to legislate by arguing that the generality of the people will best see the general advantage; that the people will readily observe laws passed by themselves, and quickly resent laws imposed from without; and that, in any case, the maxim ought to be obeyed, *quod omnes tangit, ab omnibus approbetur.* The people thus makes the laws: the people, therefore, has the institution of the sovereign. The doctrine of ultimate popular sovereignty is thus enunciated by Marsilio, and supported by arguments from the *Politics.* Yet the whole atmosphere of the argument is modern and remote from Aristotle. Marsilio seems to use arguments from Aristotle to support conclusions which anticipate Rousseau. Though he looks backward in his form, his substance is an anticipation of what was yet to come. While he anticipates Luther, in arguing that the Church is the congregation of all the faithful (and not merely the hierarchy), and that the lay power is competent to supervise and correct the hierarchy (two principles which—and particularly the latter—go deep into the essence of the Reformation), he is also the forerunner of the days of the social contract.[1] But while to a historian he must rank as a prophet of that which was to come, to an Aristotelian his interest lies in the Aristotelian form and basis of his views. It is true that he "interprets" his author, and that some of his conclusions from Aristotelian premisses might have made Aristotle gasp. The legislator of Aristotle, for instance, is a philosopher trained in political science, knowing the end of life, and guiding others by his knowledge; yet on Aristotelian principles of the collective judgment of the masses Marsilio assigns this high position to the university of the citizens. But it cannot be denied that he understood the *Politics,* and expounded or expanded Aristotle with considerable original power. His *Defensor Pacis* may

[1] It must be noted that the practical contemporary fact behind Marsilio's theory of the power of the *universitas civium* was the recrudescence of the power of the *populus Romanus* during the papal absence at Avignon. A decree of the Roman people had altered the place of imperial coronation for Henry VII.: decrees of the Roman people gave Lewis IV. the imperial crown, and took away from John XXII. the papal tiara.

almost be regarded as a widening of Aristotle to suit the conditions of modern times—as an attempt to find room, within the categories of the *Politics,* for two new things, the Church, and popular legislatures. Nor can it be said that Marsilio was cramped by thinking in Aristotelian forms. It would be truer to say that Aristotle taught Marsilio how to think. Marsilio learned from Aristotle truer doctrines of the origin and aim of the State than those which the contractarian school compounded from Roman law and the Hebrew Scriptures.

Machiavelli

What has been said of Marsilio and his relation to Aristotle's political science may be said of Nicholas Oresme and his relation to Aristotle's economics. His *Tractatus de mutatione monetarum* is based, as we have seen, on the first book of the *Politics;* and Oncken's judgment of this treatise might be applied, word for word, to the *Defensor Pacis:* "where he agrees with Aristotle, he shows a correct understanding of his views, and where he departs from him, he shows independent original reflection and a keen sense for the real truth". But perhaps the most famous author who is indebted to the *Politics* is Machiavelli. When Machiavelli wrote, the Greek text had been printed by the Aldine Press (1498); and a new translation, the first since the *Vetus Versio,* had been made by Lionardo Aretino, early in the fifteenth century, and printed along with the commentary of St. Thomas in 1492.[1] The sixteenth century is the great age of editions and translations of the *Politics;* and modern political theory, which begins with Machiavelli, is nurtured upon Aristotle from its birth. The Prince, it has been said,[2] is a commentary on the last chapter of Aristotle's book on the theory of Revolutions. Machiavelli follows Aristotle's classification of States;[3] but he is most concerned with a prince, especially a new prince or usurper, the tyrant of Aristotle. Both Machiavelli and Aristotle condemn the tyrant. For the one, he is a man without virtue, faith, piety, or religion, a man with no glory, but only power; to the other, "in no respect

[1] This translation is connected with the name of Duke Humphrey of Gloucester, the first English patron of the scholars of the Renaissance.

[2] Lutoslavski: *Die Einteilung und Untergang der Staatsverfassungen nach Platon, Aristoteles, und Machiavelli.*

[3] Or, according to Henkel (*Studien,* p. 106), Polybius' version of the accepted Greek classification.

does the tyrant fall short of evil". Yet both suggest means for the preservation of tyranny. The tyrant must show himself a lover of virtue, says Machiavelli: he must encourage his people to pursue their professions, and give them security that they will not lose their profits; he must delight them with feasts and spectacles; he must in every way exalt his city. "Better than fortresses for a despot is not to be hated by his people." Exactly in the same sense Aristotle suggests that one way of preserving tyranny is to adorn the city; to show respect for religion; not to rob the citizens, but to be a careful steward of their interests. The tyrant should always try to win the affections of his city—of all its people, if possible, or at any rate of one of its two great classes, rich and poor. Yet in spite of his concern for the tyrant, Machiavelli believed, like Aristotle, in the people. They are the best judges; though they go wrong on generalities, they are generally right as to particulars.[1] With this belief in the people, Machiavelli was theoretically an advocate of popular government. But popular government can only exist when a State has been well instituted, and is not yet corrupt. Otherwise a tyrant is needed as a "strong medicine," who by his *virtù* shall redress what is wrong. To Aristotle also a "strong medicine" was necessary for the incessant party strife of the Greek State; but his medicine is a mixed constitution in which both parties share, and by which both parties are contented. Machiavelli too believed—but academically, and for quieter times—in a mixed government which gave scope to prince, nobles, and people; but as the saviour in the stress of the times it is the prince who bulks most largely in his eyes, while it is the mixture of rich and poor in one government that most concerns Aristotle.[2]

§ 3. But Machiavelli cannot be said to be indebted to Aristotle in the same way as mediæval philosophers. His demoralised politics are the opposite of Aristotle's ethical πολιτική. His own keen discernment, directed towards contemporary politics, is his great guide. He does not lay down general principles from Aristotle, and deduce his conclusions: he col-

The revolt against Aristotelianism

[1] Discorsi, i., 47.

[2] Villari (*Machiavelli*, bk. ii., c. ii.) refuses to see any connection with Aristotle in Machiavelli's writings.

lects the facts of the present, or the history of the Roman past, and from them draws his inductions. He is to political philosophy what Bacon was to natural science, the founder of a new method of induction, which nevertheless is not new—for it was Aristotelian. But Aristotelian inductions had been accepted as self-evident principles for deductive use, and had become unreal, because their basis had been forgotten. The age needed an induction of its own, which would make its principles real. It needed to verify the commonplace, which is the eternal task of man. Along with this revolt against the deductive method and against Aristotle as its supposed apostle went a revolt against Aristotle's teleology. "Spinoza, like Bacon, found the assumption of ends, which things were meant to fulfil, in the way of accurate inquiry into what things are (materially) and do. He held Plato and Aristotle cheap as compared with Democritus and Epicurus."[1] The times of contempt of Aristotle follow on the Renaissance and the Reformation.[2] Bacon condemned the "Master of them that know" in the sphere of physical science, though he retained his political philosophy, so far at any rate as to believe in the natural origin of the State. But the *Tractatus Politicus* of Spinoza proceeds from the idea of a State of Nature and a social contract: it conceives man not as a moral agent acting for an end, but as a force, possessed of power. Yet, on the other hand, somewhat inconsistently, Spinoza conceives the State, which he regards as the sum of these forces, as intended to secure a peace consisting in rational virtue. Hobbes is more drastic. In complete revolt against Aristotle he rejects final causes absolutely, and regards man as aiming, not at an "end" of virtuous living, but at mere life. Not only does he reject—he also attacks Aristotle. One cause of the Reformation, says Hobbes, was "the bringing of the Philosophy and doctrine of Aristotle into religion by the Schoolmen"; for so many absurdities arose as a result, that the clergy gained a reputation for ignorance which provoked re-

Spinoza and Hobbes

[1] Green, *Principles of Political Obligation*, p. 57.

[2] It is a significant fact that while in the sixteenth century itself (under the impulse of the Renaissance) there were thirteen editions, six commentaries, and twelve Latin translations of the *Politics*, there was *one* translation and two reprints of old editions in the seventeenth, and only six translations in the eighteenth century (Oncken, *Staatslehre*, i., 79).

bellion. He rebukes Aristotle's doctrine "in the first book of his *Politiques*," which "maketh men by Nature, some more worthy to command, meaning the wiser sort (such as he thought himself to be for his philosophy), others to serve": it is not Nature, but consent of men, that makes such differences. "In these Westerne parts of the world," he says elsewhere, "we are made to receive our opinions concerning the Institution and Rights of Commonwealth from Aristotle, Cicero, and other men"; and they have given false notions of liberty, leading to rebellions, so that "there was never anything so dearly bought, as these Western parts have bought the learning of the Greek and Latin tongues". But the *locus classicus* comes in the chapter of the *Leviathan*, "Of Darknesse from Vain Philosophy, and Fabulous Traditions," where Hobbes sets down his belief that scarce anything can be said "more repugnant to Government, than much of that he hath said in his *Politiques*; nor more ignorantly than a great part of his *Ethiques*". It is Aristotle's Civil Philosophy which has led to a foolish contempt for monarchy, by teaching men "to call all manner of Commonwealths but the popular . . . Tyranny," and has inculcated the error "that . . . not Men should govern, but the Laws".[1]

Political Science legal and non-ethical

Filmer, in the *Patriarcha*, uses Aristotle somewhat more tenderly. "In his *Ethics*, he hath so much good manners as to confess in right down words that monarchy is the best form of Government, and a popular estate the worst. And though he be not so free in his *Politics*," yet he confesses "that the Gods themselves did live under a monarchy. What can a heathen say more?" Generally, Filmer either seeks to show that Aristotle agrees with him, or to refute him, either out of himself, or by the evidence of experience. But from 1550 almost to 1800 political science had left Aristotle. Its two

[1] Exactly the two principles which, we have seen, mediæval writers had emphasised. It is not Aristotle, but the Aristotelians of the Middle Ages, whom Hobbes condemns. But he thought he was condemning Aristotle ("I have heard him say," writes Aubrey, "that Aristotle was the worst teacher that ever was, the worst politician and ethick—a countrey-fellow that could live in the world [would be] as good: but his rhetorique and discourse of animals was rare")—and he may have been annoyed by the appeals to the authority of Aristotle, which were made by contemporary writers who belonged to the popular party: see Appendix A. (The French Revolution, like the Great Rebellion, "harked back" to Aristotle; and *citoyen Champagne* published in 1797 a translation of the *Politics*.)

schools, the Absolutists (or "Machiavellians"), like Bodin and Filmer, and the Contractarians, like Languet[1] and Locke, were thinking in other terms than those which Aristotle could furnish. In their hands, Political Science deserted Ethics; it ceased to regard itself as concerned with the spirit of man. It became a legal science. It took to itself law in the place of ethics, and radically altered its nature. One school thought in terms of contract; the other, or absolutist school spoke, as in Bodin's *Republic*, of an *imperium legibus solutum*, or, as in Filmer, of *patria potestas*. The wedding of Political Science to Roman Law was its deterioration. Law hardened political conceptions into unreality: for the spiritual will which is the basis of the State it substituted a more material but less real contract. Law, regarding the external act and concerned with the prevention of damages, made the State likewise into a force external to the individual, and merely active to protect his property, instead of an idea proceeding from man's mind, and directed to his spiritual good. By the influence of law, Political Science was, in a sense, *demoralised*. But it must be admitted that law was not by any means exclusively responsible for this demoralisation. Machiavelli demoralised the conception of the State most trenchantly, and Machiavelli seems to have known Aristotle rather than Roman Law. What really impelled thinkers to demoralise the State was, as Aristotle would say, "facts themselves," or in other words, the tendencies of contemporary history. Political science has its roots in history, not only in the sense that it represents a series of inductions from the recorded past, but also, and perhaps still more, in the sense that it represents views coloured and even determined by the living present. From 1500 onwards a process of State-centralisation was at work; the State was busied in subjecting to itself the particularist tendencies of the baronage and the separatist instincts of the Church. In such a work, said Machiavelli, it may be necessary to go to work against faith, against charity, against humanity, against religion.[2] And as absolutism demoralised the State, so,

[1] I refer to the author of the treatise entitled *Vindiciæ Contra Tyrannos*, published during the French Wars of Religion, and often referred to Languet, though it ought perhaps to be ascribed to Duplessis-Mornay.

[2] *Il Principe*, c. xviii.

too, paradoxically enough, did the revolt against absolutism. Men who rebelled against the State's authority in the name of religion, and, like Languet, used the argument from contract to rebut its claim to enforce a uniform faith, would naturally desire to limit the State's province to mere material protection; for a State limited to such functions must needs leave the sphere of religion free. Still a third influence due to contemporary politics tended to limit the State's sphere. The constitutionalists of the seventeenth century, who, like Locke, wished to limit the claims of monarchy, tended not so much to *transfer* those claims undiminished to a new authority, the House of Commons (which was the eventual solution), as to *limit* the powers of the State vested in the monarch, and to assert the "rights" of the subject against the interference of the State with the divine right of property. In all these ways contemporary politics were as much responsible as the influence of law for the desertion by Political Science of Aristotle and Ethics.

Renovatio imperii Aristotelici—**Rousseau and Hegel**

§ 4. The *renovatio imperii Aristotelici* (if it may be so called) was deferred till the end of the eighteenth century. The Reformation had liberated the State from subjection to the Church: the French Revolution introduced prominently the notion of the State as a free self-determined community. Room was given for the Greek idea of the State—as a moral agent (and not the mere defender of a Church which was itself the one moral agent), and a self-governing association of equals. At the same time the reaction from the mechanical conception of the world to a worship of "Nature," visible alike in Wordsworth, in Rousseau, and in Wolf's *Prolegomena* to Homer, brought men back to the old Aristotelian conceptions. To Germans who knew of early "folks" forming natural units, governing themselves in folkmoots and depositing gradually a folk-custom of their own, the return to Aristotle was perhaps most easy; and hence it appears in the German idealists of the end of the eighteenth and the beginning of the nineteenth century, and particularly perhaps in Hegel. But, as Professor Bosanquet has shown, German thinkers had here their forerunner in Rousseau.[1] Unlike Locke, he did not limit the State's autho-

[1] Burke is still more obviously an Aristotelian, in his respect for what has developed, and his sense of the inevitable foundations of political order.

rity, but transferred it whole and entire to a new authority, the people. Like Aristotle, he believed in the moral mission of the State. He may indeed sometimes speak of the State as a corruption from the simple state of Nature. But in the *Contrat Social* there are hints, and indeed pronouncements, of a very different theory. The State appears, not as a corruption, but as the perfection, of man, as introducing a true morality, which did not exist in the instinctive stage of Nature. It is defined as *un être moral collectif*—a definition which comes near to the Aristotelian view of the State as "an association for good life". This moral collective being has two wills—a true will, set to the collective good, which is called the general will; and a false will, set to the individual good of the several members, which is called the will of all. Just as Aristotle believed that the State must habituate its members in a good life, so Rousseau believed that the State must endeavour to force the true will upon the individual. Nor is it not only in these fundamentals that Rousseau is Aristotelian. He came from a city-state, Geneva, and the State which he desires to institute is a city-state after the old Greek model. It is, in size, to be a mean between excess and defect: its institutions, we are told, should aim at equality, but they must suit the genius of the people and the circumstances of its territory. Finally, though to Rousseau, as to Marsilio, the people is the true legislature, room is yet made, because the people do not always know what to legislate, for a single legislator (who is particularly Aristotelian in character), to supply the defects of their knowledge.

To Hegel, as to Plato, the State is a product of mind—the sphere of "Mind Objective". But Objective Mind issues not only in the State: it issues in a triad—in Law and in the Morality of conscience, as well as in the "Social Ethics" of the State. Law, morality, and political obligation are all phases of mind, expressing itself in an "ought". Here Political Science definitely returns to its old ethical connection. Indeed there is no separate political science: there is simply a philosophy of mind as it manifests itself in action, and the State is one of those manifestations. But it is the highest and greatest. To Hegel there is an ascent from law to morality, and from morality to the social ethics of a State. Law is a hard system of universal equality: it involves, as its necessary complement and supplement, the free determination of the individual will in Morality. But if Law is rigid and universal, Morality in itself is too flexible and individualistic. The two must meet and be reconciled in the moral life of a political community, which contains the objective and universal element of Law (since it is manifested as a single and visible life), and also, because it is the free expression and creation of the community, includes the element of free self-determination. Thus "in the spirit of a nation, the 'ought' is no less an 'is'" (§ 514)[1]; and "the State is the self-conscious ethical substance" (§ 535). The State being thus a living whole, its constitution is to Hegel, as it was to Aristotle, the manner of its life. It is the expression of the self-consciousness of the State. "What is . . . called making a constitution, is . . . a thing that has never happened in history." "A constitution only develops from the national spirit identically with that spirit's own development" (§ 540).

Thus to the unit of the nation Hegel applies the old philosophy of the πόλις. The essence of the nation-state, as of the old city-state, is, he tells us, a moral life; and the spirit which sustains that life issues in a constitution which is its inevitable expression. Developed "on the Nature-given unit of the family," the State is natural; and in its service is perfect *αὐτάρκεια*, because by such service there comes the fullest expansion of the moral life. In Hegel Political Science is speaking once more in its native tongue. Once more it speaks, as it were, in Greek: once more it expresses itself in terms of ethics.

[1] The references are to the *Philosophy of Mind* in Wallace's translation.

APPENDIX A

A NEWSPAPER ENTITLED *OBSERVATIONS ON THE POLITICS*

THERE was apparently a revival of interest in Aristotle as a result of the Civil War; and Hobbes' venom against Aristotle may perhaps be explained by the fact that his writings served as a basis for the revolutionaries. A newspaper [1] appeared in 1654, entitled *Observations, Historical, Political and Philosophical upon Aristotle's First Book of Political Government: together with a Narrative of State Affairs in England, Scotland and Ireland*, etc. Only six numbers appeared, and the *Observations* only extended to the first six sections of the first book. In the first number there are about two and a half pages of observations to one and a half of news: in the second there are six pages of observations and two of news. "I shall for thy direction," the author says, "present thee with this taper that I have lighted at Aristotle's bright candle, or Lamp of Reason, in his Eight Book of Politik Government, who (we promise diligently to observe the Lord Loys, le Roy) [2] (*sic*) calleth just Politik Government a lawful art". If it be objected that Aristotle ought not "to be published to common view," he urges, "truly they may as well say that the Bible ought not to be published". "I shall show the happiness of those people that live under such a government, where it is the duty of the governors to rule by Law, as the Lord Protector here hath sworn to do." The newspaper is to be "a school to teach the art of just preserving politic government: it shall also show the causes of changes in all governments since the beginning; as also rules for prevention of such changes". The author puts it "forward into the world in such parcels, because the beginning may be useful in this time of needful searching out of perfection in government, as well to temper and inlighten the minds of the people, as for information of those that shall be called to the Trust of Government". He knows that the work

[1] I owe my knowledge of this newspaper, and the opportunity of reading it, to the kindness of Professor Firth.

[2] See next page.

can only be finished, "as it is intended," in a long time; for he intends "to apply Aristotle to all history, and so get lessons thereof".

The conception of political science as practical and medicinal is quite Aristotelian; but the author does not quite rise to his conception. He is indeed anxious to inculcate the Aristotelian idea, that alternate rule and subjection is the true canon of government: "there's no such remedy against changes in a state as to change the persons that govern"—a lesson which he enforces by many instances. But on the whole he makes the text of Aristotle a peg on which to hang discursive and disjointed notes; and Aristotle's allusion to the utility of the ox leads him to remark—"how usefull is the ferret in the Cony Warrens". He follows Aristotle faithfully, except with regard to slavery. Slavery is not by nature, but "by second nature": it is a thing ingrained by cunning and might, for "man is a free creature by nature". In an appendix to the fifth number a confession is made: "the several parts of this work hath not answered that which was promised in the first part; yet it shall in the continuance". Next week there shall be a discourse "on the basis of the Papal States," and then on "all the rest of the States in the Universe": but "reader, the four parts preceding is necessary for thee to have: they show the matter and parts of which a commonwealth is". Evidently the sales were not large, as this advertisement indicates; and the discourse of next week on the Papal States was apparently the last.

NOTE.—The cryptic allusion in the text to "Loys, le Roy" refers to a French scholar who translated both the *Politics* and the *Republic.* Loys le Roy, *dit* Regius, published in 1568 a translation of the *Politics* (which he dedicated to "Henry III., King of France and Poland"), entitled *Les Politiques d'Aristote. Esquelles es monstrée la science de gouverner le genre humain en toutes especes d'estats publiques.* Along with the translation there were expositions from the best authors, especially Aristotle himself and Plato; and there were "innumerable examples ancient and modern from Empires, Kingdoms, Seignories and Republics". There was also a preface, *de la politique et des legislateurs plus renommés qui l'ont pratiquée, et des autheurs illustres qui en ont escrit.* The whole was translated into English in 1598, and this translation (the first English translation of the *Politics* that I know) was used by the author of the *Observations.* Loys le Roy, the second after Nicholas Oresme to translate the *Politics* into French, was the first to translate the *Republic.* His translation, accompanied by a commentary, and by "some other Platonic treatises touching the immortality of the soul" (to illustrate the Tenth Book), is, he boasts, "a work very necessary and useful to kings, governors, and magistrates, and to all other sorts of estates and qualities of persons".

APPENDIX B

THE LATER HISTORY OF THE *REPUBLIC*.

COMPARED with the *Politics*, the *Republic* has no history. For a thousand years it simply disappeared. From the days of Proclus, the Neo-Platonist of the fifth century, almost until the days of Marsilio Ficino and Pico della Mirandola, at the end of the fifteenth century, the *Republic* was practically a lost book. It is said of Proclus that he used to assert, that "if it were in his power, he would withdraw from the knowledge of men, for the present, all ancient books except the *Timæus* and the Sacred Oracles".[1] His wish was fulfilled. What the Middle Ages knew of Plato came from a Latin translation of a large part of the *Timæus*, made by Chalcidius in the fourth century, and from the references in Aristotle, in Cicero, Augustine and Macrobius, in Apuleius' *De Dogmate Platonis*, and in Boethius' *De Consolatione Philosophi*, the great commonplace book on which so many generations drew.[2] Something of the *Republic* was contained in Cicero's *De Republica*. Along with the praise of the mixed constitution, which Cicero had borrowed from later Greek writers, the *De Republica* contains a translation of Plato's sketch of democracy, an imitation of his picture of tyranny, and, above all, in the *Somnium Scipionis*, an adaptation of the myth of Er, which greatly influenced later thought, and was the foundation of Petrarch's hopes of heaven.[3] St. Augustine, though he had but little acquaintance with Greek literature, quoted largely from the *De Republica* in his own *De Civitate Dei* (a picture, like Plato's *Republic*, of a city in the heavens), and in this way helped to preserve the Platonic tradition. The *De Consolatione Philosophi* of Boethius is as

[1] Sandys, *History of Classical Scholarship*, pp. 366-67.

[2] John the Scot knew Greek, and quotes the *Timæus* in Latin which is not borrowed from Chalcidius; while Henry Aristippus, the deacon of Catana, translated the *Meno* and the *Phædo* in the Norman kingdom of Sicily.

[3] Burckhardt, *The Renaissance in Italy*, p. 546.

much inspired by Platonism as is the *De Civitate Dei* by what may be called Hebraism; but, though Boethius quotes the *Republic* occasionally, and especially the text "on kings becoming philosophers or philosophers kings,"[1] the theme of his book comes from the *Timæus.* And, partly because it was the one treatise of Plato which they possessed, partly because it was "something craggy to break their minds upon," the thinkers of later generations continued to cling to the *Timæus.* The legend of Atlantis became a great "matter," and Bacon's *New Atlantis* is a relic of its influence.

During the thousand years in which the *Republic* slept, its influence was not dead. The Realists who believed in *universalia* which were *realia ante rem* regarded themselves as Platonists, indebted to the theory of Ideas in the *Republic.* And there was still more of Plato alive in the Middle Ages than his Ideas. "Great part of the educational furniture of the Middle Ages . . . may be found already in the *Republic* of Plato. The Four Cardinal Virtues of popular doctrine in the Middle Ages, familiar in preaching and allegory, are according to the division and arrangement adopted by Plato. . . . It might be fanciful to derive the three estates—*oratores, bellatores, laboratores*—from the *Republic,* though nowhere in history are the functions of the three Platonic orders of the Sages, the Warriors, and the Commons more clearly understood than in the mediæval theory of the Estates as it is expounded, for example, in the book of *Piers Plowman.* There is no doubt, however, about the origin of the mediæval classification of the Liberal Arts. The *Quadrivium* is drawn out in the *Republic* in the description of the studies of Arithmetic, Geometry, Astronomy and Music, though Plato does not allow the mediæval classification of dialectic as a Trivial Art along with Grammar and Rhetoric. Furthermore, the vision of Er the Pamphylian is ancestor . . . to the mediæval records of Hell, Purgatory and Paradise."[2]

With the Renaissance came a new birth of the *Republic.* The Platonism of the Florentine Academy and the circle which gathered round Lorenzo de Medici was indeed Neo-Platonic; but in the little farm at Montevecchio, Ficino had completed by 1477 his translation of Plato's writings into Latin. It is, however, in the *Utopia* of Sir Thomas More that we seem to find the Plato of the *Republic* redivivus.[3]

[1] I., c. iv.

[2] W. P. Ker, *The Dark Ages,* pp. 26-27.

[3] *Plato Redivivus* is the title of an unplatonic work by Henry Neville (a pamphleteer who had been Parliamentarian and Royalist by turns) in the reign of Charles II. See *Dict. Nat. Biog., sub voce* Neville.

The *Utopia* has many references to the *Republic;* and, what is more, it advocates community of property and the emancipation of women. But whatever stimulus its author may have owed to the *Republic*, the *Utopia* is a different and independent treatise.[1] While in Plato there is no little asceticism, in More there is something of Hedonism; while Plato had taught that society should let its useless members die, More suggests that those who are too old or too sick to get pleasure or profit from life should commit suicide. Penetrated by a different spirit from that of Plato, while borrowing, as he does, Platonic details, More is a typical representative of an age in which, " in opposition to Christian monasticism men lived like Epicurean philosophers, and in opposition to Christian scholasticism thought like disciples of Plato ". When we turn to More's advocacy of communism, we come upon the same difference from Plato, which appears in his general outlook on life. The idea of communism may have come from Plato; its motives and its scheme are altogether different. The motives of Plato, as we have seen, are not economic, but political or rather moral: communism is necessary for the realisation of justice, and because it alone will secure an unselfish and efficient government. The motives of More *are* economic: his communism is in direct reaction against contemporary economic conditions. Plato had felt that ignorant and selfish politicians were the ruin of the Greek city; More felt (as a Lord Chancellor said at the end of the fifteenth century), " this realm . . . falleth into decay from enclosures and the letting down of tenantries ". He saw the agricultural class evicted from its holdings to make room for sheep pastures: he saw " sheep devouring men ". He saw great landowners monopolising the land, and men who would have been contented farmers betaking themselves to vagabondage and theft. Agricultural communism was being advocated among the German peasantry by the movement called the *Bundschuh;* and to agricultural communism More turned. Since private property means such lack of " commodious living " for the mass of Englishmen, and since palliatives like equalisation of property and inalienable lots are of no avail, let us go the whole way, to the final goal of common property.

More's motives are thus economic: they are motives suggested more by the evils of his own times, than by the reading of Plato. His scheme is altogether different from that of Plato. Plato's communism had only touched the two upper classes: More's communism

[1] I am indebted to the edition of *Utopia* by Michels and Ziegler, Berlin, 1895 (*Einleitung*, pp. xvi.-xxxv.).

touches every member of the State. Plato's communism had been arranged in such a way as to set the two upper classes free from all material work and material cares: More's communism is so planned, that every man must put his hand to the plough, and labour at husbandry. Plato's guardians had shared in common an annual rent in kind paid by the *tiers état:* More's citizens share in common the whole of the products of their country. Plato left the third class with private ownership of all property, and the guardians with common ownership of—nothing, except their barracks and their annual rent: More leaves his citizens with no private ownership, and common ownership of everything.[1] Of all these differences, the one which is cardinal is the difference in the attitude of the two thinkers to labour. Plato meant his communism—a communism consistent with private ownership of most things, and involving common ownership of very few things—to set his guardians free *from* labour: More meant his communism, which was real communism in all things, to set all men free *for* labour. In place of unemployed farmers tramping the English roads, he would have work for all: in place of the many drones who live in rich men's houses, he would have all men bees. In this way (all working, the lazy as well as the unemployed), he hoped to shorten the hours of labour, and to give all men a six hours' day.

It is obvious that More has many affinities with the modern socialism from which Plato so greatly differs. There are, indeed, differences between More and modern socialism. Modern socialism is generally collectivist, and believes in common ownership of the *means of production:* it is a community of *products* which More advocates. Modern socialism would not "purify" society of its "luxury"; it would only divide that luxury equally and impartially. More comes nearer to Plato in this respect; he would "simplify" economic life down to its elements of agriculture and a few necessary trades. But on the whole More has the spirit of modern socialism—he has something of its Hedonism (*supra*, p. 138), something of its zeal for a fairer distribution of this world's goods, something of its close touch with actual contemporary economic conditions. And the problem of education is treated by him in the same modern spirit. Education had been to Plato the head and forefront of his scheme: communism had been, in comparison, secondary and subordinate. Communism is first and foremost in More, and education is considered

[1] There is *no* gold in Utopia: in the *Republic* it is the guardians *alone* who have no gold.

chiefly on its technical side, and as meaning a training in some trades; for every citizen of Utopia must practise a trade as well as agriculture, and alternate regularly between the two—a suggestion which shows yet again More's modern and unplatonic view of labour.

In his attitude towards woman More is, in some respects, very like Plato. He believes in the emancipation of women: he believes that women are able to do the same work as men. As in the *Republic*, the women of Utopia bear offices: as in the *Republic*, they go to war. But it is not all who fight; and it is only the priestly offices which women can hold. Nor is there any community of wives: More believes in monogamy. There is perhaps something of Plato's physical point of view in the suggestion that bride and bridegroom should see one another nude before marriage, in order that they may know that they are fitted for matrimony; but that is the only approach towards Plato's attitude to the sexual question. There is no attempt to regulate population, except by the system of colonies, which Aristotle [1] deprecates as a mere palliative (*supra*, p. 397, note 1).

It would thus appear that More, on the whole, is Platonic in the letter, and not in the spirit. He is rather "the father of modern Utopian socialism," than an imitator of Plato's communism. His aim is equality of enjoyment for all: it was the aim of Plato to secure perfection of knowledge for the few. In Plato intellectualism leads to the philosopher king and the rule of the all-wise Cæsar: More smiles at the idea of what the King of France would say to his Utopia. There is nothing of the ascetic despotism of the Idea in More: his motto is (as R. L. Stevenson wrote)—"Let cheerfulness abound with industry". Both in the *Republic* and in the *Utopia* there is some idea of religious reformation; but the difference is striking and suggestive. Plato would reform Greek mythology into a uniform conception of God: More advocates a quiet and happy toleration of all beliefs. *Quod credendum putaret, liberum cuique reliquit.*[2]

[1] The plan on which towns are constructed in Utopia reminds one of what Aristotle says of Hippodamus (*supra*, p. 415). See Michels and Ziegler, xxi.

[2] Jowett, *The Dialogues of Plato*, iii., ccxxvi.-ccxxviii., compares the *Republic* with Campanella's *City of the Sun*, a work which belongs to the beginning of the seventeenth century. Campanella was a Dominican friar. He advocates Platonic communism both in respect of property and of wives; but his work, "though borrowed from Plato, shows but a superficial acquaintance with his writings". He knows something of Aristotle, however, and defends community of property against his criticisms. "The most interesting feature of the book, common to Plato (?) and Sir Thomas More, is the deep feeling which is shown by the writer of the misery and ignorance prevailing among the lower classes in his own time." As compared with More, Campanella is far more Platonic in the prominence which he gives to

In conclusion, it may be suggested that the history of Plato's influence on political and social thought is to be seen, not only in the history of his writings, but also in the history of the writings of Aristotle. The pupil exercised a far greater influence than his master, but the master had set his mark deeply on the pupil, and the influence of the pupil was also that of the master. If men for centuries applied the doctrine of Final Causes to politics—if they conceived of the State as a moral institution—if they distinguished selfish governments from governments that were unselfish, and taught that every shepherd should seek the "common weal" of his flock—were they not following Plato, who had first taught all these things? We have spoken of Hegel under the rubric of the influence of the *Politics;* it would have been wiser, perhaps, to detect in Hegel the fulfilment of the influence of the *Republic.*[1]

education. "He looks forward to a new mode of education, which is to be a study of nature, and not of Aristotle." A peculiarity of his system is his belief in the efficacy of allegorical paintings, with which the seven circuits of the walls of his city are to be decorated. Another feature is a system of confession to the authorities, by which they are kept informed of all that the citizens are thinking and doing. This reminds one of a casual suggestion of Plato in the *Laws* (*supra*, p. 204).

[1] Similarly, Rousseau may be regarded as indebted to Plato—the Plato of the *Laws*—in his *Contrat Social.* His attitude towards the influence of the sea, his conception of the size of the proper State, his belief in a legislator —all these find their parallels, if not their origins, in the *Laws.* (*Cf.* Morley, *Life of Rousseau*, p. 313.)

INDEX

A

B

C

D

I

J

P

R

S

U

V

A CATALOG OF SELECTED

DOVER BOOKS

IN ALL FIELDS OF INTEREST

A CATALOG OF SELECTED DOVER BOOKS IN ALL FIELDS OF INTEREST

CONCERNING THE SPIRITUAL IN ART, Wassily ww. Pioneering work by father of abstract art. Thoughts on color theory, nature of art. Analysis of earlier masters. 12 illustrations. 80pp. of text. $5\frac{3}{8}$ x $8\frac{1}{2}$. 0-486-23411-8

CELTIC ART: The Methods of Construction, George Bain. Simple geometric techniques for making Celtic interlacements, spirals, Kells-type initials, animals, humans, etc. Over 500 illustrations. 160pp. 9 x 12. (Available in U.S. only.) 0-486-22923-8

AN ATLAS OF ANATOMY FOR ARTISTS, Fritz Schider. Most thorough reference work on art anatomy in the world. Hundreds of illustrations, including selections from works by Vesalius, Leonardo, Goya, Ingres, Michelangelo, others. 593 illustrations. 192pp. $7\frac{1}{8}$ x $10\frac{1}{4}$. 0-486-20241-0

CELTIC HAND STROKE-BY-STROKE (Irish Half-Uncial from "The Book of Kells"): An Arthur Baker Calligraphy Manual, Arthur Baker. Complete guide to creating each letter of the alphabet in distinctive Celtic manner. Covers hand position, strokes, pens, inks, paper, more. Illustrated. 48pp. $8\frac{1}{4}$ x 11. 0-486-24336-2

EASY ORIGAMI, John Montroll. Charming collection of 32 projects (hat, cup, pelican, piano, swan, many more) specially designed for the novice origami hobbyist. Clearly illustrated easy-to-follow instructions insure that even beginning papercrafters will achieve successful results. 48pp. $8\frac{1}{4}$ x 11. 0-486-27298-2

BLOOMINGDALE'S ILLUSTRATED 1886 CATALOG: Fashions, Dry Goods and Housewares, Bloomingdale Brothers. Famed merchants' extremely rare catalog depicting about 1,700 products: clothing, housewares, firearms, dry goods, jewelry, more. Invaluable for dating, identifying vintage items. Also, copyright-free graphics for artists, designers. Co-published with Henry Ford Museum & Greenfield Village. 160pp. $8\frac{1}{4}$ x 11. 0-486-25780-0

THE ART OF WORLDLY WISDOM, Baltasar Gracian. "Think with the few and speak with the many," "Friends are a second existence," and "Be able to forget" are among this 1637 volume's 300 pithy maxims. A perfect source of mental and spiritual refreshment, it can be opened at random and appreciated either in brief or at length. 128pp. $5\frac{3}{8}$ x $8\frac{1}{2}$. 0-486-44034-6

JOHNSON'S DICTIONARY: A Modern Selection, Samuel Johnson (E. L. McAdam and George Milne, eds.). This modern version reduces the original 1755 edition's 2,300 pages of definitions and literary examples to a more manageable length, retaining the verbal pleasure and historical curiosity of the original. 480pp. $5\frac{3}{16}$ x $8\frac{1}{4}$. 0-486-44089-3

ADVENTURES OF HUCKLEBERRY FINN, Mark Twain, Illustrated by E. W. Kemble. A work of eternal richness and complexity, a source of ongoing critical debate, and a literary landmark, Twain's 1885 masterpiece about a barefoot boy's journey of self-discovery has enthralled readers around the world. This handsome clothbound reproduction of the first edition features all 174 of the original black-and-white illustrations. 368pp. $5\frac{3}{8}$ x $8\frac{1}{2}$. 0-486-44322-1

STICKLEY CRAFTSMAN FURNITURE CATALOGS, Gustav Stickley and L. & J. G. Stickley. Beautiful, functional furniture in two authentic catalogs from 1910. 594 illustrations, including 277 photos, show settles, rockers, armchairs, reclining chairs, bookcases, desks, tables. 183pp. $6^1/_2$ x $9^1/_4$. 0-486-23838-5

AMERICAN LOCOMOTIVES IN HISTORIC PHOTOGRAPHS: 1858 to 1949, Ron Ziel (ed.). A rare collection of 126 meticulously detailed official photographs, called "builder portraits," of American locomotives that majestically chronicle the rise of steam locomotive power in America. Introduction. Detailed captions. xi+ 129pp. 9 x 12. 0-486-27393-8

AMERICA'S LIGHTHOUSES: An Illustrated History, Francis Ross Holland, Jr. Delightfully written, profusely illustrated fact-filled survey of over 200 American lighthouses since 1716. History, anecdotes, technological advances, more. 240pp. 8 x $10^3/_4$. 0-486-25576-X

TOWARDS A NEW ARCHITECTURE, Le Corbusier. Pioneering manifesto by founder of "International School." Technical and aesthetic theories, views of industry, economics, relation of form to function, "mass-production split" and much more. Profusely illustrated. 320pp. $6^1/_8$ x $9^1/_4$. (Available in U.S. only.) 0-486-25023-7

HOW THE OTHER HALF LIVES, Jacob Riis. Famous journalistic record, exposing poverty and degradation of New York slums around 1900, by major social reformer. 100 striking and influential photographs. 233pp. 10 x $7^7/_8$. 0-486-22012-5

FRUIT KEY AND TWIG KEY TO TREES AND SHRUBS, William M. Harlow. One of the handiest and most widely used identification aids. Fruit key covers 120 deciduous and evergreen species; twig key 160 deciduous species. Easily used. Over 300 photographs. 126pp. $5^3/_8$ x $8^1/_2$. 0-486-20511-8

COMMON BIRD SONGS, Dr. Donald J. Borror. Songs of 60 most common U.S. birds: robins, sparrows, cardinals, bluejays, finches, more—arranged in order of increasing complexity. Up to 9 variations of songs of each species. Cassette and manual 0-486-99911-4

ORCHIDS AS HOUSE PLANTS, Rebecca Tyson Northen. Grow cattleyas and many other kinds of orchids—in a window, in a case, or under artificial light. 63 illustrations. 148pp. $5^3/_8$ x $8^1/_2$. 0-486-23261-1

MONSTER MAZES, Dave Phillips. Masterful mazes at four levels of difficulty. Avoid deadly perils and evil creatures to find magical treasures. Solutions for all 32 exciting illustrated puzzles. 48pp. $8^1/_4$ x 11. 0-486-26005-4

MOZART'S DON GIOVANNI (DOVER OPERA LIBRETTO SERIES), Wolfgang Amadeus Mozart. Introduced and translated by Ellen H. Bleiler. Standard Italian libretto, with complete English translation. Convenient and thoroughly portable—an ideal companion for reading along with a recording or the performance itself. Introduction. List of characters. Plot summary. 121pp. $5^1/_4$ x $8^1/_2$. 0-486-24944-1

FRANK LLOYD WRIGHT'S DANA HOUSE, Donald Hoffmann. Pictorial essay of residential masterpiece with over 160 interior and exterior photos, plans, elevations, sketches and studies. 128pp. $9^1/_4$ x $10^3/_4$. 0-486-29120-0

THE CLARINET AND CLARINET PLAYING, David Pino. Lively, comprehensive work features suggestions about technique, musicianship, and musical interpretation, as well as guidelines for teaching, making your own reeds, and preparing for public performance. Includes an intriguing look at clarinet history. "A godsend," *The Clarinet,* Journal of the International Clarinet Society. Appendixes. 7 illus. 320pp. 5³/₈ x 8¹/₂. 0-486-40270-3

HOLLYWOOD GLAMOR PORTRAITS, John Kobal (ed.). 145 photos from 1926-49. Harlow, Gable, Bogart, Bacall; 94 stars in all. Full background on photographers, technical aspects. 160pp. 8³/₈ x 11¹/₄. 0-486-23352-9

THE RAVEN AND OTHER FAVORITE POEMS, Edgar Allan Poe. Over 40 of the author's most memorable poems: "The Bells," "Ulalume," "Israfel," "To Helen," "The Conqueror Worm," "Eldorado," "Annabel Lee," many more. Alphabetic lists of titles and first lines. 64pp. 5³/₁₆ x 8¹/₄. 0-486-26685-0

PERSONAL MEMOIRS OF U. S. GRANT, Ulysses Simpson Grant. Intelligent, deeply moving firsthand account of Civil War campaigns, considered by many the finest military memoirs ever written. Includes letters, historic photographs, maps and more. 528pp. 6¹/₈ x 9¹/₄. 0-486-28587-1

POE ILLUSTRATED: Art by Doré, Dulac, Rackham and Others, selected and edited by Jeff A. Menges. More than 100 compelling illustrations, in brilliant color and crisp black-and-white, include scenes from "The Raven," "The Pit and the Pendulum," "The Gold-Bug," and other stories and poems. 96pp. 8³/₈ x 11. 0-486-45746-X

RUSSIAN STORIES/RUSSKIE RASSKAZY: A Dual-Language Book, edited by Gleb Struve. Twelve tales by such masters as Chekhov, Tolstoy, Dostoevsky, Pushkin, others. Excellent word-for-word English translations on facing pages, plus teaching and study aids, Russian/English vocabulary, biographical/critical introductions, more. 416pp. 5³/₈ x 8¹/₂. 0-486-26244-8

PHILADELPHIA THEN AND NOW: 60 Sites Photographed in the Past and Present, Kenneth Finkel and Susan Oyama. Rare photographs of City Hall, Logan Square, Independence Hall, Betsy Ross House, other landmarks juxtaposed with contemporary views. Captures changing face of historic city. Introduction. Captions. 128pp. 8¹/₄ x 11. 0-486-25790-8

NORTH AMERICAN INDIAN LIFE: Customs and Traditions of 23 Tribes, Elsie Clews Parsons (ed.). 27 fictionalized essays by noted anthropologists examine religion, customs, government, additional facets of life among the Winnebago, Crow, Zuni, Eskimo, other tribes. 480pp. 6¹/₈ x 9¹/₄. 0-486-27377-6

TECHNICAL MANUAL AND DICTIONARY OF CLASSICAL BALLET, Gail Grant. Defines, explains, comments on steps, movements, poses and concepts. 15-page pictorial section. Basic book for student, viewer. 127pp. 5³/₈ x 8¹/₂. 0-486-21843-0

THE MALE AND FEMALE FIGURE IN MOTION: 60 Classic Photographic Sequences, Eadweard Muybridge. 60 true-action photographs of men and women walking, running, climbing, bending, turning, etc., reproduced from a rare 19th-century masterpiece. vi + 121pp. 9 x 12. 0-486-24745-7

ANIMALS: 1,419 Copyright-Free Illustrations of Mammals, Birds, Fish, Insects, etc., Jim Harter (ed.). Clear wood engravings present, in extremely lifelike poses, over 1,000 species of animals. One of the most extensive pictorial sourcebooks of its kind. Captions. Index. 284pp. 9 x 12. 0-486-23766-4

1001 QUESTIONS ANSWERED ABOUT THE SEASHORE, N. J. Berrill and Jacquelyn Berrill. Queries answered about dolphins, sea snails, sponges, starfish, fishes, shore birds, many others. Covers appearance, breeding, growth, feeding, much more. 305pp. 5¼ x 8¼. 0-486-23366-9

ATTRACTING BIRDS TO YOUR YARD, William J. Weber. Easy-to-follow guide offers advice on how to attract the greatest diversity of birds: birdhouses, feeders, water and waterers, much more. 96pp. 5³⁄₁₆ x 8¼. 0-486-28927-3

MEDICINAL AND OTHER USES OF NORTH AMERICAN PLANTS: A Historical Survey with Special Reference to the Eastern Indian Tribes, Charlotte Erichsen-Brown. Chronological historical citations document 500 years of usage of plants, trees, shrubs native to eastern Canada, northeastern U.S. Also complete identifying information. 343 illustrations. 544pp. 6½ x 9¼. 0-486-25951-X

STORYBOOK MAZES, Dave Phillips. 23 stories and mazes on two-page spreads: Wizard of Oz, Treasure Island, Robin Hood, etc. Solutions. 64pp. 8¼ x 11. 0-486-23628-5

AMERICAN NEGRO SONGS: 230 Folk Songs and Spirituals, Religious and Secular, John W. Work. This authoritative study traces the African influences of songs sung and played by black Americans at work, in church, and as entertainment. The author discusses the lyric significance of such songs as "Swing Low, Sweet Chariot," "John Henry," and others and offers the words and music for 230 songs. Bibliography. Index of Song Titles. 272pp. 6½ x 9¼. 0-486-40271-1

MOVIE-STAR PORTRAITS OF THE FORTIES, John Kobal (ed.). 163 glamor, studio photos of 106 stars of the 1940s: Rita Hayworth, Ava Gardner, Marlon Brando, Clark Gable, many more. 176pp. 8⅜ x 11¼. 0-486-23546-7

YEKL and THE IMPORTED BRIDEGROOM AND OTHER STORIES OF YIDDISH NEW YORK, Abraham Cahan. Film Hester Street based on *Yekl* (1896). Novel, other stories among first about Jewish immigrants on N.Y.'s East Side. 240pp. 5⅜ x 8½. 0-486-22427-9

SELECTED POEMS, Walt Whitman. Generous sampling from *Leaves of Grass*. Twenty-four poems include "I Hear America Singing," "Song of the Open Road," "I Sing the Body Electric," "When Lilacs Last in the Dooryard Bloom'd," "O Captain! My Captain!"—all reprinted from an authoritative edition. Lists of titles and first lines. 128pp. 5³⁄₁₆ x 8¼. 0-486-26878-0

SONGS OF EXPERIENCE: Facsimile Reproduction with 26 Plates in Full Color, William Blake. 26 full-color plates from a rare 1826 edition. Includes "The Tyger," "London," "Holy Thursday," and other poems. Printed text of poems. 48pp. 5¼ x 7. 0-486-24636-1

THE BEST TALES OF HOFFMANN, E. T. A. Hoffmann. 10 of Hoffmann's most important stories: "Nutcracker and the King of Mice," "The Golden Flowerpot," etc. 458pp. 5⅜ x 8½. 0-486-21793-0

THE BOOK OF TEA, Kakuzo Okakura. Minor classic of the Orient: entertaining, charming explanation, interpretation of traditional Japanese culture in terms of tea ceremony. 94pp. 5⅜ x 8½. 0-486-20070-1

MAKING FURNITURE MASTERPIECES: 30 Projects with Measured Drawings, Franklin H. Gottshall. Step-by-step instructions, illustrations for constructing handsome, useful pieces, among them a Sheraton desk, Chippendale chair, Spanish desk, Queen Anne table and a William and Mary dressing mirror. 224pp. 8¹/₈ x 11¹/₄. 0-486-29338-6

NORTH AMERICAN INDIAN DESIGNS FOR ARTISTS AND CRAFTSPEOPLE, Eva Wilson. Over 360 authentic copyright-free designs adapted from Navajo blankets, Hopi pottery, Sioux buffalo hides, more. Geometrics, symbolic figures, plant and animal motifs, etc. 128pp. 8³/₈ x 11. (Not for sale in the United Kingdom.) 0-486-25341-4

THE FOSSIL BOOK: A Record of Prehistoric Life, Patricia V. Rich et al. Profusely illustrated definitive guide covers everything from single-celled organisms and dinosaurs to birds and mammals and the interplay between climate and man. Over 1,500 illustrations. 760pp. 7¹/₂ x 10¹/₈. 0-486-29371-8

VICTORIAN ARCHITECTURAL DETAILS: Designs for Over 700 Stairs, Mantels, Doors, Windows, Cornices, Porches, and Other Decorative Elements, A. J. Bicknell & Company. Everything from dormer windows and piazzas to balconies and gable ornaments. Also includes elevations and floor plans for handsome, private residences and commercial structures. 80pp. 9³/₈ x 12¹/₄. 0-486-44015-X

WESTERN ISLAMIC ARCHITECTURE: A Concise Introduction, John D. Hoag. Profusely illustrated critical appraisal compares and contrasts Islamic mosques and palaces—from Spain and Egypt to other areas in the Middle East. 139 illustrations. 128pp. 6 x 9. 0-486-43760-4

CHINESE ARCHITECTURE: A Pictorial History, Liang Ssu-ch'eng. More than 240 rare photographs and drawings depict temples, pagodas, tombs, bridges, and imperial palaces comprising much of China's architectural heritage. 152 halftones, 94 diagrams. 232pp. 10³/₄ x 9⁷/₈. 0-486-43999-2

THE RENAISSANCE: Studies in Art and Poetry, Walter Pater. One of the most talked-about books of the 19th century, *The Renaissance* combines scholarship and philosophy in an innovative work of cultural criticism that examines the achievements of Botticelli, Leonardo, Michelangelo, and other artists. "The holy writ of beauty."—Oscar Wilde. 160pp. 5³/₈ x 8¹/₂. 0-486-44025-7

A TREATISE ON PAINTING, Leonardo da Vinci. The great Renaissance artist's practical advice on drawing and painting techniques covers anatomy, perspective, composition, light and shadow, and color. A classic of art instruction, it features 48 drawings by Nicholas Poussin and Leon Battista Alberti. 192pp. 5³/₈ x 8¹/₂. 0-486-44155-5

THE ESSENTIAL JEFFERSON, Thomas Jefferson, edited by John Dewey. This extraordinary primer offers a superb survey of Jeffersonian thought. It features writings on political and economic philosophy, morals and religion, intellectual freedom and progress, education, secession, slavery, and more. 176pp. 5³/₈ x 8¹/₂. 0-486-46599-3

WASHINGTON IRVING'S RIP VAN WINKLE, Illustrated by Arthur Rackham. Lovely prints that established artist as a leading illustrator of the time and forever etched into the popular imagination a classic of Catskill lore. 51 full-color plates. 80pp. 8³/₈ x 11. 0-486-44242-X

HENSCHE ON PAINTING, John W. Robichaux. Basic painting philosophy and methodology of a great teacher, as expounded in his famous classes and workshops on Cape Cod. 7 illustrations in color on covers. 80pp. 5³/₈ x 8¹/₂. 0-486-43728-0

CATALOG OF DOVER BOOKS

LIGHT AND SHADE: A Classic Approach to Three-Dimensional Drawing, Mrs. Mary P. Merrifield. Handy reference clearly demonstrates principles of light and shade by revealing effects of common daylight, sunshine, and candle or artificial light on geometrical solids. 13 plates. 64pp. 5³/₈ x 8¹/₂. 0-486-44143-1

ASTROLOGY AND ASTRONOMY: A Pictorial Archive of Signs and Symbols, Ernst and Johanna Lehner. Treasure trove of stories, lore, and myth, accompanied by more than 300 rare illustrations of planets, the Milky Way, signs of the zodiac, comets, meteors, and other astronomical phenomena. 192pp. 8³/₈ x 11. 0-486-43981-X

JEWELRY MAKING: Techniques for Metal, Tim McCreight. Easy-to-follow instructions and carefully executed illustrations describe tools and techniques, use of gems and enamels, wire inlay, casting, and other topics. 72 line illustrations and diagrams. 176pp. 8¹/₄ x 10⁷/₈. 0-486-44043-5

MAKING BIRDHOUSES: Easy and Advanced Projects, Gladstone Califf. Easy-to-follow instructions include diagrams for everything from a one-room house for bluebirds to a forty-two-room structure for purple martins. 56 plates; 4 figures. 80pp. 8³/₄ x 6³/₈. 0-486-44183-0

LITTLE BOOK OF LOG CABINS: How to Build and Furnish Them, William S. Wicks. Handy how-to manual, with instructions and illustrations for building cabins in the Adirondack style, fireplaces, stairways, furniture, beamed ceilings, and more. 102 line drawings. 96pp. 8³/₄ x 6³/₈. 0-486-44259-4

THE SEASONS OF AMERICA PAST, Eric Sloane. From "sugaring time" and strawberry picking to Indian summer and fall harvest, a whole year's activities described in charming prose and enhanced with 79 of the author's own illustrations. 160pp. 8¹/₄ x 11. 0-486-44220-9

THE METROPOLIS OF TOMORROW, Hugh Ferriss. Generous, prophetic vision of the metropolis of the future, as perceived in 1929. Powerful illustrations of towering structures, wide avenues, and rooftop parks—all features in many of today's modern cities. 59 illustrations. 144pp. 8¹/₄ x 11. 0-486-43727-2

THE PATH TO ROME, Hilaire Belloc. This 1902 memoir abounds in lively vignettes from a vanished time, recounting a pilgrimage on foot across the Alps and Apennines in order to "see all Europe which the Christian Faith has saved." 77 of the author's original line drawings complement his sparkling prose. 272pp. 5³/₈ x 8¹/₂. 0-486-44001-X

THE HISTORY OF RASSELAS: Prince of Abissinia, Samuel Johnson. Distinguished English writer attacks eighteenth-century optimism and man's unrealistic estimates of what life has to offer. 112pp. 5³/₈ x 8¹/₂. 0-486-44094-X

A VOYAGE TO ARCTURUS, David Lindsay. A brilliant flight of pure fancy, where wild creatures crowd the fantastic landscape and demented torturers dominate victims with their bizarre mental powers. 272pp. 5³/₈ x 8¹/₂. 0-486-44198-9